ABOUT THE AUTHOR

Camera Reflections: Chase Studios, Ltd.

Otis L. Lee, Jr. has practiced law in Philadelphia, Pennsylvania and Charlottesville, Virginia. He formerly served on the faculties of several Midwestern and East Coast universities and as a former Director, Coordinator and contributing author to the Howard University School of Business 1980 Project to Revise and Edit the U.S. Department of Commerce manual entitled *Local Economic Development Corporation, Legal and Financial Guidelines.* His career has included serving as Trust New Business Solicitor, at Harris Trust and Savings Bank, Chicago, IL, Panel Executive for the Panel on Product Liability and Associate Director of the Center for Small Business at the United States Chamber of Commerce in Washington, D.C. as well as an Advance Underwriting Consultant for the Mid-Atlantic Region for the New York Life Insurance Company.

FROM
SOUTH BOSTON
TO CAMBRIDGE

❧

9/10/05

TO: Barbara & Joan,
Thanks for attending
And all the Best to
the both of you.

Cl

FROM SOUTH BOSTON TO CAMBRIDGE

THE MAKING OF ONE·PHILADELPHIA LAWYER

A MEMOIR

OTIS L. LEE, JR.

THE FITZGERALD COMPANY PRESS
CHARLOTTESVILLE, VIRGINIA

Frontispiece: Philadelphia Skyline with Schuylkill River, author in silhouette

FitzGerald Company Press
1126 East Market Street
Charlottesville, Virginia 22902

First FitzGerald Company Press hardcover edition May 2013

For information about special discounts for bulk purchases,
please contact FitzGerald Company Press at
1-434-293-9977 or valaw1126@comcast.net.
Visit our website at www.otislee.com

Manufactured in the United States of America

ISBN: 9781624070761
ISBN: 9781626208087 (ebook)

Library of Congress Control Number 2013936871

DEDICATION

This book is dedicated to all the forgotten and unsung members of the Lee, Penick, Williams and Moon family. Generations whose existence and toil and whose stories have not been told or recorded.

I also dedicate this book to all the civil rights leaders, the anonymous Emmett Tills, Medgar Everses, Fannie Lou Hamers and freedom fighters of the era. The meaning of their lives transcends their presence on this earth. To the known and unknown who fought the battles against segregation and the denial of civil rights for Americans of African descent, so that the lives of Black people in America and in other countries would be better, and upon whose shoulders we stand today.

Moreover, I dedicate this book to all of the Africans who were taken from their villages in West, Central, and East Africa by force and subjected to the most heinous of crimes for centuries and whose lives and stories will never be known and whose suffering we cannot even vicariously imagine.

Finally, I dedicate this book to my sons, Dr. Otis L. Lee, III, and his descendants so that they might learn about the family they are an integral part of. And the descendants of Justin Patrick Palmer Lee, Esq., whose academic achievements, I believe, have set a new standard for the entire family: Moon, Lee and Penick. Last, but not by any means least, I dedicate this book to my wife Dr. Michelle Palmer Lee, whose patience, tolerance, love, commitment and understanding through the years enabled me to accomplish so much during the decades of our married life, she is indeed the indispensable party.

And most essentially to my father, Otis Leonard Lee, and to my mother, Rosa Belle Moon Lee, whose love, caring and continued faith and investment in me over the years that went well beyond the call of duty even to this day is intrinsic to who I am. A forever thank you.

Contents

Editor's Note

One day in the spring of 2011, my office phone rang. A man named Otis Lee said he was calling the English Department at Piedmont Virginia Community College to inquire if any professors were editors or had editorial experience to help him edit his memoir.

This was not a request the head of an English Department gets every day. I was intrigued. I had long worked on academic texts, two just recently having been published, and on my own novels and short stories but had always longed to break into editing fiction/memoir. So I decided to give it a try.

That's how my professional relationship and my friendship with Otis Lee, Jr. began. Over the phone that day, we discussed my qualifications, doctoral studies, publications, teaching experiences, etc. Satisfied that I was qualified, he set up an initial meeting for us to discuss the memoir and editing project the next week.

At the end of this initial meeting in Hamilton's restaurant on the downtown mall in Charlottesville, he handed over a copy of the memoir, saying "take care of this thing, man. This is a one shot deal." He was repeating what he said in the meeting: this was a significant slice of his life story and would probably be the only book he would write. Under his fisherman's cap, his eyes glimmered with excitement, anxiousness. I said, "I will, Otis. You have my word on that." We shook hands and went home.

During the next few days, I looked over the manuscript and found it intriguing. This was a man who had much to say. Otis's story traces his family history from 1820 to the present: the history of a notable Black family in Charlottesville. From his childhood/adolescence in C'ville in the 1960s to his trials in Chicago as an aspiring lawyer to his triumphs in Philadelphia, and his return to the tranquility of his beloved Albemarle County. This is a story that involves courage, perseverance, business acumen and success, vividly described in startling detail. In short, here was a notable story with some poignant moments and philosophical insights from a variety of experiences.

At our subsequent meeting at Hamilton's restaurant, I outlined the projected time needed to complete a line-editing of the 537 page manuscript—about a year.

But was I biting off more than I could chew? Only time would tell. But I was confident that we could see it through to publication. Above all, I assured Otis, I am a "project guy"—I see projects through from beginning to end—something my mother instilled in me from an early age. I have always had a "finish what you start" mentality. All those school projects and household projects too! So after citing these examples and my professional "projects" completed, I said, "Otis. This is your magnum opus. I'll see this thing through to the end. That much I can promise you."

At one point during this meeting, I had an epiphany and said, "I want this memoir to sing the song you want it to sing." My task, among others, was to make his manuscript sing his song as vibrantly and as clearly as it could; to enliven his melody; to, in effect, make it the best it could be. That metaphor comes from my deep appreciation for both writing and blues and jazz music, and is my expression of something like how James Baldwin describes jazz music: as songs carrying personal messages—like musical memoirs—messages which the musician, like the writer, has to struggle with and strive to express.

As chance would have it, Otis has long been captivated by Baldwin too; he even mentions Baldwin in the latter part of the memoir. His Baldwin-esque prose provided a stylistic platform for me upon which to build and to add poetic flourishes to attempt to capture the true message—the meaning of his journey. Otis said he aspired to add flourishes to his prose—to achieve Baldwin's power and style. I said something like "just about every writer wishes he could do that!" We laughed. And with the conclusion of that meeting at Hamilton's restaurant, over a drink, thinking, "Now that's 'classic Otis'! This guy's got style, class," our working relationship began, as did our friendship.

As the months and the chapters rolled on, we came to find that we have much in common. I will not detail those commonalities here for sake of time and paper, but suffice it to say this literary partnership has turned into a friendship that has been deeply gratifying. A unique experience that has made the past year a pleasure and an education. To paraphrase Melville's magnum opus, Moby Dick, this memoir, this magnum opus has been "my Yale and my Harvard" in editing. Now that we have seen this into print between two covers, Otis's ship can set sail, wherever the literary winds may take it. Hopefully into the hands of readers who will appreciate the depth of the voyage within.

– Justin R. Wert, Ph.D.

Acknowledgements

I want to thank my editor and friend, Dr. Justin Wert, Professor of English and head of the Department of English at Piedmont Virginia Community College (PVCC). Dr. Wert shaped and molded the manuscript, enabling it to flow more freely and evenly. His requirement that I be more explicative and plaintive in my description of events caused me to flesh out with more detail and recall more memories than I thought I could remember. His poetic contributions to the text, in the form of epigrams, added a poetic flavor and helped to accentuate what each chapter was truly about. Our common appreciation for the role of poetry either by itself or as a part of a broader narrative made all of this complementary.

Special thanks are reserved for Faye Royster Tuck, an experienced historical researcher, specializing in Halifax County, Virginia, Southside, Virginia and North Carolina. Mrs. Tuck uncovered many gems of irreplaceable value about the Moons and the Penicks.

Amanda J. Cook of Amanda J. Cook Genealogical Services, a member of the Georgia Chapter of the Association of Professional Genealogists was the primary researcher for the Lee and Williams family histories. Mrs. Cook was able to travel to court houses in Fitzgerald, Georgia and to Macon, Georgia to uncover and reproduce court records providing primary source data for the Lee and Williams family facts outlined in this memoir.

Joye Lett Quinn, also a member of the Georgia Chapter of the Association of Professional Genealogists expanded upon both Mrs. Cook's work and Mrs. Tuck's work and produced the family diagrams included in the text.

A special word of thanks to the folks at Charlottesville Press, Inc., especially Joshua P. Smith and Scott E. Cook, for their very able assistance with the layout and cover design required to bring the book to publication.

To my youngest son, Justin Patrick Palmer Lee, Esq., thanks for your continued encouragement and enthusiasm for the project. Justin lent his support from the very beginning. While standing on an Amtrak train platform waiting for a train to take me to Philadelphia, Pennsylvania, after visiting my Aunt Louise in Mt. Vernon, New York, Justin called me from his dormitory room at law school to say he had just read the first chapter. "You've got some good moments in there man," he told me. I was at once filled with appreciation and encouragement. A smile, a grin and a quiet sigh of confidence remained with me as I reflected upon that phone call time and again over the years.

PREFACE

In part, this book arose out of my reading of the short biographies published by the New York Times to honor the victims of the 9/11 terror attacks, shortly after their identities became known. I was moved by the individual stories. And the purpose behind the biographies, which was, as I understood it, because so many of the victims left so little behind in the way of knowledge about themselves that their children could hold on to. Their deaths were so unexpected and so many of them died at a young age and left young children who would always wonder about who that person was who was their lost parent(s). What kind of person was he or she and what did they think about their world and their place in it.

When my father died I was privileged to have known him intimately for 53 years. But his death still left a void because, among other things, I did not know how he really felt about his life and the times he endured. And I do not want my children to have that void in their lives. You can live with parents, and adore them but not really know them because all of us retain an undisclosed side that unless revealed voluntarily will remain secret. And what is the purpose behind secrecy? To hide something or not reveal it because it might not reflect well upon you? My mother has often told me that her parents discussed little about their backgrounds and family histories. What she learned about her family she learned through observation.

This endeavor has also been about living a life of transparency as much as one can. I want my life's history to be as pellucid as feasible. My life is not unique or special, to be distinguished from the thousands of lawyers who labor every day in their offices to obtain justice for their clients and support their families. But each path is different and unique to that individual. This has been my path. Each path is a part of the tapestry of a family's quilt. My patch is set forth herein.

This memoir has also been a legacy project. I want to leave my family something lasting and psychologically sustaining. They will have their memories, I know but, I want to give more than just memories, I want to give them "me," in language and in deed. I want to give them my essence, the essential me, the raison d'etre, a light into the opaque, the hand that moves my clock; not just the outside but the inside as well. I want to give them something that will be transcendent in the afterlife religious culture we live in. This has been my primary motivation.

The beginnings of this project can also be traced to a conversation I had on a train ride during one of my frequent commutes from Philadelphia, Pennsylvania to Charlottesville, Virginia during the middle to late nineties and the early 2000s. I had the coincidence to sit by a White man named Joseph C. Pearce who at the time lived in Faber, Virginia. I knew nothing about him except that we sat together for the two hour ride on train #19, the Crescent. His encouragement that I should write during that interval remained with me through the years. And I have not spoken with him since that train ride until just recently. I did not know at the time that Mr. Pearce was a prominent author and has written over ten books on "human intelligence, creativity and learning." *See, www.harpercollins.com/authors/7543/ Joseph_C_Pearce/index.aspx.*

Obviously this book does not reflect my entire life, nor every event that took place in this period. And it does not reflect the latter years of my professional life: my law practice experience in Virginia commencing in 1991 which is ongoing and represents the capstone of my career as a lawyer. Neither do I discuss the founding of the Fitzgerald Company, a real estate management, investment, remodeling and renovation firm, successor to the Lee Estate's business interest: a company I founded and have run with the indispensable assistance of my wife and mother over the last twelve years. But herein, I have attempted to recall the more poignant and memorable events that occurred during the early years that shaped the broad outlines of my life and that had pivotal impact.

This slice of my life occurred during a time of racial segregation in America and in Virginia specifically. I was impacted by these events and my outlook is drawn from my experiences and informed by that history.

The names of four individuals mentioned in the text have been changed to protect their identities. Balance and truth have been weighed with truth the final arbiter of the memoir. I hope that my family will now have a written record of some of the members of our family and a credible source upon which to embark on their own research and elucidation of our family history.

I

THE WELL

OUTH BOSTON'S RUSTIC ENVIRONS are intoxicating belying the history of its confederate past. Quaint shops selling antiques populate the downtown. Frame and brick antebellum houses line both sides of the main avenues. The rough calloused tobacco stained hands of field workers with straw hats meet you as you walk about the streets. The side streets are hilly and green. Horses harnessed with plows being pulled by farmers preparing their fields for planting are a common sight. Memories that come to mind are of white and brown chickens having their heads cutoff, their torsos soaked in scalding water to loosen their feathers for picking.

Everything appears to be within walking distance. A sense of nostalgia and of the yesteryear overtakes me when I visit South Boston. The pastel pink hospital on Main Street where I was born exudes a peaceful plantation like aura—tranquil, serene and lazy.

Before indoor plumbing was installed in my grandparents' home, wide grey metal wash tubs were used for bathing. Tall wooden outhouses served as toilets, wood burning cast iron cook stoves cooperated with my grandmother and resulted in scrumptious mouth-watering meals. Manual water pumps in the shape of a backward "f" affixed on top of water wells provided our water. White metal buckets with lids trimmed in red known as "slop jars"—now referred to as "chamber pots"—would be placed in each bedroom at night and emptied each morning to rid the house of human excrement accumulated during the night. All the stuff of country life in the late forties and early fifties in South Boston, Virginia. I remember these artifacts as a chorus of song, a tapestry of hand woven fabric, an unrehearsed cacophony of the rural life made real by my maternal grandmother and grandfather as they fought to make a life out of the hard times in which they lived.

In 1795 Patrick Moon, the eldest of record, my great-great-grandfather was born somewhere near Bannister, Halifax, Virginia, now known as South Boston, Virginia in Halifax County. It is reasonably assumed based upon an examination of census records taken before 1865 that he was owned by Parham Moon, the putative slave owner, who was born in 1806 and who died in 1866 in Halifax County,

Virginia. During his lifetime Parham Moon owned 38 slaves, one of whom was a male age 26 prior to 1870. In the 1870 Census, Patrick Moon was noted to be 35 years of age. Parham Moon was one of the largest slave owners in the county at this time. Parham Moon died leaving three sons: James A., Thomas A., and Edward B. Moon. At his death in July of 1866 he left a will which recited the following, "as the slaves given to the older sons have been liberated by law."[1]

Patrick Henry Moon built the family house on College Street with his own hands. The house sat on a half-acre of land. His family lived on the tract of land before title to it was conveyed by deed to Patrick Moon's mother Elizabeth Johnson Moon on March 15, 1902, from the trustees of the South Boston Mutual Aid Society. The white frame house sat on a hill. It had a wide front porch with narrow decorative columns standing perpendicular to the porch that supported the porch roof. The front yard was small but well maintained. He kept the yards, front and right side neatly cut, using an old iron push mower with rubber tires around the wheels. There was no back yard because in the back of the house there was only land for farming. On the left side there was little grass, just black dirt and bare spots. The west side of the house bordered the Poindexter House. He painted the white wood frames on the exterior every three or four years. The red tin metal roof looked as though it had been painted even if it hadn't. The front yard had no natural boundary but simply meandered into the adjoining yard on the eastern side of the property on which another house sat that my grandfather also owned, all cut to blend in with a few shrubs and a small dwarf tree at the edge of the front yard between the two houses.

Great-great-grandmother, Elizabeth Johnson Moon, circa 1869

South Boston is a small unincorporated agricultural country town on the south side of Virginia in Halifax County, located 31 miles north of Danville, Virginia not far from the northern border of North Carolina. It is a poor town—and still is by most accounts.

I remember the warm fire my grandmother "Helen," as she was known to me during my childhood, would make in the fire place in the living room which was off to the left as you entered the house from the front porch. She would plop down with a sigh of exhaustion, dead tired in the upholstered end chair which sat on the left as you entered the living room and fall dead to sleep after a day that began around the house at 5:00 am. In a few moments she would be snoring as we watched The Lawrence Welk Show.

My maternal grandmother Helen was hard working: she was always busy washing clothes, cooking or cleaning. A slender thread of a woman, she was fair skinned and was born in 1893 in Halifax County. She was a serious Christian.

Her mother was Margaret Sue Penick born in 1861. Margaret married a "Johnson" but the date of the marriage is unknown. Her maternal grandfather, Armistead Penick, was born a slave of record in Halifax County in 1820.[2] Armistead married "Susan" who was born in 1825. Armistead was the son of Peter and Milly

Penick. By the will of Nathan Penick, his owner, probated in Halifax County Court on August 22, 1853, Armistead was bequeathed to Nathan Penick's son William Penick. William Penick in settlement of his father's estate purchased Armistead for $875.00. Armistead's brother Burwell married Isabella Johnson, the sister of Elizabeth "Lizzie" Johnson Moon, Patrick Moon's mother. The Penicks and the Moons were known to each other before their marriage 1924.

Helen Moon, maternal grandmother, circa 1965

Grandmother did a lot of walking to get to her job as a housekeeper. She walked from College Street where the family home was to Main Street near downtown, a distance of at least three miles, possibly more. This was all the way downtown every day. Grandmother was paid $5.00 a week to keep house and cook for Mr. McKinney, the local Commonwealth's Attorney. Her day began before his kids went to school, and she worked until 7:00 pm each evening. After she finished working in the house, my mother and her brother walked to meet her on most nights. They did this so that she would not have to walk from his home near downtown to hers alone at night. She suffered from a heart condition. The family was concerned that she might be attacked by derelicts or other unseemly characters. Her slight build and small frame would not enable her to put up much resistance. My mother says it was a "horrible experience" trying to meet her each night to prevent her from walking home alone at night. "It was dark," Mother recalls, "anything could have happened."

During their youth, my mother and her sisters did their share of "days work" as it is called in the Black community. Mother worked for White folks in their homes as an adolescent before she went to college. One White woman in particular, Mary Poindexter, a spinster, lived next door by herself in a large white painted frame house. The house was more than she needed for herself, but she had apparently inherited the house from her family. She had a sister Sally who tried to stay with her on many occasions, but as Mother relates, "you never heard such quarrelling and fighting as between those two, they could not live together." Mary also had a brother Henry who owned a small farm across the street, "you could see the white framed house from the front steps," said mother. The Moons got their milk and butter from Henry Poindexter.

Mary Poindexter taught Mother and her sisters the fundamentals of "good old house" cleaning. "If you wanted to learn how to clean a house, go work for that White woman" the talk was, as recited by mother. "Ms. Mary," as she was called by the local Blacks, required that my mother and her sister Louise get on their knees to scrub her floors. She made them get into those crevices around the corners and edges of walls and doorways to get the dust that was not visible at first sight, the dust that was trying to hide. Mary was frail, thin and prickly. She owned an old black Buick automobile which she drove with reckless abandon up and down College Street and back and forth from Main Street as though there was no tomorrow. Mother was asked to stay with her at night because the old White woman did not want to be left alone in her old spacious house at night. Since Mary was good enough to let them use the water she paid Mother 50 cents a night each time she stayed with her. Mother and her sisters worked for Mary Poindexter and did many chores around her house for fifty cents an hour until they left home to go to work or to college.

The Moons lived among and around White folks. At this time housing was not, in this locality, segregated by race: Mary lived on the left and Henry in front across the street from grandmother Helen's house. Before Mary had the well dug, all of the families got their water from a spring not far from the house about a block down the road toward downtown. All of them carried buckets to carry the water from the spring to their houses for cooking and bathing and drinking. After the well was dug, both families, the Poindexters and Moons, shared the well. The well was located on Mary Poindexter's property. The well was the life blood of their existence on College Street. The role it played in their lives can be better understood by a poem I have written to memorialize it:

The Well

I am the well on the lot adjoining your grandfather's house in South Boston, Virginia. The waters within me are deep, dark, life giving, sonorous in tone, nourishing and sustaining. I am reflective of many passers-by with stories of division, thirst quenching in my reprieves, my possibilities are endless. The well is my repository. I am confined by my structure but escape is not my purpose.

That which I hold is vital to your life, try living without me.

My primordial essence, my source and my life are as far and as wide as the Nile, the Niger, the Neva, the Mississippi, and the Indus rivers. I was here before any of you, before history, before the Egyptians, the Nubians, the Bubi and the Ewe. I am what you want me to be, intrepid, elastic, impervious, and the genesis.

What I do not know does it matter? I knew it all at one time. I know things beyond your comprehension. Some say it matters not, I think it matters greatly.

I am a well just across the line from your grandmother's yard. Deep, foreboding, resplendent, refreshing, urgent, boiling, helpful and inviting, subject to drying up like a twig or a limb from a dying root.

I am a well, I sit just across the boundary line of your grandmother's house. I require some effort to get to. When you come you must bring something worthwhile that will retain what I have to give. I sit at the end of a trodden path.

To get to me you must pass a wood shed on the right side of the beaten path, my nearest neighbor and friend. We share nature's wisdom of creation.

This shed is full of chopped wood, kindling, wood chips and sawdust, stored there by Patrick Henry Moon. The smell of the wood is refreshing, rustic and awakening to the senses. Here you will find the wood of maple, tulip, oak and pine.

An old ax is posited in the center of the chopping block in the center of the floor it awaits your efforts in the storehouse.

I am constructed in cylindrical shape, made of moss covered granite, sandstone and clay. I extend above the ground and below the surface to an unknown depth.

You come to me for what you need. I provide you with water the substance of life, embodied in my experiences and interred in the bones of the mortar that binds my wounds. I can heal your sores and your soul. I am the perennial elixir of life. My element flows in the blood of man, but I cannot change his heart, his beliefs, or his karma.

I am your well. Your fountain, your rock of ages, that which saves you from aridity and barrenness. I am the well of history. Drink deep, absorb thoroughly and remember.

I am green , I am blue, I am black, I am brown. I am distant yet close. I am what you make of me. What you are embodies me. We are inseparable, indistinguishable from one another. I am more of you than you are.

You are what you are and I am that which I am. Drawn from the elements of the earth and to the elements we shall return. But my existence is eternity.

— — —

Patrick Moon, my grandfather, was a carpenter by trade. He built "hogsheads," tobacco barrels. He traveled throughout the South selling and making his barrels. He earned a living sufficient to support his family from barrel making and farming. And he was a member of the Masons and the Grand United Order of Oddfellows, national Black fraternal organizations. Patrick and Helen belonged to and attended different churches. He belonged to Mt. Olive Baptist Church and she to First Baptist Church near downtown. Mt. Olive was closer to the home place.

I remember Patrick Moon sitting on his porch rolling his tobacco making his cigarettes and clearing his throat with a double "...ummm ummm." As young kids, my cousins and I would tease the old man and play hide and seek with him, except he really was not playing.

My grandfather slept in a single bed in the bedroom on the right at the end of the hallway which extended from the front of the house to the dining room in the back. He would go to bed each night about the same time in his bed by the window. The room was dark and smelled of his presence, a musty antique smell, a combination of chopped wood, split logs and old books. The bed was the equivalent of a twin bed, narrow and long, and made of metal with metal springs, with a brown metallic finish which served as a box spring, supporting the single slab of mattress. The bed was unadorned satisfying only the essentials. After years of sleeping in this bed the mattress had automatically adjusted to the contours of his frame.

My grandfather enjoyed a drink of whisky now and then as one of his delights. But his favorite drink was tea. That man loved his tea, hot and cold.

He worked hard and he drank hard. He owned a team of horses that he used to plow his fields and plant his crops. The team was located in the rear of the land in back of the house. He was the first to own an automobile in his community, a black Buick. He drank moonshine as well as standard spirits. The moonshine was distilled over in "Bloodfield," the Bowery of South Boston. Mother says that "everything went on in Bloodfield." This area was located not too far from mother's elementary school. While in his fifties and when Mother was a teenager, after drinking good whisky and moonshine for some time, Patrick Moon experienced a life changing event—what that life changing event was no one knows—one that came close to ending his life, one that almost killed him. He stopped all drinking after that and never drank again. Whatever happened, it was powerful enough to have changed his behavior, but anyone with a substance abuse problem can imagine this consequence.

Mother says she remembers her dad bringing her and her brother candy, "Baby Ruths," when he returned from town. And she remembered enjoying eating the sweet cherries known as "black hearts" that he grew on the land back of the house. She says "they were so sweet and good," she smiled when reminiscing about them. Mother also remembered the team of horses her father kept in a barn in the rear of the land they lived on.

Mother also recounts that she was named for father's sister who died before she was born. This sister was named "Rose," and she was blind when she died.

Between late 1962 and 1965, my grandparents moved in with us in Charlottesville. They stayed in my room which had twin beds, and I moved to the bedroom on the other end near the alley. When I arrived home from school, granddad would be gone. I would be curious and concerned figuring that he would wander his way back home. But when my mother and father came in, they would be frantic and start searching for him around the neighborhood me included. We usually found him near the graveyard, Oakwood Cemetary, in back of the house. My grandfather stayed with us until he passed on October 29, 1963 at 9:15 am at the University of Virginia Hospital. He was 80 years old. At long last his heart had given out.

When I would come home after school after grandfather died, grandmother would be ironing clothes and she would speak about the judgment day coming. She was convinced judgment day was close at hand. Was this because of the recent death of her husband, my grandfather, or was it a premonition about her own death that was not that far away? Grandmother moved away not long after grand-dad's death. She went to live with her oldest daughter Margaret in Greensboro, North Carolina. It was there that she finally succumbed to a heart condition in February of 1969. She was 76 years old. Though both of my grandparents are buried in South Boston, neither one died there.

When my grandfather died, my father remarked "there was nothing wrong with him, he died of dehydration."

Patrick Moon, maternal grandfather, in South Boston, circa 1953

Patrick Moon, senior, never quit. He and my grandmother, who was twenty years younger than he when they married, raised four children: two sisters of the "half-blood" that my grandmother had before her marriage to Patrick Moon and two children products of their union, Patrick Moon, Jr. born in 1927, and my mother, Rosa Belle Moon born in 1925. Both grandparents had been married before they married each other. The record is in conflict because both Helen and Patrick were recorded in the public record as having been widowed, but Patrick is known to have been divorced before marrying Helen. The genealogical records reveal that the Black families in South Boston after 1865 probably were familiar to each other. It was not unusual for these families to marry within their small community of friends and neighbors. The Moons, Penicks and Johnsons knew each other and married between the families. My grandfather and grandmother formed a successful union, because they knew what they were getting into and knew what each expected from the other and their past histories.

My mother's oldest sister, Margaret, greatly influenced mother's pursuit of higher education. Margaret taught school in South Boston during Mother's youth at the M. H. Coleman Elementary School, the same grammar school Mother attended. Coleman was within walking distance from the family home on College Street. The white frame College Street house was set on an elevated plot of land, making it a belvedere for the scene beyond. The sun having risen earlier, still shone of its variegated hues, Mother stood looking out over the plowed fields from the front porch of the house on many mornings, dressed in a sky blue jumper, dotted with vertical and horizontal plaid swatches of brown, green and yellow. Her white blouse crisply ironed by a mother who rose before dawn each week day to see that her family was cared for before she went to care for a family not of her own. With her books tucked neatly under her left arm; shoes worn and scuffed but speckled with the remnants of what remained of the polish she rubbed on them a few days earlier; her brown socks, given to her from the McKinney family, crumpled at the top, half up and half down, she could see her grammar school from her front steps. There, even at her young age she knew that her future was not in South Boston. Its circumference was too limited even for her limited vision at that stage of her life. Something inside of her beckoned her toward the horizon, like Captain Ahab in Herman Melville's *Moby Dick* to find the "great white whale" out there somewhere, but not in South Boston.

Mother relates that in 1943 she enrolled at Fort Valley State College because Margaret was there with her husband Robert L. Wynn, who was working on the campus at that time. When Mother first arrived at Fort Valley, she stayed off campus with Margaret and Wynn who were renting an apartment at the time. Mother kept Lorraine, their oldest and only daughter at the time, taking her to and from the baby sitter in between her classes. After her last class she picked up Lorraine and took her home waiting there until Margaret and Wynn came home for the evening. During her second year, Mother moved on campus and Margaret and Wynn moved to North Carolina.

Mother and Dad worked their way through college; they had to. They worked in the college dining room as waitress and waiter. It was there that they met and formed a relationship that would culminate in marriage in 1946. Mother often, upon reflection, says "Lee waited on the faculty in the faculty dining room, and I waited on the students in the student dining hall. Lee got to eat the best of the food." She says that she used her relationship with him to get him to share his good fortune with her from time to time.

During the summer of those years, Mother worked in New York in Westchester County, in Pelham, doing maid's work. She worked for a white family named Baker. Mother related that "Mrs. Baker was a nice lady. Nobody made me do this. I was self-motivated. I had to earn money for my tuition." She says she never got $10.00 from her parents to support her college education. Helen went to New York and worked at Mrs. Baker's during the time Mother was in school. To save money, she stayed with Margaret in Greensboro, North Carolina one year during her breaks before finishing college. She paid no rent because in exchange for her room and board she babysat Margaret Lorraine. She would hitch a ride home to visit her parents when Margaret drove there, and she made occasional trips by bus paid for from the money she earned working at the college.

In Greensboro, Margaret taught school and Wynn worked as a professional in Agriculture at North Carolina A&T State College. Ironically, Margaret and Mother both ended up marrying men from Georgia. Of the two half sisters, Margaret and

Louise, Margaret went to college and became a teacher; the other, Louise, became a professional caterer. Margaret owned her own home, but Louise never acquired real property. But both of them owned automobiles. Louise was the professional cook of the family and Margaret the least endowed cook in the family.

This was the life that my mother knew as she grew up. She once said of herself that, "I'm just a quiet, conservative country girl."

Hers was not a harsh life, though it was limited in its horizons, but she grew up strong nevertheless: secure in the knowledge of knowing who her father was, having his care and knowing who her mother was and having her love. She was well fed and clothed. Poverty was not her next door neighbor. When she came of age, she left these environs to get an education. Leaving behind the world known as South Boston, for southern Georgia and Richmond, Virginia and later Charlottesville.

— — —

Mother was raised in South Boston, Virginia, in Halifax County. Her father was Patrick Henry Moon and her mother was Helen Wilson Penick. Patrick Henry Moon, was a reticent, taciturn, and austere man with a Willie Stroud, Gary Cooper-esque demeanor. Patrick Moon was a tall, lean and balding American of African descent. He was the third generation of Patrick Moons whose past ancestors can be traced to slavery. A man of few words, he was dour, sullen, but also determined, and my youngest son is his namesake.

Patrick Henry Moon, my great-great-grandfather married Judah or Judy who was born in 1805. Both were born somewhere between Roanoke, Halifax County in Virginia. Patrick and Judah had three children William, Fannie and my great grandfather Patrick Moon. My great grandfather was born between 1835 and 1839 in Bannister Township, Halifax County and married Elizabeth "Lizzie" Johnson who was born in 1843. They were married in 1867. From this union , my grandfather Patrick Henry Moon was born between 1862 and 1879. Six other children were born of this union: Mary J., Madison, Rollin, Emely, James T., and Robert.

Of Patrick Henry Moon's two sisters, Louise Boykin or "Aunt Lou," (possibly Mary J.) stayed in the bedroom on the right as you entered the home on College Street. She stayed there until she died. I remember seeing her there when we visited. Emely, his oldest sister, who migrated to Hartford, Connecticut from Social Circle in Atlanta, Georgia, died in Hartford. The Moon family owned the land and the homestead before Patrick and Helen married. It was Emely that Dad did business with to safe guard mother's interest in the College Street homestead, a tale to be discussed further on. There is some confusion in the record about "Aunt Tee Ida," whether she was a sister of my grandfather. I remember this woman as a thin tall dark skinned woman. I remember her coming to the house in South Boston on occasion. She married Bernard, who Mother remembered as one of Helen Moon's cousins. Little is known about the lives of Patrick's brothers.

Patrick and Helen Moon were married on July 16, 1924 in South Boston, Virginia. Two children were born of this union, my mother Rosa Belle born in 1925 and her brother Patrick Henry Moon, Jr., in 1928. Together they raised four children, two from the union of their marriage and two children not born of that

Patrick Moon Sr. and Helen Moon, circa 1956

union, but close siblings nonetheless. Ten to twelve years separated the children of the whole-blood from those of the half-blood.

As a young child visiting South Boston from time to time during the summer and at family gatherings, I seldom interacted with my grandfather. He was present and accounted for, but not integrated into the fabric of the frolic and fun these family gatherings normally entailed. His taciturnity was emblematic of his life style. You could usually find him sitting alone smoking his self-rolled cigarettes on the front porch away from everybody else. Yet, he was responsible for the well-being and the physical facilities within which these gatherings took place. It was as though Patrick Moon was a picture on the wall, seen but silent, communicating a presence but not a focal point.

His was a life of opaqueness, stolid, productive but not completely understood. As I turn the pages of my nascent memory to recollect my thoughts about this man, I am struck by the paucity of real contacts, the lack of real time spent getting to know my grandfather. I never kissed him or hugged him or got close enough to know his smell. Not to mention getting to know what he thought about his world or the people in it. What a loss. There was no "bonding" with him that we talk about today, the expected connection between children and grandparents.

Perhaps it was not easy for older people of that generation to talk with young folks, to reach out to them. Especially if their personalities did not embrace that sort of thing. Their lives had experienced so much that the younger generation could not relate to, not to mention "bear up under." The experiences that made up his world included some of the worst of times for Black people. Maybe their world was so absorbed with the troubles they had seen and experienced that silence and introspection were their only true friends.

2

RESPECT THE WATER

N ONE OF THE DAYS during my last summer visit with my first cousin, Edwin and his close friend Al, the three of us went to the neighborhood pool, Wilson Woods Pool not far from Edwin's apartment. Edwin and Al had been to summer camps and knew how to swim, but I didn't. The pools in New York were integrated and Whites and Blacks swam together—color did not matter. It was a bright sunny day, the weather was perfect. Edwin and Al got on the diving board in the deep end and dived in. They had been used to doing this because the pool was accessible to them and because they had swimming experience. Like a babe out of water literally, I followed them without hesitation, and I too jumped off of the diving board and into the deep water with no idea about what to do next.

My exposure to swimming was next to nil. I remember going to our segregated swimming pool in Richmond, Virginia and just belly flopping in the shallow water, but nothing resembling swimming. I remember my father who had taken me to the pool, in Richmond, standing outside of the fence and watching me for a few moments before he left. I had not had any swimming lessons or instruction on water safety and that ignorance almost cost me my life. Swimming was not in the family culture, so no emphasis was placed on this essential skill. Benign neglect carries a price. Even well intentioned misjudgments carry a price. Now in the deep water without a clue as to what to do next, panic set in—a swimmer's worst enemy. Survival was at stake. I fought the water, splashing and whirling–all to no avail. The water, ever present, consumed my taut body, and won all battles to displace it in this unequal war. In the nanoseconds of this episode, my life spread across my mind in a collage of pictures. I could see everything that I had done in my short life. I was oblivious to what was going on around me. It was as though I was encased in a time warp viewing a motion picture of my life story being played for my sole attentive benefit, while the world around me was evolving, possibly observing my panic fight for life. The noises of other kids playing in the water and having fun was deaf to my ears. I forgot about Edwin and Al, Mom and Dad, and Aunt Louise, everything was in slow motion. The next thing I remember was being pulled out of the pool by a young White lifeguard. With his right forearm taut around my neck he frog kicked his way to the closest side of the pool with me in tow. With the help of his colleagues, I was hoisted out of the pool and laid onto the deck of the pool. I lay prostrate on the pool deck gasping for breath, crying out of panic and emotion with people hovering over me and one of them, kneeling over me, pumping my chest and saying "stand back, stand back." Later an older White man, an official at the pool, said in a calming tone, "he'll be alright, he'll be alright." I had not swallowed much water because I was rescued quickly and fought so strongly that my buoyancy kept me from sinking below the surface only a few times before being pulled out. I never told my parents about this incident. And to the best of my knowledge, neither Edwin nor Al told anyone about it. It is an indelible memory, planted as though it had happened yesterday.

Even though the Moon-Penick family did not "have much," the family on the other hand was well off comparatively for Black people of that era. The family was progressive, industrious, hard-working, had its "high yellow" or mulatto element, owned real property and had college educated men and women counted among its number. The patriarch of the Moon family as we have seen had a definable skill and trade. So there was a station in life that the family occupied, back in the 40s, 50s and 60s.

Six male children were born in the Moon-Penick family between 1928 and 1954. Patrick Moon, Jr., one of these six, my uncle whom I knew but never loved, was mother's only brother. Born in the next generation was Walter Cecil Parker, Aunt Willnett's only son; me, Otis Lee, Jr., Rosa's boy; Ralph, Patrick Moon, Jr.'s son; Edwin Louis Johnson, Aunt Louise's son, one of my mother's half-sisters; and Robert L. Wynn II, "Bobby," the son of Margaret, my mother's other half-sister. Though my mother's sisters were technically half-sisters none of us thought of them in that way. All of my aunts were whole aunts in all respects.

Patrick Henry Moon, Jr, or "Junious" we called him, was a man who lived an adult life of dereliction, depravity and criminality, though his younger days may have been spent more fruitfully. He was the subject of a misbegotten upbringing for whatever reason, in which alcohol played no small part. We can only speculate on what went awry, perhaps he could not adjust to the life he saw around him and the family he grew up in. Mother avows that Junious's downfall began when he started drinking with that group in "Bloodfield." Town derelicts and moonshiners congregated in Bloodfield. This area was the den of iniquity of South Boston. Patrick Moon, the elder, drank but he created no disturbance after doing so; he kept to himself. But Junious went wild and exploded as if something had gone off in him and ignited a disease that took over. Rationality was no longer a factor, barbarism ruled him after imbibing. Education was not a pursuit he reached for. Mother recalls that Junious worried his father, Patrick Moon, Sr., relentlessly to let him build a house on the lot next door to the main house. Eventually, his father relented and allowed him to build the house which he did all by himself. It was the single most important achievement in his life, a life that was otherwise characterized by miscreancy.

During his lifetime, Junious was in and out of jail on various petty and felonious offenses. We had finished a full day of play and fun at grandma's house during one of my summer stays in South Boston. All bathed and fed, Edwin and I were in bed but not yet asleep. The other adults were going about their business. It was about 9:00 p.m. Out of the blue a commotion unfolded near the front door at the upper end of the hallway. Junious came home in a drunken stupor and terrorized the house. There he was full of hell fire, brimstone and rascality, wanting to fight whoever was in his midst. We were startled by the uproar he made. It took all of Aunt Louise's savvy to calm him down. She took the lead to resolve the melee. The last criminal offense Junious was convicted of sent him to prison for several years. I remember going with Mother and my grandparents to visit him at the prison farm somewhere in south-side Virginia. It was a surreal place that looked like a tranquil garden as you approached the grounds belying what its real purpose was. I stayed in the car while the grown folks went inside to make the visit. Most of the family was afraid of Junious and kept their distance. Mother once said, "Junious would just as soon take a shot gun and shoot you as look at you," "you hated to see him coming." Mother said "she had never seen a brother like that."

While Junious lived in the small house next door, Mother was afraid for her parents. After we moved to Charlottesville, both of my grandparents eventually came to live with us out of fear that they would be harmed by him. Mother says that she never really got to know her brother, that she had little or no relationship with him because at an early age he was truant and irascible. After many years of fighting the demons within him unsuccessfully, he died alone with no one by his side in that little house he built by himself at the young age of 58.

Ralph, Junious's only child, grew up in South Boston. He was a good looking dark skinned boy with short curly black hair, an infectious smile and a handsome face—a naturally good looking face. His dark brown complexion was even and smooth, the stuff of ebony, a deep lustrous black brown mixture. Ralph had an ebullience and energy about him in his activities that was not characteristic of the other cousins in the Moon-Penick clan, and he was a "southpaw." His mother, Frances Wells Moon, was not close to the family. My recollection of her is opaque and ill-defined. I was in her presence once, at least, but I do not remember what she looked like. She was reclusive and probably did not feel that she was a part of the core grouping of the family because of her background which was murky, lower-class and because of who she was married to.

Above and right:
Ralph Moon, Jr.
(son of Patrick Moon, Jr.),
circa 1953 (above)
and 1962 (right)

Patrick Moon, Jr., South Boston, VA 1979

Three sisters, left to right: Rosa, Louise, and Margaret, Junior's house in background, circa 1955

I do not ever remember seeing Frances at family gatherings though Ralph would be there. During childhood I played with Ralph and Edwin, so I got to know them individually. He stayed with his mother, Frances, who had separated from Junious many years before his death. The house, where Frances lived, was in the Churchill section of South Boston. While we were out playing together in South Boston during a family visit, I ventured down to Ralph's house one day. His house was indistinct, dark, and foreboding, it was not on College Street. Churchill was a lower class enclave of South Boston, nothing inspiring there. Inside, the house was unkempt, mysterious and appeared unwholesome. His mother served us some food, but I did not eat it because I did not trust the cook, the food or the place where the food was prepared. My rejection of the food was instinctive not factual. I did not feel comfortable. My unease was both environmental and familial because there was a strangeness within the relationships that existed, yet these folks were family. Junious, Ralph and Frances were outcasts plain and simple. It did not have to be that way, but because of the paths chosen that is how it developed within the immediate Moon Family. Ralph was a casualty of a dysfunctional family. There was no safety net for Ralph as there had been for Skeeta, one of my first cousins, on the Lee side. Ralph's paternal grandmother, Helen, did not take him in and raise him for a multitude of reasons including because he had a father and a mother living together during this time. But during his early adolescence, Ralph fell through the cracks all the way to the bottom into oblivion.

Ralph stayed with us in Charlottesville one summer during his adolescence for a brief time. But he and I did not get along that well, and he was sent back to South Boston. It was not anticipated that he would stay permanently, but because the two of us did not make it, his stay was shortened. Ralph had habits and insights that were uncomfortable to me, insights that were ahead of my maturity. He was more mature about sex and other sexually sensitive activities than I was. Perhaps Mom and Dad were trying in vain to see if Ralph could be saved or a change could be wrought. But his manner and nature were too advanced. Even at that age he had been exposed to too much for us to overcome. We grew up together sharing many family times in South Boston, but there was the attenuation. Ralph was the black sheep of my generation. He led a life of obscurity in the dark shadows of homosexuality. An opaqueness that was penetrable only by imagination. Hence much was said but most of it remained unspoken. Ralph led a life without discernible definition. He was hardly ever heard from except when he decided to emerge from the shadows with a faint phone call to Aunt Louise. And one day he left me an obscure, indecipherable message on my phone. A life without discernible definition. How did he support himself? Where did he live? Who were his friends? What type of lifestyle did he have? Without knowing for certain, we were left to our imagin-

Otis Lee Sr. with Walter Cecile Parker, Richmond, VA, September 1970

ings and thought the worst. Even to this day we do not conclusively know whether Ralph is dead or alive.

Unlike the shadowy Junious, I got to know Walter Cecil, Aunt Willnett's son. Cecil was just the opposite of Junious: he was quiet, respectful, a smoothie and a lady's man. With his part neatly cut in on the left side of his head, and his hair brushed securely to the right, his smile was enticing. It could charm the poison out of a venomous snake. Cecil grew up in Richmond, Virginia. I got to know him while we lived there. His handsome looks hid his demons. Cecil was also one who did not pursue an education. There was little or no tradition in his family that channeled him in that direction, although there were plenty of examples in his extended family. Cecil did odd jobs to make a living: nothing substantial or of any real sustaining value. Walter Cecil liked to drive cars, he was a good driver, and could have earned a good living driving long haul trucks or as a chauffeur, or taxi cab driver, but Cecil failed to do anything with this skill or make much of himself. Years later after we moved to Charlottesville, Cecil died of diseases associated with alcoholism. "Aunt Rose and Cousin Lee," he called Mom and Dad. Cecil was a nice kid, a handsome kid, but I don't know if Cecil ever got the discipline he required because of his father's disability, but we all loved Walter Cecil, and hated that his end came the way it did. There was a void in his life somewhere that never got filled, and alcohol was a convenient but deleterious substitute. Cecil died in one of Dad's rental properties on the second floor on Grace Street in the West End where he lived for a considerable time with his second wife and his two children by her, Sandy and W.C., before his death.

Edwin, Aunt Louise's only child, was a pampered, spoiled child from birth but without privilege. His mother had no privilege to bestow on him. After all, her life was a bootstrap operation from birth as was that of her older sister Margaret, except for a big variation, with Patrick Moon their step-father, supplying both the boots and the straps. Margaret was the child of Helen Penick and Arthur Howerton who were married in Halifax County on September 25, 1911. They were married when she was born. That marriage ended because of Howerton's early death, the cause of which is unknown. Helen Moon said on her sworn marriage license that she was widowed at the time she married Patrick Moon. Louise was a child born out of wedlock the public record reveals, though during her lifetime she disclaimed this background. Aunt Louise says she was a Johnson before she married a Johnson. There is a splinter of plausibility to this claim because my great grandfather married a Johnson and somewhere down the line maybe a Johnson of that clan fathered Louise with Helen Penick, but who knows? Margaret came to live, along with Louise, with Patrick Moon and Helen Moon after Patrick and Helen married. Both were reared in his home on College Street. Though not acknowledged as

Edwin and his Volkswagon, Mt. Vernon High School, 1965

such and perhaps not appreciated as he should have been, Patrick Moon was the "black knight" to the rescue, but his armor was not "shining." It dimly shone.

Edwin was "high yellow" in pigmentation, a mulatto, but the complexion of his character was brown like the rest of us. Perhaps his skin color contributed, inter alia, to his mother's view of his "specialness." He always had special care. He had to have special food, the best toys, and summer camps when the rest of us played in the rough fields of South Boston and Fitzgerald, Georgia during the summer.

During one of several stays during the summer in the early days of my youth, I stayed with Edwin and Aunt Louise in their apartment in Mt. Vernon, New York. I got to know some of his friends, Al and Mirabel and several others. I played pickup basketball during my later stays and went swimming with Edwin and Al during my earlier visits. I played with the neighborhood kids in the local park. I played so much that I got to know the guys who hung out around there. And I got my first case of jock itch and prickly heat. Because of my height and desire I was always chosen by the kid "who had next," on the basketball court, which was not far from their apartment. I was one of the "boys." Edwin did not play. He seldom mixed it up with the neighborhood ball players, but I relished the acceptance.

Edwin started taking piano lessons, and he showed me while his mother was looking on what he could play. I was not impressed but my competitive instincts were stirred. I had been taking piano for a while and stopped but seeing him "do his thing" convinced me right then to resume my lessons. The major difference between Edwin and me was that I was grounded in a "rougher reality." I engaged more in the bump and grind of life even at that age than he did or was allowed to do. The absence of a father, who died when he was very young, I am sure contributed to his apparent timidity in certain areas of his life.

When Aunt Louise was away during the day during my summer visits, Edwin would have girls over to the apartment, and grinding the girls up against the inside of the apartment door was the central activity until the girls had to go home and the time was approaching when Aunt Louise would be coming home. The boldness of this activity and the ease with which it was accepted by the girls was intriguing to me. The girls did not know me and there was little time to get to know any of them, so all I could do was watch, though if given the chance I would have participated.

Paradoxically, in my adolescent naiveté, I was superficially envious of Edwin's spoilage with all of the "baubles and beads" that Aunt Louise showered on him. I thought that these toys and trinkets and clothes were things that I wanted.

Edwin was provided with just about everything he wanted that his single mother thought her precious child needed. Edwin's dad died when he was a young child, no older than three years old. And his mother never married again, though she probably had several chances. I am sure she felt an added burden to get it right, her way, since she was raising him without his father. His mother worked as a caterer for the "well to do" in Westchester County, but she owned her business. His mother did not attend college, but she felt the influence of education very deeply and she required that he attend college. However, there was no serious culture of academics in his family since his mother did not attend college, and his college life was short-lived, brought on by his indulgences in activities beyond the scope of normal college life. With all of his "specialness" his mother neglected to teach him how to fend for himself, to have self-discipline, and how to manage stress, how to accept and discharge responsibility, how to live independently of her. Edwin had difficulty breaking away from his mother's powerful influence, her well-intentioned but dominating influence that proved destructive of the strength required to be a man. Female dominated households with one male child present can often result in a skewed relationship between the two. I doubt if Edwin ever had a real job in his life that required him to do some serious work for a prolonged time independent of his mother. When the time came for Edwin to shoulder adult responsibilities—which included the burden of raising and supporting a young child, the pressure of getting along with the equally powerful influence of a streetwise wife who rebelled against his mother, with him in the middle—his nervous system was overwhelmed and he cracked. He developed a schizophrenic personality characterized by irrational ideation. This schism aided by a pre-existing drug abusive lifestyle caused him to have a harsh and difficult life and an early demise—before his 50th birthday. Of all my cousins, I spent the most time with Edwin. We did a lot of things together and shared many good times. I was saddened to see him deteriorate the way he did, but the pathology of his descent was predictable by those who observed his family closely.

Bobby was much younger than Ralph, Edwin and me. Bobby, the youngest of the male Moon-Penick progeny, is the only son of my Aunt Margaret and her husband my "Uncle Wynn." Margaret was the first in the Penick family to attend and graduate from college. I spent the least of my childhood time with Bobby. I did not share a deep bonding experience with him like I had with Edwin and Ralph. Nevertheless, we had, as youngsters, a solid bond of kinship and a strong knowledge of each other. Bobby excelled educationally. He graduated from a prestigious law school and made his mark as an executive in state government and as a facilitator and promoter of business deals, nonprofit organizations and a host of enterprising business endeavors. He is a success by the parameters we use to measure.

Margaret once remarked when she and her family visited us in Charlottesville, "Rosa," she uttered with a big smile, "I think Otis is the best." Bobby and several of his siblings, along with his father, were visiting our home at the time in the presence of mother. An hour or two later she then said to me directly, "Otis you know when to lead and you know when to follow." Both of these comments from her endeared her to me even though I did not dwell on them or thought for a moment that she literally meant what these statements implied. But her jovial disposition and warm smile, always congenial, made her one of my favorite aunts to be

Three cousins at the table, left to right: Ralph, Otis, and Edwin
South Boston, VA, circa 1955

around. Between Aunt Louise and Margaret, I spent the least of my time with Margaret. But the time I did spend in her presence was quality time and was not infrequent.

I enjoyed a good relationship with all of my aunts on both sides of the family; they were all nice and supportive of me. Never a harsh word was spoken to me by any of them.

As children and as young adolescents Ralph, Edwin and I could have been compared to *The Three Princes of Serendip*[3], as depicted in the novel by Michele Tramezzino in 1557. Our lives at that time were indeed serendipitous. We had everything we needed, we were catered to, and our circumstances yielded gratuitously fortunate results. But our luck changed dramatically as young adulthood and the realities of maturity extracted their price. Our fates evolved into drug abuse, insanity, madness, schizophrenia, homosexuality, ignominy, success and self-actualization all seared in travail. Ralph, Edwin and I grew up together during the same time period between 1947 and 1966 with South Boston as our root and with Moon and Penick blood in our veins. But that is where the similarity ended. We knew each other well but not intimately. And so our lives became a parody of the "three princes." We were born to different parents, raised in different places, lived in different environments, learned different value systems and morals from our parents and acquired different ethics regarding work, life, education and responsibility. Each family culture was different and each had its own ethos. Good fortune in youth became misfortune in adulthood especially for Ralph and Edwin. We were all raised under different parenting philosophies, took divergent paths into the portals of conscious experience, all by choice none by happenstance. What can be gleaned from this history is that on the Moon-Penick side when there was a strong male parent in the home who enforced the requirement of education, demanded adherence to a moral standard of conduct and work ethic, the children did well. Where these factors were absent, the children either failed or became driftwood kindling in a fire that consumed the underbrush of their lives, destroying any hope for a fruitful and productive future. While the male children in this family have not always fared well, the females did considerably better, several attaining college degrees and post-graduate degrees. Strong insightful men made the difference in the success rate for the males.

Moon family photo, South Boston, (Junior's House in background) from left to right: Otis Lee Sr., Cecille Jr., Robert L. Wynn Sr. (head turned), Esther, Bobby (obscured), Cecille, Susan Penick, Helena, Patrick Moon, Elizabeth, Helen Moon, Rosa, Otis Lee, Jr., Margaret, Willnette, Edwin, Margaret Lorraine, unknown, Louise, circa 1956

VESSELS OF DECORATION

Finally, within the Moon-Penick family there developed, along with education, or perhaps because of it, an oblique but mostly benign undercurrent of invidious competition and tacit envy. The two pillars of the family, the Lees and the Wynns, and to a certain extent the Johnsons, were implied rivals and competitors. This is not an uncommon issue in families. Unlike the Wynns, who appeared to see education as an end in itself, the Lees see education as a means to a greater end.

Mother the youngest, by ten or more years, was passive and not assertive, but the economic success of her immediate family, in her and her husband's opinion, made her the object of petty jealousy. Hence she was out maneuvered by her older sisters who were more aggressive and dominating when it came to the family "jewels"—the home place and its contents. Her parents knowingly or unknowingly aided and abetted that domination by their actions. For some reason Mother was thought to "have too much already," so her parents, particularly her mother, for this and perhaps other reasons, threw her favoritism toward Margaret, Louise, and her son Patrick H. Moon, Jr. in the final disposition of her possessions including the home place.

Did Helen Penick love her daughter by Patrick Moon as much as she loved her daughters by prior relationships? After all, she had had two children before she married Patrick Moon. We know from our own experiences that "first love" though it may not last as long as a subsequent love is by itself a "special love," where the truest of intentions are manifest. Patrick Moon was 20 years older than Helen when they married, and he had been married before and was divorced when he married Helen Penick. Perhaps she married Patrick Moon out of a need for survival. She had two kids to take care of, and he was a property owner who had a skill he used to earn a good living.

A corollary to these questions is: why did Patrick Moon, Jr. flame out the way he did? Did Helen put as much love into him as she put into her two older children? Was that void in his life, if any, filled by alcohol? Was alcohol a substitute for the love he felt was wanting from his mother? Obviously something was severely lacking in his life. What drove him to rebel in such a fashion?

He was the youngest of them all. On the other hand, perhaps Junious just fell in with the wrong crowd, as we previously discussed and could not be rehabilitated. I have no answers to these questions. But supposition leads me to believe that the truth is buried somewhere in the answers to these questions.

On October 19, 1960 Patrick Moon by deed conveyed his half-interest in the homestead to his wife Helen Moon. It is not unexpected that in most cases a husband by will or by deed would convey his interest in the marital home to his wife. But not in this case, because there were children, not born of this union, in the family. Instead, if he had by will or deed conveyed the property to his son, Patrick H. Moon, Jr., and or his only daughter, Rosa Moon Lee, children born of the marriage during his lifetime, the result could have been the possible dispossession of his wife Helen Moon of her marital interest in the home. In reality that would not have happened because neither Junious nor Mother (Rosa) would have put their mother, Helen Moon, out of the only home she had known. Moreover, Virginia law protects a surviving spouse from being disinherited, hence, in all probability the reason for the conveyance. Was Patrick Moon, Sr. aware that by making the transfer of his interest in the real property to his wife that he had given his wife the power to disinherit either one or both of his children? Probably not. There are other ways Patrick Moon could have achieved a different result and still not dispossessed his wife but neither he nor his attorney at the time, as far as we know, utilized these legal mechanisms. Patrick H. Moon, Sr. died on October 29, 1963.

By will dated October 29, 1960, Helen Moon left a portion of her estate including the contents of the home place to her son Patrick H. Moon, Jr., who was still alive at her death. Helen Moon died on February 6, 1969. Patrick H. Moon, Jr. died on March 11, 1985, more than 25 years after the execution of her will and 16 years after his mother's death. Helen left an additional portion to "Louise (Howerton) Johnson"—we know from the public record that Louise was not a Howerton—and the rest and remainder of her estate, including her half-interest in the land upon which the home place was situated to Margaret Howerton Wynn, as well as naming Margaret the residuary beneficiary and executrix of the will, meaning that Margaret would take all the property left to the deceased son Patrick H. Moon, Jr. if he failed to survive his mother Helen Moon. And, any property left to Louise if she too failed to survive Helen. But both Patrick H. Moon, Jr. and Louise survived Helen Moon. Therefore, the only legal interest in the estate that Margaret was entitled to take was the half-interest in the land and improvement, the homestead, which sat upon the land, but not the contents in the homestead. And, she had the power by will, but not by qualification, to distribute the estate according to the law in the State of Virginia and the terms of the will. The will was probated on February 10, 1969. The will had to be probated, meaning as we say "put to record" in order to transfer title to the real estate. The will was probated but without qualification,

Mother with daughters, left to right: Margaret, Helen Moon, Rosa, and Louise, South Boston, VA, circa 1950s

meaning no person or entity qualified publicly as a fiduciary, as executor or administrator, having a legal duty to answer to the court and heirs regarding the administration of the estate.

Under Virginia law, if Junior died without a will at his death, which as far we know he did, the contents in the home descended to Junior's heirs, to his wife Frances if they were not divorced and to his only son Ralph Moon. In the absence of these takers then to his sister of the whole blood Rosa M. Lee.

Clearly Helen Moon made up her mind to disinherit her only daughter by Patrick Moon as manifested by the will after we moved to Charlottesville from Richmond, Virginia in June of 1960. Perhaps in her own distorted way she was trying to affect some kind of rough economic justice. But the way she arrived at her kind of justice was unhelpful and the results painful. Any influences Helen Moon came under, undue or otherwise, if any and by whom, were exerted before 1960 and impactful 9 years before her death.

Mother was unaware of the existence of the will. But others probably were, but I cannot be certain that they were aware of its existence, even though they were named in the will as beneficiaries and took initiatives according to their interpretation of the will. This partially explains why Margaret felt she had the legal right to remove the furnishings from the home but legally she did not, even after Junior's death in 1985. Junior was probably unaware of his inheritance except for perhaps his home place next to the main house, since he lived there until his death. And Junior probably cared little about the contents in the main house although they were legally his.

Those of us who have practiced law in this area know that the best way to disinherit a child is to mention him or her or leave them "a widow's mite," as Dad would say. But not to mention them at all also results in disinheritance but can create confusion and a possible contest over the disinheritance.

But Dad was the equalizer. He abhorred the forfeiture and could see it coming. His business acumen allowed him to outwit this faction, and he protected Mother from being essentially disinherited by her parents. She was undeserving of this injustice. She had done nothing except that her immediate family, the Lee family, had accumulated more wealth than anyone in the Moon-Penick family. Petty jealously and small mindedness pervaded the clan because here were folks who aspired to greatness. Aspiring to greatness breeds competition, by definition. People start noticing what you have and don't have. Mother once remarked chauvinistically, while we were all in the car leaving someone's house after a social visit while in Richmond, "people treat you the way that they do because of what they think you have." What Mother was saying was that if people think you are well-off or have money they treat you differently, it can be for better or worse. Unfortunately for her, clearly her parents "treated her differently" for the worse because of what they perceived her to have; as a result she was the only one of the four children disinherited. Mother perhaps had arrived at this conclusion, as an afterthought, after considering how we had been treated in this neighbor's home. Maybe also her family had shorned her of her right to inherit precisely because they thought themselves more in need. The consequences of her success had both a benefit and a burden. Dad did some deals with the College Street land which resulted in him owning the entire lot including the home place. His adroit business strategy protected Mother and guaranteed that she would get a share of her family's estate, notwithstanding the efforts of others to deprive her of it.

Forty-two years later, on December 27, 2011, I received a call from Bobby, Aunt Margaret's only son. The two of us had been collaborating on a project to secure the return of treasured mementos to my mother that she had failed to obtain after the death of her mother and father.

He said, "I'm heading your way with some packages." It was two days after Christmas and I was lying in bed looking at a movie. Two hours later when he arrived, he and his wife, Millie, brought with them two packages in bubble wrap. Of course I knew and my wife knew immediately what they were. In fact when he called and said he was coming to Charlottesville to bring some packages, I knew what he was bringing. After he and Millie arrived, we talked for just a few minutes because the two of them had a long drive back to North Carolina. My youngest son Justin was home but was not quite up to speed about the issue. He would soon get a full education on the subject.

After they left, I called Mother and said, "good afternoon how are you doing?" "I'm alright" she said. Her usual stock answer, indicating that nothing was unusually wrong. I said "we will be over in two hours." I purposefully did not give her any hint about what the purpose of our visit was about.

When we arrived at mother's at about 2:30 that afternoon, we brought in the packages, and she said "what is that?" We all said individually, but almost in unison "these are some things you have been waiting to receive," expecting to fully observe her reaction to what was in the packages. We helped her open the bubble wrapped packages, revealing two 18-inch clouded glass vases. Each vase—fashioned in the form of tall Coca Cola bottles, except that each end tapered to about half of the middle diameter—was covered with etchings painted in gold and green in an assortment of flower patterns. The mouth of each vase was notched in a rounded pattern adding to the decorative character of the vases. The vases exuded a degree of fragility and elegance. Though we all knew they were not works of fine art, what made them priceless nonetheless was the sentiment attached to them.

As Mother opened the vases and her mind made the connection with our help, she exclaimed, "I never thought I would see them again, this is really, really Christmas. I can't get over it!" She teared up as her memories became sharper and the images of her childhood home in South Boston refreshed her recollection. She again exclaimed her relief in seeing the vases: "A gift, truly a gift, I never thought I would see them again in my life. I never thought I would see them again. I had given up on the idea of seeing them again. I grew up with them. Thank you all so much. It's the only thing, except for a coffee table I have, from the family. Mother (speaking of her mother) had them sitting above the fireplace, that's where she had them."

She paused for a minute to gather her thoughts and began again telling the story: "I wasn't there when they moved everything out of the house. I didn't have anything from my father. I've never been so surprised in my life." She repeated again. Her mother had passed in 1969 and her father in 1963. "I never knew where they went to after that, I had given up on them......growing ....I just grew up with them as a child. Dad put them in the home, one of the few memories of my dad and home." She repeated again her disbelief, "I never thought I would see them again, but you never know, just keeping hoping, and that makes a difference. I did get the little coffee table." She went on to say "I don't know why I liked these. It's all I can remember coming up as a child, to remember my dad."

Upon returning to South Boston, after her mother had passed and the funeral was over, Mother shed tears. Mother relates that she was crestfallen and disappointed when she opened the front door to the white frame house on the hill with its bleached red tin roof to discover the emptiness, the cavernous hollow sounds of vacancy expressed by the emptiness that otherwise in past years had been filled with family, friends and possessions. To her dismay she discerned that Margaret, mother's half-sister, had removed all of the furniture and personal items from the house, apparently to her home in Greensboro, North Carolina. It was a painful emotional letdown; Mother was heartbroken. She reasoned that she had done nothing to deserve what had happened; after all, it was she who had removed her parents to her home in Charlottesville to protect them from Junious. She was one of two natural children of the whole blood of the union of Patrick and Helen Moon. And it was her father that owned the land and built the house and enabled the furnishing of it. If anyone deserved to give out the family heirlooms, it was her and not anyone else. By will and deed her parents had completely disinherited her. Why? Regardless of what the older sisters may or may not have done, and for whatever reason, her parents were the parties at fault for the results. If we ascribe to Patrick Moon, Sr., knowledge of his wife's intentions after the deed was made, then he is as much at fault as anyone. Who knows what undue influences they came under as age and health deteriorated. Whether contrived or unwittingly done, the result was the same. The vases were not only vessels of decoration but also repositories of unrequited memories.

Moon family photo, South Boston, (Junior's House in background) from left to right: Cecil Donald Parker, Esther Parker, Otis Lee Sr., Cecil Parker, Robert L. Wynn Sr., Susie Penick, Robert L. Wynn II (Bobby), Helena Wynn, Patrick Moon, unknown, Helen Moon, Rosa Lee, Margaret Wynn, Otis Lee Jr., Margaret Lorraine Wynn, Elizabeth Wynn, Willnette Parker, Walter Parker, Edwin L. Johnson, circa 1956

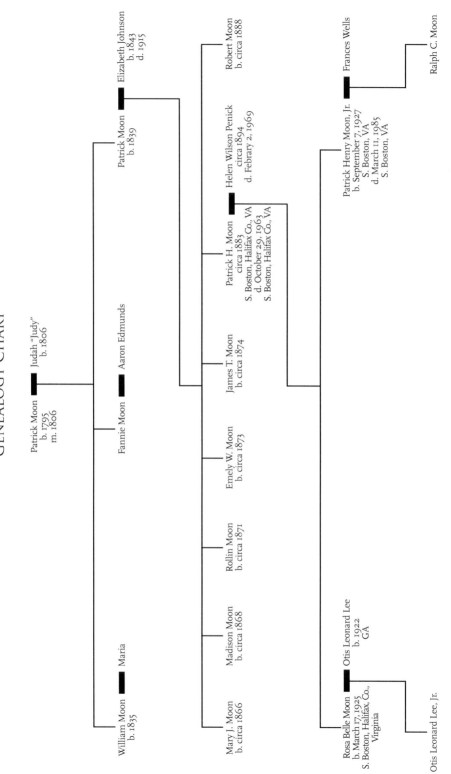

MOON
GENEALOGY CHART

PENICK
GENEALOGY CHART

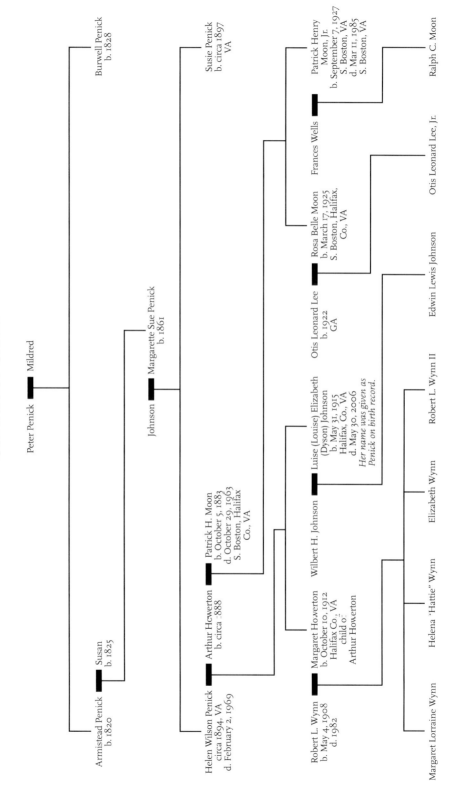

This is the old Parham Moon place. It was torn down to make room for the new fairgrounds near South Boston.

Moon House, side view

WB 54 - 89

August Court 1853

ordered to be recorded And on the motion of Elizabeth J. Boyd who
made oath thereto according to law & with William J. Ferguson &
Charles Hughes her Securities entered into & acknowledged a bond
in the penalty of £10.000 Conditioned according to law. Certificate
is granted her for obtaining probat of said will, in due form
[...] Securities having verified their sufficiency on oath according
to law

Teste W. S. Holt Clk

margin: Nathan Penick
Will.

I Nathan Penick of the County of Halifax and State of Virginia
do hereby make and ordain this my last will and testament in
manner and form following that is to say

1st I give and bequeath to my daughter Louisa Penick one feather
bed with such furniture as my other children have received
One [...] and harness and all of my other [...]

2d I [...] that after my death my executors hereinafter named
do sell the whole of my estate both real and personal except
such as is bequeathed in the foregoing clause, in such manner
and form as they may deem best and out of the proceeds
first pay all of my just debts, then to the children of my
daughter Elizabeth Robertson the sum of Six hundred and
fifty nine dollars & 30 Cents with interest thereon from the 28th
day of September 1847 until paid it being my will and desire
to divide that sum and the interest thereon as aforesaid equally
between the children of my said daughter Elizabeth to be paid to
them respectively as soon as they marry or attain the age of
twenty one years And then to the children of my daughter Judith
Owen formerly Judith Hawkins (excepting William M and Thomas
M Hawkins, whom I hereby exclude from the inheritance or
enjoyment of any part of my estate whatsoever) the sum of Eight
hundred & nine dollars & 38 Cents with interest thereon from the
28th day of September 1847 until paid it being my will and desire
to divide that sum with interest thereon as aforesaid equally between
the children of my said daughter Judith (except the said William
M and Thomas M) to be paid to them respectively as soon as they
marry or attain the age of twenty one years

3d If there should not be a sufficiency of my estate
herein before directed to be sold to pay to the children
of my daughters Elizabeth & Judith the sums herein before
bequeathed to them respectively it is my will that they shall
[...] proportion to the sums bequeathed to them respectively

4th It is my will that if there should be a surplus of my
estate after complying with the provisions and [...]

Nathan Penick will, August 1853

90

August Court 1853

before made, it Shall be divided into Seven equal Shares and I do hereby give and bequeath One Share of the Same to my Son Thomas R Penick, One Share to my Son William Penick, One Share to my Son Branch Penick, One Share to my daughter Mary Ann Smith, One Share to my daughter Louisa Penick One Share to the Children of my daughter Elizabeth Robertson, and One Share to the Children of my daughter Judith Owen formerly Judith Hawkins (Excepting her Sons William at & Thomas M Hawkins as aforesaid) to them and their heirs forever

5th. I Constitute and appoint my Sons Thomas R Penick and William Penick executors of this my last will and testament hereby Revoking all other wills by me heretofore made but hereby Confirming the division and distribution made by me On and before the 28th day of September 1847 of a part of my estate and which is not intended to be included in the provisions and bequests hereinbefore made And my will is and I hereby direct that my said Executors Shall not be required to give Security on qualifying to act under this will And I furthermore desire that no order Shall be made for the appraisement of my estate In testimony Whereof I have hereunto Set my hand & affixed my Seal this the 12th day of November 1847

Signed, Sealed and acknowledged
and declared to be his last
will and testament by
Nathan Penick in
presence of
  Thos H Everett
  James T Hile
  Edw M Carrington

                      Nathan X Penick (Seal)
                           his Mark

I Nathan Penick of the County of Halifax having made my last will & testament bearing date the 12th day of November 1847 and hereto annexed giving to the Children of my daughter Elizabeth Robertson the Sum of Six hundred and fifty nine dollars and thirty Cents with interest thereon from the 28th day of September 1847 to be equally divided between them & to be paid to them respectively as Soon as they marry or attain the age of Twenty one years; and having paid to Lucy Robertson and Lucy Owen, Edwin J Robertson and Robertson R Robertson, three of the Children of my said daughter Elizabeth Robertson their respective proportions of the said Six hundred and fifty nine dollars and thirty Cents (including interest thereon) up to the 1st instant

August Court 1853

June 1848 I do by this present writing, which I will and direct
to be annexed as a Codicil to my said will & taken as a part
thereof, revoke the legacy given to the said Sarg. Edwin &c &
Robert R. Robertson as aforesaid

And having appointed my said Wm Penick and of my executor
& Supposing that he may probably wish to purchase my
many servants who are &c hand divides to his said for certain
purposes after my death It is my will and desire that his
be appraised by three disinterested Freemen, and after him to be
Chosen by each of my three Sons Thomas R Penick Wm Penick
& Branch Penick & that my son William &c may to take
& bound him and paying the amount of such division if
his Chooses, if not the said Negro is to be sold as directed
in the 2nd Clause of my said will. The proceeds in either case
disposed of therein directed. And I do ratify my said will
except so far as the same is hereby revoked as of this is advance
In witness whereof I the said Nathan Penick have to this
Codicil Set my hand and seal this 28th day of June 1848
Signed Sealed and published by the
said Nathan Penick as and for a Codicil   Nathan X Penick (Seal)
to be added to and considered as a part of   his mark
his last will & testament in the presence of
as who have subscribed our names in his presence

 John A McCraW
 Saml Carter
 James T Hill
 E M Carrington

At a Court held for Halifax County the 22nd day of August 1853
This last will and testament of Nathan Penick decd was
with a Codicil thereto annexed was presented in Court & the
will proved by the oath of Thomas K Bennett a Subscribing
witness thereto, the Codicil proved by the oaths of Jno A McCraw
& Samuel Carter Subscribing witnesses thereto and the hand
writing of James T Hill another Subscribing witness to
the said will proved by the oath of James Young. and the
said will & Codicil ordered to be recorded. And on motion
of Thomas R Penick & William Penick who make oath thereto
according to law entered into and acknowledged a bond in
the penalty of Twelve thousand dollars Conditioned according
to law Certificate is granted them for obtaining probate of
the said will in due form without giving Security

      Teste Wm S Holt ck

WB 24 - 433

438

January Court 1855

Dr. The Estate of Nathan Penick in account Current with Thomas
R. Penick and Wm Penick Executors

1853 Aug. 22	To Cash paid James A Roberton as pr rec.d			127.64
Sept 2	" ditto " Fox & McKinney			25.00
	" ditto " Tax account for 1853			13.47
	" ditto " Benson Burgess			1.10
Nov. 15	" ditto " C. W. Atkisson			1.49
1854 Aug 23	" ditto " Joseph C. Ferry			9.27½
" 27	" ditto " Heel W.d & Co. accts			17.00
Mar 25	" ditto " Reg.d C. B. Spencer			6.00
Apl 26	" ditto " J. H. Perkins			5.63
Aug.t 22	" ditto " Robt J. Smith admr. H. A. Smith			30.14
	" ditto " Geo.d & J. B. Brown			15.00
	" ditto " C. M. Brooks 2d inst 1854			274.50
	" ditto " Clerk of Halifax			0.75
	" 5 per Cent Com.s to Execr on $4130.59			206.52
Aug.t 22	" Balance due Estate this day			3378.13
				$4130.59

Contra Cr.

1853 Aug.t 22	By Cash of Young Ferrell &c for their note			1397.27
	" " ditto on hand			13.00
Sept 7	" amt sales household furniture			42.07
22	" Cash of Wm Y Morton for first instalment for the tract of land			403.25
25	" ditto of James Bowman for purchase negro boy Jim			900.00
	" ditto " William Penick for negro man Armistead taken by valuation			875.00
1854	" ditto of Billington Owen for rent of plantation in 1853			100.00
				$4130.59
1854 Aug.t 22	By Balance due Estate as per Contra			$3378.13

Halifax County, to wit

At the request of Messrs Thomas R. & Wm Penick Executors
of Nathan Penick dec.d and pursuant to the act of Assembly in such
Case I have examined Stated and settled their account Current as executors
as aforesaid and find them indebted to the estate of their testator in the
sum of $3378.23 the 22nd day of August last as will appear by reference
to the foregoing Statement which is Submitted as a part of this report.
Given under my hand this 3d day of October 1854.

John A. McCaie, Com.r

At a Court held for Halifax County the 25th day of December 1854
The within written account Current of Tho.s R. & Wm Penick executor of
Nathan Penick Senr deceased was returned to Court and ordered to be continued
And at another Court held for said County the 22nd day of January
1855 no Exceptions being taken to the said account it was ordered to be
recorded.

Teste

Current account; estate of Nathan Penick with Thomas and William Penick executors. "No exception being filed against the account, it was ordered to be recorded, January 22, 1855, Circuit Court of Halifax County."

3

❦

"DO YOU BELIEVE IN TREATING PEOPLE RIGHT?"

OUR TRIPS TO GEORGIA before we moved to Charlottesville were epic journeys into the Deep South. I remember them as adventures. Dad often wanted to go to visit his mother, so we made this trip many times before we left Richmond in 1960. In those days, Blacks were not allowed to stop and eat at rest stops, to stay overnight in motels or hotels, or to use the restrooms except begrudgingly at filling stations along the interstate highways. On a long 13-hour trip from Richmond, Virginia to Fitzgerald, Georgia, all of this had to be taken into account before planning a trip home especially when taking the family. Before we would travel, Mother prepared for the trip a week before by baking and fixing the food we would need to eat along the way. I remember my mother making sandwiches and preparing other food stuffs that we could eat and packing the trunk of the car with these goods, so we could get at them with ease.

On one of our trips to Florida after getting to Georgia, we were on our way to visit Bud in Opa-Locka, a suburban enclave of Miami. Evening was approaching and anxiety began to take hold as we contemplated how far we had yet to drive and how hungry we were. Dad talked with Mother about stopping because they knew what to expect. So after traveling on a little farther, Dad pulled the car to the side of the road on the same side of the street as the fast food restaurant, an early resemblance to a Dairy Queen or a McDonald's, to make our assault upon the task of securing a meal. Dad went up to the window and asked for his order, three hamburgers, three sodas and French fries, the usual fare. The waiter, a young White adult with a white apron and matching hat, looked Dad squarely in the eye as though he had been preparing for this encounter all his life and responded, "we do not serve Blacks in this store, you will have to go somewhere else." But what he did not count on was the humanness of my dad's plea, that human beings were the recipients of his inhuman refusal to supply an essential human need. We were all sitting in the car, right in his line of sight. I remember Dad responding to him by saying something like "are you a Christian, do you believe in treating people right, doing the right thing?" The clerk, feeling some remorse, relented and motioned Dad to come around to the side of the building where he sold him some food through a side window. As a child witnessing this incident, I felt the pangs of inadequacy, helplessness and vulnerability. I felt that my dad was being made to humble himself and to suffer an indignity solely because of his race in order to beg food to feed his family. Dad may not have felt it demeaning. But rather, it was a matter of dealing with the culture at that time, something to be expected, something to which he had become acclimated. We were tired and hungry with miles to travel before we got to our destination, so he tried to obtain food for us. He had done what Black mothers and fathers have always had to do, suffer indignity to provide for their family. He had sacrificed his dignity for a few moments for the benefit of his family and perhaps he felt vindicated by the success he attained. Although I doubt if my father even remembered this encounter because it was probably just one of numerous slights and deprivations he experienced in his life in Jim Crow America, I never forgot this episode and the situation my father was put in. As the years passed I felt even more acutely my father's pain. And people ask the question, "why are some Black folks angry?"

— — —

Amos Lee, my father's great-great-grandfather, was the oldest identifiable paternal ancestor of the Lee family. He was born a slave somewhere in Elko, Georgia, Houston County, between 1840 and 1842; he could neither read nor write. His probable slave master was John S. Lee, who at the height of his operation in Houston County owned 1400 acres and 35 slaves. John S. Lee had two sons, one of which may have been Benjamin F. Lee who "mustered" up for the Civil War and filed for a Confederate pension. Amos Lee related to his granddaughter before his death, "that his master took him with him to do errands for him when the war was between the states." The treatment he received, she recounts, is the stuff which saddens the heart and evoked tears as he recited these facts to her before his death: "Amos was just a young boy at the time. After the war ended Amos went back to his master's farm and was a slave there until he became a man. He became partly free to go and come when he got permission from his 'boss' and also a pass from one plantation to another." Amos married Martha Laidler living in Henderson, Georgia, Houston County in 1869, and from this union twelve children were born: nine sons and three daughters. One son, John Robert Lee was my father's grandfather. A genealogical study was unable to verify all of these facts, however, this does not disprove the accuracy of the firsthand accounts of the experiences endured by a man who lived through them and recited them to his granddaughter before his death.

The legacy of defilement, meanness, savagery, debauchery, mistreatment and violence both physical and incorporeal against Blacks by a class of Whites breeds anger, animosity and mistrust. Stripping a culture from a people is equivalent to removing the marrow from the bone, leaving behind a calcified outer shell easily fractured from a lack of structure and fortification. Does this result in perennial victimhood? No. But it explains our plight and what must be overcome, and the burdens we bear in an unfriendly and unwelcoming environment. This legacy leaves an indelible mark on succeeding generations who venerate their ancestors, empathize with their unnecessary suffering and appreciate their history. It is a legacy that dies hard and will not recede until the generations who are most affected by it have expired. The residuary effects of this part of our history still redound to our disadvantage and manifests itself in less than representative academic achievement, low self-esteem, morality and values deficits, and subpar socioeconomic advancement, but this is who we are; this is a part of our legacy and our history. These stories should be retold and reiterated as a frame of reference so that our young will be strengthened, and motivated to learn their history and know the prices that were paid for the liberties they exercise today.

— — —

Emma Williams Lee Clark, paternal grandmother, circa 1959

Emma Lee Clark, my father's mother was the heroine of her family. Her first husband, John L. Lee, my father's father, was killed on September 15, 1926, by a White man, by the name of Stonewall Jackson Barron. Barron lived 11 miles north east of Fitzgerald on a farm owned by J. C. Brewer. In the early morning of September 15th an altercation arose between Stonewall and Lee over the favors of a Black woman, familiar to Lee before the incident. The woman was a cook in a local eatery frequented by railroad men and laborers. John Lee worked on the railroad. Lee was a hot head and a blow hard who could have saved his life had he been home with his seven children and not chasing some woman who had no loyalty to him. The record shows that Lee confronted Stonewall and the woman as the two of them walked down a street not far from the eatery where she worked. Lee had planned to be with the woman that night and was surprised to find her in the company of Stonewall Barron. The anticipation and expectancy of a tryst in the twilight were not easily abandoned. The ire of his wounded ego and pride could not be assuaged by the quiet acceptance of rejection. His recoil required satisfaction. When the confrontation occurred invectives were exchanged, epithets were hurled and profanity was not in short supply. Anger curdled in his hot blood and threats were made. "You mess with me and I'll blow your god damned brains out," Lee shouted to Stonewall. The men quarreled over who had the rights to "Willie Mae" that night, but Willie Mae had made her choice for that night. The two men scuffled and in the dark of night Lee reached for what appeared to be a gun in his pocket, a bulge that seemed the outline of a gun. His motion was menacing to Stonewall. But Lee had no gun. Stonewall shot first and Lee was dead. The bullet went through Lee's heart killing him instantly. Emma was now a widow with seven mouths to feed and no permanent home.

Stonewall Barron was indicted in October 1926 by a Fitzgerald grand jury and tried by jury on December 14, 1926. The jury was unable to agree on a verdict and a mistrial was ordered. At a later time the indictment was *nole prossed*—dismissed without prejudice to bring the charges again, but rarely ever done. Barron was later issued a warrant for carrying a concealed weapon. He posted a $500 bond and later pled guilty to the weapons charge. The state declined to retry Barron, probably be-cause the record shows a vote by the jury favoring an acquittal 11 to 1 on the basis of self-defense. The genealogist who researched the records provided census evidence that the assailant was a White man.

This loss set the course for Dad's life. He was fatherless at a tender young age. And the father he knew, if he remembered him much at all, he vaguely remembered, at best. Dad was four years old when his father was murdered. He never knew the truth about his father's death. Maybe someone whispered the truth in his ear when he was older, but maybe not. Nevertheless, he never found out the truth, perhaps preferring the story he was told as a child: "that his father was killed on the railroad." And this is what he believed until his death seventy-two years later. It is the story he told me until I decided to probe further. In a curious way, John L. Lee's death may have set events in motion that resulted in Dad getting an education rather than be-ing directed toward his father's footsteps to a world of coarseness, ignorance and honest but ignoble labor, a world for which he was ill-suited by temperament or physical ability to endure. I have postulated that John L. Lee's early death removed the coarseness from the family unit and allowed the nurturing side of his mother and older sister to prevail, opening up opportunities for education and the expansion of vision beyond the dirt roads of Fitzgerald. Perhaps his absence allowed a gentler and more loving atmosphere to prevail in the home, albeit a poorer home because of his father's absence, to take hold in the family emanating from the warmth and glow of his loving mother Emma. She was soft spoken and nurturing in stark contrast to John L. Lee.

His widowed mother, Emma Lee Clark, was medium height, but not short, dark skinned with a grey patch of hair on the left side of her forehead and she wore glass-es. Emma was the first Black woman in her community to purchase her own home. She purchased the house with the proceeds from a life insurance policy insuring the life of her husband, my father's father. In this house she raised her seven children and kept her family together.

Emma Williams Lee Clark was educated in the public schools of Macon, Geor-gia, Bibb County. She was the daughter of Riley and Mary McDay Williams. Emma was born November 27, 1904. She was raised by a devoted grandmother Mary Williams Green. I spent considerable time around my paternal grandmother and observed her closely. She was a Christian woman, church going, quiet, reserved, dignified with a patrician manner but without the underpinnings to support and accompany the appearance. She was gentle and soft spoken. She barely spoke above a soft monotone, just louder than a whisper. She loved to sit on her front porch on Orange Street, an unpaved orange and clay colored thoroughfare, rocking in her favorite rocker, passing the time talking with neighbors and family members. She slept in the front bedroom of the small white frame house she bought in 1926. Her front bedroom abutted the front porch she dearly loved. Being the sole support for seven children, times were tough on the Lees. Emma was literate but not formally educated beyond high school, if that. She did "days work" to make ends meet. There were no luxuries just the bare necessities.

On the Lee side, the males did not distinguish themselves, save for three, me included. Arthur "Skeeta" Davis made himself an outstanding success; obtaining a master's degree from a major Midwestern university, rising to the level of a senior state government official in Michigan and retiring from the Army Reserves with the rank of Colonel. And Daryl Boles finished college and became a salesman. These were the children of two of Dad's sisters "Cat" and "Dilo." In both cases the males were raised by females. In Skeeta's case, he was raised by my dad's mother; in the other case the male was raised by a single mother who was a teacher.

Dad was one of seven children. He had two brothers and four sisters. I got to know them all, some more so than others, but a knowledge of each was ingrained in me because of close and enduring contact through the years so much so that each of them became a part of me in some significant way. All of Dad's siblings had children.

Dad loved them all and he enjoyed being around them. He derived a certain comfort from being in their presence. When they gathered at the family home in the old days for holidays it was a raucous, partying, exercise in nostalgia. The yelling and the shouting, in and out of the front door at grandmother's house, the screen door slamming incessantly after each repeated entrance and exit. The door was so worn from abuse it no longer functioned as a door but was relegated to being a noisy passage way signaling the goings and comings of each family member—from grandmother's across to Aunt Dilo's, then over to Jean's. All day and all night long until it ended, that was the scene. The fried fish, rice and cabbage, the biscuits and the grits, the okra, collards and turnip greens, it smelled so good and was prepared exactly right and tasted even better and I ate it until I popped. Luckily for me during those days I was too young to know anything about heart disease.

"Bud" or Wesley as he was known in the family was Dad's oldest brother; Bud became a licensed electrician and traveled around the southeast region setting up the

freezer and electrical components for the Southland Corporation, owners of the Seven-Eleven stores. Bud had one biological son, Bummy, who was killed in a robbery situation. His reputation in the family was that of a "bad boy." The facts surrounding his death are not completely clear, but I remember him as an aggressive perhaps out of control young man, when I saw him, the few times I did, and that was when our visits converged in Fitzgerald before his death. Bud as the oldest was a tough cookie. He was candid and direct. He was in the army and fought in World War II. He lost an eye sometime after his service in a freak accident. Bud owned real estate and built for himself and his wife financial security. Bud did well. Next to

Wesley "Bud" Lee, Fitzgerald, GA, 1968

Dad, Bud had the most success financially, and Aunt Dilo was third in line.

Willie Robert Lee, Dad's youngest brother, was a career soldier. We called him "Junior." Junior married and had three sons. Junior was gentle, not a mean spirit in his body. His gentle quiet manner was the hallmark of his personality. A small man who spoke with a modified stutter as though phlegm covered his vocal chords. His oldest boy died in a car accident, the next oldest of natural causes and one still survives. After returning from his army service he stayed around Fitzgerald most of his days and lived in the small house in back of the main house on Orange Street. While in the service he contracted a severe case of asthma that eventually killed him. I wish that I had gotten to know Junior better.

Dad's sister Tobytha Lee Byrd was the oldest and the first to get a college education. She was responsible for inspiring Dad to do so and perhaps even Aunt Dilo. She was known in the family as "Bee." Bee died when I was 9 or 10 years old while we lived in Richmond, Virginia. Dad loved this sister passionately. I think he loved her so because of her inspiring story, coming from nothing, going to college, leaving

Fitzgerald and making something out of herself and inspiring her siblings to do the same. Having come out of the poverty that embraced that household she pulled herself up and became a college educated woman. She lived her adult life in Pittsburg, Pennsylvania with her husband and family. Bee had four kids to my knowledge, one of whom became a doctor. Her younger children made something of themselves professionally. Bad blood developed between the Lees and Bee's husband, James Byrd, after her death, because for some reason they faulted him for her early demise. I was young then and was not privy to what the adults were saying. But it was evident by their behavior that blame was assessed against him. Consequently, Bee's younger children were steered away from the

Tobytha Lee Byrd (aunt), high school graduation, Fitzgerald, GA, circa 1939-40

Lees. So neither I nor any of the other core family members' children bonded with Bee's younger children. As a result contact between Bee's children and the rest of us after her death was limited. I hardly got to know them except for a glancing moment. Her oldest child, Brenda, whom I fantasized about as a young boy had more contact with the Lees before her mother's death and because of that early familiarity continued to have a loose association with the Lee side as she grew older.

Maebell Wilcox, who was rumored not to be a Lee biologically but was a Lee in all other aspects, spent most of her life in Fitzgerald working at various day jobs and caring for my grandmother except during her very last years. "Bell," Dad called her, bore six children. Her kids called her "Madear." I spent much time around Aunt Maebell. She was a colorful deep throated lively person. It was Aunt Maebell who prepared the lunches for Wendell, Skeeta, Pat and me when we went to the fields to pick cotton and crop tobacco during summer vacations. On many occasions she went with us.

Buddy Neuman, a field hand about the size of Uncle Bud, dark skinned, actually resembled Bud in his height and demeanor. Buddy worked in a saw mill most of the time, especially in the winter. In the summer, his job was to round up the sharecroppers of which I was one during the summers that I spent in Fitzgerald cropping tobacco and picking cotton. Cotton picking season went from the first of July until the end of October. I usually left for home well before the season ended. Mr. "Buddy" Newman would pull up his truck in front of my grandmother Clark's house early in the morning around 5:00 am and shout "heylo" or something similar, alerting us that he was there and that it was time to go to the fields. Sleepy eyed

Willie Robert Lee, circa 1958

we dressed and fell into the back of his open bed pickup truck for the cold windy ride to the cotton fields or to the tobacco fields each day Monday through Friday unless you just decided not to go. I went most of the time, trying to make enough money for a baseball mitt or some other item that motivated me. It was a novelty to me to do this work for the while I did it.

The tobacco and cotton fields seem to stretch as far as the eye could see. And I wondered how any single individual could finish out a row. During one outing, when I had finished cropping out most of my row after lunch time, the owner asked me to work in the tobacco barn. I had to climb up to the loft where parallel rows of wooden beams lay from one end of the barn to the other upon which strung poles of tobacco lay row after row. My job after each pole was handed up to me was to place each complete pole across the beams for curing in the hot suffocating air. Sweat was dripping off of me like a shower, and I was scared I was going to fall having to straddle the beams to keep from falling and to balance myself while placing the tobacco poles. Jean did this work as well. She was a "stringer" usually a woman who strung the tobacco around the poles about five feet in length. After the tobacco was hung, the curing process began. After the leaves were cured they were then packed and shipped off to market.

Aunt Maebell was appreciated and loved in the family. She was the constant in the family home during essentially her whole adult life. Aunt Maebell's service to my grandmother in the later years created conflict and consternation in her immediate family and in the family at large. Because she was rumored not to be a Lee, biologically, her immediate family thought, incorrectly, in my opinion, that Maebell was being "used;" that she was the "black sheep" because she lived in the family home and was asked to take over the primary chore of looking after her ailing and declining mother. But she was not the "black sheep" in their minds she was just there: the one to whom naturally the others looked to take up the primary care responsibility. After all, grandmother Clark had given Maebell a home and sheltered her for many years when she could not do for herself. Was this too much to ask? Yes!, her immediate family thought, and after vehement and inflammatory urging from her daughters, Maebell, perhaps against her better judgment, left the family home in Fitzgerald with her ailing mother there alone and moved to Philadelphia with her youngest daughter, Pat.

Philadelphia was a place alien to her lifestyle and culture. I was living and working in Philadelphia when this dispute and transition occurred. Aunt Maebell lived with her youngest daughter until her health declined. Pat then moved her back to Fitzgerald where eventually she died in a nursing home after spending some time with her middle daughter Jean. In the absence of her presence, Dad and the other siblings tried to hire help to care for grandmother in her home. This act—the act of moving away at a time of the greatest need of her mother that resulted in grandmother having to go a nursing home where she expired—left an unrequited legacy of incompleteness to an otherwise sanguine life of cheer and hope. Maebell was above all, a hopeful, optimistic and caring person. It is unfortunate that her last acts will cause her, in my mind, to be remembered in less than the full blossom of optimism her life reflected.

Maebell Willcox, circa 1980

"Cat," we called her, Catherine Lee Graham was her full name. One of four female children born to Robert L. Lee and Emma Williams, Cat was not a refined woman but she was warm, good hearted and had a beaming smile. A mother of seven children, Cat moved to Lake City, Florida where she raised her family. "Bill," her husband and father of six of the children, left her when the children were small. I do not ever remember meeting Bill, but there was much talk about him around the "house" in Fitzgerald. Cat was a factory worker and home owner. Dad worked closely with Cat to help her acquire property and sent clothes to her kids, from the time we lived in Richmond all the way through the Charlottesville years. She was a single mother struggling to support six children not including Skeeta. Whatever support she got from Bill it did not do the job completely. Dad was moved to do what he could. His heart went out to her. Here was a woman, his sister, who had nothing, who had been saddled with seven kids and a husband, who, because of the trial of the ordeal left her to fend for herself. Dad bought an adjacent rental property for Cat, gave it to her so she could collect the rent which added to her income, and gave her some measure of financial security.

Many thought Cat had a life threatening disease, cancer it was supposed, because no one really knew rumor was our only source of credible information. I visited her in Lake City, Florida at the local hospital in route to Budd's place outside of Miami after she became ill. I had visited her before with Dad on one of many trips to Fitzgerald over the years. I was expecting a modern facility. But what I encountered was a hospital that seemed like it was a civil war hospital ward rather than a modern hospital facility. I wondered what kind of medical treatment she was receiving in this place, but somehow she recovered. Generally community standards in "Black" Lake City resembled some of the worst backwaters in rural Georgia. The place was uninspiring and left in my mind little room for hope for a better tomorrow. Her living standard then was not high with all the children to support, but she was graceful with what she had. Dad quoted Cat as saying, when referring to raising her kids, some of whom were giving her a problem, especially the young men, "let the law raise them!" she yelled uncharacteristically, in exasperation. "I've had all I can take!"

After her retirement with her home paid for, she bought a new Cadillac, which she and one of her son's Otis, drove to our home in Philadelphia for a brief visit. She paid for her home and began to live well in her retirement years. She was happy and generally in good spirits when I was around her and she enjoyed her beer. She had the biggest smile resembling the full breath of the sun when she was enjoying herself. Her heart was broken when Dad died. I believe he was her favorite. While attending his funeral, she slipped and fell on ice that covered the second floor veranda in front of her motel room. I sued the motel and obtained a recovery, but Cat died before the case was settled and I paid the proceeds to her daughter Barbara Ann. Barbara Ann, who became a teacher, acted as her executor. I can hear Cat now inquiring loudly when the family gathered in Fitzgerald, "where is Red?!"

"Aunt Dilo" I call her. Formally she was Dilo Lee Boles. She was also known affectionately in the family as "Aunt Tee." Aunt Dilo had three kids and she lived directly across the street from grandmother, on Orange Street, in a modest yellow stucco ranch style home. Aunt Dilo was probably the most unique personality of all of

Catherine "Cat" Lee Graham, circa 1980-81

Dad's brothers and sisters. The twin natures of her lifestyle of parsimony and eccentricity set her apart. Her penchant for peculiar behavior in the midst of proper protocols reinforced in many family members' minds her tendency for unconventional behavior. In my opinion, her conduct at times stood in stark relief compared to others and what was normally expected. She was the female Silas Marner of the Lee Family. She was a steady, hard-working, consistent, opinionated teacher and a devout Christian at Salem Baptist Church on Palm Street one block over from the family home, the same church grandmother attended until her death. Dilo was also a single parent during her child rearing years.

Aunt Dilo did not believe in wasting money. It was a precious commodity to her, perhaps because she, along with her siblings, grew up without it. Aunt Dilo would drive her car until you could see the road through the floor boards. And she literally tried to get the "buffalo off of every nickel."

At the end of a summer stay in Fitzgerald picking cotton and cropping tobacco, Dad asked Aunt Dilo to put me on the bus back to Charlottesville. I was about 12 or 13 at the time. School would be starting soon, and I needed to get back home. Dutifully she did that. The night before our trip to Atlanta, that is where I could get a through bus, she made me one tuna fish sandwich, which I was supposed to eat from Atlanta to Charlottesville, some 500 or more miles away. En route to Atlanta the next morning from Fitzgerald, she ate half of my sandwich and when we got to the bus station in Atlanta she put a nickel in the coke machine to buy us a coke. The machine failed to deliver the coke and she beat the hell out of the machine trying to make that machine deliver that coke. So I traveled all the way to Charlottesville with just half a sandwich to last on a 12 hour trip. Fortunately, the lady I sat next to, a Black woman, had prepared some fried chicken for herself and she offered me a piece which I gladly accepted.

The last time I saw Aunt Dilo was during a visit to Fitzgerald in the summer of 2002. I was there to review the progress being made on the renovation of several houses Dad purchased directly across the street from Grandmother's house well before he died. I was driving up Orange Street toward Palm, and no one looked to be home at the old family place or at Aunt Dilo's, but lo and behold she emerged from

Dilo "Aunt Dilo" Lee Boles, circa 1978-80

inside her house. I stopped the car and went up to the fence to greet her and to talk for a while. Two mangy looking dogs barked and howled from inside the fence, so I did not enter. We talked across the fence and it was then that she said out of the blue "when you lose your mother you have lost everything." This statement sticks with me to this day. She had been raised without a father and her mother had been dead for over twenty years. She was obviously still hurting from that loss, and she wanted to impart the wisdom from that loss to me. Who could disagree? A mother's love is unconditional, a love created in conception that transcends death.

At Aunt Dilo's funeral at the Lee family church, in Fitzgerald, Georgia, the resident minister who preached her eulogy spoke about "holding on, reaching beyond the break." The rope may break, "but reach beyond the break," he said. A profound concept. On the Lee side there is no pretension. These folks were "hard boiled scratch cooks," plain spoken. Unrefined, but good-hearted, and not ignorant. This household grew up qualitatively poorer than mother's household. They were who they were. What you saw is what you got. The honesty in these folks allowed them to be real with one another all the time. They did not pretend to be educators or elites and they knew nothing about "high culture" as it is known in some circles. Conflicts and family feuds abounded from time to time, but except in rare instances they all loved each other devoutly. There was no invidious competition. Folks were just glad to have what they had and were glad to see you have what you had. They are a family without scheme or artifice. This sense of family emanated from my grandmother who fought to keep her family together against the odds from the beginning. Though they may have been unrefined, the culture of unconditional love between the siblings was clear for all to see and witness. Serrated on the edges, this clan was industrious, and home owners except for one, all of them kept their families together in one unit despite the obstacles owing to the legacy of the female progenitor, grandmother Emma Lee Clark.

The cousins I have on the Lee side are many. But principally I grew up knowing Beryl "Wendell" Boles Mills, Dilo's only daughter, Pat and Jean two of Maebell's children, and Skeeta, one of Cat's children, better than any of the others, even though I got to know them all to a certain degree. We were misfits more than any other thing, a hodgepodge.

Wendell and I spent a fair amount of time together during our adolescence. Wendell was quite the looker back then, and she could have any guy she wanted. Dad took a liking to her and wanted to help her. Wendell stayed with us in Charlottesville during the summer one year, and we attended summer school together at Lane High School, the White high school in Charlottesville. We both flunked the classes we were taking and went out for hamburgers and milk shakes after getting our grades.

Years later, Dad, exercising his power as an administrator, hired Wendell as a teacher in Albemarle County, but it all ended in failure. A criminal charge was filed against Wendell for assaulting a White teacher. And after leaving Charlottesville, she filed for bankruptcy to avoid paying a loan Dad cosigned for her to obtain an automobile while she lived in our home on Ridge Street in Charlottesville. Dad was deeply hurt, he felt betrayed. He was disappointed and chagrined at the way the Wendell situation turned out in Charlottesville and the poor judgment that she had shown. It cost him a hit against his reputation in the county, and he was made to pay the loan Wendell defaulted on. Dad was always trying to help, in his own way, those he loved and cared for. He would have little to do with Wendell after this episode ended, though he still respected her as his sister's daughter. In his usual stoical manner, he sucked it up, never spoke of the incident after the fervor cooled but he never forgot it.

"Sis" whose given name is Tobytha, named after Dad's oldest sister, was another cousin I got to know somewhat. She is a tall, brown skinned woman whose voice ebbed and flowed from bass to treble, uniquely her own. Sis was always "out there" on her own "flying her own kite," chasing her own rainbows.

Skeeta was raised by grandmother, Maebell and Aunt Dilo. As a youth he lived in the back room of grandmother's house on East Orange Street until he left for college. A tall tan colored man with short-cut black hair, he too had a voice distinctly his own, a voice that sounded covered or muffled, never fully vibrant.

In the latter years of her life, I got to know Pat very well, Jean's youngest sister. She was a beautiful dark skinned woman with black hair. I spent a lot of time with Pat eating her cooking and talking about the family when she lived in Philadelphia while I was there. While I was in Philly, I got to know Pat better. I had spent little personal time with her before then even though I was around her in Fitzgerald. Wendell, Skeeta and Pat were raised by women. Wendell and Skeeta went to college but Pat did not. We would grow to share some memorable experiences, none more sharply etched than our shared experiences picking cotton and cropping tobacco in rural Fitzgerald, Georgia. We had moved to Charlottesville when these adolescent experiences took place.

Lee family photo, from left to right: Rosa Lee, Otis Lee, Sr., Dilo Lee Boles, Emma Lee Clark, Roosevelt McDuffy, Maebell Wilcox, Willie Robert Lee, Mae Lee, Fitzgerald, GA, circa 1979-81

LEE GENEALOGY CHART

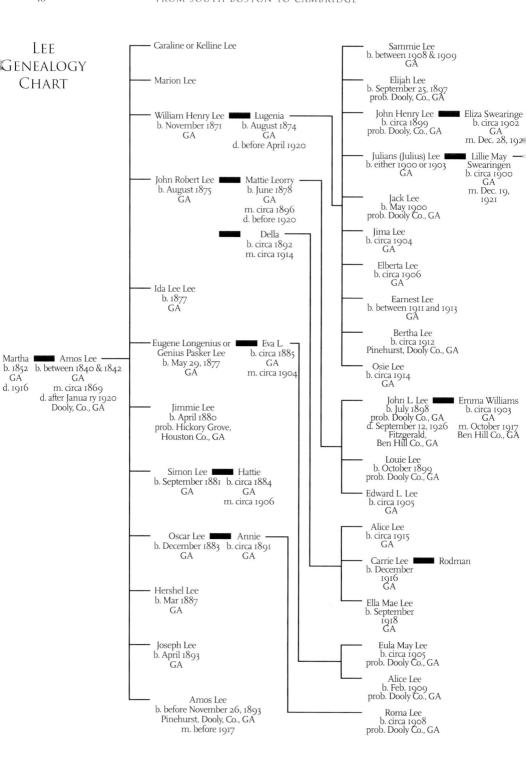

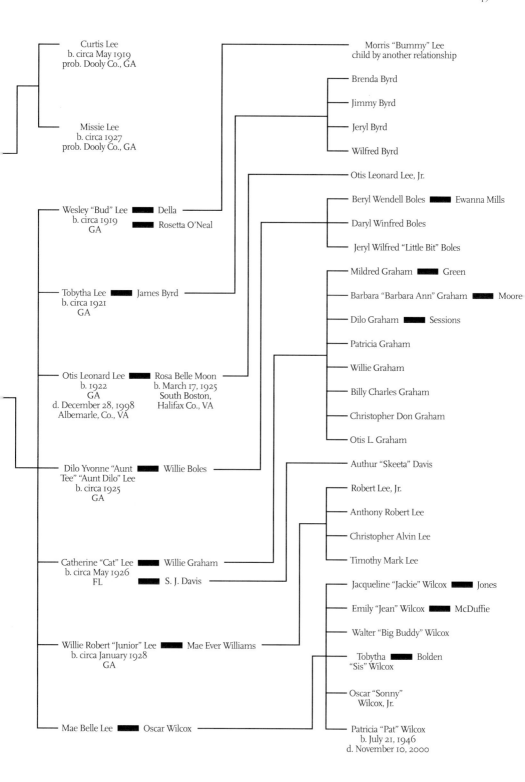

Curtis Lee
b. circa May 1919
prob. Dooly Co., GA

Morris "Bummy" Lee
child by another relationship

Missie Lee
b. circa 1927
prob. Dooly Co., GA

Brenda Byrd

Jimmy Byrd

Jeryl Byrd

Wilfred Byrd

Otis Leonard Lee, Jr.

Wesley "Bud" Lee ▬▬ Della
b. circa 1919
GA   ▬▬ Rosetta O'Neal

Beryl Wendell Boles ▬▬ Ewanna Mills

Daryl Winfred Boles

Jeryl Wilfred "Little Bit" Boles

Mildred Graham ▬▬ Green

Tobytha Lee ▬▬ James Byrd
b. circa 1921
GA

Barbara "Barbara Ann" Graham ▬▬ Moore

Dilo Graham ▬▬ Sessions

Patricia Graham

Willie Graham

Otis Leonard Lee ▬▬ Rosa Belle Moon
b. 1922   b. March 17, 1925
GA   South Boston,
d. December 28, 1998   Halifax Co., VA
Albemarle, Co., VA

Billy Charles Graham

Christopher Don Graham

Otis L. Graham

Dilo Yvonne "Aunt ▬▬ Willie Boles
Tee" "Aunt Dilo" Lee
b. circa 1925
GA

Authur "Skeeta" Davis

Robert Lee, Jr.

Anthony Robert Lee

Christopher Alvin Lee

Timothy Mark Lee

Catherine "Cat" Lee ▬▬ Willie Graham
b. circa May 1926
FL   ▬▬ S. J. Davis

Jacqueline "Jackie" Wilcox ▬▬ Jones

Emily "Jean" Wilcox ▬▬ McDuffie

Walter "Big Buddy" Wilcox

Willie Robert "Junior" Lee ▬▬ Mae Ever Williams
b. circa January 1928
GA

Tobytha ▬▬ Bolden
"Sis" Wilcox

Oscar "Sonny"
Wilcox, Jr.

Mae Belle Lee ▬▬ Oscar Wilcox

Patricia "Pat" Wilcox
b. July 21, 1946
d. November 10, 2000

4

꩜

THE EARLY TEACHING YEARS, GEORGIA

HE FRIGHT AND THE STENCH in rural Georgia of Jim Crow permeated the culture of people of color. Tears come to my eyes when I think about the story my mother tells of the time between 1948 and 1952 in north Georgia, where she and Dad began their teaching careers after graduating from Fort Valley State College. They taught school in the small towns and counties of Locust Grove, Commerce, Nelson, Athens and Pinehurst, buried deep in the rural fabric of Georgia. These areas were desolate, desiccated by Black privations. They lacked commerce and urbanity. Black school teachers during the Jim Crow era, taught Black school children often in ramshackle segregated, and dilapidated one and two room white frame schoolhouses located on dirt roads of clay and mud many with gabled roofs. This was not an education: this was a miscarriage of education, a miscarriage of the promise of freedom and liberty. But it was the social order that had been ordained by law and custom, confirmed by the courts and applied with the force of the flogger to the people tied to the whipping pole.

In those times, Mother taught school in Nelson County, Georgia, in a town called Wilsonville. There was no direct train from Fitzgerald to Wilsonville where she taught. On several occasions she was driven by horse and buggy from the outskirts of Nelson County to her school in Wilsonville. She taught school in a one room schoolhouse for one year, teaching combined grades of 1 through 6 in one classroom. She says "it was a mess." There was no teacher's aide to assist in keeping the disparate groups under control, teaching materials were scarce and chaos and pandemonium reigned except on those days when she had had enough and screamed to the top of her voice to get order, but only briefly. Her experiences were so gut wrenching that they seared her subconscious with the stark images of poor Black kids drowning in poverty, desolation and ignorance, but not hopelessness.

She remembers the White men who owned turpentine trees who would come through the Black shanty towns with rows of crudely built houses, blowing theirhorns to awaken the Black laborers, a kind of alarm clock reminding them that another day's work lay ahead. The awakened Blacks would come out of their houses disheveled and

Rosa M. Lee, mother, circa 1950

barely awake, and jump onto the back of these trucks to be hauled off to the tree farms to harvest the pulp and the sap from the turpentine trees.

She often remarked, "we just missed slavery." She was speaking reflectively, reminiscing about how hard it must have been during slavery as she could have imagined it. She was comparing her situation in north Georgia, in that one room schoolhouse with all those kids looking to her for an education, with that bygone era. The slavery era had passed, but its residue and the trappings of that period were all around her. She was overwhelmed by the depth, ferocity and thoroughness of its legacy. Mother did this work for one year, but after that she said she had had enough.

Even on weekends, my mother rose before the rising sun. She ran through the grass fields at dawn, the night still visible, to catch the local train: running with a baby in her arms, hands waving, yelling to a passing train. A train that came out of nowhere, going to a place called somewhere.

"Stop! Stop! Please stop," she pleaded to anyone who could hear her cry. Her voice echoed against the deafness of the silent night. Exhausted from the sprint, she no longer ran but walked, knowing that if she missed this train there was no certainty for a Black family that another train would come and bring with it the salvation of a better life that she dreamed of for herself and her family. The train could take her out of the reality she was in, into the embodiment of her aspiration—a vision for a better life.

She stayed in Wilsonville during the week and traveled to Fitzgerald on the weekends to be with Dad. On her way to Fitzgerald to be united with her love, she pressed on, striving not to be denied.

— — —

In spite of the deficits—no father, a single mother and poverty always at the front door—my father, the "Georgia man," made good. With the encouragement of his mother and his sister, Tobytha—the first in the family to be exposed to higher education who he loved so dearly—he made a success of his life. "Red," they called him fondly, was raised in southern Georgia: one of seven children raised by a widowed mother. He knew poverty, but not hunger. He did not lack for love and affection. He experienced loss but not the loss of hope, pain but not despair. His energy for triumph over adversity was boundless.

This Georgia man's face was round, his hair black and short but straight with distinguished grey at the peak. He wore glasses. His build was rotund but not obese, his height not tall but well above short, his complexion, a rust color or "red." His voice was southern but cracked with a discernible northern inflection unique to his persona and experiences outside of Georgia. He spoke with clarity and strength. During those days he looked like a young Mufti with his round head, short hair and horn rimmed eyeglasses.

These physical features describe the outward appearance of my father, but do not begin to describe this complex human being who had the drive of Napoleon. He was a husband, a father, an uncle, a grandfather, a son, and a brother. Professionally he was the consummate educator and within that field he wore many hats: a trailblazer, a school master, a principal, a teacher, an administrator, a supervisor, a resource, a counselor to his colleagues.

Dad began his teaching career in Douglas, Georgia in Coffee County, immediately after graduating from Fort Valley State College in 1947. After two years he was hired as the principal of Ambrose Junior High School, in Ambrose, Georgia. And from there until after I was born in 1947, he was principal of the Johnstown High School in Commerce, Georgia. I stayed with Dad in Commerce, Georgia while Mother taught school in Wilsonville, Georgia.

I remember living with him in a wooden house coarsely built but not far from where Dad was teaching and working as the school principal. He tried to cook for me and take care of me, making his famous soup of leftovers and goulash. The wood stove made of black cast iron sat in the center of the small room where we ate our meals. Even though I was less than five years old, I remember having fun with him because of his love of language. Dad taught English along with a host of other subjects back then. He would say to me at the dinner table, "Otis, eat the fragments" by which he meant the ends of the bread. I thought that was funny, and I laughed heartily at the word "fragments." It stuck in my craw. The word fragments became my new toy and I played with it every place I went. I even told Dad he had to eat the fragments. As I hopped and skipped along, playing with the kids that were around I would sing, "you gotta eat the fragments, you gotta eat the fragments."

Dad took me to school with him during those early years. Dad was the headmaster, the janitor, teacher and disciplinarian. I vaguely remember a schoolhouse, a white frame building sitting on a hill surrounded by red Georgia clay, and neighborhood children leaving their nearby homes to come to school each morning. The kids looked disheveled and poor, for these were the children of the rural south: the children of farmers, sharecroppers, and cotton pickers. No polish or brass for these folks, just the bare bones basics, overalls, scuffed up brown shoes, brogans, pressed cotton blouses underneath worn cardigan sweaters in solid colors of blue, green and brown for the girls. Yet they retained jovial dispositions. I remember the kids being happy and fun loving toward me and to Dad in spite of their deprivations. Black education was not a high priority for the state of Georgia, or for any of the rural Black Belt, Deep South states.

Teaching in these substandard conditions was all he knew. He attended these "separate but unequal" Jim Crow Schools during his early education days, and now he was teaching in them as an adult. It is the height of hypocrisy, in my judgment, that White folks speak of Black underachievement as a caste attribute when it was the White system, with "equal tax dollars" from the cash-poor Black community,

Otis L. Lee, Sr., father, circa 1950

that provided Blacks by design with substandard educational facilities. The Blacks that overcame this gross inequity should be applauded and exalted not dismissed as benign mediocrity. This hypocrisy continues today when these same White folks, who denied the existence of unequal educational opportunities for Blacks, seek to devalue the achievements of Blacks who graduate from White schools as being less than a valid achievement, calling them merely "affirmative action" graduates. If not for affirmative action, these Blacks would have been denied the opportunity to succeed. I postulate that "but for" 400 years of slavery, by a class of predatory White people and 100 years of mean spirited and evil Jim Crow and marginalization, academic achievement and the values that undergird them would not be an issue for Black people. The history of Black people is replete with stories of how our people have always overcome tremendous odds to achieve excellence.

Dad overcame the limitations of Jim Crow education. He embraced the values of hard work and education, even segregated education, and went as far with it as he could. In the process, he learned to appreciate that there was higher ground in education to be had. His objective was to help Black children see the benefit of education—to appreciate the opportunity they had albeit that it was less than it should be. After all, this situation was the rule rather than the exception. Some education was better than none.

Dad cared for me as best he could, God bless his soul. He was not much of a cook, but I did not starve and my belly was always full. He tried but he was not the most astute caregiver. He meant well and he saw that the basics were taken care of, but his efforts were not that of a mother. His were the efforts of good intentions, rough and unsmooth, caring but not fawning, protective and reassuring but not effusive in his display of love. His love for me and commitment to me was ever present in his daily activities, expressed through making sure that the essentials were taken care of. I was fed, kept warm, clean and dry. He provided all the essentials and a bit more without the frills of pastries and other baked goods during this time. When I came down with a severe cold, he took me to a nearby drugstore and had the druggist make up a batch of flavored castor oil to trick me into swallowing it. When Dad tried to pour it down my throat by holding my nose, so I would not taste it, I threw it all up right there in the drugstore. The oil was nasty tasting, thick, oily, slimy and swollen with a translucent viscosity that made it pour like molasses. It was a mixture of laxatives and who knows what else. Castor oil was the most hated of all cold medicines to kids my age. But old folks thought that when you got a cold the best medicine was to take castor oil so that it would clean you out and carry the cold with it. Dad was "old school" and thought he had hit upon a remedy, a magic portion that would cure my head cold, but he was mistaken.

During these years, Mom and Dad made my dad's mother's home on Orange Street in Fitzgerald, Georgia "their home." They met there on weekends and holidays during the early Georgia years each returning from their teaching sojourns after graduation from Fort Valley State College and the start of their teaching years in Georgia. Fitzgerald, the "colony city," if you blink your eye too quickly you might miss it. This small town in southern Georgia about 150 miles north of the Florida line is a rural agricultural town. The neighboring farms raise peanuts, tobacco, cotton, pulpwood, turpentine and tomatoes. They stayed in a small room in the rear of this small frame house with the cool in the morning, cool in the evening front porch.

The dogged, stoic personality of this man was well known to those of us who knew him well. He would endure and not complain. He bore his burdens bravely and confronted his trials with the sinew of moral valor; he embraced reality. One rarely knew how much he might have been hurting inside; such was the nature of his character. He never complained because he knew from experience that he had it good. He often said, "I came up on the rough side of the mountain." Mother urged Dad to come to Virginia. She did not like Georgia. It was too rough, backward and raw. But Georgia was all that Dad knew at the time, even though his horizons had been expanded during his college days. He was raised and received his primary and secondary school education in the town of Fitzgerald at Monitor School, and he became a young adult in the back rural farm roads of pulpwood and turpentine country. During his college years, he worked in New York and Connecticut during the summers to raise money for his tuition where he learned to play golf working as a caddy and to appreciate fine clothes. But he had never lived in Virginia. Virginia was the north to him. So the decision to move to mother's home state of Virginia was like deciding to move to New York—out of the Deep South into foreign territory. Dad felt that the move to Virginia was progress. Georgia, with its harsh segregated regimen, did not offer a long term solution about where to live, work and raise a child, nor the environment he wanted to live in long term.

5

THE EARLY TEACHING YEARS, RICHMOND

M Y FAMILY'S MIGRATION TO RICHMOND was not easy. To ease the transition, we had family in Richmond. My Aunt Willnet, her husband, Walter Parker, "Uncle Walter," and their son, Walter Cecil Parker.

Willnett Parker was the daughter of Mary Penick, a niece of Helen Penick, a granddaughter of one of my grandmother's brothers. Years before Mom and Dad moved to Richmond, Willnett married Walter Parker, a short handsome man who was dark brown in complexion and wore black rimmed glasses. The Parkers were an old Richmond family. Willnett was a cousin and a well-known and familiar family member. She was a frequent visitor to the family home in South Boston traveling between Richmond and South Boston for holidays and family gatherings. She was an Elam, an offshoot of the Penicks. Uncle Walter walked with an awkward gait that required him to lift up his deformed left leg that had braces on it in order to move his good right leg. He had been born with infantile paralysis, polio, so he used a cane to assist him as he went about.

When Mom and Dad first arrived in Richmond, Virginia between 1948 and 1949, determined to make a stand there, Dad was still teaching in Georgia, so he had to travel back and forth as time, holidays and train schedules would allow. To make ends meet, Mother worked in a restaurant in Richmond as a waitress. She and Dad rented a room from Isaac Parker, Aunt Willnett's father-in-law, in his small but sedate home on Ladies Mile Road on the north side of Richmond. After her toils at the restaurant, Mother worked at the local telephone company as an elevator operator. While Dad remained in Georgia, Mother worked in jobs outside of her occupational field, doing what was available for her to do, a devaluing exercise of her education and capability. This was just part of the price both were willing to pay, not knowing what the ultimate success or failure of the decision would be. Education was the ticket but not a panacea for Blacks during this era. All of these issues figured into the decision to make the transition from Georgia to Virginia.

Before my father mounted his entrepreneurial wings, he worked two jobs to make ends meet. He worked in a dairy, and he waited tables in addition to everything else. Working two jobs was not an uncommon plight for Blacks during this time, but these were college educated people in the segregated South struggling to make a life for themselves and their family. Without their educations, professional opportunities would have been unavailable and their horizons and expectations would have been stunted. Only menial work would have been the order of the day.

The ethos of our family culture was well established by the time we arrived in Richmond. The merger of two southern Black family cultures, one from the south side of Virginia and the other from southern Georgia brought together two people who knew hard times but who had loving intact families. Their ancestors' ignorance and a lack of education were surely impediments to their early progress, but they were not sustained road blocks that could not be overcome with diligence and an appreciation for and an acquisition of education and the drive for economic independence. The Moons were hard working, the Lees industrious. Several of the Moon-Penick children made something of themselves, but some did not. And all of the Lee children made something of themselves, barring a few. In this generation of the two families, there emerged five college graduates, one licensed electrician, a career military man, a caterer, and a factory worker. No one ever received public assistance or went hungry. They all owned their own homes except one. Self-reliance was the strong underpinning of these two family combinations. Accepting "no" for an answer or acquiescing to the status quo was not in the book for these two. They knew that the White man offered them nothing but more of what they had grown up with. So they were determined to succeed and to indemnify themselves against the caprice of White "good will" and to rise above the ever-present pall of vehement racism. Hard work, ingenuity, entrepreneurship, education, self-reliance, a morality built around a Christian faith dutifully adhered to but not fully understood, and thrift characterized the habits and life style of my mother and father. Mom and Dad aspired to appreciate high culture, not just the trite mundane ordinariness of everyday life. They wanted something better, something higher and different. They refused to settle for the limited visions Black folks often had and the limited opportunities begrudging Whites made available.

These values—inherited from the remnants of their ancestral culture and seared into them by the realities they lived, were innately inculcated by osmosis, observed from parents, and other role models, gleaned from talks with aunts and uncles and from observing and by associating with successful White folks—were indissoluble against trial and tribulation. There was no safety net for them. They were themselves, together, their only safety net. The only helping hand they had was at the end of their arms. These were the values that transcended place, time or person. The synthesis formed from the Lee-Moon combination catalyzed a synergy that empowered their aggressive assault on wealth accumulation, to attain and maintain a middle-upper class status with economic security. The bet was always placed on what was real, not speculative. Wishful thinking and fantasy were avoided, and in their places pragmatism and reality helped them navigate through a world antithetical to their well-being. What else can account for the tenacity and consistency to win in children of the Jim Crow generation?

Like a successful relay team, the values of a family must be handed off, relayed from one generation to the next and successfully employed, not dropped. This was and is the way my immediate family chose to run the race of life.

Dad is the man that had the most impact on my life. Thank God he was a good man. And mother—most loving, sincere and caring woman I know—is the woman that had the greatest impact on me. I was fortunate to be born into the breast of a family with the values enumerated above.

My parents along with other Blacks were able to acquire homes in Richmond, Virginia because in 1948 the U.S. Supreme Court in *Shelly vs. Kramer* (1948)[4] made unenforceable racially restrictive covenants which were in popular use in Richmond at that time. During this period racially restrictive covenants in deeds were common. These covenants barred Blacks from buying real estate in certain neighborhoods. These contracts, which had kept Blacks out of certain neighborhoods, had been tacitly approved by the U.S. Supreme Court in 1926, in *Corrigan Et Al. v. Buckley* (1926)[5], notwithstanding its earlier decision in 1917 which struck down local laws that promoted residential segregation.

However, their first attempt to buy a home in 1950 fell through. The North Avenue home they would later acquire was a chance encounter while passing through the neighborhood, still searching for the right buy, and seeing the "for sale" sign out front.

North Avenue Residence, Richmond, Virginia, circa 1957

In 1952 a deal was struck. Dad was 30 years old and Mom was 27. My parents purchased their first home on the north side of Richmond, known as Barton Heights. Barton Heights had been an exclusive all White north side community for generations prior to 1948, when middle class Blacks started migrating into this section of Richmond. Blacks began moving into the north side as the Whites migrated to the surrounding suburbs. Black professionals, teachers, doctors and lawyers, hard-working office types, firemen and government workers populated the area. The house cost $10,000 in 1952, which was a large amount to them, and they paid $49.50 a month on the mortgage note. This bought them a two story, four bedroom white frame colonial on North Avenue, where the Ginter Park city transit bus stopped on the corner for easy access to public transportation. My mother would ride the segregated Ginter Park bus, standing when no seats were available for Blacks, nearly every day to and from work for many years before we left Richmond. After returning home from school each day, I remember watching that bus as it made its way up the block to the stop nearest our home to see if my mother was on it. My heart was gladdened to see her exit the bus and walk to our home in the middle of the block. It would not be long, before she would be preparing dinner, and I would be sitting at the kitchen table telling her about my day in school.

We lived in this colonial style house on the north side of Richmond for eight years, from 1952 to June 1960. This was my first home, the house that encapsulated my world. Our home had a large living room, dining room and kitchen on the first floor, four bedrooms on the second floor, hardwood floors throughout, a large backyard, a corrugated tin garage with a dirt floor situated on the left side of the back yard. The front yard was rectangular, of moderate size and was enclosed by a three-foot high red brick retaining wall that Mom and Dad had built. A cement walkway ran parallel to the front yard and extended around the house to the back yard. The walkway in front of the front steps was perpendicular to the city sidewalk. The house had a long wood front porch that extended across the length of the front of the house.

Mother, with a hint of wistfulness, recites the saga of how she struggled after she and Dad moved to Richmond and purchased the house on North Avenue. After buying the house, we had no dishes and no silverware. Many times when talking about those days, Mother would remark: "We didn't have nothing! We didn't have nothing. We bought a house but we had no furniture, no dishes, nothing." Then she said, "but we did have an education and we worked together."

In search of dishes and silverware, Mother went into the tin garage with its dirt floors. There, to her relief, she found buried in the dirt some old porcelain dishes and silverware, their silver-plating barely visible. The dishes and silverware had been discarded by the prior White owners. She brought these dishes into the house and washed the plates, forks and knives so we could have eating utensils. In the early days, Mother and Dad rented out the upstairs to Aunt Willnett and Uncle Walter, and later they rented out a room to other tenants to make ends meet. It was Aunt Willnett who assisted Mother and Dad with buying the first furniture for the house from Haverty's Furniture Company in downtown Richmond. Aunt Willnett had an account with them and lent her reference to Mom and Dad, so they could open an account and buy their first pieces of furniture.

One day Mother had a verbal blow-out with a male tenant as he went upstairs to his room. She stood in the living room looking up the stairs. "Mr. Jacobs," she bellowed, "we do not allow drinking and women in this house without our permission, and your rent must be paid on time if you intend to stay here or you will have to move." I stood there right beside her, innocent as to what this was all about, as the exchange took place.

"Mrs. Lee," he responded. "I pay my rent and I am a grown man and if I want to have company I'm going to have them!" he shot back. She quickly retorted "not in this house you won't. I suggest you pack your bags and get out immediately!" I was amazed at her strength and fight. Mother "ruled the roost." She could be stern when she had to. You did not want to tangle with her when she was ready to do battle. Mother had been waiting for this man to come home, so that she could confront him. I do not recall seeing that tenant much after that.

Growing up in Richmond on North Avenue between 1952 and 1960, I lived in a middle class neighborhood amid a corridor of single family two-story, three and four bedroom homes. The houses in this neighborhood were built during the 1920's in a similar colonial style. Each house was built on a deep lot with a front yard and a back yard large and deep enough for the neighborhood kids to romp, wrestle, play hide and seek, and dwell in the kid's world of imagination. In keeping with southern tradition, each house on the block had long front porches for lazy sitting on summer mornings with a coffee royal; in the afternoon with ice tea; and in the evening with a Jack Daniels. Some houses had garages in the rear like ours with a backyard that sat adjacent to an alleyway that ran parallel with the wide-paved street in front of the houses.

During this time, I was oblivious to the wider racial events unfolding in Richmond, Virginia. Richmond is the old capital of the confederacy and a city as bigoted and racist in its relations with people of color as any southern city. But inside the world I lived in Richmond was different. Richmond was a city with a thriving Black middle class, a city with some sophistication, a progressive Black community and a Black community of educated elites. My family and many others were a part of that Black educated middle class. Richmond had Black lawyers and doctors, educators and funeral directors, ministers and business owners—an entrenched Black middle class.

Mother, unable to secure a teaching position in Richmond, was hired for a year as a teacher in Fredericksburg in Stafford County, 50 miles north of Richmond. During that time, she took me there with her, and we lived in a rented room during the week while she taught during the day. I went to school with her each day and was put in the first grade teacher's class as a favor to her. Teachers did that for one another, back then. We would stay in Stafford until Friday and would go home on the weekends back to Richmond. Mom and Dad and their colleagues were the *Brown vs. the Board of Education* educators. Black educators whose careers were just taking off when that decision was handed down, and whose career tracks were forever altered by the decision.

When Dad, who was teaching in Georgia, would leave to return to Georgia from Richmond, my memory recalls the scene at the Broad Street train station. The three of us gathered together, saying our goodbyes, awaiting the arrival of the train on which Dad would depart. When the train arrived, I would burst out in a sea of tears crying for my dad not to leave me. I had lived with him in Georgia just a few years earlier, and I sensed the loss of his leaving and the pangs of that loss made me sad and tearful. I cried uncontrollably and could not be consoled, creating quite a scene until the tearful spasm had passed. Dad's haste to end his career in Georgia was caused in part by these continuous outbursts of tears every time he left to return to his home state. He often remarked that his heart could not take this kind of emotional assault for long.

In Georgia he was somebody, but in Richmond he was on the outside looking in. With a mortgage to pay and no job in the Richmond vicinity, Dad returned time and again to Commerce, Georgia. But his family required his presence, and he could no longer rationalize being in Georgia when we were in Richmond, just because Georgia offered him the recognition that he deserved. To him, family was more important and the time for separation was ending. It was not long before Dad finally left Georgia, that he found a position as principal at the H.H. Poole Junior High School in Stafford County, his first teaching position in Virginia.

Running around the North Avenue neighborhood, I was hard charging. Playing with reckless abandon, full throttle, all out, sometimes without thinking because I felt safe in my environs, knowing I was "in my home." Because some of the neighborhood kids lived across the street, we all ran across the street maybe two or three times a day. North Avenue is a wide street which served as a major artery to downtown Richmond and other points on the north side of town. About midday during one of these unthinking moments, I darted out in front of an oncoming pickup truck near my house. My fleetly little legs could not out run the truck.

On this particular afternoon when all else was calm, the mothers that were home were in their kitchens preparing dinner or looking at the soaps on TV, their "stories," thinking that all was safe in this little slice of Black tranquility. But then the abrupt, frightening sound of screeching tires, cries of panic, pain and fear and the terrible thud of flesh smacking up against metal. I am sure the grown-ups, in their heart of hearts, all dreaded the possibility that their child could be struck by a car or truck that went up and down this busy thoroughfare all the time.

Without considering the risk and not thinking, I darted out and was struck by the left front end of a pickup truck. I was thrown from the point of impact, which was in the center of the road, all the way to the other side or opposite side of the street from where my home was. I remember being dazed, scratched up, bruised and more frightened than injured. I was shaken and totally disoriented when all of the neighbors came out to comfort me and to see if I was all right. The cries and the anguish and the sorrowful mourns were all expressed, but what mattered most was my physical condition. That would determine whether or not this would be a truly mournful occasion or just a temporary sorrowful event. Regardless, that was a teachable moment for all the kids and parents in the neighborhood. As I lay too shocked and stunned to move, everyone tried to comfort me without moving me. An ambulance came, my mother was fitful and distraught, but retained her equanimity in the midst of the squall. Dad was away. Later in the evening that day, I recall being in a hospital room with my father standing over me saying he was going to spank me for getting hit by that truck, a spanking I never got. There were no broken bones or internal injuries. My supple frame reflexively bounced off the front end of that truck, causing me no permanent injury. The truck was apparently not going fast enough to put more hurt on my young fragile body. Divine intervention was at play this time, and as it turned out would be at play in several of these life threatening events.

During one of these early years, I was given a dog. We named him "Sparky." A mixed breed Dad got from somewhere. He was a small brown dog with white patches in his coat. His breed was that of a hound of some sort. I remember playing with Sparky, but Mother was the family member that kept up with the dog as far as feeding him and caring for him was concerned. I was much too young to do this with any regularity. My parents wanted me to have a dog for some reason. Maybe they thought it was a middle class entitlement. Or maybe they thought because I was an only child at that point, a dog would keep me company. None of the other kids in the block had dogs.

Sparky's time with us was limited. He became sick. He started making coughing noises like something was stuck in his throat that he could not expel. He became sick and his misery could not be relieved by our collective meager knowledge of dogs and their maladies. His behavior became so erratic that Dad and Mom made the decision to get rid of him before he went mad and something awful happened. How they did it, I do not know. He was probably put to sleep. But Sparky was no longer a part of our lives. I often think of Sparky in the context of what he symbolized to me and to my family. Did he represent a misguided attempt to do something my parents envisioned but really did not know how to do? Or was Sparky just an aberration, a lark, something that was imagined but not really embraced, a whimsical adventure by parents who visualized the middle class life but were not really ready to deal with its fullest dimensions by White or elite Black standards. In any event, having a dog in my life may have had an effect on me for the better. My compassion for Sparky and experiencing the loss of that pet that I was trying to make a friend of, was an example of what life teaches us—that loss is inevitable. They did not make a second attempt at having a dog in the family.

As much as they tried, neither she nor Dad could crack the Black hiring clique that walled them off and held sway over the hiring of Black teachers and principals in the Richmond segregated school system. Even though Mom and Dad had college degrees, and Dad was working on his master's degree at Virginia State College in Education Supervision and Administration they still could not crack the system. There were many more college-educated Blacks in Richmond than in rural Georgia. Plus, Virginia State College, which was outside of Richmond, and Virginia Union University, which was in the city, were turning out new college graduates every year. The competition was strong in this city. The Black elite of Richmond drew from Virginia State College and Virginia Union University.

Dad was a gregarious fellow but very analytical, and above all he was blessed with vision. Dad was the educator entrepreneur; that was the business model he employed. Years later I would copy that strategy and become the lawyer entrepreneur, Dad could see beyond the immediacy of his situation. He had a vision of the future he wanted for himself and his family, and he had a strategy for how to get there. And he vowed that he would never be poor again. He was always considering things as he went about his daily routines. He was in a hurry to get ahead but not in a rush. He made friends easily. He kept company with old teachers and principals, as well as White and Black real estate professionals, business people and his friends.

Ora Newman and Pearl Peters were Black educators in Richmond during this time. Ora was high-yellow and a principal of an area school. Pearl was short and brown skinned and was a teacher at Randolph Elementary School where Mother worked as the dietitian. Pearl used to say that Blacks "were not late in getting an education but were long in getting it." I used to hear Dad say this all the time, and I wondered what he and she meant. Back then educated Blacks were always talking about other Blacks and education.

Pearl was a good friend of a distant family member, a lady name Geneva Johnson who lived with her husband George in Highland Springs, Virginia, a suburb of Richmond. Geneva may have been a Penick. Her facial features and pigmentation resembled the Penicks, but where she came in is unclear. Mother says Geneva was in the family by some connection but that "the old folks never discussed it." Geneva had long graying hair, was light skinned in color with a soft manner. Her aristocratic appearance belied her middle class status. By contrast, George, was short and dark skinned, smoked a pipe, wore glasses and was quite affable.

The Johnsons owned a beautiful farm spread out over seven or more acres of land. The house set well back from the road that ran in front of it. The neat little brick house was picturesque in its quaintness with a manicured lawn that extended about 100 feet from the front of the house to the edge of the road. I remember the acres of corn growing in back of the house, a wood storage shed darkened by age and wear, partially dilapidated but still sturdy enough to hold the farm implements. The shed set to the left just below the two rows of grape vines growing parallel to the house. Mother and Dad would take me to stay with Ms. Geneva on several occasions. During one of my stays—there was some celebration with guests all around—I got stung by a wasp right in the middle of my back while picking grapes on their farm. It was a painful sting. It hurt so badly that I remember the incident exactly as it happened 53 years ago. I always thought that Ms. Genera was a family member, because of her place in our lives.

The Johnsons were raising a girl, who was the daughter of one of their children. Her name was Shirley, a brown skinned, medium-height girl with indistinct facial features. She was a mystery to me. I never got to know Shirley. Neither her father nor her mother was ever around when I was there, even though I stayed there many times. "Ms. Geneva," we called her, would call out to Shirley, "Sherleee! Come peel the apples." She called her to clean out the pantry, do this or do that, every order being a household chore. Shirley would bristle as the orders came in. Shirley did not work in the fields, but she would reluctantly comply.

Ten years later the Shirley mystery would be solved when Shirley sued Dad because the Johnsons left their farm to him. Apparently somewhere in the relationship Dad loaned the Johnsons some money and they were unable to pay it back, so in satisfaction of the debt they left the farm to Dad. Dad was always doing deals and when money was involved he always covered his bets. Shirley was aggrieved when she found out that the estate bypassed her, and she sued Dad for her part out of the farm. Dad settled with her. Terms of the settlement were not disclosed, but Dad did alright, enough to leverage the proceeds from the settlement into another real estate investment that proved hugely successful.

Dad was a sociable guy and people took to him. This coterie of friends and family was part of the social, political and economic rounds he made to advance his prospects of being hired in Richmond, which he never achieved, and to teach and learn the ins and outs of the middle class Black community in Richmond.

Dad had a penchant for making friends and he learned plenty from his associations. It all began in the days of his youth when he would spend time with Fannie Fears, his "Aunt Fannie," his mother's sister. She lived in a little house down the road across the railroad tracks in Fitzgerald. She and her sister were raised by the same grandmother. Fanny had a two-bedroom frame house that sat on cinder blocks with no foundation. The wood siding revealed its age from the weather beating it had taken over the years, but it was hers. She owned it, she paid no rent. And although it was modest, it was the cradle of her security and peace. He sat at her knee as the fire warmed his body in his clean but frayed clothes and learned everything she had to teach him. His search for knowledge for sapience began when he was a boy. That was his way. He learned from old people, he treasured their wisdom. With no father to lead him, the elderly were his fount from which he acquired his wisdom. That's probably where he learned all of his old sayings.

Dad was also aggressive, a pusher, a striver, a hunter gatherer, eager to make his mark in education and real estate. Dad was a man on the move. But he was not my favorite during those elementary school years. I preferred my mother. This would change drastically as I grew older. My father would, in time, become my best friend. "Is he coming back again" I snidely remarked to Mother one day while she was cooking, with the tone urging that he not come back. Dad had gone to the store or to run an errand, and we were left alone.

"Don't let me hear you say that again you hear" she demanded.

"Yes ma'am," I sheepishly said with eyes downcast. Her words were spoken with such command: as though she had spanked me without laying a hand on me. The affect lingered and was real. I felt remorse for my remark. I loved my father during that time, but in my kid's world he was not a playmate; he was not fun. He didn't make jokes. I never saw him enjoy himself except when he and Mother were playing cards with some of their friends. Around me, it was always work. I do not remember him laughing that much around me. Back then he was always serious, was impatient and had a temper.

He took me with him on many occasions when he drove from Richmond to Petersburg to take his classes at Virginia State College as it was known back then. The trip was long—seventy miles round trip. Dad didn't talk too much during our trips, perhaps his mind was on his studies. I probably gabbed on about school or my friends and he just said, "uh-huh, uh-huh." I do not remember anything unique about the commutes except Dad's driving was not the best, but somehow we always made it to and from safely. On one occasion I remember sitting on a bench on the campus talking with a student Dad had asked to look after me while he tended to his business. We talked about everything. I am sure I wore her out being the loquacious kid that I was. We talked about parents and grownups for a while until he returned for the trip back to Richmond.

I remember his graduation ceremony in June of 1956. It was held in a large auditorium on the campus. I was seated in the audience when the graduates marched down the aisle. There were so many people I could hardly see anything and I did not see my dad. I was just there, it was all a huge undertaking to me.

The august ceremony was well attended—the auditorium was packed. The music was loud "Pomp and Circumstance" bellowed through the sound system. The graduates, those that I saw, walked briskly down the aisle all dressed in their graduation regalia, but I could hardly see them. I just knew that my dad was among them. It was as though I was a midget surrounded by giants, tall people all of them. No one lifted me up so that I could see, perhaps I was too heavy then, in 1952. I knew what the occasion was but barely remember if there was a guest speaker or what the order of service was.

When Dad socialized, he played cards, enjoyed his drinks, puffed on a cigarette on occasion to be sociable, but he did not inhale the smoke. He abhorred low behavior and vulgarity. He played the piano and worked hard at whatever he decided to undertake.

We took piano music lessons together. I do not remember who started taking lessons first, him or me. I remember accompanying him to his lessons. He took lessons from a fellow named Daniels who lived somewhere in the West End of Richmond. Daniels was a bespectacled Black man, short in stature, dark in complexion and he spoke in this stammer cadence and he called the piano, the "pie-ano." I did not accompany him to his piano lessons with anyone else at any time thereafter.

As we entered this man's quaint little apartment, the room smelled of musk, a kind of smell in cedar closets where fur coats are hung and protected. The instruction room was decorated with old world figurines and drapes. It was as if we had entered a time warp and entered a male version of Ms. Havisham's cloistered world from Charles Dickens' "Great Expectations." Daniels was not married and he lived alone. The upright piano was at the rear of his living room which faced a window looking out into the street. The piano sat neatly centered between the dips in the draperies that hung over a cornice along the top of the windows. Dad went to the piano and started his lessons, and Daniels would correct him as he went along. I sat in a chair a few feet back from the two of them and observed the instruction. "Mr. Lee," he would say in his herky-jerky cadence "you are not playing that right, sir! Go back to that line now, now, now, go back!" And so it went, week after week as the two of them tolerated each other in the name of each advancing his art. Daniels must have been, as so many music teachers are, a frustrated virtuoso unable to achieve the dream of playing the piano at the highest of levels. Playing the piano for Dad was his hobby, the way that he relaxed.

Years later, I asked Mother what prompted Dad to take up the piano. She had no answer. He just simply must have appreciated the instrument and wanted to learn at his age how to play it. He was not into classical music rather he liked to play the old Baptist hymns and some old folk favorites. His favorite hymns were "My Hope is Built on Nothing Less, The Solid Rock," by William Bradbury; "Blessed Assurance Jesus is Mine," by Mrs. Joseph F. Knapp; "The Old Rugged Cross" and "Rock of Ages, " by Thomas Hastings; and "Nearer, My God To Thee" by Lowell Mason. The folk tunes he played came from a piano book authored by Maxwell Eckstein. Dad loved to play "Jeanie with the Light Brown Hair" by Stephen Foster and "Beautiful Dreamer" another Foster song.

He beat these songs out week after week, so often that they became family favorites. The songs set the tone for our home. His error prone and inaccurate playing was accepted because we loved his sincerity, the purity of his effort and the homeliness of his art. Dad later followed up his piano training by studying under William Beller, an instructor at Columbia University in New York at his Sherman Square Studios. Father was there in New York during one of his summers renewing his teaching certificate in the early 1960s while contemplating an assault on the Ed.D in education.

Many years later, Dad was awarded in 1995-96 an Honorary Doctorate of Humane Letters, from Virginia Seminary College, the first post-civil war college, in Lynchburg, Virginia.

These experiences were my introduction to the piano. I started taking piano lessons about this time in or about 1956 from a woman who rented a white frame house from Dad on Garland Avenue around the corner from North Avenue where we lived. The lessons were given on Saturdays before noon. The teacher was a light brown skinned woman with a gentle not strict approach. The lessons for whatever reason did not last very long. After a few sessions it was over.

I then began taking piano lessons, in earnest, from Bernice Williams, a music teacher who was a member of our church, Ebenezer Baptist Church. Ms. Williams was a school teacher by profession. A short sophisticated Black woman with two children of her own with a no-nonsense disposition. This neat, strict and stern woman started me on my music journey. Upon my return from school most afternoons, I walked around the block, in the opposite direction from my first teacher on Garland Avenue, to her home on Barton Avenue. First, always looking to see if her car was there to see if she was home, hoping against hope that she was not. If not, I was on my way back home, smiling and skipping all the way having escaped another piano lesson. But she was there more often than not, it was not even close. She was there all the time except for one or two occasions.

Mrs. Williams was tough on my fingering and she tapped me on my fingers with a pencil to make me concentrate on getting the fingering right. She was tough but good. I played the piano continuously from this point until I graduated from high school save for a brief pause attributable to youthful myopia—my exasperation and exhaustion with the instrument. During most of my stay in Richmond, I played some kind of musical instrument the piano or bass violin, which I played in upper elementary school as part of a string quartet.

It was during these early elementary school years that I began to be sensitized to the differences in learning readiness: "The smart kids versus the dumb kids." The teachers began to distinguish among us, by patent capability, putting us in groups separated by performance or some diagnostic test. It bothered me even then not to be put in the "smart group." Why the educators chose such a track escapes me?

Vincent, light complexioned with straight black hair, straight nose and a mole on his face, who lived one block up in a rental duplex unit was seen by the teachers as a "smart kid," he was always moved ahead. I was not. We played together every day before and after school. For the first time the seeds of inadequacy, not being like "the smart kids," was planted. It did not bother me deeply, but I was affected. Back then the school administrators were skipping kids to another grade level if they were achieving above grade level or higher. The slow or average kids were left to progress normally. By this time, *Brown vs. The Board Of Education of Topeka* (1954)[6] had become the law of the land, and it was tenaciously resisted by the political forces that governed the state until cooler heads prevailed in subsequent years. However, Brown had no effect on me or my education that I could notice. The Richmond school system retained its duality of segregated schools for several years after we left Richmond. Not until almost 1972 and thereafter was full city integration achieved in the Richmond city schools and surrounding suburbs. By that time I had graduated from law school.

Playing marbles with my schoolmates in the school yard before school started was a young school child's equivalent of a high schooler's pick-up basketball game. Childhood virility and maleness was at play in these games. When purchased, the marbles, round clear glass with various designs and different colors inside, were sold in a little draw string sack similar to the way uncut diamonds might be sold to a jeweler. These glass objects were our "jewels." Kids that played the game, mostly boys, collected various sizes, types and designs of marbles similar to the way one would collect and trade baseball cards. There were "cat eyes," "big moes" and other real pretty marbles and your "toy," the one you used to win other marbles.

A circle ten inches in diameter was drawn in the dirt and all the players placed a marble in the circle, usually one they could afford to lose. Each kid took turns shooting his player called his "toy" into the pack to knock one of the marbles in the circle out of the circle. You kept shooting as long as you kept knocking marbles out of the circle. In games for "keeps," you kept each marble that you knocked out of the circle. We treasured certain marbles, the cat eyes especially. This was serious kids business; you didn't mess with a kid's marbles in those days. In the currency of kid's play, marbles were money. I played hard at marbles. I was all kid, 100 percent.

Mother was finally hired in the Richmond School System as an area cafeteria manager, stationed at Randolph Elementary School, a school across town. Her friend Cora Lee, no relation, helped get her the job. Cora Lee was already doing the job, when she learned of the opening and got Mother hired. Mother was responsible for the hiring of the kitchen help, designing the daily lunch menus, ordering the food, supervising the preparation and cashiering when the regular help was not there. Mother managed three schools in her district. Though she took her college degree in Home Economics, cafeteria manager was not what she had in mind as a career. Her degree in Home Economics, though not intended to be used this way, gave her the knowledge to function in this job. She did not particularly like the job because it forced her to be around food all day. And that environment caused my mother to eat more than she preferred. But this was a job in the system. After moving to North Avenue, I went to school with Mother at Randolph Elementary where she had been assigned. During a summer session there, a group of us kids attending the session to upgrade reading skills gathered around a circular table playing a game of Scrabble to strengthen our vocabularies. The teacher had two letters on the tray an "i" and a "t". Without thinking I said, "I got it! S-h-i-t!" The teacher looked at me with puzzlement and amazement. The precociousness of my unthinking remark caused the teacher to exclaim, "Wait till your father hears about this!" While walking home across a bridge that connected the North side to where the school was located, a car pulled alongside of me. "Get in this car boy!" his voice grumbled in a stern and demanding tone. He was seething with displeasure. It was Dad. He immediately started swinging at me, but because I was in the back and he was in the front he had to keep his eyes on the road, so he kept missing me. Like a basketball player, I used the rear seat as a backboard to prevent being hit. He finally cooled out by the time we got home, and I was banished to my room for the rest of the evening, as far as I can remember, without food or water primarily because I was too afraid to ask for it.

I entered the first grade at Albert V. Norrell, the neighborhood elementary school, which was within walking distance from our home. This small all-Black elementary school was the magnet elementary school for elementary school kids from the Barton Heights, North Avenue, Garland Avenue area. It was a magical time in the life of a young child. I was protected and secure in my ethnic community.

From Albert V. Norrell Elementary School, I went into the sixth grade to Baker Upper Elementary School near the Jackson Ward Section of Richmond, the Black community where our church was also located, which was not within walking distance. I had to take a city bus to get to this school or walk a long way across a bridge to get to the part of town where the school was located.

One day I took a pack of playing cards to school. And my elementary school teacher, Mrs. Mosby, caught me showing the cards to a classmate and embarrassed me in front of the class. "What do we have here Otis? You can't get your homework done, but you can find time to bring these evil cards to school. I'll see that your parents hear about this. Go to your seat," she commanded.

I had found the cards in the top drawer of our dining room server. What was the big deal? I was treated like a criminal. I was chastised. I had "sinned." I knew I was in for a beating when I got home after this incident. Well, "what the heck," I thought to myself, "a day in the life."

Having a penchant for petty mischievousness, I would come home after school each afternoon and against my parents' instructions watched television. I most remember watching "It's Howdy Doody Time," "Mickey Mouse and The Mouseka-teers," "Amos n' Andy" and the "Little Rascals." Of these television programs, the program that haunted me the most was "Amos n' Andy" with its negative portrayals of Black men and women. There was Amos the "Kingfish," a balding irascible conniver always seeking to pull the wool over his friend Andy's eyes. Andy was the rotund, big eyed gullible pretender led by the nose by Kingfish his intellectual master. Then there was Algonquin J. Calhoun, the lazy, befuddled and inarticulate lawyer, and Saffire was the pigeon- headed, loud mouth, protruding-derriere, high-octane firebrand. For some reason this program penetrated my impressionable brain and planted a seed for an unfavorable and unhealthy image of Black people. The program was funny and quizzical. While I laughed at the buffoonery, I drank the poison of Black deprecation. Counter balanced against the positive images I saw of my people in real life, a shadow was cast where there had been only light. Doubt about self-image was seeded. A fight, where none had existed before, between the good and the bad in Black people consciously and invidiously began.

While attending Baker Elementary School, the last school I attended in Richmond before moving to Charlottesville, I played the bass violin. The instrument was too large to take home every evening, so practice at home was impossible. The school owned a limited number of instruments; as a result two students took these lessons together, my classmate Chris and I. Chris was a dark skinned fellow with black hair with a brimming personality who wore dark black glasses. He was shorter than I was, and he appeared to have more confidence with the bass than I did. He seemed to play the instrument better than I did as well. He may have practiced more, how I do not know, but the teacher favored him more than me during our practice sessions together. My exposure to this instrument was interesting, but it did not make that much of a musical impression.

In those days, throwing rocks was a common childhood activity. And I liked throwing rocks. I took pride in my accuracy. At heart, I likened myself a country boy from South Boston, and country boys liked to "chunk" them, we used to say. One day while out frolicking, this kid and I, Harold Scott was his name, started throwing rocks at each other. Harold was a tall lanky awkward fellow from my school who lived a few blocks over from my house. He always had money to buy candy bars, especially Baby Ruth candy bars. And because he was lanky and awkward, the kids in the neighborhood all wanted to see if they could best him in a tussle. Urged on by some neighborhood kids, he and I began trying to fight each other. It was not a real fight. We were not angry with each other. Our entanglement was just a burst of youthful energy being expended. We were wrestling and throwing punches none of which hit their mark or did any damage.

After the physical contact ended, we separated ourselves and began to throw rocks at each other from a distance as we each made our way back home. In the midst of it all, I picked up a small piece of glass, a small shard of glass from a Coke bottle. As unlucky as I could be, my usual good aim resulted in the missile hitting its mark. It cut the kid near the right side of his lip. The lip bled profusely. I ran home and so did he.

I didn't really dislike this kid, but the rock throwing got me in trouble. When word got out back to school the following week that Harold had been cut by my having thrown that glass, it was the first time I ever felt afraid and ashamed. When my teacher was told that I was the culprit, she looked at me with eyes of admonishment but she never spoke a word to me about it. My body became as pliable as a wet noodle, and I slid down in my desk almost to the floor, trying to disappear. I felt like a wanted man, a fugitive. That feeling of guilt, responsibility and embarrassment occasionally comes back to me even today, as a strong incentive not to break the law—to behave myself at all times. Worrying about wrong-doing is uncomfortable. I hated that feeling then, and I hate it today.

Mom and Dad had to pay for the kid's medical bills I believe, because Harold's parents or their representative visited my house. I saw them sitting in the living room discussing some issues related to the incident. And I believe a White man came to our home to talk about the matter. I do not know what they talked about, but I was scared. Surprisingly, Mom and Dad never discussed the matter with me, and I did not get a whipping for this. Why I don't know.

I had great friends when we lived in Richmond. These were the halcyon days of carefree bliss. Rocky was my best friend, the only son of our next door neighbors, Oscar and Kitty Blake. He was funny as could be, a natural born comedian. A brown skinned curly-head boy. We cracked jokes and laughed all the time, looked at cartoons on Saturday mornings together and just had fun. We laughed heartily at the cartoon character "Dr. I Am Nuts." Rocky lived next door until his family moved to Hawthorn Avenue a few blocks over from North Avenue, but that did not stop us from getting together. Rocky had two sisters: Brenda, the oldest and the one I grew up with, and a younger sister, Brigette, born near the end of our stay in Richmond or shortly after we left.

Then there was Marcellus Easter. A light skinned kid with short black hair. His family was different. His father sold Watkins Products a line of toiletries and cleaning products and had a big old black Packard automobile that he kept parked in his garage in the back of his house. To my knowledge, during those days, Marcellus and his sisters seldom received toys or clothes on Christmas day. It was rumored that his parents always waited until after Christmas to get him his toys. He had two sisters Priscilla, the younger sister, and Arnez, the oldest. Marcellus could not come out to play as often as Rocky, but often enough. I liked Marcellus, or Marcel as he was known in the neighborhood, he was kind and gentle and soft spoken. He was the emotional part of my being at this time. Until he was threatened, I did not know that I could feel an emotional response to someone else's pain. We had been running from Battery Park, the neighborhood recreational park at night after a dance. We were probably too young to have been there but we were. When the ruffians from across town started the ruckus, Marcel and I began to run home but he fell behind.

As we crossed a small plot of land shaped like a triangle that separated the rows of houses on opposite sides of the street, where neighbors could sit or walk their dogs, Marcel fell and the gang of bad boys descended upon him like vultures on vulnerable prey. They pounced on him and began to beat him. I slowed up several yards in front of him and saw, through the shadows reflected by the street lights, the blows as they were being delivered and heard the moans and groans of young boys fighting. As each blow was struck, I felt the throb in my heart. My best friend, my playmate was on the ground with several guys hitting him time and again. I was unable to assist because I was outmanned—too afraid and ill equipped to provide assistance.

Unbeknownst to me this was probably the first sign of my high empathy.

Neighborhood kids, North Avenue, circa 1954, from left: Otis, Marcellus Easter (Marcel), Oscar L. Blake, Jr. (Rocky), James Byrd, Priscilla Easter

When we played we always used to say "you gotta eat dirt before you die." Never a truer phrase was spoken. But, we actually put dirt in our mouths and tried to swallow it to no avail. When we wrestled each other to a standstill the question was asked "do you give?" If you said "yes," the kid on top of you would get off of you. It is amazing how the wisdom of life finds its way into the play of children.

This was a kind and gentle period. And then on to the next adventure. In the summer, sliding down the side hills in Battery Park on the sides of flattened cardboard boxes made slick by the dead grasses that had turned brown over the weeks. In the winter, sleigh rides down those same hills. Those hills became gathering places for the neighborhood youth, especially in winter.

It was during this time that I proclaimed to my parents, while sitting at the dinner table one summer afternoon, I was going to "cut a record" and be a pop singer. As I walked and played along the avenues of the North side, I could hear the refrain from the Drifters popular hit song, "There Goes My Baby... moving on down the aisle," echoing from the car radios, home radios and record players, restaurants and bars that served the "fast" crowd in the neighborhood. The song reverberated in my memory and was popular during these times. The nature of the song seemed to characterize and capture the late 50s social climate of that period. The young Black middle class men and women in this community all knew this song. It was a song of their generation.

As we ate, Dad said something to the effect "that there were many people like you standing on the corner wanting to cut a record." I took no offense. My feelings were not hurt because I sensed that in reality he was right. Many people remarked that I had a good voice, and I guess all that went to my head. My hopes were not dashed, but I do not remember mentioning it again. I was a singer nonetheless, singing in the choir at First African Baptist Church, Aunt Willnett's church which was within walking distance from our home on North Avenue. I would go there for Vacation Bible School and Sunday School when Mother and Dad did not take me to Ebenezer. It was my backup church. Y.B. Williams was the pastor then.

I played hard in the neighborhood, romping, wrestling and running. One day I came barreling through the back porch door and sat down at the dinner table. Thirsty and out of breath I was looking for some of mother's iced tea. Without thinking, I grabbed a glass half full of a brown looking liquid that looked like it had tea in it and immediately started drinking it down. All of a sudden I spit it all out! It was cooking grease. What a mess, the mixture was horrifying to taste and repulsed me at once. Mother all excited shouted, "Otis put that down, that's not for you to drink!" But she was too late. My tongue told me that, before she had time to warn me. The thick torpid brown and beige color liquid that had the remnants of fried droppings from the last frying pan moved at the speed of molasses, had the taste of castor oil and the feel of eating cloth. I rinsed my mouth out as quickly as I could with water to remove that horrible taste, but it took time to rid myself of the taste. From that point on, no matter how much of a hurry I was in, I always looked into the glass to see what was in it before raising it to drink its contents.

Mother, on occasion, would send me to the corner market across the street known as Marty's Market to get an item or two she needed in the house. The store sold sundries of one kind or another. But most often, I went to buy one of my favorite summer treats: a frozen "grape iceberg." These icebergs came in 5-inch long cups that we dug out with a two inch wooden spoon. The deeper you dug, the sweeter and richer the grape juice. These were the favorites of the neighborhood kids and they only cost a nickel.

One evening after dinner, a knock was heard on our front door. Not expecting anyone to come by, we all wondered "who could that be?" Strangely, when Mother answered the door, there stood an old White man begging for food. He was gaunt, bent over, and unkempt in appearance. Mother was surprised that a White man, the embodiment of oppression, the "hammer" whose policies sought to strip us of our dignity, was at our door asking for food. Apparently his condition was so dire that he did not care from whence his help came. Perhaps he had been on the receiving end of the "hammer" just as we were. After gathering herself and looking to Dad for some reassurance that her instincts were right, she had him remain on the front porch while she went into the kitchen to gather some ham and biscuits, leftovers from an earlier meal. She wrapped the food in paper towels and put the contents in a brown paper bag to give to the man. Mother is a caring soul, a good spirit, who always, regardless of her plight, wanted to "do the right thing" as she would always say.

Before we moved to Charlottesville, one of Dad's friends whom he met commuting back and forth from Richmond to Louisa County invited us to Sunday dinner at their farm. Kate Allen was her name. Kate was a teacher and was married to Joe Allen, a farmer who was rough around the edges. Kate and Joe both worked the farm, but Joe was the real farmer. Joe was short in stature but a real man's man: tough, hard, no nonsense and real. Joe and Kate had one natural son from their union. Kate was a tall, full-figured dark skinned Black woman who wore thin yellow gold-rimmed eye glasses. She spoke with a funny cadence: part stammer, part stutter with a spasmodic hesitation and a raspy tone. Kate was strictly from the "old school." Kate and Joe kept foster kids. It seemed to me that they kept these kids to help them work their farm in addition to the money they received. They worked the hell out of those kids. I didn't get to know them too well because they rarely were allowed out to play. But not long after Dad was hired in Louisa County, I did get to know one kid, "Andy," after Kate and Joe bought the house next door to us.

One Sunday afternoon, we embarked on our trip to Kate's farm in Louisa. All was pleasant and we had a good time as we drove west on 250 out of Richmond into Louisa. As we turned into the farm road from the highway, the clouds burst and it rained as if Noah would come again and build his ark. It rained so hard the dirt road of clay began to emulsify into a thick convulsing mud. To get to the farmhouse from the road, Dad had to drive up a hill. There was no way we were going to make it in these conditions. The car got stuck in the mud. As he pressed down on the accelerator, the car went back and forth, the wheels spun rapidly going nowhere and spit out mud, digging ourselves deeper and deeper into holds made by the spinning grinding tires.

Soon the realization set in that we were in trouble. A gloom descended upon the three of us as we sat there thinking of our immediate future. How would we get word to Kate that we were even here at the bottom of the hill? We had no cell phones back then. To me it was great fun. Dad didn't seem to be too disturbed, but Mother was fit to be tied. She was always anxious about driving and especially Dad's driving, and even more so about driving in bad weather. Well, what to do. Someone had to get out of that car and walk up to that farmhouse to let them know we were stuck. Dad was elected and he got out and immediately sunk six inches down into the thick brown muck of mud. As he did so he was drenched and soaked by the rain that continued to fall. We had no umbrellas or rain coats, boots or galoshes. As he tried to advance after immediately exiting the car, he was fussing at Mom in frustration. They were yelling and fussing about the situation we were in. But on he went, one step at a time, pulling each leg from the suction cup of mud in each step. The shoes he wore were only good for covering his feet. His socks only provided a covering for his ankles and lower leg; they both were ruined.

"Lee, be careful!" she exclaimed.

"Rosa calm down I'll be right back." Mother was always the nervous type. After an hour or so, we saw Dad riding in the back of an old open trailer attached to an old dilapidated tractor soaked wet in discomfort. He was cheerful as he led Joe to the car. Mom and I were still dry but that would soon change. Joe detached the trailer from the tractor and backed the tractor up to the front of the car. He attached a hitch to the front bumper of the car and began to pull the car up the hill. It was no go. The rear wheels of the tractor began to spin. The incline of the hill made it difficult for the tires to get a grip in the thick mud. Mom and I had to get out of the car and get onto the back of the trailer, which he attached to the tractor, in order to get to the farm house. The car would have to be pulled back near the roadway rather than up the hill when the rain stopped.

Down into the mud Mother plunged her stocking feet just as I did. Our misery was made worse by the endless pounding of the rain. We were wet well beyond our zone of expectation. Dad began to find the whole matter funny as he surveyed the expressions on our distressed faces. Mother's stocking covered legs and feet had been assaulted by nature without recourse, no pity and no shame. Mom with her proper sense of decorum was out-done, exasperated and angry. To her the whole exercise was a useless adventure with nothing in return to compensate for the aggravation. As for me, I liked riding on the back of that trailer up the mud soaked hill to the farmhouse for dinner in the country. "All of this to eat dinner on a farm in the country," I could hear her murmur, "was not worth it."

"Lee let's go home!" she exclaimed, her sense of purpose for this undertaking having been long exhausted. The rain continued to fall. We got so soaked that our clothes felt like an extra layer of skin. Joe pulled us back to the farmhouse, all three of us in the back of the open trailer. We felt and looked like three rain soaked hoboes in search of shelter. Joe later went back to pull the car out of the mud pit it had dug for itself. After putting on dry clothes that didn't fit, we settled down for a real home cooked country meal prepared by a genuine country cook. The food was great, and as the stress dissipated and nerves calmed down, we had plenty of laughs recounting the ordeal. We had been humiliated by nature, an act of God, in search of a country meal, covered up to our chins in the mud of Virginia clay and lived to tell about it.

Reminiscing several years later, in 1962 Mother remarked, "I have never been so wet in my entire life from then until now."

Dad was a devout Christian, but far from being a saint even though he took his religion seriously. He hardly missed a Sunday service, and he held strong feelings about the order and process of religion. Dad was used to a "silk stocking" church, a middle-class church, but had to settle for the "country church" level of religious service in Charlottesville. Every Sunday Dad would get all "noxzemered up" with every strand of black and grey hair in place and go to Ebenezer Baptist Church for Sunday service. Our church home was a "silk stocking church" located in the

Jefferson-Ward section of Richmond on Leigh and Judah streets. This church set a standard for intellectual preaching, high tone singing, a formalized sophisticated order of service with some good looking Black people in attendance. I was baptized in this church by Rev. Eugene Everett Smith, one in a succession of high-end Black preachers. Tan in complexion, small of frame and bespectacled with wire thin gold rimmed glasses and short cropped curly black hair, "E. E." as he was affectionately referred to, set the standard for me at an early age for what I would come to look for in a minister. He was the embodiment of a sedate, moderate, well educated, unpretentious, yet dignified and classy Black minister. Revered Smith exuded a reverential quality seldom seen of late in Black preachers. But Rev. Smith had it, and he could preach. Dad admired him greatly. I remember attending his funeral service in the packed sanctuary of the church when he passed.

"I baptize you in the name of the father, the son and the holy ghost," and with one hand in the small of my back and the other on my forehead, swish, E.E. dipped me into the baptismal pool on my back. Thirty seconds later with water dripping from my face and all of my garments, I was back on my feet. A newly minted Christian. I was nine years old.

Forty-five years later, I would reunite with my home church. On the day I re-joined, the right hand of fellowship was extended to me, my wife and young son, Justin. It was the most heartwarming and welcoming embrace of my religious life. Tears swelled up in my eyes. I could not resist the tears of joy and communion that I felt when finally coming home.

What makes Ebenezer a great place to worship are a set of qualities that are enduring: high standards are set for the pastorate. For example Revered Smith and his successors exude a quality of sincerity, reverence, religious substance and dignity. These men always kept their dignity; staying in character is the key. They were and are conservative in their nature, bearing and disposition and have a natural or trained ability to preach the word from an intellectually logical as well as from a practical and biblical basis. Excessive histrionics are unwelcomed, and avoided but true excitement and emotion is fully expressed.

High standards are set and maintained for the choir, the music program and order of service. A business-like operation is essential for any organization that expects to endure the economic storms of business life. And vision, not myopia and small mindedness, though common in all congregations does not always prevail though these attributes may be manifest in some members.

An affiliation with the academic side of theology, in Ebenezer's case Virginia Union University, encourages substance over shallowness and demagoguery. And lastly, an enlightened, welcoming and loving congregation sets the tone for the sublime to enter, lifting one from the mundane and the trite to a higher place that you need to go to embrace the Holy Spirit: a congregation that demands that high standards be set and adhered to and know what those standards should be without compromise.

Religion is difficult to accept in all of its dimensions but these standards make it easier to open one's heart to the greater meaning of spirituality. This is why I think fondly of Ebenezer Baptist Church, because it exemplifies more of these qualities than any other church that I have joined. Some come close but none captures the essence of these issues like Ebenezer.

Life was good for us in Richmond, even though the jobs for Mom and Dad were not what they wanted. I remember going downtown with Mother to G.C. Murphy, a large variety store in the nature of a five and dime store but bigger, situated on a corner on Broad Street. When Mother would take me there my eyes would bulge at the sight of the big round size cookies that shown through the glass show cases in the pastry department. Chocolate chip, sugar and butter cookies, they all looked so good that I wanted to eat them all. My eyes were bigger than my stomach but that did not stop me from begging Mother for them. And worrying her to buy me cookies to the point she would get angry with me. "Will you stop whining about those cookies, Otis. I am not going to buy you anymore cookies! Every time we come down here you do the same thing," she exclaimed. But in the end I got at least one cookie out of her, but she was peeved by my insistence.

Dad on the other hand loved to shop at Green Trees, a top of the line men's clothing store. But I rarely went with him when he shopped there. I went with them alternately to shop at Miller and Rhodes and at Thalheimers where they bought linens and household goods. Thalheimers was the largest department store in Richmond during the 50s.

Dad was beginning to make his moves economically, and Mom and Dad had a great social life. They had their pinochle parties, the backyard parties, the Christmas parties, the church going, family and friends. This was a special period, although a segregated period, but Black people in this community evolved positively. Black people in our neighborhood had a community of shared values and standards. They were all contemporaries, the Black middle class of the 1950s. It was an idyllic time for me; I knew no difference. My world was North Avenue, Ebenezer Baptist Church, Albert V. Norrell Elementary School, Baker Upper Elementary School, my friends Marcellus, Rocky, and Vincent. The neighbors all knew each other and each other's children.

The blissful days of my youth in Richmond were unfettered by worries of race, grades, self-image, or competition, even though the seeds of all these factors were being planted and allowed to grow. Looking back, my parents' perception of middle-classism was flawed. Though they did appreciate many important values, they did not fully appreciate the signal importance of these issues in their fight for economic security.

Instead my father and I built cement steps together in front of one of his rental properties on East Grace Street. I was not by any means deprived of anything. He bought me everything I needed and some of what I wanted. When I was with him and he was buying something for me such as an article of clothing, he always told the sales clerk that he wanted the "cheapest." I cowered in embarrassment when he uttered those words. They had an effect on me unbeknownst to him. I didn't like to hear him say that, but he was trying to save money. It made me feel unworthy.

While we lived in Richmond, Dad took ill suddenly. Apparently he had an attack, an inflammation of his appendix, and he had to have his appendix removed to save his life. He was hospitalized for an appendectomy. In those days, the hospitals were segregated. I remember visiting him at the Richmond Community Hospital. A Black hospital founded by two Black physicians. When I visited him, he seemed well, a little drawn perhaps but glad to be alive, nursing the scar in the middle of his lower abdomen where the incision was made to remove the infected organ. He recovered unremarkably, and life resumed its normal course. Mother also suffered some serious discomfort during those years. She was a smoker back then. She fell victim to a severe back ailment requiring her to sleep on wooden boards for a time before she regained her health.

Once we moved to Charlottesville, Mom and Dad longed for Richmond and lamented the move for many years, even though they achieved professional and economic success in Charlottesville, and the move was good for me. My parents mourned the loss of their friends and contemporaries, the warmth and camaraderie of their neighbors, the sense of inclusion rather than exclusion, the "silk stocking church" both of them adored, and their professional friends.

Dad's closest friends were mostly other educators, teaching in one school or another, like Sapp, a dark skinned chap and fellow teacher and Brown, a math professor at Virginia State College, they were Dad's "hanging buddies." Usually on Saturdays they would come by the house in Richmond and pick Dad up and drive away.

"Come on Lee, you ready to go" Brown would call out.

"Yeah, I'll be there in a minute," Dad responded. "Rosa I'm going out with Sapp and Brown for a while," Dad would say before leaving. "I'll be back in a while," he was telling the truth but not the whole truth.

"Alright, tell Emma I said hello if you see her," Mom acquiesced in her high pitched voice. Emma was Brown's wife, also a professor at Virginia State College.

"OK," Dad said as he left the house and got into the car where Sapp and Brown waited for his anticipated entrance. Once, while walking up the avenue, I looked across the street where the ABC store was located and I saw the three of them parked in front of the ABC Store where they must have just bought their favorite brew and were about to consume it.

Cora Lee and Doc were friends Mom got to know through her work as a cafeteria manager for the Black schools she managed. Cora Lee was her colleague. She was a dark skinned stout but very pleasant woman with black hair. Doc was lighter in complexion with a hoarse voice. Cora Lee and Doc played cards with Mom and Dad. Often Mom and Dad would go over to their place which was a few block over. They lived in "a twin," a house attached on both sides by adjoining houses. Ruth and Jimmy, another set of friends who lived two doors down on North Avenue, on the same side of the block, were our immediate neighbors. They were also cardplaying partners of Mom and Dad. Ruth was light-skinned and Jimmy, well he was similar to Doc in complexion, but Ruth and Jimmy were older. Both Doc and Jimmy were jovial characters who liked their drinks and their cards. Pinochle was the game of choice and each of these folks enjoyed their drinks as they passed the time "taking the weight." Mom and Dad enjoyed these associations. These folks were unpretentious, easy-going contemporaries that enjoyed each other's company; Black people who had reached a level of peace with themselves and where they were in life.

Unable to find suitable professional work in Richmond after relocating, Dad drove to Louisa County every day to principal a school. It made no difference that Mom and Dad were college graduates and that he had a Master's degree, they were outsiders in Richmond.

6

"THE PATH,"
CHARLOTTESVILLE

"There are no beaten paths to Glory's height,
 There are no rules to compass greatness known;
 Each for himself must cleave a path alone,
 And press his own way forward in the fight."

from *The Path* by Paul Laurence Dunbar

W HEN THE TIME CAME TO MOVE to Charlottesville, it was the summer of
1960. For all we knew Charlottesville might as well have been Charlotte,
North Carolina which was named for Queen Charlotte of England. I
was thirteen years old, having finished the sixth grade at Baker Upper Elementary
School. My father was hired by Paul H. Cale, the superintendent of Albemarle
County Schools, to be the new principal of a new Black elementary School, Virginia L. Murray, being completed in Ivy, Virginia, about 15 to 20 miles west of
Charlottesville off of route 250 west.

At the time of his hiring, Dad was commuting from Richmond to Louisa
County daily as the principal of Z.C. Morton Elementary School. In 1960 I knew
nothing of Charlottesville; neither did Mom or Dad. Mom's work in Richmond had
not gotten any better. The opportunity to end the commute, close out the fight to
get into the Richmond schools and to get Mother into the classroom and out of the
cafeteria were strong incentives to take the offer extended by Paul Cale.

Though Dad had the Napoleonic drive to succeed, Charlottesville was not his
Waterloo, not even close. But Albemarle County-Charlottesville—where he fought
many battles professionally and in business—was his own "Elba," where he is interred, and where he suffered a kind of elected exile away from friends, family and
professional aspirations unrealized.

One Saturday morning in June of 1960, Dad and I drove to Charlottesville to
look for a new home. We were taken aback by the provincial uninspiring nature of
the city; the paucity of upscale modern housing for Blacks that met our standards.
Compared to North Avenue in Richmond, Charlottesville was drab, antediluvian,
rustic. At its core Charlottesville was and to some extent still is, a small racist southern college town living on the history and living out the legacy of its "patron saint,"
Thomas Jefferson. The contrast between the Black community of Richmond and
the Black community in Charlottesville was the difference between the sophisticated
and the provincial. Richmond's Black community was vibrant and alive: that community had a wealth of Black lawyers, doctors, teachers and principals, preachers
and funeral directors because it was a larger city with a progressive Black culture.

Charlottesville in early 1960 was a stagnant languorous place, with only the University of Virginia and Skyline Drive as its calling cards. There were no Black lawyers in Charlottesville at that time. There was only one Black doctor who made house calls without hospital privileges at the University of Virginia Hospital. One dentist, three funeral directors, enough Black teachers to teach in the Black schools and enough Black principals to manage them. Black businesses in Charlottesville were more than rare: besides two nondescript neighborhood variety stores and three funeral parlors there were no other Black businesses except for two local realtors. The standard of living for the average Black in Charlottesville was not high. The small Black middle class—consisting of the few professionals listed above—lived better than the lower classes, but Richmond had a critical mass of such Black professionals.

The real estate agent showed us small frame and stucco houses in the northwest Black section of town near West Street and Page Street, but we declined any interest and moved on. Those houses were small, antiquated in design and accouterments, and lacked inspiration. The streets were narrow and the houses close to one another. There were no grand boulevards, with wide streets traversed by city transit buses and statuesque houses to entertain our fantasies.

Later in the day we were shown a stately red brick four bedroom house on a wide street in the southeast section of town on Ridge Street, near the corner of Elliott Avenue and Ridge, not more than three miles from the center of downtown. This was a White area just beginning to change over. Several, but not many, middle class Black families lived in this section of the city. Dad liked the house. It satisfied his ego and when he asked me if I liked it, I said "yes I like it." Amidst the uninspiring, this house touched the imagination. Mother had not seen the house, but she trusted Dad's judgment. We knew that if we liked it Mother probably would, at least we thought so. But mother's heart was still in the house on North Avenue. It was her first house and she dreaded the day she had to leave it. Several weeks later we were moving our furniture and our futures to Charlottesville.

Dad knew what he wanted out of life when we moved to Charlottesville. He learned the game of success in Richmond, having been tutored by some of the best. By the time we moved to Charlottesville, Dad already owned four houses including our home on North Avenue. So Dad got ahead of Charlottesville before Charlottesville got ahead of him. When Charlottesville looked up, Dad had made his mark and was cruising. Charlottesville was not accustomed to the presence of an aggressive Black man of Dad's ilk. Dad charged through Charlottesville like Sherman swept through Atlanta, only he didn't burn everything in his path; he tried to acquire it. The powers that be in Charlottesville were more used to a "hang dog," "yes man" type of Black man. An "accommodating" Black man with no vision, a captive, dependent on the system. Not one out to "beat the system." Dad was anything but an "accommodationist". He tolerated the beast of discrimination, but he did not accept it. Dad was not a flag waver or a protest marcher. He couldn't be; he was a part of the system he fought to overcome. Rather, he was a social conventionalist, single minded in his determination: a Black man with a plan to achieve economic security for his family and professional satisfaction for himself. He played the game the way he saw it, as a Black man "trying to play an inside straight." They didn't know it, but the power brokers in Charlottesville and Albemarle County had a guerrilla fighter in their midst, a secret agent.

As the moving van left the wide boulevard of North Avenue, my mother cried. She did not know what to expect in Charlottesville but knew what she was leaving in Richmond: her friends, her church, her family relations, the familiarity of a place she had grown to know over many years and the resultant "community of neighbors," and of course the house she had made our home.

Mother cried all the way from Richmond to Charlottesville. The tears kept coming, her heart had been touched by memories. Each flashback evoked more memories and more tears. What was the problem? People are often stirred by the memories of their beginnings, the genesis of it all. For mother, Richmond was the substantial beginning of her family life, a place where we were all together under one roof. The place where the ideal, albeit imperfect, was transformed into reality, if just for a while. A place where imperfection was present, but that which was perfect was good, fulfilling and treasured. It had been a special time in all our lives.

— — —

This was the Charlottesville of my youth at age thirteen as seen from Vinegar Hill, a Black enclave of small white masonry buildings containing small retail stores of one kind or another lined one beside the other abutting the side walk as it descended into downtown. Vinegar Hill was located at the vertex, of Main Street, east and west, Ridge Street to the south and McIntire Street to the north, one entranceway into the city of Charlottesville in 1960.

Charlottesville was a "country" town in 1960, yet it was the largest thriving city between Richmond on the east, Harrisonburg on the west, Washington D.C. on the north and Danville on the south. The country folks from the surrounding counties of Greene, Madison, Fluvanna, Orange, Buckingham, Culpeper and Louisa came to Charlottesville on Saturdays to shop. The red clay on the treads of their tires, the roughness of their attire and coarseness of their demeanor testified to the rural nature of their being.

As the crowd formed to observe the dance, the smell of salt pork and freshly slaughtered pork bellies drifted through the air. Followed closely by whiffs of alcohol, from wine, beer or liquor and moonshine held in bottles and cans of different shapes concealed by brown paper bags folded down to reveal the mouth of each container. The hands that held the bags were dark brown, black and white with traces of ash noticeable between each fold of rough skin. The nail beds of the fingers that held the paper bags were pink rimmed by a dark grey band of dirt underneath each nail. The hands of farmers, cooks, dairymen and janitors.

The dancer's stature was small, diminutive, short and thin. He wore rumpled blue jeans, with the cuffs rolled up, a plaid shirt that was torn in spots and threadbare. Black shiny shoes on his small feet. The complexion of the man was dark, leathery, shiny to a gloss, and smooth as freshly tanned rawhide. He danced a jig, and sang his song, "ace, king, queen, jack, good looking nigger, but you sho' is Black." They threw coins at the man's feet as he danced, pennies, nickels and dimes. The more they threw, the harder he danced. With a small top hat on his head, his movements were swift and exact. He knew his steps; he had performed his routine so many times. Those of us who witnessed his show admired his artistry but disdained what he represented. The Whites liked to hear him sing his song and threw him nickels and dimes the more he danced and sang. The Blacks were entertained, yet shamed and embarrassed but they laughed at themselves knowingly. *Tippy Rhodes*[7] was his name, Charlottesville's version of the Vaudeville minstrel Steppin Flechit, the Blackman, the buffoon. Defeated by an alien system, a fool, reduced to a caricature of his noble self, whipped down by the legacy of Jefferson's Monticello and its residue.

As the evening approached and his daily routine wore out its welcome, he would disappear into an alley not to be seen again until he reappeared the next day to do it all over again. Tippy danced up and down Main Street until he got enough money to make it worth his time.

The Black neighborhood of Vinegar Hill would be removed a few years later by what political leaders called urban renewal, but what John Lassiter the author of *The Silent Majority: Suburban Politics in the Sunbelt South* (2006)[8] calls "Negro Removal."

I had never seen anything like this in my short life until I came to Charlottesville. Tippy danced across my face, and he danced on my evolving self-image. Still harboring the images of Amos and Andy from television, now I saw the caricatures in person. This was the race culture of Charlottesville during those days. Tippy's act was a metaphor for the subjugation of the Black self-image by a system that enabled and perpetuated the indignity. Less than three miles to the east at Court Square slaves were bought and sold. And to the south east was Monticello, an historical edifice that slaves built, the home of Thomas Jefferson, the personage whose legacy of intellect, impiety, ethnocentricity, racial and moral duplicity pervades the culture. This was part of the way of life in Charlottesville during those days.

"You better have your money or know where you're going to get it if you go to Charlottesville," so my mother and father were told before moving to this town. "There are only two kinds of folks in Charlottesville, the rich and the poor" the commentator opined.

Charlottesville was a locked down segregated city when we moved here. The races were polarized and severely segregated well before the explosion of the civil rights momentum that invaded this hamlet in 1962-66.

We worked hard during the summer of 1960 to get our new home ready for our long-term stay in Charlottesville. Dad and Mom were set to begin their careers living in Charlottesville but working in the Albermarle County Schools in the fall. The Ridge Street home is an all brick statuesque house, but at that time it was in need of some major overhaul. We did all of the painting and cleaning and restorative work ourselves. Our neighbor Mr. Sturman provided us with advice. He knew something about construction, way more than we knew, which was next to nothing, so his advice was welcomed. Mr. Sturman owned two properties, his home and a rental property, two doors north of our house. Mr. Sturman, was bald and had a heavy foreign accent. He was muscular in his build but short and he wore small wire-rimmed glasses. He came over each day advising us on what to do. His advice about how to remove the wallpaper and prep the walls for painting and repapering were invaluable. He did this kind of work for himself and some others. I got to know him a little bit over the months and years that ensued. His wife was seldom seen but we knew she was there. She kept close to their home.

The Ridge Street house has a long and wide front porch made of cinder block and cement painted dark red with a red brick wall railing system that surrounds and encloses the porch, similar in style, but not in construction, to the porch on North Avenue. Four, four-foot high brick columns rest on the porch wall, each stationed at opposite ends and at the center where the entrance way to the house creates an alcove affect that supports the porch roof. On the first floor, the front door opens into the living room area, which includes a small working fire place; there is no "center hall plan" as Dad would say. In addition to the kitchen, there is a dining room, living room and a second sitting room. The kitchen is a large eat-in kitchen with a pantry in the right rear corner. There was also a small half-bath on the right near the front entrance to the kitchen, and a small back porch on the opposite side of the pantry separated by a wall.

On the second floor, four large bedrooms await and a full bath all centered around a small but somewhat wide hallway; one for mother, one for Dad, one for me and a spare bedroom. Their bedrooms faced Ridge Street, mine faced the "Monticello mountain"–the distant view from the back of the house. High masonry ceilings and walls with crown molding in some of the rooms and hard wood floors throughout attest to the quality of construction. A new heating system was installed. All the walls in the bedrooms and living rooms were scraped of their existing wallpaper and repainted. The floors were cleaned, waxed and polished.

Ridge Street Residence, circa (1964), with Otis Lee, Sr. (Dad) in front

A new roof was added. A four-foot high brick retaining wall in front of the house abuts the side walk, in back of which was a shallow front yard, but the backyard is deep and wide. The extended wall sets the front boundary line for the property except for a narrow two-foot strip of sidewalk that runs parallel to the north alley side of the house and extends to the rear property line. An unpaved alley separated our home from our next door neighbor's house on the north side. The ground level of the house resembles a Greco-Roman facade. Large mature evergreens, "boxwoods," planted perpendicular and parallel to the porch front and along the walkway, obscured the front porch from public view. The backyard had a small gold fish pond with no gold fish in it at that time.

Mom, Dad, Andy and I worked tirelessly each day during this period. So much so that Dad broke out in hives two weeks before school was to start. His sensitive skin rebelled against the dust and glue that suffused the air, so that his face became red and puffy. It looked like a beehive pocked, swelled with red bruises and contusions. We all wondered what kind of impression he would make on the first day of school with his face so irritated and inflamed. He had gotten this skin disease from all the plaster and dirt unleashed by peeling the wallpaper from the masonry walls, sanding the floors, applying polyurethane and waxing them afterwards, cutting grass and hauling trash. We worked from sun up to dark for two straight months.

We brought along with us Andy, one of the foster kids being raised by Kate and Joe Allen. Andy was about my age, with a tanned skin-tone with short closely cut hair. He and I had gotten to know each other having lived next door to each other on North Avenue. We played together sometime but not like I played with Marcellus and Rockie. Andy had a sense of humor and we enjoyed each other's company. Andy was there to work and to be company for me. Dad must have worked out some sort of deal with Kate and Joe to loan us this kid to help with the work or to be company for me. He was used to hard work. Either way Andy stayed with us the remainder of the summer and worked with me in the yard, cutting grass, peeling wallpaper and waxing floors. It was good to have Andy along since I had no friends and school had not yet started. Andy was my co-worker and my playmate.

My father did not believe in spoiling the child. If you hung around him, he would put you to work. In Richmond when my friends would come around to see if I could come out to play, he often tried to put them to work with me if I was working when they came around. He used to always say "you better work while you got somebody working with you because if you don't, when they leave, you'll have it all to do by yourself."

After the bulk of the work was completed, we settled down into our new home and schools. In September I enrolled in Jefferson Elementary School in the city, Mother went to Benjamin Franklin Yancey Elementary in Esmont and Dad went to Virginia L. Murray Elementary School in Ivy. All of these schools were Black populated schools, one hundred percent. Life was good in Charlottesville. No more commuting for Dad, Mom was back in the classroom, and I began a decade-long search to find self-definition and determination, and in the process answer the question, who was I? Moving to Charlottesville was good for me and for my family in many ways. Mom and Dad had professionally appropriate jobs. The city was quiet. The crime rate was low and the economy of the city, at that time, facilitated Dad's investment strategy. We all did well here. I thrived within the confines of this world and so did the family.

The Charlottesville of the 1960s, 65 miles west of Richmond, on route 250 west, was a one horse town according to mother, and that horse was a white horse. Black folks did not ride that horse; instead it trampled them under its hooves as it galloped from historical period to historical period. Black folks worked as cooks, maids and butlers, where slaves were once sold at auction in Court Square north of downtown. This city was, and is not today, a friend to Americans of African descent. Back then, and now, the University of Virginia located west of the city was the beacon of attraction and the *raison d'etre*. During the 60's the bitter, caustic culture of racism was blatantly advocated by governors and state political leaders of that day and vehemently enforced by many local leaders who ran for city council. The heavy hand of racism upheld segregation unfailingly in the schools, businesses, hospitals, and neighborhoods of this city. The Whites, as you would expect, had the best of everything in Charlottesville at this time: schools, playgrounds, movie houses, restaurants, clothing stores, and medical care.[9]

Back then, as now, the "gold coast" was along the 250 West corridor which begins at the corner of 10th street and west Main St. The business, property and institutional owners along this wide swath controlled politics in Charlottesville. Sections such as Bellaire, Ednam, Boar's Head, Farmington and Flordon are the highbrow neighborhoods. In recent years, many celebrities have moved to the area giving it a cachet that the elite of the community nourish and work hard to maintain. But at its core, stripped of it flourishes and highbrows, I find Charlottesville to be a "provincial" town as that term is defined by Webster's Dictionary: "illiberal, unsophisticated, rustic, narrow and parochial, yet inspiring to the nouveau riche." A bastion for the "old boy" network where wealth is preserved for those who traditionally have had it.

7

"Forward in the Fight"

S IX YEARS BEFORE we came to Charlottesville, after the Brown decision, Black citizens of Charlottesville began the arduous task of integrating the Charlottesville and Albemarle County public schools. "Massive Resistance" was the White strategy for defeating integration of the public schools. Prince Edward County closed its schools for five years rather than accept the mandate of the Brown decision. John Lassiter in his cogent presentation of the problem in his book *The Silent Majority*, states the case: "Governor Lindsay Almond closed public schools in three communities that faced immediate desegregation mandates. The enactment of the massive resistance program deprived thirteen thousand White students of public schooling in Norfolk, Charlottesville and Front Royal. In Charlottesville, upper-middle-class White mothers opened temporary facilities to prevent local segregationists from converting to a permanent system of private education." In order to defeat integration, the Whites, in closing the public schools to keep the Blacks out, were forced to deprive their own children of a public school education during this time. The system did not care what happened to the Blacks, so long as the Blacks did not, even under court order, attend their schools.[10]

On February 4, 1959 Venable Elementary and Lane High School reopened, after being closed because of the aforementioned state and local policies. On September 5, 1959, the federal courts ordered 12 Blacks transferred between Lane High School and Venable Elementary School. And the rest of the schools were opened on a desegregated basis on September 8, 1959. The Charlottesville City Council continued to appropriate taxpayer money for tuition grants for Whites to attend private White academies to avoid attending schools with the limited number of Blacks allowed to attend at this time. The council continued this policy until the federal courts invalidated the policy in 1965.[11]

This was also an eventful year in the fight for school integration and political enfranchisement. The decision in *Baker v. Carr* (1962)[12] ushered in the demise of "the Byrd Machine" in Virginia by realigning the power and voting strength of the rural areas and replacing it with voting power in the metropolitan areas and the suburbs. The subsequent passage of the Voting Rights Act of 1965 and the shift to "one man, one vote" allowed the cities and not the hinterlands to decide electoral politics. Hence Blacks and progressives from the cities began to change the voting dynamic in elections that resulted in the defeat of rural segregationists and massive resisters. It was not ever thus that Blacks would continue to be disenfranchised, their voting power diluted and their voices muffled by the chicanery of depraved White supremacists making their nefarious deals in the back rooms of electoral politics. The end had come.

So in effect, although the public schools were eventually integrated for the benefit of Blacks, public school education as we know it was "saved" for the greater benefit of White students. The consequence was that Blacks got to attend White schools as mandated by the Brown decision, "with all deliberate speed, " in *Brown II,* 349 U.S. 249 (1955 USSC), which meant, according to Judy Jones and William Wilson in their book *An Incomplete Education* (2006)[13], "sometime in the afterlife." White folks took the approach of "gradualism and individual meritocracy" as a way to comply with the law and save public education.

White folks have seldom, if ever, done anything to improve the lot of Black people solely for the moral reason to "right a wrong," but have done so to achieve other goals that had incidental and coincidental benefits for Blacks. There are numerous examples including the integration of the Armed Forces by President Harry S. Truman in 1948. Michael J. Klarman, a prominent law professor now at Harvard University School of Law espoused such a position—which I fully embrace—during a lecture at the Miller Center at the University of Virginia in Charlottesville, during its celebration of Black History Month on January 10, 2008. Simply put, there is no overriding morality that influences White decision-making as it relates to Blacks, and what we get, if we get anything, we usually get second-hand.

When we moved to Charlottesville, the worst of the fighting over integration had subsided. What remained was the residue: the implementation, woven through the dense webbing of an entrenched segregationist mentality. The movement to integrate the schools was a riptide moving through a sea of historical race hierarchy, a legacy of Jeffersonian elitism that had come to expect Black docility and servitude. As long as Blacks stayed in their places, washing dishes, waiting tables, cooking, cleaning White folk's houses and emptying their bed pans, nursing White babies and caretaking their lawns, the White community was satisfied. They appreciated the "hang dog Black," not the head-held-high Black. Why the hatred? All Black folks wanted was to be treated decently and with respect. A chance to get a good education for their children, which their tax dollars were paying for.

The indigenous Blacks from Charlottesville and the surrounding counties, the home-grown Blacks were largely myopic in vision, except for a rare few, lacked uplift and sophistication. Their horizons, standards and expectations were parochial in nature. The poor Whites, of which there were and are many, were not much better off except their brethren, the rich Whites, controlled the capital and resources of the area including the administration of the University of Virginia. They determined the winners and losers in the marketplace, and Blacks were channeled not to win in Charlottesville and Albemarle County.

The language of hate hurled at Black men and women who attempted to make life better in Charlottesville during this time was filled with paroxysms of vitriol characterized by ignorance. Blacks were beaten and bloodied and some permanently injured including Rev. Henry Floyd Johnson, then minister of Zion Union Baptist Church in Charlottesville on 4th Street, trying to integrate "Buddies" a popular White restaurant on Emmet Street.

My cousin Wendell and I played a very minor role in integrating the old "Mountain Bowl" bowling alley off of Old Ivy Road, a place frequented by the university community. One summer evening during this time, we casually entered the bowling alley without thinking and proceeded to sit down at a bowling lane. As we paid for our shoes and bowling balls, we were not conscious of "what we were doing," and we were greeted with shock but not animosity. It seemed that management made adjustments on the fly and just let us proceed to bowl that evening. Apparently management felt there was no need to resist since integration was breaking out all over the community. We knew at the time that we were integrating a bowling alley, but it was all by happenstance.

8

"Each for Himself Must Cleave a Path Alone"

I BEGAN MY CHARLOTTESVILLE EDUCATION at Jefferson Elementary School at 4th street NW and Commerce Streets, just off West Main Street. Jefferson Elementary School was at one time a high school for Black students before Jackson P. Burley High School, the high school I attended the next year, was built. Jefferson is a sprawling red brick building of at least three floors whose campus occupied half of 4th St. Trimmed in white with long wood windows, nine-over-nine, and white fascia boards, the building is handsome.

For the next year, each day I walked to Jefferson School from our house near the corner of Ridge and Elliot, north on Ridge Street past old two story red brick colonial houses on both sides of the street. There were other Black sections in the city but none as prominent as Ridge Street. On the east and west side streets that ran perpendicular to Ridge, such as Diggs Street and Dice Street, the streets were narrow, the buildings quaint and uninspiring. Various degrees of modernity existed in the houses, some lacking all modernity with dirt underlayment overlaid with wood planks for flooring, dilapidated porches and steps. Many of them were ramshackle structures, mostly frame houses badly in need of repair, but all with television antennas on their roof tops. Back then Charlottesville did not have its own television stations. The T.V. stations received in Charlottesville came out of Richmond or Harrisonburg. The picture was snowy and not viewable unless you had an antenna. Many of these structures were southeast of Main Street and within easy walking distance of downtown.

As I continued my walk to school toward the end of Ridge, at the Lewis and Clark statue, I went west on Main Street to 4th Street and turned north at the corner where Inze's Store was located. Mr. Inze was a rotund copper-colored Black man with a nice smile who operated this small variety store for many years. His was a prominent Black family in Charlottesville. The school kids, including me went there for candy and gum and the usual nick-knacks. There was nothing extraordinary about the store, except that it was owned by a Black man. Mr. Inze was always cordial. He wore a long white apron over his clothes and looked more like a baker than a store clerk. The store shelves were sparsely filled, and one had the impression that he never felt the need to overstock the shelves with goods of any kind.

When I entered the 7th grade at Jefferson, I was placed in the "B" group. Why? I do not know. Perhaps my grades from Richmond did not warrant placement in the "A" group. But this is where I stayed during this school year. Charlottesville had this clannish tacit favoritism that was practiced throughout the segregated school system by the Black teachers and administrators. They had their favorites, and I was not one of them. I had to earn whatever favoritism I received. This one year was uneventful except for a few happenings that stand out in my memory. First, it was during this time that I resumed taking piano lessons. The lessons were given across the street from the school at the old Zion Union Baptist Church, a Black church on 4th Street. With the permission of the parents, those children taking the lessons were permitted during school hours to go across the street and have the lesson and then return to school. My instructor Mr. Robert Smith, a White man, formally educated in piano, easy to get along with and at all times encouraging, was a career music teacher and church organist. He would be my music teacher for the next six years until I graduated from high school. Under his instruction, I would achieve my highest level of musicianship with the piano.

At Jefferson I was selected to play a lead role in the year-end school play "Laughing Star of Zuni." It was an operetta about an Indian tribe, composed by Lily T. Strickland in 1946, the theme of which escapes me. I played the role of the chief of the tribe. A local theater group either at the high school or in the city said I was a good actor because "I stayed in character throughout the play." I did not realize that I had done anything special, or noteworthy. And in celebration of Black History month I was asked to recite the poem the *The Path* by Paul Lawrence Dunbar. I recited the poem with such vigor and conviction that my teachers asked me to recite it more than once, even after Black History Month had passed.

I had my first girlfriend while at Jefferson, Brenda Payne, a vivacious little girl bubbling with personality. The relationship lasted only a week, if that long. I bought her a cheap ring from a local jewelry store downtown. I gave the young girl the ring, and it created quite a stir among the kids. But the next day or so I decided that I wanted it back because I no longer liked the way the girl dressed. I remember that her slip hung below the hem of her dress the day or so after, and that made her look sloppy, not neat, and my infatuation soured. I no longer liked the girl. But during this aftermath, in the process of reneging in the gift-giving exercise, I had the strange feeling of not liking myself very much. My self-image was reflected in her, and I rejected the reflection. Neatness and sharp lines satisfied my ego and defined my self-image, not the unkempt look. Seeds of an unconscious poor self-image had grown and sprouts were emerging. Perhaps my over exuberance was too much for me to handle at that age.

And during that maiden school year in Charlottesville, I severely sprained my left ankle while playing a pick-up game of touch football. A group of us guys gathered on a bright sunny Saturday morning over at Dickie Moon's house for a game. Moon's house was one block east of Ridge Street, separated by Oakwood Cemetery. The Ross brothers were there and some others. We were having a whale of a time when all of a sudden, during one of the tackles, I got caught underneath the pile, and my left ankle twisted. I knew immediately that I was hurting. I could not walk and had to be helped home by the guys playing the game. I spent the next three hours in the emergency room at the University of Virginia Hospital. My ankle was placed in a modified cast, and I had to walk on crutches for the next several weeks.

When Dad took me to school the following Monday, I walked with my crutches under my left shoulder for support. He carried my books. The kids peeked out of their classrooms on the 7th grade floor to observe the event. To see a parent in the building during the day was an event in its own right, and to see the new kid's parent was certainly worth watching if only for a moment. They all saw me with my father and knew of my situation. There was something special about it. I felt loved by him especially at this time because he had taken the time to take me to school. He had his own school to run but that did not matter on this day.

9

"No Beaten Paths to Glory's Height"

URING THIS FIRST YEAR, Mom and Dad mourned the loss of Richmond. We would drive back on most Sundays for church. Most of all they mourned the loss of the socialization with their friends and family: the Blakes, Ruth and Jimmy, Cora Lee and Doc, Sapp and Brown, Aunt Willnett and Uncle Walter, all the connections that made Richmond home. These folks were not likely to drive 65 miles for a visit with us. If the relationships were to last, especially the friends, Mom and Dad would have to make the trip and they tried for a while. But in the end the relationships suffered and ties were loosened to the point of not being connected. Everybody's life moved on and so did ours.

After a while I realized I was not receiving any more spankings or whippings, just chastisements, admonitions and blandishments. I never got too many spankings anyway, but I got my share. The spankings and whippings had become as deciduous as the leaves that fall from the trees. Hands-on punishments were no longer needed; their season was past. My age and perhaps my parent's acknowledgment of my evolving maturity dictated an end to this approach to change my behavior. Also at this time Dad was beginning to work on me psychologically with his many sayings that held real truths. Dad waxed poetically about almost everything. He had an aphorism for all situations. He loved odd word formulations. He was a conscious malaprop when he wanted to be. For instance, one day we were talking about stereo speakers and he called them "sound boxes." Looking at me peevishly, he knew it was funny when he said it. He said it for effect, to evoke laughter in me and it did. Dad would do things like that all the time. He liked words and the play on words. He used the word "peach-osh-a-bosh-osh" to mean a young person. I don't know where he got that one from. Yet he was a stickler for the proper use of language and grammar. At the dinner or breakfast table he would always correct you if you misused the English language. The teacher in him was never far off.

Dad's penchant for words and language made this tactic a natural evolution. For example, he would say most often "a hard head makes for a soft behind." A warning that if I did not behave, firm discipline could be in order. He would also say "I got my eyes on you, after a while I'll have my hands on you." Another warn-

89

ing shot fired across the bow to keep me straight was: "You make your bed hard, you have to turn over that much more often." Dad was full of old sayings. In the words of Dr. Bergan Evans the vocabulary expert, "you call him wise, but I think he's only sententious, full of old sayings, maxims, or proverbs." Dad was both wise, quirky, and an odd ball at times and full of old sayings. He used them to make his point and enjoyed the wisdom of the sayings. The sayings were repeated so often that I took pride in them and absorbed them practically by osmosis.

During his later years he would say, "if you live like the White folks you got to pay like the White folks." He expressed this sentiment after paying real estate taxes on his home and after paying real estate taxes on his investment properties. He lived well and he knew it. He repeated it often, so often that this expression became a part of the family lexicon. He was conscious that his life style, while not ostentatious, was well above middle class and wanted me and Mom, but especially me, to know that it cost money to live well. And his point was that if Black folks expected to live well they had better be prepared to pay for it. He spent large sums of money acquiring the material things that made his lifestyle reflective of his station in life and his economic success.

"The only thing black about us is the color of our skins." Dad recited this mantra pridefully because he recognized that we didn't live like the typical Black family. He was chauvinistic about our family and the way we did things, how we thought about life in White America, the strategies we used to beat the odds against Black success in this country. He was expressing his elevation and appreciation for the standard of living and the values our family embraced. He was not disparaging Black folks, because he loved Black people, but he did not, and neither do I, embrace all aspects of Black culture. Dad was relating our family values to the higher values culturally associated with Whites but not exclusively "White" by any means.

"I'd rather sleep in a hollow log and drink muddy water before I let you go from man to man" a phrase from a Muddy Waters blues song famous during Dad's time. Here, he was expressing his love for mother. He jealously knew that "mother was the jewel in the crown" his jewel and he loved her deeply and dearly. He fought to protect her even from her own family. He would repeat this phrase when he was having fun, joking and playing around with Mother and me. He had a recording of the full song in our record collection. Mother would blush with affectionate pride at his attention when he teased her with this song.

"My time is now, your time will come." He recited this phrase when he was tired of me inquiring into his business. He loved to kid with me. Dad often took pride in his accomplishments and had fun kidding me and joking with me about life and people in the community. When he would tell me this, my attention would speed forward to the future and my immediate attention on him would be deflected. In effect he was saying to me "move on to something else kid." I felt that one day my time would come, as it did.

"If you see a Black man with it, he deserves to have it." This phrase was recognition that it is hard for anyone to achieve success in this life. And it is especially difficult for Black people, especially Black men to successfully manipulate the system to the point of success. So, as he said, "if you see a Black man with it—meaning money and wealth—he deserves to have it" because you know it wasn't easy for him to get it. You have to respect the accomplishment.

"We don't know what the future holds, but we know who holds the future." He enjoyed this expression because to me it demonstrated his belief in God and the faith he held that everything would be all right one day. Dad was indeed a man of faith. Not a zealot but a God-fearing man who served a risen savior. This form of expression was an integral part of his personality. When talking to me, when he had a point to make, it would not be long before an apt saying would be used to drive home the point. And whatever saying he used made it stick.

"Nothing goes over a horse's back that does not buckle under his stomach." Meaning everything comes out in the wash. What goes around comes around. Nothing you do will remain secret for long.

"Fish and guests stink after three days." Don't overstay your welcome. The oil magnate Rockefeller would charge his guests for the use of his utilities, room rent and food when guests stayed at his house.

"Familiarity breeds contempt." The longer you know someone, the more you are likely not to like them.

10

HIGH SCHOOL DAYS, THE BEARS OF BURLEY

THE SUMMER BEFORE HIGH SCHOOL, I went to Lane High School, the White high school, for a summer program in biology. We dissected frogs and worms. I enjoyed the experience. This was the first time I had a White teacher. All of the teachers at Jefferson had been Black. The White teacher was kind and nice and made favorable comments about how careful I had been in preserving the spine of the frog during the dissection. I had my first good experience with a White student who was also in the class. He loaned me his bike to ride home to retrieve a book I had forgotten even though he did not know me. A Black kid refused to loan me his bike even though he knew who I was. This was insightful and stuck with me the rest of my life.

After the summer program ended, my next school year was at Jackson P. Burley High School, home of the "Mighty Burley Bears", in the 8th grade, in the fall of 1961. During this time, integration was being implemented gradually in Charlottesville, but all of the Black educator's children of my age, with a few exceptions, continued to attend all Black schools. These post-Brown Black educator parents did not rock the boat by sending their kids to the newly integrated high school; it would have been too provocative. They all played it safe. The kids in the vanguard of integration who attended the newly integrated schools were from non-educator families for the most part. I can think of only one exception and this student was several years younger than me.

I walked northwest past Lane High School to get to Burley on 4th street, then on to Preston Avenue, and then west to Rose Hill Drive. I would do this every day until I graduated from Burley in June of 1966. Burley is a sprawling red brick building at the corner of Henry Avenue and Rose Hill Drive in a Black section of the city northwest of town. It is trimmed in high-grade off-white cement blocks at its entrance, illuminating the red brick façade—a striking contrast of colors. The building is an imposing structure, but the education it produced was suboptimal and not as impressive as its outer fascade. Both city and county Black high school-eligible students attended Burley for high school. The school was built to keep the races separated.

During the integration era, 1962 to 1966, I remember Governor J. Lindsay Almond went on television to demonstrate how poisonous and pervasive integration of Blacks would be to White society by pouring black ink into a six-ounce glass of clear water to dramatically demonstrate how Black Americans would destroy the White public school system in Virginia if integration took hold. I remember watching this dramatization on television with my parents. I was fourteen years old. My mother and father looked at the newscast with awe and amazement at the crass, vile and disheartening demonstration. Governor Almond and many other Southern governors of the era, except for Linwood Holton who succeeded Mills Godwin, were "massive resistance" advocates. These leaders of the White population closed the public schools in several counties in Virginia rather than integrate them.

"That's what we're up against in Virginia" my dad said. Mother responded, "well he didn't have to do all that, what he just did was ridiculous." "But Rosa" Dad retorted, "you know how Virginia is." Dad always called Mother by her first name and she always called him by his last name Lee. This must have been some kind of southern thing that Mother got into long before I was born. "White folks have never had anything for Black folks to do, they have always had their foot on our necks," Mother declared with a sense of resignation. Then in the same moment as though switching gears seamlessly she said, "Otis go set the table for dinner." Off I was sent just when it was getting good. I wanted to hear the rest of the conversation.

The symbolism of this racially offensive demonstration by Governor Almond was dramatic and indelible, forever etching a negative vision of White people and further helping to erode the delicate fabric of my self-esteem and self-image. Were we really that bad? What were these racist politicians thinking or did they think at all? Theirs was an appeal to the lowest common denominator—the least among them. The aggrandizement of racism at tremendous cost to a vital tax-paying, but disregarded, segment of the population.

As stated earlier, Lassiter demonstrates that it was the "open schools movement" of White middle-class mothers that saved southern public education in Virginia and in the rest of the traditional South. Quoting Lassiter, "the limitations of the Southern Leadership Project are clearer: a desegregation consensus forged through the race-neutral rhetoric of White self-interest, rather than deeper examination of the meaning of equality in the context of the burdens of southern history, all too often represented not the first step of a good-faith process, but instead reluctant acquiescence to the minimum requirements of the law. A full decade after Brown, the political failure of massive resistance had brought secondary school desegregation to every southern state, but the structural legacies of the dual educational system and the fundamental inadequacies in the moderate approach to race relations meant that almost 98 percent of Black students remained in segregated institutions." (Emphasis added). This was my experience in Charlottesville and that of many other similarly situated Black students who suffered from the effluent of racism.

Upon entering Burley, I found the place to be hospitable. The teachers were cordial, all Black and easy going. Many of the teachers were expatriates from Farmville, in Prince Edward County, where the schools had been closed under "massive resistance" enforcement, these teachers found jobs at Burley. The 8th grade was uneventful, nothing significant occurred. Our freshman class was divided into the vocational tract and the college-bound tract. I was of course, in the college-bound group. That meant that I was scheduled during the course of the next five years to take algebra, and higher math, several years of a foreign language, French; several years of English, world history, typing, biology, chemistry, physics and the usual college preparatory curriculum. However, no sense of urgency or seriousness of purpose was evident in the scholastic culture of the place that I could discern. Everyone just went along and did their work without thinking about tomorrow and oblivious to what White students or even more sophisticated Black high school students in Richmond or in the Tidewater region of Virginia were accomplishing. All of us were in our own little cozy Burley High School world. The only time competition was front and center, clearly manifested and on everyone's mind, was in athletics, when football and basketball season would start, then we all became animated about beating the other team, especially Dunbar High School in Lynchburg and the high school from Campbell County. That is not to say that there was no attention paid to academic performance, there was, but it just was not the dominant culture of the school. However, there was an active academic honor society on campus. Discipline was not an issue: everyone behaved, there was no fighting, and drug use was unheard of. The kids were older and more mature.

For the first time, we changed classes, which was exciting and "grown up" for the eighth graders. There was no tension or pressure, just warmth and pleasantness. The hallways were long and clean with lockers on both sides. Each student was given a locker. Franklin Bowles, a student from the county, out near Rio Road and not far from Earlysville, who would become, perhaps, my closest friend at that time, had his locker next to mine, on the first floor not far from the principal's office. We shared this communion our entire time at Burley. The upper class students kept to themselves.

The auditorium was vast like a theater with a large stage for plays and assemblies. As the years passed, I spent a fair amount of time on that stage. And the cafeteria was large and roomy enough to accommodate, the various classes at their lunch periods. The gym was big and expansive. The library was quiet and as far as I knew, adequately stocked with periodicals and books. I never spent much time in the school library. I spent more time in the city library on Market Street. I had never gone to a school up to then with a full gymnasium with enough floor space for a full-court varsity basketball game with bleachers and ropes for climbing and glistening hard wood floors. Outside was a full football field with bleachers and a sound system along with bright floodlights for night football games. Burley was "the real thing."

This was truly a "high school" for us freshmen. Burley was not just a high school for Black students: it was a Black community nexus, a meeting place, a point of reference and identity for the marginalized Black community in Charlottesville and Albemarle County. It was the largest and only institution that Black folks in Charlottesville and Albemarle County had some control over. As I began the ninth grade, my self-awareness increased. I was 15 years old now and I was concerned about my looks, girls and sex. I was also impressionable and fell in love with movie and television stars, all of whom were White. I loved Haley Mills and thought about her lots of times and fantasized about her as my girlfriend when I watched the television series she appeared in. I felt the pain of Jean Simmons, the mysterious brunette, when she was forced to live only momentarily with a man not of her choice in the film "Spartacus." Beautiful, quiet and petite, my embodiment of beauty. To my mind, she was too delicate to be spoiled like that. She was my movie star of choice. I experimented with bleaching cream to lighten the color of my skin, and I tried to comb my hair in such a way as to make it more wavy and straight using different kinds of hair creams and products. I did not get very far with the makeover and soon abandoned the effort.

My mind had enveloped consciously or unconsciously the White image of beauty, and I was attempting in my own incompetent way to make it personal, to incorporate the images into my own world. There were no images of Black people that rivaled that of the Whites in my orientation.

My parents had no idea what was going on with me during this time. I would have flunked the test made famous by Dr. Kenneth B. Clark, the New York psychologist in the Brown case where he demonstrated that Black kids who were shown Black and White dolls to choose from, chose the White dolls as more attractive and the Black dolls as being "bad." Dad's White image of beauty was represented in Heddy Lamar, the White actress of his time he often mentioned in passing. And Mother often spoke of Tyrone Power as her image of White male beauty. It seems we were all indoctrinated by the culture of "Whiteness."

Fighting was not something I was used to. In fact, I had never had a meaningful fight with another kid before I came to Charlottesville. I did not have to fight to survive as a "student" in Richmond or as a playmate. Aside from the melee I experienced with Marcellus and the glass-throwing incident with Harold Scott when we were kids playing in Battery Park and along North Avenue, I had not experienced the fright, anxiety, fear or bullying associated with school fights. But in Charlottesville I would have to fight whether or not I liked it or wanted to. It was the nature of this community. My exposure to the "bad boys" of the community began slowly between Jefferson Elementary and Burley High School. I remember being in the same room when Eddie Hawkins, a brown skinned medium-build kid, who had no distinct characteristics other than being "tough," and John Vest, a taller lighter skinned male with black hair, who lived off of Ridge Street. These two took turns punching each other in the chest as hard as they could to see who could withstand the beating the longest. They were taking the measure of who was the toughest. Then there was a kid from the county, Sherman Brown was his name. Dad taught him at Virginia L. Murray Elementary in Ivy before he came to Burley. Sherman was short, built like a wrestler with a menacing demeanor. He was branded as a tough guy, and I instinctively avoided him. Then there was "Bumble Bee," another fighter with a reputation for being mean. I steered clear of him as well. Bumble Bee was another short, brown skin, otherwise nondescript guy whose brand for fighting and intimidation was well known by all the students.

My first personal encounter was with John Vest. Since Vest lived off Ridge Street, we ended up walking home together which was unusual because I did not associate with him. He was not in my "crowd." But on this one afternoon we ended up walking home. Somewhere along the route, as we neared Main Street, he started bullying me, threatening me. I foolishly bluffed him back not thinking that this guy was used to calling bluffs, and mine was all bluff. All of a sudden he started punching me in my chest at short-range, the impact of the punches striking my chest frightened me. I had never been hit in the chest before, and the books I was carrying dropped to the asphalt, scattering everywhere like glass shattering upon impact. My new books were all neatly covered in new book covers, some of which I had just received from a special order. I started crying loudly. That was the only reaction I could muster. My cry did what my absent punches could not do. The suddenness and loudness of my cry must have startled him. His point had been made. He stopped hitting me and went on his way, while I stayed behind and wiped the tears away and picked up my books. Ironically, one of my book covers had a rhyme that said "the only helping hand is at the end of your arm." We were alone so no one saw me cry myself out of the incident. There was no embarrassment. I did not see much of Vest after that incident, but many lessons were learned. I had to fight. I could not just cry my way out of these fighting contests. And no more bluffing! Either say nothing when sat upon, or when you do speak, be prepared to fight.

It seems as though I was beset from time to time with bullying and intimidation. Was it because I was new or appeared different or was tall? What was it that made other boys want to challenge me, to fight me? My family culture did not embrace fighting and belligerency. I was not accustomed to this mode of operation. What was I doing to incite these attacks? I had no brothers or sisters, uncles or aunts to come to my defense. I had to deal with it as best I could.

A year later, again while walking home, another kid, Otis Sowell, started hassling me and making threatening gestures at the corner of Ridge and McIntire. We were fighting because we both had the same first names: the fight was to prove who was the toughest "Otis." I did not know this kid. I may have encountered him in the cafeteria, but he was not one of the guys I associated with. But this time there was a crowd and they circled around us and urged a fight. "Get him, get him," Sowell's guys talked. "He ain't no good, beat him" they continued to urge. But this time not knowing what I was doing, the fury of no retreat, the mindless, unthinking response controlled the moment. I fought. My long arms and tall stature kept him away from my face. Although the punches were wild and gangly, he was reluctant to engage but so much. He never hit me, nor I him, we just kept swinging at each other and jostling back and forth. The crowd was satisfied they had their fight and something to talk about. My goal was achieved. He could not say I did not fight back, and I thought better of myself for having fought back albeit awkwardly. Even the guys who talked trash about such things started teasing me about having fought Sowell. My swagger was slight, if nonexistent, but to the kids on the block I wasn't a pushover anymore.

My next encounter was with a guy named "Hester." Hester was his last name. He was a guy who lived somewhere in "the Bowery" of Charlottesville. He was a tall unkempt rough looking fellow with a country crude demeanor. Brown skinned with black hair, he was after me for some reason. I had done nothing to this guy. During my travels through the neighborhood on 4th street near the old Bell store, he started at me with mean talk and gestures but I eluded him and fled safely home.

Wherever I went around town, he was stalking me, hoping to catch me and beat me up. One late evening, after I had finished my work at the Youngmen's Shop on east Main Street, I was walking past Diggs Street which ran perpendicular to Ridge on my way home. I had on a new black overcoat. As I walked past the opening to Diggs Street, Hester and his henchmen sprang on to Ridge Street. One of them said, "we got him now." As I turned to face them, I could see him winding up to throw a punch, a "haymaker," but he missed. I took off my new coat so I could maneuver better and remember regretting having to lay my coat on the dirty sidewalk. But I had no choice. I had to fight this guy once and for all or he would continue to stalk me until I did. I was tired of trying to avoid him, always looking over my shoulders to see if he was around. His hangers-on formed a circle, and Hester and I started throwing blows trying to hit the other, none of which hit their mark. We circled each other. He was looking for the knockout blow, and I was trying to keep up my nerve and hoping someone would come by and stop the fight, but no one did. In the words of Coach Jones, the football coach at Burley High School, "one was scared and the other glad of it."

The ritual of throwing blows and hitting nothing continued for a while. All along he was talking trash about how he was going to "kick my ass real bad." The gallery of on-lookers urged more action, but all resulted in nothing. Hester turned out to be a big bag of wind when I no longer ran at the sight of him. Finally confronted, he saw a foe ostensibly ready to take him on. Standing up to these bullies was half the battle, but I did not see it that way then. I just saw each fight as an intimidating moment—one that I wanted to avoid. I was not a fighter. I did my best to avoid these confrontations, but they always seemed to occur. Charlottesville seemed to be full of these "bad guys" who wanted to fight or beat up other people. The class of homes these people came from was low, uneducated, almost poverty stricken and devoid of any social standing. Most of these fellows were truants, bedevilers and guys who had no future. They all wanted, it seemed to me, to beat up the guy who was not home-grown, the new kid, the kid that did not have as many friends, who largely walked alone. Perhaps this was a class thing, but class was not bantered about, maybe it just exuded itself by the way I carried myself. By the reputation that my family had made in the community. To me I had nothing to attract this enmity. But I think the root cause was not having any roots in the community. And I was tall, a tall guy who couldn't fight, a trophy to the bully. Moreover, I was not a known commodity. By beating me up, these "tough" guys could add to their reputations, their legend for toughness at my expense. There were several instances of verbal harassment, mean threats hurled at me that fortunately did not end in fights. I do not know what it was, they just did not like me. I was of a different ilk.

The worst of it occurred on a balmy summer night on Ridge Street south of Langford Avenue. First Baptist Church was having a party for juniors who would be graduating next year. I asked Mom and Dad if I could attend. They were hesitant but I assured them I would be all right and that I would come home early. I went to the party but did not care for the goings on, so I left. There was something in the air during this time that did not favor me or my family. We were not a part of the "inner community" of the old Black families of Charlottesville. Some parents who were educators and business people did not allow their children to associate with those in the hinterlands because of this lack of acceptance by the "regular folks."

But there was always a historical class difference between the middle class and the *hoi polloi*, the common folk in Charlottesville. This difference applied more so to the Blacks than to the Whites. It resulted in teachers dating waiters, and cab drivers. There were not enough educated people for those who were educated to find mates, hence the social disparity in dating relationships among the Blacks. I left early because there was jealousy in the air at the party. I didn't quite fit in with the "in crowd." I was not being treated well. I had no real friends at this party. I felt alone. The clannishness of the students, their lack of inclusion of me into their inner sanctums heightened my sense of exclusion, so I said to myself, "let me leave and go home," it was not happening for me there. It was not so much what was said, but what was not said that spoke the loudest. I was always trying to fit in.

The stretch of road between Langford Avenue and Hartmans Mill Road was dimly lit, and some of the folks sat out on their porches to cool themselves from the heat of the night. I could vaguely see them and could hear them talking as I went by. I was by myself as usual, walking along with my hands in my pockets when this fellow came out of the shadows and wanted to fight. I did not know him. He was younger than me and lived several doors down from the site of the altercation. We exchanged a few words, the normal back and forth about fighting. He reached down and picked up a piece of broken cinder block lying beside him on the right side of the shoulder of the roadway where we stood. The cinder block had lain dormant, lifeless crushing its weight against the dirt beneath it. Making its foot print with the dirt bugs and worms crawling underneath it. But in the hands of a derelict, this inanimate object became a missile of destruction. I remember telling him if he wanted to fight he should put down whatever he was holding in his hand. All of a sudden without warning, unable to see because of the absence of street lights, something hit me in the face with the force of a blunt instrument.

I was stunned, shocked, horrified. A rough two inch gash was opened on my left cheek right below my eye. I did not know it at the time but my jaw bone was broken in several places. Blood gushed down my face and onto my shirt and trousers. The perpetrator ran away, and I hurriedly walked home holding my hand against my face to retard the flow of blood.

This perpetrator was Cecil Loving, a truant and juvenile derelict. Loving was a short, mouthy, out of control bully. If he had wanted to fight a fair fight, I was reluctant but willing. But Loving preferred to "steal me" with a brick in the dark of night. What had I done to deserve this? I did not deserve it. I was the recipient of an evil unthinking act by a depraved youth. For God's sake! I was leaving a "church" sponsored event. This just goes to show, that you do not get what you deserve in this life, you get what you get and that's that.

Mom and Dad were sleeping when I entered the house that night. I woke them telling them that I was hurt. My mother looked at me and lost it. Her emotional state could only be calmed by Dad's cool reaction to get me to the hospital. He assured her I would be all right. She started immediately trying to stop the bleeding with cloths pressed up against my jaw. Dad put his clothes on and took me to the emergency room at the University of Virginia Hospital. Silence overtook us all out of disbelief that someone would do this to another person for no reason. I was treated in the emergency room for several hours, where they determined that I had a broken jaw. The gash required several stitches.

Dad hired a maxillofacial surgeon, Dr. G. Slaughter Fitzhugh. Dr. Fitzhugh was a member of an Otolanyngology, ear nose and throat, medical practice under the name of Hedges, Fitzhugh, Humpries and Crigler. The concern was that I would have a permanent scar on my face and have the look of some criminal type.

Dad and Mom wanted to avoid that if at all possible. Rather than the usual procedure of wiring my jaw, Dr. Fitzhugh wrapped the jaw in a twill that fused the bone. My jaw was swollen and my eye was bruised and blackened. The usual stitching was limited to avoid a pronounced scar and special ointments and salves were applied as well as cocoa butter to reduce the scarring. Black skin tends to bruise and heal more colorfully than light skin so the concern about my appearance was real.

I stayed home the balance of the summer for the next six to eight weeks while the jaw healed and the swelling reduced. The packing around my jaw had to be removed and I was unable to eat foods that required chewing. When the day came for the packing to be removed, I remember sitting in front of the doctor as he pulled the wrapping from around the jaw bone inch by inch. The white gauzy like material was brown and beige as it exited my mouth. It felt like a coarse rubbing between bone against bone and it smelled terrible. The worst of the healing was now over. A post nasal drip of mucus that would lodge in the base of my throat and caused me to hack and spit to clear my throat was the permanent residue, along with the noticeably faint scarring that eventually blended into the surrounding brown skin remained below my left eye. It is still noticeable today upon close examination. This was a physically traumatic experience, but strangely it was not a mentally disturbing traumatic experience. But I did have some traceable fear of people getting too close to my face especially in threatening situations.

Dad pursued criminal and well as civil charges against Loving for the injury. I remember going to the old red brick Settlement building at the corner of Ridge and east Main Street, across from the old Mt. Zion Baptist Church for a hearing or meeting before Judge John M. Hamlet, Jr., the Juvenile Court judge. The judge was White, short and bald, he used crutches to get around, and he wore glasses, a somber looking fellow who seemed not to take the matter that seriously, but I could be mistaken, since this was Black-on-Black crime except for the fact that my father was a principal of a school in Albemarle County. I was too young to know what happened, but I think the issue of Loving's family being poor had something to do with their inability to pay damages. Neither Mom nor Dad discussed the details of the court proceedings with me. The whole thing, over time, just melted away into the fabric of daily life after that.

Not long after healing up, I remember trying to resume a normal routine, and going to a football game at Burley for the first time after the incident. I was there with my girlfriend Roberta Harris, a cute light brown skin girl with a round face with short reddish brown hair and a gap in her front teeth. When some bullying loud mouth shouted and made a threatening motion toward me as we were leaving the game, she stepped forward to defend me. Roberta who was tall for her age and well-built for a girl—she played sports and was my steady girl for a long time during those years—told the fellow that if he tried something she would beat him herself. The fellow went his way and no more was heard from him. The news of the incident made its way around the school, but not much was made of it except the occasional tease from some students who could not resist picking fun at my expense.

My last encounter happened in my senior year at Burley in the school cafeteria. I went to the lunch room as I usually did without anything particular on my mind. At Burley there was a group of guys with nick names like "Cow Brown," and

"Sights" who always kept something going on. They were witty and provocative at the same time but never got into fights. Some of the guys were jocular and had the swagger of tough guys, but did not fight. They talked a lot, kept a lot going on but avoided physical contact. These guys were always teasing about "your mama" and making jokes about the sex they were having or boasting about the sex they wanted to have. There was something about my wanting to belong, yet I was not really one of them. I tried to be, but never really made it.

In reality that was good because the culture that most of these fellow students lived in was not the culture that motivated me nor was it the culture I was being reared in. My family culture was not better, it was just different, more progressive and more visionary to an extent. Perhaps in reality it was better because I was neither born in nor reared in the Charlottesville mentality. One day, I had purchased my lunch and was about to sit at a lunch table. As was customary, guys who hung together ate lunch together. But this time I sat at a different table with boys who were not traditionally in my group. It just happened that way.

A fellow student, Tiffany McCullough sat opposite me. He was tall, light skinned, heavy set, bigger than me and full of loud bravado; he was at times an intimidating fellow though kind hearted basically. I do not remember Tiffany ever having a real fight with anyone. He and his family lived on Ridge Street near Langford Ave. Doing his usual thing, Tiffany began jiving with me about some topic that was aggravating. He made a crack about me just about the time he was about to start eating. He said something to the effect, "they say that Otis Sowell got the best of Lee" he laughed and joked with his friend sitting next to him, then he said "Lee can't fight anyway, he's a mama's boy." Back then among the guys, the cracks were always about someone's mama, but he made no remark disparaging my mother. Without warning, I grabbed my carton of chocolate milk, which was fully opened, and threw it on him. "You jackass, keep your mouth off of me," I shouted filled with the tone of exasperation and out of character. Perhaps I was tired of being looked upon as a patsy. He was shocked and jumped up from the table creating a big stir. Everyone took notice and looked at our table, anticipating that a lunchroom brawl was about to begin. Tiffany looked at me with menacing intent, thinking to himself whether or not to engage me by reaching across the table and swinging. He was startled because he did not think I had the gumption to challenge him. The harm I momentarily caused him was not physical, it was psychological. He was a proud guy. We stared at each other but nothing happened. His restraint probably saved me from a beat down. Chocolate milk was all over his shirt, but he did not know what to think of me after that; I had become unpredictable. This became known as the "milk carton" incident.

Cow Brown as he was known, was a slight built, medium-height light brown-skinned fellow with short cut black hair, but with a "big mouth" that he used comically. He made one of his notoriously funny retorts to something that had been said to him by Bridgeforth, "Sights" we called him because he wore eye glasses. Sights was a light-skinned tall fellow with black hair who was gentle by nature and a good basketball player. He played on the varsity basketball team. "Mr. mother fucker" he said and went on …and we all just burst out laughing. There were several of us standing in the lunch line when the exchange took place. Brown was funny as hell. It was the way he said it, the intonation and spontaneity plus the language that made the remark so humorous.   Burley was like this, easy going and humorous. There were so many different characters, all with individual personalities, all characters in a high school play.

GETTING THE LAY OF THE LAND

AFTER DAD GOT HIS BEARINGS IN CHARLOTTESVILLE, he started to buy real estate in the city. He began by buying the house in back of us: 528 Ridge Street. Sometime after 1961, Dad began to earnestly make his move on the Charlottesville real estate scene. He buddied with the Black real estate brokers and investors of this time such as Rev. E.D. McCreary, a short dark skinned preacher who had been playing the real estate game well before we got to Charlottesville. Rev. Mc-Creary owned several properties in Charlottesville and was the colorful minister of Ebenezer Baptist Church on 6th St. N.W. Dad liked Rev. McCreary because he was outspoken. He liked the old man because of the religious connection and his quaint, direct style. Rev. McCreary appreciated those who sought to go against the grain. His wife was the librarian at Burley when I attended there during this time. He had two sons: one was a prominent minister in Richmond and the other a minister in Phila-delphia whom I would meet in later years. Thirty-one years later, I would become a member of Rev. McCreary's church, and my youngest son would be baptized there.

In addition to Rev. McCreary and T. Arthur, Dad befriended James Fleming, an-other realtor and real estate investor in the city. A rotund, fast talking copper-colored man, Fleming was a licensed realtor and appraiser. Fleming sold us our home on Ridge St. Dad's relationship with Fleming was elastic; it would expand and shrink over the years. Dad dealt with all of these characters, a makeshift bunch of fighters and iconoclasts, but of all of them I think he enjoyed his relationship with T. Arthur

Barbour more than any. T. Arthur sold Dad several properties, and his easy going, "under the radar" approach fit more squarely with Dad's demeanor and strategy.

Dad's venture into the real estate market in Charlottesville was not by happen stance, but that of an invader with a ravenous appetite who knew what he wanted before he got there. Being in Charlottesville, back then, was similar to being in a candy store and marveling at all the treats that were available for one with a vision. Before we moved to Charlottesville, Dad had purchased several rental properties in Richmond. One on Garland Avenue, on the Northside, not far from where we lived on North Avenue. Another on east Grace Street and a property on Broad Street on the east end of Richmond. Dad was gifted with good business acumen but had absolutely no mechanical ability. Dad was applying the same lessons to Charlottes ville he learned earlier when we lived in Richmond. He got to know local realtors in Richmond and picked up pointers about the real estate investment game from these people. He did this with Mable Jones Connelly a White, well-to-do woman, distinguished looking with grey hair and aristocratic bearings; a realtor from whom he bought several rental properties and whom he mentioned often.

At that time in Charlottesville, the people were not sophisticated, tenants did not demand much and the city had not reinvented itself into the university-centered up scale retirement community it later would become. As Mom said, "Lee bought prop erty in Charlottesville because it was cheap." At one time Dad owned over 35 rental properties in the city. He purchased raw land in Fluvanna County, sold properties, rented properties, built a new six-unit apartment building on Ridge St. He was an "unlicensed realtor" and a formidable investor. His appetite was not quickly satisfied and he bought property almost until he died in 1998. In fact, near the end of his in vesting life, Gary O'Connell, the then city manager, met with Dad and me to request that Dad not buy any more properties in Charlottesville, an explicit acknowledgment of the city's view of his real property ownership position. He believed in putting his money out there to work for him. He nurtured banking relationships with bankers who would loan him money on short-term notes that he rolled over when he needed to, and he developed relationships with local real estate and non-real estate lawyers with whom he did a slew of business. He created his wealth in the typical American way, up from the "bootstraps." As she reminisced, Mother said, "Bootstraps!? We didn't even have shoes to put on!" He and Mother invested their money, lived mod estly and worked continuously.

Dad eschewed debt. He felt it was a trap for the unwary, a kind of bondage that could make him vulnerable to control by outside forces, but he knew how to use it in moderation to advance his investment objectives. He paid off all of the homes we ever lived in. He believed in being debt free. And he paid off all the mortgages on all the investment properties he bought. This ethic regarding debt has become a family economic value, and I have tried to practice it when and where I can. Paradoxically, he was demonized by the press, local housing advocates, housing inspectors and le gal aid lawyers because he did not borrow money to fix up what the naysayers consid ered his substandard houses, and by doing so play the "inside game" which required "sucking up" and pandering to city officials and his detractors giving them leverage over him. He did not play the political game to assuage their ire. Every investment he made in his properties was self-funded. The press made hay painting him as a slum landlord but gave a free pass to the tenants who destroyed and vandalized his property, lived like dogs in his property and left owing him over $100,000.00 dollars in unpaid rent, bad debts and judgments. He received no credit for being, in effect, the landlord of last resort, for poor Blacks in Charlottesville. He kept many people from sleeping on the streets over heating grates. He lent money to those who asked because they did not qualify for bank loans. And he put money back in the Black community by hiring Blacks to do much of the repair work. He was wheeling and dealing. He often remarked when talking about his dealings and paying income taxes, "when they come for me just have them give me a padded cell." But the hypocrites, the do-gooders, the jealous, the naive and the mendacious saw only what they wanted to see. He rented to those who would not otherwise qualify to rent an apartment, but in the haste and fervor of an attempt to destroy him this gratuity was ignored.

His only limitation was that he was a public school official and that would cause an undertow amidst his tide of good fortune. He operated below the radar for many years, quietly buying properties and adding to his estate. Because no one knew him, he had free reign for a while, the powers that be not seeing him as "a dog in the manger" at that time. But that would change as the years rolled on and his real estate exploits became more visible to more people.

With prominence comes scrutiny, jealousy, envy, the things of small town fodder. A big fish in a small pond: being Black, nonconformist, progressive and determined to do it "his way" in spite of the conventions of the era and the culture of the region inevitably resulted in an attack. Too big too soon, too Black to be controlled and too proud to buckle under. These were the attributes that characterized Dad's *modus operandi* in that environment. There is a price to be paid for everything; nothing is free. The acquisition of wealth is not free, but the price he would pay, partly self-inflicted but mostly orchestrated, set the tone for part of his legacy.

Dad's status as a principal of a county public school, hence a "public figure," made him different from all the rest. It distinguished his efforts from those who were not public figures who acquired real estate such as McCreary, Barbour and Fleming. Dad's status made him a lightning rod, a point of contention and an object of attack. When the attack fully blossomed years after I had left Charlottesville and was living in Philadelphia, Dad had worn out his welcome with city bureaucrats charged with regulating state building codes in the city, along with the patience of the local legal aid society that represented his tenants. Years of back and forth fighting, harassment and resentment, though manageable in the past, now found its way through concerted action to an accommodating press. Because of his status as a public figure, the press took license to inflame the community and libel him with impunity using the shield of the First Amendment to the United States Constitution and the Supreme Court decision in *New York Times Co. v. Sullivan* (1964)[14]. It was the Times decision that gave the print media the protection to go after him relentlessly because that decision held that a public figure had to prove actual malice, in effect, that the publisher knew before printing the article that the statements were false, before a suit for libel or defamation could succeed.

I doubt if Dad really knew what he was up against when the battle began. He knew that the housing code folks were on his case, and he knew that the press was out to get him. To some extent, he reveled in the media attention that portrayed him as an out of control slum landlord because race played a role in the press's caricature of him. Dad was an anomaly in the Black community. His profile was higher than most because of his status as an educator: his appearance before the county board of education many times kept him in the public eye and created enemies more Black than White. He was a prisoner of his profession and of the assets he had on the ground. It was not so much the parents of his school kids, they appreciated what he did for their kids. The White folks didn't really care what he did as long as it did not interfere with his school duties. Many White folks respected what he was doing. It was only when they were made to inquire into his activities that his real estate business aroused their ire. The Whites had to be led into it. But his Black professional contemporaries in the school system were jealous and envious of his position. This extra layer beyond the community folks heightened and increased the pressure on the school system. He was respected but not liked by them. It was the Blacks who cared the most. The Black strivers who look for and took full advantage to turn the sword of envy into his removal as the prominent Black principal in the system who was also amassing wealth as a real estate investor. The Blacks used the press and the system to bring him down. It was a "throw the ball and hide your hand" collaboration informally extended to the government by way of the use of housing inspectors and representation by tax-paid legal aid society lawyers that represented his tenants.

Once a month he had me come up to the master bedroom to receive the money from him to make the monthly mortgage payment on the property he bought behind our house at 528 Ridge St. He would go to his bureau as I entered his room and tell me to "stay back" in a tone mixed with sarcasm, irony and humor, and beckon me with his left hand in sequential hand motions indicating for me to come no closer. He liked to count and handle his money in private. This eccentric behavior was characteristic of Dad. That was the message. I was not allowed to get any closer than six or seven feet or so from him while he went into his bureau and put together the money for me to take to Mr. George Gilmer to make the monthly mortgage payment before going to school. Dad was being funny again. He loved to do quirky things just to be an odd ball and to make me laugh. Dad was not a petty person. He was broadminded and visionary. If you played him cheap, you would lose.

Back then Gilmer's office was on the ground floor in a red brick corner building across the street from the county court house in Court Square. The act of paying that mortgage each month made an impression on me. It taught me about paying mortgages, something that would come to be a common practice in my later life. And it created an image in my mind of a secure private business man taking care of his business, quietly and unobtrusively. I liked the way Gilmer ran his business. When I would enter his office to make the payment, he always seemed to have muddy shoes or boots on with red clay on them as though he had been outside surveying some property or something similar. He was always there alone. And he had a rustic country manner, self-employed, yet secure in his own eccentricity and in his own private business. I took mental pictures of Gilmer and carry them with me to this day.

Dad's acquisition of Charlottesville real estate went on aggressively from 1961 until 1995 when he purchased his last rental property. When Rev. McCreary died sometime after 1967, Dad had the opportunity to buy all of the properties in McCreary's estate. Fleming brought the deal to him, and it sat on his desk for several days before he declined to take it. I remember him thinking about the "buy," but in the end he let it go because he already had too much, and the thought of him acquiring so many additional properties would put him out of the education business and squarely in the real estate business full time. He was already getting flack from several quarters: the water was rising and the undertow of his real estate adventures was making the surface waters uneasy. Had he acquired McCreary's property and proceeded further, it would also have inflamed an already jealous undercurrent, and invited closer scrutiny and further attack.

As it was, word was beginning to trickle in at Burley about my family and the real estate. In a small city such as Charlottesville, with a captive intransigent Black population, word travels fast. I do not think he wanted the kind of increased public attention the acquisition would have garnered nor did he want to leave his profession at that time. He prided himself as an educator and did not want to cease being one then. Before these events, he was invited to deliver a paper at the National Association of Secondary School Principals convention in Chicago. Mother, with her conservative approach, lobbied against it as well. So he turned it down, opening the door for an arriviste, a social climber and parvenu, to enter the competition.

As in all endeavors, there is a precipitating event that cascades into a reckoning. For Dad it was the renting of an apartment between 1982 and 1983, on Ridge Street to a new, young Black teacher from out of town. Apparently the new teacher was unhappy with the condition of the rental unit. The specific complaint was that the unit did not have a refrigerator. When Dad was notified about the problem, he had one delivered. But by then the teacher had called a Black female principal who had an ax to grind with Dad who complained to the superintendent, who in turn suspended Dad for conflict of interest and other ethical violations related to the incident. It is not always the White man who is the villain in matters of race. There are many Blacks who dislike each other for various reasons and will turn the knife just as painfully, if not more so, than any White would do. Ironically, the very people he tried to help were pivotal and instrumental in his undoing. Blacks fighting Blacks, Hispanics fighting Blacks, minority fighting minority, all doing the White man's bidding. When I sat with Dad and he told me the facts, as a lawyer I knew he had potentially crossed the line. Dad could have retired before all of this happened, but he stayed on because he felt no need to retire.

One cannot be sure that this event was the essential cause of his eventual separation from the Albemarle County School System. Dad rose to prominence in the system over three decades. He worked with three superintendents. He was appointed principal of four different schools, both elementary and middle, and rose to be an Assistant Superintendent for Records and Reports in the central office: a position created when integration came into the county. At that time, they did not know what to do with him, so they created this position and brought him into the central office. Mother remained in the classroom teaching the third grade, but was transferred to Stone Robinson Elementary School.

Perhaps Dad's greatest legacy to the school system was his recruitment of Black teachers to the county. At the time of his unfortuitous entanglement with the county school system, his primary duty as assistant superintendent was to head a minority recruitment task force. He singlehandedly brought in dozens of Black teachers to a county that did not aggressively recruit them nor sought them out especially, but he did. He went to many of the Black colleges in the South and recruited the teachers, some of whom still remain in the system today or have since retired. He brought in music teachers who worked in the county schools and led local church music pro-grams. During the period of the dual school system, Black teachers were recruited by the central office because they needed them to teach in the segregated schools. But after integration settled in, in the middle sixties, there was no need for these Black teachers. He almost found himself without a job, except for the tenure he had earned from years of service. The post *Brown vs. The Board* educators were displaced by integration all over the South, many untenured Black teachers were "integrated out of a job." Black teachers were whipsawed by Brown before and after. Schools were closed to prevent integration and closed to enable integration, causing Black folks the loss of jobs and schools—in the name of improved education. There was an abundance of White teachers to fill these jobs, but Dad brought in Black teachers to fill some of the vacancies.

His against-the-grain style of leadership, coupled with his perceived feisty vain-gloriousness and his supposed grandiloquence, none of which was his personality, probably did not sit well with many of his professional contemporaries. It angered some and it made others jealous, so when he handed his adversaries an opportunity "to get him," by dint of his poor judgment in this case they leaped to it and dismissed him. The result was a ten million dollar lawsuit filed against the county school sys-tem for wrongful dismissal, *Otis L. Lee v. The Albemarle School Board and Carlos Y. Gutierrez, et al.,* U.S. Dist. Ct. of Virginia Civil Action No. 84-0038-C (W.D. Virginia 1986), which drove Carlos Gutierrez, the first and only Hispanic superintendent up to this time from his job, who instituted proceedings against him—an administra-tive dismissal hearing, which I helped his counsel handle, and his subsequent resig-nation. A mistake of judgment brought on by hubris was his undoing. Did he really care? Probably so, but knowing Dad as I did, he did not mourn too long because he took solace in his discomfort because he had made it "to the finish line" in all that was really important to him.

The legal team he assembled to fight this battle initially was centered around a young enthusiastic Black lawyer from Richmond, who along with a seasoned, older, and highly esteemed Black lawyer Samuel Wilbert Tucker, made up the team. But the younger Black lawyer was killed tragically and unexpectedly in circumstances that were dubious and Mr. Tucker, the older more esteemed Black lawyer's health precluded him from asserting himself vigorously in my father's case. As a result, Dad turned to local lawyers whose advocacy was cavalier, not as zealous, nor their performance persuasive. Race was not the issue. Once the young Black lawyer from Richmond died, Dad's legal fate was sealed. I accompanied Dad to the appeals hear-ing at the Fourth Circuit Court of Appeals in Charlotte, North Carolina. Dad had lost the first round of court hearings when the local Federal District Court judge granted the school board's Motion for Summary Judgment. In other words, the judge found that there were no "material issues of fact" in dispute and based upon the application of the law to those undisputed facts, the school board was entitled to have the case dismissed, which the judge did. Dad then appealed that ruling to the Fourth Circuit Court of Appeals.

When the appeals court hearing began, Dad's lawyer was immediately flustered, when one of the appeals judges fired the first salvo asking him "where's the race?, where's the race?" What the judge was really saying was, unless you can show that the dismissal from his position was race-based you're out of here! There was no "race", just poor judgement in this instance and malevolence. In the frenzy, the lawyer hurriedly fumbled through the brief to find the section detailing the race issue but could not find a section or a response to deflect the volley. Any lawyer who has ever argued a case or tried a case hates to be put on the spot like that, then to go looking hurriedly through his or her papers, which are unorganized and disheveled, trying with much disconcertion to find a response, which in this case there was none to be found. The case was over right then. I told Dad, as we sat together observing the proceedings, that it was good we were not at a hanging, or we would be mighty sad and solely disappointed.

Ten years before his death, I was fortunate to have the opportunity to help him fight some of these battles. I assisted him with his dismissal hearing. As mentioned earlier I went with him to the Fourth Circuit Court of Appeals. After moving back to Charlottesville in August of 1991, I fought his real estate battles in the court system relentlessly until a truce was achieved and a rapprochement settled in. I saved him much grief and tens of thousands of dollars in attorney's fees and beat back an attack that had been designed purposefully to cause him further harm and to drain assets from his estate. Being of service to my father is one of the noblest achievements of my life.

His was a recrudescent reputation, one that fed upon itself. As a leading Black regional educator and a wealthy man with substantial real estate ownership, people either knew him or knew of him. He is remembered not so much for the "precipitating event," but for all that he did prior to that event. He is remembered fondly, even by those who fought him. As his son and like many sons I have inherited his reputation, and I labor to continue and to improve upon this legacy.

Last Albemarle County School Administrative Team
Serving in the Old County Office Building – 1981
Left to Right: Mr. Thomas W. Hurlburt – Assistant Superintendent for Personnel,
Mr. John W. Massie – Administrative Assistant to the Superintendent, Dr. Clarence McClure, Superintendent,
Mr. Otis L. Lee – Administrative Assistant for Personnel and Administration,
Dr. James R. Myers – Assistant Superintendent for Instruction

12

"It was the Best of Times, it was the Worst of Times"

—from A Tale of Two Cities *by Charles Dickens*

I N THE SPRING of my tenth grade year at Burley, life began to change and it happened as a lark. Student council elections were about to begin and my hall locker neighbor and friend Franklin Bowles, a loquacious, comedic, easy going, but capable friend and I joked about running for president and vice president of the student council. Franklin was medium height, he wore his hair short, as we all did back then, and his skin tone was rust colored not brown or black, a greyish brown tone. I ran for president and Franklin for vice president on the common-man ticket and platform. Franklin's mother worked in the school cafeteria and he had a sister, Barbara, who was in our class as well. We thought that too much attention was being paid to the favorites in the school, to the students who had become teacher's pets. The teachers at Burley favored certain students and families for that matter, over others, and realistically that was true. It all depended on your reputation and your family. If you were seen as smart, the teachers perpetuated that aura. The favored students did their work better than we did of course and were encouraged by the teachers, while the rest of us were not taken seriously I believe. But to convince the teachers you were deserving was not easy. To break into that mentality was impossible. Of course the students who made the honor roll continued to make the honor roll and went on to become members of the Honor Society. It became a self-perpetuating mentality for the favored few. We less-serious students continued to receive the average grades that we deserved. Black folks are like that. So we entered our names into nomination and at the assembly where each of the candidates spoke for a few minutes to explain their reasons for wanting to be president of the student council, my time came. And to everyone's surprise, including me my oratorical skills were high, very natural, fluid and well beyond what anyone expected. Words seemed to roll out of my mouth with facility. I had never spoken publicly before an assembled crowd. But you would have thought this was something I was used to doing. I was a natural. The kids liked what we had to say, they identified with it and we won! And so began a three year odyssey of extra-curricular achievements with sporadic academic improvement. From obscurity to high school prominence all in one week. Fortuitously, I was propelled into a leadership position. I had gained the attention of the faculty, but like Bowles, high school for me was a happy go lucky experience I did not take seriously.

My grades left a lot to be desired and there were tense moments at home on report card day. But all of that began to change over the next two years as my personality emerged, like a duckling breaking through his eggshell to birth; crack by crack the shell broke open and I was a different high school student than I had been before.

Perhaps it was the absence of rigor and palpable competition in the classrooms at Burley that enabled me to go off on my own in search of knowledge that interested me, who knows. But surely all of this was extraneous to Burley High School. There was no summer reading list handed out at the end of the term, and no summer school. You were left to your own devices.

By this time I was reading books on my own without advice or recommendations from any teachers and with no instruction from my parents. I read *The Group* by Mary McCarthy, *The Spy Who Came in from the Cold* by John Le Carre, *Catch 22* by Joseph Heller, *The Ordeal of Major Grisby*, by John Sherlock, *Andersonville* by MacKinlay Kantor, the French classic *Madame Bovary* by Gustave Flaubert and *The Affluent Society* by the Harvard economists John Kenneth Galbraith and a few others. *The Catcher in the Rye* by J.D. Salinger was handed around in school, but I never read it. I was already familiar with such classics as *Two Years before the Mast, Cyrano de Bergerac, A Tale of Two Cities, Silas Marner, Les Miserables* and several others through my large collection of classic comic books. All of this was self-motivation and untutored reading, stuff I was doing on my own.

I also went to the public library and read sections of one book on sex for beginners, which was interesting reading. I received no sex education at home. The closest thing I got to instruction was a blurb by my mother—a cross between a Victorian and a Puritan—when she quipped, "if you don't know what you're doing with it, you better leave it alone." Well, what did that mean? On another occasion Dad asked to look into my wallet one evening. As it turned out, earlier in the day Bowles had given me a condom, which I initially did not want to take, but he said "Lee go ahead take it," so I did and put it in my wallet, even though, I did not know how to use one, nor did I have the prospect of using one. Dad, thumbing through my wallet, came upon the condom and said in a shocked but stern voice, "Ohhhh! You're using these now." "No," I said honestly, pleading my innocence, "I'm not using these, my friend gave it to me." I do not know whether he believed me or not, but nothing else was ever said about it again. An excellent opportunity to discuss sex was missed because he chose not to and the matter passed.

I learned more about sex outside the house than inside and learned nothing about it from school. If I had been more educated about sex and had more experience earlier, I probably would not have married as early as I did. But naiveté always finds its victim. I was told by strong implication "not to do it" but not instructed about it in such a way as to know why not to do it and what the issues were about "doing it," or how it was done. Burley did not have sex education classes when I went there. Premarital sex was a taboo, but an activity that many teens were engaging in and some girls got pregnant. All I knew was that my sexual desires were strong and I was curious and I liked grinding against the girls but I knew nothing else. It was the luck of my ineptitude, not my attempts to have sex, my desires or my opportunities, that kept me from impregnating a girl in Charlottesville. Thank God that I didn't.

I got out a book on How to Study, but I never read it. What a difference it would have made had I read and absorbed that book. I was going in the right direction. I had the right ideas but no guidance. There is a science to proper studying. It is not something you are born knowing how to do.

Dad made perhaps one of the biggest and most profound improvements in my academic life when he ordered and brought home to me the vocabulary building and enhancement program by Dr. Bergen Evans out of Chicago, Illinois. I learned and mastered all 500 college level words in the series and did all of the exercises and memorized many of the sentence examples he used to define the words. This knowledge has lasted a lifetime. It was also during this time that I began the life-long habit of dictionary reading. The dictionary was both the source of words and an encyclopedia. Malcolm X is recited to have learned much of his knowledge from reading the dictionary. The dictionary became my favorite book and continues to be so.

During the spring semester of that year, as president of Burley's student council, I attended the state student council annual meeting in Martinsville, Virginia. Virginia's dual educational system divided everything along racial lines. There was one state student government association for Blacks and one for Whites. At the annual meeting I was exposed for the first time to progressive students from other sections of the state. And the opportunity to run, unexpectedly, for state student government president was first introduced to me. The vice principal of Burley at this time was a medium-height brown skinned Black man with a crooked neck sealed in place due to some injury he sustained years before I met him. His name was Mr. Samuel Griffin. I liked Mr. Griffin. He was very encouraging and we became good friends. He was the faculty advisor for student government and it was he who took me and another student to Martinsville and ushered us through the meetings. At one of the final sessions, we were all assembled in a convocation theater at the school where the meeting was being held, and I witnessed the existing state president address the delegates. He was smooth, poised and confident. I was impressed. I said to myself I should be up there doing that. So before the conclusion of the meeting, elections were to be held for the next state president and Mr. Griffin urged me "to throw my hat in the ring," he said. That was the first time I had heard that expression. I did, and made my pitch to the delegates and won! Our delegation was ecstatic, for the first time in Burley High School history we had a state president from our high school. Winning meant several things: I would be a delegate to the International Student Burgesses convention held annually in Williamsburg, Virginia. State Presidents were automatically invited along with international student guests from foreign countries. Dorothy Gordon, a NBC, national radio personality at the time conducted her national radio Youth Forum Program, consisting of student leaders discussing certain issues from the Burgesses convention. Next I would be a delegate to the National Student Council annual meeting in Lexington, Kentucky at Transylvania University.

Of course, all of this was exciting to me but it did not, as I remember, create much excitement at Burley. It appeared that most students and faculty did not even know the event had occurred. It created more envy among some students than anything else. I had made an end run around the entrenched clique of "name brands" and achieved my own distinctive persona. I was somebody in spite of the clannish mentality that pervaded the culture of Burley. An outsider had made good who was not in the honor society. All of this opportunity carried with it one restriction; I could not leave the state for the one-year term of my presidency I was told. This restriction was not researched to determine its scope but was accepted at face value. That put my desire to attend the Milford School in Connecticut in contention with my new status as state student council president.

I attended Lane High School one final time during the summer of 1963. The school was officially integrated by now and no repercussions ensued because we attended. In contrast to the earlier experience after leaving Jefferson, this time it was an unwelcoming experience. I did not like the smell of the place for starters. The White students were unfriendly and uninviting. My cousin Wendell and I went there during the summer; she stayed with us while her mother was finishing up her teaching duties in Norfolk, Virginia. Nothing positive was gained from this brief experience. Both of us flunked our courses and went out to eat some hamburgers after getting the summer reports. Neither of us told our parents about the failure, and we did not lament the poor grades. We knew it did not count and we discounted the effort and immediately moved on. That was it for Lane High School and me. The school I walked past every day to go to Burley might as well not have existed as far as my educational experience was concerned in Charlottesville, save for that one summer early on when things went really well. A warm teacher and an accommodating environment.

I led the student council the next year and perhaps the one after that. At the same time, my music lessons were beginning to bear fruit. I continued taking piano lessons but this time the lessons were taken in the private residence of the Yancey family, a Black family who made their home available on Rose Hill Drive, a block and a half south of the school. The lessons this time were given before school not during school hours.

In February 1964 at the annual local Lions Club piano competition, known as the Virginia Lions Club Bland Music Scholarships Piano Competition, my music teacher entered a few of us in the competition. We were all seated next to each other in a small auditorium. A hush fell over the room. Each music student had practiced his or her piece to perfection for weeks in preparation for the contest. As I waited for my name to be called, my right leg began to twitch and shake uncontrollably, and the palms of my hands were cold yet sweaty. The parents and city music teachers sat on the other side observing and critiquing each student. The piano was up on the stage. Each student, after his or her name was called, had to walk from the seat each was sitting in below the stage and walk up to the piano, face the audience, announce the piece to be played, and play the piece. You could hear a pin drop in the room. Throats were cleared, but no words were spoken. All the piano pieces were performed from memory. After each piece was performed, the student got up from the bench, turned to face the audience and bowed, then left the stage the same way he or she went up to the piano.

"Next we will hear from Otis Lee, Jr." the announcer called out with the sternness of a disciplinarian. I got up and crossed over the young girl that was sitting on my left, walked up the center isle and went up to the stage. I tried not to think, just act. I kept all of my thoughts straight ahead. When in front of the black upright piano looking straight ahead, I was afraid to look at my parents. I said, "I shall play a *Muzurka in F Major* by Chopin." This was a tricky piece, but not difficult. If I could get through the most difficult passages, the rest of the way was clear. We were trained that if we made a mistake to keep on playing. I got through without too many errors and finished the piece. It was over, now I could relax. I did not care about the results; I just wanted it over with. When the results were announced, no one was more surprised than me that I had placed second. It was the highest I ever placed in the Lions Club competition. This was the Black music student's competition.

A few of the Black families who could afford it began to consider sending their kids to private schools outside of Virginia. One prominent minister was sending his kid, and a local teacher was sending her son. This may have been in reaction to segregation even though integration was at hand. But the small mostly unnoticed movement was in response to status and separation from the masses and perhaps the quality of the schools. Dad and Mom considered whether to send me or not. I went to St. Ann's Belfield School, a local private school in the county, to take the Secondary Schools Admission Test. Not knowing how I did on the exam, I began to dream as only a kid could do, about how it would be to go to a private school out of state. I was both intrigued and fascinated by the prospect. I had no idea what it would be like nor the costs. I took the exam in the Spring of my tenth grade year and received notice sometime in early Summer that a trial admission was offered to the Milford School in Milford, Connecticut. The issue was front and center at home, but still recessed, discussed but not fully debated in my presence. I was kept in the dark about the real issues underlying the crucial decision. I dealt in dreams and my parents dealt in the realities.

Dad saw to it that I learned how to work. I could not be raised being afraid of work in his scheme of things. But the trips to Fitzgerald, Georgia picking cotton and cropping tobacco ended after my ninth grade summer, though we still went to Fitzgerald as a family at least annually. Dad spoke to a local jeweler, the owner of Jay Jewelers downtown on Main Street about my getting a job in his store after school. How this came about I do not know, but one day he sent me down to meet with Mr. Janow (spelled phonetically), the owner, and shortly thereafter, I began working at the store after school cleaning up the place. Mr. Janow was a short, dark haired Jewish man with a swarthy complexion. Charlottesville has a noticeable contingent of Jews living in the community. My job was to clean the jewelry counters, sweep the floor, clean the outside store windows and do whatever else Mr. Janow deemed necessary.

Prior to working at Jay Jewelers I had a paper route, delivering the Daily Progress along a route I obtained after Dickey Moon moved on to other things. On one really cold and snowy afternoon it was so cold and snowy that I chose not to deliver the paper. My clients called and complained about not getting their paper. Mother had to drive me around so that I could make my deliveries. It was not long after that that I quit the route. And I built the road between our home and the house next door leading down to 528 Ridge St, the house Dad bought in back of us from George Gilmer. I also mowed yards, dug up trees, waxed floors in our home and whatever else Mom and Dad saw fit for me to do. Many of the kids had part time jobs after school. Some worked at the UVA Hospital as orderlies, custodians or on the food staff. One of my fellow students at Burley, Clarence Nicholas, worked across the street at a competing jeweler doing the same thing I did. We would often acknowledge each other as we cleaned the outside windows of our respective stores. Janow and I got along well, but on one occasion he pulled me aside and said to me "you're not that good, you're not that good" and went on to lecture me about life. What brought that on baffled me. What had I done? Apparently he thought that my attitude and approach to the work warranted the rebuke. He must have thought that I thought I was doing something "special." But I did not think that way. When I did my work, my mind was usually a thousand miles away. Why was he trying to bring me down? I was just a lowly teenage Black student janitor, but I must have exuded an attitude that he felt needed to be nixed. In retrospect perhaps Janow was on the right track with me. Instead of putting me down he may have been trying to help me by getting me to realize that I had a lot to do to be as good as I thought I was by attitude at least. An expression comes to mind that a dentist said to me when I was late getting on a tourist bus, "you are so far behind that you think you are ahead." In reality that was the truth.

I kept an after school job from the days I worked at Jay Jewelers 1962-63 until I graduated from Burley in 1966. After Jay Jewelers, the next job I got was at The Youngmen's Shop, a block west of Jay Jewelers but still downtown. The Youngmen's Shop sold good conservative, quality men's and women's clothes. I plotted to get this job because I knew the fellow that was quitting and asked him to recommend me. This was another janitorial job, but this time I was working with a senior janitor, a fellow named Wilbert. Wilbert was unique in all respects. A short, rotund, brown-skinned fellow with big, bulging black eyes. Wilbert was colorful, hard-working but a sad case. He talked often about the troubles he had with his "old lady." But Wilbert made his biggest impression on me with his famous saying that he was doing something "not for the season but for the reason." I worked there every day after school and at least a half-day on Saturdays. The owner, Mr. Omansky, was a kind gentleman. Omansky was a short Jewish man with grey hair and a hump in his back. He smoked a pipe all the time.

Omansky knew that the job was not a career move for me. Dad let him know that if I needed to be off for school-related events, that was going to happen. With Wilbert, I put up stock, swept the floors, cleaned the bathrooms, washed windows and cleaned up the sales floor as needed. Wilbert was the full-time janitor. He did the bulk of the work, and if Omansky really needed something seriously done involving stock or cleaning, he was the man. I observed the White gentry of Charlottesville come in to buy clothes, try on the sport coats, suits, overcoats and look at the ties. University professors, university students with their girlfriends, giving advice on what looked nice and what did not. It was the culture of Charlottesville. Blacks seldom bought clothes in the store. The clientele was essentially all White and middle to upper class. The White privileged shopped in this store. I gained an appreciation for quality men's clothing: the different types of shirts and collars, different types and styles of sports jackets, trousers, ties and sweaters.

However, I complained to Dad about cleaning up the bathrooms. He reminded me that if I did not want to continue cleaning bathrooms, I had better get an education. That stuck with me.

Dad made the decision not to send me to Milford based upon "his calculus." If I had been asked, I would have traded in my state council presidency to attend the Milford School, but I was not asked. In retrospect, his decision lacked enlightenment. His normal visionary perspective failed him on this issue and consigned me, as a result, to a struggle against mediocrity in my education. Launching me into the world ill-equipped to make the lofty dreams I envisioned for myself a reality without much trial and error. His inability to appreciate the benefits to be derived from attending a private White school reflected his exposure to White schools which was non-existent. After all, he had been educated in all Black schools. He did not realize the benefits to be gained. His background was far from being that of an elitist. He did not see himself as an elitist in this sphere of life, but he did in all others. He did not know what elitism in education required. In that regard he was *soi-disant*, self-styled, in his aspiration to be. Therefore, as the son, I suffered from this lack of complete appreciation, in that I was not seen, perhaps in his eyes, either as deserving of, or entitled to the sacrifices required to secure an elite educational experience. It was not a priority for him. The schooling I was getting was sufficient. After all, in his reasoning, I was not maxing out the school I was already in. I just needed to work harder and make the most of what I had.

The vision of the parent, determines the direction of the child's life. But it seems to me, that in spite of the mediocre grades, the budding talents I was now exhibiting required a broader perspective. Why could they not have made the sacrifice to send me to that school is beyond me? I had been accepted! What a difference it would have made in my life. Why not go the extra mile? Take the chance and expose your son or daughter to these potential opportunities if it was within your means to do so! It was for a good cause: education. Though education was important and essential, an elite education was not. It was not as important in his scheme as investing in rental real estate to secure his and the family's economic future, an economic decision which was clairvoyant. He had grown up poor. His drive was for money and property, not elitism in all its dimensions. Pragmatism, culture and upbringing informed his decision. He felt he could get the job done of educating me without the intervention of a private school, notwithstanding the nascent talents that were being exhibited. Dad said to me that he thought I was too "green behind the ears" to go away to school. He also said to me many times, "you gotta go to the upper ten, the upper ten." What he meant was the "Big Ten" schools like Ohio state, Northwestern, Michigan State and University of Illinois, Penn State and University of Wisconsin and others.

But what was I supposed to go there with? Not a Burley High School education! I do not know whether or not Mother fought for me to go or not. She did not speak on the issue with me at all. Years later she remarked with pregnant irony, "we wanted you to get the best education we could, we did not know about that Harvard stuff." Therein is the answer, their visions and experience did not encompass "the White school thing." They were not aware of the breadth and depth of benefits to be derived.

The decision to go would have been a "game changer" even if it did not work out completely. For one thing, my self-image could have been strengthened and enhanced. Instead of having to struggle mightily just to pull myself up academically; to throw off the shackles of familial and systemically imposed mediocrity;

OTIS LEE JR.

Student Named Delegate to Burgesses

Otis Lee Jr. of 526 Ridge St., a Burley High School senior, has been elected one of t w o Virginia delegates to the ninth Williamsburg Student Burgesses in Williamsburg Feb. 12-16.

Lee will represent the Virginia Student Participation Association, of which he is the state president. He is also president of the Burley High School tudent body and he is interested in dramatics, debating and music.

He is a native of Richmond. His father is principal of Virginia L. Murray School at Ivy.

Virginia's other delegate is Ken Elsea of Bristol.

Theme of the Williamsburg conference is "Protest: A Right and a Responsibility."

The Student Burgesses, an educational seminar, will attract high school leaders from 50 states and 36 foreign countries. It is sponsored by Colonial Williamsburg.

Speakers will include Ambassador Leitao da Cunha of Brazil, a former Brazilian prime minister, Brooks Hays, consultant to President Johnson and former special assistant to President Kennedy, and Rep. Patsy T. Mink of Hawaii, first woman of Japanese ancestry elected to the U.S. House of Representatives.

and to beat back the beast of the inferiority boogeyman, I would have been exposed to rigor, in depth reading, self-discipline, real academic competition, competent teachers, first class facilities and a culture of academic achievement. My horizons would have been opened to this new world.

Who knows what affect that would have had on an aspiring imaginative young mind. Instead of dealing with the trite, worn out Jim Crow policies of mediocrity, a new paradigm was in the offering. My path could have been much easier. I would have learned these lessons earlier had less disappointment, self-doubt, uncertainty and potential self-destruction. Instead of seeing myself as "less," I would have seen myself as "more." The private school experience had the potential to catapult me to another level of self-image, and put me on a glide path to high self-esteem and academic achievement. Some of us need more not less to make us right. Our sensitivities are different; our reaction to external stimuli is different. I was one who needed the extra academic reinforcement. It is a parent's responsibility to perceive these needs and if possible to address them.

Years later, I was determined within my means that my youngest son would not suffer from this lack of insight. And I stressed to my oldest son the importance of hard work and diligence in his studies and encouraged him to persevere. One should not speculate too much on what might have been. I may have gone up to Milford and become discouraged, or maybe I would have learned a few things. One thing is for certain: my view of education and my approach to my studies would have changed forever. The exposure would have been invaluable and life altering, and the negative consequences of my struggle to become academically competitive might have been avoided or lessened.

Courtesy Daily Progress, Charlottesville, Virginia, circa 1964

13

✥

"BRING ME ALL YOUR HEART MELODIES"

IN THE SUMMER OF 1964 it was time for my piano recital. The socially conscious parents of one or two kids that took piano lessons wanted their kids to
give a recital. The activity was purely voluntary. My recollection is that only one
other student was presented in a recital during this time, though there were many
other students my age taking piano lessons. Of course, one needed to be somewhat along in the process, not a beginner certainly. It is a coming out party for the
parents as well as the student. Similar in purpose to a cotillion for debutantes but
in a much lesser sense. The recital is a chance for the parents to showcase their
child and his or her musical prowess and the family's social status. The music
teacher is fêted as well since it is his pupil that is on display.

Usually these events take place in the afternoon in the student's home, a semi-
private affair. The family as well as the music teacher invites fellow students and
members from the community to come. Dad was especially engrossed in this affair. Mother looked forward to the recital but took it all in stride. Her role was to
prepare the home for the event including the refreshments that followed and be
a gracious hostess. In preparation for my recital, my music teacher and I selected
a list of ten piano pieces that I would have to learn by memory for the recital and
learn them well enough to play them in public for a listening small audience.

Preparation for this event began six months before. Formal invitations were
not made. All of those who attended were invited by word of mouth. On the adult
side, I invited Erma Carter, a short round faced brown skinned middle-aged woman with whom I often sat and talked. Erma lived on the corner of Ridge Street and
Lankford Avenue in a big white stucco house with a large side yard. She used to
say that I had a "gift to gab." I spent many afternoons talking with Erma Carter
about everything under the sun. Erma was an adult friend, a nice lady related to
my girlfriend's family in some way. Dad invited the minister of our church, Rev.
James B. Hamilton of Mt. Zion Baptist Church to the affair. He also invited family
and friends from Richmond, Virginia who came up for the Sunday afternoon: the
Blakes, Aunt Willnett and Uncle Walter. Mr. Robert Smith, my music teacher, a
tall White man with brown hair, and a disarming personality, arranged for several

of my fellow music students to attend. Three or four showed up. Dad had a local photographer, Mr. Scott, the father of a distant classmate take pictures.

Mr. Smith and I rehearsed the music and practiced until I was sufficiently proficient to go public with the selected music. I enjoyed taking music from Mr. Smith. He was kind and gentle. He never scolded me but he would always say "Otis you got a good start on this piece," meaning I was doing well, but I had plenty of distance to travel before I was proficient in performing the piece. He was always encouraging, and never demeaning. It was rumored that Mr. Smith went to the Peabody Conservatory of Music at Johns Hopkins University.

I was getting near to the pinnacle of my piano music experience. I had been taking piano lessons, on and off since about the middle 1950s. My interest in music was deep. I was given a stack of old classical 78's from some antique collection. I loved the classics, and became familiar with all the favorites and some of the esoteric. I went to Cabell Hall at the University of Virginia to hear various artists from time to time.

On one occasion I asked a girl I was trying to make headway with to go to a concert at Cabell Hall with me. She was also a student of Mr. Smith's and begrudgingly agreed to go. She was a hard sell. But I had not completely cleared the date with Dad. I had mentioned it to my mother, and she had tacitly given me permission to go but Dad was still not on board. On the night of the concert, I got all dressed and proceeded to go out, when a fuss commenced with me and Dad. "Where are you going and do you expect to drive my car?" "Yes," I replied, looking for help from my mother which was softly provided. "Yes Lee, I told him he could go," she said. A "manhood thing" was taking place. I felt man enough to be able to go, but was not and Dad was the "man." Dad was clearly annoyed, but reluctantly he assented. It was a school night and that did not fit well. After easing past that "trip wire" I went outside to go. We had two cars at that time, an old 1960 blue and white Oldsmobile and a newer gold metallic Buick. One car was parked in front of the other on the east side of Ridge Street about twenty feet north of the house. There was no street lighting, the area was dark. The Oldsmobile, which I was allowed to drive, was parked in back of the Buick. I was a new driver and very much unsure of myself. As I sat behind the wheel of the Olds, I put the car in reverse to back up and go around the Buick, I thought, but the car was still in drive and as I pressed down on the accelerator it lurched forward and struck the Buick on the rear bumper, denting it. I tried it again, this time I tried to go around the Buick but misgauged the distance striking it again on the rear bumper hitting the Buick so hard that it went up onto the sidewalk. With my tail between my legs, I went back into the house to explain what had happened. All hell broke loose. Dad said, "you did what!" "I wrecked the back of the Buick" I said sheepishly. Dad went outside in the night and examined the wreck. It wasn't that bad, but as far as going to the concert, that was dead. And as for the girl, I never got close to taking her out again.

Dad bought me a new black suit for the recital, and all of us were dressed in our finest. We assembled in the living room as you entered the house. Chairs and our sofa were arranged so that everyone could be seated directly in back of the piano. The piano, an upright, sat against the back wall in the living room about ten feet or so from the front windows. A few guests sat in the dining room which opened to the left of the living room. Mr. Smith assembled the guests and announced the opening of the recital: "Otis Lee, Jr., today will present a recital of music this afternoon for your enjoyment. Otis you may begin." With that introduction I entered the room from the kitchen which was in back of the dining room and walked to the side of the piano, since there was not a lot of room to stand beside the piano stool. I sat down and proceeded to go through the first part of the program. I do not remember being too nervous, though nerves were always a problem for me. But the atmosphere was calm and pleasant and I was among friends. I played well. But the *Mazurka* was always a tricky deal for me. I made the mistake I dreaded. I peeked at Mr. Smith who was seated to my right. He had heard the mistake, of course. But I gathered myself, kept playing and took another assault on the passage, nailing it this time and finishing with confidence.

The music pieces Mr. Smith and I selected were pieces I had played and learned before the recital was planned. We added a few additional selections, but the crux of the program was well known to me. The music program was not complicated. It was balanced for an intermediate level student: no real hard dense pieces were selected but levels of difficulty were there for me. Mr. Smith wrote out the program in my music notebook. When the time to play arrived, I announced each piece before I played it:

"First I shall play, *Prelude in C Major* by J.S. Bach; next I shall play *The Last Movement of the Sonata in "G"* by Beethoven, next, I shall play Frederic Chopin's *Prelude in C Minor*, next I shall play *Muzurka in F Major* by Chopin, next I shall play *Indian Sunset* by Gustav Klem and incidentally this piece was written by one of Mr. Smith's music teachers at college."

Then after an intermission, the next group of songs was announced:

"First I shall play *Rustic Dance* by C.R. Howell, next I shall play *Flower Song* by Lange, next I shall play *To a Wild Rose* by Edward McDowell, last I shall play *The Black Hawk Waltz* by Walsh. My last selection will be *Nocturne in E Flat Major* by Chopin."

The afternoon was a success. After the program I accepted congratulations on a job well done. Mom and Dad were proud. The guests sampled the refreshments. Mrs. Blake and Aunt Willnett helped Mother serve the guests. We all mingled and talked for a spell. Mr. Scott took a series of pictures of our guests and family to memorialize the event then gradually everyone left. The afternoon had been a success for the family.

Later that fall, I was invited to compete in a music contest held at Burley at night sponsored by the Omega Si Phi fraternity. I had been working on my signature piece, a nocturne by Chopin in E flat Major. The piece was intricate with long passages of melodic scales. The Nocturne required that I feel the love expressed and my intrinsic high level of empathy was evoked by its passages. So I worked on this piece. It drew me into a world of imagination, of love and torture, sacrifice and pain. At times when I played the piece, I felt that I could feel Chopin's mood and the longing he may have felt for an unrequited love. I worked on the piece with Mr. Smith for some time and at times had success but at others frustration was my reward. My problem was practice. Each morning, while I lay asleep in bed, Dad would yell "Otis! get up and go practice," and each morning before school the ritual was repeated over and over again. He constantly hammered me to practice, which I did but not enough to be really good. Allen Iverson responded during a news conference challenging him over his reluctance to show up for basketball practice sessions: "You talking about practice man, practice!"

I had a talent for interpretation, I could feel the music, but not a talent for execution. Like a basketball player, dribbling the ball is fundamental, but your dexterity with the ball and your ability to pass the ball determines the level of your creativity. It was the same with the piano; fingering and technical knowledge was where I fell short and needed more skill. And that could only be attained with dedicated practice and more practice and study.

On an autumn night in the fall of 1964, I experienced an exalted moment of both execution and interpretation. It was special, and I have never been able to encapsulate myself in the music so well during a performance, to lose oneself, such that the externals no longer matter. It was as if I was at home playing by myself. But several contestants preceded me. The event was staged in the auditorium at Burley. This large room with theater-seating had reasonably good acoustics. A large black Steinway Grand piano sat in the center of the stage. The lighting was dim and the glow subtle and unobtrusive. Everyone was quiet because there were only a modest number of patrons present. I announced my selection, sat down and began to play. I was removed psychologically from my surroundings for the moment during this time and lost myself in the piece. I played it flawlessly for the first time in public. The suppleness of my body and the freedom of my spirit allowed me to sway and weave with the requirements of the music. The Nocturne and I were one, like lovers in a full embrace. I felt a lust for the haunting melodies in the music. It was a *tour de force* for me. Never again have I been able to duplicate the atmospherics that characterized that evening at Burley, not to mention my performance. It just happened so unexpectedly, and I won first place.

I was then invited to compete at Howard University in historic Rankin Chapel against other winners from local contests throughout the region. Perhaps in retrospect, the performance at the contest was not all that great, but for me it was the best I had ever done.

To Howard University we went in the spring of my graduation year. I had never been to Howard, and I do not remember knowing much about the university. Little did I know, I would end up attending Howard University for undergraduate studies and law school. Divine providence was playing a role here. All of the contestants assembled in Rankin Chapel. A majestic red brick building well preserved with dark woods accenting the accoutrements. In preparation for the contest, I practiced but not as intensively as I should have. I was obviously familiar with the Nocturne but there was never any guarantee with the Nocturne that I would manipulate its curves and crevices adroitly, and if I did not confidence would be lost.

I had a bad case of the nerves that day on the big stage. My lack of intense preparation showed up, and I finished near the bottom. I had gone out "with a whimper." It was an embarrassment for them to whom it mattered, but not to me. I was not up to public performances. My skill level was not adequate if the practices were not there. The pressure, the nervousness and all that went with it was not to my liking. My piano music career ended that day, but it had been one hell of a ride! I had gone as far as my skill level and preparation could take me. To go to the next level required more natural talent than I had. Neither Dad nor Mom was a musician and no one in my blood line had exhibited any musical talent that

I knew of. Everything I learned was from what was inside of me. I had to work at it to be good, and I did not have the determination and discipline, or the innate ability to take it further. But I continued to play at student assemblies from time to time when invited to do so. After the competition at Howard, mentally I waived goodbye to an instrument I love and appreciate. It was my "adieu to the piano" as Beethoven had written many years before. Henceforth, I would let the grandeur of my expectations be fulfilled by my imagination.

In the summer of my eleventh grade year I went to Lexington, Kentucky as a delegate to the National Student Government Association annual meeting at Transylvania University. There I was exposed to thoroughbred racing horses for the first time. We toured horse farms in the rich Kentucky countryside and saw how the rich lived. I was impressed with the expansive ranches but was struck by the fact that the owners did not live any better, based upon their furnishings, than I did. It was eye opening.

In the fall of my eleventh grade year, in 1965, I attended the International Student Burgesses meeting in Colonial Williamsburg. Student leaders from all over the United States and around the world from 35 different countries were invited to attend. The most significant event to occur at the meeting for me was being selected by Dorothy Gordon, an NBC radio personality, to participate in a youth forum discussion broadcast nationally from the forum center. I remember her as being a short blond haired woman bubbling with personality. How I came to be selected escapes me, but my recollection is that throughout the meetings the sponsors were looking for delegates that stood out from among the others, for some reason, and those they selected were invited to participate. Several illuminati were in attendance including U.S. Representative Patsy Mink, a Democrat from Hawaii. I had a bad cold during that entire meeting, but it did not stop me. The weather was rainy, full of clouds and dreary. I met several wonderful people including a Laotian student Charkery Cun Seng Dao, (spelled phonetically) a short happy fellow. We took tens of pictures together. He asked me to send them to him but I never did. And I met a White student from Rhodesia, now Zimbabwe, whom I would meet again years later in Chicago while crossing Monroe Street on my way to work at Harris Bank. He recognized me after all those years and I him. We talked for a while then went our separate ways.

After my arrival home from the meeting, I told my parents about my selection to be on Dorothy Gordon's program. When the program was about to air, we all gathered around the radio in the living room huddled together with great expectation and listened to the program and my contribution. When the moderator, Dorothy Gordon, came to me I expressed myself well but I was stuck on the word "prerogative" and kept using it several times, it was all very fascinating. Was this my 15 minutes of fame?

Courtesy, Charlottesville-Albemarle Tribune, 1964

Piano recital living room view, circa 1964, courtesy Scott Photography
Robert Smith and fellow music students

Piano recital parlor room view, circa 1964, courtesy Scott Photography
Left to right: Ms. Upshaw, Otis Lee, Sr., Alexander Scott (principal, Burley High School), Rev. James B. Hamilton
(Pastor, Mount Zion Baptist Church)

Piano recital front porch view, circa 1964, courtesy Scott Photography
Left to right: Otis Lee, Sr., Rosa M. Lee, and Otis Lee, Jr.

Piano recital, circa 1964, courtesy Scott Photography, father and son

14

"BRING ME ALL OF YOUR DREAMS YOU DREAMER"

T IME WAS APPROACHING to wind up the high school experience. As the outgoing state student council president, I had to preside over the annual state meeting and give the keynote address to end the session. These were the turbulent Civil Rights years. The March on Washington took place on August 23, 1963. We watched it on television, but I really wanted to be there. These were also the Kennedy years. Dad was a great fan of President Kennedy. When President Kennedy was assassinated on November 23, 1963, the beginning of my ninth grade year, I remember all of us gathered around the T.V. watching his funeral procession. It was a sorrowful time.

My farewell speech to the delegates would be my concluding speech and exit from the leadership of this state wide assembly. The concluding activities were held in Martinsville, Virginia at Albert Harris, its Black high school. In preparation for my concluding speech, Mother and I bought a book of President Kennedy's speeches and I borrowed heavily from them as we crafted the speech. By now, I was used to talking before an assembly and presiding at assemblies because I had that duty at Burley as student council president. Dad, having heard about my exploits at Burley from me and others, decided to see for himself. He showed up one day unannounced at a Burley assembly to witness; he wanted to see what all the chatter was about. In Martinsville I borrowed from President Kennedy's lines "ask not what your country can do for you, but what you can do for your country" and adapted it to the student council program. I also borrowed his phrase about the "problems of man are made by man and therefore, can be solved by man."

As I arose to deliver the farewell speech, I looked over the hundred or more assembled students and imagined how they must have felt watching me as I had felt watching my predecessor. I took my time, gathered myself, which included holding my breath to a count of ten—a practice I never forgot in my trial practice as an attorney years later. It is amazing how long ten seconds can be in the mists of anxiety, but the pause calmed me down, and I delivered a good speech. I received a rousing ovation. Mr. Griffin was very pleased and the other teachers who were assembled also thought well of the speech.

I remember sitting at the kitchen table on Ridge Street listening to WINA, on the radio, playing its country western, folk music and an occasional soul record while my mother and I selected the excerpts from President Kennedy's speeches and made a speech for me to deliver to the assembled delegates from across the state. But now, my tenure as president was over and college loomed on the horizon. The world I experienced at Burley would follow me the rest of my life, but a new reality beckoned.

Even more than speech making, debating was my charge in my eleventh and twelfth grade years, 1965-66. Eugene Williams a young, Black, English teacher from outside of Charlottesville started the debate club at Burley and was its sponsor, the first debate club in the school's history to my knowledge. Mr. Williams was brown skinned, pleasant looking with a receding hairline. He had a welcoming personality and was very decent. I got involved and so did my erstwhile friend John Ragland. John was a naturally smart student who was raised by a family of smart people. He had a penchant for science and had a studious mentality. Tall and thin with a light brown and yellowish skin complexion. John and I took a liking to each other and embarked on the debate experience together.

Mr. Williams rehearsed us and guided our research efforts. The topic for debate was: "Resolved: that the Federal Government should adopt a program of compulsory arbitration in labor management disputes." I took the first negative position, and John took the second negative position. We practiced and practiced, then practiced again, even recorded ourselves as we practiced and listened to ourselves to perfect our elocution and presentation styles. We typed out our positions on three by five index cards. We were only allowed to work from these cards during a debate.

I remember two significant debates. The first was in 1965 against several White schools in the Tidewater region of Virginia, the most significant being Hampton High School. We had never debated against a White team in a White school on their turf. It was an exhaustive experience. They were tenacious, aggressive and relentless. John and I stood up well under the attack, but I remember being very tired after the rounds were completed. I was worn out. The Hampton High faculty advisor said something to the effect: "Wait! Wait! You guys," raising his voice above the decibels of our yelling, "you're going too fast, hold up, stop!, stop!" he shouted. Like race horses galloping at a fast pace being pulled back and made to halt, our verbal combat slowly halted and we listened to him. He was shouting at his team as well as us. We had gone at each other with a vengeance, determined not to give an inch to the other and not to be out done. They may have won the debate, but I am not sure. Why was the tenor of the debate so richly competitive? I do not believe the White team had ever debated a Black team before and we certainly had never debated a White team. It was indeed a tune up for the Second Annual Inter-Scholastic Debate Tournament in March of 1965 at Norfolk State University, in Norfolk, Virginia where the final debate tournament was held. Before going to Norfolk State we went to Hampton University. I do not recall debating at Hampton, but I do remember talking with a student who accompanied us on campus. He asked me what my name was. I didn't answer right away and he immediately said "did you have to think about it," after a few seconds I said "no" my name is Otis Lee and that was the end of it. His rapid fire question so punctiliously posed had taken me aback. I did not expect the question, nor the way he asked it. This student was a member of the Hampton University Debate Team.

The English Department at Norfolk State sponsored the tournament. There were several rounds of affirmative against negative until the best affirmative and negative teams were left standing. We were the negative team that made the finals.

The final round was held in a small banquet room on campus before dinner was served. The two teams sat at the head of a horizontal table in front of the room on opposite sides of the lectern. Faculty members and the other debate teams and their teachers sat around the other tables vertically alongside each end of the head table. The chair of the English Department, Dr. Robinson, presided over the event. He was a light skinned man of medium build with black hair that seemed almost straight. He wore a dark suit. The contrast between the black eyeglasses and his light skin made his appearance jump out at you. He selected other faculty from his department who acted as judges.

John and I debated the topic with splendid confidence. We out shown our opponents by using carefully crafted arguments and phrasing practiced in the heat of debating battles with White teams and school practice sessions. We won five out of five debates and beat Phoenix High School of Hampton in the final round. We had won the tournament, "Best Negative Team in the State 1965-66, champions 1966-67." I was awarded "Best Speaker" of the tournament. John and I each received $125.00 scholarships to Norfolk State College. When we arrived back at Burley, The Daily Progress, the local newspaper, came to the school and had us hoist the trophy and took our pictures. We were state champs!

Trophy for Burley Debaters

Members of the Burley High School debating team display the trophy they won Saturday in the third annual debate tournament at Norfolk State College. From left are Eugene Williams, English teacher and the team's coach; James Wood, a junior; John Ragland, a senior; Otis Lee Jr., a senior; Ocenia Jordan, a junior; and Alfred Carter, a junior and student coach. The tournament topic was Resolved: that the federal government should adopt a program of compulsory arbitration in labor management disputes in the basic industries." Ragland and Lee took the negative side and won five out of five debates, then defeated Phenix High of Hampton in the finals. Each won a $125 scholarship to Norfolk State. Wood and Jordan took the affirmative side and won three out of four debates, receiving awards as outstanding debaters.

Progress photo by McKown

Debate Trophy, 1966, courtesy Daily Progress

During the extra-curricular travels of my last two years at Burley, I met several young women. There was Joanne Goldstein a Jewish girl, whom I met at the National Student Participation Association meeting in Lexington, Kentucky between 1965 and 1966. This was my first interracial relationship, and it was significant for me and I feel sure it was just as significant to her, because neither one of us had dated people from outside our racial groups. As I remember her, she was a short, perky, red headed "White girl" with freckles from Mason City, Iowa. We took to each other for some reason right from the start and proceeded to hang around together at the conference and we walked hand-in-hand down a public street in downtown Lexington, unaware that I was perhaps taking my life in my own hands by doing so. Because Lexington was a college town, the culture may have been more liberal. But these were halcyon days. The days of "anything is possible." Race and the confinements of being Black were not on the table for me then. We were innocent and unthinking naive young students who had found an attraction regardless of race. I do, however, remember getting some strong stares from some of the passersby and feeling slightly uncomfortable but not enough to turn back or quit holding hands. When the convention was over, we corresponded some. She sent me an invitation to an event in Clear Lake, Iowa that she thought I would like to attend. But there was no hope of me going. I did not even mention the invitation to my parents, although I thought about her often and lay in my bed dreaming of what it would be like to attend such a function. As the years passed, I wondered what happened to her. I wondered whether what we had momentarily experienced was worth holding on to, or was it an aberration? Possibly so. Time and distance brought an end to the speculation.

I met another very charming woman in Martinsville, Virginia at the last annual state student council meeting. She was brown skinned with beautiful long, black shoulder-length hair. She ended up going to Adelphi University. I often thought about her. We had clicked but distance made further association unavailable. I did not follow through as I should have. My naiveté about such things cost me good opportunities to know some good women. And there was another young Black woman that also got my attention from Corpus Christi, Texas that I met at one of my outings. She too was charming and inviting. Each of these women was different and our attractions were based solely on honesty. I was myself and they were themselves, unadulterated fondness. We were students of a certain ilk: we shared, albeit momentarily, a class of common values. These women all had finesse and even at my young age I was attracted to that quality. I could recognize it when I saw it. They were leaders themselves in their high schools and were out to make something of themselves. Relationships could have developed out of each of them. I especially regret not pursuing the woman I met in Martinsville.

The Black girls I associated with in Charlottesville, however, were undistinguished by and large, narrow-minded, had little vision and were cloistered, as some of them should have been. They were not open to my entreaties. They were not of the same class as the women I met on the road. My horizons had been expanded from what was available in Charlottesville. And I was not a favorite of the females in Charlottesville anyway, except for one relationship with one of my best friend's sisters, Roberta Harris, as mentioned previously, who was a round-faced light-skinned young woman with a boyish manner and short brown curly hair. Roberta was my senior prom date. We had a long relationship without sexual intimacy, not for lack of trying, however. Otherwise, I sputtered and had several halting superficial relationships with the girls that I was attracted to. There was another local girl that I wanted to date, that I thought worthy of my attention in earnest, but she was unwilling and unresponsive, aloof and uncooperative, so that nascent desire withered on the vine and passed into a faint recollection. In retrospect my alien and aloof relationship with the girls and many of the guys in Charlottesville was for the best. Because it allowed me to avoid mistakes that could have dimmed my family's dreams for me and my dreams for myself.

My high school graduation was now at hand. Many in my class would either go to work, college or the military. Those that did not go to college faced what their predecessors faced in the Charlottesville tradition, a market place characterized by retail and service work: cooking in the kitchens of restaurants and private homes, cleaning and janitorial work; or orderly work cooking or cleaning in the university hospital; or cooking and serving at the University; a life of waiting tables as a "busboy," or washing dishes. A Black person could expect to be a groundskeeper and maybe a secretary in the city government or maybe at the university; odd job construction work and barbering offered possibilities. Charlottesville never had anything for Black people to do except to do the servile jobs traditionally held by Blacks in this area. Michael J. Klarman, the highly regarded law professor, refers to these jobs as "Negro jobs."[15] Progressive Blacks left this area after finishing high school or college. Very few stayed around. Even college graduates who wanted to work here faced the prospect of little or no employment but under employment was a certainty except for teaching in the public schools. I often wonder why Blacks would remain or come to Charlottesville. There is little or no industry, light or heavy, that working people can be employed in to earn a decent living with a high school diploma.

I dreamed of becoming a lawyer. I didn't get the idea in my head by seeing real lawyers do their thing during my youth in Charlottesville, for I did not know nor did I see any lawyers Black or White. There were no Black lawyers in Charlottesville during my entire educational experience here. My aspiration to become a lawyer came from T.V., but not Perry Mason, a popular program that had little or no effect on me. No, it was a British movie that portrayed the lawyer as an aristocrat that excited my imagination.[16] Years later I would lament that the closest thing to freedom a Black man can attain is to be a lawyer and to acquire wealth. That was and is my view. Regardless of the times it seems that Black lawyers of a certain ilk feel the same. By now I had an exalted view of myself, and becoming a lawyer fit my self-image—what I expected of and from myself. But I had no idea what I had to do to make that dream a reality.

I fantasized about going to a number of colleges: Bowling Green State University, in Bowling Green, Ohio and Ohio State University in Columbus, Ohio come to mind most prominently. I watched a lot of Ohio State University football games when Woody Hayes was the football coach. During the fall of our senior year, several faculty members gathered a few of the college bound students in the twelfth grade class into a first floor classroom. We were about to be visited by an admissions officer at the University of Virginia. He was either on the admissions staff or a professor there. He essentially said to us "don't apply," for we stood little or no chance of being admitted. That is what we took away from his visit. No one in my class of 125 applied for admission to UVA. Gregory Sampson, the smartest kid in the class, who scored over 600 on the math section of the SAT's, when scoring 800 on each section was the maximum you could get, chose not to undertake the humiliation. Here we were in the backyard of the most prominent public university in the region, less than 4 miles away, and yet not one of us was good enough to enter this local White university, the embodiment of liberal democracy in higher education. We were not good enough. Why? Was it our color or the quality of our education that kept us out? I am sure that neither the White kids at Lane High

School nor those at Albemarle High School were told "not to apply." Rumor had it that Gregory Sampson was offered admission to an Ivy League University, but in order to be admitted he had to repeat the twelfth grade at a private school somewhere. He took the deal, and as far as I know, later enrolled at Cornell University. One Black female graduate was accepted to a White elite female college, but to my knowledge she did not enroll. The circumstances or conditions surrounding her admission were not made known to me.

Neither we, nor our education, were respected by the White schools. Ironically, they knew something we did not know at the time. Only the Black colleges understood our plight and were sympathetic to our cause, because they knew our history, they were our history. To my knowledge, empirically, less than 40 percent of my graduating class applied to colleges and of that number less than 20 percent enrolled and graduated four years later. I say this modestly and without foundation but to the best of my knowledge I may be the only lawyer to come out of Burley High School in its history; I do not know of, nor have I heard of, any other.[17]

There were some teachers at Burley that I remember fondly because their impression was singularly lasting. Mrs. Gladys McCoy, my French teacher, for instance. She spoke often about West Virginia State College, a school she knew well. The only French I know today I must attribute to her teaching. I think of her often. Samuel Griffin, the Assistant Principal was a kind man and very encouraging. He, of course, was instrumentally important during my student council adventures. Mrs. Cammora Snowden, my physics teacher lived a few houses down and across the street from us on Ridge Street. I do not know any Physics today, but she said something and kept repeating it so much that it sticks with me to this day: "Live above the law and you do not have to worry about the law." Mrs. Snowden was a smart woman.

And of course Eugene Williams, my debate coach. Mr. Williams for a time lived in our lower level on 526 Ridge Street. He was supportive, encouraging and forward thinking. Mr. Williams went on to receive a Ph.D. in English some years later. The only teacher at Burley, to my knowledge, to have done so. I ran into him at Howard before I left there in 1972 when he was appointed to the faculty. These post Brown v. Board of Education teachers were good people who did the best with what they had.

Jefferson's imprimatur on Charlottesville left this city with a quiescent genteel aristocracy, occupiers of the "pole position" when it comes to real politics in Charlottesville. The University of Virginia, long a bastion of sexism and racism that had to be dragged kicking and screaming into the age of civil rights so that White women and some Blacks could attend the school, is the power behind Charlottesville. The university is a separate city within the county. A figurative "Vatican City" within the county and city. It is the repository for the elite whose cachet extends beyond its boundaries but dissipates and fades into obscurity when filtered through the deep layers of poverty and ignorance in the hinterlands that define most of the population in this area. The annual operating budget for the university is tens of millions of dollars larger than the annual operating budgets of the city and county combined. The university is the region's largest employer.

In the modern era the university is touted as an elite university, one of the "public Ivies" though it still retains an invidious seam of racism woven into the fabric from its founding. The old, established, indigenous, silent, White middle class go about their business maintaining the status quo which excludes Blacks, oblivious to what it means to be Black in Charlottesville. Not until this class was forced by progressive external forces of society—the Civil Rights Movement—to allow Black folks into some of the limited benefits of living in Charlottesville was this movement actually allowed to happen here. It is this class, expanded by new arrivals, characterized by well-to-do retirees, immigrants from the north who have allowed this city to be sold as a beacon for the nouveau riche, in the nature of a Georgetown in Washington D.C. or Soho in New York. The only hope for the future are the immigrants from the North. It is they with their liberal leanings that can change this historical culture of servitude.

As a general rule, a culture of exceptionalism does not exist for Blacks in Charlottesville, save for a few Black emigrants who work and teach at the university. These folks are not part of the basic fabric of Charlottesville society outside of the university. Within the greater community, exceptionalism exists only in rare individual anomalies attributable solely to that individual's genius. Neither the culture nor the educational system facilitates greatness in Blacks; this was especially true during my school days in Charlottesville. The question is why does it not exist here? Is it something in the water, the culture, history, politics, the social fabric? What is it? Is it the reflection of tradition, the disembodied spirit of Thomas Jefferson? Yes, it is a neocolonial Jeffersonian ethos. A tradition of racism—almost a birthright, an inheritance, if a locality can have one. What does exist for Blacks in Charlottesville and Albemarle County are uninspiring banalities of mediocrity. An abundance of "hot air" abounds freely given by the White elite to those Blacks who trade on sycophancy, pander and peacock for their own self-aggrandizement: none of which matters in the slightest to the political power structure, the moneyed aristocrats and the entrenched revisionists who determine the culture in Charlottesville and Albemarle County. Nonetheless, Black folks are stakeholders in Charlottesville and Albemarle County, but that stake is subservient to the dominant stake occupied by the larger and more powerful White culture.

The irony in all of this is that there is a substantial body of historical research led by historian Mario de Valdes y Cocom and others that espouses that our fair city is named for England's Black queen. Charlotte Mecklenburg-Strelitz, the Queen consort of the United Kingdom as wife of King George III, known as the "mad king." She was known as Queen Charlotte Sophia. Her mother was Songhai, (West African), a noble lady whose parents gave permission for marriage to the visiting German Duke of Mecklinburg, Germany. It is postulated by some that her mother or a maternal ancestor was Songhai. She married King George III when she was 17. They had 15 children. Queen Elizabeth II is her great-great-great-grand daughter.[18]

On a trip to England in 1999 with my wife and youngest son we visited Windsor Castle outside of London. Our tour guide made a passing reference to "England having a Black monarch." I was intrigued by the remark and felt there was some truth to the statement because this particular tour guide was very knowledgeable. A quick trip to the British Museum the next day yielded me nothing. There was not enough time to research the issue thoroughly because I did not know where to look, nor did I have the time. But many years later, the mystery was solved by a

Queen Charlotte Sophia, mother was a Songhai (North African), noblelady whose parents gave permission for marriage to the visiting German Duke of Meckinburg Germany. She married King George III when she was 17. They had 15 children. Queen Elizabeth II is her great-great-great granddaughter courtesy Edward Robinson, Attourney at Law, Philadelphia, Pennsylvania

referral to me by a lawyer historian, now deceased, Edward Robinson from Philadelphia, Pennsylvania. So we go back to the central question, why is and has Charlottesville over the years developed the culture of Black marginalization? It should be just the opposite but it isn't.

Blacks are on the periphery in a White culture that is anathema to African or Black American culture. An environment that does not promote, fund, accentuate, sponsor—except for the very recent renovation project for Jefferson Elementary School that will house an African American Museum—or embrace the culture of things Black. Sure, there are some museums containing African art and Black art at the university, but those few cultural antiquities are not reflective of the at-large community's sponsorship and embrace of that culture. No, these are academic exercises intended to showcase an egalitarian, inclusive approach to learning, art and history. The Whites have no "Black problem" in Charlottesville. The Black population is less than 20 percent of the total population in Charlottesville and Albemarle County. "Black Power" as defined by Stokely Carmichael and Charles V. Hamilton is nonexistent in Charlottesville. Being few in number and largely untrained, they are harshly dealt with for violating the law and they are priced out of most good neighborhoods where the new White arrivals want to live—within the highest performing school districts.

Their cultural and political institutions either never existed or were integrated out of existence. John Lassiter, the aforementioned author of *The Silent Majority*, recites the case of Charlotte, North Carolina, which is also the namesake of Queen Charlotte Mecklenburg-Strelitz. His description of Charlotte captures in my view what Charlottesville and Albemarle County are about precisely. He says

"...the present and past political and business leadership is dedicated to the (unwritten) goal of a racially and economically segregated city." "Charlotte's progressive mythology flourished by allowing affluent Whites to maintain a liberal façade [...] because of their physical and social distance from the problems of race and poverty." This description of Charlotte, North Carolina has appropriate application to Charlottesville and Albemarle County.

Racism hangs over the head of Charlottesville and Albemarle County like the Sword of Damocles, denying it its "true place in the sun"—a community unhampered by the issue of race. The underbelly of the area are the poor Whites, the poor Blacks and the Black middle class. The poor Whites cling to the last vestige of White privilege as a basis to hold their heads high, but in reality they are no better off than the Blacks, except for race; locked out of the better life by a lack of money, education and "cavalier values." The Black middle class, a reed so thin as to be invisible, microscopic in appearance, their number few and tenuous, find their way inconspicuously through teaching jobs, low-level government careers, the postal service and in quasi-secretarial and administrative placements here and there.

And finally the poor Blacks, compelled to be tolerated in subsidized public housing and in trailer parks by an indigenous presence, are maintained to provide a servile workforce for the aristocracy, the moneyed class and the business elite. The poor Blacks are subject to few substantive career opportunities and depend upon the largess of philanthropic Whites who cleanse their guilt by helping individually and through charitable organizations to the extent that they can. An insidious decadence spawned by this lack of opportunity, poor education and exclusion from the mainstream of the region gives rise to debauchery, drug abuse, crime and immoral acts. Nihilism, a pathology rich in historical causes, some all too familiar, barely begins to explain the reasons.

During this time, Mother and Dad had to renew their teaching certificates by taking teacher education courses periodically at intervals specified by the state department of education in Richmond. Dad applied to the University of Virginia to take his required courses but was denied admission even for that! He went instead to Columbia Teachers College in New York. Mother did not even apply to U.Va. She went all the way to Petersburg, Virginia to Virginia State College to renew her certificate.

From what I observed back then, some of the first Black students at U.Va. were from the Tidewater area of Virginia. When these students first came to Charlottesville, they were treated like celebrities among the common folk. Local Black students were admitted later. Those Black students that attended the White schools in Charlottesville after integration became the norm, but not the Blacks from Burley. The Tidewater schools were deemed more competitive than our local Black schools. Burley closed the year after my graduation and remained closed until converted in later years to a county middle school.

Uncle Wynn, God bless his soul, took me, along with several of his kids, my cousins, on a marathon trip to East Lansing Michigan to visit Michigan State University during my junior year at Burley. Michigan State had been an instrumental institution to him in his profession as an Agricultural Extension Agent in North Carolina. He was going there for his own reasons, but suggested to Mom and Dad that they allow me to go since I was at the point of choosing a college. He was trying, as he always did, to help family members, especially the kids, improve their educational opportunities. A few weeks before he came to Charlottesville to pick me up, I was playing in the back at 528 Ridge Street and stepped on a rusty nail. The treatment for which was soaking my foot in a medicinal solution to promote healing and to take the soreness out. I was doing that every day until he came to the house. I was just about finished with the treatment when he arrived. Mother was a bit cautious about my going in this condition, but reluctantly felt I was well enough along to risk it, so I went. It was a long car ride all the way to Michigan in his Dodge. We ate hamburgers all the way there and all the way back. By the time we got back to Charlottesville, I had had enough hamburgers to last a life time. But the trip was good. It expanded my horizons because I had never visited a college for the sole purpose of evaluating the suitability of a college for attendance. The closest I had come were my visits to Hampton Institute and Norfolk State as a part of the first and second debate tournaments.

After arriving at Michigan State, we took a brief tour which included the football stadium. It was gigantic, so modern and precisely detailed and marked. The green smooth artificial turf and immense stadium seating, and the striking white goal posts was something I had never ever seen before, coming from Charlottesville. I was overwhelmed. Next, we went to the dormitory where I stayed. Again, I was put in awe by the size and scale of the building, but I was underwhelmed by the small size of the rooms and bunk beds that were used for student sleeping. I remember saying to myself, I will be lost in this big maze of facilities so far away from home. I would literally be a speck on the wall in this humongous place. Uncle Wynn took me to the admissions office so that the officials there could review my credentials for possible admission. I do not recall what credentials they reviewed, nor for that matter what credentials I took with me, if any, for them to review. But after the review of whatever I had and what they could get, I received a small note rejecting my application. I was not bothered by the rejection because I had not really entertained the prospect of going to Michigan State anyway. This was Uncle Wynn's initiative.

I was admitted to Howard University on March 15, 1966. I ranked number 21 out of 125. I did not consider Hampton Institute, Virginia State College, Norfolk State College or any of the less prominent Black colleges. Dad must have chosen Howard because I do not remember knowing anything about Howard before playing in the music contest there earlier that year. Howard was viewed as more progressive, having more to offer, and broke the plane of normality and predictability that characterized Black aspirations in Charlottesville. One other student from my class was accepted, but she did not enroll. Dad said to me before I left for Howard in the summer of 1966, "if you do not have any sense by now, you won't ever have any" and off I went.

When I graduated from Burley High School and left Charlottesville in the summer of 1966, I was a virgin in all respects: no sex, except for grinding at school dances on occasion, no alcohol, no cigarettes, and no drugs. All of this would change during the next six years.

The same inconsistent, desultory, undisciplined, and at times shallow approach to my school work, along with "moments of brilliance" which I always exhibited from grade school through law school, is the same approach I took to Howard University because I had not learned better. Ironically, I had done so much at Burley that I retreated into complete anonymity at Howard. I chose not to get involved in any student activities. The breadth of my intellect allowed me to use only what I needed to "get over" but not to excel. I never utilized the depth of my intellectual capacity. I didn't know how. This is what I had to learn. I had to get more out of myself, work harder and dig deeper. I had gotten away with "half stepping" for years, but the end to that discredited approach was now in the offing. I began to study better at Howard, but in many instances I still "got by." It was not until I attempted to enter professional life that the "chickens came home to roost." These unlearned lessons had to be learned and learned well. The opportunity to acquire this discipline was delayed for almost 8 years when the Milford School decision was made. After that decision I was on a problematic path to achieve excellence. It would not be until I took my first Bar Exam that I would face the rigor that, because of my approach, would become an existential experience.

Dad was a rich man by the time I graduated from Burley High School in 1966. He became richer by the time I finished college and graduated from law school. Dad was probably the wealthiest Black man in Charlottesville and Albemarle County at one point between by 1972 and 1998. Along with his penchant for language, he also enjoyed fine clothes, southern cooking, good preaching and high-end living in all things he touched. He was far from perfect, in fact he had many foibles, but his character was well made of virtuous timber. Mother remarked early on while we lived in Richmond that, "people treat you the way they do because of what they think you got!"

My father was not one of pure and exacting finesse all of the time, but his tendency toward and his embrace of finesse ensured the qualities of his approaches. And though his efforts at times may have missed the mark, his knowledge of what was proper, as well as his vision, strength and drive always put him over the top. Dad was an aristocrat in bearing, temperament and wealth. If he had been born to money and education and high culture, he would have thrived under those conditions as well. So he made himself into the aristocrat that his birth denied him. He educated himself, mastered his profession and built a successful real estate business that sustains the family today. Dad associated himself with people of class and with common people. He enjoyed them all and he learned from each of them. His humble beginnings energized his approach toward life. He was a hunter gatherer. The Lees were not born elites, how could we have been? We were the progeny of slaves. Our origins are humble, but as we have gone forward with uncanny vision we have acquired many things through hard work: entrepreneurship, high educational attainment, wealth, values and diligence. Over an extended period of time, across generations, the acculturation took hold, the adornments and the trappings of the elite class have been acquired.

My high school life was important. Just as important, or more so, in molding my personality and congealing the prism through which I would see myself during my college life and during my professional life. And it was that self-image that refused to give up when my search for success encountered significant but not insurmountable headwinds. It was the platform upon which all else rested. My high school life set the tone for the image I would carry of myself for the rest of my life, modified and woven into by other life-forming experiences. My achievements in high school were a skein of affirming events that shaped the person I eventually would become. After all, no one put my dreams in my head but me. I had to make it happen. I did not plan to have an "ordinary life," intuitively; mine was to be beyond the ordinary. Whether or not I would have an "extraordinary life" is another question. I do not believe my parents expected nor intended for me to have an extraordinary life, they may have wished it so, as all parents do, but that would be up to me. But then how do you define extraordinary?

Charlottesville for the Lees is a "prickly heat" environment. We were respected by the Whites but the Blacks were by and large envious though friendly. We were at times controversial and at other times at peace. In our home we danced the night away when we got our first high fidelity stereo system, a Magnavox. The three of us danced to Martha and the Vandellas, The Four Tops and many more until I got a large splinter in my left foot from dancing with only my socks on against the wood floors. Nat King Cole and Mahalia Jackson records were Mom and Dad's favorites and they bought them on occasion.

As our real estate holdings expanded and our wealth increased, Charlottesville became more hostile toward us. We were seen as elitist Blacks who owned a lot of real property in the city. The city government, especially the housing inspection department at times harassed Dad and caused he and Mom much angst. This department became a tool for the jealous and adversarial forces bent on creating difficulty and assisted in a program to dismantle or destroy what remained of Dad's reputation. At times the family did have friends, but as the years wore on the friendships died out and were not replaced, so it seemed as if we were in a new town. Our church affiliations were stronger during those early years than in more recent times. Some of the newer ministers are akin to dabblers in the field of religion not, in my opinion, true theologians. So it's been a mixed bag. A difficult track, a troublesome journey but a rewarding and beneficial place to live overall.

Our family is a family of "heavy lifting," taking on the system, taking on challenges, not bowing down but fighting to the end, building mansions and estates. Setting a standard, not officially but, for ourselves and others who choose to follow or observe, and there have been a few. We have not run away from the big job. We stand our ground and try to make providential decisions. This is not a tale of bitterness toward Charlottesville, nor a saga about struggle exclusively. The trend for Charlottesville, thanks to the out of state retirees is progressive. For there were and are many enjoyable and memorable moments with family and friends that Charlottesville made possible. Charlottesville is our home, we will be buried here, and we strive to see this place in a positive light. I say that the disease of Charlottesville is that it makes us all seem more important than we really are because of its size and the nature of its politics. That, perhaps, is a good thing if managed properly. But as it is said in today's vernacular "it is what it is."

15

❧

THE BISON YEARS

M OM WASHED AND IRONED my clothes hurriedly upon our return from
a trip to Georgia and packed my suitcase, a large blue sky-colored case
filled with clothing and personal items to see me through my first
months living on my own at a university, 125 miles north of Charlottesville. Dad
did not accompany me on this maiden voyage. "If I did not have any sense by now
I would never have any." Dad's statement echoed in my mind as I stood in front of
the Mordecai Johnson Administration building, a large red brick building planted
in the center of a main street that bordered the western boundary of Howard University. There I stood as though transported by a particle beam toting a heavy suitcase with my admission papers in one hand and the other wrapped sternly around
the handle of my suitcase. I entered Howard in the summer of 1966 and would
graduate 3 years later in June of 1969.

Howard University is a predominantly Black University located on Georgia
Avenue in the upper northwest section of Washington, D.C., in the urban core of
the city. Howard has a beautiful campus with a mix of old and new buildings many
of which are placed along the perimeter of the main campus. The center of which
is a courtyard with cement pathways leading to different buildings on opposite
ends and directly across from each other around the rectangle. Howard is named
for Oliver Otis Howard, a General in the Union Army who was appointed commissioner of the Freedmen's Bureau after the Civil War by President Andrew Johnson.
The Freedmen's Bureau was established to help freed slaves establish themselves
after the Civil War in a region hostile to their newly won freedom. Howard was an
incubator for me, a place of refuge and support. Were it not for Howard University,
I would not be a lawyer today. Howard gave me a chance.

If I could characterize my matriculation at Howard during the undergraduate
years it would be, brash, unabashedly brazen and bold; studious enough to "get
by" or "get over" as we used to say in those days, but lacking the necessary tools to
excel. In retrospect a missed opportunity.

I did not have as an objective to graduate in three years, I just did it. I went the
year-round, every summer, every spring and every fall semester. I usually took in

excess of 15 hours each fall and spring and 6 hours during the summer session. My best grades were made during the summer sessions. I would have been better served to have taken fewer hours and made better grades. There was no reason for me to be in a hurry, none at all.

My roommate the first year at Howard was Oliver Morgan. Oliver had been raised by his grandfather. They were from the Tidewater area of Virginia. Oliver was a decent guy, relatively tall, dark skinned but his eyes seemed not to be as white as they should have been. His eyes had a yellowish tinge to them as I recall. We were living on the first floor in special dorm rooms furnished and maintained similar to hotel rooms in Drew Hall. Drew Hall was a tall, bright, red brick building at the end of a block across the street from a reservoir. These rooms were for special guests. I got into the rooms because Dad knew the Assistant Dean of the men's dorm, and based upon that he assigned me to one of those rooms. But this dean was a whacky guy, eccentric and a fuddy duddy. He threatened to put us out if we made any disturbance on the floor.

Oliver was more mature than me. He studied harder and made better grades, but he disappeared on occasion without explanation usually at night possibly to see or be with a girl. I never knew what to make of his whereabouts from time to time. I did not hang out with Oliver during the school day, but we usually got together in the evenings in the dorm room. Near the end of undergraduate school Oliver applied to Howard Law School and got in without a hitch. I had to have an interview because of my poor grades in Russian. Dorsey Lane, general counsel for the university and a Torts Professor at the law school, conducted the interview. Bespectacled, of short build and slightly rotund with his "ever-present bow tie, Professor Lane was a shrewd lawyer and was nominated or mentioned as a possible judge in the D.C. judicial system. Oliver either knew about my interview or had contacts with people who were on the committee, because he told me I was going to have an interview. Upon my admission to law school but before the second semester ended, Oliver died suddenly of causes unknown to me. There was speculation his death may have been caused by some drug related issue, but possibly not. I was never told the exact cause, if it was ever determined. Oliver was easily admitted to the law school and I had to fight to get in, yet he died before ever getting to attend. After his death, I met the grandfather who had raised him—a gaunt, short Black man with an easy-going personality.

My intellectual curiosity had no bounds. I was unafraid to take upper level classes, perhaps because I did not know what I was doing, nor the danger I was in. For example, in my freshman year I took political geography, a senior-level class, from geography professor Anthony Reyner. I was in over my head but somehow with the assistance of the professor and a fellow student, a handsome Asian Indian named Mikel, a light brown skinned, black haired mustached senior in the Geography Department, I delivered the final paper which discussed how *Nehru Seizes Goa, Bombay and Diu* (1963), the title of a book that served as my primary reference. Goa, the city of my interest, was a Portuguese colonial city on the western coast of India. Ironically, but perhaps not so, I would visit that city 42 years later because I had learned about it back then and would bathe in the calming blue waters of the Arabian sea.

I enjoyed the Humanities and the Social Sciences. I stayed away from math and science except for freshman Biology. "Death Valley," a section on campus where most of the heavy sciences and math were taught, had an apt name because many students failed to survive their stint down in the valley. Students who aspired to attend medical school but could not get in on the first try would get a Master's degree in some science and reapply. Many had success usually on the second try. I had no confidence to tackle these areas and knew instinctively that to venture in I would certainly fail.

I felt most comfortable with the classes I took in Frederick Douglass Hall. An old classroom building diagonally across from the administration building. This old brick building with its creaking floors and wood trim was comforting to me. I made my best grades in classes that I took in this building. I most disliked and felt the most discomfort in the "New Classroom" building across the court yard from Frederick Douglas Hall. In this red brick stainless steel building, I always encountered trouble of my own making, of course. I had my hardest times academically in that building.

My choice and assignments of roommates was not particularly beneficial to me in regard to learning from others about how to study. My associates were not the most studious of students. All of my closest friends during those days were from New York City or its immediate suburbs.

Pugh, a dark skinned black haired fellow with a charming personality, was a good dancer. He could do the African Twist better than anyone in the dorm. My closest friend for the shortest amount of time was "Shelly," another New Yorker. Shelly and I hung out together laughing and partying most of my freshman year. Shelly was a short brown-skinned male with bulging eyes. His gait was long for his size which gave him an awkward look as he strolled along. What Shelly and I had in common was a similar sense of humor. We could make a joke out of anything and that we did. We laughed at people's last names, and all sorts of odd situations. Paul Wallace, another friend, was a light skinned rotund, short fellow with short black hair who roomed with me for one year. Paul followed me to the New Classroom building to make sure that I, as he had done in accounting, failed my Russian III class. He was a "misery likes company" guy. Paul and I had the longest and most personal relationship of all my freshman acquaintances. Our relationship would last beyond the Howard years and extend to the post-Chicago years. After that period we drifted apart, never to engage as closely again. Only one of my freshman friends, Melvin Williams, a tall handsome brown skinned fellow whose speech pattern was strictly New York style, became a medical doctor. My relationship with Mel would extend to the early Philadelphia years and then trail off, never to be resurrected after that.

Momentous events in my life occurred while I was a student at Howard. I met my first wife, my first son was born, and I avoided the Vietnam War draft with an assist from an ROTC commander. A fateful decision to become a lawyer rather than a minister was made right in the court yard as I looked across the yard to the School of Religion and then across at the School of Law. I chose not to become a minister because I did not want to be a hypocrite. Not living the life of piety I thought such a career would require. And, I came to grips with failure for the first time. All of these events were maturing events. My ability to work hard academically was stirred, but the "giant" in me was still not fully awakened. What would it take?

All freshmen were required to take Physical Science. I wound up in a class filled with sophomores and second semester freshmen. The instructor was Dr. Joshua Henary. Dr. Henary was a man of slight build and he walked with a cane. His hair was cut close and he had eyes that curled in his face making his expression when he smiled hypnotizing. There was a deviousness that surrounded his persona. His skin tone was copper colored. He was the entrepreneur professor engaged in outside projects beyond the university. Dr. Henary was rumored to be gay, but no one knew for sure and the students joked about it whenever his class was in session.

My grades were not good and I began to feel the pressure of failure. Word was that Dr. Henary wanted a student to help him grade papers. A ruse perhaps to engage a student in homosexual activities it was thought, but maybe not. I took it upon myself to go to Dr. Henary's house one evening, not his office, by myself. His home was located near the Bethesda, Connecticut Avenue line in upper northwest D.C. The house was a red brick Georgian style abode on a quiet tree-lined street. I was there to volunteer for the job of grading papers in the hope of improving my grade. When I arrived at the house, it was dark around 7:00 pm. A big muscular Black guy, his helper and possibly his lover answered the door. His presence was intimidating and I immediately felt and sensed I was in over my head, but I had gone this far.

"Dr. Henary!" the man yelled. "There's a student here who says he is here to grade papers." From what I could see from the front door, Dr. Henary was in the kitchen either cooking or working on some other project. He told the man "let him in." I walked in and was ushered into the kitchen. "What is your name, son?" he asked in a gentle voice. Dr. Henary was not a rough man but a gentle creature. I said "Otis Lee, I'm in your 10:00 am Physical Science class. You said you needed someone to grade papers, I thought I would volunteer." He thought for a moment, probably saying to himself, "what do I have here? Is this a setup, a potential one night stand or a naïve student?" The big Black guy was standing in the doorway blocking my exit. I was now in the lion's den with no way out. I thought to myself, this was probably a bad decision. After a few moments he told his helper to take me upstairs to a room and give me some papers to grade. The helper escorted me upstairs to a bedroom, and I sat on a bed and reviewed some student's papers but I really did not grade them. I was up there for over 2 hours without seeing anyone and without a word being spoken. The whole event happened in an eerie, bizarre highly unusual atmosphere.

It was getting late and I thought of how I was going to get back to school as well as my concern for my safety. Would I be attacked, sodomized or otherwise molested by these guys. All kinds of thoughts ran through my mind but nothing happened. Sometime during the 10 o'clock hour Dr. Henary and his helper came upstairs and Dr. Henary said "are you finished? It's time for you to go." I left the papers on the bed and went immediately to the front door and walked back to the dormitory. I had been scared, not knowing what I would encounter. Dr. Henary probably did not know what I was there for other than what I had said. I certainly was not there for homosexual activities, but I had the courage to naively expose myself to whatever would occur. Thank God Dr. Henary had more sense than I did. He knew that if he had attempted to molest me, a scandal would have erupted and his professional life would be ruined. But he also knew that I had explored and took him up on his request for a student grader. That took guts.

This whole episode has never left me for several reasons. It symbolized how far I would go not to fail and how my fear of failure controlled my irrational mind. And finally how much of a risk taker and how naïve I was to even try something like that. All I really had to do was to buckle down and study the material, but I did not know how and was undisciplined enough to realize what I had to do to save myself. The risk of expediency got me a "B" out of the class.

In April of 1968 a shock to the heart and consciousness of Black people occurred when Martin Luther King was assassinated. I was in my sophomore year when his death happened. Previously I made sure I attended his address on campus and now, along with other students and members of the urban community surrounding Howard, I was caught up in the riots. Earlier in the day there was no hint of things to come. The day of his death was passing as so many others had before it. Students went to class and professors lectured. Mid-term exams had come and gone and all eyes were on the end of the semester. Nothing unusual distinguished the weather on that day from any other day during that spring season.

Howard was the citadel of protest during the last half of the decade of the 60s. We had protested the military being on campus and the requirement of compulsory ROTC for the men. Sit-ins in the administration building occurred. Stokely Carmichael was on campus; in fact he had also been a student at Howard. Muhammad Ali appeared on campus and so did Leroi Jones, a.k.a. Amiri Baraka, the poet of protest, who held court whenever a few students gathered around him. Amiri was an electrifying orator of protest. Dick Gregory was the political comedian who mixed humor with sarcasm and politics. I remember listening to one of his albums where he talked about Christopher Columbus discovering America. Gregory said "how can you discover something that had already been discovered?" Other notables of the time included, H. Rap Brown, a firebrand who was noticed, as was Angela Davis who was on trial in California for alleged criminal acts. Angela Davis was defended by one of the law school's noted professors, Red Morris, an Evidence Professor, the only professor at that time with a S.J.D. degree, Doctor of Juridical Science.

Our blind eyes and uniformed minds were opened and awakened during this era. For the first time we saw and heard perspectives that none of us had heard before. We were wilted flowers in an uncultivated garden in need of water. Once watered and fertilized we stood upright and blossomed into our full glory. It was the era of the Civil Rights Movement. Black power was the slogan of choice. Dashikis and Afros were worn by everyone who sought to be identified with the struggle. I was one of them, but I was not visible or vocal. I was one among many anonymous, silent standees in the crowd. I was one of those who gathered around Amiri to hear him talk, who was there when Ali stood in front of Frederick Douglas Hall to protest his induction into the military and I was one who participated in the riots in the wake of Martin Luther King's assassination. The chant could be heard often, "What do we want? Black Power! What do we want? Black Power!

Smoke discolored the atmosphere, and the color of the night was dark and sandy. Colored from the smoke and haze and sandy from the reflection of the overhead street lights that illuminated the dust particles in the air. People were going wild, the urban equivalent of the "running of the bulls" in Pamplona, Spain. The sound of glass breaking was strange because normally one would not hear glass being shattered along a normally quiet commercial strip. Folks were coming out of stores with crates of orange juice, racks of sweaters, furniture being toted on their heads, televisions weighing them down but being carried nonetheless. Pure chaos, bedlam and social disorder prevailed.

A group of us rode around in a car to survey the chaos. Whose car it was I do not remember. But I do remember riding around with several other students through the affected area watching in amazement as people ran wild. It was a sight that had to be witnessed to be believed. We did not get out of our car but some of the contraband made its way into our possession. I told the guys, "why don't they take the riot down where the White folks have big businesses," down where the Hecht Company had a department store, where Winthrop and Lothrop had their department store? Down below P Street where the real power was instead of confining the riot to the U street, Florida Avenue, upper 14th Street and Georgia Avenue corridors. We were burning and looting our own neighborhoods.

Walter Washington, a conservative mild mannered and cultured Black man, was the mayor-commissioner at the time. Julian Dugas, a light skinned dark haired patrician, who was a part time professor at the Law School ran the federal enclave on a day to day basis. These guys were dangled on a string and held in check by the master puppeteer, the Congress of the United States. Marion Barry had not made his debut into D.C. politics but he waited in the wings at stage left. President Lyndon Johnson in consultation with the leadership of the District called out the National Guard to quell the disorder. But though order was restored, the political lethargy of the "colonial city" had been stirred and would never be the same again. I remember seeing the troops as they marched down Georgia Avenue in formation. No one, I repeat, no one, got in the way of these guys. We all just stood aside and watched.

It would take almost seven years after the riots before the District would obtain a form of self-rule. For the first time citizens of the District elected their own mayor and city council. This transition scared White folks and many of them moved out of the District when the chant then became "D.C. the Chocolate City". It would take almost 30 years before the burned out neighborhoods would be rebuilt and upgraded with gentrification as the engine.

During my sophomore year I had a girlfriend from Michigan. Her name was Janet Welsh. Janet was a copper colored light version of brown skin, short, but well-built with black hair that was attractively long, but not that long. She was in the honors program and we hung out for a while. But she later took up with another guy who was in the School of Engineering. I noticed them together and felt the loss but soon got over it. In my junior year I went to a dance in the Quadrangle, the female dormitory. The dance was proceeding smoothly when I asked a young lass to dance with me and she obliged. She was slight of build, with black hair, she wore glasses and was quiet, pleasant looking and receptive to my advances. The fact that she was receptive and did not resist my advances enabled the relationship to proceed. Had she been more difficult I probably would have abandoned the effort and sought love elsewhere. Romance ensued and within the year we were married. Everyone's life took their own turn based upon the decisions they made.

Unlike my friends I had taken the turn to marriage and all that it entailed. Delma Frances Terrell became my first wife. A year later my first son was born. I now had a wife and child, and my senior year in undergraduate school to complete and law school to finish if I got in. There was a time during law school that I considered quitting but fortunately I did not. The responsibilities of marriage and fatherhood were real and manhood had to arrive quickly. I rose to the occasion with the help of my parents who had not tried to prevent the marriage though they knew that it threatened my education. So they did the next best thing. They bought a duplex on Gallatin Street north of Howard for us to live in while we both completed our educations. The euphoria of young love would probably have made prevention of the marriage difficult. This act of parental foresight took the pressure off and allowed me to continue with school.

Delma and I were first to each other in all aspects, in purity of heart, sanctity and fidelity. But as in all things that are initial, that state would not last. Ours was a marriage of misadventure, born out of a need on her part to escape and mine to ingenuously explore pure affection from another, the avoidance of rejection. We were at first cooperative and friendly with each other, but not communicative enough to understand what each other truly wanted out of marriage, because we did not know, at that time, what we wanted. We had not experienced emancipation from school and parents. We were yet to be born into the thoughtfulness of maturing adulthood, where values are reconciled and the depth of communication gives rise to the potential for resolution of discord. As Randy Crawford sings so tenderly, "All the king's horses and all the king's men could not put our hearts together again."

My eagerness to take on challenges reached a climax with my assault on Russian. I went through Russian I, II and III without much strain but I could not, at least on the first try, get through Russian IV. I took Russian solely because I was intrigued by it. My ego was stimulated by it. I should have taken French. I would have had better success since I had taken French in high school. Oooh...oh no, I had to take Russian. I did not so much take Russian as Russian took me.

My Russian teacher, Mrs. Flaume was a tough old bird. She never missed a class in two years. She was a nice older Russian lady, with greying blond hair, cut short. She was short in stature and stern, a no nonsense woman. I had met, at this level, my match. My shoddy study habits would not pass her muster. Flaume was an expatriate from her motherland. She had taught me in all my prior Russian classes, and probably had a good gauge on by knowledge of Russian and where I should have been in this last class. She flunked me and another male student. He was pissed off as he could be because he wanted a military career and was a popular lad on campus. He and I had to take Russian IV over again from the same teacher. She was the only instructor teaching it. Having flunked Russian IV, my graduation was now in jeopardy because Howard required two years of a foreign language. So I got a tutor, an albino with black beady eyes, that moved back and forth in a nervous rhythm. His name was Scott. Scott was smart, he knew the stuff and I tried as best I could to learn as much from him as possible, but I was still struggling. In the end it was a chance encounter with Mrs. Flaume in a Giant super market where both she and I were, coincidentally, grocery shopping at the same time in the same store. Delma was with me pregnant as she could be. It was this encounter that convinced Flaume to let me pass the class. Upon seeing her I went up to her and said, pointing to Delma, "this is what I have to take care of," with my plea of sincerity plainly obvious she begrudgingly acknowledged my plight by nodding her head. She passed me on the final exam with a "D" and I was a happy soul. No more Russian for me until many years later.

In addition to my struggles with a new marriage and admission to law school, my bout with the Vietnam draft during this time was probably the most pivotal. Because, if I had not obtained a deferment via the ROTC program at Howard, I may not have lived to tell this story or I could have been severely maimed fighting in that conflict. In 1966 ROTC was mandatory for men at Howard. During my freshman year I was enrolled as an Air Force cadet. I had a choice between the Air Force or the Army, and I chose the Air Force thinking that this branch of service was not as rough. We had to assemble at dawn several days a week for drill on the football field. In 1965, shortly before the Vietnam War erupted and American troops began to be deployed, universities were under attack for requiring mandatory ROTC for men under pressure from students and the politics of the issue in the academic community nationwide. It was a hot button issue and Howard was a tinder box of volatility on the issues of the day: Civil Rights, the Vietman War, Equal Rights for Women, etc. Under the pressure of these protests, the university discontinued compulsory ROTC. I and many others dropped out of the program immediately. I had no further thoughts about the military since college men were automatically deferred until they finished undergraduate school. But when I finished undergraduate school in three years I was no longer deferred and I was then placed back into the draft lottery and subject to the draft. If I had taken my time and graduated in 4 years or longer, as most students did, who knows maybe I could have avoided the military side of things altogether. The war was not close to being wound down in 1967 and 68. But I had been smart about school but dumb about manipulating the draft. I had out smarted myself, subjecting myself to the draft at least one year earlier than necessary.

Charlottesville is a small town and the draft board in town was sending every Black kid for sure to the military. We all knew there was no way I was going to get around that draft board. Dad opposed the draft system as much as he could. He talked to draft board members, lobbied as best he could, all to no avail. My lottery number was very low and I was now classified as "1A", prime draft material. The volunteer Army was several years away.

When I received my draft number with the loss of my deferral, I knew I had to do something. I was not the military type but in times where life and limb are at issue I became the military type. I had to save myself. Dad had done all he could to keep me from being drafted but his efforts though well intentioned fell short. Sensing that it would not be long before those White men in Charlottesville would be issuing a draft notice to me, I sought out the Army ROTC program at Howard. I was accepted into the ROTC program, but I had to have a physical first to complete the process and to be properly enrolled and receive a deferment until law school was completed.

Captain Wille Gore, a Black man, tall and muscular with brown skin was compassionate in his demeanor and bearing. Captain Gore was the recruiter and freshman instructor as well as an administrator in the detachment; he was in charge of the day to day administration of the program. After Captain Gore processed me into the program, I was sent to the Pentagon for the officer's physical exam. I was examined by a White medical officer probably in his early 40s. He examined me, and though I did not have a relationship with him beyond or before the examination we seemed to communicate, so I felt I could relax around him. Then I had a thought, what if I complained about my stomach, and any other ailment I could think of, and played sick? Perhaps I could get out of the whole thing by being physically unfit. So I complained, "Doc my stomach hurts all the time. I have to bend over to keep it from hurting." I had this ailment when I was young, so it was easy to make the complaint sound authentic. I complained about headaches and dizziness. So he said, "Well Mr. Lee I believe you will not qualify to be an officer in this Army."

"Great!" I said to myself. "I have beaten them. I will not have to go into any kind of army, be it ROTC or otherwise."

I went back to Howard and spoke to Captain Gore carrying with me my medical rejection papers and told him what I thought was my good news, not necessarily to him, but certainly to me. He said "Otis," as he glanced down to read the papers, "you have flunked the officer's physical exam, but you can still be drafted because the physical standard for officers is higher than for draftees. So you can and probably will be drafted nonetheless." I said to myself, "Oh hell! What have I done?" I was in panic mode. I said "What? You mean I can still be drafted?"

"Yes, you can," he said with a smile that betokened the view that I had outsmarted myself after he had tried to save me. The look on his face, that of puzzlement, spoke louder than his words.

In a rush and a panic I went right back to the Pentagon immediately, as they say "in a New York minute," catching the first bus available. And as fate would have it, I ran right into the doctor who had examined me as he was walking down the hall from the examining room. I said to him, "Doc, I was lying. I feel great, I don't have any problems with my stomach and I don't have headaches. I was just trying to get out of being drafted."

He said "Ok, let's take another look at you. You mean all that stuff you told me was a lie?"

"Yes sir," I said reassuring him of my fitness. I now wanted him to pass me on the physical because that was the only way for me to avoid the draft. The doctor willingly reassessed my condition and passed me. It was getting late in the evening but most of the officers were still at the detachment, and I went back again to Captain Gore showing him my papers and he said, "OK, you're in, classes begin Monday at 2:00 pm for new entrants. Report on time!"

"Yes, Sir!" I said with an excited military flourish.

I completed my ROTC duties in 1971, and was commissioned a 2nd Lieutenant. I was assigned to the Adjutant General's Corp, the secretariat of the army. I escaped the troubles of Vietnam. Eventually I was promoted in the inactive reserves to the rank of Captain. I would not see Captain Gore for 39 years; he was career military, part of the regular army and had been promoted by this time to Colonel. It was in the summer of 2008 by happenstance that I would meet him again in his hometown of Southport, North Carolina. We were reunited as fortuitously again as we had been in 1969.

16

The Chicago Experience, The Harris bank

THIS PART OF THE STORY is about life in the big city, reality, naiveté, the glass and steel skyscraper which housed Harris Bank and Trust Company on Monroe and LaSalle Streets in Chicago, Illinois and the value of self-worth laid bare through my passage to become a lawyer. This part began in the warm humid summer of 1972.

The shadows of the evening hung over the trees and light posts that lined the short cement walkway from the Illinois Central commuter rail station to my apartment building on South Lake Shore Drive. The resulting silhouette was dark, grey and haunting. I lived at 2345 South Lake Shore Drive on the twenty-third floor in a one bedroom apartment overlooking Lake Michigan. On this particular evening I dreaded that walk, I loathed the prospect that awaited me.

More than thirty years ago I relocated to Chicago, Illinois immediately after graduating from Howard University Law School. My father opposed my move, he thought it unnecessary. I am an only child, and I had always been a loner. When the crowd went one way, I always went the other. I was always good at one-on-one basketball, but in group play I always got lost in the play. I marched to my own drummer and followed my own intuition. I liked people and made friends easily, but the move to Chicago would be a solo flight without the help of a copilot or a navigator. I was recruited and employed by the Harris Trust and Savings Bank to work in the trust department. The "first" Black man hired to work in its heralded individual trust department. Its reputation then and now is celebrated in the national banking community. Before joining Harris Bank I knew nothing about banking and had not considered making banking a career. In law school, I had fallen in love with the arcane law of estates, wills and trusts. A visiting law professor from Louisiana fascinated me with the French pronunciation of estate law terms and made the subject seem wonderful. But it was a real property law professor, Irving Ferman, who advised me to pursue the offer from Harris Bank when it came. I remember him saying, "Otis you will be one of a few to go into this field of law in banking." Harris Bank managed tens of millions of dollars in personal and corporate trust assets. The bank was a leader in investment research and personal-trust asset management. It ranked in the top ten of trust departments in the United States at the time I worked there. Harris Bank was a family owned bank that began as a farm loan bank to down state farmers in Illinois by the Harris family. The bank's motto was "honesty and fair dealing," a principle that stayed with me and has guided my business practices to this day.

In the summer of 1972, the bank moved my family and me to Chicago. The biggest city I had lived in prior to that time was Washington D.C. With the able assistance of my mother and father who put up the down payment for the purchase of our first house, my college wife Delma, my son Otis III and I moved into a three-bedroom split-level bungalow in a middle-class neighborhood on Kimbark Street on the South Side of Chicago known as "Mary Nook." The bank made me a small loan to buy furniture to round out the furnishings we brought with us from Washington D.C. Our street was quiet. All of the homes in the neighborhood were similarly constructed. The lawns were neatly cut and the hedges trimmed. We had good neighbors, friendly neighbors, several of whom became close friends. Our house sat next to a passage way leading to Avalon Park, a popular park on the South Side. The back of our yard bordered the grounds of the park. When I picked Otis up from nursery school after work, our usual route home was through the park up to the passage way around the corner and to the house.

I was tall, literally dark and handsome, aggressive and full of confidence. I had never been defeated, a babe out of water. A newly minted law graduate from a renowned and highly esteemed law school. I was hired as a Trust New Business Solicitor. Which meant that I was hired to bring in fee-producing trust business for the bank through trusts, wills and other estate planning vehicles. But, being Black, where was I supposed to get this "new trust business?" Back then, White folks were not accustomed to talking to Blacks about their money, never mind giving trust assets to a Black to be managed by a bank. The confidence level was not there. Prejudices and old stereotypes had to be overcome, even if the Black worked for a major White bank. Black folks were out of the "loop" when it came to the uses of trusts and wills and the tax treatment of life insurance, many of them were not thinking in those terms. For Blacks, drafting a will was a big deal, and estate planning...are you kidding!? At this time I was the only Black trust professional in Chicago at a major bank. Before any business would come my way, I had an educator's job to do; first both in the White professional community and in the Black community. Each trust officer had their own contacts and was expected to bring in business through those contacts or through their own ingenuity. New business production sheets came out once each month listing each solicitor's production for the month. Each piece of business brought in had a value attached to it determined by the amount of money to be managed in the trust by the bank, the amount of life insurance payable to an insurance trust or the value of an estate the bank was expected to settle as corporate executor.

Though I took my place in the "goldfish bowl," where I was the only person of color on the floor and all eyes were on me, I was undaunted. The staid uniformity of Harris Bank culture was not objectionable to me. The Personal Trust Department was on the 4th floor of a 30 story steel and glass high rise. Our desks sat behind one another, three to a row. The sides of each desk were made of Black enameled steel. The desk tops were burnished hard wood with a glossy polyurethane finish with wood trim and high gloss polished steel legs. Everything was first class. After all, this was where the real money was. At the end of my row sat Jim Seitz, a blond thin haired assistant vice president, a veteran of the trust department, a German I supposed. Behind his desk was a wall of floor-to-ceiling doubled-paned glass overlooking LaSalle Street. Our entire floor was glass enclosed. You could see the downtown "Loop" area for miles from these panoramic windows.

The executive guest dining room was on one of the upper floors above the 4th floor. The executive dining room was used to entertain our guests. Only those employees of a certain rank had access to the dining room. There we would ply our guests with breakfast, lunch or an early dinner to sweet talk them into giving us their business be it loan, trust or other significant bank business. The dining room was impressive. It too was glass enclosed overlooking the Loop. It would have been a five star restaurant had it been a stand-alone restaurant establishment. A tuxedoed maitre d' greeted you at the door. Reservations had to be made in advance and the service was by foreign waiters—no Blacks—with linen tablecloth and linen napkins. The food was excellent and the waiters were servile and courteous. I practically lived on this floor. For one thing, I enjoyed the food and the service. During one of my parents' visits I invited them to have lunch with me in the dining room. The cuisine was of the lobster bisque and of the demi-glace variety. I saw the dining room as an extension of my self-image. And I used it to impress my guests as well as myself that I was somebody. A somebody that could entertain selected guests at no cost to them at this level. I entertained many lawyers up there. The tab for the meals were sent to the department vice president and factored into your cost effectiveness when measured against your business development.

Back then bankers usually dressed like funeral directors except on the occasional day when nerve exceeded established decorum. I usually wore tailored suits, not custom made suits. A habit I acquired from my days as a youth working at the Young Men's Shop. I wore white and sometimes blue dress shirts with an occasional French cuff with solid, striped or paisley ties. Tall and slender, my clothes fit me with an air of elegance when it all worked. I looked the part and seemed to have a natural business inclination.

The stolid day to day drumbeat of nods, winks, sighs and half-smiles all conveying nothing pervaded the social discourse, no one really knew you. That was the way it was on the 4th floor of Harris Bank building. I fit right in except for the probing questions from the racially ignorant mid-western trust officers with whom I worked.

"What do Black people want?" my associate Paul Lawless, a bespectacled trust officer in my division asked me one day in the lunch room. Lawless could have passed for the cartoon character, Dr. Doolittle. The shape of his face, his demeanor and oversized black rimmed eyeglasses contrasted sharply against his white skin. Except for his accomplishment of being a CPA no one would expect him to be particularly astute. I responded with a question "what do White people want?" Is there a difference? I was black as night in a white goldfish bowl. I was a new phenomenon to these people, one to be probed, plotted and observed. Back then it was a chic "Black thing" to be a "first." Today being a "first," though still anomalous, has lost some of its glow. Every Black should experience being a first at something. It makes you feel special when in reality you are not special. This "pseudo-speciality" that is felt is a perverse effect of racism.

As the days passed, the novelty of the goldfish bowl existence loss its appeal. The competitive nature of the job with its learning curve was fraught with traps and unpleasant surprises. The reality of my unrealistic expectations coupled with the back-biting superficiality of my fellow employees and the paternalistic approach of the senior executives made my stay at Harris shorter than it could have been. But I was unable to accept that I had indeed blazed a path: I had proven that my skills made a Black will and trust market potentially profitable to the bank and that a professional Black man could indeed do this job just as well as his White counterpart. I was blinded and shamed by a bruised ego because of my lack of success with the bar exam, myopic insight and the fear of losing that specialness that had been my sole province at the bank. My productivity resulted in more, instead of less, competition for me when another Black trust development solicitor was brought in near the end of my stay at Harris Bank. But my perceived loss of stature, entangled struggle with the bar exam, caused me to look upon my success through the crystal of a glass half-empty.

Before I left the bank, I brought in over 9 million dollars in new trust business. None of it was "active fee producing business," millions of dollars to be actively managed immediately to produce fees, but it was "future fee producing business": estates with wills naming the bank as executor and insurance trusts naming the bank as trustee. The way this business worked was that Lawless, and a few other like-minded trust officers and executives who had been getting what Black business existed, directed their contacts with Black clients to throw their business to me. Sympathetic contacts would refer their Black will and trust business to me. I developed contacts in the insurance industry and with stock brokers and with accountants and other prime movers who were influential with Black citizens. I gave talks to insurance groups and local business organizations on the importance of planning your estate. I had a special meeting with John H. Johnson, the late-publisher of Ebony and Jet Magazines, in his new office building on Michigan Avenue. I knew Crillo Macswain a prominent south Chicago entrepreneur when he was a leading life insurance salesman. I partied at an affair given by Don Cornelius, the Soul Train founder, though I was just one of many who had access to the affair. I was called and given a heads up that maybe I could get Jesse Jackson's estate plan, but it was rumored that Amalgamated Bank got the business, a competitor bank.

Chicago was a city in the mode of recovery in the wake of the civil rights marches, boycotts and sit-ins. Martin Luther King's foray into Chicago had not gone well. Oak Park, Cicero and other suburban areas of the city had strenuously resisted integration. Chicago was a racially polarized city attempting to open up after being jolted by the awakening of its progressive and highly professionalized and the nonprofessional Black community. The civil rights movement in Chicago had emboldened the Black community to assert itself and to demand a piece of the Daley pie. Banks were feeling the pressure from the American Bankers Association and from federal regulatory agencies to integrate their ranks.

Otto Kerner, the 33rd Governor of Illinois and Chair of the Advisory Commission on Civil Disorders (The Kerner Commission), was prosecuted for corruption by James "Big Jim" Thompson, the U.S. Attorney for the Northern District of Illinois during this time.

Back then middle class Black people in Chicago lived predominately in two areas of the city: the South Side and the West Side. On the South Side were the lower-middle, middle-middle and upper-middle classes. On the West Side were the lower classes. On the South Side two prominent subdivisions were most popular, Mary Nook where I lived and Chatham. Mary Nook was for the "up and comers" and Chatham was for those who thought they had already made it. A few of the nouveau riche Blacks were scattered in Hyde Park near the University of Chicago and along the gold coast on the north shore of Chicago.

Roland Burris, a Howard Law graduate and an attorney, was a banker at the time at Continental Bank—the bank that had originally recruited me. A friend at the time, Roland handled the settlement on my home in Mary Nook. Roland lived in Chatham and had purchased the home of Mahalia Jackson. After Roland became a political power he invited me to meet with him for a job opportunity, but because I was late for the meeting the opportunity was lost. I have always regretted that.

The Black community in Chicago had cohesiveness to it. The people were friendly, cordial and nice. Friendships were easily made. Many of the Blacks in Chicago migrated there from the South. The food was good and the ribs and rib tips were succulent. Chicago is a big Southern "cow" town. The night club scene was largely peaceful, though one had to always be mindful. One night after studying, I went to a popular bar on Stoney Island Avenue. While sitting at the bar and imbibing a few drinks, I was playing with my tongue and twiddling with my mustache, a bad habit. An ominous looking Black man dressed in a long fur coat with dark glasses, who had been sitting across the bar from me with a woman on his left side, came over to my male friend with whom I was sharing a drink and said to him "tell your friend to keep his tongue in his mouth." I was taken aback. Apparently he thought I was making a sexually suggestive gesture to his lady friend seated next to him. I wasn't.

A rich social vibrancy permeated the South Side. The Nation of Islam had their main edifice on the South Side. The Nation also had some restaurants on the South Side, and I remember eating one of the best fish salads I ever had in one of them. On many occasions, especially on Sundays, folks on the South Side would eat at the Queen of the Sea—a popular soul food eatery.

The Black community was on the verge of breaking through. Grass roots community organizing was happening. A political sophistication and coalescence was dawning. This would give rise years later to the election of Harold Washington as mayor.

I was recruited to the bank along with several other young Black college graduates in 1972. We all worked in various departments within the bank, the commercial loan department, consumer banking, real estate, economic forecasting and trust. Some of us had more success than others. The individual adjustment of many of the young Blacks was difficult and some failed. Let's face it; this was an experiment.

My minority colleagues at the bank, some of whom became friends and others, who remained only acquaintances, were in a high rise menagerie of black steel and glass windows and carpeted floors for all the world to see. Their backgrounds, purposes, professions, and individual objectives were as varied and complicated as the weave in an oriental rug. There was, for example, Gene Deramus, a thin obscure dark skinned Harvard MBA. Gene sought a place in the commercial loan department, a tough department to make it in. He looked good in his crisp white dress shirts and fancy ties. Gene was all business and did not associate much at all with the other Black bank employees, it might have interfered with his upward mobility or he might have been so serious that associating with us was not a good use of his time. He might as well have been White as far as the other Blacks were concerned. We talked about him and kept up with his progress through the proverbial grapevine. We all knew that Gene would make it. He was all business, bank business that is, and he did.

Then there was Al Washington an African American[19], another commercial loan department member. Al was older than most of us young recruits. At least Al seemed older. He was married and had two young grade school age boys as I recall. Al was medium complexion, not high yellow but not real brown or dark. A gusty, tough guy who took nothing off of those he didn't like at the bank, Whites included. Al made commercial loan officer before I left the bank, and I remember him saying after some us made our way to his office to congratulate him: "I earned it, man. I earned it." We all knew what he meant.

There were other personalities: Ed Williams an Asian American, a long time bank employee; Cecil Coleman an African American, with closely cropped black hair and an outwardly smooth personality. Every hair was in place on Cecil's head. Cecil's suave demeanor appeared to be more of an affection than real. When I first met Cecil he was a personnel junior executive. There was something I liked about Cecil—his smooth, controlled manner, every word modulated—but also something I distrusted: my perceived lack of sincerity on his part. I was never quite sure what side Cecil was on. Before I left the bank, Cecil was transferred from personnel to the personal trust department, another Black to share the stage with. Instead of seeing this as flattery I saw this as an ominous sign.

A fellow I had considerable contact with was L.J. Simmons. An African American from down South. L.J. as we called him was a nice guy. Tall, rough around the edges with a flashing smile revealing a gold trimmed tooth in the front of his mouth, but an aspiring man of class. L.J. was smart but unschooled in the ways of the sophisticated corporate culture. His dress never quite made it until later in his tenure, and he wore his hair in a style that in my judgment did not become him. L.J. had the bell-bottom platform shoe look, however modified for the bank, but never quite the classic banker look. L.J. made his mark in the real estate department and became quite good at it. We often talked a lot about what it took to make it at Harris and whether or not the sacrifice was worth it. I used to tell the group that "if it was worth it to you, you would make the sacrifice." L.J. wanted me to be honest with him about what I thought he needed to do to improve his lot. I did not want to tell him because I did not want to hurt his feelings. People rarely want to hear the truth though they often say they do. I liked L.J, so I told him: "You need to wear more conservative suits, man, and fix your hair in a more becoming style and adopt a business like demeanor." He retorted, "Bull shit man I'm not changing the way I do my thing! What's wrong with the way I dress? You think you're better than me? You're a phony with your suits and business manner. Who are you to tell me?" He got over it sooner than later, and we maintained our friendship. Several years after I left the bank, L.J. was killed by an irate motorist at a Chicago gas station. Apparently something was said by L.J. on the roadway before arriving at the gas station that angered this man who then followed L.J. to the gas station and pulled out a gun and shot him dead. What a loss.

The senior vice president, who headed the entire trust department, was Jim Mandler, a tall, distinguished aristocratic gentleman with a full head of flowing blond and brown hair, brushed to the side—a soft spoken man with a gentle manner. Jim Mandler had been with Harris for many years before I got there, and he had the final word on my being hired. However, I had few interactions with Jim except during the Christmas holiday season. I would pass him occasionally in the hallways or see him in the elevators. Nothing substantive was ever discussed between us except when he would come around to the side of the floor where our division sat and handed out crisp $10.00 bills to each of us for Christmas bonus money just like they were gold nuggets. I was impressed the first time this happened but after that it was a joke. Especially when my classmate at the law firm Jenner and Block was getting a holiday trip to Acapulco for her Christmas bonus. But when he handed out those $10.00 dollar bills you had better act like you were pleased and happy and make a big deal about it, or otherwise word would get out that you were not happy about the bonus money and that would not reflect positively on you. I reacted coolly one Christmas and I heard about it within the next hour: "Otis isn't happy with his bonus...What's wrong Otis were you expecting more?" Mandler said as he reacted to my understated exuberance and acceptance.

"Oh, no, everything's great. This is good," I made sure I said, even though it was all fake.

Herbert Ullmann was my immediate boss, the vice president of my division. Herb was a different sort of guy. Short and bald except for the black hair on each side of his sparkling shiny head. Herb walked like a general, head up high, arms swaying back and forth, speaking with confidence and firmness—a tough, all-business individual. I misunderstood Herb for a long time. My dealings with him were largely fair. On one or two occasions, however, our paths collided to my chagrin. One day Herb asked to see me at his desk which was in the vertex of two adjoining walls, providing him a panoramic view of the floor center and the city scape. He could look east and west on Monroe Street. I went over to his desk. He was seated behind it. I was standing up. He said, "are you having problems with your checking account?" I nonchalantly said, "No," shrugging my shoulders and gently moving my head to the left, not thinking anything was up. "What's this?" He handed me a piece of paper on which was printed a listing of a few bounced checks from my checking account.

"How can you advise other people about their money when you cannot manage your own." The logic of that statement hit like a brick. "You're right," I said. "I'll get this corrected right away." I had been naive. I did not know that to avoid this type of thing most bank employees had their checking accounts at other banks. I later switched my checking account from Harris to another local bank. The issue I had with Herb was his style of springing the surprise on you, the "I got cha." He already knew the answer to the question when he asked you about something that was not right. It was as though he was always trying to trap you. If he knew what was up, and he always knew it because he was the one bringing the issue to you, then just come out and say "look this is the problem," rather than setting you up for the sucker punch.

One cold wintry day when the temperature must have been several degrees below zero, which was not uncommon in Chicago in the winter, Herb came bustling on to the floor "Burr-r-r! It feels good out there." I said to myself, "this guy must be crazy, it's cold as hell."

There were twelve new business solicitors and trust officers in our division and five secretaries, everyone did their own thing. Kathy Quainton was my secretary. A White female in her late twenties, Kathy was a bright, effervescent, energetic fast paced young woman. I detected no reservation in Kathy's handling of my business at the bank. All the business came in through written instruments, trust agreements or will documents. Each of these documents had to be examined by lawyers in a section known as "trust counsel." This section only hired lawyers that specialized in the legal particulars of wills and trusts, the real know-it-alls. They were there to protect the bank's interest and to make sure that outside lawyers drafted documents that met minimal standards of competence. I worked closely with Ron Mora and Terry Netsky. Ron, a suave medium height blond haired man was smooth and polished, practiced law with Terry. Terry was dark haired heavier set and more vocal. Between these two lawyers I received most of my business. These guys were wired into a few sophisticated Black insurance general managers and agents like Leo Burnett of Mutual Benefit Life Insurance Company who had his own insurance agency on the South Side and John Lassiter of Prudential Insurance Company, who gave me the book *Business as a Game*, by Albert H. Z. Carr (1971), a book I treasure to this day. I also made my first contact with a New York Life Insurance Company general manager who became my source for my later introduction to the Advanced Underwriting Department at New York Life Insurance Company in New York City where I would work ten years later. New York Life flew me to New York City for an interview. While there, Phyllis and I saw the premier of the movie "Paper Chase." I gave talks at general agency meetings on trusts and wills and went out on sales calls with certain agents from these companies. I developed special friendships with some of them.

Ellen Rowizer, a pleasant looking White female attorney in the trust counsel unit, befriended me. She and I talked many times about the bank and lawyering. Ellen was a grader for the Illinois Board of Law Examiners, an elite position with the bar reserved for only the best legal scholar insiders. A careful, polished woman, she always kept her distance when it came to discussions about the bar exam, careful not to be drawn in to conflicted discussions about the exam. She knew I had taken the exam and failed, but she offered no help or advice. After finding out that Ellen was a grader I was tempted to ask her advice, I wanted to know what I was doing wrong. But, I held off instinctively, knowing that to ask these questions might invite her rejection of my inquiry as being unethical and out of bounds for a grader, at least I thought it would. Still, it took a lot to restrain myself from asking the questions that I needed answers to, but in retrospect, maybe I should have. I admired the people in the trust counsel section because they were the brains of the outfit.

The most genuinely jovial co-worker of mine in the trust department was a tall, round-faced gravelly-voiced White fellow named Paul Lynne. I liked Lynne, he was an older fellow and we talked often about the politics of the trust department, law practice and the bar exam experience. Lynne was always pleasant and he accomplished something that made all the other members of the department envious.

The trust department was anxious to get some of the Florida vacation crowd and winter immigrant business. Many of the well-to-do crowd in Chicago had Florida homes or went there in the winter. Talk had begun around our division about someone from our division going to Florida and setting up a branch or correspondent trust department relationship. Lynne stepped forward and agreed to go to Florida, take the Florida Bar Exam and be the point man in Florida for the bank. Lynne kept some of us posted on his progress but never divulged too much inside information about the deal the bank made with him. I remember the day he got the news he had passed the Florida Bar, and off Paul Lynne and his wife went to Florida. He did it all very quietly and unobtrusively and always with a smile. I think his age had a lot to do with it. He smiled from ear to ear. His tall frame and black glasses seem to stand out even more as he walked along, looking down as he reread the letter exclaiming his success. Lynne was a nice guy anyway and I was happy for him. The pleasure of his satisfaction showed on his face as he proudly told the news to the department. He was quite excited. I don't think too many of his colleagues expected him to succeed at his age, but now he had something the bank wanted and needed: Lynne had leverage.

My best and most influential friend in Chicago was Kenneth Bowe. Ken lived in my building on the South Side of Chicago with his young wife Sheryl who was a graduate student in mathematics at the University of Chicago. Ken was a smart guy. A graduate of the University of Chicago in Mathematics, and Ken worked on economic modeling and forecasting, all that heady economic stuff at Harris Bank in the Economics Department. During this period Beryl Sprinkle, a nationally known economist, was the bank's chief economist. His department was the think tank of the bank. Nobody knew what those guys actually did except the truly economically informed bankers. Interest rates, inflation rates, euro dollars and exchange rates were some of the subjects they explored. I don't remember exactly how Ken and I met. Whether it was at the bank or at the apartment building, anyhow we hit it off keenly. Ken was a Bahamian, who was from Nassau Island in the Bahamas. He had sophisticated European mannerisms and a Caribbean accent. Apparently his family was big time down there at least that was the impression he gave me from many of his comments. Ken was my color a rich brown, average height with an emerging baldness. He was quick witted, dominating, demanding, discriminating and did not tolerate fools too gladly.

On Sunday mornings we would jog along South Lake Shore Drive and have breakfast in Hyde Park near the University of Chicago's campus. He introduced me to champagne before breakfast which I enjoyed—it stimulated my appetite— and to the American Express card, after he received a dunning phone call from them one day while we were talking in his living room. "Lee," he would say after surveying my bar preparation regime, "you read intensively but not extensively," with his Caribbean accent. At a later time he would declare, "I do big favors and

I ask big favors," and when we talked of leisure he would say "I work hard and I play hard."

Bowe was the continental Black man, the consummate man of big ideas. Bowe iterated his view of marital negotiation this way: "it's either my way or the high-way." His marriage ended before I left Chicago. Sheryl, a quiet soft spoken woman, must not have been enamored with his approach to marital bliss. Bowe and I continued our relationship well after I left Chicago in the summer of 1975. We discoursed again in Washington, D.C., but after that time our paths separated and though I think of him often, we remain out of touch.

17

THE CHICAGO EXPERIENCE, KENNETH STREET

I EMBARKED UPON MY PARALLEL CAREER as a real estate investor and property manager for my own account in Chicago in 1973. This was something I wanted to do, and Dad was always supportive when it came to investing in real estate. Dad was into the real estate thing big time in Charlottesville and was going full throttle. I aspired to be a successful real estate investor as well. Before graduating from law school in Washington D.C., Mom and Dad bought a duplex for me and my new wife to live in after I got married, while I was finishing law school. It was a smart investment decision to make. We had to live and they were determined that my early marriage was not going to interrupt my schooling: I had to finish school. The duplex was on Gallatin Street in upper northwest Washington D.C., ten blocks south of the Silver Spring, Maryland line. This was my first venture into the world of being a landlord.

On one of my regular visits home from D.C., my dad chewed me out about not taking care of business on Gallatin St. He hurt my feelings and I began to cry. I was tender then, green as an apple. I had a young wife and a new baby. My wife at the time, Delma, not knowing how to react or what to do in this situation, found a hiding place on the front porch. Dad said sternly in his peremptory tone, "you get up there and put those bastards out you hear, and take care of that business, do you understand!" Dad could be mean when he wanted to. "Yes sir," I said as tears ran down my cheeks. In a commanding tone, "You're too soft!" "Get some lead in your pants!" After the tongue lashing, I went out on the porch where Delma had gone to hide from the commotion. I attempted to veil my emotions. She made no attempt to console me. She may not even have known about the tongue lashing. Perhaps she thought it best to let it pass.

After graduation from law school in 1972, we moved to Chicago and Dad sold the building on Gallatin Street. He later took to me to the Peoples National Bank in Charlottesville and cosigned with me on a note for $3,000.00 to borrow the down payment for the purchase of the Kenneth Street apartment building, an eight unit multifamily building on the West Side of Chicago. The seller took back the first mortgage, in effect financing the purchase price. In the business this is known as owner financing or a purchase money mortgage. His banker at the time, Mr. Thacker, loaned Dad various sums of money over time for his real estate ventures. Thacker lowered his head, leaned over his desk, looked at me over the rims of his bifocals, and said in his typical Southern drawl, "son are you ready for this?" "Yes sir," I replied with enthusiasm. I did not even know enough to know that I was not ready. "Ignorance is bliss," they always say.

"Sign right here" Thacker said. "He can handle it," Dad volunteered, attempting to bolster my naive bluster. But Dad was a sink or swim man. He believed in throwing you into the fray. He always said, "the job will make you." He meant that, if you were not fully qualified for the job at the start, if you did the job well, the job would qualify you.

The purchase price was $25,000.00. The seller, an old Jewish man name Merzel, owned the building for many years. Unbeknownst to me, Merzel had sold and resold the property several times before I became the next sucker, making money off of each unschooled buyer who failed to right the ship. Merzel was short, gaunt, rumpled in appearance. The stereotypical big city landlord who owned old broken down buildings and rented them to poverty stricken inner-city Blacks. Merzel resembled an older version of the TV character "Columbo." I was going to be the new version of the inner-city landlord, the "do gooder," the landlord with the social worker mentality, the "do good banker."

Nathan Slutsky was Merzel's attorney. Slutsky was Polish and slick as slime with a receding hair line and wire rim glasses—the old school headmaster look. Slutsky was the classic big city solo practitioner, confident with a loyal following of clients like Merzel. He knew the ins and outs of Chicago Law; he was an insider. He and Merzel had worked their magic many times before. Any experienced real estate investor needed a lawyer like Slutsky, and he was a pro.

The building was a partially dilapidated structure with one and two bedroom units, centrally heated with oil. It was a corner property in a decaying neighborhood but not a completely ruined neighborhood. Across the street was an unattended vacant lot. No one would bother you if you were on the street. But it was not the South Side along the Lake Shore and certainly not "Mary Nook." As you entered the building a dim light flickered from a bulb overhead, just enough to illuminate the mail boxes and the old mosaic floor that hid the ancient secrets of a once proud building. The grimy stuccoed walls belied their color of either grey or stale pastel green. The hallway was small, large enough for tenants to get their mail and turn around in, but too small for any long winded conversations. The mail boxes were on your immediate left as you entered the building. Five feet ahead of the entrance door was the stairwell that led up to the four stories with several apartments on each floor.

Keeping up the mortgage payments to Merzel and to the bank were nearly impossible. I was subsidizing the whole operation. Keeping oil in the tank for fuel was nearly impossible especially during the long and cold Chicago winters and maintenance was non-existent. During one of our infrequent meetings, after I had owned the building for a while but before I left Chicago, Slutsky said to Merzel, "he owes everybody in town." Slutsky was cracking on me because I was having problems making the mortgage payments. He probably knew that because he knew everybody in town.

I thought I could turn this building around, but I was mistaken. I would go over to the building some days after work in my suit to check on things. I was as out of place as a man could be. Those tenants paid me no attention, they were hard core. Merzel was the only one they respected. I was the owner, but he was the one who could get the rent out of them. The tenants knew they had a chump by the short hairs and they worked it. It wasn't that I bought the property from Merzel; this was a joint venture between Merzel and me. At the time, I did not know it, but Merzel had more invested in the building than I did. I went to the building on a Saturday, not long after having purchased the building, to clean up the place. The tenants had thrown garbage from the back porches of their units onto the back steps and yard below. There were heaps of garbage from days of tenants dumping empty bottles of soda and milk cartons, open tin cans of left over beans, greens, and other solids; discarded newspapers and magazines; boxes of Kellogg's Corn Flakes, empty egg cartons, scraps of bones and rotted meat, that only a dog might find attractive. Mounds of rotten and rancid leftovers from meals scraped off plates and dumped over the bannister railings as if the back drop was the in-house garbage pail. All merged into black dirt and soil after days of baking in the sun of summer. The flies, the filth and the stench were deterrents in themselves.

An old bedraggled White drunk was walking down the street on the same side as the building, dragging a grocery cart behind him filled with bottles and junk.

I said to him "hey you wanna earn some money?"

"Yea," he said.

"Come around back. I need this garbage raked up," I said. "Can you do that?"

"Yep," he said. That old man and I worked liked dogs together all day to clean up that mess, only for it to be thrown right back there again by the next week.

"The hell with this," I said. I gave up. I could not change the mentality of the Black folks living in that building. No amount of "do-good" social work made a dent. The tenants in the Kenneth Street building were dyed-in-the-wool urban survivors.

Then there were the harsh Chicago winters. The building was centrally heated with oil, supplied and paid for by me. It was a nightmare trying to keep oil in that building. As cold as it was in the winter, some tenants had their windows wide open and my precious oil heat was going out of the window. When, on one occasion, I left Chicago to go home for a holiday, I asked a female real estate agent to manage the building for me and to buy oil for the property during the days of the winter month that I was out of town. The agent failed to buy the oil and the pipes froze. Water burst from frozen pipes all over the building, and I'm back home thinking "all is well." It was a mess, a panicked mess.

During the whole time I owned this building in Chicago, my first solo real estate venture, I never went to Landlord Tenant court, and I do not ever remember receiving a housing code violation. How could you be in the rental real estate business and never deal with these issues. Maybe Merzel took care of all that stuff. Merzel and Slutsky were black ice on the winter roadway in Chicago, and I knew nothing about driving in the winter in Chicago. How these issues were handled I haven't the slightest idea. I just know that I did not handle them. And yet these issues should exist in most localities. Merzel and Slutsky may have worked their magic, or maybe there was no magic to be worked.

I eventually left Harris Bank and started work for a less esteemed employer, a situation I will detail later. My ego was trending down and my morale was low. I no longer had the prestige of working for a major bank. I now worked for a small minority business consulting firm, Talent Assistance Program (TAP) on the second floor of an office building on LaSalle Street around the corner from the Bank. In a quick walk I could still join my old bank colleagues in a cup of the "muddy" during the mid-morning coffee break. After a year or two the new job venture ended disastrously, and I was on my way back to the East Coast within a year.

The new job though less esteemed promised more time to concentrate on studying the law. Hugh Turner was my boss at TAP. I was the associate director; he was the executive director. TAP was a small business minority technical assistance organization. We provided technical assistance to minority businesses that qualified for it in Chicago. Hugh Turner was nice but he lacked confidence. He spoke in a herky-jerky cadence, and his thoughts seemed to be slow in developing. He recruited me to be his second in command because of my persona at Harris Bank. I did not know anything about business consulting, but I did have a natural affinity toward the business side of things. Neither one of us had ever run a business, but we were the experts. I took the job because I was on the rebound and dangling for life by only one or two chords. Hugh gave me gobs of time while on the job to study for the bar exam.

During that time I came to know a Black lawyer named Daniel Smith, most folks that knew him called him Dan. Dan had an office in the same building. Dan was dark skinned, grey haired and wore lots of jewelry including several rings on his fingers. But Dan had a softness to his style and a quiet office where he let me study in his conference room during the day. I studied there for hours and even went to court with him on occasion. He had graduated from Howard several years before me.

My exposure to Dan was key because, through him, I met other Black lawyers including Ernest Lafontant and several others. I began to engage in another dimension of this reality. One Black lawyer told me "keep at it until you see it as a whole, you got to get that vision." His remark to me was tantamount to the military phrase, "don't fire until you see the whites of their eyes." One day one of my law school classmates, Diane Kinard, came by Dan's office and saw me studying. Diane had passed the bar the first time and had finished third in our class and was working at Jenner and Block, a medium size law firm located in the Loop. Diane was smart and she was from Chicago. A short brown skinned woman with short reddish brown hair, a chain smoker and a hard hitter. I admired Diane and tried to keep in contact. She was doing what I wanted to do. But I could only imagine the legal world she operated in. Otis she said "you have to read that stuff, the full outlines, not just the summary outlines." I looked at her, not in amazement, but I was puzzled. I thought that was what I had been doing. Her advice was well taken though. It meant, from her perspective, that my preparation had not been thorough enough.

Before leaving the bank, my first marriage ended in divorce. The divorce took such a toll on me that I lost twenty pounds. My clothes hung off me like an ill-fitting clown costume on a coat hanger. These were the coldest days of my life. I threw myself into the pursuit of the bar to assuage my anxieties of which there were many and to camouflage the emotional costs the decision to divorce exacted on me. It was a cold time in the "Windy City." I was alone by choice. I had no extended family to go to for consolation, only wine, women, song and my studies.

My marriage to Delma ended two years before I made the fateful decision to go my own way. We married after my junior year in undergraduate school at Howard University. The bonds of trust that held us together in the first years of the marriage were shattered into a thousand shards of pain carried over from the latter years of our stay in Washington D.C. I felt I had been wronged by events that took place while Delma worked at a branch location of the University of the District of Columbia. Her conduct during that time caused my innocent heart to hurt. Real or imagined, the perception of the wrong broke my heart, and our relationship was never the same after that. We both married young, too young actually. The need and the urgency to marry sprang from a source peculiar to newly enfranchised love: the intoxicating love letters during the courtship expressing a reciprocal love expanded the energy already present in the dream. Neither one of us had yet experienced the vices of the world. Delma married me perhaps to separate herself from her family and to be independent. I was naive about marriage. I had not been to "marriage school." I was driven to marry by love, however naïve, and sexual exploration.

After graduating from law school I stayed behind in D.C. to pack our belongings and manage their shipment to Chicago. Delma went ahead with Otis to take a job that had been identified through the efforts of her cousin Vickie. By the time my college friend, Paul Wallace, and I completed the fourteen hour drive from Washington D.C. to Chicago, I was "out of the house." We were more estranged then than before she left. When I arrived in Chicago, I stayed at a local YMCA before we settled on the house in Mary Nook. Delma and Otis stayed with her cousin Vickie and her husband Larry. There was little or no contact between us for several weeks.

In my mind, the death of Delma's mother while I was in law school changed her. Her mother was a kind and sweet woman. A caring woman and the soul of Delma's family. Her loss was a watershed event in Delma's life and consequently mine.

A college love can be a most enticing love because of its innocence and the virginal quality of the initial experience: attraction and commitment. But reality often trumps dreams, and heartbreaks do occur. The love of youth sours under the steady pains of individual maturity and expanding horizons. When the bonds of trust no longer hold and the innocent become more worldly, and when discordant values become manifest, separation becomes inevitable. The fidelity and sincerity of the initial and beginning marriage years were never in question. The corruption of that placidity occurred after about three years of marriage. The bonds of trust now cast aside my heart, and my heart was again available to be captured. The beckoning of a new world was hard to resist.

When decisions of self-interest are made, there are always casualties. In this case my first son Otis III was the casualty of my decision to leave his mother. I hated that consequence. Delma remarked during one of our pre-separation conversations "who is going to talk to Otis?" My son and I were close. I had never been separated from him. I had cared for him as both father and mother during his infancy while Delma worked. I was at home during the day studying and attending law school. Otis and I talked all the time. We were buddies. But my love for him was not sufficient to sustain me in a marriage I had out grown and lost faith in. The pull of this new life was strong. My errant search for love and bourgeoning lawyer-ego coupled with a new found burst of self-appreciation by exposure to the trappings of the big city made my nascent decision to leave confirmable. My infidelities became manifest and the results were painful and disconcerting. My behavior just before the actual separation in Chicago was dishonorable.

On the day I decided to leave Delma, I called my father from my desk in the bank and told him the news. I said, "Dad I'm going to separate from Delma." He did not have much to say about it except "oh yea, are you sure this is what you want to do?" "Yes," I braved on. The conversation was short. I could tell he did not approve. Dad was a traditionalist and not experienced in this area. By this time, he and Mom had had an intact marriage for over twenty five years. I am sure he was hurt by the news. Both of my parents had gotten comfortable with Delma and Otis. Mother babysat him many times while we were in college and some of the neighbors thought Otis was their baby. We were a family. It had taken me quite a while to get up the courage to take this step, but I had fallen in love and it was this new love that helped me on. As my high school football coach would always say, "one was scared and the other glad of it."

I never saw Delma but once or twice after I left. Years later my Aunt Louise would remark to my father, "whatever it was (speaking of Delma) I would have made it right." Delma did not fight to save the marriage, and after I left I did not look back. She did not try to persuade me to come back home. She may have wanted it over, just as I did, but said nothing. It was as though she acquiesced in my decision.

George Karkazus was my divorce attorney. George was a tall handsome guy with thick wavy black hair who had a small law firm in the Loop within walking distance from the bank. I selected George because he and I got along well on the trust and will side of things. I referred him a few cases, and he agreed to do the divorce without fee, one of the gratuities of the inside trade. When he called me to tell me that the divorce decree had been entered there was no celebration only resignation and relief that I was free. I did not feel the economic pinch of the divorce settlement because I ended up deeding my interest in the house including all the furniture in it to her in exchange for a complete settlement. There was little equity in the house at that point since we lived there only two years or so before the divorce. While having lunch with a local prominent lawyer in the executive dining room at Harris Bank I discussed my marital situation with him. He said "you would not be in this situation if you had kept her in an apartment." He was right, but I was young and naive and did not realize the value. And that was not the way our family did things. Had a divorce been contemplated, an apartment instead of a house would have been the order of the day. In any event, it didn't matter to me, perhaps it should have, but I was not paying attention to equity and savings and all that stuff. My head was in the bar exam trying to make real this lawyer thing, and I had the solace of a new romance.

After the separation, I moved into my apartment at 2345 South Shore Drive a medium sized high-rise apartment building on the South Side on a top floor overlooking Lake Michigan. The apartment was a refuge. The front of the build-ing had a large canopy extending over the driveway that faced South Lake Shore Drive. When you entered the apartment a narrow hallway greeted you. The hall closet was to the right and the kitchen, a Pullman kitchen, was to the left. The corridor through the kitchen led to a sitting area and ended at a side window where I took my meals and where I studied. The window provided a view of the thoroughfare below. That window would play a part in my self-discovery months later. The sitting area expanded to reveal a large living room area with a large pane of glass that extended to the ceiling from a ledge it was mounted on. This window extended from the north corner of the room to the south corner. Through the window the horizon of Lake Michigan was captured. Large rocks and boulders along the shore line were clearly visible below. The next room over was my bedroom. A medium size room with a large window pane that continued the panoramic view of the lake.

I stayed in this apartment until I left Chicago in the summer of 1975. The apartment was romantic. I awoke each morning to the sounds of undulating waves crashing against the large rocks below that sang to me as though a bird chirped a rhythmic melody outside my window each morning. During the day the unending sight of water as far as the eye could see kept my attention. I passed many days gazing at the horizon soaking in the halcyon that shone in my apartment daily. I was lulled to sleep many nights by the sounds of the crashing waves. The froth that formed on each wave disappeared quickly when the wave reached the shore and collided with the rocks. With no lights on, an eeriness pervaded the bedroom and living room when the moon light ricocheted against the still darkness from the plane of the lake below into the apartment. The movement of the waves back and forth, the high and low tides were a frequent occurrence. When winter came I followed the slow steady formation of ice on the rocks and watched the ice melt just as slowly in the spring time. The music of the waves soothed my soul and caused my imagination to run wild. I had always imagined myself the seafarer with my fisherman's hat aloft, sailing the seas into some exotic port of call. My vision of myself was that of an old man of the sea–my Walter Mitty incarnation. Like sailing a ship on the tides, I experienced the highs and lows of my life during my remaining time in Chicago in this apartment. It was also the first time I had paid rent. I loved it.

A new love was in my life. Contemporaneous with the divorce, I became en-raptured in a significant love, a female law student at Northwestern University. My relationship with Phyllis Jackson, who became my second wife, was a bridge love. A bridge over which I crossed from a love of discordant values, a naive virginal love, into the bright light of release and freedom, self-realization, professional aware-ness and awakening. An adult love, a true love with all the possibilities for the full retinue of family life, but choices made averted that possibility. I will always be in-debted to Phyllis for the fidelity she demonstrated and the courage she undertook by forging a relationship with me. My struggles within myself to face the realities of my deficits, having for the first time to come to grips with that reality, was an ego emaciating experience. My relentless pursuit of self-fulfillment–coupled with the pressure of distance, divorce and self-assessment of my real needs I wanted ful-filled by a woman–was too intrusive on the fragile bonds of a transitory love I had discovered on my circuitous pathway to maturity, however valid and well meaning. The hurts were too great to resurrect anything.

Phyllis Jackson, a light skinned woman of slender build with closely cut black hair styled as an Afro, was "too hard." Her edges, though refined, were nonetheless sharp. Her lawyering acumen was keen, an admirable quality. She was very smart, smarter than me. But I needed a "scratch cook," a warm breast, a softer femininity and a more accommodating domestic state of mind. Through this relationship I gained exposure to a premier university that became the center of my post-law school study of the law for several years.

18

THE CHICAGO EXPERIENCE, THE BAR EXAM

N AVIGATING MY WAY through the rigorous and highly competitive Illinois Bar Exam was rough. I had not encountered an academic obstacle like this before: unyielding in its demands for a universal standard. The collateral damage from this epic struggle had caused a naive young man from the South to reassess hard lessons glossed over and unlearned—to examine the value of self-worth beyond professional accomplishments. And to accept responsibility for the consequences of the separate but unequal secondary education foisted upon me by the decision of my parents, the land of my birth and my role in past educational opportunities unfulfilled.

My ritual for preparation usually began six to eight weeks before the exam. When I first took the exam in the fall of 1972, I did not know how to prepare, nor what to expect. The bank was generous; they paid for my bar review fees and they had high expectations that I would be successful the first time out.

I read the short outlines and reviewed the long outlines from Bar Review Incorporated, BRI, a private bar preparation company operating in almost all states preparing bar admission applicants for the bar exam. Similar to the Scholastic Aptitude Test, SAT preparation classes for college admissions and other professional licensing exam preparation systems. I practiced answering many of the practice exams in the review manuals.

I was not successful the first time out. But two things happened that were important. Upon returning home after the first sitting, I rested in the lower level of our three bedroom split level house in "Mary Nook," and I said to myself "Otis you can do this, this is not beyond your capability." I knew then that I had what it took to pass this exam or any bar exam. Next, for the first time in my life, I felt the sting to my ego of public disappointment. Everyone in the section of the trust department that I worked in knew that I had taken the exam and eagerly awaited my results, or at least in my mind I thought so. The news was not what these White mid-westerners expected from their "first."

By the time I took the next bar exam, I had begun maturing about what it took to get up to speed. I could no longer withstand the shame and perceived disappointment from my colleagues at the bank. My ego had been stuffed back into my shirt after these failed experiences. Two years after this comeuppance, I left the bank after finding fault with bank politics and my unrealistic view of my lack of progress toward being promoted to Trust Officer within the trust department.

I handled the public relations part of this struggle improperly. Rather than keeping my struggle quiet and to myself, outside forces got caught in the mix. The bank, the friends I knew in Chicago, my public. It would have been far less burdensome if I had undertaken this project unobtrusively and quietly. The pain of disappointment, though just as harsh, may have been less pronounced, confined only to me and my immediate family and perhaps just one or two friends.

I redoubled my efforts for the next time with a greater resolve and more in depth study, but without success. I was still not competitive enough in my knowledge of the law, issue analysis, writing under stress or in my preparation for the exam; something was just not clicking. What I did not realize was that I had not really studied the law as seriously as I should have in law school. My grades were OK but not exemplary. I had glaring bare spots that needed covering. Sure, I had had my usual moments of brilliance, but all through my academic career my core had never been pressed. My standardized test taking skills were substandard. I was now in the "big leagues" competing in a major market with law school graduates from the top law schools in the country. Students from Yale, Harvard, University of Illinois, University of Chicago, Stanford, Columbia, the University of Virginia, and Northwestern University. Even one of Mayor Daly's sons was sitting for the exam. All of these "would-be lawyers" from all over the United States were taking the exam. Along with a few "also-rans," second and third-timers taking another go at it. All of my formal education would converge in this exam, the mis-education, the under-education, the moments of brilliance and the inconsistency. They would all be measured in this pedagogical theater of mental stamina and intellectual attainment for the aspiring lawyer. This was the way I looked at it from my perspective. But the exam, though important, may not have been viewed that way by other persons. But the results, the test results, determined whether you would be "held back" or as we use to say in elementary school or "promoted" to go on to the next level, and it felt like that.

We all filed our way into the large gymnasium where the exam was administered. I was a country boy from a segregated uncompetitive high school in Charlottesville, Virginia; an uncelebrated graduate of a major Black university and law school—where many luminaries had graduated—who had "gotten over" but not excelled, trying now to compete with the big boys for the big prize.

All pretensions now gone, I began to look deeply within myself to search for my truth. What was I really made of? Did I really have in me what it took to overcome this unyielding obstacle? Introspection, evaluation and self-absorption were my state of mind. I read books I neglected to read while in college. I absorbed myself in self-help books. I strengthened my memory. I sought tutoring from Ronald Kennedy, a "star," the boy wonder, the wunderkind, who was at that time a newly appointed assistant professor of law at Northwestern University Law School. Ron was tall, light brown skinned, with neatly brushed black hair, a rising star in the law school at Northwestern. Hence his early election to its renowned faculty. This erudite young Black attorney was counsel of record for the lawsuit filed against the Illinois Bar by me and a group of other unsuccessful applicants between 1973 and 1975, alleging race discrimination in the grading and treatment of Black bar admission applicants.

The local branch of the NAACP took up the cause and put together classes to help those of us who were struggling. The branch provided tutors and sample exam questions administered under test conditions with graders like Kennedy to polish our test-taking, writing skills and techniques. And I attended and practiced the exercises diligently. I would do anything. I waged this war with zeal. I was undaunted. I remember sitting in Kennedy's office one day at Northwestern as he critiqued my answers to the sample exam questions. He corrected my use of language to describe various doctrines in the law; small lapses that subtly identified the test taker as Black or as lacking the depth the examiners required. The pass rate for Blacks even without deficits was small and paltry. Blacks were known to do more poorly on standardized tests than Whites. So I purchased a sample multistate bar exam kit from Yale Law School. I found out about this kit while walking through the halls of Northwestern University Law School and reading the bulletin boards on my way to the law library for my studies. Once I received the test kit I practiced under test conditions in the law library using my watch as a timer to time my completion of each section in the time allotted. The "Multistate" is the standardized portion of the bar exam that each applicant is required to pass with a certain score designated by the Board of Bar Examiners. Upon completion of the test I sent the results to Yale to be graded.

On the day of the exams, small desks some wooden and some made of iron were lined one behind the other in a file twenty-five to fifty deep, ten to fifteen rows across. One of my friends from the University of Chicago remarked that he had to have a drink before coming to calm his nerves. The red meat of tension was so high, that if you could have cut it with a knife, blood would squirt from the incision. It was time for academic war. Many casualties were taken and I was among them.

The pressure of studying for the exam got me fired from my job at The Talent Assistance Program, TAP. When I left the bank, the job of associate director of this minority business consulting program, funded by the U.S. Small Business Administration became available. The executive director left to work at a major industrial firm. The existing associate director, Hugh Turner, moved into that slot leaving vacant the number two position, and I sought the opening and was hired. During my interview with one of the board members I remember him saying "this guy is the only guy I know who knows the questions to ask and has all the answers." I was taken aback by this retort but I was hired nonetheless. Working in this job with its bare-bones accommodations was a real come down from the plush offices at Harris Bank, but in time I made the adjustment. At least I did not have to contend with the professional peer pressure from my colleagues at the bank. At the same time between 1973 and 1975 I taught as a part-time instructor at several local colleges and universities.

After one intense bar preparation session I blew up at Hugh Turner, the executive director of the organization, over his chastisement of me about taking so much time off to study. He was willing to look the other way, but he felt I needed to be reined in. Hugh was an unmarried middle aged Black man with curly black hair cut close but not short. He had some advanced education, possibly a college degree, but he was not a hard-nosed experienced businessman. He spoke in a nervous cadence, not stuttering but haltingly uneven especially when he was under stress. I had taken the measure of him and I knew he was intimidated by me. When a lawyer works for someone who is not as well educated, the imbalance breeds cynicism, condescension, competition and fear between the parties. I knew I added prestige to the program. That's why he hired me and feared me.

After arriving at the office sometime before 3:00 pm after studying for a while, Hugh beckoned me to his office: "Otis you have been spending too much time away from the office, not getting your work done. The secretary tells me that you have been out of the office more than you have been in the office," he instructed. I responded by saying, "What are you talking about Hugh, I thought we had a deal, that as long as I took care of my duties you would look the other way, that you would allow me to study for six weeks."

"No!" he responded. "We had no such understanding. No I did not agree to any such thing!"

Then I exploded. The little respect I had for him evaporated and I tore into him, "I'm the one who keeps this office going, all you do is collect a big check and parade around like you are the big boss, you're over your head and everyone knows it!" Once I exploded, he went ballistic firing me instantly. I had disrespected him and he would not allow me to make things right. "You get your things and get out of this office right now! You're fired! Get out, get out!" he repeatedly commanded. Then finishing up saying "You ungrateful son of a bitch," he muttered underneath his breath, as I dejectedly turned and walked out of his office and back into my office for the last time with a one way ticket home.

The pressure of preparing for the bar exam had caused me to lose my cool. My ego, self-esteem and confidence and yes, arrogance, all of which had been suppressed because of my past failures, took control of my rationality. These feelings could not flow and now that I was working for a rinky-dink, two-bit, fake, minority business program with offices that were unflattering, it all came to a boil. Like a wooden match from a wooden match box struck against sand paper, I ignited in a flash of uncontrolled yelling. It was so unexpected he probably did not know what hit him until it was too late for me. This situation could have been handled differently if I had not yelled at him and in the process berated him. But in my heart I do not believe I had much respect for him. He didn't really know anything about business consulting and with the little I knew, I knew more than him. This was the age of minority business "set asides," or MESBICS, Minority Enterprise Small Business Investment Corporations, licensed by the federal government. We were not a MESBIC, but we were paid to help minority small businesses stay in business by helping these firms improve their business practices. I used to say that most of the firms that were our clients "got just enough money from the federal government to go out of business."

Hugh had been good to me. And my actions showed ostensible ungreatfulness. He had allowed me to study for the bar exam while being paid. He valued my presence in the organization. And when Hugh left I could have replaced him as the executive director. Now because of this intemperate irrational act, all I had left was exhaustion, exasperation, wounded pride, remorse at blowing a "good thing," my savings and my part-time teaching job at Chicago State University. The old say-ing of "don't bite the hand that's feeding you" had proven correct. Hugh saw me as ungrateful, perhaps even arrogant. He had done so much and had intentions of doing even more. Or, perhaps this was an opportunity for him to get rid of a threat or dead weight that he knew was only using his employ as a way station while I pursued my real love. On the other hand, he could have been getting stress from the Board for allowing me so much time to study. I do not think this was a factor but who knows. Nevertheless, though I literally begged for his forgiveness, he re-fused to allow me to make it right. He would not meet with me inside or outside of the office; in person or on the phone. The line went dead.

I was so tightly wound from the pressure of the time schedule I had imposed on myself that a gusher erupted relieving that built up pressure but consequently creating conditions for other pressures to occur. The peer pressure from seeing guys pass this exam, who were no smarter than me, yet they found a way to get by, was embarrassing and ego deflating. I was essentially a wreck at this point. I was spent. I have always remembered this incident and vowed not to repeat it. There were many lessons to be learned. In my memory I call this episode the "Hugh Turner Incident."

Though I did not realize it at the time I had become a gorilla-fighter. Before the start of the next exam, I bought several bags of groceries to last for six weeks. I studied in my apartment day after day, day and night. I made a schedule of all the subjects that I had to cover before the exam. Everything from the law of personal property, to conflicts of law, federal income taxation, the Statute of Ann in the law of real property—an Illinois real property rule—and the "race notice" rules, among many, many other rules of law. The days I was not in the apartment, I drove to the law library at Northwestern University Law School on the north side where Phyllis was in her second year. I was in the library at 8:00 am, and I studied until it closed. I did not even want to take time to eat lunch or dinner. An older White man at least twice my age was always there when I got there, his head buried in the pages of the BRI Outlines. I would see him reading intensely turning the pages as he read, head transfixed to the page. He was always there when I left. He could not be out-studied. He was there for the "reason and not for the season." He was a man who knew the value of passing the bar even at his age. It occurred to me how amazing it was that some White folks who already had the world on their side could out work the average Black man working who needed it more. White folks know the value of what money and accomplishment can do for them because they are more used to the privileges and immunities that money and status affords them. White folks often know what it takes to be successful, the sacrifice required to achieve certain goals, and to be excellent. Some White folks are aggressive, greedy and relentlessly competitive. They have an insatiable appetite for money and power; after all, so many of them have had it and they never have enough.

My confidante during this time was my friend Michael Smith. A Chicago na-tive and a Howard Law School graduate. Mike was my guru. The figurative Af-rican-American Rastafari, my muse. The only thing bad about Mike was that he always kept me waiting. Mike seldom showed up on time. He was a grass roots community organizer and he was married. He lived in a shadowy world of con-nections in the community. How he made his living I do not know, but Mike was always into something community oriented. Mike was with me when I spoke with LJ about the bank. He said to me, "Otis I like what you said to those guys. It made a lot of sense." "Well," I replied, "I was just telling them what I thought. It was up to them whether or not they wanted to make it at the bank." Mike had had his problems getting past the Illinois Bar Exam even though he was a native Chicagoan. When I would daydream about what it would be like on the other side, he would say "don't look past it, don't look past it." I would remark sometime to him that "I don't really want to practice, giving myself an excuse for not passing the exam." Mike would reply, "that's what everybody says until they pass the exam. *you* want to practice!" I nodded acceptingly, then echoing "you're right." I admired Mike's shrewdness. He was a man who could get things done. He had his ear to the ground. After he flunked the exam, he told me that he went to see Morrissey, one of the bar examiners who worked for one of the big law firms. Morrissey was a White man, rotund with a round face, with a black receding hair line and approachable. He said Morrissey told him something like "he was close to getting by," and in his disgust he said he almost threw Morrissey out of his office window before the meeting was over.

After I flunked, I took Mike's lead and went to see Morrissey. Morrissey pulled out my exam paper and began to explain my errors. He gave me a similar story: "you should have passed. You are right there, you're very close, practicing law is a lot of pressure," he said. And I immediately responded by saying "I can take the pressure, I can take the pressure," I repeated, trying to convince him of my suitability. His patronizing statements only fostered disgust in my mind. If I was so close, why the hell didn't I pass? Morrissey's comments stirred up more emotions than they quieted. The meeting did not advance my cause. I thought of Mike's encounter, but like Mike I too did not throw Morrissey out of his office window which was twenty stories up in a high rise building.

Mike was always having some encounters with the police. He lived a life of intrigue and incognito. I asked him how he expected to be admitted to the bar even if he passed the bar exam. Mike said "many arrests but no convictions" that was his mantra. Mike passed the exam before I left Chicago and remarked to me that none of this practice stuff was new, "it had all been done before." There was no mystery in it. Mike always said, "the law is a fickle mistress." I always held on to this expression because it is truth.

My exposure through Phyllis to Northwestern University Law School was important. I met many of her law school friends. I camped out in the law school library. It became my "away from home" study center. On my breaks I walked the corridors of the law school and came upon an old saying, "lessons hard learned are lessons long remembered." This expression seems to hold so much meaning for me. I had finished law school, so many of them liked to discuss legal issues with me and I felt no hesitation.

The day was hot and muggy. A typical late Chicago summer day. After a long day at the office, I hopped a Chicago Transit bus to the South Side to my apartment. I was traveling on Cottage Grove Street, a wide boulevard heavily traveled by city commuters going north and south through the city. The bus was crowded, standing room only. I hung onto an overhead steel bar and braced myself as the bus made its way south stop after stop. Work that day at the bank had been tiresome. I was weary and fatigued, my mind a thousand miles away. I had been standing for a spell when I noticed this petite, short black haired, Spanish looking woman looking at me. Because my mind was transfixed, I had not noticed her until I looked up. She smiled as I acknowledged her gaze. We kept smiling back and forth at each other without saying a word for several minutes. Though we said nothing to each other for several stops, it was as though we were talking non-verbally. The smiles back and forth continued until she got off of the bus at her stop. I also got off at her stop which was not far from my stop, and we began a conversation. She told me her name, Maria Cotto. She worked as a secretary in an office in the Loop. She refused to give me her home phone number but did give me her office phone number. I gave her all my information not holding back anything. We agreed to talk later.

The next day I gave Maria a call, but she was not available. I left my phone number and told the receptionist to have her give me a call. Before leaving work that day Maria called back, and I suggested she come to my apartment so that we could talk and get to know each other in more detail. I was intrigued by her, our meeting had been such a happenstance.

My apartment was a short, not out-of-the-way distance from her route home and to work. She came by the next evening and so began a relationship that would continue until I left Chicago and resumed momentarily when I searched for her in Washington D.C.

Maria was a Spanish beauty. Short, she stood about five feet three with shoulder length black hair, and a gap in her front teeth. She had a beaming personality. Maria was a breath of fresh air for me. Maria was typical of many women in Chicago: Nice, kind, unpretentious, not college educated but every bit a woman. Maria was a break from the usual women I dated. Not being Black or White she was different. She spoke with a Spanish ascent. She looked at the world differently and what she felt about me and for me was earnest and real without pretense. What she was offering was herself, nothing more. What you saw was what you got. Maria was a mood changer. She got me out of my usual pensive, self-absorbed self and got me to laugh and look at life positively. But unbeknownst to me, she took the relationship as far as she could. She did not confide in me what decisions she was making and the consequences she faced from different aspects of her life. She did not let me in but so far.

When Maria met me, she had been living with a guy who was the father of her child, a little girl aged three. Maria's little girl was spoiled "to the nth degree." Maria loved this child so much. She catered to the girl's every need. A rotund bundle neatly groomed with every hair in place, she occupied a big space in her mother's world.

One evening while Maria and I sat on my sofa, I played with a penny. I flipped the coin in the air and caught it. "See," I said, showing her daughter the penny, then handed her the penny and said "do not put this in your mouth." Maria and her daughter sat on opposite sides of me. The next thing we knew the girl was choking and gagging uncontrollably. She had done just the opposite of what I had asked her not to do. Within a second, she turned red as a beet. Her eyes buckled, you could tell she was in an uncontrollable state and did not know what was happening to her. Maria panicked and began to cry. The little girl was choking and gurgling, her eyes were recessed and bulging, she was spitting and crying. "Do something, do something!" Maria exclaimed. The little girl seemed near to passing out. Without thinking I grabbed the girl by her ankles turned her upside down and shook her furiously. One, two, three! Hard shakes vertically up and down, back and forth I went. After a couple of hard jerks, the penny tumbled out of her throat. The crisis was over. Maria was forever grateful for my intervention. I had saved her daughter's life perhaps. Though the moment was fraught with danger, I thought little of it after the event passed.

While we were together, I was invited to an annual social event, a gathering of business men and women, insurance agents, lawyers and community leaders. Maria wore a sleek black gown with matching black pumps. Her long black hair draped over her shoulders, shapely legs, frame and voluptuous physique, making me the envy of the men at the affair. Heads turned when we entered the room. I remember feeling triumphant. I had the best looking woman on my arm in the place. The guys wondered "who is that guy with the beautiful woman?"

Life was good during those days. Maria would come to me each morning before she went to work, prepare my breakfast and leave me with the nectar of life with which to begin my day. Her eggs were not that good, but she gave it a good try. After one of my failed attempts to pass the bar exam, Maria exclaimed in her tortured English "what are they doing to you? Those people must be out of their minds, you worked so hard." The caring expressed in her tone masked the Spanish accent in her tortured English. She was hurt by my pain.

Then one day Maria disappeared. She never returned to me. I grieved for her return. She just vanished. I did not know where she lived in Chicago, and I dared not venture too near the neighborhood she frequented for fear of running into her estranged boyfriend; she said he was a cop and that put even more fear into me. I didn't see her again in Chicago. I do not know why she left. Rumor had it that she was diagnosed with cancer in her uterus, but the truth of that I never determined. When I moved to Washington D.C. a year or so later, I found her in the Hispanic section of "Adams Morgan" a neighborhood in the upper northwest quickly being gentrified by young White urban pioneers. The neighborhood had a large Hispanic community. We talked briefly. I had married Phyllis by then, and I told her that I had done so. She nodded with a smile on her face quietly accepting the reality of what that meant but still holding on to her reality that she still did not fully disclose to me. We parted after that brief encounter forlornly, the after-effect lingered for many years. But in her cheerfully truthful but tortured English cryptic style she said, "you had to have it right by your side didn't you!"

Sometime during the course of my study, I began to study with a buddy, named Houston Burnside. Houston was a Howard Law grad and a nice guy. He was from Illinois, exactly where I am uncertain, but when I encountered him he was living in Chicago. We studied together for days. He and I memorized almost verbatim the entire 200 page BRI summary outline. "A negotiable instrument is an instrument in writing signed by the maker and payable to the order of..." etc, etc. I have to admit that I literally taught Houston the outline and practiced him on it and he did the same for me. We seriously studied the material. We rehearsed each other on the rules, we exchanged and discussed proposed written answers to the essay questions, and we did this intensively over several weeks. Houston was in the Illinois National Guard or one of its reserve units at the time and he occasionally showed up with his fatigues and army boots on at my apartment where we studied after his weekend warrior exercises were over. We became good friends during that time. And the memory of the trench work we did together in preparation for the exam is indelibly etched in my memory. This preparation effort would be my last gallant effort to pass the exam.

The hiatus after the exam and before the reckoning was a twilight period. Lazy days could be spent on the pristine North or South Shore beaches. Catching up on overdue correspondence and social calls filled some days. A return to the daily routine of life was the norm for most aspirants of the bar. A sigh of relief that "it was over" was the common lament. My determination to overcome was heightened. I had survived the ordeal and knew I had the ability innately to compete. After all, I had made it this far and I was not about to be denied. Through this struggle I had found a new love, been exposed to a higher vision and had my horizons expanded. I realized that the gaps in my background were not insurmountable, that I only needed to face up to the bare spots, summon up the latent discipline dormant within and put a plan in place to bring myself even with the competition.

The news broke soon thereafter that the bar results were out. A chill went through my spine, my knees buckled. Though I did not know at this time what it felt like to have a heart attack, I could have had one by the symptoms running through my body: a light sweat, a palpitating heartbeat, an increase in my respiratory function and a near panic attack, all a fleeting response to the stress of anxiety to the news. I was indeed over wrought. My emotions were as volatile as a ship tossed about in a perfect storm. The highs of imagining a bruising fight successfully concluded, cozy thoughts of a newly minted lawyer with head held high, juxtaposed with the stark realities of what a negative result would portend. The feelings of depression, of inadequacy and low self-esteem, even thoughts of suicide darted in and out of my mind, but what a waste that would have been. I did not take my usual route home that day. Instead I detoured to a local watering hole.

Not wanting to face the collision that lay ahead, which I intuitively knew awaited me, I drank. "Let me have a shot of Jack Daniels on the rocks," I told the barkeep. Down the hatch the first one went, then another and maybe one more. By now, I thought I was fortified to make the journey home and face my reality, but instead I was actually making myself less stable and more vulnerable to my emotions. A sense of inevitability, dread and a foreboding aura of defeat were paramount in my thinking. Intuitively I knew I had not made it. It hurt but somehow I knew without going home what the result was. I had studied so hard that I memorized several outlines on the subjects tested. I had drilled my study companion so hard he referred to me as the "teacher." I knew the material. After the shots of bourbon, I caught the Illinois Central home. I was distraught, so much so, that I went way past my stop and ended up in suburban Indiana. The conductor came back to me and said "young man where are you getting off? We are at the end of the line."

Disheveled, I realized I had gone to the end of the line and would have to go back to my stop and go home. In a quasi-drunken stupor, I exited the train. I gathered myself, staggered to my feet and righted myself for the walk home. Ostensibly fortified by liquor against the impending pain I knew was coming.

As I walked along that shaded pathway, I could see through the glass doors of my apartment building. The yellow gold mailboxes reflected through the glass vestibule from the crystal chandelier that glowed brightly from the ceiling. I opened the doors and went to my mail box and opened its door. Sure enough the thin beige letter from the Board of Bar Examiners was there. The thinness of the envelope foretold of its contents: "We are sorry to inform you".........that is all I needed to read, the rest was of no value.

I made my way to my apartment, threw myself onto the couch and cried. What else could I do? The pain of rejection was real. I called my parents that night and let out such mournful, maudlin sobs and crying "What had I done wrong?" "Why can't I pass this exam?" I had done everything right, obeyed the rules, what was it? What had I done to deserve this? I had been a good citizen, kept myself clean did all the right things, what was the reason for this? "Why?" I cried and cried. I bellowed with anguish the pain I felt both mental and physical. My anguish was palpable and real, my heart hurt. It seemed as though my entire life's sojourn was encapsulated in this exam. The narrow vision of my mind made me feel that my self-worth and my self-image were at risk. I had nothing to fall back on for solace or strength. The thought of religion did not enter my mind. It must have been terrible on Mom and Dad to hear their only child lament with such passion a 1,000 miles from home. I was so distraught I thought of jumping out of my apartment's side window twenty-three stories up, but common sense prevailed. For the first time I had run into an unyielding brick wall that said "no!"

When Houston passed the exam that time and I failed, salt was poured into the festering wound of my broken heart. My life changed after that night. Everything just crumbled.

Had I betrayed myself by not studying as hard as I could have during my earlier school days? Had my parents betrayed me by not sending me to that private school I had a chance to attend while in high school? Had the system betrayed me with its segregated and unequal schools I attended in Virginia? Was my failure after filing suit against the Illinois Bar, the recoil of that impolitic decision? Was my failure the sum total of the collective betrayals resulting in this forfeiture? Perhaps, had my nose been rubbed in the academic rigor required to meet the standard at an earlier time, this comeuppance could have been avoided. Certainly the failure to win was not for the lack of a work ethic. What was it then? Was this experience the price I was paying to become the first lawyer in my family, second generation college graduate, first generation lawyer? I had no coach to school me on how to play this game. The demand note had been called in, the overdue debt had been in arrears for a while. Pay up or get out was the message! Payment was now due. All I knew was failure at this pursuit and the failure was painful. I had failed at something I wanted more than anything in this life except perhaps life itself. At this time nothing else mattered. I had tried my darndest to pass, but had failed.

Unbeknownst to me, however, were the politics involved. I was in a state that I had no history with. I was only there because of employment. I was not born there. I had not attended any school there. There was nothing that really tied me to Illinois. I had an attenuated nexus to the state at best. I was unaware that if there is any discretion to be given, states reserve this discretion, if any, in favor of their own people over outsiders on professional licensing exams. I was not a favorite son, and I had had the audacity to file suit against them. As a consequence my head was in the proverbial lion's mouth. Would my head now be snapped off with the facile alacrity of the guillotine? Yes! I had nowhere to turn and no place to go. Filing suit had been a viable suggestion at the time in the midst of a search for a solution, though an impolitic decision. I, along with four other plaintiffs, filed the suit which focused attention on us. We could expect nothing more than the same old gruel. It was a dog's breakfast.

The next day I discussed my dilemma with a friend, Ted Sherrod. Ted worked for Chaplin and Cutler, a large law firm on one of the upper floors of Harris Bank building. Ted was a medium build dark skinned fellow with short black hair. He was obviously smart to be at Chaplin and Cutler, and he probably was the only Black there other than a secretary or two. Ted suggested that I consider other states. An old quote rang true: "failure is not a dead end street but a detour." I had not thought of this before. I was not a quitter. I was one of those who would keep butting my head against the wall until either the wall shattered or my head fractured. I was determined to fight on, but in my present mental condition the suggestion made sense.

My father ordered me home, and I finally acceded to his advice, enough was enough. The next day I caught a flight home. When I exited the plane and walked down the ramp to the tarp below a light illuminated my consciousness. I felt as though a burden had been lifted from my shoulders. As he greeted me with his arms out stretched, I sank into his warm breast, his consoling arms wrapped around me soothing my pain and assuaging my ire. The familiar smell of his cologne was comforting and reassuring: a respite from the battle was finally at hand.

The fire that burned so brightly at the start of my Illinois campaign in the summer of 1972 was dimmed. My sojourn at Harris Bank, the Kenneth Street real estate venture, my marriage and new home, and the prospect of becoming a lawyer, had lost its luster and I was left with only the dull residue of smoldering embers of a pyrrhic victory. The debacles lay against the tenuous spine of my fractured psyche. The ash pile of my ego still flickered beneath the banked fire that glowed with the resilience of my drive to still obtain what appeared to be and was now slipping out of my grasp.

Nothing worked for me in Chicago, the bar, the marriage, and the real estate venture fizzled. Merzel had Slutsky write me from Chicago threatening foreclosure on the Kenneth Street property or as he recommended, I could give him a "deed in lieu of foreclosure." I chose that path since it was the option with the least resistance. In any event, my mind was not on Kenneth Street any longer. To save myself I had to leave. Get out. I even went back to Chicago after being in D.C. a few months and took the exam again. I didn't study this time. I did it just to say "fuck em." I didn't give a shit anymore, I didn't care. I did it to make a statement; to say, this is not over, you have not beaten me! It was, however, my last at bat in Illinois.

When I left Chicago in the summer of 1975, a frustrated, worn out, divorced, wounded veteran of the bar exam wars, I returned to the city that had been my launching pad three years earlier.

A thought was born on that flight east that said in essence, "you are worth more than the results of a bar exam. There is life beyond passing the bar. You are capable and you will persevere." I did rejoin the battle and achieved a good result.

What had started out as a 100 yard mad dash for professional empowerment became more like a four-minute mile. Little did I know, this journey had just begun. I had come to Chicago as innocent and naive mush but had emerged from the Chicago experience congealed in my maturing manhood: a wiser more knowledgeable man about the ways of the world and the gamesmanship required to succeed in it.

And so on a bright sunny morning in June of 1975 my stay in Chicago ended three years after it began. Ron Gafford a friend of long standing, a dark skinned fellow who had the prettiest girl friend whom I discreetly admired, helped me pack up my belongings and loaded them into a U-Haul truck to begin the trip East to Washington D.C. The U-Haul truck broke down somewhere between Indiana and Ohio. Ron and I had to off-load the entire truck and reload everything into another truck to complete the trip to D.C. After arriving in Washington, we unloaded everything and for his help I purchased him a one-way airline ticket back to Chicago. Ron had been a good friend. In fact, I made several earnestly good friends while in Chicago. I would not be as lucky in the future.

19

THE INTERREGNUM: "WHAT HAPPENS TO A DREAM DEFERRED?"

"What happens to a dream deferred?
Does it dry up like a raisin in the sun?
Or fester like a sore then run?"

—*Langston Hughes*
from Montage of a Dream Deferred

WAS BEING HUMAN MY DILEMMA? It is human to dream, is it not? And yet still not know what it takes to make dreams reality? Where did this dream, this aspiration of mine to become a lawyer come from? There were no Black lawyers in Charlottesville in the 60s when I was in school here; Had I heard about the exploits of Thurgood Marshall? My parents did not push me in this direction, and I don't remember them ever dictating any particular field of study or profession to pursue. My goal had been to become a lawyer since high school. My vision of being a lawyer, as best I can remember, came from seeing a British lawyer in an English film. The lawyer was a figure of authority; people looked up to him, he was respected and catered to; his manner was regal and aristocratic; he was a man of means, knowledge and influence. This portrait agreed with my nascent self-image.

All of this was an exaggeration of course, but to an impressionable youth it informed my vision. "I want to be like that!" my inner voice must have said. Perhaps we would dream fewer dreams if we knew the price for making our dreams reality. Our dreams and aspirations would then be limited to only those dreams we were sure we could achieve. Should our dreams and aspirations be limited solely to our abilities; and who determines that? But wouldn't this myopia stifle the progress of mankind? We would be nowhere if each step we took was a measured step, a step we were always sure we could make. We must dare ourselves to be great and put ourselves to the test to achieve it. Heraclitus, the Greek philosopher is quoted as saying that "character is destiny." Heraclitus also said that, "Good character is not formed in a week or a month. It is created little by little, day by day. Protracted and patient effort is needed to develop good character."[20]

My ancestors would have achieved little if they had not dreamed of a life of freedom, and fought to make that dream, that aspiration, a reality: not knowing what the ultimate cost of the battle would be to realize for their progeny a better life.

Beehive
by Jean Toomer

Within this black hive to-night
There swarm a million bees;
Bees passing in and out the moon,
Bees escaping out the moon,
Bees returning through the moon,
Silver bees intently buzzing,
Silver honey dripping from the swarm of bees.
Earth is a waxen cell of the world comb,
And I, a drone,
Lying on my back,
Lipping honey,
Getting drunk with silver honey,
Wish that I might fly out past the moon
And curl forever in some far-off farmyard flower.

THE BEEHIVE, WASHINGTON, DC

My earlier flight home to finalize my return to Washington had been concluded with arrangements between my father and myself on where I would live. Dad told me to find a building to buy in D.C. He felt, I think, a desire to help me heal. I think he knew in his heart the pain I felt and his good heart and magnanimity expressed itself in the choices and finance he contributed to help me come home. My last agonizingly woeful phone call made in the midst of my last failure rang loudly and resoundingly in his mind I am sure.

I found Alba Gardenia, meaning the white garden, the name I gave to the apartment building at 1340 Peabody Street in upper northwest D.C. The building was in the Petworth section of D.C., ten blocks or so south of Silver Spring, Maryland. It lay between Georgia Avenue on the east and 14th street NW on the west, northeast of Rock Creek Park. I named the building Alba Gardenia during the turmoil that ensued after my breakup with Linda Herring, my roommate at that time. The building was a handsome red brick structure, a Cape Cod/Georgian style four-unit apartment building. The building sat twenty feet back from the sidewalk fronting Peabody Street with its own square lot surrounded by a cement circular alley. Apartment buildings lined the south and north sides of Peabody Street between Georgia Avenue and 14th St. NW. Working class Black people employed by the D.C. government or off shoots of the federal government populated the corridor.

I entered my apartment through a side entrance gained from an adjacent parking space next to the alley that encircled the lot. Two Black wrought iron railings stood at opposite ends of a five foot square cement porch of the two-step walk up. As you entered the unit, the front door opened into the living room and an alcove appeared large enough for a dining room table and chairs. Perpendicular to the alcove was a small bedroom that contained a twin bed and book shelves that hung parallel to each other around the room to form a library. At the end of the alcove to the left was a full bathroom and adjacent to that was the main bedroom. Beyond the alcove was a Pullman Kitchen and beyond that a screened in back porch.

The Peabody Street property was a real find. D.C. was evolving from direct federal government rule to home rule in the summer of 1975, and many Whites who owned property in Black neighborhoods were getting out. The Black power chant of the Civil Rights era "look out Whitey Black power is going to get your mamma," taken from the 1967 book by Julius Lester of the same name, intimidated many Washington D.C . Whites especially when closely followed by the move to home rule less than eight years later. Many Whites left the city. When I bought the property, Margaret Dhillon, a White woman, had been living in the building for many years. Dhillon was a thirty-something. She lived on the right side of the building in the first floor unit directly opposite my number with her twelve year old son. I lived on the left side of the building and had a parking space in front of my door. Dhillon knew the ropes of being a tenant in D.C. and she vowed, "I was living here before you came and I'll be living here when you leave, my friends are legion."

After settlement on the building, I threw myself into the task of rehabbing and refurbishing the property. I worked like a man possessed. Possessed of what? The energy of a person glad to be rescued from a foreign land hostile to my survival and success.

During the summer of 1975, my mother came up to stay with me for a while, and Delma sent Otis there for a visit as well. While I worked on the renovations, Otis spent his time playing with the neighborhood urchins who gathered each morning in front of my door to see if Otis was coming out to play. Otis was a tender sort, not used to battling his way with the rough-housers of the block. This group of four youngsters controlled the alley playgrounds and back yards behind the apartment houses not meant for child's play in the neighborhood.

The leader of the pack was a round-faced, brown-skinned, scrappy boy named Beanie who played hard and never knew when it was time to go home. He seemed always to be out front and bossed the other kids around. He was a natural leader, had a mind of his own and demonstrated his nascent intellect from time to time. His moments of brilliance were demonstrated when the boys would huddle to plot their next escapade for the day. Also in his group was Dante, a fair-skinned mulatto, a quiet boy who kept mostly to himself. Chauncey, another member of the group, was essentially orphaned from birth, estranged from his father, an alcoholic and sometimes criminal, and had little or no relationship with his wayward father. Andre, the youngest of the group, had piercing dark black eyes and was silent but resourceful. He avoided conflict. He would never contest for the leadership. He was "Mr. Congeniality."

Each was no more than nine years old and all within a year or two of the other. Where they each lived could never be specifically determined; they just appeared each morning, always dressed about the same. Dingy short pants, tee shirts, and unlaced tennis shoes some with a hole poking through the front toe. Otis went out to play with his friends each morning and would be gone a few hours, when all of sudden we would hear some yelling, and they would all be running one after the other chasing after Otis. When Otis would get to the front door, where his safety was assured, the other kids would stop their chase.

"They want to fight, they want to fight" Otis said, out of breath, panting steadily.

Beanie replied, "he threw a rock and we want to get him."

"I didn't throw no rock," Otis defended, "Chauncey did."

"Uh uh, Otis did it," Chauncey chimed in.

My mother, being the traffic cop, blocked their entrance and instructed, "didn't I tell you, Otis: no throwing rocks, somebody could get hurt."

"Yes m'am," Otis nodded to his grandmother, knowing his safety was no longer at issue.

"Now go on out and play and don't come back here running from a fight," she sternly warned. I chimed in, "Do not be afraid of getting hit, you have to take a hit to give a hit."

For the next several days, the energy of the summer was expended on renovating and refurbishing the apartment building. I was a contented man. My mother was with me helping me set up my house and my son was with me. The next day Otis came running home again all out of breath with the same story. One of the kids was after him and wanted to fight. I told him he had to stop running and fight these kids. I told him he could not allow these boys to run him home every evening. My mother agreed. So as the boys stood around waiting for us to quell the moment, I took Otis outside my door and said "look, ball your fist up and go out there and fight Beanie right now! Do it!" Reluctantly, Otis put his dukes up and began swinging at Beanie with reckless abandon. Beanie, always in control, pranced around and took a wild swing missing Otis by a mile. Otis took another swing also missing by a mile. The other kids just giggled and laughed as if witnessing a clown show of their own making. As both boys continued to play at fighting, the point had been made. Otis no longer ran from the gang of four, but had finally gathered up his courage with the backing of his family to confront the bully of the neighborhood boys.

I extensively renovated my unit: we painted the walls, and put down new carpeting throughout. I bought house plants and Dad and Mom helped me to buy new furnishings to supplement what I brought from Chicago. I put in asphalt for my private driveway, painted the central hallway of the building and put in new carpeting for the hall stairway. When we bought the building, the neighborhood folks were parking their cars on the lawn in front of the building. I had these vehicles towed away. It took several days for the violators to get the message.

Dhillon fought me all the way as I renovated the building and raised the rent. During this time, the D.C. government passed a rent control law. This law was antithetical to my view of ownership of private property. I found it hard to accept. The nerve of the city to pass a law that told a property owner how much he could charge for rent galled me. The rent control law created a bureaucracy and a complicated process for raising rent on existing tenants, and Dhillon, through her legal aid lawyers, knew the process; she hit me over the head with it at every turn. I found myself battling law students from Antioch School of Law, a local new law school, and legal aid lawyers who were using me for a training ground in landlord tenant law. The law students filed all kinds of motions and petitions challenging my every move at Dhillon's behest. I had no experience beyond my time in the Law Student's In-Court Program I participated in while a third year law student at Howard Law School. These guys were applying practical law to a spongy theoretical lawyer. I was out of my class and intimidated. The pressure they brought forced me to start acting like a lawyer. Before this struggle would calm down, I had to hire several lawyers. I was armed only with my conviction that the city had no right to tell a property owner what he could charge for rent. No tenant would control a building of mine. I paid the taxes, not the tenant. But D.C. was close to being a socialized city at this time of rent control. I won a victory or two along the way, but it was always a struggle with the same old foes.

"GETTING DRUNK WITH SILVER HONEY"

Two years before I was admitted to the Bar, my moment of grace was tainted by a harrowing paralyzing neurotic episode brought on by drug use, stress, being overwrought with anxiety, mild depression and an emotional fight with my room-mate, Linda. The confluence of these factors exploded into a psychosis, a form of psychoneurosis.

Had the cumulative effect of all this wear and tear finally caught up with me? The unsettling sediment from the confluence of the recoil from the bar exams, the drug use, and the Peabody apartment battles, the fight with my live-in girlfriend and the stress of teaching at Morgan State was all just too much. Had my determination to succeed run against an unyielding standard? These clashes had slowly and insidiously dismembered the fabric of my self-perception, which was not that solidly anchored to begin with, leaving me nowhere to go except into oblivion. Religion did not save me though it did reveal itself in my encounter with the doctor who failed to perceive my plight. The irresistible force had met the immovable object.

My sense of self fought to survive the attack of this trick. My ego was being submerged and my being would not accept it. Repressed ego reverberates in the psyche and manifests itself in many psychologically destructive ways. The psychosis caused my ego to explode in the opposite direction, all of which could have ended in disaster, but for the grace of God it did not.

My opiates of choice were *cannabis sativa*, the "weed of wisdom," and liquor. Paradoxically, the weed became a major factor, if not the sole cause or at least the prime facilitator of my mental illness. The use of marijuana had been in my lifestyle since my third year in law school at the persistent urging of my New York roommate: "Lee you should try this stuff." "I'm not interested," I responded on several occasions. I even threw a joint away he gave me to try. I rebuffed his over-tures many times. "But Lee this is some good shit man," he persisted. In a mo-ment of thoughtful curiosity I relented and smoked my first joint. It took a while for me to feel the effects but slowly the high became real and I liked it and so it went.

My use of the drug began in late 1971/early 1972 during the time of the break-down of my first marriage to Delma. My addictive personality caused me to find solace in the use of the drug, it filled my lonely spots. The drug became my friend and heightened moments of introspection. I enjoyed listening to music while be-ing high. My New York friends socially smoked the drug and it was viewed as a "cool" thing to do and a way to leave that "oil" alone, the hip word for liquor. Liquor was viewed as old school. I carried this lifestyle to Chicago after law school and back to D.C. and continued my use there. I was an idle time recreational user, not a chronic user. My use of the drug did not interfere with my work or school. The drug enhanced sex and sleep and I enjoyed both.

That volatile mixture of degraded ego, drugs and stress ignited by a violent fight with my girlfriend exploded into a form of psychoneurosis, as I mentioned earlier, temporary madness, temporary insanity for which there was no warning. I was never officially diagnosed, but it happened. From this clash of stressors the miasma emerged. My experience was confined to a small circle of people most of whom were unaware that I was going through this trial. When it manifested itself, it was characterized by megalomania, visions of grandeur, manic and reckless behavior. The psychosis caused me to feel like I was a king, exalted somehow. Was this schizophrenia? I didn't know. The balance of the psyche is not to be taken for granted. In my case a delicate balance had been disturbed in an intensely high strung individual. The mania controlled my mind for months after the initiating event though the intensity of its affects attenuated over time. The residue of the mania would remain in the recesses of my mind for many years, awaiting a triggering event. And one additional innocuous episode did reoccur years later. The mania would not be completely eliminated until those factors giving rise to the psychosis were completely extinguished.

Somewhere in my subconscious, as a youth and as an adult, I must have had and maintained a strong self-image. A self-image of power, dignity and self-worth. And when the world that I was in would not allow that self-image to be exhibited by my achievements as personified by the bar exam, it was insufferable and unacceptable to me psychologically; hence the implosion, the boomerang, and the mental regurgitation expelled from my psyche. The beat down I experienced from the bar exam process and my ill-considered refuge into marijuana was a volatile ad mixture, the combustible elements of which were ignited by these varied stressors.

During my third year in law school, the pain from the gradual dismemberment of my youthful marriage to Delma, may have galvanized what was already a latent addictive personality. I was going through quite a lot during that time: finishing up my studies, keeping Otis III and working part time, while Delma worked and tried to recover from the untimely death of her mother. Delma's restlessness during this period caused me to doubt the wisdom of our early marriage in 1968. A hurt I had not experienced before a loss of innocence. I booked my first room in the heartbreak hotel. But little did I know that my tenancy in that room would be for a term of years, rather than for a day. In fact, over the next eight years, I would frequent this hotel so much that I got my room at a preferential rate. The innkeeper always kept a light on for me. He knew I would be back.

My first marriage had been true. There was no premarital sex or pregnancy that drove us to marry, just a true virginal love albeit a naive love. After Delma's mother's early death she began to change. One of her unexplained absences from our apartment during this time coupled with my emerging objection to her expressed desire to ask more of my parents than I thought was required or expected, what I felt was exploitation after all that they had done, caused me much unease. Since there was no explanation for the unexplained yet troubling absence, I was forced to accept the probability, that the trust between us had been broken. I turned to my New York friends Paul Wallace and his girlfriend Bunny for solace, support and respite. Philosophical differences over values simmering below the surface emerged and our youthful marriage never recovered. By the time we moved to Chicago, to say our marriage was on the rocks was an understatement; it was essentially over.

During law school days, my stress level was moderate and my marijuana use was infrequent. In fact my use did not begin until my 3rd year. Except for my estrangement from Delma, my ego remained unchallenged. The competitive stress of the professional world had not yet entered my orbit when my initial use began. Unbeknownst to me, however, was the insidious effect on the central nervous system of continued use of the drug on a highly sensitive, highly empathetic individual.

The high empathy that characterizes my personality can manifest itself in pangs of deep feeling for a hurt real, imagined or feared in the future, such as the dreaded death of a loved one. Or simply just relating deeply to the pain felt by someone close to me or even just another human being. Marcellus Easter's beating after a party at the neighborhood playground at Battery Park went sour is one such example. My heart went out to him. This was my first experience with high empathy. These emotions when they come can be wrenching on my being and may result in a tearful expression of feeling.

Being an only child I lived in my dream world all the time. My ability to be self-contained was strong. I enjoyed my solitude as a youth and as an adult. The use of marijuana fit into my world of isolation and heightened the pleasure of it real or imagined. For my personality it would have been better had I never been introduced to the drug. There were too many complementary negatives.

Since I liked getting high, I continued to use the drug moderately. Having reasoned that smoking was harmful to my health I curtailed my use of cigarettes as my use of marijuana became preferable.

Tension between my compulsive side and my healthy side emerged as I continued to smoke. My compulsive nature urged me to use, yet my inner voice of restraint and self-preservation fought against it constantly in the spirit of a nagging reminder that kept my use limited and moderate. This tension never went away and caused me to waste money by buying the drug, smoking some of it and then throwing the rest away in a fit of guilt, flushing it down the commode more often than not.

Knowing innately that my use of the drug was harmful, I kept myself as informed as possible with as much medical information as I could and subscribed to the magazine "High Times" to get more information about the adverse health effects. Dr. Robert L. DuPont a leading authority in Psychiatry and drug abuse at that time was a key player in the debate about the harmful effects of marijuana use. He talked on television about a study about the continued harmful results of marijuana. I remember him saying when being interviewed, paraphrasing, "if I used it, I would use the least amount as infrequently as I could." That statement caught my attention. I even went so far as to order a medical study from the National Institutes of Health on marijuana's health effects. My guilt and paranoia about what I was doing to my health was a persistent drag on my use, but it did not stop it.

"FLY OUT PAST THE MOON, BALTIMORE"

Before Phyllis reentered my life in D.C. in the summer of 1976, I met Linda, a young female college senior from Morgan State University in Baltimore, Maryland. The first job I got was as an instructor/adjunct professor in the Department of Business at Morgan State where I taught Personnel, Management 101, and Business Law. I was teaching three classes and commuted to Baltimore four days a week. My preparations for classes required extensive reading and preparation of outlines and syllabi. The toil of this effort was hard, but I enjoyed it. I felt like was earning an MBA with all the business textbooks I had to read. My knowledge base expanded considerably. I had secured this position because of my law degree and my prior college teaching experience in Chicago. The most rewarding aspect of this teaching experience was the colloquia that formed with a small group of African-American and African students that met in the late afternoon: these sessions were less formal and filled with jocularity and humor.

Linda came to my attention by way of introduction from a student in one of my classes. She was a tall, good looking woman with a closely cropped Afro hair style. We soon became fast friends and it was not long before we were living together.

When my parents found out that Linda was living with me, my mother fired off a salvo. "How could you do a thing like that?" she exclaimed. Her Victorian values had been violated by her beloved son. Dad, though curious, did not seem to care one way or the other. It was Mother who caused the furor. After fussing about this for several minutes on the telephone, I said to her "well what are you going to do, cash in all the chips?"

"Cash in what chips, nobody's cashing in any chips, what are you talking about!" she retorted briskly. From her tone I knew she was angry. But I didn't care at that time. What I was asking them was whether or not they would withdraw their support because of my new roommate?

The fuss passed and Linda and I went about our daily routines, she to her classes and I to my teaching and studying for the Pennsylvania Bar Exam, until that fateful evening.

Linda and I had been together for a while. Maybe a year or more. My friends had gotten to know her and she them. We had gone out together many times, and she had graduated from college by the time this impending event happened. Her mother came to her graduation and met my parents as well.

As Linda and I sat drinking Ballentine Scotch Whisky, smoking and rolling some joints in the alcove at the dining room table, a fight began about some nonsense. The fight began slowly but grew in intensity as each verbal blow was hurled. Before the fight began, Linda had shown me a picture of her deceased father. In a burst of anger, for some unknown reason, I grabbed the picture from her hand and slapped her with a back hand across her mouth that swelled and distorted the left side of her lower face. As the violent anger continued, I tore up the picture into bite size pieces and threw it at her face. She stormed out of the apartment and went to the window on the driveway side and threw a rock through the library window shattering it and scaring me to death. I thought she was trying to kill me.

After all the money I had spent rehabbing and refurbishing the building, I was further enraged at her audacity at destroying my property. The fight turned into rage. She came back into the unit and grabbed a knife from the butcher block, and I grabbed one as well. The scene was frightening. Dope, liquor, stress, fatigue, anger, and discontent merged at a crucial moment. We stared at each other, knives pointing at each other raised as if to strike at daggers point and breathing heavily. The sweat from our brown-skin foreheads moisturized the anxiety of the moment; one was scared and again, the other was glad of it.

In the pit of despair, and for a return to partial sanity, we retreated. Realizing the extremity of my actions and knowing that my conduct was an aberration, contrition overtook me and I dropped my knife. Immediately I dropped to my knees in a supplicant position and kissed her feet, licking each toe and begged her to forgive me. As I kissed her feet, she just stood there motionless without uttering a word and went outside. I was doing the Jesus Christ thing, in effect washing her feet, attempting to show the ultimate regret for what had occurred. In the melee she left and I never saw her again. For several days I looked for her forlornly, inquiring of our mutual friends without success. She had been put out with only the clothes on her back. Where would she go? What would she do? Who was she with? I did not know. A phobia about kitchen knives haunted me for years after this event.

After the stand-off, I flipped into the high gear of temporary insanity. Was it megalomania? I threw out all of her clothes onto the grass and concrete driveway outside. Not concerned with her modesty, I threw out her bras, her panties and every other piece of clothing she had in the apartment. At this moment I didn't care. It was one hell of a mess. The next thing I know there was a stern knock on the front door. Linda had gone.

"D.C. police open up," the voice said. When I opened the door, two burly White D.C. cops with night sticks in hand were standing at the entrance. The lead cop, a short rotund figure, asked what was going on. They said a neighbor called. I did not know at the time that Margaret Dhillon called the cops. She apparently heard the ruckus through the wall separating our apartments.

The lead cop looked at me with alarm—a tall Black man seemingly under control—and I at him. I was out of my mind, but somehow the lawyer in me took control. The repressed lawyer emerged to save the day. Now was the time, to show what I knew and to get those cops out of my apartment. I knew that I could be jailed for anything they saw in plain view that was illegal. But for some reason, after studying all that law, I let the cops into the apartment. They came in looking all around. Peabody Street was just a stone's throw from the Petworth police barracks, less than two miles away off Georgia Avenue. My revulsion at my behavior in this melee caused me to recoil against the marijuana. I instinctively took all the dope and threw it into the toilet and flushed it down several minutes before answering the door. Somehow I just knew because of the nature of the commotion and the explosive character of the incident that I was in trouble. Out of control, I had gone too far. The cops walked through the apartment beating their night sticks into the palms of their hands intent on quelling the dustup as they took each step. They looked into the small room I used as a guest room and library. The shelves of law school books and college books weighed down the side wall. I said to the cops, out of my mind, attempting to intimidate them, "I know everything that is in those books." The lead cop looked at me with puzzlement. He knew that I was either crazy or smart. He was puzzled on which applied. They left. I had survived the moment.

After the cops left, I blew out a deep breath, a sigh of relief. I called a law school friend who lived not far from the building just south of Silver Spring, Maryland and asked him to come over. I had known this fellow when we were in law school several years earlier. He was a mature man several years my senior with a wife and two children. Jerome Harris is his name. He came to the apartment and looked around in amazement. I said "she tried to kill me!"

Jerome, looking bemused said "uh huh, she tried to kill you, huh?"

"Yes," I demurred.

"And just how did she try to do that Otis?"

"She threw a rock through the window!"

"Well you need to make a police report for the record if you want to, to protect yourself," he said in his usual southern drawl. I said the police have already been here. "Well, he said, in that case why don't you try to get yourself together, maybe things will work out."

"Work out! How is it going to work out, Jerome. This woman tried to kill me man!" I repeated with even more force the second time, but with the tone of exasperation. I no longer felt like explaining the incident to anyone else. Jerome could sense that the situation was not what I had sought to convey. He could see the ridiculousness of it all, but he was trying to be gentle.

When Jerome left, my head was spinning out of control. Self-preservation took over. I got into my car, an orange 1975 Volvo I had purchased soon after returning to D.C., and drove to a Holiday Inn on Georgia Avenue in Silver Spring not far from the building. I got a room and tried to sleep. I don't remember whether I slept at all that night.

The next day I checked out of the hotel and drove back to the apartment. As I drove up I saw all of Linda's clothes strewn about the side lawn. At that moment I burst into tears crying as never before, weeping with great intensity. The windows in my car were rolled up. No one saw me as I wailed uncontrollably. What had caused the gulf of emotion is unknown.

As I sat behind the wheel in the mists of this tearful mourn, Prather, the slightly obese, bald-headed, bearded janitor from the building next door, was returning to his apartment. He saw me crying. Through the glass he hollered, "what's the matter, what's the matter with you, what's going on?" Though I saw him, I could not answer. Prather and I had befriended each other over the last year or so that I owned the building. He was an okay guy, but the one thing I remember him saying to me was that "women are to be used but not abused." I had clearly violated his sacred principle. I did not acknowledge him. I just kept on crying and crying without stopping for several minutes more. Realizing that he could make no sense of the situation and had no control of it, he left. I remained in the car for several more minutes until I regained my composure.

I got out of the car and went inside the apartment. Things were a mess. Dishes in the sink unwashed for several days. Beds unmade and liquor bottles half empty on the table. I hadn't slept there the night before, and the night before that all hell had broken loose. Embarrassed by the sight of Linda's clothes thrown about the lawn, I gathered them up and took them inside. But my altered state of mind was still in control. When I turned on the television, I thought that the commentators and news casters were talking directly to me. I heeded their signals and messages as if in a secret code that only we understood. I felt I was being guided by a force beyond my being. I thought I was being prepared for some high government assignment, CIA, State Department or something like that. I had to pledge my allegiance.

My semester at Morgan was over, but I was attempting to get summer employment. I drove over to the campus to discuss a few things with a few contacts there. A job possibility loomed but when time came for me to make a pitch, I told one official "if they wanted me, let them come to me." The insanity of my arrogance, the reemergence of a repressed ego had skewed the reality of the hiring protocol. My ego was so out of control I felt like I was the man! And I left the campus in my orange Volvo to the tune of "Breezin," the popular song by George Benson.

Traveling on 95 south from Baltimore to D.C. a reckless fearless impulse entered my troubled mind. I wanted to see what would happen if, while going sixty miles per hour, I immediately shifted the car into drive two or even drive three. Tractor trailers were passing me on the left, but I feared them not. In the next moment without hesitation I down shifted the car throwing the car into a tremendous convulsion, a high screeching noise emerged and startled me as the engine adjusted to the sudden gear shift that had been made without slowing down or coming to a stop. Why had I done this, did I want to be killed? My mental state caused me to take risks I otherwise would not have taken.

Music was my companion during these days. I thought I was receiving messages through this medium as well. In fact I enjoyed my music so much that I went to the Volvo dealer to have two speakers flush mounted in the rear of my car. The dealer needed two days to complete the job and gave me a loaner until the job was completed. I drove this loaner, another Volvo, all over town and to Maryland back and forth. On the final leg of one of my trips when I was about three miles from my apartment on Georgia Avenue, I noticed that the car started making strange sounds as if it was going to stop on me without notice. I pulled to the side, my mind elsewhere. I figured that something mechanical had gone awry. I called the dealer and told him to send someone out to check the car, that it had broken down. The dealer sent two mechanics out to look at the car. They checked and they checked and could find nothing wrong. It turned out that the car was simply out of gas.

Back to the apartment I went. I looked all over D.C. for Linda to no avail. I wanted so much to make right what I had done. I had wronged her, in a fit of high intoxicated rage and my guilt made my search even more intense. But I was not a detective. I had no way of really finding her. Essentially my efforts were trivial and fruitless. She was not to be found. I talked to everyone I knew who might have known her; to see if she had called or made her whereabouts known. There was no success. My heart was aching. I wanted to make amends, but was prevented from doing so. She probably did not intend to be found at least by me. Rumor had it that she had befriended some guy and had found refuge with him. I knew nothing of this mysterious guy if he existed. This had been the most inhumane act I had ever exacted upon another human being in my life. I was contrite and deeply hurt by my behavior. And I was never able to make it right.

As the hours passed into days, my condition worsened. I walked down 14th St. N.W. bare footed near P street looking at the ground and picking up trash and old newspapers looking for signs and clues and for direction from this mysterious force that was directing my life to tell me what to do next. As I walked past a stately white marbled church near 14th and R St., I picked up a pair of old sunglasses that had been thrown in the trash. I threw my treasured college class ring into a field nearby as an act of commitment to the force leading my life. I was willing to do anything to prove my fealty to this new power.

A White cop passed by me on the sidewalk, walking his beat. He looked at me curiously and suspiciously but kept walking. His eyes looked into mine, his night stick dangling from his hip ready for use. I cleaned up my act enough to pass muster for the moment and to avoid any unnecessary attention. I felt threatened by his presence as he passed, but I was stealthy; I did not give myself away and we passed each other warily.

I walked into the emergency room at George Washington University Hospital, the best place for me. The admitting nurse, a mild-mannered Black woman, sent a young doctor in to talk to me. After he entered the room and sat down in front of me and began to ask me questions, I put on the sun glasses I had just found on the street and looked at him. I saw Jesus Christ, blue eyed with blond hair sitting right before me. He looked so much like the embodiment of Christ that "I knew I was on the right track." He asked me a few perfunctory questions and made his conclusion that I was alright. Again I did just enough to avoid being detected. I asked the admitting nurse a question, "does holding your breath help you calm yourself down?" She said "yes it does, it causes you to think about something else." They let me go, I was off again.

I was stark-raving mad, a victim of an undiagnosed nervous breakdown. But for some reason I was able to operate through two chambers of my mind. One plane allowed me to function fairly normally in the real world. The other chamber was guided by a virtual reality of delusions of grandeur. When I walked downtown in D.C., I looked over my shoulder and saw a long black stretch-limousine following me as though beckoning me to get in. In my virtual world, I was someone important. A high end government official, I was supposed to be chauffeured around. My car was waiting.

Next, I proceeded to a gun shop on Georgia Avenue, near the downtown area. As I walked in, I asked the man behind the counter for a gun. I had a boom-boom in my mind. I didn't know what caliber to buy or how to even buy a gun. The salesman, a White middle aged man with thinning grey hair, approached me from behind the counter. A cigarette dangled from his mouth and smoke oozed from his nose. He noticed that I was a troubled man looking to buy a gun and asked me what I wanted to do with the weapon. I had no answer. He pulled a drag on his cigarette and exclaimed, "I'm not going to sell you any weapon; get out of this store young man and don't come back." This guy probably saved my life.

When I listened to the radio on WHUR, Howard University Radio, "Breezin" was playing and it became my theme song. Whenever I heard the song, I would kick into gear. I thought I was breezing. When I read the newspapers and my horoscope, I thought I was being directed and given messages. As I was being directed, I went about certain of my duties as if I was following through on the "plan." What plan? Where was I supposed to be going? And to what end?

One of my friends called my father in Charlottesville and urged him to come to D.C. Dad was away in Richmond when he got the message and quickly got himself to my apartment in D.C. He noticed that I was clearly high-strung, but I was well enough again to make sense to him. He did not know or could not discern because of the duplicity of this schism in my head that I was either having or on the verge of a nervous breakdown. The mania was not all encompassing. He asked what had happened, and I said a girl had offered me some sex and I took advantage of it. He understood that. Dad was a man's man all the way. To me he did not seem too concerned at what he saw and heard from me. I had no way of knowing how he was gauging what he was seeing from me. Later that evening we went to dinner and we talked. When the dinner was over, he wanted to pay for the dinner but I did not want him to. I wanted to pay. My father was so used to paying for everything for me, but I wanted to pick up the check as a statement of my own independence. We hemmed and hawed until finally he relented, and I paid the check.

This episode also encompassed subliminally, a psychological desire to break away from my father who had been such a dominating force in my life. Although misguided, I was asserting my manhood, yet still needing his presence and the security of knowing he cared. I believe Dad sensed, though, he did not show it, that I was in a troubled state. But the strength of my mind kept just enough sanity floating about that the extent of my aberrations were hard to gauge by intermittent appraisal.

In the midst of the turmoil with Linda during this manic episode, I filed court papers against Dhillon to put her out of the unit. I didn't know what I was doing. I was just doing. Her legal aid lawyer defended against the legal action and asked me why I had done such a thing, since my basis for doing so was not on solid legal ground. I replied "in defense of ownership rights." I was hell bent on standing up for my legal rights as a property owner even in my weakened state. As I waited outside of the courtroom for the judge to appear, I was absorbed in my state of mind. Judge Fred B. Ughast suddenly appeared donning his black judicial robes, a short man with distinguished grey hair, he was presiding over Landlord-Tenant court during this time. These were the days of Herman Miller, the king of Landlord tenant practice in the District. Herman Miller was a short stocky White man, possibly Jewish, who wore glasses.

The judge emerged from his chambers walking down the hallway toward the court room followed by his coterie of assistants and court personnel.

When I saw him I immediately sprang to my feet out of respect for his position, it was as though I was in court. By popping to my feet so attentively it signaled to him that I was either crazy or I knew the power of his position. I was like a shell-shocked soldier, reflectively imagining what I was supposed to be or do but in reality I was not doing it. I was acting out the role of a lawyer. My intent was to show the judge that I respected him even in my weakened state of mind, even though I was not, at that time a licensed attorney. As I sat on the bench right outside the entrance to the court room, the young White female legal aid lawyer sat on my left. The judge entered the court room to begin court proceedings. The judge walked near us before he entered the double doors into the court room. He looked directly at me, as if to say, "Is this a troubled man or what?" I thought he was trying to discern what was up with me. But these thoughts were in my mind. He may not have thought anything close to that. I knew instinctively how to perform the obsequious acts of the dutiful lawyer. In many respects I resembled Don Quixote, Miguel De

Cervantes' fictional character swinging at wind mills as though they were dragons. But I had no Sancho Panza, a trusty servant, to steer me back when I veered off line in my illusory search for sanity and redemption, justice and direction. I sought only the misguided imagination of a mania-driven illusion.

In one incident I was accused of perjuring myself on a rent increase form filed annually with the Rental Control Commission. The city attorneys summoned me to court for this transgression, branding me as a potential criminal defendant for the first time in my life. The thought of this rebuke increased my anxiety. This misstep had the potential to be a problem. I had not taken the rental form seriously and had haphazardly filled it out; not respecting the bureaucracy or the process that generated it. Why had they come after me? With all the landlords in town filling out rental increase forms, not exactly accurately. Was this another one of Dhillon's operatives at work? When I received the notice that the city was taking me to court, I called my father. He said "hire yourself a criminal lawyer of some repute and pay him." I followed his advice and hired a lawyer recommended by the real estate agent who sold me the building. On the day of the hearing, Phyllis accompanied me to court. I was relieved when, outside of the court room, my attorney told me the matter had been dismissed. This lawyer was shrewd and I was thankful.

I was so distraught during this period that I wanted to get away from Peabody St. New condominiums were being built and sold in northern Virginia. Before Dad came, I went there and talked to one of the salesmen about buying a unit. Just the thought of living somewhere without the stress of Margaret Dhillon was comforting and soothing to my mind. I was searching for peace. I convinced the salesman that I was a willing and able buyer even though I had no money with which to buy. I looked at a two bedroom unit with a view and was ready to write a check for the deposit. I was serious, I wanted out. I had had it! Before Dad left we drove over to the unit and I showed it to him. He liked it but made no commitment to support my efforts. He did not know the depth of my situation or the extent of the mania that was pushing me to the extremes I was reaching. After we finished talking with the salesman and looking at the unit, I drove Dad back to Charlottesville. As we drove along the highway, there was a car in front of us. I said to Dad "that's a cop in front of us." And he said with his usual abject frankness, "Well if it's a cop, why don't you just get behind him and follow him." I said ok, and I drove behind this cop for several miles down 29 South until he pulled off of the road. The mania was still in control.

Within the next week or so after I returned to D.C, I moved all of my possessions to Charlottesville and moved into the second floor at 526 Ridge St. My cousin Wendell was living on the first floor at the time with her husband Ewanna and their son. I wanted to get away from Peabody Street, so I moved home. I stayed there two weeks before realizing that I didn't want to be in Charlottesville. It had been a laborious job moving to Charlottesville, now I was moving back to D.C.

"CURL FOREVER IN SOME
FAR-OFF FARMYARD FLOWER"

During one of my exalted moments, I called Phyllis in Chicago and asked her to marry me. Phyllis had returned to Chicago after a brief visit to the city earlier. I saw Phyllis as my queen sitting beside me as I sat on my throne. I was persuasive and she was still in love; she accepted my proposal and made plans for our wedding. My proposal to Phyllis was a cry for help to someone I trusted, who knew me. We were married in Charlottesville that summer in front of a few close friends of my parents. No one else attended. My sanity remained cockeyed, but I was still able to function somewhat. After our wedding, we flew back to Chicago where Phyllis wrapped up her clerking duties with her judge. While there, one of Phylliss's friends Neville remarked "I don't know why Otis didn't pass the bar. He certainly has the vocabulary." We had lunch with the judge Phyllis clerked for in a high end club: his farewell gesture to her. I struggled throughout the lunch because I felt I was being led by my mysterious handlers, and I lost confidence in my eating skills, where to put the knife and the fork and that stuff. I was not all there—only a part of me. It was miraculous how the illness would ebb and flow, come and go.

Each day I would see the white post office trucks with the blue and red striping along the side and top, coming and going all over D.C. And I just knew that inside one of those trucks was my admission letter to the bar. The mania kept me visualizing the mail man bringing me my letter. Every time I saw one of those trucks anywhere in the city, this was the thought that went through my mind. I was fixated on the mail. I knew it was coming.

These earlier failures ignited and revived an array of emotional, repressed racial and political inequities. Revealed ignored gaps in my maturity, my schooling and in my recognition and acceptance of reality. My naiveté had been patent. Except that I had learned the harsh realities of what it took to be competitive academically. Up to that point, my vision of learning had not been deep enough. It had been superficial and shallow, not deep and penetrating as it needed to be. I had been allowed to get by, but not anymore. "The die had been cast," "the chickens had come home to roost," and my fragile mentality was their repository.

These occurrences spawned a new birth. The birth of a committed competitor. I was always good at one on one basketball at 5th Street Park in Charlottesville against any willing opponent that chose to play me. That was my first introduction to winning, beating someone directly and personally. My most frequent opponent was a school friend named Gordon Miller. Gordon's skin color was blue black. The dark rich hue of his skin color glistened and made him a standout in a color-conscious world of Whiteness, high yellow and brown skinned Blacks. Perhaps his sub-Saharan skin color affected his personality as it has done with so many people of color. But, Gordon was a charming fellow, quiet and unassuming. He once defended me when a ruffian threatened to fight me one day at the basketball court. But one look at Gordon, and he was frightened off. He did not know what he was in for and left that pursuit on the court. I befriended Gordon because I instinctively knew he probably had few friends. And playing basketball together was an outlet for him and me. We played many games and got to know each other well. It was through him that trying to beat someone at something first emerged.

Competition, though it existed in college and in law school, was not openly discussed, except by those who knew what the game was about. I didn't. But in the mists of this frustration the sweet bird of competitiveness was expelled from my bosom like a fetus extracted from the womb of its mother, crying as it emerged into the bright reality of its new world of life, no longer shielded by the opaqueness of the womb. For without understanding the role competition plays in the world and how it operates, my success would be limited. The desire to win, heretofore latent though it had been and lacking in definition and recognition, was now front and center and henceforth would occupy my being like no other character trait learned late in early adulthood through hard experience.

THE WELL OF WATER ROSE

Though my Chicago sojourn had been an enervating experience, I discovered within myself a resiliency. I found out who I was. I had been far away from home with no support system except from within. I had thrown myself into the world of big business, divorce, urbane sophistication and elite academia and survived. I took the knocks, absorbed the blows, weathered the storms and kept standing, and in the process I had learned the law. The old Northwestern University Law School adage that hung on the wall outside the law library that said "lessons hard learned are hard forgotten," rang true.

In the process I unbridled myself from a premature marriage; true though it may have been, the marriage should have been delayed for several years. I began to live my life expansively as a young professional adult for the first time. I discovered a discipline, a sacrificial discipline required for high achievement that I had yet to fully appreciate; a toughness and joy of learning that had not shown itself before except in spurts, bits and pieces and moments of brilliance. I needed to harness these sparkles and fashion them into a constellation of continuity for sustained excellence if I was to achieve my goal and be fulfilled. Passing the bar didn't require all of this. But this is my personality, an unrelenting satiation for things pleasing to my sensibilities, that are attractive to me, drove me in this direction. This characteristic also manifests itself in other behaviors, both good and bad.

The strenuous efforts to climb this mountain was the epic struggle of my academic life, it was the culminating event. Nothing else really mattered until this score was settled. That is why no commitment to any woman could be sustained until this was finished. Would I free myself from mediocrity or would self-inflicted and systemically enforced mediocrity define my world? This was what this battle was all about. Unfortunately for me however, because of many prior judgments and the law of unintended consequences, the price of winning was perilous.

Lawyers are not by definition academics, but there is an academician in every lawyer. A renaissance academically, intellectually and scholastically was happening to me for the first time in my life.

The twin evils of naiveté and systemically imposed mediocrity mattered no more. I had contended resolutely with this two-headed monster and had finally prevailed. It had taken several years, two divorces, one child left in the breach, and a neurotic episode to shed this disease.

The nightmare struggle against the legacy of the 1896 Supreme Court decision of *Plessey v. Ferguson*, a separate but unequal segregated Virginia education; parental decision making though well intentioned albeit misguided about the direction of my secondary education; and my self-inflicted ignorance and naiveté about what it meant to be competitive academically was over. I had pulled myself up by my proverbial bootstraps, overcome my deficits through sheer determination, hard work, diligence and perseverance which yielded its return.

My pedigree would not allow me to be defined by the mediocrity that enveloped my academic life. My genealogy and my class laid claim to the station in life to which my vision had attached. My ability to achieve the vision was always present.

The bottom line: it was all my fault. No school had failed me. I had failed myself by not working as hard as I could with the opportunities that I had. It was my responsibility to make my dream a reality. Nobody forced me to want to be a lawyer. The gulf between the dream and reality would be as wide and as long as my naiveté, my strategy, my preparation, my test taking skills and my energy for persistence. I had to find out what it would take to climb the mountain step by step. If there was no one there to guide me, I had to find my own way. If my vanity kept me from being plaintiff about my short comings in the arrogant world of legal elitism, that was my problem. I had to recognize the problem, deal with the issues and resolve them, and that is what I did.

Passing the bar for some law graduates is no more difficult than stepping over a three-foot wall. Some wear their britches out attempting to scale what to them is an eight-foot barrier. I was somewhere in between. The wall separated me from an unrequited passion for achievement and self-actualization. Many of my colleagues went through this exercise unscathed, while others got caught in the net. A segment of this population fails to overcome for one reason or another. Still others choose not to endure the ordeal, accept their law degree as simply an academic achievement, and move on to other non-law practice endeavors. There are many hushed horror stories of applicants for the bar who have failed to pass the bar. Lives have been wrecked, and changed. Lives have been redirected and I dare say there are many who have suffered psychological problems because of this obstacle.

One Texan, a tall heavy set dark skinned Black man not unusually obese, with a bellowing voice, and who had been the victim of several failed attempts to pass the bar, roomed with me while we both took the Pennsylvania Bar Exam. His famous mantra was, "if they won't fuck, they won't fight!" Why this expression was so important to him is still a mystery to me when I think about him today. But this is what he was always saying. I often wonder what happened to him. What did this expression have to do with passing the bar exam? He didn't make it and it was apparent that he had been severely damaged by the ordeal.

An insurance man from the Mutual of New York Insurance company (MONY) with whom I worked between 1975-76 after leaving Chicago but before I went to the U.S. Chamber of Commerce, was a neurotic basket case because he could not pass the bar. As a result he had to sell insurance for a living. He carried peanut butter in his car with him wherever he went, making peanut butter cracker sandwiches sitting in his car that left his car smelling of peanut butter with cracker crumbs all over the floors and seats. He had failed to live up to his father's expectations.

For a law school graduate, not passing the bar exam is similar to being left behind, not being allowed to move to the next level. A repeat of this result is a fractured ego and shattered self-esteem. There are no subsidies such as minority set-aside programs and affirmative action when it comes to professional licensing exams in medicine, accountancy, law and engineering, though politics does enter in. You either pass or fail. But the vestiges of slavery and Jim Crow are ever-present in the American system of "equal opportunity."

Society scorns and sneers, and makes distasteful jokes about law graduates who are unsuccessful at the bar; there must be something wrong with them. Those who don't pass don't like to talk about it. This is damaging to law graduates because they already think they know everything and view themselves as high achievers; as highly-wound stallions eager to hit the ground running.

This tortured path is littered with the remains of crushed egos, broken hearts, shame, neuroses, psychoses and self-pity. As I have said, I recall some buddies whose lives were changed for the worst because of a failure to get past this exam or to finish law school. The bar exam tests the competence of law graduates, and as such may discourage some law graduates who are not truly committed to becoming attorneys; it separates the wheat from the chaff; it winnows out the weak in the interest of protecting the public.

No one owes you anything in this world. You have to take responsibility for making out of yourself what you envision for yourself. It was my decision to engage in destructive behavior by smoking marijuana to fill some psychological need. Perhaps my personality and my manner of dealing with rejection and defeat opened a pathway for destructive behavior to surface. Regardless, this had been my passage.

The road of life by definition is filled with disappointment, failure, detours, obstacles and vexations. Character is determined by how we cope and manage our way through these travails. Unchartered ground such as what I encountered as a first generation lawyer can make the road particularly rough but not impassable. I had made the mistake of equating passing the bar exam with my self-worth. Rather than realizing that passing and flunking exams is a passage of life for any aspiring professional, not life itself.

My plight was aided by vanity, lack of insight, no consistent mentor, poor gamesmanship and not learning from others, tongue in cheek. I was a second generation college graduate, and my parents were educators not lawyers. What I was experiencing in my case was first generation lawyer blues. Someone in my family had to learn how this game was played.

One tear had become a creek, another a stream, and as each tear fell the well of water rose until it had engulfed me. As I approached the banks of this undulating river of tears, each drop had taken a piece of my heart with it and reflected the cost that had been paid for that tear. I could see the future I wanted on the shores of the other side. The waters that separated me from the beckoning shores glistened with the translucent hue of blue, muddy brown and green inviting me to venture in and to cross. There would be no hesitation for I had been shorn of the shackles that bound my mind for many years before. I strove to the other side by crossing the twin bridges and in so doing shed the yoke of mediocrity and pierced the veil of naiveté.

I remember an aging actor, when receiving an Academy Award, uttering the biblically textured phrase "the Lord's delay is not the Lord's denial." Certainly that had been my case. I always had a deep inner faith that I would make it. I didn't know when, and I didn't know how, but my inner voice was sure. I was stretched to the breaking point but had not broken, at least not irreversibly. And I had enough sanity, drive, energy in reserve and love for the law that I embraced my future with the fermented effervescence of a dream deferred.

In the words of the great gospel singer Mahalia Jackson, "my soul looks back and wonders how I made it over."

Thirty years ago, after relocating from Chicago, Illinois, I lived in Washington D.C, and it was there, in the fall of 1977, that my bar admission letter arrived without fanfare but with great anticipation. I opened the letter gingerly, my heart throbbing and my hand shaking. My blood pressure rose and my breathing became staccato in length as my eyes hesitantly gazed down to read the writing. State Board of Law Examiners, Supreme Court of the State of Pennsylvania, "we are pleased to inform you that you have successfully passed..." That was all I needed to read. For me it had been an arduous task breaking through. I had moved from Chicago two years earlier when the bar results came in. Several years of struggle had finally come to an end. I had become a lawyer by sheer persistence, a refusal to quit, a glutton for pain and a relentless drive for self-actualization.

The euphoria of that moment intoxicated my mind like no drug could ever achieve. I sat down on my couch, holding the letter in partial disbelief, and exhaled so deeply I could feel my stomach muscles straining to touch my spine. It was a cleansing exhalation. Now past the fright of disappointment, I relaxed and read the letter word by word savoring every syllable with no fear, knowing that the conclusion was a fact and would not change. I had striven for this result for several years, realizing how the writing on this parchment would change my life forever. Healing could finally begin. I became what I had sought to become.

If this episode had been equivalent to a pro football draft, my passage would be equivalent to being taken in the 5th round. This was my moment. When I called my friend from Charlottesville to tell him the news, he said "I can't beat that." I did not call him for him to "beat it," I called him to share a personal moment of success that I thought would be received empathically. Instead my friend looked upon my triumph as another competitive leg up. You cannot expect people to feel your pain or your joy to the extent you do regardless of how close you perceive them to be to you. The highs and lows of life we share with one another are all shared vicariously.

On this day I had become one of the fortunate ones. I had made it to the mythical other side. I was finally a lawyer. I could have caved in, thrown in the towel, but something inside of me would not let that happen. Black folks in the legal community in Chicago often said, "You ain't a lawyer until the White man says you are a lawyer, regardless of how much law you know."

I stayed up all night reveling in this outcome. I called my parents, my ex-wife and a high school friend. My parents were ecstatic, for they had gone through some of my trials with me. I am sure they remembered, and perhaps reflected upon, the crying and out pouring of emotion months earlier while I was in Chicago. Parents set the table of values for their children. If the table is set properly and reinforced through example, the child will eat continuously from those values for the rest of his or her life. I had learned from my parents the values of hard work, perseverance, energy, ambition, dignity, love of family and respect for property. Even though they could not fully appreciate the deep psychological relief I felt, at this moment, they shared as much as parents could in my elation.

I called my ex-wife Phyllis because we shared a connection that resonated from the struggle we went through alone and together a few years earlier in Chicago. I was never jealous of Phyllis. Our relationship was on a much higher plane; she epitomized what I was striving for. She was smart, competent and on her way to achieving success. Here I was, stuck, spinning my wheels in the mud of anguish. She said upon listening to my news, "well, you made it in." I said "yes! It finally happened." She had little to say beyond that. For her it was anticlimactic after what I had put her through in Chicago, not including our most recent troubles. The ink had yet to dry on our recent divorce decree at the time this news broke. She was happy for me but not ecstatic. The sincerity of her love was never at issue. She was more than decent, and I had and still have a great respect for her.

After moving back to D.C. from Chicago in 1975, Phyllis also found her way there for a short stay. After finishing law school, she clerked for a local judge in Chicago. She was highly regarded in the legal community she worked in. She now clerked for a prominent judge in the D.C. Court system. The breakup between Phyllis and me had been particularly painful because of the distortion in my personality wrought from enduring the peaks and valleys in our relationship and my professional ups and downs. And my gradual realization that my selfish needs from a marriage did not match what Phyllis was offering. I had come to realize through all of my trials what I really wanted in a wife. It was gratifying to me that Phyllis was a lawyer, and we had many common interests. She had been a bridge over troubled waters. But deep down, I wanted something else. Perhaps more softness, more compassion, more femininity and a willingness to do the mundane chores required of being a wife. The embers of that relationship still smoldered. Even though we were physically apart, she knew my plight, having witnessed it first-hand. There would be no rapprochement this time; we had hurt each other too much and been through too much. Better to let sleeping dogs lie.

The balm to quell and to repair would now come from a healthier lifestyle, good lawyering and hard-won success in court, having a client thank you for a job well done or a judge commenting that, "you did a good job on this case." Slowly the negatives of the past would be ground into the strengthening cords of character. The accolades, over time, would heal the wounds and make this painful experience only a fading memory relegated to the dust and ashes of the past. One among many battles won and lost in a successful career.

20

THE PHILADELPHIA PRACTICE

"Law, the secular god"

A S THE MANIA RECEDED in its intensity and my mind righted itself, was I any different than I was before all of this happened? Yes, I was! I knew what I had been through. An indelible experience that would always remain in the recesses of my mind had seared my consciousness and given pause to any excesses in my lifestyle caused by the combination of stress and dope, or stress alone. I had been to the mountain top and looked into the depths of the abyss, and hadn't liked what I had seen. I had peered into my personality and witnessed an ego that was unrelenting in its thirst to be satisfied, an itch that had to be scratched. And if it had meant my destruction to satisfy that thirst, the price, I believe, would have been paid.

It was as though my unthinking autonomic nervous system had taken control of my being. And it had. But in the process, I had been transformed. My New York friends no longer mattered and were no longer in my life. I eschewed the small-minded people from my home town and no longer embraced, even momentarily, the triteness of their *modus vivendi*. I had made new friends when I returned to D.C. from Chicago, renewed some old relationships, and made them better. It was as though, through this process, I had been made ready for the new journey I was about to undertake. I now knew my limitations—and knew them well.

Mel Williams, a friend from undergraduate school who had become a doctor, re-entered my life during this time and we renewed our friendship. We began to hang out and I felt security in his presence. I met several of his doctor friends and they became daily associates of mine. Mel was living with a woman who many believed was unsuited for him, but I didn't have a solid opinion on the issue, for she had always treated me decently.

Shortly after leaving Morgan State University in Baltimore, Maryland in the Department of Business, and later as director of an economic development project at Howard University I secured employment at the U.S. Chamber of Commerce. When the Pennsylvania Bar results came in, I was working at the U.S. Chamber of Commerce as a Panel Executive for the Panel on Product Liability and as Associate Director of the Center for Small Business. The U.S. Chamber is a trade association that represents the business community in the policy making apparatus of the U.S. Government. Pennsylvania had granted me my professional life and in years to come physicians in Philadelphia would save my life.

Not long after the bar results came in, I resigned my position at the U.S. Chamber of Commerce and had a goodbye luncheon with the Vice President of the chamber and my immediate boss. They were very gracious and wished me good luck, but regretted my leaving. I made plans to go to Philadelphia. There was never any thought of relocating to any other city, even though there were several small, pleasant Pennsylvania towns closer to D.C.

Months before resigning from the chamber, I took several trips to Philadelphia to scout out apartment buildings. My plan was to buy a building that I could both live in and rent out, and that could also serve as an office–the same formula as I had used in Washington.

When people asked me, "Why did you go to Philadelphia?" or, "What brought you to Philadelphia?" I would lie and say I had relatives there and business associates I knew from the chamber. In fact, I went there simply because I had passed the bar in Pennsylvania. That was the main reason, even though there were other factors as well.

But there was another. When my colleagues at the chamber and on Capitol Hill asked me why I wanted to go to Philadelphia to practice law, they claimed that there was nothing exciting there. As one said, a friend who worked in the office of a prominent senator from Pennsylvania, "All you'll do is the same old stuff, over and over again." Well, that "same old stuff" was fascinating to me. I hadn't done any of it yet. And I wanted to get into the fray, to be a functioning lawyer in a city where I had the power and stature of a law license. I wanted to taste how that felt. I wanted the experience and nothing would keep me from having it. As Jack Johnson, the Black heavyweight fighter who took on "the Great White Hope" said, in a movie of the same title "I got my chance to be the champion of the world and got to take my turn."

On my last trip to Philadelphia before leaving the chamber, a real estate agent drove me down Germantown Avenue in northwest Philadelphia, between Upsal Street to the north and Johnson Street to the south. I had no idea where I was; it was all new to me. He showed me this nice four-unit building facing the avenue with a sizable front yard and deep back yard. I particularly liked it because it had a recessed facade from an old storefront.

The building was stone and masonry trimmed in wood—an ornate architectural style that reflected a baroque influence. However, with all its charm, a gothic mournfulness emanated from it. Despite this, it had a reception that was dignified in appearance and seemed quite suitable for my plans. It was attached to another building on its north wall and had originally been a single family house. At one time or another, it had been divided into apartments and old White folks reminiscent of the Dutch and German settlers who had originally settled the area in colonial times were the existing tenants.

Of all the buildings I had seen on my trips to Philadelphia, Germantown Avenue was my second choice. My first was a stately building on Tulpehocken Street several blocks south. But that deal didn't go through and I lamented the loss.

As the agent and I toured the Germantown Avenue building, school children were coming out of school and walking home. I was so impressed by how nice the

Germantown Building, 2008

children looked, dressed in their plaid school uniforms, little girls with their hair neatly braided into quilts of squares lubricated with hair oil glistening from their heads and skinny brown legs with white socks folded above the shoe line. They were an idyllic vision of how school children ought to look. In my mind, I was contrasting them with what I had grown used to seeing in D.C.–an undisciplined rag-tag of ghetto youth looking to be warehoused for another six hours.

This area of the city seemed bucolic and genteel to me; rustic and quiet. The buildings were huge, with large, cavernous rooms and constructed of old stone and masonry. The neighborhood looked like a place in which I could make a home, gain some quietude, and make real my vision of what I wanted my life to be practicing law in this town. This was one of my first impressions and it would remain my lasting impression except for the intrusion of the urban ghetto around the edges that characterizes most neighborhoods in the city, especially where unorthodox housing designs and patterns are allowed by the local zoning board.

The move to Philadelphia in June 1979 turned out to be a real *auto da fe*, a public declaration of judgment that I passed on myself. My dad's tussle with the Albemarle County School Board was at an end. His career as an educator was coming to a close and mine as a lawyer was beginning. Mom and Dad drove to D.C. from Charlottesville. Dad had his trunk filled with office supplies and stationary. He had cleaned out his office for me.

As Dad and I drove around D.C. talking and shooting the breeze, he said a few things that have always stayed with me. He said, "You deserve watching!" By that he meant I had made it. He was giving me a compliment, an acknowledgment of my achievement. But did he also mean that I would be observed by him and others as I played the game? Or was he saying that I had become somebody of interest to those who had an interest?

His words turned out to be true "You deserve watching": a haunting expression, awkwardly put, and one of Dad's many cryptic, yet comedic expressions, rich with meaning.

This was a new thing for the Lee family and especially for Dad. He had labored hard in the vineyard of life and had a lot to show for it. He had gone far from his humble beginnings in Fitzgerald, Georgia, where he had been one of seven children raised by an uneducated but not illiterate mother, and with no father. But I had stepped up the ladder from him in real terms. Dad had dealt with lawyers in his business and professional life, and he knew something about what this achievement could mean for me. It was a good thing. He also told me, "try to be as thorough in your work as you can. If you work at it for ten years, it will take care of you for the rest of your life."

How did he know that? I don't know. Perhaps he had garnered his perspective from his dealings with real estate lawyers, all those court sessions he had attended where he had played lawyer, and from the bankers he had dealt with in his business.

By the eve of my departure, I had signed a contract on the Germantown Avenue building, but had no job and nowhere to stay. I had expected to close on the building within a few weeks, but the weeks turned into months.

Meanwhile, Mel's roommate planned a going away party for me. She bought some fruit and made some cakes. She did everything except provide the place. All my new acquaintances came for the feast in my apartment on Peabody Street. We had a great time laughing and joking and just generally enjoying the merriment. It was a great day! Through some odd set of circumstances, I had found protection within a new group of friends who had come together at this particular time to render solace and comfort to me. I often wondered whether or not they knew what had happened, that perhaps someone had told them, or just how did this new coterie of friends develop? I had always wanted to hang out with this type of crowd, but never seemed to rate. All of a sudden, I was one of them; I was accepted. What had begun as a retreat now ended with a new beginning, a new offensive. That for which I had given so much would not disappoint me in the return on my investment, the pain in its application, nor in the richness of its reward.

I packed my belongings and moved to Philly. I knew I had to drive up Interstate 95 to get there, but that was about all I knew. I was stepping out in faith, just as I had done when I left for Chicago in 1972.

In order to gain a perspective on life in Philadelphia, I asked a Black cab driver. He gave me a dour outlook, saying "Philly is a dope-infested town...Everybody in Philly is on dope." Perhaps this represented his way of life. I didn't know what to believe, or whether to believe, but was not too discouraged. I had a few contacts in the suburbs from my days at the chamber. However, when I called on these folks, they let me down. They had encouraged me to come to the city, but now that I was there they had nothing concrete to offer me. I was suddenly on my own; I didn't even know how to get to Germantown Avenue.

My parents had suggested I call some relatives who lived in Philadelphia to see if they could put me up for a few days until the closing on Germantown Avenue. But my father's cousin said, "Oh, no! You can't stay with me." As a result, I spent my first few nights in the International House in West Philadelphia. This was a big building that comprised several small, pleasant housing units. I had a single; it was small but safe and comfortable. The whole place was teeming with activity and students. People were moving and grooving all over the place.

The University of Pennsylvania operated the International House and mostly foreign students stayed there, but there were American students living there. I was alone. I knew no one and did not know which way was up. After being assigned a room, I remember lying on my slender twin bed staring at the concrete walls and wondering what to do next.

When I relayed the news of my predicament, my family told me that my cousin Pat was living in Philly. I had not been aware of that when I arrived, so I called her and she was receptive and engaging. She had been living in Philadelphia for some time when I arrived, so she knew how to get to the International House. She jumped in her car, drove over and picked me up. She let me stay in her small spare bedroom in her apartment in North Philly until I had settled on Germantown Avenue.

Pat was the fifth child in a family of six. Overweight but pretty, she had a charming personality. Her skin was ebony and her hair jet black. I knew her from our days together in Fitzgerald, Georgia. We had grown up apart, yet shared a common family relationship: her mother, Maebell, was my father's half-sister. As kids growing up, we had picked cotton and cropped tobacco during the hot summers in the long farming fields of Fitzgerald. We had gained a familiarity with one another over the years forged by my father's dedication to ensure I knew the people of his family through repetitive summer visits to their home.

Pat moved to Philadelphia several years before I ventured there. She went to live and work with her sister Tobytha, who we called Sis. Unbeknownst to me at that time, Philadelphia was a place that many in the Lee family had gravitated to in generations past. The Lees went to Philadelphia from South Georgia and did well there. They had owned a retail outlet in a section of the city; were principals in the criminal court system; ran for elected office; and generally made progress. So perhaps, in the scheme of things, my gravitation there was not solely of my own doing, but was a place of destiny set down for me by the souls of my ancestors.

Pat's apartment sat atop a funeral home, a distinctive corner brick building attached on its right side to an adjoining building, a row-house office building. It was built in the typical style of Philadelphia—a cavernous, two-bedroom unit with high ceilings and crown molding. Bleach-dried ceramic tiles rimmed a chair rail that circled a kitchen littered with antiquated appliances and an old kitchen sink, all of World War II vintage. But it was certainly adequate for our purposes. Pat had saved the day and was my Black knight in shining armor.

Ostensibly, Philadelphia is "the city of brotherly love," the Liberty Bell, Independence Hall, Benjamin Franklin, the first capital of the United States and the capital of American history; hoagies, and of cheese steaks.

The dilapidated storefront exuded the odor of fried onions on the grill, with slices of thinly shaved steak frying on top of the onions. The onions were diced and stirred in with the sizzling, frying steak. My mouth began to salivate. My cheese steak was butterflied and provolone cheese slices layered on either side. Then the roll was spread on top of the heap of meat and onions face-side down. With a spatula, the cook swept up the frying steak strips and onions onto the Amoroso roll and flipped the mix right-side up as steam emanated from the sandwich. A Philadelphia cheese steak was born! Add a dash of salt, pepper, catsup and pickles, and something to wash it down and we were ready for the game—any game. The Phillies, the Flyers, the Eagles, the 76ers, or the renowned Philadelphia Orchestra. And for dessert, how about a Philadelphia Tastykake? It is a city where good food is the rule, from such diverse points as Independence Mall in the east to the Philadelphia Airport in the south.

In reality, Philadelphia is the city of "cut the jugular vein." A city of hardball tactics. That's the way the game is played there. Within the last forty years or so, the urban poor who inhabit its streets are unable to maintain the antique homes of their White forefathers. The economics are beyond their reach. And the city government faces a huge challenge to reverse the trend of decay and dilapidation. It would require at least a billion dollars to restore and rebuild some of its neighborhoods, and even that might prove to be only a drop in the bucket.

Philadelphia is a mix of discordant strands lingering from the erstwhile glory of the colonial and Victorian eras, the modernistic economic development of the cityscape, the rot of racism, drug abuse, excessive taxation, a dwindling tax base, and the misguided education of the poor. It is a city where the public schools are so bad that a mature private school industry sustains itself by catering to the children of the enlightened. It's a city where Jews have a disproportionate influence on the body politic; where public schools are closed on Jewish holidays, but not on significant Black holidays, excluding only Martin Luther King's birthday; where politics are king, the labor movement is queen, and the unions are the knave.

Philadelphia is a giant oak tree with its roots deep in the soil of American history. From Center City, its branches stretch out to the south, north, east, and west in a tangle of neighborhoods: The Art Museum, Independence Mall, Center City, the Northeast, Chestnut Hill, Germantown, West Mt. Airy, East Mt. Airy, East Falls, Roxbury, West Oak Lane, East Oak Lane, North Philly, South Philly, Old City, the Main Line, Manyunk, Roxborough, Wynnfield and West Philadelphia, and many others. Old buildings of the seventeenth, eighteenth, and nineteenth centuries populate the neighborhoods, buildings with lavish ornamentation that are massive in size. Many of these magnificent buildings were built by early German, Swiss, Austrian, and other European immigrants who settled in Philadelphia between the seventeenth and nineteenth centuries. The houses have stone exteriors, slate roofs, masonry walls, high ceilings with crown moldings, chair rail moldings, parquet floors with marquetry made of pine, oak, and other hard woods, oval transoms, and built-in dining room servers. But so many of these Victorian and colonial structures are now crumbling and in decay.

The Poles, the Jews, the Blacks, the Irish, the Italians all have their own neighborhoods, along with their own political clout and patronage positions in city government. It is also a union town–the unions control all organized labor in Philadelphia and can bring the city to a halt. Philadelphia is a small Chicago and it suffers from all the same ills. Ethnicity, race, acculturation, and money divide the city.

Head hunters have labeled Philly as unattractive to job seekers. Could this be because of the drab aura that pervades certain sections of the old districts, lingering from before America became the United States? Or could it be because of the ubiquitous graffiti scrawled on boarded-up buildings that stand beside trash strewn vacant lots where cars have been abandoned to await final dismemberment.

The old elite of the city is still composed of cold and arrogant sophisticates, urbane and cunning, suave, and dressed in haute couture, fashionable dress. But the people in the hinterlands are the exact opposite. They are the ones who welcomed me with a certain naiveté and were politically unsophisticated but did not remain; they are the common folk, looking for a respite from the toils of Philadelphia life; they are the blue collar people, those who had made Philadelphia what it was–a vibrant, colorful, hip, religious city that was slick, hardcore, and tough. These people give no quarter and let the chips fall where they may.

When I arrived, most Blacks were unable, except for a limited few, to attend the elite University of Pennsylvania, though their population numbers dominated city demographics, and they were also largely excluded from the other major universities that surrounded the city. The White population refused to surrender its control of the city and fought to hold on to what was dear to them: Center City, their neighborhoods, police and fire departments, city government jobs, and the nexus of commerce.

The city suffered from a virulent form of racism expressed through the trumpet of Frank Rizzo and the Rizzo machine, which was condoned and acquiesced in by the White community that kept Black Philadelphia in its place for years. Frank Rizzo, the embodiment of Philadelphia racism, was police commissioner from 1967 to 1971. He was elected mayor in 1971 and served two consecutive terms. He ruled Philadelphia with an iron fist and viewed Blacks as animals–and treated them as such. Blacks were unable to coalesce against his tyrannical rule until the seeds of Black political sophistication emerged in the late '70s and early '80s. Harold Washington's election as mayor of Chicago portended the political changes that would occur in Philadelphia a few years later. On 3rd August 1979, a US District Court charged Rizzo and eighteen high ranking city and police officials with acts of police brutality, although the charges were later dismissed.

The ethos of the city was reflective of Rizzo's racially polarizing politics of "keep the Niggers down," which reverberated throughout the fibers of the city and made for some tense moments between the police and the Black community. In years to come, this backdrop of racial discrimination and containment caused a whole neighborhood to be destroyed in a conflagration of historic proportions.

I didn't know Philadelphia in the heyday of the Rizzo era. I was there at the tail-end and eventual termination of that era. Horror stories about police brutality, overzealous cops and overt racism abounded in Philadelphia history, yet the city was also known as a beacon of liberty for freed slaves and had led the way in establishing minority set-a-side programs instigated by the federal government in the construction industry, the forerunner of modern affirmative action.

Lang and I often wondered how God was going to solve the Rizzo problem in Philadelphia, but in 1979, the corrupt "law and order" maverick was succeeded by William (Bill) J. Green III, who appointed the city's first Black managing director, W. Wilson Goode. In 1983, Frank Rizzo ran again for mayor but lost in the Democratic primary to Wilson Goode, who went on to become mayor–the city's first elected Black mayor.

In the fall of 1986, Rizzo ran for office one last time, this time as a Republican. In the primary, he fought against Ronald Castile, the Philadelphia District Attorney. If he won, it would lead to a final face off with Democrat Wilson Goode in the general election in November of 1987. During the campaign, Rizzo beat up on his opponent, asking, "What's the deal, Castile?" which became his slogan. It referred to a cozy yet unclear relationship between Ron Castile and some big-government-connected Philadelphia law firms. Rizzo won the Republican primary but lost to Goode in the general election. However, he remained a colorful figure in Philadelphia politics and many Blacks were fearful that he could get back into office. There were many Whites in north and south Philadelphia who liked what Rizzo stood for and the Rizzo mystique haunted Philadelphia until July 16th, 1991, when he suddenly died, the rumor was, of a massive heart attack caused by ventricular tachycardia. His death finally lifted a veil, bringing to an end the politics of racial hatred and alienation that had crippled Philadelphia.

I had come to the city near the end of that period, when police brutality and outright subjugation of the Black minority characterized the politics of Philadelphia. But finally, the Rizzo era was over. A new day was dawning. Philadelphia was on the verge of changing for good. Bill Green, the man who first beat him, was a White aristocratic Philadelphian whose father had been a big man in Philadelphia politics, so there was a regal quality about his ascendancy to the mayoralty. And with his ascendancy, Philadelphia left behind its legacy of Jim Crow, Northern-style. Philadelphia has a way of saluting its blue bloods, its royalty, its Princess Grace types who rise up from old Philadelphia money–and Bill Green was one of them. He was a beneficent change from the old style politics of Frank Rizzo's overt racism. The city breathed a sigh of relief and welcomed the change. It made us all feel better about our home and its prospects. A new era had begun.

Bill Green brought innovation and a new breed of democrat into Philadelphia government. Besides appointing the first African American Managing Director of Philadelphia, W. Wilson Goode, he supported Joe Coleman as President of the Philadelphia City Council. Coleman provided another breath of fresh air after all the scandals and unsavory backroom dealings that had previously characterized Philadelphia politics.

Operating in full view at this time was the "Abscam scandal." This was a bribery scandal involving the city council president and several councilors. The federal government was prosecuting this case, and it spread like wild fire through the city of Philadelphia. Philadelphia has a political history of "pay to play"–if you want to play in Philadelphia politics you have to pay the money. Being a political animal, but eschewing any thought of participating in Philadelphia politics, I was just an interested observer. Labor unions, politicians, some crooked judges, the mob and the like made for a rich mixture of brine and sorghum.

21

"LIFE FOR ME AIN'T BEEN NO CRYSTAL STAIR"

P HILADELPHIA HAS ALWAYS BEEN KNOWN as the beacon of liberty: where the Liberty Bell sits, where Independence Hall is located, where the Continental Congress first met, and where the Declaration of Independence was drafted and signed. But for Blacks this is historic irony.

Blacks fled to Philadelphia on the freedom train during slavery and after Reconstruction. And they migrated to Philadelphia from the South during the Great Migration, under the mistaken belief that they would be escaping racial discrimination, isolation and marginalization. Instead, they ran smack dab into it. Sure, Philadelphia was better than Virginia, Mississippi, Alabama, Georgia, Florida and the Carolinas during those times, but it was far from a panacea. Northern Whites discriminated against Blacks insidiously. The racially gerrymandered election and school districts were geographically based upon housing patterns and White flight. They denied Blacks access to quality education and hence entrance to the city's top universities and jobs.

Philadelphia still is one of the most racially segregated and viscerally racist places in America, unless your economic situation allows you to rise above the obvious or you belong to the professional class that gives you some entre into White Philadelphia. To be a Black Philadelphian is to know your place in the city and the nature of what makes Philadelphia the city that it is: a sophisticated east coast city; at one time, the fifth largest market in the nation, after New York, Los Angeles, Chicago, and Dallas-Fort Worth; a big city with teeming skyscrapers and professional sports teams and world class universities; a big city with a small-town mentality; a city of neighborhoods and racial boundaries and at one time the city that published more medical textbooks than any other city in the U.S.; a city of poor Whites and poor Blacks each living in their own enclaves.

My instincts directed me to the northwest section of the city: the communities of Upper Germantown and Mt Airy. Here, all races interacted with one another and this section of the city was probably the most liberal area of Philadelphia. Upper middle-class Blacks and progressive Whites populated this area and intermingled with relative freedom.

Blacks in Philadelphia, in my view, are divided into three tiers. The elite is composed of the professional class, including those who claim heritage as far back as the Mayflower in 1620, of which there are a few, and the Boule, who also include some Black "firsts"–the first to be admitted to the University of Pennsylvania, the first to have hospital privileges at a Philadelphia area hospital, the first to pass the Pennsylvania Bar, the first to be appointed a judge, and so on. Many of these folks dwell in West Mt. Airy or the higher end sections of West Philadelphia.

The second tier, the middle class echelon of teachers, insurance agents, bureaucrats, small business entrepreneurs, police officers, firemen and politicians, generally live in Wynnefield and some parts of West Mt. Airy, East Mt. Airy, West Oak Lane, and East Falls, and Old Town.

The lower classes are essentially illiterate in one way or another; street smart but far from being learned individuals, they comprise the day laborers, blue collar workers, construction types and those receiving government assistance of one kind or another; they are the city-slick, ruthless in their survival techniques. These are the ones who live off lawsuits; they are the hustlers and those thrown into the cauldron of urban life without a raft, the *hoi polloi*, the common people, scorched by the burning flame of high taxes, poor education, drugs, crime, and murder.

Exclusion and subjugation from all sides make for a cruel breed of inner city Philadelphian. These folks live in North Philadelphia, some parts of West Philadelphia, lower Germantown, and in housing projects located in various parts of the city where the guiding light has yet to shine. They are the ones clamoring to move up and want out. W.E.B. Dubois's description of the "Philadelphia Negro" perhaps provides some historical background.[21]

Not everybody in Philadelphia was a lawyer, thank God, nor a politician or a big shot, as seemed to be the case in D.C. In Philadelphia, you got what you produced. If you became a professional, you were allowed the rank of a professional. If you worked in the trades, then that was your position. There is no artificial subsidy built into the Philly system. You were what you became. I liked it that way. The competition, though stiff, was not so intense. You were allowed to spread your wings. The marketplace determined your worth.

When I arrived, rumor had it that a Black had not passed the Pennsylvania Bar exam in years. One of my law school buddies, who is now a prominent Philadelphia lawyer, was among several who sued the Pennsylvania Bar and broke through the barrier that had existed before me. I began my professional life in the city by attending a "Bridge the Gap" legal education seminar held at Dickinson Law School in York, Pennsylvania for newly admitted lawyers transitioning from being law students and for older lawyers wanting to keep up. Soon afterwards, I found my way to my first law office in the Robinson Building on the corner of 15th and Chestnut Street in Philadelphia's Center City. I gave no serious thought to obtaining a job in a law firm. Instead, I would become a solo practitioner, even though I had never imagined myself in that role; it just naturally evolved. I had worked for other people, but now I wanted to work for myself.

Solo practice is for the Lone Ranger type. The last of a dying breed. Yet for many, and for me in particular, it is the only way to practice law. It is difficult and burdensome, but for those who have problems getting along with others, taking orders from other people less endowed intellectually, and who like to be their own boss, I felt it was the only way to go.

Surprisingly, although the sole practitioner is often referred to as a dying breed, lawyers continue to practice in this form, one way or another. I reasoned that I was too "old and ugly" for the law firms. After all, I had not distinguished myself in law school. Even though my grades were good, they were not exceptional, and I had no particular legal specialty, except for my familiarity with estate planning and the law of wills and trusts. I had no clients to trade on and nothing to bargain with; in effect, I had nothing to sell. No one wanted me: my stock was not on the "buy list."

As I pondered my fate, I kept hearing my father's old rejoinder, "Root hog or die poor." For me, becoming a lawyer "ain't been no crystal stair." It was all part of "hanging out my shingle." I had to make my own job, create my own demand; my success or failure would not be about "luck, it would be brought about by "pluck." And the sections of the law in which I had some background would soon distinguish me from many fine Philadelphia lawyers.

There I was, a practicing Philadelphia lawyer in Center City, Philadelphia, with no one to practice on; no clients, no stationary, no way to pay the bills. No one knew me. I didn't know the city and I had no reputation. No friends or enemies. But I did have good instincts and a natural acumen for business. And I knew the syllogism of the law: facts, law, analysis, and legal conclusion.

The logic of this approach had been drummed into me from my past experience and I knew it had to be applied in every case. As a distant old Black lawyer, as I mentioned before, had once told me in Chicago, "The closest thing to freedom for a Black man is being a lawyer." To which I added, "and having some money." I was finally in the bosom of that freedom.

My transit from the wilderness to the Promised Land, that Middle Passage, had left scarring where there should have been the skin of virginal unfettered confidence. What I had internalized from my bar experience now played a role, even if only occasionally, in my day-to-day outlook; it was a fleeting shadow, not a constant plight, but if stirred up, it caused anxiety. And, as a further consequence of my past experience, I developed a brittle, tough mentality, and I didn't except "no" for an answer to anything. I was resigned to the fact that I would have to do everything by myself. There would be no helping hand, except at the end of "my" own arm. No one was going to give me anything without a price being paid. With that understanding, no one could discourage me or intimidate me, except the occasional judge, but this too would evolve.

Was this an inevitable rationalization of my situation, or was it how I metamorphosed my experience? Or was it a consequence of being an un-mentored neophyte lawyer in a big, mean, unfamiliar city seething with greed, avarice, arrogance, self-interest, and sophisticated lawyering–a city with a long, rich and glorified tradition in the practice of law? I had arrived at the mountain top, so what else mattered? I had paid the price, so what else was new?

I had some good experience in banking and knew the will and trust business; I had been a business consultant, a college instructor, a real estate investor, and a junior political executive at the U.S. Chamber of Commerce. My maturity was growing. The cumulative years of education and work and experience were there. I knew what I knew and no one could take that from me.

These were my advantages. I could not be frightened. I accepted the fact that I didn't know anything about the real-world practice of law and would have to weave my tapestry from the whole cloth of my own experiences and mistakes. But, as Ross A. Webber of the Wharton School at the University of Pennsylvania said in his book, *Management, Basic Elements of Managing Organizations* (1975)[22], "Decision-making is 90% information and 10% inspiration." What I lacked in information about Philadelphia and the practice of law I made up for in inspiration.

The road I was about to travel was a "road less traveled," in the words of the poet Robert Frost. But whether it would turn out to be the road to professional fulfillment, the road to domestic tranquility, or the road to financial security, I didn't know at the time. However, I intuitively knew that I was going in the right direction. And I knew that you didn't abandon the road because it was rough or had sharp curves, slopes, unexpected blind spots, or pot holes. As long as the road I was on headed in the right direction, even though I might not be able to see the end of it, I had to stay on it. That was my approach.

I had always pushed myself beyond the expected. Expected more from myself than I had a right to. I constantly criticized myself and always wanted to do a task better the next time. I was driven to achieve some measure of excellence. As a result, my problem was not the fear of failure. I had proceeded beyond that boogeyman. I was brimming with confidence–all chuckles and smiles. This confidence may have spawned from naive bliss, but it enabled me to go further and achieve more than normality ordained in my Charlottesville community and more than the system prepared us for or expected. I had not been detoured, defeated, or discouraged in my youth.

On the other hand, I had only known success on one particular level and in one specific environment. I was in a state of closeted and youthful exuberance. Sure, I had chosen not to be mediocre, but I didn't know just how hard it would be to rise out of my mediocrity in a world that constantly wanted to push me down. When I left Charlottesville in 1966 and went to college, those naive smiles faded as the real world entered in. And now in Philadelphia, the world kept coming in and kept coming in, until the rain started to pour on my parade.

Where did my youthful, exuberant mentality come from? This brazenness to excel, to be different? I was always reaching. I had no fear, I was confident in my innate ability. In another instance, while I was running on a track in Silver Spring, Maryland, one day, a friend met me there. He ran one lap or two and then quit. I asked him, "Why don't you try to run further?" He demurred. His life had been that type of experience, settling for less. I pushed on further and ran a mile, perhaps more.

Where did I get that bigger-than-life drive, that resilience, that energy to suffer in the service of achievement, that desire to be the best, to win? My father had great energy and a capacity to withstand a lot; he had withstood abject poverty and mediocrity in his education, but he had emerged a determined visionary. It was in the genes. And vision is more important than skill, though skill is essential to implement the vision.

Because Philadelphia was a cold, uncaring city when you had no inside track to run on; because it was a thicket of insider trading, in both business and politics; and because I was not a native son, I had to stay firmly on the beaten path. Stand on firm ground. However, this was extremely difficult for me because I was an outsider. And my predicament was exacerbated by the absence of any mentoring confidante in the profession. I had no-one to talk to or help me through.

Professional pride and vanity played a major role in an anxiety that could at times embolden this issue for me. It became a stark and painful choice. How much ignorance should I admit to and how much supplication should I endure to get help from someone I didn't know, in a profession of the all-knowing? This would be one of my dilemmas.

Confidence is a state of mind, whereas competence is an objective standard applied to the professional in the community in which his profession is practiced. Competence enables confidence. The latter is derived from the former. But how could I be confident after having endured my daunting trek to lawyerdom? I had to forget all that. It was history. Gone, past. And the path makes a big difference to a professional's confidence whether he is a neophyte or is experienced. For the neophyte lawyer, his burden is heavier; the experienced lawyer has an advantage.

This issue could not be resolved until I had gained ample experience in the bowels of the pit, in the muck and mire of all the legal battles that had to be joined. Like sediment that settles to the bottom of the river bed and is aroused by agitation, confidence and competence would only become issues when things didn't work out. In order to destroy, to eviscerate the baggage built up from those bar years, I would have to fight and win my legal battles, and by so doing, prove my mettle to myself and to others. I had to grind the vestiges of that period into a powder so fine that the past would only be a fleeting memory unrecognizable to the inattentive. To do that, I had to protect my psyche–at least, the remnants of the seeds that remained.

However, the emerging seedling of my fragile psyche was trying to force its way up through a jungle of bigger plants that were trying to block or otherwise dim the rays of sun on my emergent professional life. It was no place for the faint of heart, the tender soul, or the fragile shoot. I had to find a protective casing, a greenhouse that would protect and encase that seedling in an impenetrable capsule, so that the onslaught of the world I had chosen to enter, with its many prickles and thorns–all pointed at me–would do no further damage as I undertook the formidable task of making myself into a successful, competent, practicing Philadelphia lawyer.

The German adage, "That which doesn't destroy me, makes me stronger," had application here. My mind was actually stronger than the vulnerabilities I had imagined. What had happened to me in those bar years was both an aberration and a warning. It brought to my attention my limitations, and told me that I would have to respect them–or suffer the consequences.

I faced three problems that persisted for every practicing lawyer: the court, the client, and the bar. It was within the context of balancing all three that my success would be measured. They consisted of parallel sets of consequences, which were not always in sync with one another–and more often than not, were at odds with one another, either on the human level, the secular level, or the ethical level; and they all played out in front of the public and were placed on the record in what the French called the Theater of the Absurd.

The law is filled with road maps, pathways, and instructional briefs for how to do things and get things accomplished. It is an exact science, the logic of which is scripted and expressed in language and legalese understood only by those in the profession. It is an exact science in an inexact world of uncertainty with costly consequences affecting liberty and property. The law is a traffic cop, regulating human behavior offering a forum for the redress of grievances, in the mad scramble of people trying to feather their nests and fill their rice bowls–plenty for the elite and scarcity for the bedraggled poor. Like ants bumping and grinding, pulling and pushing in a gridlock of organized chaos, society gropes and lunges forward. Law and religion, though polar opposites, offer a respite to the weary. If religion is the platform upon which spiritual life is built, law is the chassis upon which society is built. It has become our secular god.

Ross A. Weber's book, *Management* (1975) again rang true to me: "Time is a dynamic process for achievement-oriented people." This phrase stuck in my mind. I never forgot it. And though I didn't consciously apply it in everything I did, the meaning of that phrase reverberated in my approach to my work. I threw myself into the task of building a law practice from scratch in a city of no brotherly love. No one, at this time, referred any cases to me. I was given no help whatsoever to understand the Philadelphia Court system. It was an up-from-the-bootstraps operation.

It is every individual's job to make something out of himself, if he chooses to do the work and pay the price. Hopefully, it will be affordable. Becoming something is not self-executing. It doesn't happen by itself. My journey and my challenge was to make something out of myself, to "do the best with what I have to work with," within the context of my world and my dynamics. So my new job was to make myself into a competent lawyer, do some good, and make some money–the enabling ingredient.

The Robinson Building is a twenty plus storied high-rise in the middle of center city at the corner of 15th and Chestnut Streets. With marble floors and revolving steel doors at its entrance, a lobby small by comparison with other buildings of its size, four steel elevators zipped you up to your floor. The hallways were sullen with brown dark wood paneling with matching commercial indoor and outdoor carpeting inlaid in each hallway. Because of its proximity to city hall, this building is a popular office building for lawyers, court reporters, process servers and an array of commercial small businesses providing aid and comfort to the legal profession. This cottage industry typifies Philadelphia's legal community. Many small businesses exist to provide services to lawyers. Philadelphia is a lawyer's town, just a hop, skip and a jump from city hall, where the various courts of the Philadelphia Court of Common Pleas are located. The Robinson Building is a known address.

The lease holder of the small office I rented—on August 1, 1979 for six months for $150.00 per month at Suite 1212 Office No. 4, Robinson Building at 42 South 15th Street—was a lawyer from my law school, Richard McDaniel. His friends called him Rick. McDaniel was older than me by five or more years and had been practicing law as a solo practitioner in Philadelphia for several years before I arrived. A short man, quick witted, somewhat rotund with engaging eyes; a churlish demeanor with brown skin and short black hair. He always dressed like a lawyer, good suits, polished shoes, white shirts and silk ties and he moved with haste. Rick wasted no time. He never raised his voice, and he always spoke in a whispery hoarse tone. He is a wily shrewd Philadelphia lawyer. Though he was not my mentor he had the capacity to be. But either because of his demeanor or my reticence, the right hand of fellowship did not extend much beyond the rent check. That is not to say that from time to time in the midst of his hurried pace, he did not offer timely insights into various practice issues, but I was not under his or anyone else's wing. He never showed me how to do anything nor did he offer me any substantive practice tips. But from time to time by the mere fact of being in his presence, I was on the receiving end of a pithy remark here and there, crumbs from the master's table.

What I learned from Rick McDaniel, I learned purely through observation. It was all business with Rick. When he spoke to you, it seemed as if you had become his client. He always spoke in an instructional voice. "Well, you see, it's done this way." Or, "What you're going to encounter is this..." Most of the time, McDaniel left me on my own. He owed me nothing and I should have expected nothing. Rick is a decent individual and an honorable man, but not very charitable. The relationship we established 30 years ago is still based upon the same chemistry of facilitative benefit and hard-won mutual respect. We get along well.

In the Robinson Building, Rick's office suite consisted of two large offices of comparable size and one small office at the end of the suite. The two larger offices were next to each other and connected to the open space that stretched the length of the suite where the secretarial bay was housed. The small office also connected to the open bay area. Dark wood paneling with matching brown indoor and outdoor carpeting was inlaid throughout the office. He offered me the small space in the back of his office of about 350 square feet. The office had a desk, a chair and a phone. There were no pictures or paintings on the wall, no file cabinets or typewriters, file folders or stationary, pens or pencils, not even my diploma or bar admittance certificate. It was bare bones. If you wanted those things, they had to be purchased. Robert Redmond, another young lawyer also rented office space there. Redmond had one of the two larger offices and McDaniel occupied the other. There was one secretary and she worked for McDaniel. If you wanted her to do any work for you, you had to pay her and get Rick's permission so that his work would not be interfered with.

McDaniel appeared to be at that time a process-directed lawyer. He knew his way around the court system. He knew how to practice law and had been in many battles.

When I told him where I was living, with my cousin in North Philadelphia, he groused, "Man, that's where most people are trying to get out of." McDaniel thought I was some poor kid who had gotten his break in life through the law. I didn't do a thing to disabuse him of that perception. Most of my associates in Philadelphia would come to ascribe this same perception to me—a poor boy who worked hard and who had some smarts. They were all mistaken. But that mistaken perception worked well for me.

When I left for work each morning from Pat's apartment, I would shower, put on my suit, walk to a corner bus stop on Diamond Street and wait for the bus. During the summer months the heat was oppressive and beads of sweat trickled down the side of my face early in the mornings. I knew I was in territory that was not used to seeing a Black man dressed in a suit and tie with a briefcase in his hand.

I felt that many eyes were on me. Survival in the inner city is an art form. No staring, keep your eyes in front of you and act like you know where you are going. No one bothered me and I traveled to work for eight weeks this way with no incidents. McDaniel offered me a ride home one day, and I could tell he was ill at ease about going into the neighborhood. Not knowing much about Philadelphia, I was not as keenly aware of the reputation of "North Philly" as McDaniel was. People from Philadelphia viewed North Philadelphia as the poster child for ghetto. But for years before the ghettoization of North Philadelphia this was the place where immigrant Whites, lower, upper and middle class Whites lived and worked. The three-story, faded, orange-colored brownstones with their high ceilings and masonry walls were classic neo-gothic constructions from the turn of the century. These old brick buildings were for the good livers back then, and were within walking distance of Temple University and Center City. The block to the bus stop was lined with old, three-story twin buildings with a stoop out front. A local Black doctor had his sign out announcing his office hours.

Lawyers often rented more office space than they needed and then subleased the excess rooms to other lawyers—to reduce their overheads and encourage other lawyers to join their firm. Lawyers who do this often hope to build a firm or an association of lawyers who want to be together without a formal fee-sharing arrangement.

Before I signed my lease, Dad came up for a visit, and I took him to see my proposed office. He agreed to pay my rent for the first ninety days to get me started.

Redmond was more intriguing to me than McDaniel. Redmond was my contemporary. His iconoclasm and handsomeness were attractive traits. He was a man of medium height and build with short wavy black hair and an aquiline nose. He had a rich copper brown complexion. Redmond was well educated. He had a business card reciting that he had a PhD and a JD. As best I could discern he went to Georgetown University Law School in Washington D.C. As I began to observe Redmond more closely, I noticed some of his methodology for the practice of criminal law. Redmond had a desk file of 3x5 cards on every Pennsylvania Supreme Court case on the Fourth Amendment and search and seizure; on the Fifth Amendment self-incrimination; on the Sixth Amendment, the right to counsel; etc. Redmond was the real deal, a student of the law and an intellectual. Not being simply process-oriented myself but substantively directed, I learned something from Redmond. I begrudgingly allowed my ignorance to show in order to learn. There was so much I did not know. I did not feel ashamed because there were things I did not know. If there were issues you were not knowledgeable about, then as a lawyer you were expected to get into the books and find the answer.

But the learning process can be made so much easier if someone just told you either where to look or showed you the way. But some lawyers are unwilling to do that especially in the world of solo private practice where every solo lawyer is in competition with every other solo practitioner. Grabbing for all they can get and protecting their turf like a mother hen. Knowledge is power and knowledge costs money in the legal world. Legal insight and information is closely guarded. My eyes were opened and I felt a kinship to Redmond's approach. We gravitated toward each other and developed a warm relationship. I cared for the guy. I do not know what Redmond thought of me, but he seemed to have some positive feeling toward me. I knew Redmond was a substantive guy and that I was not up to his speed at that time. So my pride kept me from completely revealing how empty my hand was.

Our relationship did not extend beyond the office. Redmond kept a certain distance and he kept his private life to himself. Redmond would tease search and seizure issues out of every criminal case he undertook, whether or not the issue existed on the face of the facts. It was just his method. He would file an omnibus pre-trial motion challenging the stop, the arrest and the search in every criminal case. And he would always tell me "never to stipulate to anything the D.A. wanted you to, always make them prove everything." I embraced his approach and I followed his advice in my cases. He was right.

Redmond characterized McDaniel as a schrewd capitalist from a bygone era because McDaniel was all about making money. McDaniel was the legal entrepreneur. Redmond called the clerks in city hall "drones" because of the repetitive nature of their work, docketing court filings and stamping in court papers, much of which required little or no thinking. He also advised "that every client was a potential adversary." No truer phrase was ever spoken in this profession. I learned more from Redmond than from any other single lawyer. Instead of dressing up, he dressed down. He preferred the "Harry the bum look." Redmond was not pretentious and he was smart. That is why I admired him. He was unafraid and was a student of the law. Redmond said, "There's no such thing as permanent friends, just permanent interest." I had an "intellectual" love affair with Redmond, and months after I began renting office space from McDaniel, we left.

As I began to "get my legs" in the practice, while renting office space from McDaniel, I started advertising my legal services in the Philadelphia Daily News for divorces, criminal cases and personal injury cases. Little did I know, what I had started would last for twenty years. It was surprising to me that as a newcomer to Philadelphia and to the practice of law that I would have the vision to start advertising when Redmond and McDaniel had been practicing many years before I arrived and had not ventured to do this. My phone began to ring. I got business and they noticed right away. Now I had to learn how to do what I was advertising that I knew how to do.

I always believed in investing in myself. So I bought the books I needed and attended the legal seminars on the subjects that interested me. And I took my first shots. One of my first clients came into my small office and paid me thirty dollars to start on his divorce, my first fee. I put some of the money in the bank and with a few of the dollars I bought my first Fisherman's hat at Wannamakers Department store on Market Street. I became a fisher of men.

Next, I wanted to launch my estate planning business. Not knowing any insurance agents in Philly, I went through the yellow pages and made a list of life insurance agents that I thought would be amenable to a solicitation to work together in this field. I knew from my days in Chicago that this was a way to get off the ground in this area. In Chicago I worked with lawyers to bring trust business into Harris Bank and with many like-minded insurance agents. Leo Burnett, the general agent for Mutual Benefit Life on the South Side of Chicago, introduced me to John Hill, one of his agents, who often amused me by telling me the tale of the "old bull and the young bull" both standing on the slope of a hill admiring a herd of cows below.

The young bull wanted to rush down to the herd, scaring them away in the hope of catching one or two cows and having sex with them. John would say, "The young bull said to the old bull 'Man, lets go down there and get them all.' The old bull replied, 'Slow down there young man. If we take our time we can get them all, one at a time.'"

"I LOVE THIS CULTURED HELL THAT TESTS MY YOUTH!"

"Although she feeds me bread of bitterness,
And sinks into my throat her tiger's tooth,
Stealing my breath of life, I will confess
I love this cultured hell that tests my youth!"

From *America* by Claude McKay

To GET STARTED IN THIS BUSINESS I had to get referrals. I was able to get McDaniel's secretary to type the letters. He had given her orders not to do any of Redmond's work or mine without his approval. He paid her salary, we did not. The secretary was a brown skinned woman with a high school education who was totally controlled by McDaniel. She could be persuaded because she had a certain naiveté typical of young Blacks who came from a "north Philadelphia" environment, who somehow learned to type either in high school or on-the-job training and could begin to see some hope for themselves through the secretarial path. Working for a lawyer in Philly was considered a good job. With his consent and my payment, she typed up fifty letters or so introducing me to the insurance agents, expressing my knowledge and desire to work with them in the estate planning field, and I mailed them out. I received some phone calls but only one visit from an agent. His name was Lang Dixon.

Lang worked as an insurance agent for the General American Life Insurance Company in Philadelphia somewhere between 1979 and 1994. But he was not just another insurance agent. He was the quintessential insurance agent and the recipient of many high achievement awards. He didn't finish college, though he did attend for a year. Humble beginnings epitomized his early start in life; he was raised by his grandmother. Lang was a tall, handsome, African American, sub-Saharan in skin color, with small, thin pink lips. He wore gold-rimmed eyeglasses, kept his black hair closely cropped and often styled it with a comb, particularly after removing his hat. Lang was an attractive man, garrulous and full of life. He was interested in world events and so we shared that interest. Also, he truly loved Volvos.

While launching my estate planning balloon, I was advised by lawyers in the office to get on the judges' appointments lists. Back then, judges assigned to the criminal division, known as Quarter Sessions Court in Philadelphia, were allowed to appoint an attorney on their list to represent an indigent defendant. These lists were added to the court system's list of attorneys who could be appointed to represent indigent defendants.

To get on the list, a lawyer had to solicit the judge and request to be put on. But, before adding a lawyer to his list, most judges wanted to interview the lawyer to get a feel for his depth of knowledge. This was to ensure that a green, neophyte lawyer was not appointed to a homicide or rape case, where his inexperience would mean justice would not be served.

Politics entered into the process of selecting lawyers for these lists because all judges had their favorites, whom they appointed to their cases. For example, homicide cases were usually handled by a select few lawyers on each judge's list—every judge reserved those cases for his favorite qualified practitioners. These cases also paid the most.

Curiously, Howard University and Howard Law School were well represented in the judiciary in Philadelphia. A representative group of its alumni sat on the bench and practiced law in that city, probably because Howard is not far from Philadelphia. Many aspiring law students who could not get into the Philadelphia law schools considered Howard as their next best alternative. There is something in the air between Howard University and Philadelphia, which was a good thing for me. It made me feel at home and lessened my burden of proof in the city and within the legal community.

Young and old lawyers maintain their names on the list for the same reason: to earn fees. But young lawyers like me also got on the list to obtain experience. Trial experience is what every young lawyer worth his salt wants to attain. The appointment to a judge's list allows you to learn the court system, visit the jails and prisons, earn some fees and learn how to practice criminal law.

Court appointment fees are considerably less than a lawyer would expect to be paid if privately retained, but who was going to retain an unknown, untested lawyer in a criminal case who has never tried a criminal case before? So I made the trek to City Hall to visit the local judges in Quarter Sessions Court to get on their list for court appointments for indigent criminal defendants. Some judges obliged without the need for an interview, while others insisted upon one. So off to City Hall I went to meet with the judges, briefcase in hand, tie and coat smartly in place.

City Hall is a mammoth structure located in the center of downtown. It is a U.S, Pennsylvania, and Philadelphia landmark constructed in 1860 in a similar style to the Old Executive Office Building in Washington, D.C. Its clock tower rises 510 feet above the sidewalk. It sits on its own circular plot of land and stretches an entire block. The corridors of the hall are at least 70 meters long in each direction. Every December, the city's Christmas tree was installed in the inner courtyard. The building is so large that one can enter on the north side and exit on the south side of the city. The same can be said for the east and west sides of the building. The gray hue of its stone exterior, with William Penn affixed on top, makes for a striking entre for anyone entering Philadelphia. Around the promenade near each oval entrance stands a statute of a prominent Philadelphian—either a soldier on horseback, a full frame figure, or a bust. The building has a courtyard at street level with oval entrances that intersect at the north, south, east and west with several cross-streets that divide the city. Located in what was once known as Center Square, but is now called Penn Square, the building is exactly in the center of Philadelphia.[23]

City Hall houses the Philadelphia Court of Common Pleas and several of its divisions, including the Prothonotary's office—the main clerk's office. The Pennsylvania Supreme Court sat there as well, when in session in Philadelphia. The courtrooms were of various sizes. Each had a sign hanging from the transom of its door. Some courtrooms were large and expansive with high ceilings, huge windows, and a large public sitting area. The large courtrooms echoed your voice and the judge's bench was elevated high above the floor and wrapped in rich dark woods emanating majesty and honor. Below, to the left or right, a smaller bench was reserved for the court crier, court clerk and court stenographer. Behind the judge's bench were his chambers, usually a large room where his valet personnel and his secretary tended to his needs. These large court rooms were ornate and had old oil paintings of famous judges placed on the walls inside those court rooms over which they had presided in their day. Overall, a rich judicial tradition was commemorated and preserved throughout the courtrooms of City Hall.

Scattered between the government offices on the first floor were several courtrooms where misdemeanor trials were conducted. The Prothonotary's office was located on the second floor. The third floor contained felony court rooms, misdemeanor trial rooms, the Motion Court, the file rooms, and other court administrative offices, including judges' chambers. The fourth floor was reserved for the Orphans' Court, where estate settlement issues were resolved. The remaining floors had felony courtrooms, the holding cell for prisoners awaiting transport to a courtroom, file archive rooms, the tower, and the clock level–eight floors in all. The Mayor's Office and City Council offices and chambers were also located in the same building.

McDaniel, the ever present busy lawyer, was always on the move but very secretive about his movements. Lang on the other hand was energetic but tentative. Lang was looking for an anchor and a partner; we needed each other to advance.

One day, McDaniel, taking a moment to lecture me as he kept working, asked me, "What is going to be your primary practice area? Because whatever it is, you'll begin to get referrals in the area you practice most." I thought about that question, but I didn't dwell on it. I went ahead and pushed forward on all fronts, not having the luxury to be a specialist just yet. But what I knew most about was estate planning. So I launched my estate planning career, with all the peril that it entailed. I was on several judges' court appointment lists, and I began advertising for no-fault divorces.

Meanwhile, Lang was always on the attack. He never stood still without something to do. And most of what he did concerned his insurance business. Lang was a go-getter. He had just moved his family from Madison, Wisconsin, where he sold life insurance under a General American Life Insurance Company general agency. Now settled in Philadelphia, he was anxious to push ahead in the estate planning business. He had a wife and three children and had recently purchased a home in suburban Philadelphia, so he needed to make some money.

Upon arriving in Philadelphia, Lang affiliated himself with a Black casualty insurance brokerage firm, Watlington & Cooper, Inc., selling car insurance, fire and liability coverage. The firm was an upstart Black group. Black businesses in Philadelphia were rare in 1979. Philadelphia lagged in Black entrepreneurship, one of the regressive features of a city light-years behind other major cities when it came to progressive Black overtures in business and politics.

The casualty brokers Lang affiliated with had just started their firm when I moved to Philadelphia. Lang was not a casualty man, but the firm offered him an office and a place to start. Their vision was that he would enlarge their business by selling life insurance to their casualty customers. He knew from his experience in Madison, where he sold the concept of estate planning to Oscar Meyer meat packing executives, how the business could sell. I drafted wills and trusts for his clients and he sold them life insurance to fund the trusts.

Thus, we established our own system by creating an "estate planning team," a concept I learned from my days at Harris Bank in Chicago. Our team was made up of a lawyer, an insurance agent, and a trust officer. I had been the trust solicitor in Chicago, but now I was the lawyer.

We were a hit. We worked with many prominent Black doctors and higher-ups in middle-class Black Philadelphia. I built my reputation as an estate planning attorney on the basis of Lang's referrals, as he built his reputation as an estate planning life insurance underwriter. This was new to Black Philadelphia. In Philadelphia, there had never been a Black twosome like us. Just as in Chicago, Blacks had been relegated to the lower rungs when it came to estate planning, money management, and trust services. The average insurance agent didn't sell this business in the Black community, even though successful White and jewish agents made big money selling these services to their clients.

Lang was one of the best and brightest in Philadelphia at what he did. Even though he had been foreshadowed by a fellow named Ted Tillman, an agent with New York Life Insurance Company who sold this business, Lang began to far outdistance him by his sheer tenacity, energy and reach. Lang made it into all the top clubs in his industry, including the Million Dollar Round Table, and became a leader in Black insurance circles.

Meanwhile I began to gain a reputation as an estate planning attorney. One of a few, if not the only one, in Philadelphia at this time who knew more than one side of the business. I went to all the trust departments in Philadelphia looking for an affiliation. I found them in Girard Bank and Provident Bank. I used the same system I had used in Chicago: I used the executive dining room in the bank to get business, entertain clients and close the deal. Many Blacks had never been above the first floor in most banks. They had never seen what a trust department looked like and I introduced them to this new world. The world that I knew.

However, this was not all plain sailing. I suffered from serious inner turmoil. The causes of this self-doubt were the professional ramifications of the work I was doing. Even though I was working with Lang, as an attorney I was flying solo; I had no back-up, no firm of lawyers behind me. I was by myself, a solo practitioner.

To protect myself, I kept to the trust system, which I knew well, and put all my documents through the counsel section of each trust department to which I submitted documents. My documents were then reviewed and corrections suggested for my consideration. This gave me some sense of ease that my work was being reviewed by other professionals.

But I had to stay on the "beaten path." I didn't know enough to be creative. Creativity breeds errors. The one thing you learn from being in the lawyering business is there are gradations of knowledge. Your level of expertise only equips you to go to a certain point and no further. In most instances that point is far enough beyond the knowledge of most lay and professional people that you can add value and guidance to the undertaking and make money. However, as the French say, "For every smart one, there is one smarter." Knowing where to get off and when to bring others more knowledgeable in is crucial. As Christopher Hitchens recites in his book, *god is not Great*[24], "Knowing the extent of your ignorance is the definition of an educated man."

Lang didn't have to be concerned with these issues. He was only focused on selling insurance. I had to be concerned with the bigger picture: how this plan was going to work in practice. Lang would brag about my drafting prowess, but I didn't. He was the salesman; I was not. Perhaps he really thought my work was good, or maybe it was just his way of puffing us up in front of a client to make the sale. Whatever his motives were, it worked. We got a lot of business.

I was always reminded as I went forward of a quote my daddy would often repeat when I was growing up in Charlottesville, "Nothing passes across a horse's back that doesn't buckle under his stomach." I knew I was responsible professionally for what Lang and I were implementing for these families. I couldn't get too lightheaded on the hyperbole. This was not a game, though Lang and I certainly enjoyed our success. So my glee was always tempered by reality. I didn't lose a lot of sleep over this issue, but it was one of the many stressors that added up as the load got heavier.

After every signing and execution of documents, I would leave the bank and walk the streets of Philadelphia, west on Chestnut Street then back east up Market Street, past the boutique shops and the maddeningly impersonal crowd and wonder to myself, "is this really real? Am I really doing what Terry Netsky and Ron Mora had done in Chicago eight or nine years ago? Am I really implementing that experience? Am I embodying that same idea?"

The answer was, yes, I was. I had come full circle. And it was immensely gratifying to me, a personal triumph after my nightmarish and heartbreaking experience in Chicago. I was now making money from that trauma.

But I still had a lot to learn. On one occasion early in our practice, I gained a valuable lesson about patience, professionalism, and how to handle the collection of fees from a client. Lang had sold his estate planning idea to a prominent Black Philadelphia architect. I had drafted the documents and we set a signing appointment at Girard Bank. We sat around the rich, mahogany, glass-covered conference table on the fourth floor in the trust department. When all was done, I asked to be paid and the architect balked. For some reason, a heated discussion resulted and barbs were exchanged between the client and me.

I said, "Chuck, the fee is $600 for the will and the trust agreement and I would like to be paid now," nervously pretending to be confident.

He said, "Otis, it's not my custom to pay on demand. I will pay you in due course!"

"What the hell do you mean by 'due course,' I expect to be paid now, man!" I responded, totally out of character.

I had let my insecurity about being paid outdistance my character. Had I forgotten where I was? I had lost my dignity and lessened the elevation of the moment and the caliber of the work that had been completed, all for the sake of money. Had this really been what this was all about? It was a mess and totally unprofessional from everyone's standpoint. Had chauvinism replaced dignity and class? For the moment it had.

I learned a valuable lesson from this encounter. Young lawyers have their biggest problem with charging and collecting fees. The confidence to charge for your work is a bridge that must be crossed and if there is trepidation, the client can smell blood and push the lawyer around. Subliminally, such timidity is a sign of a lack of confidence in your skill level and in your work. The hardest thing to realize in this profession is that, even though the quality of your work may be good and the disappointment may be great in the way clients perceive its value, you must be discreet and maintain your dignity when it comes to fees and money. You can equate the quality of your work to money, but you can't let a client's view of paying fees equate with the quality of your work.

Some clients balk at the fees, or may have no intention of paying you, even from the get-go. So the likelihood of receiving payment must be taken into consideration before you start on any assignment. That is why many lawyers insist on a deposit paid up-front, a retainer, and once that initial payment has been exceeded, they will expect the client to continue to contribute as the case goes along. It took me a while to appreciate the value of that approach. It prevents a lot of arguments and misunderstandings.

I should not have argued with that client over fees, even though he knew I expected to be paid after the signing. The trust officer was absent that day; had he been present, his objectivity would have prevented our lapse into crassness. Collecting fees is a science and an art in the lawyering profession.

23

"HER VIGOR FLOWS LIKE TIDES INTO MY BLOOD GIVING ME STRENGTH ERECT AGAINST HER HATE"

LANG AND I CONTINUED TO WORK in the estate planning business until his death many years later. In the interim, I was busy pursuing other facets of my practice. After sharing an office with McDaniel for a year, Redmond and I decided to strike out on our own. Redmond liked the idea of advertising for no-fault divorces and wanted to get in on that business, so we left McDaniel.

Redmond and I got along well, but he had a certain arrogance about him, and though we could have been much, much closer, he chose, for whatever reason, to keep me at a distance. So the love didn't last. Even so, I was still able to observe how he operated and take a closer look at how the law business worked.

Redmond could write the law reasonably well, and he always viewed the parameter of a lawyer's writing as a good determinant as to whether or not he or she was any good. In fact, Redmond was hired by other lawyers to write their briefs, which was a real eye opener. He didn't get the work because those lawyers couldn't write the briefs themselves, but because it was more cost efficient to hire someone else to do it. The quality of brief writing can make a difference in the outcome if the facts and the law are present in the record, otherwise draftsmanship is not an issue except to the naive, who think that everything had to be done from whole cloth by the lawyer himself. What mattered most was that "the work got done," the client's rights were protected, and the court was satisfied.

To some judges, Redmond was a good lawyer, and to others he was a nuisance. In one pivotal case, when he was defending a criminal defendant, he pushed the nuisance button too far. While arguing a Motion to Suppress, he refused to follow the judge's request to "move on."

Taking a deep breath and exhaling cautiously, knowing all eyes were on him, he continued in his deliberative style, questioning the witness *ad nauseam* and making little progress on a legal point he felt would sustain his motion.

The judge admonished him again: "Mr. Redmond, if you continue with this line of questioning, I'm going to hold you in contempt."

"But your honor," he implored. "This very important issue will prove that my client was illegally searched."

The judge responded, "I have heard it all before Mr. Redmond, and for the last time, you either move on to another issue in your motion, or I'm going to dismiss the motion."

Defiantly, Redmond labored on, arguing that he was not going to abandon the point until the witness had given his full testimony.

I admired his bravery, but not his politics. He had failed to consider the temperament of the judge and his proclivity to be obstinate. He was before a seasoned, older, Black female judge, one of the first to be installed on the Court of Common Pleas bench. She ruled with an iron hand and had little tolerance for fishing expeditions that yielded little substance. Exhausted of patience and sensing Redmond's obduracy, the judge lowered the boom. "Mr. Redmond," she said with a stern voice, implying that 'I'm the ruler of this court not you,' "I have warned you that unless you get to the point I will hold you in contempt!" Not long after Redmond had resumed his examination of the witness did the gavel slam. "I am holding you in contempt. Bailiff, take Mr. Redmond into custody to the cell block," she commanded sternly.

The Black, muscular bailiff came forward and put Redmond in handcuffs. Redmond didn't resist. Momentarily bereft of dignity, and powerless to change the course of events, he was hauled away like a common criminal. He was embarrassed and shocked, his courtroom strategy had forever been shattered. His client looked on in amazement and disbelief as the bailiff escorted him with his head bowed, his suit jacket crumpled by the twist of the handcuffs, his tie dangling from the loosened collar of his white shirt, down the long and lonely corridors of justice.

The elevators at the end of the hall went up to the seventh floor. There, he was led to the cell block where prisoners were waiting to be taken to their courtrooms for hearings. As he was led away, I thought about my childhood friend Marcellus Easter on North Avenue in Richmond, Virginia when I felt his pain as the boys beat him. Each blow reverberated against my body as though I was being hit.

Once again, my empathy was in high gear as I ascended to the cell block to visit him and to offer to be of service. At this point in my career, my comfort level with visiting inmates in jail was still forming. As I entered the cell block and the turnkey motioned me to come forward, I loathed the look of the place, the smell of urine, the wildness. The detainees resembled animals caged by a power they were unable to overcome. As the clang of the heavy iron grey bars slammed behind me, locking me in, I momentarily thought how painful it would be if I couldn't leave this place, but had to stay. The reverberations of the cell door locking behind me sounded an alarm in my own inner sanctum: "But for the grace of God, there go I."

The guard brought Redmond out. He was sullen and visibly shaken by the experience. He was chastened, but not broken. As I gazed upon his countenance, to my surprise, I experienced a deeply existential moment. Several thoughts went through my mind: "Would this have happened if Redmond had been White? Why would a Black woman judge treat a Black male lawyer in this manner? Was it necessary? Were his actions so egregious that this level of heavy-handedness was required? Do Black folks really love and respect each other, or was this "brotherhood thing" just a synthetic affectation easily rejected when self-interest and ego predominated? Black folks should be ashamed of themselves for the way they treat each other, knowing – if they do know – what most of us are up against. Do Black folks really care? Why are we so keen on enforcing a system that brutalizes us?

I often remind myself of a scene that kept circling back and forth in my mind over the years. It arose from an experience I had while I was completing my basic training in ROTC in law school. The Reserve Officers' Training Corps is a college elective that focuses on producing officers by instructing them in military leadership development, problem solving, strategic planning, and professional ethics. It was during basic training at Fort Indian Town Gap in Pennsylvania that our unit had been out on maneuvers all night. And as we settled down for a few hours as the dawn approached, I positioned myself against a tree not far from the White captains and colonels and other officers who were leading the operation. The darkness of the night obscured my presence and they spoke freely. As I lay there I heard them say derogatory words to effect that, "these Black recruits, it doesn't matter how good they are, they'll never count for much."

As I heard their discourse, I realized that, as far as those White officers were concerned, this whole ROTC exercise was a joke. All our striving was a joke. As far as they cared, for Black people, it wasn't worth it. They totally took our lives and efforts for granted. It didn't mean a thing to them. Our lives didn't matter. This is certainly not true in all regards and there are many exceptions, but at this time that was the impression I was left with by those officers.

In a few moments, I was disabused of all my naiveté about America and the sacrifices White America expected Blacks to make. And, in response, I became disillusioned, cynical and confirmed in my disbelief. Why the heck should I give my life for something that America doesn't have true regard for? In my view, I valued my life and sacrifices more than America did.

On reflection, I now realize that this is a very complex question. Yes, I had given my soul to make a "Faustian" deal with the devil to accomplish the goal of becoming a lawyer. But was it, in fact, to be a lawyer that I had sold my whole being? Or was becoming a lawyer just a metaphor for being accepted as an equal–as a smart, intelligent, and accomplished human being who could be proud of himself and be the embodiment of the vision of being a lawyer that I had for myself; to be what I knew I could be. It was all of that. I had never been the type of person to be defeated by mediocrity, or to accept an "Amos and Andy" type education. I was better than that! I didn't go to law school because I wanted to help people; I went because it was a statement about me, about where I saw myself in the world. I was born with this lofty impression of myself and had shown manifestations of my talent, but I was fighting against malignant and benign forces that were determined to reinforce their vision of a caricatured Black man wallowing in poor self-esteem and deflated ego. This thing about helping other people only came about when I was able to help myself, to prove that I had the capability to be what I had shown myself capable of becoming–exceptional.

As I watched my partner talk to me from the other side of the cell window, my attitude toward the lofty purposes proclaimed by this system and espoused by its promoters, enforcers and protectors was being changed and recalibrated. This was a sobering picture, a glimpse at the underbelly of the reality of the nothingness, the triteness, the arrogance of a system I had to finesse. What had I paid such a heavy price for? Was it worth all the hoopla? Did the client, after all this, even care?

Redmond disclaimed any fault for his circumstances and berated the judge for an overzealous reaction to his conduct. His use of invective toward her was justified and he merited a chance to reclaim his dignity. My heart went out to him. Was this job really worth all this? Was Redmond's act a badge of courage or a badge of disgrace? Does zealous advocacy include going to jail for your client? Putting your own freedom at risk? I think not.

I knew then that my advocacy, though spirited at times, would immediately be curtailed when I sensed, either that I had gone too far, or that the futility of it all made it not worth the effort. That is perhaps why I never saw the law as an end in itself, but rather as a means to other ends. I have respect but really little faith. And I don't believe in the absolute fairness and the unblemished integrity of this system.

Redmond, as I would have done, hired McDaniel, who was a more experienced lawyer, to get him out of jail. McDaniel filed a motion to vacate the contempt citation and for release of Redmond from jail. The motion was granted. Redmond stayed in jail at least the balance of that day and perhaps maybe overnight, until the contempt citation was lifted. He never discussed the matter with me any further.

I believe this experience changed him. It took the fight out of him, which was unfortunate because he was just trying to do his job. I don't believe he was ever the same fervent advocate he had been prior to being incarcerated. It takes courage to be an advocate in court, fighting against a system that intends to have its way unless rationally persuaded to do otherwise. Criminal defense attorneys and trial lawyers both in the civil and the criminal bar get burned out, washed up, and fatigued doing battle day after day, usually against insurmountable odds.

That is not to say that lawyers don't make a difference; they certainly do. But sometimes their victories are in degrees and far apart, slotted in between many defeats and partial victories. In this business, if you are to keep your sanity, you have to define many partial victories or deals with the other side as a "win." You seldom get an acquittal, but the advocacy may be successful enough that it keeps your client out on bail for as long as possible. Perhaps you even get some of the charges against him or her reduced or thrown out. Perhaps you even obtain a reduced sentence. Maybe you manage to block and obfuscate the legal process long enough and slow it down–even deliberately bog it down– that it buys your client enough time and you are able to force a better settlement from the opposition. All of these results are "wins" in the criminal defense and plaintiff world.

After his brief incarceration, Redmond and I continued to practice together for a while, but the old street adage of "no pushing the dealer," is what Redmond failed to adhere to. Know your limits and stay within them. Lawyers have been known to push the envelope but caution must always be exercised even in a system that embraces zealous advocacy. Lessons were learned by all involved with Redmond in this episode—most of all by Redmond himself.

24

MICHELLE, MY BELLE

AS I WENT ABOUT MY BUSINESS between June and September of 1979, I was still waiting to close on the Germantown Avenue building. What was taking so long? Taking matters into my own hands, I went to the Jenkins Law Library, which was for members of the Philadelphia Bar Association, and reviewed some reference materials on the Department of Housing and Urban Development Regulations. After reading some pertinent regulations, I drafted a four-page letter to the loan company threatening to sue them if the loan was not forthcoming. I was tired of living in North Philadelphia and wanted to complete my move into the new building and get on with my new life in Philadelphia. Shortly thereafter, I received notice that the loan had been approved. Dad came up for the closing.

However, a glitch developed before the closing, which required me to pay some additional money. Dad remarked, "There are always some burnt edges on any toast." The last-minute development was of no moment, and my glee could not be robbed by this occurrence. So I returned to D.C. to move my furniture to Philadelphia. On move-in day Pat came over, smiling broadly, being her usual jovial self and carrying some items in her hand. She was excited that a Lee had purchased such a building in this community. It was a joyous day indeed.

I was always so impressed with the old-world antiquity of the buildings in Philadelphia, the stone exteriors, the high ceilings, the slate roofs, the rounded arches and heavy use of wood trim, the stone construction and masonry walls. The purchase of this building would turn out to be the *elan vital*, vital force of my financial and professional life in Philadelphia, my flagship property in the city. The vision to see the role of that purchase in my life in Philadelphia was clairvoyant. I had a fortress as an anchor, from which I could build my career and on which I could start my new life.

My financial world began to congeal. I now owned two buildings in prime locations with a total of eight rental units. My entrepreneurial juices began to flow and the vision was becoming more real.[25]

It was during this period that a female acquaintance from Charlottesville who had moved to Philadelphia several years before me, heard that I was in town and invited me to her house for a party, and to meet one of her female friends, who was single.

Shortly before this, I had started teaching an economics class at Pierce Junior College in South Philadelphia. Several well-meaning friends, some from Charlottesville, wanted to find a mate for me. I suppose I was an eligible bachelor, but I had my own vision of what I wanted in a new spouse. I was not new at the dating game. Some of these folks were setting me up with women through the church I was attending, but I didn't care for any of those women and was not impressed with what Philadelphia had to offer—at least, not in the circles I was moving in.

The best Black women were in insulated, middle-class households and were secluded and unavailable to men like me who were on the prowl until the appropriate introductions had been arranged. But I was excluded from those circles because I was not an indigenous middle-class Black Philadelphian. I was an outsider.

I was still going back and forth to D.C. and seeing a girlfriend, Susan, who I had picked up in an adult education class I had taught in suburban D.C. Susan was intent on making things happen between us: she was a nursing assistant at Walter Reed Army Hospital, not far from my old home on Peabody Street in Northwest D.C. But I really didn't want her total package, which included two young boys from a previous relationship. Susan had her good points, but I was not sold. Little did I know that I was about to meet a woman who would forever erase the woes of my melancholy heart.

I was twice divorced. My first marriage had ended in Chicago at age 27 during my complex pursuit of self. The next had ended because it wasn't a good fit. There were many reasons why that second relationship could have lasted, but there was not enough symmetry in timing, marital values and my deeply held, though evolving, aspirations of what I wanted in a wife, causing it to fail. It was unfortunate for Phyllis.

Now, all I wanted was what I had envisioned all along, a physically attractive woman with values in keeping with mine and a solid home life. A woman who was not afraid to be a woman. And who was not reluctant to do the types of things a woman must do to make a home work.

As I began to dress for that evening's party, I thought seriously about what to wear. I didn't know any of the people that were going to be there except my acquaintance from Charlottesville. I wanted to look good, but not over-dressed. My sartorial purpose was simple. To look confident, but not ostentatious. So I chose one of my old favorites: grey wool slacks, a white turtleneck sweater and a blue Burberry blazer, double breasted and double vented with brass buttons. Standard fare for an up-and-coming, well-dressed lawyer.

I was tall and slim, and my grey widow's peak shone with distinction – the result of a family gene on my father's side. Overall, I felt that my presentation was authentically me, both mentally and physically. There was no façade. My earnestness was evident.

I arrived at the small townhouse on Independence Mall in the historic district not nervous but somewhat ill at-ease; not knowing what to expect. These folks all knew each other from Swarthmore College, an elite small college in southeastern Pennsylvania, and other White schools, but I didn't know them at all. I was a "field Negro" who had worked long and hard to earn his way into the "big house." At this time in my life, I was highly sensitive to the line of demarcation that separated those Blacks who had gone to White schools and those who, like me, had struggled up from Black schools. Perhaps none of this was real, but this was all part of the residual baggage I still carried in my mind.

After I knocked on the door, my friend greeted me graciously. "Hi, Otis come on in. Make yourself at home. I'm glad you could make it."

It seemed to me that her whole speech was merely pretense. But at this point I think her intentions were genuine. She had known I was going to make it to her event, but the social graces required her to be nice. There was music playing on the stereo and a fire burning on the grate. The atmosphere was cozy and comfortable. But I was aware as I looked around and took stock of the place, just how small the interior of the house was. All of the quaint buildings in this historical block were attached on both sides, in a row of adjacent houses. At the front they each had a small, three-step stoop with a wrought iron railing to assist you as you climbed to the front door. The streets were cobblestone and the sidewalks were brick. My place on Germantown Avenue was less historic but more spacious and inviting.

I sat down and tried to make conversation with the people on my right and left as best I could. I made the effort, even though making small talk was not my strong suit. But I was on a mission to meet the woman for whom this whole party had been planned.

Time passed and some folks began to dance. Then this woman caught my eye. She was as high yellow as any Black woman I had ever seen. I had seen many light-skinned multiracial people before and not really fancied them, but this woman was not only high yellow, she was real pretty, with long, black, flowing hair. If she wanted to, she surely could have passed for White.

I thought about Dad and his derisive remark he used to make at the house in Charlottesville when the issue of skin color arose in family conversation: about mulattoes and the historical conflict between them and their darker-skinned brothers, a fiction, that one was perceived to be better off than the other.

A few more of the guests began to dance, but there was only really space enough for two couples at a time. The music was a silly kind of off-beat, phony rhythm and, in my general cynicism towards the whole event, I reckoned to myself that this must be the way Blacks danced who were trying to play sophisticates. I was not impressed, and I was certainly not motivated to dance. The music didn't raise any emotion in me, nor did it stir most of the attendees to dance.

This was a total waste of time.

I gathered myself, took a position by the mantlepiece and rested there. A woman drifted towards me and tried to make conversation, but I was hardly interested. Then the hostess came over and said, "Otis, I want you to meet my friend Michelle Palmer. We were classmates together at Swarthmore."

Michelle was standing behind her.

"Hi," I responded, not wanting to put too much emotion into my response, as I casually and rather indirectly looked at her from stem to stern. Then our eyes locked into each other's with a resoluteness and seriousness of purpose, and I felt something very special had happened.

Michelle went through a few pleasantries, then to my surprise and chagrin, moved away. She didn't linger with me for long. We had looked at each other and made our assessments. Michelle later remarked to me that I had that "Frederick Douglas" look, grey hair and all, whereas I felt that she was comely. Her exquisite beauty, though discernible was modestly displayed. She stood away, as if preoccupied with her golden, embroidered, brocade-looking blouse and black slacks draped neatly over her well-proportioned frame.

The previous woman came back to resume her conversation, and I obliged her but my glance and my attention were focused on Michelle, as she remained in my direct line of vision. Her poise made a very attractive silhouette. I thought to myself, "Well, well, I think I'll make a play for this woman. I'll have you for me."

I was particularly impressed by the nape of her neck, how well-groomed and attractive her hair was as it swirled around her beige-colored shoulders in a French Roll. The strands of her lightly brown hair and her golden necklace made a big impression on me. She was a work of art, and I wanted to possess it, I wanted to make it mine.

Michelle stood erect, gracious but not bothered. She had no way of knowing what I was thinking–or so I thought at the time–but I kept my eyes on her the rest of the evening as she moved back to an inner room and resumed her conversation with her friends. Her mission had been accomplished. And I was determined to make the next move. I have always been the type to know when I have seen something I like. It is an instantaneous feeling of pleasing sensibility.

After another hour or so, I had had enough and was ready to leave, but not before saying a proper goodbye to Michelle and asking if I could see her again. I found her in the back area talking with her friends. I went over and boldly interrupted the conversation. "Excuse me, could I have your phone number? I'd like to give you a call, if I may?"

"Sure," she replied, and gave me her work number. I gave her my card. Then I said my goodbye to the hostess, told Michelle I would be calling her, and left.

As our courtship began, it became obvious that to capture one heart, I had to break another. I knew instinctively that I had met the woman I was looking for. The pieces were all coming together. But to be free and honest, I had to let go of the other woman in D.C. It was painful to do, but it had to be done, so I called Susan in D.C. and told her that I had met someone who interested me greatly and that our relationship was at an end.

Susan had been a gamer; she had tried hard and she knew what she was losing. She had even visited me in Philadelphia and had met my parents. But it was not to be. I told her that she had met the master and that the game was over.

As I got to know Michelle better, her situation became more clear. She had been reared in humble circumstances and believed in self-reliance. She had pulled herself up by her bootstraps. She was a female Horatio Alger in search of gravitas.[26]

Twenty-nine years later, after giving birth to one son and raising him, as well as helping raise another, Michelle would achieve and acquire that gravitas by earning a Ph.D. in Health Service Organizations and Research from Virginia Commonwealth University. It had been important for her to earn the Ph.D. because it finally gave her the status she had always wanted , to be taken seriously in her field, and to make manifest her love of school by getting to the finish line academically.

We were both underdogs. Me with my Rudy-like "pursuit of happiness." Her with her good values that had surpassed her economic underpinnings. In her sojourn through life, she had overcome significant privations, but had been blessed in the way she had been raised and had been careful with herself. We were ideological soul-mates, birds of a feather. She was exactly what I was looking for. But this unlikely Victorian spinster was about to get involved with an urbane Lothario who had a strong conservative bent, yet liberal views on the nature of justice.

Although my demeanor sprang from a wellspring that was significantly more well-heeled than hers and my worldly experiences were more expansive, we formed a relationship that immediately felt as if it had a seriousness of purpose. Her hard work to make something out of herself and not fall victim to the mundane undertow of her blue collar community of Chester, Pennsylvania and my struggle to reach my goals made us two peas in a pod. Philosophically, we were conjoined twins tied at the hip. And we were determined both to do well in our domestic life and master our chosen professional pursuits as a couple.

Our common values were of the old school: self-reliance, hard work, and thrift. These transcended the throw away, easy-come, easy-go attitudes of the times. We were intent on achieving something and appreciated not just the price, but the value of things. This table of values from which we now ate had been set by our parents. During our youth, we were both made to eat from those plates until they were inculcated into our very beings. When we became adults we applied them to our lives, and we would apply them in the future education of our children.

Michelle's parent had clearly inculcated these values in her. We started by not taking each other for granted. Tacitly, we knew what we had in each other. The school of hard knocks made us two souls seeking redemption in the social market place. We both supplied each other with what we needed. She was supportive, thrifty, loving, and a willing worker, pleasing to my sensibilities. And I more than reciprocated and supplied her with fidelity and commitment born of prior failures in the marriage game, as well as protection, love, strength, stability, and economic security. As our affection for each other grew over the next several months, our love simmered to a steady boil with the lid always on. As our romance continued, I would often be reminded of the Curtis Mayfield song "So in Love".

Our wedding took place at 10 am, 10 August 1980, nine months after we met. It was a bright sunny Saturday in Michelle's home town church, Spencer AME in Chester, Pennsylvania. My father was my best man. I asked him to do this for me because he was, in reality, my best man. He had fun at the wedding and we drew even closer together.

We planned our wedding and paid for it ourselves. As older adults, we could not expect our parents to pay for it, so I borrowed some money through a contact at one of the local banks to help defray our costs. Aunt Louise came down from New York with Edwin's son Akin. A close friend of the family and Louise's close friend Lil also came down from New York. Mom was there. Pat was there, and Lang attended. Tom Dunlevy, the silver-headed vice president of the Trust Department at Girard Bank, sent a card and a gift and spoke of his desire to attend but was unable to do so. Steve Holderness the trust officer with whom I had been working so closely attended. Michelle invited many of her friends from Swarthmore College and her friends from her job and from high school. I invited Mel from D.C., a friend from the old days, and he attended.

The day and night before the wedding, all my family gathered at my apartment on Germantown Ave. A practice walk-through was scheduled for later that afternoon, so Dad, Mom and I went over to Spencer Church to attend it.

Patsy, a friend of Michelle's, was practicing a song we had selected as our theme, "We've Only Just Begun", by Karen Carpenter/The Carpenters. I told Patsy she was sounding good, but I needed to hear a few more bars to be sure. Everyone laughed at my brashness. The church was decorated with signs that read "Otis and Michelle." I was actually surprised by how much decoration Michelle and her helpers had hung. My other weddings had been very modest affairs with little or no fanfare.

That night my party laughed and played games into the wee hours. We had a great time. But as time for the wedding approached, I grew nervous. This was my third time down the aisle. What if it didn't work?

The old brick building of the church had an eight-foot wrought iron fence surrounding it. It was rich in tradition, having served its congregation for many years as a focal point in this small Black community. Rev. Hardin, a quiet, dark-skinned and rather reserved, gray-haired man of many years was the officiating minister. His dignity and reverence exuded a sanctity reminiscent of days gone by when ministers were the bestowers of blessings sincerely conveyed upon approved events within their churches. He was one of "the old school."

Michelle wore a two-piece, cream-colored suit. With her hair in a French roll and her feet neatly tucked in matching pumps, she was resplendent. In the words of the Isley Brothers, "There is no place I'd rather be than with you. I was drifting on a memory, no insecurities within; I had paradise within, a new horizon was coming into view; I was living for the love of you."

Having been abandoned by her father at an early age, Michelle was given away by a close family friend. I stood at the front of the church in my gray pinstripe suit with the chain of my pocket watch hanging across my vest, looking like a farmer with a pitch fork in his hand, waiting for his mate to join him—somber, serious, and forthright. My father stood next to me and beamed confidently.

Michelle and I exchanged our nuptials, paid the minster his fee, took the customary pictures, and retired to the church's recreation room for our breakfast reception—something a little different and unusual. Such an early meal allowed us extra time to drive down to Ocean City, Maryland, for the start of our honeymoon. The breakfast was catered by a local caterer Michelle knew, with mouth-watering hot rolls, a special egg dish, and flavorful breakfast meats. However, we were both so anxious after the ceremony, neither of us could eat. The emptiness in our stomachs was disguised by the tension and excitement of the moment.

Despite our inability to eat, the occasion was joyous for both of us and was a grand day in our lives. My empathy told me that Michelle's heart was epitomized by the ballad, "As Long As He Needs Me". And, for my part, I knew from the first moment I saw her that I would need her for the rest of my life. Here we were, two well-meaning hearts fortuitously and appropriately united in love, common need, and purpose.

I had learned some hard lessons from my marriages to Delma and Phyllis. Both marriages had occurred at times of unreadiness. But this was different. Many of my trials were over and much baggage had been tossed overboard, never to be heard from again and I soberly knew what I wanted this time.

I had gone through a lot of pain dealing with women before I met Michelle. She took away the pain. Every man has to "settle." Men relish the view of having as many women as possible, but that is impossible–though I certainly had my share. I was fortunate and happy to have "settled" with Michelle. For a man to finally settle, he must find a woman who, in his own mind, has a proportionate amount, subjectively speaking, of intelligence, sexually attractive physiognomy, caring and common values. Michelle was the embodiment of that vision, of what I wanted in a woman, and I felt lucky to have her. The sustaining beauty of her quiet elegance maintained an enchantment in my mind when moments of reflections on her reoccurred.

For the first time, I was able to approach a relationship with a clear head, unclouded by the youthful coercion of sex and the novelty of infatuation, nor beguiled by an ill-defined neurosis, real or imagined, engendered by unrequited self-actualization, as I had experienced with Phyllis when I married her five years earlier. So, at last, I was fully myself, not limited by naiveté, vision or accomplishment. A level of maturation had taken place over the years. Growing pains had come and gone, and I felt I was operating in a state of grace. The gods of providence were smiling their approval. All I had to do was to take my woman and go–no looking back. The past was no longer the prologue of my life; now, it was the future.

That Christmas, I purchased five bottles of my favorite sherry, "Dry Sack," and delivered one bottle to each of the trust officers I had done business with that year. It was my way of saying thank you for their support.

The overture was well received. No one had done this before and certainly no Black lawyer had done this before. All the recipients were pleased and it sent notice that I knew how to play this game. Philadelphia is such a parochial city, in spite of its presumed urbanity. So many segments of its society are reserved for only a select few, untouched by minority representation. The staid world of the trust department was reserved for only the genteel of the Philadelphia White banking and law community. The conservatism of the discipline and the moneyed interest it represented made it an exclusive enclave. What I did with Lang's help was splash into that closet and open it to Black representation. What I was learning along the way was that estate planning was a good "loss leader." Even though it had been lucrative and portended to be even more so, the big money was in estate settlement work. Estate planning got you in the door, but estate settlement allowed you to eat from the table.

I received an invitation through a contact to attend a reception in Harrisburg at the Governor's Mansion. Members of the governor's cabinet and members of the Pennsylvania Supreme Court would be there. The occasion was an art exhibit of some kind. Michelle and I decided to attend. The week before the event, I bought Michelle a lavender and white silk and chiffon dress from Wanamakers Department store in Center City. I loved the dress as soon as I saw it, and I knew she would look beautiful in it. As a young married couple, buying clothes for each other was a learning experience that was not always successful, but this one was a hit. She liked the dress.

We drove over to Harrisburg in the early afternoon and arrived on time for the reception. It was the second time I had been to Harrisburg—the first was when I went there to visit Phyllis' family before we got married in 1976.

As we exited the car a breeze stirred and a magic moment was revealed. The undulating breeze sauntered under the dress after Michelle got out of the vehicle as she stood erect and lifted the dress above her knees illuminating her beautifully sculptured legs—a striking component of her natural beauty that she modestly tried to conceal. As I looked upon her face in that fleeting moment of her embarrassment I thought, no greater beauty had God created. The freshness and scintillating handsomeness of her frame and countenance brought pleasure to my aesthetic sensibilities. It was reminiscent of the Marilyn Monroe moment when the actress stepped onto a heating grate and the hot air blew her dress above her knees and revealed her beautiful legs. Unforgettable.

When we entered the mansion, we were amazed at how plain and lacking in ornamentation the house looked. The rooms in the public sector were sparsely furnished and the accouterments were few and scattered. The interior of the house was unremarkable, Pennsylvania plain–quiet, but substantively appointed. The Dutch and Quaker influences inspired the unpretentious embellishments. Perhaps the taxpayers didn't feel that the governor needed a lavish environment in which to conduct the state's business.

We toured the public sector of the house, walking around and being careful of our movements and looked at the paintings on the walls. As we made our way around the rooms, we encountered Justice N.C. Nix, the lone Black associate justice on the Pennsylvania Supreme Court. He would later become the first Black Chief Justice of the Pennsylvania Supreme Court and the only one in the country at that time. Justice Nix was the scion of the late Robert N.C. Nix, a Black congressman from Philadelphia who served his district for many years with distinction. The Nix family is an old and revered family in Philadelphia politics. Justice Nix was sitting on the bench when I was sworn into the bar three years earlier in Philadelphia, but he didn't remember me.

We spoke briefly and he asked me, "Young man, in what profession are you?" As we admired the same painting, I responded that I was a lawyer and he said, "Well, I suspect that in the coming years you will be buying your beautiful wife an ermine coat."

I nodded my acquiescence, not knowing what an ermine coat was. I suspected it must have been something expensive.

After our honeymoon, it was back to the realities of my practice. As Redmond often remarked, "There are no permanent friends, only permanent interest." And my interests had diverged from his as I had developed my self-interest into other areas. Redmond wanted to work in the divorce business with me; that was the impetus for our joint move in the first place. He wanted to make money and I had shown him the way. We were doing well for a while, but not enough to overcome other factors which persuaded me to go with Lang.

25

PHILADELPHIA FIRE

If We Must Die
by Claude McKay

If we must die, let it not be like hogs
Hunted and penned in an inglorious spot,
While round us bark the mad and hungry dogs,
Making their mock at our accursed lot.
If we must die, O let us nobly die,
So that our precious blood may not be shed
In vain; then even the monsters we defy
Shall be constrained to honor us though dead!
O kinsmen we must meet the common foe!
Though far outnumbered let us show us brave,
And for their thousand blows deal one deathblow!
What though before us lies the open grave?
Like men we'll face the murderous, cowardly pack,
Pressed to the wall, dying, but fighting back!

FOR THE BALANCE OF THE YEAR, Redmond and I resumed our practices, but my work with Lang continued apace. The Abscam scandal forced the city council president to resign and other high officials ended their careers in disgrace. But the Rizzoites were still in control of City Hall and the police department. In Philadelphia, there was always another scandal just around the corner waiting to be uncovered. That was the nature of the city's politics. Every scandal-prone politician was looking for a sinecure of one kind or another. It was only a matter of time before federal prosecutors uncovered the graft and prosecuted the culprits.

Meanwhile, the police department had several nasty confrontations with MOVE, a Black counter-cultural movement founded by John Africa. MOVE was based in the Powelton Village section of West Philadelphia and its members were characterized by their dreadlock hair. In my mind, the inspiration for the group's views and the life style of its members resembled the Rastafarian traditions of Jamaica. In the Amharic language traditions of Ethiopia, Rastafarians believe Africa is the promised land and that the Messiah was Prince Tafari, the late Haile Selassie I of Ethiopia. Modern-day Rastafarians believe there will be an Armageddon in which Babylon will be destroyed as part of the epic battle between good and evil. John Africa could have been a dreadlock Rasta.

The group espoused a philosophy that sought to stop industry and government from poisoning the environment and repressing the people. The "system" was seen by MOVE to be at fault for the woes that afflicted and enslaved the people. Its supporters sought to live in harmony with nature, and their programs attempted to help the homeless and ex-offenders, eliminate child abuse and wife abuse, as well as drug addiction and alcoholism. The group was a back-to-nature organization.

Rizzo abhorred the group and his surrogates attacked them relentlessly in 1974 and 1975, using the pretext of law enforcement to legitimize their actions. However, on 8th August 1978, during a raid on the MOVE compound, shots were fired and police officer James Ramp was killed. This event transformed what had been a series of battles and demonstrations into a "war" to eliminate this group. A timetable was set for a cataclysmic conflagration. The MOVE folks would not submit to Philadelphia's White ethnocentrism, racial condescension, ambivalence and intolerance. In the midst of it all, our day-to-day living continued.

When several MOVE cases came before the judicial system, the court sent word that it wanted court-appointed attorneys to come forward for these cases, but not too many lawyers volunteered. The veterans knew the downside and wanted no part of it.

One day in the office, when Redmond and I were chewing the fat, he asked me whether I was going to step up and take on one of those cases. I responded emphatically, "No!" because I knew instinctively that it would be professional and mental suicide to get involved in these endless battles between MOVE and the city. Plus, I was too green in the practice for that kind of load.

Wilson Goode was elected mayor in 1984; Philadelphia was proud to have its first Black mayor. Goode was touted as being a good manager. His predecessor placed him in the position to win and to ascend to the mayoralty. Even though it was the Black community that was responsible for putting him in office, from the beginning Goode always seemed to cater to the public opinion of the White community more than to the Black community. Before becoming mayor, Wilson Goode as the City Managing Director, made conciliatory gestures toward MOVE, meeting with them and researching their legal claims to unjust treatment. Other city officials such as D.A. Ed Rendell were not as accommodating. The issue continued to boil above and beneath the surface. On May 11, 1985 Common Pleas Court Judge Lynn Abraham signed arrest warrants on charges of disorderly conduct and related offenses against MOVE members and the stage was set for Armageddon.

The Osage Avenue in the Cobbs Creek section of West Philadelphia was unpretentious in its outward manner and internal construction. Row houses and a few single family homes characterized the housing available in this community. Black working class blue collar Philadelphians populated this community. The community knew it had a problem with its neighbor MOVE, but they were content as long as MOVE did not go beyond the truly unthinkable, to live and let live. This Black community was not about to destroy itself or the MOVE compound because White folks felt threatened by their rhetoric and political stance. Sure, they were not happy with the way MOVE lived in their community and perhaps wished to be rid of them, but it was not to such an extent that they would destroy all that they, as lower middle and middle class people, had worked for all of their lives to attain.

On Monday, May 13, 1985, the police forces of the city of Philadelphia attacked the MOVE compound. Police and fire authorities were fully deployed to arrest those persons wanted in the arrest warrants and they, under color of law, intended to do all that was necessary to bring those people into their custody. MOVE would have none of it. The MOVE attack was the precursor of the ATF attack on the Branch Dividivian compound in Waco, Texas that the federal government led many years later. A full military assault was launched against the MOVE rowhouse. An array of military weaponry not limited to the following was used: tear gas, water cannons, C-4 explosives, automatic rifles and handguns were all used to subdue the MOVE compound and the people inside of it, including women and children. How could these people expect to survive an attack of such magnitude? They could not and they did not. The full measure of the police system was brought to bear against these people. The question was, was all of this required? The simple answer was no! Over 10,000 rounds of ammunition were fired into that rowhouse. A bomb made of high military type explosives was dropped on the roof of the row house when the people did not flee the compound which incinerated the MOVE house and everything in it including the entire corridor on the side where the MOVE rowhouse was situated. The neighborhood had been changed forever. Lives were destroyed, careers ruined.[27]

But Wilson Goode said he was a "good manager." How then, Wilson, did you let this happen to Black people? I'll tell you how, by managing from afar. Not being on the physical scene where the conflagration was taking place. There was no "hands on" management of the crisis. The mayor was not there in person to tell the cops not to do certain things, to restrain their inhumane proclivities toward Black people. Instead, it was reported at the time, and I believe it to be true based upon my knowledge of the facts having lived through the event, that Wilson Goode was bunkered down in his command center managing the crisis from afar in Center City and not at the crisis site. Leaving the dirty work to his police commanders who had it in for the MOVE people. The police ranks were still filled with the remnants of Rizzo-era people still seething from the defiant recalcitrance of MOVE people to accept the Philadelphia orthodoxy on race. Why did this "manager" leave the management of the city's most horrific historic challenge to systemic racism to someone else to manage? A Black mayor leaving the destruction of Black people to White racists?

A Black mayor of a city known for its intolerance of Blacks and other minorities – a city whose history reeked of mistreatment of Black people by the police – let known racist cops and firemen heap the motherlode of destruction on the objects of their racism. What Wilson Goode mismanaged was tantamount to a starving man, famished from a lack of nutrition and the foodstuffs he needed to feel good about himself, to eat a four-course meal from a menu of his own choosing, to satisfy that thirst, that hunger for suppression and subjugation: a curious quandary, for the city's first Black mayor and tragic irony of race and politics. In default of strong moral leadership, this incident demonstrates what can happen if evil forces are left to their own devices.

Do you think this would have happened in the upper class White Art Museum district, in Chestnut Hill, or in the Independence Mall area? No! Of course not. It happened because the subjects were Black people and the community was a Black community, that is why. It was the "get even battle," between the city and MOVE. In the eyes of the perpetrators of this fiasco, these people and this community were expendable. Sixty homes were destroyed, six adults and five children were killed. Was the execution of an ill-fated warrant of arrest worth all of this? I don't think so. You judge.

What happens when myth succumbs to reality, when reputation evaporates in chaos? Is the residue a heap of ash, the pulverized remainder of pretense and orchestration? What happens to human beings who rely on these myths, give their lives in service of these myths, those who are subsumed by the perpetuation of these myths, are they fodder for the power elite, those who are successful at the art of manipulation but whose core is as hollow, porous and vapid as the most common of man when the trappings of elitism and power are stripped away? Can they be relied upon to act ethically or virtuously. Our leaders, the people who send us into war, the judges who sentence us to prison and the death chamber, the folks who exercise power over life and death in this and other societies, are they worthy of our trust? Do they even merit our trust? Do they believe in truth? Are they seekers of truth or are they seekers of self-aggrandizement? Or are they chameleons camouflaging their lack of morality and strength of conviction when it comes to dealing with people of color in the greater public interest? How say you to this? What would we be if we were not who we made ourselves into without the help of others and the providence of fortuitous events along the way? Intrinsic worth, that "thing" that makes us real; *That* something, that is the foundation of character, the building block upon which all else rests, must be real. If that something is not real in its natural state, no artificial affectations will ever make it real. That realness and devotion to truth must be there in its innate form before the trappings of adornment and the harness of society's many avenues of creations are added.

The charred remains of unidentifiable bodies lay strewn about like planks of charred wood unrecognizable save for the remains in the oral cavities. The corpses lay where they dropped dodging the fusillade of bullets flying through the house like a whirlwind and they fell where they exhaled their last breaths. The smoke and toxic fumes emanating from the burning inferno of the MOVE house and that of their adjoining neighbors smelled of flesh, memories, picture frames, family bibles, family memorabilia, scrapbooks, diplomas, irreplaceable family objects. Wood burned and steel and plastics melted; couches burned, mattresses were engulfed in flames, livelihoods and peace eviscerated. The forks and spoons, knives and dishes were trampled into the ash-laden dirt of disregard and indurate callousness for the sentimentality and preciousness of the owners' memories contained within them. A community's composite of family histories each precious in its own right forever destroyed by the indifferent negligence of a city gone mad in its pursuit of a few misguided, dreadlocked "back to earth people." MOVE was not without blame for some of this, but on balance the weight of the blame must rest with those who sold us on their competence and their ability to act in our best interest, and were in the superior position to have changed the outcome. This was Philadelphia's holocaust.

Post-mortem investigations of the catastrophe in judicial and non-judicial forums exonerated all public officials involved. No one lost a job or paid a fine. The city tax payers paid for the reconstruction of that which could be reconstructed, the bricks and the mortar. Some recompense was eventually made to a surviving member, Ramona Africa, due solely to her dogged pursuit through litigation to obtain some justice. It was a pittance when compared to the losses she sustained. This was justice in the city of brotherly love.

By now I was beginning to get regular criminal court appointments. I started out with misdemeanor assignments which were tried and or settled in the city hall court rooms where the cases were docketed. Felony cases were sent to area police districts for preliminary hearings, and if I received an assignment to one of these cases I had to make my way to the police district to conduct the preliminary hearing. The best thing to do before going to the police district was to go to the Clerk of Quarter Sessions, the criminal court clerk, and ask to look at the file, so at least you could see what the charges were and read the police reports before meeting your client for the first time at the district for the hearing. This was not always possible, however.

In one of my first misdemeanor trials I represented this defendant on a "receiving stolen property" charge among other charges. I tried the case before a senior judge as a bench trial: that is without a jury. As I questioned one of the prosecution's witnesses, I kept repeating the questions over and over again getting the same answers over and over again without making any headway. Running low on patience the old trial judge groused, "Mr. Lee I am not going to keep allowing you to keep asking the same questions over and over until you understand the facts in the case, we know what the case is about!"

"Yes, your honor," I meekly acknowledged.

No one taught me how to prepare for a trial. I knew nothing about preparing a trial brief, a trial outline, how to analyze the evidentiary issues, how to develop a theory of the case and fit my evidence into that theory. I would learn these skills through the rigors of trial and error and study. I was also aided by being a keen observer while in court watching experienced trial lawyers do their thing and hanging onto every tidbit of advice. All of this eventually added up to a base of knowledge that would enable me, in time, to be a formidable opponent in court.

The police districts in the city were based on the locations of police stations. The courtrooms inside these district police stations were old, mean, utterly austere concrete structures, shorn of any trappings of comfort. There was nothing warm or cozy in these police district courtrooms. This is where police officers assigned to these districts did their business. Only serious business took place in these stations. You didn't tarry when your business was done.

On many mornings, I rose at 7 am to travel to police districts like "Broad and Champlost," in northwest Philadelphia, the home of the northwest precinct detectives. This district is in a Black middle-class area north on Broad Street and close to both West Oak Lane and East Oak Lane. It was also south and west of "Harbison and Levick," another police district I often frequented for hearings located in the northeast, which is a White middle-class area surrounded by row homes and strip malls. Then to "Germantown and Haines" in Germantown, north of Chelten on Germantown Avenue and less than five miles south of my eventual office. This is a busy Black shopping district for the working class Black community in Germantown.

Small shops and neighborhood stores populated the area from Chelten Avenue east to Chew Avenue, west to Wissahickon Avenue, north on Germantown

Avenue to Mt. Pleasant, and south to Berkely Street. The owners of these shops were Chinese, Koreans, Japanese and Asian Indians, the new purveyors of sugary and high sodium sludge, and high-fat foods with little or marginal nutritional value, belly filling but not heart-healthy. They hawked a variety of cheap Chinese dry goods and overpriced sundries of one kind or another.

It is a bustling community with an indigenous vibrancy unique to a cultural diversity of Caribbean, West Indian, African American, and Caucasian. You can find anything you want in the varied shops on both sides of the intersection. The inhabitants and the merchants are foreigners to one another, and each is from a divergent culture and speaks a different language. One half of the population barely understands the other half, yet these people, thrown together in an urban cauldron of circumstance and self-interest and a common driving need for economic survival, each seeks benefit from the others.

Inhabitants of these communities led truncated lives cut short by poor health, internecine crime, predatory commercialism, callous and exploitative capitalism, low academic achievement, and limited horizons. Yet these were my people, the people of the hinterland that made my neighborhood law practice thrive. I grew to love and respect those who became my clients and developed an appreciation of their culture and community.

We were all in the same boat. The hard scrabble of urban life in a tough, unforgiving city made all of us grist for the ever-churning mill of life. And so I discovered my nobility of purpose as these travails continued. My practice was to be "a lighthouse for the blind," as I termed it, especially for those in the community who needed the benefit of my vision to help them better their situation. I saw this as my ministry. Sure, I didn't always know everything I should have known at a particular time, and if I didn't know the answer it was my duty to find it out, but I always did my best with what I knew in each situation, legal or otherwise.

I went to these police district courts always hoping to get a win, but seldom did so. The DA's office assigned an ADA (Assistant District Attorney) on a rotating basis to each police district to go through the list of cases and complete the preliminary hearings. "Probable cause" is the standard of proof required for the ADA to prevail at a preliminary hearing: a low threshold. At one such hearing, a fellow Howardite called Mr. Green, who was an ADA at the time, was doing his usual prosecutorial thing: working his way through the list of cases. When he was confronted with some doubt as to whether or not to proceed with a particular case, or to continue it, his inclination was to proceed because the case was continued before. This was strange, because the ADA said to the judge, "Your honor, I don't think I should proceed with this case."

The judge stared at him nonplussed. "Well, Mr. Green, if you don't think you should proceed, why are you doing so?"

Mr. Green had no answer.

During one such case against a client of mine, he looked across at me in search of help, but I certainly had none to offer him. He didn't have his witnesses in court and would have lost the preliminary hearing if he proceeded. The judge sensed his dilemma but couldn't tell him what to do. The man's judgment was on the line. He had to decide whether to risk losing the case or to ask for a continuance to a later date. But had this case been continued before because of his witness's failure to appear? If so, the case was ripe for a motion to dismiss. If a case was marked "Must Be Tried," it meant that the case had been continued before for some reason not chargeable to the defendant. If the ADA tried to continue it again, the likelihood was that the case would be thrown out on motion. This is the culture of a "big city" criminal law practice.

My success was rare but in these fights my goals were realistic: to get some of the charges thrown out or reduced because there was not enough evidence to support them; to get the charges dismissed outright if the complaining witness, usually the victim, failed to appear after several listings; or to set the case up for dismissal at the next listing if a key witness, usually the victim, failed to appear.

In Philadelphia, judges were always admonishing lawyers when they felt it appropriate, regardless of the emotional impact on the person concerned. Lawyering in Philadelphia required you to have a thick skin. You had to take it as well as give it out. This was all part of the intimidation game between the bench and the bar. Those cases where an ADA prevailed were "held for court," meaning that probable cause had been established. The defendant would be tried in a criminal court after an "information" (list of charges) was filed against him or her. Philadelphia used a grand jury system for felony cases, but also allowed for "filing of an information" in lieu of an indictment in routine felony cases.

Redmond had advised me early on "never to stipulate, but make the DA prove every issue in his case." This was good advice. Put the ADAs to their proofs. Don't make their jobs easy for them.

I used this advice consistently to the end. Rarely do defense attorneys have much success at preliminary hearings because the burden of proof is too low. Prudent defense counsel rarely, if ever, will allow a defendant to testify. It serves no purpose and is harmful, unless you have a good shot—I mean a real good shot— of getting the case dismissed, which in all likelihood is not going to happen. For example, in some jurisdictions, Virginia being an example, even if a case is dismissed at the preliminary hearing, the defendant can still be indicted by a grand jury.

So the whole process operates as a discovery hearing for the defense. I did dozens and dozens of these hearings during my career in Philadelphia. The more you do them, the better you get at it. What makes the difference is getting over the intimidation. Seeing all the police with their badges and leather boots and side arms neatly strapped to their waists. The seriousness of the procedures, the officialdom and the stern way in which business is conducted was a sobering encounter every time I experienced it. These trials make a man out of you, legally speaking.

From the police districts to the preliminary arraignments, to the arraignment, and then to the trial. It was all part of the criminal process. And I participated in each phase. Trying to understand Pennsylvania statutes and the criminal codes was a Kafkaesque experience. There was so much to learn and read and try to understand. I had to peruse the statutes two or three times to make sure I understood them. There were the Pennsylvania Statutes Annotated, Purdon's Pennsylvania Statutes, and I had to understand how state law and the Philadelpia Code was organized in conjunction with the Pennslyvania and Philadelphia Rules of Civil Procedure. The Philadelphia Rules of Court is a voluminous tome that outlines every cause of action imaginable in every division of the court system in Philadelphia.

This book detailed what the lawyer had to prove and file in order to appropriately file an action in court. For the practicing lawyer, this book was the Bible. Finally, there was the Pennsylvania and Philadelphia Rules of Civil Procedure.

Because of its size and volume of cases, Philadelphia has several non-trial disposition arrangements, especially for minor drug offenses and first-time, non-violent offenders. Learning how to incorporate these diversions into my criminal defense framework took me some time, but proved essential if I was to offer my clients the least threatening choice for resolution of their problem.

One bright sunny Monday, I bounded into misdemeanor Courtroom 295 of City Hall to try a drug case. I thought I was following the correct procedures and doing my lawyerly thing when, out of the blue, the presiding judge yelled at me, "What's wrong with you, I'm going to report you to the bar association. Why didn't you object to that evidence, that question?"

I was so startled and disconcerted that I had no reply.

The judge continued to rant and rave and mumble under his breath about his exasperation with me. I was writhing with embarrassment. Had I been White, I would have turned red, orange, and yellow—the variegated flames of a crackling camp fire. Instead, I suffered a palpitating heart beating as fast as it had ever done before in my life. My chest felt like it was on fire momentarily as the embarrassment made its way through my system. I was so shocked I couldn't think. A feeling of panic pervaded my being and elevated my blood pressure high enough to pop a blood vessel. I was nonplused, consumed with public embarrassment.

The judge's rebuke had been over the top, injudicious, and had taken years off my life. But in his callous way he had been right and, as a consequence, he taught me a very valuable lesson about being a lawyer: I had failed to object to inadmissible evidence. It was my job as the lawyer, the protector of my client's rights, to object to this kind of evidence. My failure to object was not singularly dispositive of my client's guilt or innocence, but the rebuke was a warning shot fired across the bow of my nascent trial court experience, signaling that I had to delve deeper into the Law of Evidence, especially the Hearsay Rule; recognizing hearsay is not always easy.

When the case was over, I became invisible. I couldn't look my client confidently in the eye, and I was embarrassed to look into the gallery for fear of what those impersonal observers might be thinking about me. With my head bowed, I tried to sneak out of the courtroom and disappear.

The sting of that rebuke lingered. I mulled it over for hours and days after it occurred. The experience became ingrained in my bones. I thought of reporting the judge to the Judiciary Review Board, of writing him a letter explaining myself, but the better course was to leave it alone and let it die a natural death. However, I promised myself never to make that mistake again. In the words of Bob Marley, I would "Get up, stand up, stand up for my rights!" From now on, I would be up on my toes objecting to anything I remotely thought was inadmissible. I had to 'act like a lawyer.' That was what the public expected. So I had to make doubly sure I revisited the Law of Evidence, especially the Hearsay Rule. I had come to realize that I was a gatekeeper. It was my job to keep out inadmissible evidence and not to let it into the record, a fundamental act of the lawyer.

I never fashioned myself a criminal lawyer, but I cut my teeth in trial practice in criminal law. It was in this area that I learned to handle myself in court and to apply the law and rules of evidence. My civil trial practice was steady but small for the most part and mainly tried in judicial arbitration hearings, which was the second stop on the Philadelphia civil trial ladder. I did not get any block buster civil cases, only smaller personal injury cases on either the defense or plaintiff side. The civil business was good, but it came in small bites.

In one of my court appointed criminal cases, I was appointed to represent this Black fellow who was accused of stealing a boom box from another man whom he knew and apparently had had a relationship with. My client owned the radio before he forcefully took it back from the fellow who possessed it; thereafter charges were filed. My client was short, dark and obscure in his look and demeanor. He looked like a bug that had crawled out from under a rock. Nevertheless, regardless of how he looked or what I thought of him, it was my job to represent him and the case was real. The D.A. was moving ahead to put my guy in jail for robbery, theft and related charges. The case was listed as a jury trial before one of Philadelphia's seasoned trial judges Abraham Gafni, the great intimidator. Judge Gafni was a respected jurist in the Philadelphia Court of Common Pleas. He would later emerge as the trial judge in charge of the "call of the civil trial list," where lawyers appeared each day to have their civil cases set for trial or given a trial date. This was my first jury trial.

As the case progressed and the evidentiary issues were worked out between the D.A. and me, we were finally ready to impanel the jury. This D.A. fellow that I was up against was an odd ball. Unkempt, scruffy, he looked like he slept in his clothes all night, and the clothes he wore were his only clothes. I was always taken aback by this guy. I did not know it then, but I would see this fellow again before my Philadelphia practice days were over. I was in a bit of a tizzy, as the jurors filed into the jury box. Panic struck my nervous system, as I realized this was the system in real life. I was about to have a jury trial. I was in awe and intimidated; simultaneously, outwardly I exuded calm and poise, but inside my stomach was in knots until I kept saying to myself, "be calm, be calm you can handle it, this is what you have been wanting." Jury selection and qualification, called "Voir Dire," is a complicated process and requires much preparation. I knew something about it but was unschooled in the niceties. I did not know how to keep track of the jurors as smoothly as I would have liked. I had no system and no prior experience to rely on. I was scrambling to keep up but I managed. Judge Gafni remarked sternly, looking down over his bifocal glasses, and he quietly said to me, "Mr. Lee, you need to get a better handle on jury selection, are you ready to proceed?"

"Yes," I quickly responded with alacrity as I jumped to my feet, masking my lack of confidence, knowing full well he was right on the mark. In later years I would become more adept at this practice. My most important task though was to establish a theory of the defense. I went over the facts, talked to my client about what had happened, and he told me that he and this fellow, the victim, knew each other from past dealings; that he had given the fellow the radio which was his, to use, but not to keep in exchange for a sex act. They had a fight over this bargain, and when my client asked for the return of his radio, the victim refused, so my client took it back. My client was either dissatisfied with the sex act, or the victim failed to perform. The victim was of the mistaken belief that since my client had not paid for the sex act, albeit incomplete, that the radio was his to keep.

Into the books I went. Scrambling and searching furiously for a theory that would provide my client with an "out," and me, with a credible theory to argue to the jury and one that would be acceptable to the court. I came up with the common law theory of "claim of right." It was an old common law legal theory that said, if one owned the personal property that was the subject of the theft and rightfully took it back from one who adversely possessed it, the taking was not an unlawful taking hence not a theft. "Solid on down!" I exclaimed to myself. I had it. A novel legal theory but one cognizable by the law and ingenious for the young "out of school" lawyer. What I had just done was extremely important. I had found through legal research a theory of law that explained my client's conduct and was a legal defense of that conduct. Now I could explain in plausible terms my client's conduct and perhaps create "reasonable doubt" in the process. A maturation point was reached. The "light bulb" went off in the quiet of my office. I felt good about my chances and my confidence was unbounded. By just sticking with it I had learned something early in my practice that some lawyers never learn about the practice of law. Arguing over the facts is not enough. Finding a legal theory for the defence, if possible, is the Holy Grail. I was prepared with new enthusiasm to win my first jury trial.

The next day, after the jury was seated and all challenges were exhausted, opening arguments began. When my time came, I made my opening statement and the jury was intrigued and no objections by the court or opposing counsel could be heard. But no sooner had I finished my statement and a break was taken, than the victim, the complainant, disappeared. He was gone, nowhere to be found. The judge was angry and everyone was shocked, the D.A. was embarrassed for the Commonwealth, the jury wondered what had happened to the case they were to decide. The fullness of the criminal law system had been invoked, and the victim had no respect for it or the costs involved and had simply walked away. I won the case without having to try it. My theory of the case had intimidated the victim because it was the truth, and he did not want to be confronted with that truth in court, so he absconded. The judge issued a bench warrant for his arrest, but I never heard any more from my client or the case.

The Commonwealth should never have brought this case in the first place. There wasn't any case. It took a Black man who was not afraid to call "a spade a spade" to get to the bottom of a worthless endeavor and a waste of taxpayer's money.

As I gathered my possessions to leave city hall, the judge's law clerk approached me and commented on my theory..........um "claim of right, huh."

"Yes," I said. "And I have cases to cite," I responded proudly, acting as if I was lifting my weight. He gestured his approval and walked away realizing he had just learned something.

"Interesting," he muttered.

26

ONE BALA AVENUE,
THE MAIN LINE

I WAS STILL WORKING WITH LANG on estate planning, but he wanted to move from his offices on Erie Avenue in Germantown and recruit me to share office space with him and another insurance agent.

As I said before, Redmond and I got along well enough, but it was not a love affair any more. He was secretive and arrogant and our offices were sparse and not worth hanging on to. We had two adjoining offices with just a door separating our offices in a building that was sorely in need of repair. We were only able to afford the rent because the building was sub-par and in need of tenants.

On one occasion, Michelle came to the office for a planned visit. We were going over to Jewelers Row to purchase our engagement rings. When Redmond saw Michelle, he had a reaction. As she sat in my office waiting for me to finish my business before leaving, he motioned me to come over to his office for a moment. I walked through the door to his adjoining office. He closed the door behind me, and then he said, "Is that who you're going to marry?"

"Yes," I replied, puzzled by his inquiry. What was behind his question? It was difficult to figure out. Perhaps he was shocked at my good fortune and couldn't believe it.

This was the first time Michelle had visited my office in Center City. And Redmond, though he ostensibly disdained convention as he sought to be above it all, was still competitively curious and observant of what his contemporaries were doing. Michelle was a step up in Redmond's mind, and in his view he wondered how I was able to find favor with her, when guys like him, who were conceiveably more handsome and smarter, could not. In later years I saw Redmond in court on domestic relations matter of his own, and I saw the woman he was involved with and I was disappointed. I thought he could have done better. But when I put it all together, perhaps, as in many things, people appear to be more than what they are; hence the aloofness, the secrecy, and the feigned arrogance. All designed to create an impression, to keep me off guard, take advantage of my naiveté and build themselves up. Fortunately for me, despite my naiveté in the law, at that time, I came to Philadelphia with my world of experience and could see through the faux veneers that were often projected to create appearances. I always kept to my core beliefs and feelings, and instincts about important matters irrespective of the pressure to follow the crowd. Nevertheless, Lang's persuasive powers won out, and I agreed to quit my office with Redmond and move to new offices with Lang in Bala Cynwyd.

Moving day eventually arrived. Lang and I rented a suite of offices on Bala Avenue in Bala Cynwyd, a western suburb on the north side of City Line Avenue. City Line Avenue separates Bala Cynwyd in Montgomery County from Philadelphia County. City Line Avenue is also known as the "main line," the gold coast. Our offices were within walking distance of St. Joseph's University, a main line staple.

This was my third office in less than three years. Moving was getting tiring. Our new offices were at One Bala Avenue on the second floor. We had two separate offices and a secretarial front office and lobby area. The other insurance agent backed out of the deal, so Lang and I had to carry the whole thing for the term of our one year lease.

I continued to advertise for no fault divorces in the Daily News. Lang referred wills and trusts for me to draft for his clients, and we made it without much stress financially. I continued my interest in teaching and was hired by the School of Business at St. Joseph's University to teach several courses in the business school.

Teaching continued to be a side interest of mine stemming from my days in Chicago. In contrast to my Chicago State University teaching experience, both the Morgan State University teaching position and the St. Joseph's experience were the real teaching deals. I was asked to teach Marketing and Advertising and Business Law, my specialty. The dean of the school was an ex-University of Virginia professor who was interested in bringing me on as a full-time faculty member. What I had in mind was a Business Law teaching slot and continuing my law practice.

I had gained several years of teaching experience by now, but what I encountered at St. Joseph's was different. There, all my students were White and middle class. They were not used to having a Black man as their instructor—technically I was an adjunct assistant professor.

The White students seemed to be more volatile, snickering under their breaths, not genuine in their approach to me except for one student who befriended me and became my student assistant. Black students were more respectful, easier to handle, more cooperative in their manner and eager to learn what I had to teach them, but they were not always a pleasure to teach, they could be problematic as well.

My approach was non-racial. I was just there to teach them. I was not there to prove anything to anyone, but just to do my job and leave. Though some of the students showed their hostility, it was of no moment; I was unaffected. My mind was not into being a part of the full-time faculty, nor part of the university community. My heart was still in the practice of law, and teaching was just another way for me to earn money and perhaps build up a steady part-time teaching job. However, my plan was foiled. My model had been adopted by many guys before me. They had all the business law slots filled and were not about to let go. Lawyers who had an eye for this type of thing always secured the Business Law teaching jobs and held on to them as long as they could.

I didn't enjoy teaching Marketing and Advertising, though I did learn a lot during my preparations. I most enjoyed teaching the *Legal Environment of Busi-*

ness, i.e. business law. My new office was just a few blocks from campus. The most enjoyable aspect of teaching at St. Joseph's was the ease with which I could get to and from class, grab a lunch, and then finish my day. It was a nice set up.

The business model for my economic success in Philadelphia was forming as a result of the St. Joseph's job. I developed a triangle model. The law practice formed the base of the triangle and on each opposing side was income from my real estate investments and my teaching jobs. Together, I assumed I would be able to keep enough cash flowing in to sustain my economic objectives through these three sources of income, and it worked.

I was steadily building my practice and gaining more clients, but they were still mainly Black. Only rarely did a White client ever appear at my door. One of these I remember in particular.

I was sitting in my office at the end of a long week when a White woman in her 30s entered and waited for me to stand up and greet her. She was clearly a little perturbed. Before we got too far into her divorce case, she said, "I didn't know they had Black lawyers in Philadelphia. I didn't know you were Black." Apparently, she had read my ad in the Daily News, called to make the appointment, but didn't think for a minute that she was dealing with a Black lawyer. After all Lee is a name often associated with Asian ethnic groups.

I replied, "Yes, there are Black lawyers in Pennsylvania."

Her jaw dropped and her embarrassment was hard to conceal. She muddled through the consultation, paid me the $35.00 fee, and I never heard from her again. Obviously, she preferred to do business with a White or Asian lawyer and that was her right.

Even though I was shocked at her naiveté, I felt no harm, nor foul. The fact of the matter is that most Black professionals, especially in law and medicine, and perhaps in other fields as well, end up working, not exclusively, but mostly within their own racial community because this is their natural constituency. That is why many Black professionals do better in areas where there is an active Black clientele from which to draw.

Sure, I got some White business, but it was far and few between. I would never have been able to feed my family on the White business that I seldom got.

Strangely, the opposite was not true for White lawyers. Because racial politics always redounds to the benefit of the racial majority, they end up getting both Black and White business. To get White business, the Black lawyer must have a crossover appeal and practice, or his competence must be perceived by Whites to such an extent that they feel comfortable using a Black lawyer. This certainly happens, but in my experience it occurs most frequently on the criminal court side of the practice though it occasionally applies to the civil side as well.

At the end of the first semester at St Joseph's, I was confronted with my student evaluation forms. I had not encountered this at Morgan State, and I knew that these White students were going to write me up big time. I didn't lose any sleep over it, but the dean and I discussed the students' perception of me. In effect, he said not to let it bother me. He knew that this was a grand experiment.

Next semester, I taught the Business Law II class, but after that my teaching career ended at St Joseph's. By then, I knew that teaching was not what I wanted to do full-time, or even part-time, unless it was under different circumstances. Teaching had always appealed to my academic side, but I was not a true academic. I was more of a lawyer and perhaps more of a businessman than a lawyer.

The money from teaching was not good and the work was demanding, plus student politics in the White schools made it an onerous endeavor unless it was your passion. It was not mine. The drive to teach came from my parents' profession as educators, a natural tendency to want to share what I knew with others, a desire to be seen as an intellectual expounding on various topics, and a yearning to become an authority on a subject. But the fibers of my being were not woven in that direction. There were aspects of it I liked—dealing with the Black students was especially fulfilling, inspiring them to achieve, setting an example. But fighting the real academic wars of writing treatises and papers, doing research, and reading books without end—even though I'm an avid reader—didn't appeal to me. From that point on, I de-emphasized teaching and reemphasized my law practice and real estate investments.

HANGING OUT THE SHINGLE

As the year of our lease drew near to a close, Lang and I decided we would not renew it. I decided that, since I had my own building, why not set up my office there, stop paying office rent, and settle my practice down permanently? Soon, the decision was made. I would move for the final time to 6412 Germantown Avenue.

The knock against having an office in that community was that clients preferred to see their lawyers, especially Black lawyers, in Center City rather than my locale. Being in Center City connoted success. That was where real lawyers were supposed to be. But I challenged that conventional wisdom. I didn't agree with it. To me, it made sense to have a community law office—a "light house for the blind," a lawyer for the common man, the proletariat.

Parking would not be a problem because I was in the middle of the community and people could more easily get to me. Why travel downtown with all those hassles and parking fees when all you had to do was go to your neighborhood lawyer? I reasoned that, if I decorated my office sufficiently, so that my clients didn't perceive it as inferior, and if I was honest and hard-working, I could make it work.

It would be several years before I could confirm this theory completely, but the concept made sense to me and I knew it would allow me to be in charge of my own economic destiny. And it would also put an end to the endless rent paying pressure and enable me to plow all my long-term resources into my own building and practice. There would be no wasted effort. I had to start somewhere. Wasn't that why I'd bought the building in the first place?

On the night of December 9th, 1981, Mumia Abu-Jamal lay on the dark cold asphalt streets of Center City with a bullet in his chest. Police officer Daniel Faulker lay a few feet away dying from gunshot wounds inflicted from a firefight between the two men. The altercation occurred after Faulker scuffled with Jamal's brother, whose car had been pulled over in Center City.

Mumia Abu-Jamal was a highly regarded Black Philadelphia journalist. Police Officer Daniel Faulker was a White 25-year-old newlywed. The city was riveted by the event. Throughout 1978, Jamal had produced in-depth coverage of the MOVE/

city confrontation and had sought to get to know what MOVE was all about. Having experienced Philadelphia through the Rizzo years, Jamal's race-conscious approach to Philadelphia life was front and center as he exposed the city's police department for what it was. Blacks in Philadelphia knew what to expect from a Philadelphia police officer.

The police officer was ostensibly doing his duty, making a routine traffic stop of a Black man late at night on a dark Philadelphia street. However, the Black man's perception of the stop was that it was unwarranted persecution and unfair. Past and present perceptions clashed—victims of wrongheaded perceptions of race, motive, and intent.

As the blood of the two combatants slowly ebbed toward each other on the midnight street, it mingled into that strange distilling kettle called Philadelphia. Unable to be fermented into anything resembling a unified and caring community of mixed races, the resulting concoction was a toxic brew of divergent perceptions of race. These ill-conceived perceptions were based upon distortions of history, mistrust, and demagoguery. White society has so contorted and distorted the issue of race so that the Black man can hardly find a way out.

The trial of Mumia Abu-Jamal came to term several months after the shooting. Those in the Black legal community knew what to expect. No prominent Black defense attorney stepped forward to take the case. The lawyer finally assigned did his best, but those in the know realized that his advocacy would be more procedural than substantive, more histrionic than real. No one was surprised by the outcome, though few knew the actual details. The Black community had a sense about these things, and we knew instinctively which way the winds of justice were blowing. As my father would always say, "Color clouds justice."

Philadelphia is a microcosm of America; it symbolizes freedom, espouses liberty, but masks deep racial intolerance. How could the poetic beauty of the English language and the lofty principles of human rights and natural law of our Founders', as espoused in the Declaration of Independence, the Constitution, and the Bill of Rights–those enabling documents of the American republic, drafted in this great city–coexist amid the squalid conditions that defined the reality for people of color?

Historically, the trampled, sweaty backs of Blacks, loaded ox-drawn wagons with picked, sorted, and baled cotton; tobacco barns filled with freshly cropped tobacco, strung on five-foot poles and hung on beams lofted high in barns waiting to be cured; cut, cured and distilled sugar cane, refined to satisfy the taste buds of White Americans and Europeans. This thirst for material wealth was born of greed, competition, and the hunger for social status. In order to maintain a way of life imposed by an artifice purchased with the blood of human beings. The Founding Fathers saw Blacks as a means to an end, as chattel. They sought to rationalize their omissions and dehumanize, in their minds, the practical effects of ignoring the humanity of Black people, to trade off the obvious plight of their Black brothers for the political expediency of an immoral compromise.

As a result, the documents that incorporated America treated the humanity of Black people as inconsequential, a process made easier by notions of racial superiority, indelibly staining the virtuous promises of America and turning the otherwise pristine birth of a nation into stillborn ideals.

Only in America could such a hypocritical conundrum exist. The cataclysmic Civil War of 1861 merely shed light on and stopped the most heinous aspects of that barbarism. It would take more than eight generations of Black suffering and deprivation before the promises of those who fought for the end slavery secured the Civil Rights Act of 1964 and began to right the injustices. Every legislative enactment, every court decision, every societal advance that has dealt with the issue of race has been a prospective attempt to retroactively remove the crimson stain of Black blood in service of America. Each one has been an attempt to make right that which was initially wrong—to get back to the purity of the starting point, to the beauty of the enlightenment that gave birth to the ideal of America, to finally reconcile the theory with the reality.

Through overt contrivance and covert policies, proponents of America's false pretenses worked to ensure that the freedom and liberty so brilliantly spoken of in the enabling documents never applied to Black people. What say you then America? The insidious hypocrisy of these acts of co-mission and omission yielded unwittingly conscripted soldiers into this ferocious war fought throughout the various communities of America.

The difference between the treatment of Blacks in the South and in the North can be analogized as the difference between a switchblade knife and a butcher's knife. The butcher's knife makes a bigger, more jagged wound, the switchblade a neater incision, but they both cut, maim their victims, and can be life threatening.

Blacks in the South thought they were worse off than their brothers in the North. In the South, they were forced to swallow the racial pill with a taut hand across their mouths to muzzle protest, force ingestion, and metabolize the poisonous venom. Southern Blacks grew stronger because they knew what they were dealing with and could see it plainly. Southern Whites more rabidly implemented and enforced the racial caste system created during the slavery-era and continued into the Jim Crow era. Blacks who migrated to the North, however, expected better from the Northern Whites. Unaccustomed to the stealthy policies of racism administered intravenously, Blacks were hoodwinked into believing that things were different in the North, when in fact they were not; they were actually worse in many respects. And so there on a street darkened by night, the intravenous drip, drip, drip of racism into the arm of the body politic of Philadelphia had claimed its latest victims.

While I moved my office into 6412 Germantown Avenue, Lang relocated into an office complex in Fort Washington, one of the northwestern suburbs of Philadelphia. I wished him well, but never looked back. I was ready to move on and up. I hung my shingle on the front porch between two small pillars to the left of the front steps: "Otis L. Lee, Jr., Attorney at Law," with my name and phone number in big black letters readable from the sidewalk and the road twenty feet or more away.

Michelle and I occupied the first floor unit as living quarters and I worked upstairs. I hired my first secretary, bought my first copier, and began meeting a payroll for the first time in my professional and business life. My office was at the top of the stairs in the second floor rear apartment. The outer area was a large room with an oval bay area and my office in the rear of the unit was paneled in wood to give it a rich, textured look. I installed a new drop ceiling and there was a small kitchen at the front of the room with a door separating it from the main room. I

(left) Reception area

(below) Two views 6412 Germantown Attorney's Office

had a bathroom off to the left down a small hallway, and my secretary's desk was immediately in front of the hallway to the left.

This was to be my office until I left the New York Life Insurance Company four years later. Michelle would call me to come to dinner each evening, which would end my day. My practice continued to grow, my divorce advertisement was still running, and I remained on the court appointments lists. I was handling a variety of matters at this time, from support to bankruptcy, wills, and trusts. I was mining and trolling for new business in areas with which I had some familiarity. Word continued to spread about my estate planning prowess. Lang sang my praises whenever a selling opportunity presented itself, and he did a good job. I continued to advertise for divorces, child support cases, personal injury cases, and all the bread-and-butter matters community folks need help with. My practice was growing, but what I failed to do, out of naiveté, was to sift and winnow my new prospective clients.

My new business travels took me to the Small Business Administration Regional Offices located on City Line Avenue. I had handled small business issues while at the U.S. Chamber of Commerce and had visited the agency's headquarters building in Washington, D.C. many times. I had even met with the director while soliciting a job there. I had also worked on small business issues while in Chicago as Assistant Director of the Talent Assistance Program, so I thought that, by getting familiar with the small business community in Philadelphia, I would be helping myself along.

However, it turned out to be quite the contrary. While visiting the regional offices, I met a Black gentleman who worked as a career bureaucrat in a middle management position. His name was Elvin Pierce. Pierce was light-skinned, with dark black hair, rotund, but not excessively overweight. He wore a mustache and black eyeglasses. He might even have had some Hispanic blood in him.

As Pierce showed me around the building, we exchanged light banter about small businesses, and I let him know about my law practice. He befriended me and indicated that he might be able to refer some business my way. Indeed, he asked if he could come to see me one afternoon about a problem he was having within the SBA. I said, of course.

A few days later, Pierce called at my office. He arrived at the appointed hour and began to talk about his problem. The SBA had offered him either a transfer to Houston, Texas, or told him he had to resign. Apparently, the SBA was "rotating out" some of its people from its regional office and Pierce had been targeted. He had resigned, but felt he had been pressured into doing so. He was experiencing cognitive dissonance. He asked me to work to rescind his resignation, and I agreed. I wrote a few letters to the SBA asking for a review of his case and requested an appeal. I thought that by writing a few letters, the matter could be resolved. But it turned out to be just the tip of the iceberg. Even though Pierce's limitations period had expired within the agency, he had the right to an appeal with the D.C. Court of Appeals for the D.C. Circuit. Federal Government employees are able to protect their rights to their employment through the Merit Systems Protection Agency, a government agency established for that purpose and the D.C. Court of Appeals for the D.C. Circuit. This court has jurisdiction over matters that are appealed from this agency. I didn't know this when I became involved. I had unwittingly stepped into a pile of dung. Because of my dilatory efforts writing letters to the personnel office of the SBA, trying to reverse the matter administratively, the time for filing his appeal with the D.C. Circuit expired. This was a complex matter requiring specific legal expertise.

I associated myself with outside counsel as the case went along. I hired Steve Ivey, a bearded, overweight White gentleman who knew his way around the federal government's administrative system and had a stronger civil law background than me. As a result we secured for Pierce an appeal hearing before an Administrative Law Judge in the Merit Systems Protection Agency appeal. Steve took charge of the case and did a good job. We took depositions and sought out experts on the issues that Pierce claimed made his resignation coerced. He had claimed he could not move to Houston because his daughter suffered from a rare medical condition and that medical treatment would not be available for her there. This proved not to be the case because Houston was a large metropolitan area with a sophisticated medical community, and he could have secured good or comparable care for his daughter, if he had wished. As a result, the SBA's personnel action was deemed reasonable, and Pierce lost his Merit Systems Protection Appeal. Aggrieved, he then sued me for legal malpractice. What complicated matters was that, not long after the administrative hearing and in a matter completely unrelated to the Pierce case, Steve encountered difficulties with the state bar for an act not in compliance with the rules of professional conduct. As a result, the state of his practice was in jeopardy.

My naiveté was exposed on several fronts. First, as every lawyer eventually learns, never take a case when the facts indicate that the statute of limitations has expired or is about to expire. It's better not to get involved at that late stage. Second, be wary of a wolf in sheep's clothing. Pierce befriended me knowing I was new to the profession of law. He was trying to get in on the cheap after suffering cognitive dissonance and regret about his earlier decision to resign. Next, stay out of areas you know nothing about. Unless you can clearly see the road map of how a certain matter is to be handled, leave it alone or refer the matter to another lawyer who knows the field better. It was not that this area was difficult—it wasn't. It was just that, unless you work in the area of employment law or represent federal employees, you're probably are not going to know what this area of the law is about. It is a specialized niche field. And do not "do any favors"; either practice law the way it is supposed to be practiced and charge appropriate fees or leave the matter alone.

What hurt most about this episode was the betrayal by my client, a person who had befriended me and who I thought meant me some good. Much earlier during my time in Philadelphia, Redmond admonished me that "every client is a potential adversary." Those words became more than rhetoric: henceforth they became, in my mind, the crux of my practice mentality.

The malpractice lawsuit was another matter. It was difficult facing up to the fact that I was alleged to be incompetent in this case. Facing service of a complaint alleging malpractice and being sued for potentially thousands of dollars was emotionally wrenching and was extremely tough on my psyche.

Coming from where I had come from, you would expect that the psychological pressure of accepting service of the complaint and having to acknowledge personally, as well as publicly, that I had allegedly committed malpractice would be damaging to me emotionally, but it was not. Once the predicate for suit was analyzed and the evil behind it uncovered, I didn't feel nearly as bad. The important thing was to learn from this misadventure–about the capriciousness of clients and to become more savvy about how to practice law and screen clients.

Though I had been a poor lawyer on this issue, I was a good businessman because I carried legal malpractice insurance. In the early '80s, legal malpractice became an attractive field of practice for hungry lawyers looking to feed on their colleagues—a kind of professional cannibalism. As ruthless as the business is, it wasn't unexpected that some lawyer looking for a buck would try to take a shot. I had read a book years before about going into private practice titled *How to Go into Private Practice without Losing a Meal*. In this book the author said, "You can expect to be sued for legal malpractice at least once during your career," and he was right. So I had purchased legal malpractice insurance almost immediately after setting up my office during the McDaniel days. However, the experience had still been draining.

Pierce's case was, at best, a nuisance case. It had little chance of success, but it had to be defended. My insurance company hired a big law firm to defend me and the case was settled before trial for a return of the fees Pierce had paid me for services rendered, which amounted to $2,000. The insurance company paid the claim. Twenty years later, I would be the moving force behind and the plaintiff in a legal malpractice suit against a small mid-Atlantic law firm, that was settled for twenty times that amount.

I had learned valuable lessons about human nature and the practice of law. I had also learned that I was operating in a pool of sharks. The standard required by the law in this and other malpractice cases was known as "the case within the case: e.g. but for my actions, would Pierce have succeeded in overturning his resignation? The answer was, no he would not. His burden of proof was too high. His resignation was an unforced, un-coerced volitional act and it was final.

Pierce malevolently tried to take advantage of a young, untutored lawyer. Had I charged him what an experienced lawyer would have charged—something like $50,000—or a sum more closely resembling what the fees should have been, he would probably have accepted his fate. My father, who was my muse on many issues in life, used to say, "Don't accommodate before you're able." I should not have tried to do a favor that I could not afford.

27

❧

LIFE WITH NEW YORK LIFE

IN 1981, the New York Life Insurance Company hired a new Mid-Atlantic Regional Vice President for its Mid-Atlantic Regional Office in Philadelphia, Pennsylvania. The vice president managed all the general managers in the Mid-Atlantic region, which stretched from northern New Jersey to Wilmington, Delaware, and west to Pittsburgh, Pennsylvania. For the first time, they hired a Black man for the position. In addition, the Regional Advanced Underwriting Consultant who worked out of the same office was promoted and sent to the home office in New York.

His promotion left a vacancy for a new regional consultant. His job was to manage and work with the trainers and training managers who staffed the general offices. The job of the consultant was to handle advanced cases that trainers and agents encountered when making sales of insurance, that involved taxation of life insurance, business planning, and estate planning. In this region, the company employed hundreds of insurance agents scattered over more than ten general offices. The new vice president wanted someone in that job with a background in estate planning. He heard about me from his contacts in the city and asked if I would meet him to discuss the job. I agreed, but at the time had no intension of leaving my law practice.

As I talked with him about the job, I told him that I had been recruited by the company several years earlier when I was in Chicago. He inquired at the home office and, sure enough, some of the older advanced underwriting consultants still remembered the trust solicitor from Harris Bank who had flown out to meet them several years before.

I went to New York to meet and obtain the blessing of the Corporate Divisional Vice President, Walter Ubel, a young White suave, blond-haired, mid-level executive on his way up who headed the Advance Underwriting Division. I was predisposed to accept the position, because I knew it was a special opportunity, but the question in my mind was how to keep my law practice? But, as we talked in the company's executive dining room, I forgot about this conundrum and told Ubel, "I wanted the job and that I did not want to just do well, but I wanted to excel at the job because I had not, up to this point, had a chance to be an elitist." Where that idea came from, I don't know. It was totally unplanned, unscripted and unexpected. It was just one of those "excited utterances."

Flattered by the comment the young man smiled, took my comment in and said, "You're on your way. I hope you can handle it."

These were special jobs. There were only ten or twelve of them in the entire company nationwide, one or two for each region. They were for specialists in tax law as it related to wills and trusts, insurance, business, and estate planning. They held a lofty position in the insurance world. And I would be the only Black regional consultant. The job was mine if I wanted to take it. But what would I do with my practice? I never believed that I would be one of the "fair-haired boy" of corporate America. I had been through that at Harris Bank. I knew I would end up being a "gray-haired boy" instead.

I thought about my options, then decided that perhaps I didn't need to make a choice between my practice and this new opportunity after all. Realizing that this would be a great opportunity to further my knowledge in a field that few Blacks knew anything about, and since I knew the business from several vantage points, I took the job without any plans to dismantle my other businesses. Instead, New York Life just became another client of mine that I worked for five days a week. That was my mind set. This time around, I was playing to win, not to lose.

On a late summer evening, during the twilight between evening and night, Cassius Williams, a young, yet mature rising star in the New York Life executive system and the recent hire for the Mid-Atlantic Regional Vice President's job, was driving his new vehicle in an unfamiliar part of South Philadelphia. He had meandered into the badlands that, as a newcomer to the city, he didn't know to avoid. As he tried to get his sense of direction, a shot rang out. It was fired from a street weapon, a .22 caliber pistol.

Blood splattered upon impact when the bullet smashed into the soft flesh of his neck and spurted blood and bits of flesh over his seat and windshield. His head slumped over the steering column as though his neck had been broken. Blood oozed from the wound in his neck. It was so close to his carotid artery that it suffered damage. The jugular vein was nicked, but not severed, which saved him from an instant demise. Some passerby or observant neighbor called for help. An ambulance arrived and Cassius was rushed to the emergency room at the Hospital of the University of Pennsylvania (HUP) for immediate surgery. The surgeons fought to save his life from what should have been inevitable death.

"Fools enter in where angels fear to tread," is the old saying. Cassius had paid a heavy price for being unfamiliar with the violence and opportunism that characterized the city and not knowing which areas to avoid.

Word of the shooting quickly spread throughout the New York Life community in New York City and Philadelphia. I was notified. Michelle and I went to visit Cassius at HUP as soon as visitors were allowed to see him. He looked seriously unwell, as though he was still teetering on the brink of death. The precarious condition of his health was paramount in all of our thinking, because we knew that a neck wound was particularly ominous.

A few weeks after this incident, I went to the corporate home office for training in New York City. It was housed in a huge gleaming skyscraper, a "glitter dome," at 51 Madison Avenue, which was in the heart of the city. The building had many stories, probably forty or more, containing the offices of one of the world's most revered insurance companies.

The agents called this place the "puzzle palace" because of all the corporate intrigue and games played between the power brokers and those wannabe power brokers trying to move up the ladder. The company put me up at the Doral Hotel a few blocks away. While there, I trained with a guy from Delaware. He was not a lawyer, nor was he a regional consultant, but rather a trainer in one of the Delaware general offices. Jim Musser was White, short, bald and rotund. A nice guy, but a Christian advocate bent on proselytizing me when he felt it benefitted him.

During one of our dinners in the hotel after a day of training, he led the dinner prayer and invited me to join him in further prayer. I thought this guy was either nuts or was trying to one-up me during the training, since religion was his strong suit. At the next day's session, the instructor, my predecessor, a lawyer, was reviewing the Law of Future Interest, an esoteric arcane area of the law that few lawyers understand and have much less use for in the real world. But nonetheless we went through it, and this fellow tried to be smart, spouting off comments and got hung up so badly that I could hardly contain my laughter. The trainer tried to straighten him out on the Rule in Shelly's Case and the Rule against Perpetuities, both eccentricities in the law, but he tried to be smart, but without the background he was hopelessly lost.

The training session ended after a week, and I returned to Philadelphia. It was snowing heavily that evening and the snow was deep in Philadelphia by the time I arrived at the Chestnut Hill West Upsal station for my walk to our apartment on Germantown Avenue. The mortgage processing for the new house we wanted to buy had been ongoing during my stay in New York. The deal was not completed, but it was well on its way by the time of my return. Michelle met me at the train station and we walked together holding hands up Upsal Street to Germantown Avenue and to the building. There was a surreal feeling to that whole episode. My arrival back in Philadelphia after being away, walking in the night time with only the glow of the street lights to lead our way, snowflakes falling, deep snow on the ground and the walk home in the quiet of this night snow with my wife, it all felt very good. It had a New England feel to it, George Rockwell like, something out of a story book.

But we were comforted by the smothered, insulated clanging of the trolley cars as they made their way down Germantown Avenue. The depth of the snow reduced the sound and made the otherwise familiar noise soothing and comforting to a light sleeper like me. The quaint old-world style of the trolley cars was the identity of Germantown and drew the neighborhood in, making it a community.

I took my place in the regional office in Center City Philadelphia, one block east from city hall, at 1234 East Market Street a modern high-rise building overlooking south Philadelphia next to the old PSFS (Pennsylvania Savings Fund Society) building. Our offices were on one of the upper floors. Nothing particularly special characterized the space; we had a four room office suite. Each regional executive had an office, and we had a secretarial bay near the entrance door to the left. The regional Vice President was housed there, so was the regional marketing executive, the regional finance guy and me. My office had a lovely wide window overlooking south Philadelphia.

My boss and I got along well. He relied on me for more than the advance un-derwriting skill, he often sought my legal advice on a host of matters. My advice came in handy as he tried to navigate the rocky waters of the New York Life head-quarters puzzle palace of politics. I had his back and he had mine. It was good. We often commented to each other that it was unlikely that the home office would keep us together for long because we were too Black, strong and savvy for New York Life to allow for long.

I traveled around the region giving seminars for agents and holding training sessions with trainers on various subjects. I went out on occasion with our best agents to help on big cases and offered assistance as needed to any other agent who wanted to integrate advanced underwriting into his or her sales approach. My exposure to the agents was enhanced by the seminars put on by the regional office and home office advance underwriting sections. The agents liked all the razzmatazz that we presented to them about premium offset, minimum deposit or "mini dip pop," side funds, trusts, stock liquidation trusts, buy-sell agreements, key-man insurance, marital trust, insurance trust, irrevocable trust, deferred com-pensation, qualified and non-qualified retirement plans, recapitalizations, etc.

My oratorical skills stood me well when speaking before large and small audi-ences of agents from across the region at our seminars. Many of the agents were fascinated to see a Black man articulate about this stuff with fluency. My discourse would spark their interest but only for a fleeting moment. Then it was back to selling insurance the same old way over and over again for most of them. Trying to stimulate their intellectual interest to elevate their minds about the higher uses of life insurance and how it could, if effectively applied, increase their sales, and reduce their lapses was an uphill job for the most part. Agents had to be shown by concrete example and get paid a first year commission from such a sale to believe it was possible. Agents endeavoring to sell insurance the advance underwriting way had to have a commitment to study in order to move into these areas to experience the benefits. For those who used this knowledge they prospered in the business.

Lang Dixon was an example of an agent who "bought the whole loaf." Most insurance agents back then were just high school graduates, some had a year or two of college but very few then were college graduates. The insurance business is difficult, but it is one of the only businesses that a high school graduate or a col-lege graduate can go into as his "own business" without any equity capital, have control of his own time and make good money, become a professional, get a pen-sion and do well. There must however be an entrepreneurial inclination in the individual to succeed at this business. Agents are by nature gossipy: they keep up with everyone and talk about everything. They are also highly competitive. Their business fosters this attitude by having a "top club" that only the top agents can get into and through a rewards system based upon the volume of insurance sold in a year. Keeping up with how much money an agent is making or the technique he or she may be using to make money becomes the folklore of the office. Top club agents are revered and looked up to. Management treats them with high regard because they produce an income stream that generates thousands, if not millions, of dollars over the years for these companies.

Black people for many years were only sold burial insurance by debit agents: agents who went door to door collecting premiums. The owner had a little white three by five card folded in the middle on which was noted each premium payment, which was in effect a savings plan that accumulated just enough money to bury a loved one. Ordinary insurance, that is, insurance sold in larger amounts and for multiple purposes where the premium was mailed in by the owner and where cash value was created was not always available to Black people. Just like everything else in American society second-class citizenship begot second-class treatment in the financial services industry. Not until these companies, Harris Bank included, realized that middle class Black people could be a market for these products and that they could make money selling these services did insurance companies and banks hire Black agents and Black bankers to go after this market.

My time at New York Life as an Advanced Underwriting Consultant was particularly beneficial in many ways. My knowledge of the financial services industry was greatly expanded and I learned to see money in more than one form. My vision about finance, insurance and taxation were expanded. My natural tendency to embrace these areas was nourished, and I became a business oriented lawyer that dwelled in the integrated fields of finance, tax, bankruptcy, real estate, estate planning and the moneyed areas of small business. I knew my way around these fields not as the quintessential expert but as a very knowledgeable professional able to appreciate money in its various representations. In years past I had many opportunities to go into the insurance business as an agent. In law school I helped an agent sell financial services opportunities to my classmates, and he paid me for each lead. I was recruited by Connecticut General Life Insurance Company after leaving law school to work in "their" advanced underwriting section, but the opportunity failed to materialize. I was licensed as an insurance agent by Mutual Life Insurance Company of New York (MONY) after leaving Chicago and relocating in Washington D.C. My association with this end of the business was long.

In the waning years of my association with New York Life, the regional office was dismantled as the company consolidated its regions into fewer regions covering wider geographical areas. My boss took a general manager's job in a big general office in Atlanta, Georgia. I was assigned to the Southeast Regional Office located in Arlington, Virginia. On a day to day basis I was housed in the Philadelphia General Office in Philadelphia in Center City and went to Virginia once a month for meetings. This lasted about a year after which I was reduced in rank but not in pay and made a training manager in the Philadelphia General Office. Advance underwriting was a popular field for insurance companies for a long while, but the cost of maintaining an army of consultants was proving too costly for the sales conscious bottom line actuaries that cost accounted for every penny of premium dollar generated by the agents.

The Philadelphia General Office was one of four general offices in Center City and on City Line Avenue that the company maintained. Our general office was located in the Girard Bank Building next to Girard Bank which later merged to become Mellon Bank. Our offices were housed in a modern skyscraper made of grey granite extending 30 stories into the sky, smack dab in the middle of Center City, on the 15th and 16th floors. Michael Penecale was the general manager. Mike was a short stocky White man of Italian descent. Mike was nice but on the bubble about me. He did not know quite how to handle me. Mike was one of these "what have you done for me lately types." His main man was another short stocky White man of Italian descent, Eddie Dirado. Eddie was the trainer. He was "ok" but Eddie had a problem answering to a Black man who was not a heralded insurance salesman, which I was not. You see, in that world the only thing that mattered was your insurance sales bona fides. I was an intellectual trying to make it in a sales environment.

As you entered the office, there was the business counter where agents turned in their business and processed their new life insurance applications. Three or four secretaries sat behind the counter and the office manager had a small separate office in the rear of the counter area, where he could look out into the counter area observing all that was going on and have privacy to transact his business as needed. Down the hall on the left was a large assembly room where office meetings and training sessions were held. On the right were individual offices for sales managers and agents in a vertical file against the exterior wall of the building. The general manager's office was at the end of the L-shaped corridor sitting perpendicular to the corridor on the right. His office was large and well-appointed with a separated outer-secretarial space for his private secretary. A five foot-wide winding stairwell got you to the floor below. Agent's offices lined the outer and inside walls. A large office to the right at the end of the stairs was reserved for our top club agent, Bernie Klazmer: he had what amounted to a suite of his own. He out-produced everyone else, so he got the biggest suite. My office and that of the trainer was at the opposite end of the top club agent's office. Both of our offices were large and comfortable but without a bay window overlooking Philadelphia: that luxury for me ended with the demise of the regional office.

My problems began in earnest after this transfer. The agents became jealous because of my elevation over the existing trainer who was from the old school of agent training and a close friend of the general manager. Many thought I was practicing law and being paid to be in the office at the same time, which was not entirely true. They began to monitor my phone calls and watch my out-of-office routine, all of which was born out of envy.

The securities industry beckoned the insurance industry, and all big insurance companies began selling variable products and affiliating themselves with stock brokerage firms and investment banks. They wanted their agents to be licensed to sell certain types of securities and variable insurance products. I organized the training for the agents in my office and took the licensing exam myself and secured a National Association of Securities Dealers (NASD) securities license, to sell limited partnerships, tax sheltered annuities, mutual funds, real estate limited partnerships, variable annuities and insurance. I made the highest score on the exam of those taking it from my G.O, but this was not unexpected, and it also was no big deal. I tried to interest the agents in taking the exam and I set up training sessions. Some of the agents got interested, but the bulk of them shied away. My vision was to make the office into a quasi-stock brokerage firm with agents keeping up with the stock market, acting like stock brokers who sold life insurance. I put together a billboard showing the money market rates and stock quotes daily to give the appearance of a money market atmosphere. This was a heady time but all during this time I kept my law office open with a secretary in the office in Germantown who did all of the business that I oversaw on weekends. I never lost sight of "what time it was."

As the years passed, my reputation continued to grow among the Black insurance agents in Philadelphia. Lang was quite well known for his continued use of estate planning in his sales approach. Our affiliation became almost mythic. I received calls from lawyers in New York and other cities asking for help with estate planning clients. One female agent who worked and lived in west Philadelphia introduced me to one of her clients who was in need of a lawyer because her existing lawyer, who had served her well for many years, was dying and she needed help.

Wendy Bee was her name, a middle aged handsome Black woman. A small business entrepreneur with an engaging personality, a graceful woman full of southern charm, humility and warmth. If I had not had a mother, Wendy by virtue of her charm, would have been a good candidate. The irony about Wendy and me was that we were both immigrants to Philadelphia. We were "birds of a feather" to a large extent. We both liked money and were willing to take chances, she much more than me. We were both from the South, loved our families and knew that race was a factor for good—for profit and for misuse. To us it appeared as though the native Black Philadelphians, those that were home grown, were more interested in "being" than in "doing," more interested in the "sizzle than the steak." They were hung up on whose family came over on the Mayflower, whose family was this or that, whose skin color was light and whose was dark and who was the first to go to the University of Pennsylvania, the first to be admitted to the Pennsylvania Bar, the first to be appointed a judge; more interested in the superficial titles and appearances than on building wealth and businesses and political power.

Wendy had built her business from the ground up through sheer business acumen, hard work and instinct. She loved money and knew how to make it. What started as an introduction by an agent of a client to me would endure for many years and continue until Wendy's death. She would become such an important part of my life and my law practice that it would prove difficult for me to extricate myself from her or her business, until years later when her death did that.

The clock was ticking on my time with New York Life, but I had a quiet eureka moment one afternoon sitting at my desk and pondering my tax situation after receiving my tax returns from the preparer. I had made my first six figure income that year! I had crossed the threshold into financial security. It was a watershed event, privately appreciated, for it meant that I could have financial security if I played my cards right. From all sources I was now in the circle of green. What an accomplishment for a guy who came to Philadelphia with a small stake and no roots in the city. Pure hustle was all it was about. Getting out there and getting it done. The income achievement was not narrow in its meaning; it carried with it the most important aspect, wealth accumulation. I was not only making money but I was also amassing wealth albeit small, in comparison to macroeconomic scales, on a fairly rapid scale for a young man not overly talented or inventive. This was not by happenstance but it was my design—my design.

Jealousy, envy, race, the economics of the business were working against me. I knew from the start that I would not have a twenty year career with the company. I also knew that I was not going to leave Philadelphia and my home and law practice. After all, I had fought too hard to chase rainbows at my age. I was not fooled by the corporate carrot dangled at the caprice of big business. The office hierarchy in the general office was led by a general manager long on sales experience: that's why he was the general manager. But he was short on education and equivocal on race. I had little or no support behind closed doors. The general manager's team, the office manager and trainer were all White. There was one Black senior sales manager who did not support me as far as I knew, so my tentacles in the business had a short reach—at best. The culture of the office was on production of "net paid premium," not estate planning. In the real, I was expendable because I was superfluous. I was not really needed for the essential purposes to be served. If I helped an agent do something spectacular or made money for the office my stock went up, but if I did not people wondered why I existed. Higher learning was not the divine purpose of the general office. I was the only lawyer in the office—a lawyer whose work was not necessary to the bottom line of the business. My legal training, though nice, was not required. The "why" of my existence became the cause of the conspiracy for my ouster. Rumors became half-truths and friends became indistinguishable from enemies.

I was offered a job in a general office run by a Black general manager in Westchester County, New York. I knew I was not going to take the job when it was offered, but I played along and went to New York for the interview. I enjoyed the day, the weather was nice and the general manger was cordial. I enjoyed the walk along Broadway and played the hide-the-dice-card game on the street with the street hustlers that always attracted a crowd of on-lookers mostly visitors. The general manager said to me "if you want the job it's yours." I made no commitment because I did not want to lead him on. He was a decent fellow, and he sensed the situation. He was a "for real" guy. I knew what I was going to do. Go back to the full time practice of law. My first and only career love. When companies want you out or want to test you, they offer you something they know you are not going to take: that something usually requires you to make a big sacrifice to show loyalty. Ultimately, they want complete control of your economic destiny. I would have none of that.

The agents in my general office were not interested in what I had to offer. They just wanted to sell insurance anyway they could to get paid. Expediency, not substance, was a sale already made. Securities licensing, estate planning, stocks and bonds intellectual growth and advanced underwriting and all of that was nice and sexy, but not their primary interest. They were side issues at best, not the main attraction. During my heyday, I helped one male agent Darrell Washington, a curly black-haired Black man who wore glasses, with beady eyes, make a top club through the use of Keogh plans with insurance to fund the death benefit. His manager was excited and pleased and so was the head office. So much so that they put our stories into Nylic, the company monthly magazine. And the company made a video sales promotion piece out of the sales approach. Next, I helped a female agent, Betty Tillman, the widow of Ted Tillman, a New York Life agent who used estate planning to sell insurance before Lang and I arrived on the scene. Betty had been in the business for a while with only mediocre performance, but she made a top club the year I worked with her using Key man insurance and other advance sales techniques. The sale was made to a prominent lawyer and radio entrepreneur, Regan Henry who represented a prominent congressman, Bill Grey who was the minister of Bright Hope Baptist Church a prominent Black Baptist church in Philadelphia, the church Betty Tillman attended. I had other successes as well. Prior to the sounding of "taps"—the end of the job—I was invited by a local radio program for the blind to discuss estate planning issues blind people should be familiar with. I was pleased at the opportunity and I rose to the occasion. But in the "what have you done for me lately" world, my time was up and I was out. I was given a small luncheon attended by a few agents and a 21-inch Sharp portable color television set as my goodbye gifts. I was not angry and I was not sad. I was resolute and accepting.

28

⚜

A New Home, a New Son, and an Old Son

OR A WHILE NOW, we had been looking to move to a larger house. Finally, we found one to our liking. It was a Victorian twin in East Mt. Airy on Sedgewick Street, ten blocks north of my law office. When I first saw it, I fell in love with it. The house sat close to the street only fifteen feet from the sidewalk. It was three stories high, had five bedrooms, and three full baths when fully renovated. The house was attached on the east side, but the west side was unattached and had a wide side-yard full of ground covering pachysandra and two dogwood trees. The lot was deep, stretching south all the way to a back street.

When I entered the house, I was captivated by the high ceilings and large rooms. It had a tremendous amount of character, with wooden motifs, crown moldings, wainscoting, hardwood floors, chair-rail molding, parquet floors and marquetry. This magnificent building was one of many that had been constructed in the 18th and 19th century by European immigrants who had settled in this part of Philadelphia for their summer homes. A masonry constructed house, it was bold, stately, and had the charm of the Old World.

The house appealed to both my ego and my sense of antiquity, with all the ornamentation associated with a building of this vintage. It was shown to us by a realtor just in passing as an aside, to see if we might be interested. The house was for sale, but the sale was tied up in a complicated court case. The owners were in litigation because of the untimely death of an only son, to whom the property had been deeded before his death. Upon his death, the surviving wife inherited the property and the son's mother, who also survived him, an elderly woman who lived in a nursing home not far from the house, sued the surviving wife to reclaim ownership of the house.

To get this house, I would have to get involved in the litigation, but I decided it was too good of an opportunity to miss. So, to shake the house loose, I attended the court hearings when the case was being argued by the attorneys, sat in on the arguments, and spoke to one of the attorneys about my intent to purchase. I knew that, if I wanted the house, I had to help the combatants reach a compromise. Well, money talked, and our purchase offer resulted in a settlement that both parties could live with.

The house required substantial renovation. The heating system needed to be replaced, as did the windows; the porches had to be redone; it would eventually need a new roof; the floors would have to be sanded in the near future; and the lower level required remodeling. A number of other projects would eventually flesh out its beauty, but the house had the essentials. It met our needs with its space. It had dignity, was within walking distance to the office, and was very, very special. It would be a place we could be proud of.

We moved into the house in the middle of the winter of 1982. Snow was on the ground and it was cold outside. It took all day to move our belongings from the first floor unit on Germantown Avenue into Sedgewick Street. Michelle and I, as well as the movers, were so tired after completing the task that we all moaned a sigh of relief when we were finished. The movers were cordial and good natured about it all, so I bought them a fifth of bourbon and we sat down and had a laugh and a drink.

Our first night was eerie, cold and spooky. Our bedroom was on the third floor. Michelle and I thought we were hearing stirrings on the floors below, but nothing was there except our imaginations. The Sedgewick Street corridor ran perpendicular through Germantown Avenue on the west to Chew Avenue on the east and was filled on both sides with large, single family Victorian homes all constructed of stone masonry, some that were semi-detached, some that were not. The block had as many White people as Black. All the families were middle class, including teachers, lawyers, retirees, business people, and business executives. The block was clean and exuded an air of success. When I looked upon these houses, I knew these people were well-settled and had some resources.

However, one block north or south of the corridor, the neighborhood changed for the worst. Urban blight was never more than a stone's throw away. The encroachment of the evils associated with this blight caused our corridor to experience break-ins from time to time and the theft of automobiles, porch furniture and plants by those who passed through the neighborhood and sought to prey on their better-heeled neighbors. Hence, we could never really "live" in peace in the house, without worrying constantly about crime.

As time passed, we made the improvements we needed to turn the house into our home. During this time, my oldest son and my first-born child, Otis III, arrived from Norfolk, Virginia for a summer visit. Otis's mother had experienced some hard times after we divorced in Chicago in 1973. She had moved back East and bounced around several different locales until coming to rest – at least temporarily – in Tidewater, Virginia, her original home. My father maintained contact with her during this period. She called him and he responded to her when she requested it.

My Dad was concerned about Otis and always urged Delma to "send the boy to live with his father." Being my first-born and my parents' first grandchild, they stepped into the breach left by my decision to divorce. As doting grandparents, they bought him clothes and anything else he needed, if his need was made known to them.

My life in the interim years had been ill-suited to raising a child. I was still trying to raise myself. I had last spoken to Delma when I lived on Peabody Street in Washington, D.C., during the horrid times of my disequilibrium.

I always loved Otis, but had never felt willing to fight the battle of leverage Delma held over his custody. I would have taken him earlier had she been of the mind to let him go, but she never was. Delma never asked me for, nor sued me for child support. Our divorce settlement made no mention of it, or of visitation. She bore this burden herself after the divorce and before she turned Otis over to live with me. I was not even aware of such issues at the time of the divorce. I viewed the settlement, which included giving her the house and all of its contents, as encompassing all of these issues. Maybe it did and maybe it didn't. A rough kind of justice prevailed.

Delma notified me by letter that Otis would arrive on an afternoon Greyhound bus from Norfolk. When the bus pulled in and Otis walked down the steps, I looked at my son and wondered what had happened to him. I had not seen him for a few years, not since he last visited me on Peabody Street several years before. He was gangly, tall, thin, and looked forlorn, bereft of care. An aura of sadness heightened the quiet countenance of his naturally handsome face, and I wondered whether providence had finally allowed me to get myself together for the noble purpose of saving my son. Otis would reveal later, only partially, that some of his mother's male friends were not too kind to him from time to time and beat him.

Whatever caused Delma to let him come to me, the time was right. He needed to be with me. I sensed a call to duty, a time to perform. This was a mission that rivaled the other essential missions I had to accomplish. Saving Otis would be a reclamation project. Aside from purchasing his bus ticket to Philadelphia, Delma didn't expend one additional cent on Otis's support from then until he was emancipated. It was all left on me and the Lees. Likewise, I had not expended any money when he was with her after the divorce. So perhaps it was fitting the way it turned out.

Seeing him again, after my travails had come to an end, I thought of that newly born little boy that Delma held so lovingly in her arms, had cradled so gently after giving birth to him, as she emerged from the blue rambler I owned at the time, bringing to an end her stay at the Washington Hospital Center in Washington D.C. I remembered the way I had stared at him continually as we made our way to the second floor flat on Gallatin Street in northwest Washington, D.C., where we lived at that time. I thought of his rosy little cheeks and happy smile as he ran around the apartment in his walker with reckless abandon struggling to stay upright. I thought about the toddler I had stayed with and cared for while attending law school, the diapers I had changed and the meals I had fed him while his mother worked during the day. I thought of the lad with whom I had talked for hours, discussing nothing important, but talking nonetheless when we lived on Kimbark Street in Chicago. I thought of our walks together through Avalon Park in back of that house, where we strolled and played after I picked him up from nursery school and we ambled home. I thought of the young kid who had visited me in my apartment in Chicago after I had left him and his mother, and of his mother's remark to me, "Who will talk to Otis after you're gone?" I thought of Otis standing in front of the side steps of my parents' home in Charlottesville, dressed in a yellow summer suit they had bought him for Easter, posing for a photograph one Sunday morning. All of this ran through my mind in a collage of our history together.

But now I had a new wife, a new son, and a new life.

My father made sure that I fully disclosed to Michelle that I had a son before we got married, so there were no surprises for her. But she hadn't expected that he would come to live with us so soon after our marriage. However, she rolled up her sleeves and we both went to work to save this boy. You might have thought that Michelle was an old married woman with many years of experience raising kids by the way she embraced Otis and sought to be his surrogate mother.

Otis was just shy of fourteen when he came to stay with us. Delma and I had raised him together the first five-and-a-half years. His mother had raised him exclusively for the next eight-and-a-half, with occasional visits to my parents and to me, and I had him exclusively for the remainder of his youth.

We settled Otis into his room at the top of the back steps on the second floor of our home. It was a large room with a high ceiling and deep closet that faced the back yard. He had plenty of room to grow and develop. He had the use of his own bathroom, so long as no one was visiting. All of us worked to make the room comfortable. We painted it together, sanded the floors, worked on the walls and decorated it for him. Otis would live in this room until he left for college.

Otis's grades from his last school year in Virginia were poor. His mother led us to believe that he was doing well in school, but when we reviewed his report card we were shocked at his low grades and wondered whether his mother had seen the same results we were looking at. We immediately enrolled him into St. Theresa's, a Catholic middle school that operated a summer program and was within walking distance of our house.

St. Theresa's is a modern, red-brick building that fronted Upsal Street, and was ideal to get him back on track. We worked with him all summer to strengthen his reading and math skills. I put him through Dr. Bergen Evans's vocabulary building program, which I had mastered when I was in high school. Otis learned the words, but he didn't master them. Not then, at least. He would eventually learn them well enough and would continue this effort years later in his academic studies.

In addition, Otis's table manners were below what we accepted. We had to retrain him to hold his utensils the way we expected and to sit and eat at the dinner table in a manner acceptable to us. He seemed to have been hungry a lot and would eat hurriedly as if the food was about to disappear. We had to slow him down and assure him there was more where that came from.

Otis was disciplined. I spanked him from time to time when he disregarded his school work and didn't take his studies seriously. He had under-performed in school while with Delma and this was unacceptable to us. The importance of his academic work was made clear to him. Otis was a child at risk, a risk that I intended to reverse.

Otis was a casualty of my naiveté in love and self-knowledge, a casualty of my avarice for self-fulfillment, an orphan of the impertinence of love, death, dishonor, and a breach of trust, along my disorderly evolution to maturity. He was owed an opportunity to succeed. As his father, I had the responsibility to give him that opportunity, and I was determined at last to repay my debt. I had read a long time before that, "if you are worried about a responsibility, the only way to remove that concern is to discharge that responsibility." Otis was not at fault for any of this. He was conceived during a time of naive love. He was, at that time, the "innocent and injured" child. The fault lay at my feet and at the feet of his mother.

Enrolling Otis in school in Philadelphia was the next big step. We pulled his school records together with the help of his mother, and I took them to the neighborhood middle school, Houston, which was north of Sedgewick Street and off Germantown Avenue to the west. But for the slipshod manner in which his school records were handled by the school staff and their cursory reading of them, Otis should have repeated the seventh grade. I kept my mouth shut and let the school officials make their uninformed and negligent adjustments, and he was placed into eighth grade. He did well the next year, and, under the Philadelphia school system's scheme, was able to apply for a high school of some rank. Michelle and I were unprepared for this. Why would a student have to apply to go to high school? This approach was new to us.

This was the Northern U.S. and the object of the scheme was to "track" kids and channel them out of the college preparatory track. I was appalled and upset. When we purchased our house on Sedgewick Street, we didn't consider the school district the house was in. It was not a concern on our radar, not a factor in the purchase decision: after all, Otis wasn't staying with us when we bought it. But it should have been a concern, because this was Philadelphia.

The Philadelphia School District system is not for the unwary. There are only a handful of schools in the entire district worth sending a child to if you expect him or her to receive a competitive college preparatory education. And because of that, a cottage industry of private schools has carved out a market and continues to expand its clientele because of the cronyism and politics that are involved in getting your child into one of those better elementary or high schools. This system, in my judgment, is a fraud on the taxpayers.

The irony was that several Philadelphia school teachers lived on our block, all of whom sent their kids to private schools while they accepted paychecks from a school district not good enough for their own kids. What an indictment!

Graduating middle-schoolers had to take a high school entrance exam. Based upon their score on that exam, the student is either accepted into one of the "good" high schools or is tracked to what can only be termed a "warehouse" to complete high school. I was determined that my son was not going to be placed in one of those warehouses. I was prepared to send him to a school district north of Philadelphia and pay the high fees required to avoid what Philadelphia had in mind for my child, if that became necessary. But fortunately that expediency was not required. Otis's score on his exam was not high enough to gain admittance to the top high school, Masterman, but, it was high enough to avoid the warehouses to which he was initially directed. And, with my intervention, I was able to get him into a school with a good academic program.

Michelle and I tried earnestly to fill in the bare spots in his background as much as we could. But we couldn't fill in his emotional deficits. And we knew they were there, though Otis tried as much as he could to conceal them. I felt that I understood Otis's emotional state more deeply than she because I was his father and I knew more about his background. Michelle's intentions were honest and good, but I had to temper them with empathy. We often quarreled intensely over methods, rather than intentions. I was referee, umpire, and head linesman during many of these heated battles.

Michelle worked with Otis consistently on his homework. She cooked for him, worried over him, supported him emotionally and washed his clothes. She often lamented that she wished she was his natural mother so that she could remove any hesitation, if any, she had to care and love him more fully.

When she uttered these words, words she spoke more than once, I felt the depth of her compassion and her caring as well as her frustration. Michelle never once complained to me about the burden of child-rearing so soon into our young marriage, if she ever felt one. I am sure she didn't expect this duty, this obligation to be thrust upon us so soon. Perhaps in her mind she was reminded of her experience of having only one parent in her life.

We had many good times watching Otis grow and develop. We enrolled him in swimming classes, piano classes, and the college-bound program at Swarthmore College. He made fast friends with guys his age on the back street and they liked him: Howard, Suleiman, and others. These boys were all from middle-class homes. We had cook-outs in the back yard and Otis invited them all. He went to his senior prom with a beautiful date and drove a rented car that we fretted about until he returned home safely. Michelle and I encouraged Otis to continue these relationships because we thought they were healthy and Otis needed them.

When Otis began piano lessons, he was eager to learn, but was confronted with having to play beginner's songs, such as "Mary Had a Little Lamb" and "Lightly Row". He was embarrassed that he had to start from this point, but had no choice. It was as though he was a teenager sitting in on a first grade elementary class. I had to admonish him that anything worth doing was worth doing right and that if he was not going to do it right, he should not do it at all. He had to accept the fact that he was a beginner on the scales of piano music. But he didn't want to accept it and so he soon quit. He learned to drive and got his driver's license while in high school.

He did all the normal things high school kids do, we saw to that. He didn't miss out on anything that we thought he should partake of. He did well and became a student writer for the Roxborough Times, a local community newspaper published in the area surrounding his high school. He qualified to enroll in honors biology. We were so proud of him. We took two family ski trips to the Poconos and stayed in Hersey Hotels. Lang Dixon and his new girlfriend joined us on one of our trips. We all had a glorious time.

He was baptized at our home church—the Grace Baptist Church in Germantown—and I made it my purpose to teach him intrinsic values, a strong work ethic, and not to cheat on himself. I wanted him to give more than he received—to work hard and appreciate hard work. I instilled in him a culture of reading, of respect for academic achievement, of self-reliance, diligence, and discipline. I taught him to appreciate quality things and not be lured by the superficial, the cheap, and the obvious. I wanted him to have real, enduring values. Above all, I wanted him to know that I loved him and cared for him, hoping that one day he would understand that what happened between his mother and me was not his fault. He bore no responsibility; it was just an act of life.

One Saturday morning early in our lives together on Sedgwick Street, before we began our work routine, I opened a piece of mail from New York Life Insurance Company that had been written by one of its senior executives. In it, the executive said, "A man truly becomes a man when, in this competitive world, he realizes that his fate is in his own hands." This phrase struck me as being profound, and I made Otis remember it and recite it back to me many times. It became his mantra for many years. And he realized he had to embrace the reality of those words if he was to make a life for himself.

As Otis grew older, the shadow of his discontent grew larger. He stifled his anger at me and Michelle for what he perceived as the injustice of his situation. He repressed his rage because he could not vent it fully, though at times he did blow up at us. I continued to enforce a strict discipline to keep order and respect above all else during this period. Even though the situation was not perfect, it was well-intentioned and his home life was good by any standard.

We were doing our best, realizing that we were working from a disadvantage. We had his best interests in front of us at all times, but our task was not an easy one. It is hard to raise a child during his pubescent years who has suffered from mistreatment at the hands of others and feels the loss of what he believed he was entitled to and had missed. Perhaps he felt the pain of his mother's loss as well– not only her physical absence, but the loss of not having me in her life during all those years and the difference that would have made for both of them. And he was right. Had I stayed, her life would have been vastly different.

Perhaps he mourned the life he had experienced after our separation. Only he knew what his mother had endured during those unstable years after I left in late 1973. Nonetheless, the slow boiling anger, the resentment and frustration continued to simmer and gradually his need to rebel began to manifest itself in acts that were unbecoming of him.

Otis was and is a good person. He has a great heart, feels his emotions deeply, cares sincerely and has an empathetic nature. He is a likable young man, soft and gentle. He worked in my law office and helped me clean the real estate properties I was acquiring during this period. Perhaps I went too far in this direction but my intent was to instill an appreciation for the work ethic and respect for real property. Many of my clients thought he was sure to become a lawyer. He filed court papers for me, interviewed some clients on matters within his capability and the clerks in City Hall would often mention him to me when I was there. We made sure he had plenty of clothes and all the basics–that his physical needs were met. He had all the toys and popular gadgets of the time: a Walkman, a bike.

On one occasion, Otis was scheduled to fly to Norfolk, Virginia, to visit his mother, whom he had not seen for several months. She sent him a plane ticket to take his first ever flight. He was excited and looking forward to the trip. He thought he was going to fly on a jet plane similar to a 737, but instead it turned out to be a small prop twin engine plane for short hops, and I think he was a little disappointed.

I told him that before he could travel he had to read a book titled *Andersonville*, by Mackinlay Kantor. The book is approximately 400 pages long and is an upper high school reading level text that had been in my possession since I was in high school. I had read most of the book, but not all of it. The book is about the treatment of Union soldiers by the Confederacy during the Civil War. I gave him ample time to read the book, but on the day for his examination with me he failed because he had not read the book. He tried to bluff his way through, but it didn't work. In a huff, I ordered him back to his room to read the book if he wanted to go see his mother, hoping that he would be highly motivated to obey. I was trying to get over to him the importance of reading and the discipline required, but again he failed.

I was not to be disobeyed or ignored, so I reinforced in his mind that he was not going to be allowed to travel unless and until he had read that book. However, as the time approached for his flight I relented, which I knew all along that I would do, and let him travel. I could only trust that he got my point. Only the ensuing years would tell.

On January 21, 1987, Otis was accepted into Lincoln University, which is near Oxford, just outside Philadelphia. He graduated from high school a few months later, finishing in the top half of his high school class, 65th out of 140 students. Lincoln University has a good reputation for academic excellence, and both Michelle and I thought we made a good choice for his higher academic studies. Thurgood Marshall and Benjamin Nnamdi Azikiwe, the former Prime Minister of Nigeria, had both graduated from there.

Lincoln was within a commuting distance to Philadelphia. Lincoln has a beautiful campus with lush green lawns old colonial brick buildings and Georgian stone structures on 350 acres on a secluded and enclosed campus. A small college with a modest enrollment of under 3,000 students, the environment was fitting for a young person trying to find his way, we thought. Lincoln University was named for Abraham Lincoln after his assassination in 1866. Horace Mann Bond a former president of Lincoln wrote in his book about Lincoln that "Lincoln University was the first University established to teach students of African descent the arts and sciences." Ironically Dr. Bond served as president of Fort Valley State University between 1942 and 1944 while my father and mother attended that college. My parents were privileged to have Dr. Bond visit our home in Richmond, Virginia when we lived there in the 1950s.

Sunday August 6, 1987 was a happy day for all of us. Otis was excited when we drove to Lincoln University on his first day of enrollment. We were all jubilant. We thought of enrolling him at Howard University, my alma mater, but I thought Howard would be too fast for him. He needed to be close to us and have a slower pace. Months later, on our first Parents Day, on Sunday March 20, 1988, we traveled to Lincoln to visit with Otis and to have discussions with his teachers about his progress. We met with several of the faculty and they expressed cautious optimism about his future work. But something was missing, we never saw Otis the entire day. We were supposed to have lunch together and enjoy the day. But it never happened even though he knew we were going to be there. We were embarrassed and disappointed. After a few more hours of walking around the campus and wondering to ourselves about what had happened to him, we left for home.

His first year grades at Lincoln were mediocre at best. But that simmering unrest and anger reared its ugly head and got the best of him, and he withdrew after his first year. For whatever reason, he did not have the vision to see the green paths to his opportunity at Lincoln. Perhaps his early past made him more vulnerable to his demons within. He briefly returned to Philadelphia and to Sedgewick Street only to disappear again. He figuratively bolted from the house leaving jagged edges in his wake. But this time he committed a series of bad acts some of which were violations of the law, not of record because I chose not to make them of record. I chose not to involve the police authorities in his misdeeds, for if I had, his young life of adulthood and later professional life would have been ruined and his future progress forever tainted. Why ruin that which you have striven so hard to perfect and build? He was family and I couldn't and I would not do anything to irrevocably harm him, regardless of how hurt and angry I was at what he had done and how he did it. After all, I truly loved this boy from the day he was born.

I restrained myself and accepted the angst, the hurt of the boomerang. It had all come back on me, the "blowback." The job I thought I had done to salvage a life that I was responsible for had not been as good as it looked on paper. Reality had to have its accounting, its reconciliation. The acts of the past had to be paid for, the clean-up of the past would not be that easy.

Drugs and alcohol were players in his misdeeds, but they were not the sole culprits. He needed to accept the facts of his reality, and to accept the fallibility of human beings, that of his father, his mother and of his stepmother, and of himself. We were and are all fallible, these truths were also at play. He was experiencing growing pains. It was as though he was the mother and the child. He was in labor, and his passage through the birth canal of maturity was difficult. He was out of control and our prideful family no longer could conceal the disunity that had invaded our household. Life had Otis on the run. Our pastor tried to get involved, but I kept him at a distance. I would not reveal, even in the nature of a confession out of stubborn pride and a strict need to protect the confidences of my family, what the true facts really were. I appreciated his desire to help, but my suspicions about his need to know and his ulterior motives for wanting to know innately kept me from allowing him to enter my confidence. I suspected that our pastor, though a good man and a man that I admired, was more curious about what was happening for personal reasons than he was spiritually concerned for our well-being. Maybe I mischaracterized the quality of his desire to know. But, I was protective of the family's privacy.

29

"So Don't You Turn Back"

Mother to Son
by Langston Hughes

Well, son, I'll tell you:
Life for me ain't been no crystal stair.
It's had tacks in it,
And splinters,
And boards torn up,
And places with no carpet on the floor—
Bare.
But all the time
I'se been a-climbin' on,
And reachin' landin's,
And turnin' corners,
And sometimes goin' in the dark
Where there ain't been no light.
So, boy, don't you turn back.
Don't you set down on the steps.
'Cause you finds it's kinder hard.
Don't you fall now—
For I'se still goin', honey,
I'se still climbin',
And life for me ain't been no crystal stair.

OTIS FOUND HIMSELF back in Norfolk, Virginia, with his mother after leaving Philadelphia on unsavory terms. I was resigned to let him go. He had abused my trust. I imagined it was part of the price to be paid. Against my better judgment, I didn't intervene. He needed to get whatever was bothering him out of his system. Parents can only go so far, as imperfect as we are.

After his second year at Lincoln University, Otis enlisted in the army. Apparently, his mother, with whom he was staying at this time, felt that an army experience would be his best bet for recovery. I would not have chosen the army for him, but I was out of the loop when that decision was made. The first Iraq War, "Desert Storm," was waging and I worried about him as I read each account of the war's daily events. Through happenstance, Otis avoided duty in Iraq. He stayed in the army for three years, got the anger out of his system and began to accept life on its own terms being thankful for what he had. Far from home and in harm's way, he realized, perhaps for the first time, that we loved him and that he had an important place in the family. He stopped mourning over what might have been and began to think of his future. He pulled himself up and did not wallow in the puddle of self-pity. His innate desire to make something out of himself resurfaced. Though I would not have chosen the Army for him, the Army was the best solution and the Army probably saved his life.

Upon his honorable discharge from the Army in early 1991, Otis reunited with me and Michelle. The elasticity of unconditional family love expanded to welcome him back into the family with open arms: all was forgiven, and he was extended the right hand of fellowship once again. He came to realize how blessed and fortunate he was to have such a loving and caring family. With the help of a family friend who was working as a professor at Howard University at the time, we secured his acceptance into the university and Otis continued with his education at Howard University. The family resumed its financial assistance to him so that he could finish his degree. Given the opportunity, Otis proved to me that he could be trusted, seized the opportunity and restored his integrity within the family. As I told him later, if I could not trust him how can I use him? Otis is a man's man, a guy with a big heart. In many ways, he is a true representative of my inner-consciousness. He was and is the type of guy you could crawl into a foxhole with and know he would fight to the death for you.

After you have done all you can do, taught and coached all you can teach and coach, the child must be left alone to find his or her own way. The world becomes the school and life the teacher. The "academic bug" and the "values bug," though latent in expression, were securely planted. Otis became a striver, always grasping for the brass ring.

Otis's mode of operation heretofore had always seemed to lead him on a circuitous route. He had always gone on a roundabout way to get to the "right place," but he had always gotten there in the end. His task was "to get there" without the need for the trial of experience to always intervene at whatever cost to correct his path. But it is human to err and he was entitled to make his own mistakes, as are all of us.

Otis graduated from Howard University with a B.A. in History, then went on to do a master's degree in Education from Old Dominion University and an Ed.D. from Bowie State University in Maryland. About a year before he completed his doctorate in education, I asked him whether he was "winning" at the game of life. Looking surprised at the unexpected question, he hesitantly replied "yes." However, dissatisfied with his uncertainty, I answered my own question by telling him emphatically, "Yes, he was winning!" Otis's challenge was to use good judgment founded on good decisions that allowed him to move forward; learning from the past and making good decisions for the future. His success at this would determine whether he ultimately won or lost. I wanted Otis to earn his doctorate so that he would have the dignity that he long sought, a dignity that would agree with the image I perceived he had of himself. The attainment of his doctorate was not only a high academic achievement, of which we are all proud, but it was most importantly, to me, a vindication for him of what he could do with all the properly applied values in place.

— — —

Justin, the younger of my two sons, was born on April 25, 1983. A cherubim incarnate. The embodiment of my hopes and dreams, of second chances, of the chance to "do it right" this time. When in the early morning hours of April 25, 1983, nature brought forth its fruit, a twelve inch clump of pinkish brown flesh oblivious to the world he had just entered, my household was complete. His birth marked the completion of a household built more solidly on purpose, on the portent of success, hard work, and ingrained values. Oh! that day was grand, though it felt understated, perhaps because of the huge responsibility now thrust upon my broad, but as of yet, unproven shoulders.

Michelle made sure that Justin was assiduously cared for. No-one would out do this American mother of African descent when it came to nurturing. He was cleaned and bathed more than he could tolerate, dressed more warmly than he could withstand, and watched over as if he wore a halter cardiac monitor for his protection. Justin turned out to be Michelle's only child. She advocated for a brother or sister for him, but she knew that I was hesitant about taking on more child rearing responsibilities, so Justin was it for us.

I knew what I wanted but I had yet to prove that I could make it happen. A resurrection was taking place, bit by bit by bit. When I returned home that morning from the hospital and told Otis of the birth, we were both excited and we went to breakfast at, of all places, Dennys. For a father who loves deeply, takes responsibility soberly, and is determined not to repeat past mistakes, the birth of a child embraces so many values. Progeny for your legacy is an opportunity to put in place an antidote for sick spots self-diagnosed from past engagements: a chance to put it all together, a sublime reflection by two people who just completed one leg of a long, four-legged journey.

As the weeks and months grew into years, Justin lived the life of an only child. His older brother was 14 years old when he was born and was essentially out of the house most of his growing years. Justin was a jovial child. His laughter was infectious. He was happy. Not a care in the world. His plump, rosy cheeks were always in demand for squeezes and kisses, and I made sure I got my share. "That's enough!" he would cry as he pushed me away after I repeatedly kissed his fat cheeks. Life was good.

As Justin grew older, kindergarten became first grade, first grade became fourth grade. T-ball became "coach-pitch" baseball, and coach-pitch became little league. Swimming and soccer leagues took the center stage of Justin's attention and kept his mother and I thoroughly occupied trying to keep up with all of his schedules.

We enrolled Justin in Suzuki piano lessons. His mother did a good job for the first year or so as long as the lessons remained within her knowledge of the music. But as the music became more advanced, I took over. But Justin had to be made to practice. He demonstrated no innate musical ability, and I tired of fussing with him to make him practice. His teacher also tired of his desultory approach to the lessons. So the piano lessons ended. He was made, however, to study a musical instrument from the fourth grade until he graduated from high school: he chose the saxophone, an instrument his mother played in high school.

However, not all was progressing as smoothly as we led ourselves to believe. One day Michelle and I were summoned by telephone from the principal of the private preschool program Justin was enrolled in, The Ivy Leaf School. "Are you available to come to my office within the next hour or so to discuss your son with me?" the principal asked in a commanding tone.

"Yes, of course. We'll be right over," I responded energetically.

Michelle and I had been sitting in my office reviewing regular business when the call came in, so we stopped what we were doing and scurried right over. We thought all was well. We had not heard or seen anything to put us on notice for what we were about to hear.

The principal was a middle-aged, self-made Black woman, austere in her manner, presumptuous in her tone and a prominent member of our church, but not an aquaintance. She began to impart to us that Justin was devious, had a tendency to use profanity, lied to his preschool teachers during class sessions, and was mischievous. As we sat there in shock, the preschool teacher entered the office. Her slip was hanging below her dress and she looked haggard and downtrodden. She didn't make a good impression on us at all. This was the first time we had met her and now we were doubly shocked—at both her untidiness and our son's presumed conduct. But there was something wrong with this picture. The incongruities jumped out at us.

"You are not talking about our son," I retorted. "He has never done any of these things around us," we both responded as though we had synchronized our thoughts and sang as a choir of two. "Yes I am," the principal affirmed sternly as she looked us in the eyes. "This is your son. You need to get control of this boy." Thoroughly flabbergasted, we thought this woman was off her rocker. She was condescending and her approach was unprofessional. And she was treating us like some of her low-class parents she was used to dealing with. After all, we were both professional people. We were offended by the abruptness and her temperament but rudely awakened to the prospect that our cherubic incarnation might be the personification of Mephistopheles.

"What was the problem?" we thought. Justin has never heard us use profanity before. He's only five years old. Where did the cussing and lying come from?

Nonetheless, we knew we had a problem and we talked about it frequently without any concrete plan to solve it. The boy lied about everything. We would ask him if he had done this or that and he would say "yes," and we knew he was lying. Justin didn't seem to understand the importance of telling the truth.

We were no martinets. We chastised Justin for the usual juvenile mischievous acts: watching television when he was not supposed to; sneaking around in our dresser drawers; wearing my clothes to school without my permission, and so on. But the consistent strand that ran through all of his behavior was his prevarication. It was impossible to get a straight answer from this kid. Even Otis, with all of his shenanigans, either told the truth or simply failed to answer when confronted with the truth.

Meanwhile, Justin revealed a stubborn streak that only added fuel to the fire. To be kind to him, you could say that this demonstrated a character trait of determination and persistence. But he used it to doggedly stick with a lie, even in the face of clear proof to the contrary. This development was deeply troubling to Michelle and me. The combination of lying and stubbornness made for a dubious mixture that foretold only bad things if these issues were not corrected in time. We thought of sending him away to a military school if his conduct didn't change, or a Christian day school, where strict moral values would be instilled into him. We made sure Justin attended Sunday school and church from an early age and he was dedicated in the same church, but baptized in another church. We talked and lectured to him about the importance of telling the truth, but the deceit continued. He would lie about his goings and comings. He intercepted the mail to keep us from receiving any negative missives coming from his school. He forged my signature on his report cards. Our exasperation continued.

I spanked him when he needed it, but not excessively or abusively. His mother and I believed in the old adage "spare the rod and spoil the child," but we preferred it the other way "spoil the rod and spare the child." There was no abuse, but I was intent on "bending the sapling" while it was young, pliable, and tender.

We began to surmise that Justin's repeated lack of candor about simple things was indicative of a defect in his values—if he actually had any during this time. Perhaps all of our emphasis on Justin's physical and psychological development had failed to address his needs for a moral compass, and for him to trust us.

Was Justin's reluctance to tell the truth symptomatic of his lack of faith in the love we held for him. Did he not trust in us, in our love? Did he expect that, if he told the truth, punishment would be administered? Or was it just easier to lie and avoid the consequences? Had he, at his young age, decided to politicize his relationship with us to just 'get along,' rather than take the tough road of truth telling and all that would ensue? It was baffling to us.

If he was not redirected, he could become a criminal, and with this stubbornness and determination, things could really get bad. What to do? Telling the truth requires above all else, courage, it also requires strength, trust, and self-reliance—a willingness to go against the grain, to stand alone if need be.

Justin's lying didn't end quickly. It lasted until his second year in high school, and it was a gradual evolution. Not imperceptible, but incremental and piecemeal. He was given little rewards for bits of truth, reaffirming that he was on the right path. He received proportionate punishment for wrongs committed, but always with a discussion to solicit his understanding as to why a punishment could not be avoided: that he would be received with more respect because he faced up to his doubts and his conduct. We reminded him that any punishment would be worse if we later found out that he had lied. Which path was the course of least resistance? Let him make his own decision and then pay the price, we thought.

Along with the lying, during his late middle-school years and early high school years, he developed, for some reason, an aversion to us, his parents. He was ashamed of us—a typical, youthful immaturity. He did not want us around during school events such as band concerts and other public school events that parents usually attended. Was he ashamed of us or just immature? After these events were over, he was slow to acknowledge us. When other kids would run to greet their parents after these events, Justin was nowhere to be found. We would ask ourselves, where is Justin? He knew we were "there for him." But he acted as though we were not. His conduct regarding us during this time was an abrasion to our feelings. How could he treat us this way after all the love and caring we were putting into him. Where did this come from? We confronted him about his treatment of us, and of course he denied any wrong doing. This conduct receded as the months and years passed. But these episodes discolored our otherwise unfettered love for him and set a marker that would always keep us on guard about whether this kid really cared and the extent of his caring. Though these events occurred during his youth, the episodes still lingered and helped fill in some rough brush strokes over the emotional portrait we painted of him in our eyes.

We preached, lamented and labored with him over the issue of truth, lying and trust, because this was important. We explained that telling the truth was the simplest and easiest way to solve a problem: it made you feel better, it made life less difficult. We also said that truth telling would not absolve one from appropriate punishment, but by telling the truth one earned self-respect. Everything cost, telling the truth cost. And by acquiring the truth-telling habit, the discipline of accepting responsibility for one's actions would become second nature. Lying to others and to oneself is nothing more than the veil of avoidance of responsibility, a retreat from reality rather than an embrace of it. I told my boys, "at least be truthful to yourself."

We stressed to Justin that by continuing to deceive he was ruining his credibility within the family. How could we trust him with the family car if we could not trust him with simpler things? I explained that, even within families where unconditional love abounds, family members still have to deal with the politics of their behavior and have to earn their credibility within the family. How will you be received within the family?

One day, while reading the newspaper, I glanced at the television and listened to a child psychologist discuss lying by young children. He said that it "was indicative of high intelligence and an expression of their creative instincts." I prayed that this was the case with Justin. It gave me pause, but didn't allay my fears.

We have never dissected how Justin reconciled those incongruities within his being that finally led to the elimination of the need to lie and use the expedient way. However he resolved these perplexities, his mother and I are thankful. At last, a moral code had taken hold.

Before Justin graduated from high school he had to finish "my" high school which meant no television Monday through Friday with the exception of the sports games on Sunday afternoon. He had to read *Andersonville*, which he did, and to master the 500 college vocabulary words of Dr. Bergen Evans which is a family tradition including how to spell them. And on this task he was rigorously tested by me. He did very well on the vocabulary training. He was given tutoring by an outside tutoring center on how to study and prepare for class. These tutoring sessions lasted for several weeks, and I reinforced this training at home with supplemental books on the subject and review sessions with him, even though he tried on many occasions to "B.S." me. I wanted to make sure that he knew the science and not just the art of studying. I had always felt that if I had known, really known, what the academic game was all about I would have done a whole lot better in school, and been able to take earlier advantage of my abilities. I did not want him to labor under that ignorance. Next, he had to read and discuss with me *The Autobiography of Malcolm X*, by Alex Haley, *The Souls of Black Folks*, by Dubois, *Invisible Man* by, Ralph Ellison, and Professor Harold Bloom's book *How To Read and Why*. Dr. Bloom recited that reading was a monastic experience to be enjoyed by the truly disciplined. All along the way Justin was given books to read for Christmas presents and birthday gifts. During his earlier years when kids enjoyed cartoons, his mother and I sought to acquire the old cartoons of Rocky and Bullwinkle, that we thought were more intellectually challenging and tried to interest him in them. But what he really liked which was his favorite was a compilations of Garfield cartoons which he seemed to have internalized and made his *modus vivendi*, his way of life. Finally, I required that Justin write down a list of the old adages, aphorisms and sayings and quotations that we have enjoyed as a family for years. Such as "a fool and money soon part," "reading is to the mind what exercise is to the body," etc. His list may have contained at least nine or ten of these sayings.

My "high school" education for him would not be complete without a trip to Europe. We began to travel with Justin years before he entered high school. By the time he entered the 8th grade Justin had already been to Disney World twice, Mexico, Jamaica, Puerto Rico, touring Old San Juan and new San Juan, and to Italy where we toured Rome, Florence, Venice and Milan. Justin had already traveled to more places as a youth than I had as an adult by this time. I wanted to make sure before he left for college that he had certain experiences that kids on his economic level were having. And I wanted him to have them at a time in his life that would be meaningful, memorable and leave a lasting impression. So I began planning a family European trip for his junior year in high school. We toured many places in England and in France. From the Cotswolds to Avon and to Oxford in England. We were in Paris on Bastille Day which we planned, and we celebrated with the Parisians on their national day of celebration. We went to Normandy Beach and to Reims, just to name a few places. Since we had already been to Italy there was no need to return at this time.

Early in his high school career, Justin was instructed not to associate with any student in high school unless he or she was on the honor roll. These instructions were given to him to make sure he only associated with kids who were trying to make something of themselves. But he violated the rule, and we knew it, so the rule was restated over and over again and kept in front of him until he got the point: leave the bad guys alone. Only associate with people you can learn something from.

As his grandfather vouchsafed on many occasions, relaying graciously, as he often did: "He that maketh many friends, maketh his own destruction." This epigram was repeated to me many times when I was in high school until I got the point. And I hoped that Justin would get it too. Justin was told early in his academic life, around the dinner table, that in today's world it was nothing special for a Black man to attend a White college, but that, in my view, it was something special for a Black man to excel at a White college. I urged him to take the DuBoisian approach "to beat them" at the academic game and to adopt DuBois's routine for study and work, up early and retiring late.

Justin's talent was revealed in due course. He was bred to win, his pedigree was good. He was the third generation of the Otis Lee clan to attend college, and his mother and I made sure he got what he needed to succeed. Justin finished the University of Maryland as a College Park Scholar with distinction, Dean's Honor List, Phi Beta Kappa, Gamma award winner, highest G.P.A. in his junior class and *Magna cum laude*. Three years later he graduated from Harvard Law School with distinction, including being awarded by his fellow students The Barack Obama

Award. Justin's achievements are important because they not only demonstrate his talent but manifest the effort his mother and I put into him to help Justin make himself a success. His success is a flagship for our family.

So perhaps the psychologist was right after all. Justin became my intellectual alter ego. He received the kind of intellectual coaching from me that would have made a big difference in my academic life had I received that kind of intensity from my parents, and he did the hard work.

Most important, I raised two sons and both are doing well and on the right track. My sons are the left and right ventricles of my heart. I cannot make it without either one, but with both I am whole. I would not want to raise these sons all over again: it was too much work. But, if I had to, I would still resist the contemporary, the fads, and the fashionable. Instead, my emphasis would be on the old school, the traditional bumpy road less trod, and on character building. In that way, I am a relic from the past.

— — —

I used my retirement savings accumulated during my tenure with New York Life to remodel and refurbish the downstairs apartment on Germantown Avenue and move my law office from upstairs into the newly renovated office. The unit downstairs had been rented during the time I was at New York Life, to a section 8 tenant—a nice Black woman with one child, age 10. I hired an architect, got the required building permits and zoning approvals for the work to begin. My neighbor on the south side of the building filed an objection to my use permit application that was resolved without much difficulty. An occupancy permit was eventually issued by the city. My neighbor held a grudge against me from the time I handled his ex-wife's divorce during the very start of my practice in Philadelphia, in 1979. Perhaps it was a mistake to have taken her case, but I jumped in and made an enemy out of my neighbor in the process.

Michelle and I were excited about the new office and the plans we implemented. The architectural plans sketched out the office to use all approximately 1,500 square feet of space which ran from the front porch of the building to the back porch. Michele and I lived in this apartment when we were first married. As you entered the outer vestibule, you encountered a white colored steel door electrically controlled from the office which denied or permitted entrance into the inner hallway of the building. Immediately to the left after entering the small hallway was a heavy solid wood door with eight vertical strips of wood extending from the middle of the door to the bottom. Above the door knob was a small window rectangular in shape and large enough to allow me or my secretary to see who was at the door before opening it. An intercom in the outside vestibule with a door bell instructed the client or visitor to announce him or herself before the electrically controlled lock would be released. Being able to clear a person for entry gave us a needed buffer of protection that we would often need and use.

As you entered the office, a large reception room and secretary's desk greeted the visitor to the immediate left. A counter to the right of the of the reception and outer office extended three feet from the bathroom. The counter started at an open computer room and secretarial station on the right. It was built to a height of five feet, and extended from just beyond the front door three feet past the bathroom on the right to the doorway separating the attorney's office from the reception and computer room. The counter ran parallel to the right side wall. At the end of this eight-to-ten foot hallway, with the open area above the counter top to the left, was the computer room, a free flowing open space. High ceilings in both of these rooms added additional space and roominess.

Through the door into the attorney's office was a large room, one could call it a "great room." This room housed my office. Behind my office was the kitchen, converted into a storage area for file cabinets and additional book shelves. The place looked great! A *chef d'oeuvre*, a masterpiece in office design in my opinion! I had realized my vision. The office gave me the stature that I envisaged for myself; it represented me. It had the feel of a Center City law office with the ease of access of a community law office. The walls were painted light beige, and drapes and sheers were hung from the long windows. I purchased new office furniture and installed a state of the art phone system with an inter-office intercom system. New computers were in place and a dictation system given me by Dad was wired into the secretary's desk where her computer sat so that my dictation went straight to her for transcription. I purchased several paintings from Lucien Crump, a local art dealer on the avenue and hung them in the office.

Upon entering my office to the right were two sets of hand-made wood book-shelves six feet high and permanently mounted to the walls. These extended from the door to the front of my desk situated perpendicular against the right wall. A boxed ceiling rectangular in shape was built to replace the existing high ceiling and allowed for the installation of recessed modern lighting. This gave the office a living room feel and a soft ambience. To the left was a five-foot deep oval that revealed a three-windowed bay. The distance from the oval to the windows allowed enough room for a round conference table and four chairs. In the back of the room were two wooden, wall-mounted bookcases with a credenza beneath. A brown carpet was laid throughout the office suite.

On opening day, we were ready for business, except for one thing: the phones didn't work. Michelle and I went into a panic. What to do? We called the phone company and determined that the relay box in the basement which controlled the phone system had a glitch in it. After several anxious hours, a repairman appeared and the problem was solved. We were finally ready to receive our first new clients.

I bought sets of books and volumes of texts on various legal subjects: all the statutes of Pennsylvania and the Encyclopedia of Pennsylvania Law, form books, hand books and continuing legal education books. For a solo practitioner, I had a good library. Since I was not near Center City and the Philadelphia Bar Association's Jenkins Law Library, I wanted to have enough resources at the ready so that I could, at least, get to first base on most legal research in my office.

I arrived for work each morning tie and coat affixed—the "uniform" I called it—by 9:00 am and worked until 6:00, most days Monday through Friday. I also had office hours on Saturdays from 10:00 am to 2:00 pm. The benefit of being in the same place for a considerable period of time is that people get to know where you are and what you can do, come to depend on you being there. I had gotten used to the way Philadelphia lawyers practiced law, which is to out lawyer you, intimidate you and beat you down. Everything is contested in Philadelphia. This time around I had internalized many lessons, and I understood more clearly the business of practicing law. Cash flow was the secret; getting it and keeping it coming was the challenge, in addition to executing the work required. And getting a result that would make a satisfied client into a repeat client.

My naiveté and eternal optimism about human nature continued to be eroded by the duplicity, hypocrisy, callousness and shades of nuance in the conduct of my dealings with other human beings. My ability to have tenure in my practice was predicated on my ability to master the attorney-client relationship and, as I matured, to learn how to manage client expectations. The confidence to charge fees commensurate to the size and complexity of the task required balance, maturity, girth and insight. To know how to use the fee as a defense against your inability to say "No!" was tricky.

I remember reading in an elementary American history book while in Jefferson Elementary School in Charlottesville about the president and his "kitchen cabinet," a group of informal advisors who were unofficial and detached, but whose advice the president would seek out to aid in his decision making. To survive as a solo practitioner, without the benefit of a legal confidante or office associates to bounce issues off of to "chew the legal fat with," is not to survive at all. I had to have some people I could call if I had a question and most importantly, who would be responsive to my needs. A dependable array of legal confidantes was not easy to find, not being a Philadelphian, and with vanity, money and time opposing the unrequited need. But I managed to put my cabinet together.

For criminal law questions, I relied on my friend Jack Myers, a true veteran of the criminal law business. Jack is a good guy, a man's man—a true advocate with a great sense of humor. Jack always called me "Mr. Handsome," with a smile, a tease that always put us on good terms when we met. I first met Jack when I first came to Philadelphia while still at the Chamber of Commerce trying to meet the requirements of the District of Columbia Bar for admission to that bar. Jack was Jewish and a friend of my cousin in Philadelphia, Eddie Lee, who at one time in his career rose to the position of the Clerk of Quarter Sessions Court, the criminal division of the Court of Common Pleas. My relationship with Jack continued from there. Whenever I was in need of advice on criminal matters, I gave Jack a call or went to see him. He was accommodating, respectful and always pleasant. We teed off against each other in a contested divorce matter which enhanced our relationship, having gained a mutual respect for each other through this legal contest.

In civil matters, I called on the defense lawyer I met who defended me in the Elvin Pierce case. We had gotten to know each other reasonably well, and since my "rear end" was already exposed, so-to-speak, there was no pretense about asking him questions on matters I did not understand as well as he did. This relationship only lasted for a brief period. For estate settlement matters I developed a rapport with the chief law clerk of the chief judge of the Orphans' Court. This judge assigned me to a court appointment to audit a trust, a rarity in Philadelphia for Black lawyers especially. As a result, his office looked upon me as a lawyer to work with. This committee I formed was not perfect or always limited to these people, but I developed a relationship with a small cadre of folks who allowed me the freedom to reveal my ignorance and learn something from people who had more experience than I had. This was not an easy accomplishment.

For the most part though, I kept my own counsel and learned by reading, doing and attending CLE classes, Continuing Legal Education classes. My daily work in the salt mines of every day legal issues confronting the human experience in the working class and middle income strata kept me busy. This work had no end to it and continued uninterrupted except for the business of my "big" client, Wendy Bee, who offered me a varied menu of legal issues to solve. I was working for Wendy practically every day in one way or another. Her business came to anchor my practice. I spent endless hours both during the day and at night trying to solve her tax problems, filing and defending claims against her catering hall and schools and helping her elevate her vision and back office operation, negotiating with the city and the neighbors, the zoning boards and a host of entities; "bailing water" to keep any one of her many adversaries from bringing her down. I was, in effect, her general counsel. I referred matters to outside counsel and/or I jointly handled matters with outside counsel on many of Wendy's issues. In all events she relied on me, she trusted me and I her, as I managed the cases. She looked to me to get the problem solved and to choose the right outside lawyer if needed.

For Wendy, "the tax man cometh"—in the form of the federal government and the city of Philadelphia, these entities were the 800 pound gorillas in the room at all times. It was not the tax on income that gave her the headache; it was the social security withholding taxes on wages, one of the most sacred of all taxes in the tax system. Through this tax on employers and employees, the federal government funds the social, health and welfare programs it pays to the citizens. Though Wendy had many other problems, her failure to get these problems finally resolved and under control caused her much anguish. The problem was keeping up with the payments, the never ending payments of taxes on employment wages, social security, etc. The taxes, the penalties and the interest, the liens, the accounting, the record keeping were tremendous burdens on this client. I remembered the remark of an old friend from the Chicago days, as mentioned before, that "minority businesses make and obtain about enough money to go out of business rather than into business." Experience had taught me that no matter how good a business person might be at making a particular widget, if they do not know how to run their back office operation—i.e. the accounting and record keeping—they will not long be in business. This rule applied to Wendy. She knew how to make money and she loved money but mastering the bookkeeping and paying the taxes were her undoing. And the way the tax system is designed, your failure to adequately address these issues or your neglect of them will result in a loss of equity in everything you acquire. You look up one day and own nothing. The government owns it all.

I now had two secretaries, one full time, one part time and Michelle as my clerk when she worked for me, which was not consistent except when she was between career postings from time to time.

Wendy's business needs kept me on the move. Between helping her out and pushing my other cases, I always had something to do. The divorce business was good. I was settling contested divorces with real estate and pensions in the marital estate. I was doing name changes, real estate closings, incorporating businesses, drafting powers of attorney and simple wills, all the fodder of a community based law practice. As I peered out over the savannahs of this never ending plateau of unfurling needs, demands, pressures and stressors, I knew for the first time—

heightened by my concern about the stress that I was under—that I did not want to die in Philadelphia chasing this elusive mantle of success. What was success anyway? Hadn't I achieved it? What more do you want? I could not answer that question; I just kept going and going and going.

After one particularly stress laden court encounter in city hall, I walked over to Sansome Street just south of Chestnut Street to a bar in the Oyster House, a landmark restaurant in Philadelphia where I often treated myself to lunch. They served some of the best seafood in Center City. I sat down, sighed a deep breath of relief and ordered a drink, a double Jack on the rocks. It was not long after midday. As I exhaled I mumbled to myself, "another hearing is over. I am going to survive this and I will use whatever methods I reasonably need to succeed." I was always under some kind of stress in this job or self-doubt, wondering about whether I had prepared enough, anticipated enough, knew enough, always concerned about whether there would be some case or rule of court that I may have overlooked or that I did not know. Were these normal feelings felt by other lawyers? I needed a psychotherapist. I was always searching subconsciously for someone nice and kind, a sympathetic ear: a nice person, someone to understand my insecurities and professional needs. Or was I "looking for love in all the wrong places?" Better yet, was this the quiet calling for the warmth of my mother that I was yearning for, the reassurance, the need for someone to "take it easy on me" to be gentle not harsh, caustic with everything being reality based? Her comforting arms always gave me that security.

But I had to realize I was in the big leagues now in a major market, and as one lawyer told me "when you practice law you take your license in your hand each time." What was it about me that sought out the kind hearted but encountered the mean spirited, arrogant and pompous individuals? This was not my normal relaxed mode. I was not arrogant or pompous, but I had to "put that mask on" and keep my head up to keep from being battered and wounded by all the players I had to contend with in this city of "brotherly love." I said to myself then, and I would repeat it to myself from then on as long as I remained in this business, "expect the unexpected": this became my motto. I would always say that to myself before entering the court room because there was always some unexpected event, a case or a rule or some other thing, that would occur at trial or during a hearing that would put a wrinkle in the proceedings; it was a rare event if that did not occur. I knew I was in this by myself. It was a lonely somewhat isolated feeling, but not a feeling of hostility, to know that I really did not have any "friends" in this business, as in Chicago. I was still flying solo.

The Criminal Division of the Court of Common Pleas required, along with the regular court appointment, that appointed lawyers also take on a certain number of PCHA's, Post-Conviction Hearing Act cases each year. Under this system criminal defendants usually had twenty days to file appeals of their convictions under this act, and the court would appoint an attorney to review the trial record for errors and file post-conviction motions for a new trial in the trial court where the conviction was first obtained. Upon filing these petitions the trial judge would rule on the petitions, issue an opinion and then the case would be ready for an appeal to the Pennsylvania Superior Court. I dreaded these appointments, as did every other lawyer on the court appointment circuit, except those with an appellate bent.

When I received these appointments, I had to go down to city hall or over to the municipal court building and get the trial transcripts, which could be voluminous, read all that stuff, prepare a brief on the errors as determined, file the petition and go through a hearing. Most of these cases were losers and seldom resulted in a different result, but you had to go through the motions. My approach to this work was to hire a researcher who would assist me in reviewing these cases and drafting a brief. After several reviews and consultations, we would decide on which issues were worth briefing and go from there. I did not look forward to these cases, they were time consuming, paid little money and usually resulted in nothing.

But on one occasion it was worth the effort. I was appointed to a PCHA case involving a Black man who was convicted of robbing an office at the University of Pennsylvania, a simple enough case. The defense counsel had made some errors by not objecting to and introducing some evidence, and the trial judge made erroneous rulings on jury instructions which all resulted in a botched trial for this man. I prepared the brief and went through the hearing. The PCHA judge overruled the petition, and we filed an appeal. I argued the case before the Pennsylvania Superior Court before a three judge panel, the first time I had ever done this. I was nervous but I kept my composure and answered their questions. My usual confidence in my oratorical skills served me well, and I had a good experience. This was the only time that any one of these cases I handled ever went that far. Surprisingly, when I got the appellate opinion back, the court actually agreed with my argument and sent the case back to the trial court judge for a rehearing on several of the issues we pointed out. It was a victory! I had actually made some law.

30

"TOO BUSY SHARPENING MY OYSTER KNIFE"

"Even in the helter-skelter skirmish that is my life, I have seen that the world is to the strong regardless of a little pigmentation more or less. No, I do not weep at the world—I am too busy sharpening my oyster knife."

–Zora Neale Hurston, *How It Feels to Be Colored Me*

I SAID TO MYSELF when I began my business life that "I want to retire when I reach fifty-five years of age." To retire at that age would require an economic strategy that would be profitable and whose fecundity would be sustaining. I chose investing in multi-family residential real estate to get me here. I had grown up around real estate. I had observed my father and worked with him: I painted houses with him, built steps with him (though he was no carpenter and the steps we constructed would never have passed inspection), built roads, cut down and dug up trees, and later implemented many of his strategies. When I was a little boy, my friends were too scared to come to my house to play because they were afraid they would be put to work. I was embarrassed.

But from whom did Dad learn the real estate business and acquire this "entrepreneurial thing" he started in our family? From his rich White friends and associates that he sought out, and from whom he took coaching, and from his research and reading on the subject; coupled with his determination not to be poor. When Dad was working his way through college he did a lot of caddying, and I am sure he heard his White patrons talk business, and he was exposed to the finer things in life. He grew up poor. As he said, "I grew up on the rough side of the mountain." In addition to this exposure the Lee genealogy has a business and industry gene buried in the fabric of our DNA. All of his family members, whether educated or not, made something out of themselves and demonstrated some kind of ingenuity in doing so: combining his effort with that of my mother, whose father Patrick Moon owned the land on which he built the family home and was also a tobacco barrel maker, made for an assiduous effort to satisfy an insatiable drive to shield himself against the poverty of his youth. As an adult he became an inveterate hunter gatherer. This partnership of thrift, hard work and conservative skepticism of White good will, insured that they would fortify themselves against poverty and guaranteed that his family would control their economic destiny.

I watched my dad do his real estate thing and do his thing he did: "nothing succeeds like success." Somewhere in my being during those years that I observed him, I acquired the insight, and perhaps I, too, inherited a gene from my ancestors. I also gained the courage to pursue what would turn out to be an avocation that would predate my work in the law, run parallel with it and out distance my work in the law. Real estate was, for many years, the bedrock of my family's financial underpinnings. It was a natural proclivity entered into without a moment's hesitation or a second thought as though it was intended or self-ordained. For the poor man especially, it is the way to accumulate wealth, *faute de mieux*. All wealthy people own real estate because of its unique investment characteristics. However, it is not a job for the faint of heart if you are an active rather than passive investor. It is a brutal game and takes no prisoners. It is an investment that is capital intensive, requires good money management skills, vision and a long term investment strategy.

My mother once remarked when we were sitting around in the living room talking about real estate and money matters, "when the Black man was brought over here he didn't have anything and the White man has had his foot on his neck ever since." In the 50s and 60s when I was growing up some Blacks in conversation with my dad and others would refer to poorer Blacks as "not having a pot to piss in nor a window to throw it out." When you talk about poor Blacks the question is, where would they get the wealth from? Blacks back in the days of Jim Crow fought hard to have "something" for themselves and those that had the vision and pulled themselves up by their bootstraps were protective of their status and accomplishments. It was not arrogance or condescension but a competitiveness that manifested itself in other areas as well such as in education. Here, educated Blacks back then were heard to say, "I got mine and you got yours to get," referring to other Blacks trying to reach that level of education. Even among the downtrodden, capitalism and its competitiveness affects all classes.

Blacks have always had to play it safe. They could not take risks. They had to rely on what they could touch and feel. That probably explains why I never attended a White school when integration came into our community. My parents were distrusting of the White schools, their orientation was with the Blacks—with what they had known all their lives. They stayed on the "Black hand side." It is analogous to choosing between investing in a stock or a bond. The stock has tremendous growth potential but is full of risk; you could lose everything. Whereas the bond is relatively safe, though it may return a lower rate of interest, it is sure. It would take the next generation to move into these unchartered waters. So my folks, like many other middle class Blacks, played the game to win, once they got a "toe hold." As Dad mused repeatedly during these days: "if you see a Black man with something, he deserves to have it." Economic gains by Black folks were hard won gains. Blacks now, are barely sticking their noses in the macroeconomic tent in a multi trillion dollar economy. We are just beginning to live the middle class life in sufficient numbers to make a difference in our children and grandchildren's lives in the transfer of wealth game.

From my family's perspective, Blacks have to work for themselves, quit depending on the White man for everything. Use the example of the Jews and the Asians: they go into business for themselves because they know the White man has nothing for them to do. My parents went into the real estate business because they knew that their tenure, even as school teachers, in the segregated South, was tenuous and uncertain from year to year. They could not depend for their economic security and freedom on the caprice of the White man. They had to indemnify themselves against his capriciousness and the whims of race in White America. Dad often remarked "that there was nothing Black about us but the color of our skins." By this he meant that our lifestyle and values that we operated under were not that of typical Blacks, not that we were better than other Blacks but that our thinking was different than many: we looked at life through a different spectrum.

The entrepreneurial spirit is the vital force behind any investor's desire to separate him or herself from the mundane, ordained, regularized carbon-copy way of life prescribed by our society as a pathway to happiness. When in fact that route it is not a pathway to economic success but a pathway to an uncomplicated life with a predictable outcome. For some people this is fine. They are better off working for somebody, making money for the boss. I want to be the boss. That kind of life is in effect like, "three little boxes living on a hill top" all imitating one another and continuing the debtor culture of consumption that is perpetuated to sustain the moneyed class. To break that mold, one must be willing to be different—to take risk. Just like in the card game "Wis" that I played in college, the entrepreneur must but be willing to bet on the "kitty." Like in basketball, to be the "most valuable player" in the game and most importantly in the economy, you must be able to "make your own shot," to be imaginative to create wealth, to "get to the basket off of your own dribble". Then, you can "make other people better".

That is the life I envisaged for myself. I have never been able to work for anyone except myself for any length of time, and I have never been a team player except on the team I created. And I have always instinctively marched to the sound of a different drummer: when the crowd is going one way I am going the other. I tired early on in my working life of looking for jobs, glad-handing on the job, bowing and scraping, not having job security, trying to be the fair haired boy, knowing that was impossible. So I made my own job, created my own economic security based on my skill level, work ethic, ingenuity and individual savvy. I bought a piece of the market when I moved to Philadelphia rather than being subject solely to the market. That is why I fought so hard to become a lawyer to have that independence and singularity.

It all began for me shortly after my marriage to Delma in 1968. I was a junior at Howard University. Once my parents realized that I was going to get married, they decided to purchase a rowhouse in northwest Washington D.C., north of Howard University, south of Silver Spring, Maryland, for Delma and I to live in, so that my education would not be interrupted. Bemoan as I have about my perceived parent's lack of insight into my earlier educational needs, but their love, clairvoyance and fortitude to buy a building in D.C. for us to live in after we were married and to continue to pay my college tuition until I graduated from undergraduate school was more than recompense for any earlier defaults, if any, and went well beyond the call of duty.

My parents continued to give and to give and they kept on giving as long as I was making progress. It is my family's ethos that we invest in our children provided that they earn that investment by positive performance, in citizenship, education and responsibility. When my mother and dad gave me $10.00, I tried to make that $10.00 into $100.00 dollars. And when they saw this effort and the results attained, they were encouraged to keep investing in my stock, a growth stock.

During the Howard days, my parents purchased a two-story building at 625 Gallatin Street. It was an undistinguishable single family brick rowhouse that was divided into two apartments. Delma and I lived upstairs and rented out the downstairs apartment. I had no equity in the property. I didn't even know what equity was at that time. This was my first real estate management experience, and Dad was tough on me about my management skills. After I graduated from law school, he sold the building and recouped his investment, a good way to invest in a child's education.

From Gallatin Street in 1973, as mentioned before, I invested in a ten-unit building on Kenneth Street on the West Side of Chicago. It was my first equity investment and a true urban inner-city management test. I was earnest in my attempt, my heart was in the right place, but I was green in the middle, sappy, indecisive, and timorous—a combination unlikely to succeed in such a rugged environment. I was too green to handle the rough ride of managing a task as big as Kenneth St.

Dad's view of investing in real estate was that "you had to buy it right." By that he meant, buy underdeveloped property, not property someone has already developed to its highest and best use. Where is the growth for you? If there is any, it will be long and slow. I call that buying property with "some life in it": a property that needs work, perhaps a goodly amount of work, but one that is not completely gone so that you can derive some income from the property while you make the required repairs to maximize the income flow. To implement this strategy you end up buying old buildings. Buildings that require a lot of management time and can soak up millions of dollars in maintenance costs and repairs; but, if you can handle it, "there is money in them thar hills." There must be an upside to the building that you, the new buyer can ride. Buy buildings in a contiguous area so that when you go to manage the properties you do not have to go all over town to get to them. You would be surprised at how many times an owner/manager must visit his or her property to correct one thing or another.

The real estate game is a long term game, as I played it, and as many others have and continue to do. It is usually not a get rich quick endeavor unless you are playing the speculator's game, which requires a different mindset. From a swimmer's standpoint I was a distance swimmer, not a fifty meter hot shot. I was aiming for endurance not speed. From an outfielder's view, I would rather play further back and have to run forward than play too short and have to run backward. My approach has never been the short term play. I am a "long distance runner." I don't run the short sprints. I want long term financial security not short term capital gains. In 1975, rebounding from the Chicago wars, Dad and I purchased a four-unit red brick building in upper northwest Washington, D.C., at 1340 Peabody Street for less than $50,000.00, the place where Margaret Dhillon almost drove me nuts. This building was a refuge. It was as though a life raft had been thrown to me to save me from drowning in choppy waters too deep for an inept swimmer. The Whites were fleeing D.C. at the time because of the imminence of "home rule" which meant "Black rule." Dad bought the property and turned it over to me; his largess was unending. This is really when the real estate game began in earnest for me. The lessons learned from Kenneth Street in Chicago were well learned and applied. Plus, I had had the Gallatin Street experience while in college. Dad borrowed the down payment, and I paid back the mortgage loan and repaid him his down payment money. I worked hard to make this building a success and it was. I managed it carefully and got some grit in my pants to stand up to tenants and unruly neighbors and government regulators. This building presented many challenges to me. I had to conquer the building, and get control of it. That is to say, I had to become the master of the building and everybody in it. The resistance Dhillon put up almost drove me out of the building. I had to learn how to work within the rent control laws that the political system and legal environment had established as well as do the work necessary to renovate the property. When I moved to Philadelphia this building became the anchor of my burgeoning real estate business.

Living in a building while you are renting out other units is a way to minimize your individual living costs, but you get no peace in the process. You never get away from problems and unruly tenants. There is no escape. I don't recommend this approach, except for short durations with specific goals in mind.

One morning while soundly sleeping in my first floor unit on Peabody Street, I was rudely awakened by a loud scratching, spiking noise from someone walking with high heel shoes on hard wood floors over my head that were uncovered with any kind of floor covering such as a rug, carpeting or vinyl. The tenant was apparently getting dressed for work and she stomped and strutted all over that floor so loudly that it was unbearable. Angered, I rushed out of my unit and confronted her as she left for her morning commute to the Justice Department where she worked, unaware that she had awakened me from a sound sleep. I laid into this woman about being insensitive to the people living beneath her. She was an older Black lady probably a secretary or clerical employee, and I felt bad about accosting her so abruptly but she had been so disrespectful of my need for peace and quiet in the morning hours, and I was high strung. She was so angered by my approach that she threatened to get some kind of warrant issued for me at the Justice Department. She quickly moved out after that. In these owner occupied buildings, always take the unit on the top floor, so that no one is living over your head. You will save yourself a lot of aggravation! I refinanced this property at least three times pulling out gobs of equity after each refinancing, then splitting the proceeds with my father, none of which was taxable income. Eventually, selling the building thirty years later for six times the original sale price. This, after having positive cash flow and tax deductions that lowered my taxable income, saving me income taxes in untold amounts over those thirty years, especially during the years when my professional income was escalating. But to accomplish this many, many hours of aggravation and management time and cost were incurred. The profit I made was subject to long term capital gains taxes, which included the recapture of some of all the "soft and hard dollar" deductions taken over the years. Moreover, there is this concept of "phantom income," in real estate investing. This type of income occurs when, as an owner, you hold a building long enough to use up all of the depreciation to which the building is entitled. Once these "soft dollars" are exhausted, the investor starts picking up phantom income that would have been otherwise deductible. The intricacies of real estate investing embraces more than what may be obvious to the unsophisticated investor.

Buying a commercial property "right" means more than buying property that can be developed with a good upside; it means financing it properly. Since real estate is a long term investment the financing must be long term and predictable. The property must be able to pay for itself. The cash flow from the rental units should be able to pay the note on the building as well as all of the carrying charges. But in reality it rarely happens. Most owners end up subsidizing their units in one way or another. That is why when you get into this business, you must know "from whence your money comes." I call this being able to afford your investment. Professional investment advisors call it being able to take and accept the risk of loss. You will lose your shirt in the real estate business if you do not know what you are doing. On the other hand you can make good money and secure your financial future if you play the game right. Borrowing money to buy real estate is the preferred path because of the tax advantages and leverage.

Gimmicks, such as no-money-down loans and interest-only loans and even adjustable rate loans are of no value to me, although I am sure many would disagree. I prefer straightforward fixed rate loans as the best source of long-term, secure financing. And you must put money down on these purchases, which buys immediate equity, so that you tailor the debt service to the cash flow of the building. If you put the minimum down, which has its place in the game of finance, you can expect to pay a larger monthly mortgage payment, which may outstrip the cash flow from the building and, when combined with all of the other carrying charges, such as insurance, taxes, and routine maintenance, you are in a hole called "negative cash flow" that will not change unless you refinance your loan.

Loan-to-value ratios that lenders use to determine the amount of money they will lend you to buy a property is a measure of the risk they are willing to take to protect their interest in the property, not yours. The difference between that amount, the mortgage loan, and the contract price you agreed to pay for the property is, in part, your down payment: the equity, the money you need to raise to do the deal and additional equity based upon the contract price and the appraised value of the property. Commercial deals usually require at least 20 or even 30% down payments. The lenders protect themselves by ensuring that, if you fail, they can recoup their money because they have loaned much less money against the property than a conservative appraisal estimates it to be worth. You need to know something about this area. Commercial buildings carry a lower loan-to-value ratio than single family properties for home use. When you get into the commercial loan area, the game is more vicious and less accommodating to the unwary. The loan requirements are stricter and more stringent, and the credit requirements are higher.

There are many ways to finance real estate, and if you go down this route you need to know something about the various financing methods available to you:

conventional loans, purchase money loans, wrap-around loans, and a host of others. The point to remember is that structuring the loan properly is the first step in the "buy." Finally, "location, location, location" is pivotal for long-run capital appreciation. Location is the *elan vital* of real estate acquisition. It is important for so many reasons, including safety, tenant selection, appreciation, basic value and resale capability. Getting into an investment is one thing but being able to get out of an investment is just as important. A poor location may prevent you from getting out of the property what you put into it. It may limit your appreciation and prevent you from selling the property when you want to. Properties must compete against one another in the market place and the best property from a value, location, and cash value (including cash flow) standpoint always wins.

One Sunday morning in July of 1981, while lying in bed reading the Philadelphia Inquirer, Michelle, knowing that I was looking around to buy another building, saw an advertisement for an eight-unit building for sale on Greene Street in the Logan section of Germantown. "Eight units," I muttered. "...um, I just may be interested in that," I said to myself. The next day I made my inquiries and made a site visit to the building. I had previously purchased 6412 Germantown Ave., a four-unit building where my office was housed two years earlier in September 1979. And I already owned the four-unit building in D.C. The Greene Street building was an odd shaped building. It was rectangular in configuration with the front of the rectangle facing east on Greene Street. The back of the building faced to the west to a back wall separating it from a city social services neighborhood building. The north side of the building had a wide sidewalk area that allowed tenants who lived in the two side units on this side to enter their units from this side. The south side of the building was attached to an auto body shop.

The owners of the property were two elderly White people, a couple. They had owned the building for many years and were getting out of the rental business. The exterior was stucco painted white. The property was a tri-level building with eight one-bedroom units all with Pullman Kitchens that opened into a living room space not separated by walls. Each unit was small by comparison—not more than one thousand to eleven hundred square feet of living space. The bathrooms and kitchens were furnished with old World War II vintage appliances. One long hallway from the front and rear provided access into the interior of the building. On the ground floor in the front to the left was one first floor front unit and there was one large basement unit. On the second floor there were three units. On the third floor there was one large unit by itself at the top of the stairs, and two side units, totaling eight in all.

I made the owners an offer to buy the building for less than $40,000.00 with a 25% down payment, with the owners holding the mortgage for ten years amortized at 6%. They accepted the offer and we closed on July 14, 1981. Dad secured the down payment monies. I managed the building and serviced the debt. In keeping with my strategy, the building came with several units already rented. And I got to know two of the existing tenants before one of them died. The other eventually moved out. One of the two was Ms. Adele Lamb, a really nice elderly White woman who lived in the middle second floor unit for many years while the previous owners had the building. She had a deep raspy voice, smiled a lot and was sincere in her desire to be cooperative. She made it her duty to keep me informed of all the goings-on in the building. Ellis, a tall, brown-skinned Black man who lived in a side unit looked in on Ms. Lamb. Ellis was a decent guy, but his unit reeked of an offensive smell that turned me off every time I got a whiff when I visited him to inquire about any complaints. I always stood at the door, never entering any further for fear I would be overwhelmed by the noxious stench.

All of these old buildings including Peabody Street were heated by a centralized oil furnace. Dad and I realized early on that no money could be made in this game when the landlord furnished wasteful tenants who cared little and had no appreciation for the costs involved in furnishing utilities—especially heat. To make money and shift the burden of supplying heat to the tenants who were using it, all of our buildings had to be converted to individual heating units. This would be a costly capital improvement that would pay big dividends over the life of the building. Some tenants were observed walking around in their apartments with the windows up, their shirts off and bellies exposed, and the heat on 80 degrees. Oil prices were not as much of a concern back then, but the aggregate costs and effect on cash flow of owners supplying utilities to tenants, dealing with the meanness and fickle nature of oil suppliers who in effect extorted money to supply oil was too much aggravation to endure. Therefore, in succession I converted Peabody Street soon after acquiring that building, then Germantown Avenue and finally Greene Street. On Peabody Street the conversion resulted in four individual heating units and four hot water heaters. On Germantown Ave each unit had electric baseboard heaters installed, but I didn't separate the hot water. On Green Street electric baseboard heaters were installed in each unit and eight hot water heaters were also installed, as well as eight apartment-size electric stoves.

I have found that every building, without exception, has its unique maintenance personality: some problem that vexes the mind, defies solution without a great expenditure of money, and is a constant concern because of its reoccurrence. You don't know a building until you've gone through a winter with it, gone down and dwelt in the "belly of the beast," the basement, and made yourself comfortable down there. The basement is where the brains of the building operate: the heating system, the hot water heaters, the sewage system, electric panels and, in some cases, where the gas meters are located. If you are afraid of dark, dimly lit, dank, smelly, cobweb-infested basements, you will never be a small business landlord.

On Peabody Street, the vexing problem that lasted for years was the basement toilet and sewage backup that bubbled up in a toilet and flooded the entire basement with raw sewage, ruining everything in its path. I renovated the basement level into a nice cozy unit with wall to wall indoor carpeting and new kitchen appliances, planning to expand the number of units to five, when one day the sewage backed up driving the tenant into hysterics and me into bafflement and a lost investment. I could never figure out what was causing this to happen. Years later it turned out to be a tree root had grown into and obstructed the sewage pipe. When women in the building flushed feminine napkins and other tenants used excessive toilet paper, down the commodes, eventually the matter would clog up the pipes and cause an overflow. It would be years later before a fix was applied to this problem, not long before I sold the building.

On Germantown Avenue, the problem was another periodic sewage back up. The curb trap four to five feet below the cobblestone street at the edge of the sidewalk would get obstructed from time to time, causing the basement to overflow with raw sewage that smelled up the interior of the building. The problem would persist until the line was rooted out and freed. To this day, the problem is a concern, but I had the curb trap replaced and the vexing problem was resolved.

On Greene Street it was a stealthy roof leak that emanated from the flat roof area above the second floor middle-unit and went down into the first floor front side unit. Regardless of what I did to correct this problem, it would always reoccur. A gutter that was beneath the roof surface that caught water from the pitch of the roof would clog up from leaves and debris was cited as the cause but never truly diagnosed. I never solved this problem. It drove tenants mad and me speechless trying to find a fix and explain it away. Problems never solve themselves, and if you do not deal with them they get worse. Problems have to be solved by direct action, and they can never be "wished away." You have to face your problems and confront them head on. You cannot run from them; you must embrace them. As I sat on the attorney's bench after introducing a fellow lawyer to be admitted to the U.S. District Court for the Eastern District of Pennsylvania, a Federal Judge told the group of new admittees "face your problems gentlemen they will not go away unless you solve them."

Adele Lamb and Ellis were good friends. Ms. Lamb spoke in a low frog-tone but always with a smile. She had a cheery disposition, in spite of the fact that she lived by herself for many years in a one bedroom apartment and suffered from some debilitating illnesses. She was a woman of humble means but she always paid her rent on time. Whenever we spoke, she always wanted to talk for a while. One time, she asked me, "Mr. Lee, what are your plans for the building? We need to have a light in that lower hallway because its gets dark in there at night." I took the time to engage with her to let her know that she was appreciated and that her opinions about the building were being factored into my thinking. When she became terminally ill, I visited her in the hospital. I respected and liked Ms. Lamb.

Ellis was similar in many ways. His tall frame, wide grin, and pleasant manner made for an easy encounter with him each time we talked. He never complained much about his apartment, perhaps because he didn't want anyone going in there. During the entire time he lived on Green Street, I never went beyond the entrance way to his unit to look at anything. I suspected that Ellis may have been gay, but I had no proof and it made no difference to me. He was a nice guy and I liked him.

I made improvements to all the buildings I owned. Conditions were made better for the tenants, and I added value to my investment. I was, and still am, a "hands on" manager. I believe in getting my hands dirty by touching and feeling the *terra firma*. Knowing the building gave me a certain reassurance. I allowed no abstractions. I had to know in my mind exactly where things were to be found. By that time, I had four mortgages, four fire and liability insurance policies to pay, and fifteen units of rental property in three buildings. I had fifteen toilets and kitchen sinks to go bad, four leaking roofs to repair, a law practice and a home. In my mind, my stature, income, and wealth were increasing. I was beginning to build the economic foundation I had envisaged. The weight of my responsibilities was noticeably increasing, but I enjoyed my feelings of accomplishment, even at this stage of my progress.

The law business was ongoing; it never stopped. My divorce practice was moving ahead, cases of all sorts were coming in, and the court appointments kept coming. Wendy Bee and I were continuing to fight the good fight. Lang and I talked often and worked out together in a suburban athletic club he joined.

After a hard day I would either walk or drive down the street about two blocks south, to a corner bar known as Murph's for a drink. The bar was located on the corner of Germantown Avenue and Pomona Street just south of the office within walking distance. In Philadelphia each neighborhood has bars for the community to hang out in. It is a cultural feature of Philadelphia—the neighborhood bar. Murph's was owned by two brothers, their last names I never knew. The fellow I referred to as Murph was White, a short rotund bald headed man, confident talking, and gregarious, who always engaged me in conversation when I came in. Johnnie was the other brother. He was nervous and a bit shaky, and he was not as outgoing as Murph. Murph and I got to know each other over time. I usually ordered my usual Jack Daniels on the rocks and he always poured a little extra to let me know he appreciated my business. They served food in Murph's, but I never order any because I did not trust the level of the hygiene in the place.

"Otis", he would say, "how's it going today?" He liked to engage me because I was a lawyer. People like to talk to lawyers to pick their brains or just to engage. Not too many lawyers frequented his bar, and he admired or looked up to lawyers as so many of the public do. I would say, "Murph, it goes slowly, my man. It was a mixed outcome today," in my tone of reserved resignation. As he walked back and forth doing his chores behind the bar, he said "well you know, Otis, you got to keep at it in this life."

The bar was nothing to write home about: it was poorly decorated, it had no signs of modernity about it, and I looked askance at the food they prepared for others to eat. Although I didn't eat there, I drank there. It was a watering hole for me after closing up the office.

My resort to Murph's on occasion was my search for a respite at the end of some of my hectic and harried days. When I sat down at Murph's or at the bar on Sansome Street in Center City, I was lifted momentarily into the mental cubicle of peace where stress could be exhaled deeply and privately. And for a moment, if I imagined it strongly enough, I was transferred to the mellifluous virtuosity of Andre Watts playing Rachmaninoff's Piano Concerto #2 in C# Minor. I likened these moments at Murph's to sublime moments amid the chaos: not quite as soothing as listening to a concerto but fulfilling that same need.

One day Murph asked me "if I trusted anyone?" I thought about this question as I raised my glass to my lips to imbibe another shot, and I said "I don't know, perhaps a few people." He said, "Otis, you got to trust someone, you got to trust someone—that is what life is all about." He said this in his confident and assertive manner, the round rotund little fellow with his balding head standing in front of me, his white apron improperly affixed, with food stains thereabout, looking directly at me for a response. His admonition stuck with me and remains to with me to this day, the issue of trusting people. Murph's declaration caused me on many occasions to reexamine my view of trust and love. Trust and love are mutually exclusive; you can have one without the other. Trust and reliance however are closely related. Can you trust someone without relying on them? No.

Can you love someone without trusting them? Maybe. Can you trust someone without loving them? Yes you can: it is done every day, especially in business. But in matters of the heart, trust and love are inclusive of one another. Trust is hard to extend in the ordinary sense; it must be earned before it is granted. Once extended, it must be nurtured and maintained, for if it is ever breached, it is virtually impossible to restore to the fullness of its initial level. Whenever you trust someone, is there not some modicum of "love" involved? The only people I ever trusted were my mother and father and Michelle, and as my sons mature I trust them more each day.

Did I trust God? My definition of God is still evolving. I do not and did not know enough about God to know whether or not I trusted him or her or it, unless I relied on blind faith. But I have relied on that inner voice that one could say is God and I have seen his interventions in my life. My father was the only man I ever trusted and believed in. And even in accepting and rationalizing that trust and belief in him, my illusions about him and his imperfections as a human being underwent a whittling scrutiny. All of these appraisals must be seen and factored into the quality of the faith that leads us to trust and believe. Nothing and no one can be allowed to escape the rigor of scrutiny, and the searching inquiry into the consistency of their behavior and the logic of their pronouncements. No one! No person, no dogma, no belief system, no country!

In spite of all of this, if we choose to love and to trust, we just do. We ignore the imperfections and look upon the whole person, the overriding good in the thing or the individual. We look to see the good that exists: we do not look for perfection because we know in our hearts and in our minds it does not exist, even though we aspire to it and want those we love to personify it and to live it. In the end we trust people and love them because of what they have tried to do for us, the standards they set for us and vision that they have inspired in us. In my view only a limited few are worthy of this faith.

The practice of law and the rental real estate business are poor endeavors in which to find trust in people, but they are excellent laboratories in which to examine the nature of human beings. For through these occupations and businesses, you get to see people when they are enthused and want something from you and their expectations are favorable, and you also get to see them when they are under stress and despair the consequences of their own conduct. The combination of these two businesses, if you are not strong, can destroy your faith in people. One could become a misanthrope. You get to see people at their worst in these businesses: how they live, their respect for you and for property, their willingness or unwillingness to accept responsibility for their actions, not to mention the arrogance, pomposity, hypocrisy and duplicitousness of the many players and some of the principals. Fortunately, along the way you get to know people who are worthy which allows you to continue to retain some faith in mankind, to counterbalance the distortions that occur more often than not. But judging people must become, for a private legal practitioner, and a business man or woman, a science. One must constantly pick from among a varied garden of human flowers, deceptive in their beauty, alluring in their in their attractiveness, but prickly to the touch, stinging to the emotions with disappointment. In order to succeed, this task becomes an imperative.

When Murph would ask me how I was doing, I would reply with my old Harris Bank learned reply "fair to middlin." An old Midwestern expression that Paul Lawless, a co-worker of mine at Harris Bank, said that old farmers would retort when they were asked about how they were doing. Their response, in effect, said that they did not want to get out ahead of what might be around the corner. Murph, on the other hand, would say when asked how he was doing, "Man, I'm living! Man I'm living!" He was able to say this phrase with such vitality and self-assurance. I was always more reserved but I wished I could bring myself to say spontaneously when asked how I'm doing: "Man, I'm living! Man I'm living!" It's all in the self-confidence in the gut, I imagined, or at least the ability to project that self-confidence. I was not always lacking in self-confidence, just in verve. By nature I am understated.

By now my practice experience was gaining critical mass. I began to know what I was doing process-wise at least, and I was doing it with confidence. I was still not addressing the law in its fullness from a substantive stand point, nor had I gotten to the point of applying the cases and black-letter law to the matters I had before the court. My bent was in that direction, but my need to keep moving and be facilitative of my business did not allow me the time to slow down and apply the substance of the law to all my cases, although I was keenly aware of some of the important cases that controlled my legal work. I was still dancing on top, being intimidated by the system and by some of the judges. I was not "taking it on" with courage and know how, being fearless in my approach, getting in the "face of the judges," looking into the "whites of his or her eyes," but that would come. My natural oratorical skills when summoned could always rescue me, but these natural skills would have been enhanced had I combined them with more substance consistently. My job was to keep reading, keep imitating the good lawyers, trying to be like them, seeing how they did it and keep trying to be more substantive to delve into the minutiae of the law to do it better each time. For someone who had no mentor to speak of and was essentially self-taught, I was learning fast and catching on. Just "keep your head down" and stay on the "beaten path," I said to myself in my many moments of reflection. And these words became an unwritten philosophy that I strictly adhered to. "Stretch it when you can," push as much as your confidence on a given day will allow, but be gentle on yourself. "You have no one to help you"; this became my internally driven mantra. I always knew what I was up against.

In spite of it all, my reputation was congealing as hard working, consistent and fair. No one could doubt my earnestness and sincerity when it came to the discharge of my duties, win-lose-or-draw, and in the end my sentimental side often led me to believe that this was what people were paying for, "your best efforts," win or lose. But in the real world of a "results" oriented society, you must show progress to retain the faith of your clients. You must win. People do not really care about your best efforts; they are paying their money and they want results. Efforts are for losers and sentimentalists in this harsh, cruel and evil world. The public demands results, a good heart is nice to talk about but clients want the "money," results. I did not realize it until much later in my practice life, but the job of the lawyer is to manage the client's expectations. Because the management of expectations makes the lawyers's job easier. The lay public generally has no idea what the requirements of the law are and are even more clueless about how a judge is going to respond to their position in a particular case. It is the lawyer's job to anticipate how the court will respond, and this of course is determined by the law that controls the case. But needless to say, it's like baseball in a sense: it's easier for the infielder and the outfielder to play further back, to give yourself a chance, than to play too close and misjudge the ball, its flight and distance. It's better not to be overly optimistic in your expectations, if you want to handle a hard hit ball, because it's easier to run forward than to run backward.

My vision and strategic plan was fully focused now. I was 36 years old, but I wanted to retire at age fifty-five and by then I wanted to own as many rental units as my age. To achieve that objective I had to buy a building a year on average, each with at least three or four rental units, to be where I wanted to be 19 years hence–and that is exactly what I did.

THE REAL ESTATE BUSINESS

31

"To Fling My Arms Wide in Some Place of the Sun"

Dream Variations
by Langston Hughes

To fling my arms wide
In some place of the sun,
To whirl and to dance
Till the white day is done.
Then rest at cool evening
Beneath a tall tree
While night comes on gently,
Dark like me—
That is my dream!

To fling my arms wide
In the face of the sun,
Dance! Whirl! Whirl!
Till the quick day is done.
Rest at pale evening...
A tall, slim tree...
Night coming tenderly
Black like me.

I NEVER LOOKED at the law as an end in itself, but as a means to other ends. My other "end" was financial security. That is why I was never hung up on being the "best," compared to who? I just wanted be a "good lawyer" respected by my peers, by those who knew me and clients that had dealt with me, respected by the judges and as a lawyer who knew his way around a courtroom. A journeyman lawyer not a perennial apprentice. And I wanted to have a base of satisfied clients who would come back again and again to me for repeat business. I was into building a business, a law practice business so that I would have the security of knowing that when I went to the office the business would be there because of years of consistency and stability. A lawyer people could rely on. That's what I wanted! That is why the Germantown Avenue office was so vital to my practice life. I owned my own building; I was in control of my business destiny. My law business would form the anchor for my nascent real estate business, and my real estate business when matured would secure my future as a lawyer in practice. The law was my love, my ego, my intellectual side, but real estate was my financial anchor: my security blanket, a family tradition, something we knew about that had proven its value over time. I was never going to be the top lawyer in Philadelphia, but I could be one of the well-heeled ones when the deal was over and among a few who were financially secure from practicing law. It was all about how I chose to use my income from my practice. The real estate business was where the long term money was. The cash flow, the long term security. The law/real estate combination would cross fertilize each other, feed off each other, and plant roots deep in the ground in the community I called home, that I loved, and it did.

The front of the Apsley Street building in Germantown faced east on Apsley Street which ran east and west. This building is a long rectangular building and the north side of the building is what fronted onto Apsley St. Of all the buildings I owned except for Peabody Street, this building had the best and largest rooms. The building was made up of four units: one efficiency, one large one bedroom and two large two bedroom units. When I purchased the building it was heated by one central oil burning furnace located in the basement. My first job of course, keeping true to the strategy, was to decentralize the heating system including separating the hot water system and electrical system, a major systems overhaul. I had done the same thing to Greene Street just around the corner from Apsley Street and all the other buildings up to this point.

I paid just under $30,000 for Apsley Street, and I financed it with a traditional mortgage loan from a local savings and loan bank. In negotiating the deal with the seller, I always made sure that I bought the building well below market or that the seller took back some of the mortgage. This allowed me to save as much of my cash as possible in order to finance the systems overhaul that would make the building more financially viable. When I got the building where I wanted it, systems-wise, the cash flow would then allow me to anticipate the seller's or bank's note, and get them out of the picture so I could move on.

These old buildings I was buying carried with them many, many problems. I often said you could spend a million dollars on an old building, and you still will have an old building albeit a fixed up old building. The plumbing systems in these properties were made of old galvanized lead pipes. After years of use they get clogged up with corrosion from sediment and sewage. After a while they become brittle, crack and leak. Poor insulation in the exterior walls and in the basement causes the pipes to burst during the winter months. Sewage backs up in the basement spewing gunk and garbage, a putrid and poisonous mixture, flooding the basements. The windows all need replacing. Old roofs with shingles and tin decades old, crack and tear. Then seams develop and the roofs leak because they have never been replaced completely, always a patch job. The soffits and fascia boards around the roofs are usually rotted out and are home to pigeons and squirrels. Every plumbing fixture in the building could be replaced but who can afford to do that.

Even worse, lead paint is usually what's on the walls in these old buildings and this is a scare and an extreme expense if a city agency finds out about it or if some streetwise tenant knows about it and reports you to the city or worse yet, sues you claiming that her child has eaten lead from the apartment's walls even though they were present while the eating was going on; and that is why her child is doing poorly in school; this happened to one of my clients.

Many tenants will vandalize a property because they are angry, angry about their situation, about paying rent and about being evicted. It is a way of getting back at the landlord. I have had them pour cement down a sewer drain. Dig the masonry from the walls of a unit so much so that it destroys the entire apartment. Break holes in dry wall, clog up toilets with everything imaginable, break out windows whatever. You name it, I have seen it. One day while I was in Philadelphia Municipal Court, on a landlord tenant matter, one of my regular hangouts, this eccentric judge, Judge Krase, he was a nice guy after you got to know him, remarked to me, after having had me before him on many occasions: "Mr. Lee, you are a nice guy, why do you put yourself through this?" I had no answer except I muttered to myself, as I left the courtroom, "to make a few bucks."

In Philadelphia you are liable to be sued for "anything" real or imagined if a lawyer thinks he can make a buck. This is especially true if the tenant concocts or feigns some injury attributable to the landlord's negligence or thinks that he or she has some basis for getting out of paying rent or to recoup all the rent they paid you in a year or more. Liability insurance premiums are high because of frivolous claims, high litigation costs and the litigious culture of the city. People live off of lawsuits in Philadelphia; it is an industry. And finally the tenant's best friend when they are having problems with their landlord is the Department of Licenses and Inspections—the housing code enforcement authority. The "big pay back." The government's regulatory agency for landlords and every landlord's bane to a halcyon albeit fleeting moment in this business.

All tenants live differently. Some have nice homes and take care of their possessions, taking pride in their homes. But others live in filth and have no regard for themselves or your property. I used to say that the only things human beings have in common are breathing, sleeping, eating, excreting and procreating; there is no homogeneity when it comes to values or standards of living. Some folks sleep on a mattress on the floor, others sleep on the floor in a sleeping bag. I have seen tenants put newspapers up on the windows to act as blinds, while others hang a blanket across the windows to act as curtains. My market demographic perhaps lent itself to poorer standards of hygiene, but not necessarily. Many lower income people maintain nice homes and have high respect for property. The difference lies in the destructive element that must be weeded out, if at all possible, but always disguises itself and finds its way into your residences. Seeing the way some tenants live makes you feel that, if you did not know they were human beings, you would think they were some lower cast animals. You can have your heart broken by the way some tenants will leave your property. I have seen housekeeping sights that are indescribable. Brace yourself Cleaning up behind human beings is a dog's breakfast, it's a tough job, one that I left to others to perform, but I always inspected the aftermath. Garbage strewn vacant apartments left by tenants, with mattresses on the floor, bed sheets nailed across the window frames and newspapers pasted to the windows to cover the windows , closets filled with dirty clothes from the floor to the window sill, rotting food in the refrigerators, and feces in the toilets were not uncommon. The stench from spoiled meat and garbage required at times that you put a cloth across your nose to retard the noxious odors: some of the filth left behind is indescribable, to the uninitiated.

Then there are those who leave behind good pieces of furniture, items that can be used and should be retained by any family, especially a family trying "to have something." Then there were tenants who left the premises the way they moved into to them, clean and free of debris. All people have different levels of hygiene, none of these encounters ever met my standards, but who am I to judge, but I was always put off by what I saw. The real estate business is a good business *faute de mieux*, but there are easier and less aggravating ways to make money.

My home base for legal work in the landlord tenant business was the Philadelphia Landlord Tenant Court. This court met each week at 9:00 am on Monday morning and again on other days during the week in the Municipal Court Building on the fourth floor on the north side of the building, between 10th and 12th street between Market and Chestnut Street in Center City. I was a regular in this court. When the court officers saw me enter, they would immediately pull my cases to the front to be called in sequence with when I entered the court room. I would take my place in front of the bar of the court and await my time to be called. In this courtroom, I developed a good relationship with a court crier named "Don." I never knew what Don's last name was, but we got to know each other well over the years. He would kid with me about my chances of winning my cases by giving me the thumbs down gesture when he felt things were not ordained in my favor, humorously to needle me, and we exchanged light banter and sarcasm about the system. We chatted often while walking in the hallways, about his retirement, the personalities in the court system, etc. Don was White, round faced and bald, a decent, mild mannered guy, not out to make waves. He just wanted to get his time in so he could retire from his boring routine that was his lifeline.

Don was like so many other "faceless individuals" I encountered working in the court system during my practice life in Philadelphia. Faceless yet with a face. Seen but unseen, familiar but unfamiliar transient shipmates navigating a swirling sea of quarrelsome disputations. We were shadows in the light, reflecting the transitory nature of these relationships. Yet these people were important to any lawyer trying to manipulate the court system as frequently as I attempted to do. I knew these people only in the context of the court. I never saw them on weekends only Monday through Friday. There were only a few like Don. People who seem to share with me a common affinity that caused us to amiably respond to one another, yet we never really knew each other. Another such person was "Tiny," an overly obese Black man who worked in the Prothonotary's Office of the Court of Common Pleas, whose personality was as broad as his waist line—a jovial fellow, always with something to say usually positive. These were people I saw regularly, pushing court papers, stamping them in on the court dockets, doing their perfunctory court officer jobs.

Then there were those faceless people whom I saw on the street almost every day, either going to work or leaving work. These folks were even more remote. Familiar only in the sense that I saw them on the street, in passing. People who would stare me in the eye but not speak, displaying an arrogance and an aloofness that bothered me because of its premeditation. But as DuBois asserted when he encountered these types of people on his way to work at the NAACP headquarters in New York, "the burden was not on me to be the first one to speak." And so I endured these irksome yet very minor human irritations from people that just seemed to dislike me without knowing me. You cannot make any more out of these relationships than what they were: temporary, fleeting, and limited to the depth and the space of their birth and environment.

Some lawyers have made a career out of Landlord Tenant practice, such as Herman Miller in Washington, D.C. In reality it is "down the road a piece" in terms of its complexity, yet it is an essential part of the real estate law area. I made it my job to master this area of the law since my livelihood depended on it, but I never thought of this practice as an elevated area of the law to practice in. But its essentiality, for those in the residential and commercial rental real estate business, far outweighs its perceived lack of reconditeness. Many judges unless they sit in landlord tenant court regularly do not understand Landlord Tenant Law. And just like lawyers who think there is nothing to "drafting a will," many feel they can routinely try a landlord tenant case and win, but it ain't that easy. This area of the law involves the law of contracts, real property, collections law, money damages, and premises liability.

I did my own lawyering in this court the entire time I was in Philadelphia. I might not have known how to hammer a nail or how to level a two by four, but I did know how to represent myself in this and related courts having to do with the rental real estate business. By handling these cases myself I saved tens of thousands of dollars in attorney fees over the years. Some lawyers charge as much as three or four hundred dollars per case to represent landlords. This is a loser for the landlord especially when you have already lost hundreds of dollars perhaps, even thousands of dollars on the tenant to begin with.

I appeared in this court so often I should have a room named in my honor. One judge remarked "we should have a special day just to hear Mr. Lee's cases." In Philadelphia, the Municipal Court uses a Trial Commissioner to cull through the list of cases, to whittle down the list of the contested cases that require a judge to decide. When court is convened, the trial commissioner takes to the bench, usually a court employee who is favored by the court hierarchy and is appointed to this "lofty job," a chance to play judge for a few minutes each week. He or she calls the list. It doesn't take long before these trial commissioners start to take on an air of superiority and start throwing their weight around. Defaulted cases are disposed of, i.e. where one party fails to appear and the case is either thrown out or a judgment is rendered against the party at fault; continuances that are requested are usually granted and contested cases are left for the judge. Most often cases are settled by agreement. In this instance when the case is called, the trial commissioner asks the parties "if they would prefer to see if they can settle their cases with the attorney by agreement." But what the Trial Commissioner fails to tell the tenant is that by signing a Judgment by Agreement, the tenant is giving up his or her right to appeal their case. The lawyer takes the tenant into a conference room, and they work out a payment plan and reduce it to "a writing." The beauty of this approach is that once the agreement is signed by both parties and entered upon the record, it is a judgment just as if a judge had decided the case but not subject to appeal. And, if the agreement is not adhered to by the tenant(s), the landlord can immediately proceed to an eviction.

I used the L&T Court as an extension of my management system. By being aggressive more often than not in filing these cases, I placed myself in the position of controlling the life of the tenant forfeiture. It also gave me the leverage to manage the case on terms favorable to my interest in being paid or vacating the unit to cut my losses as soon as possible. Time is money in this business. Threatened by the eviction process, tenants should realize that, as I have said to many tenants, "I am not in the eviction business, I am in the rental business." Every landlord including me would prefer for tenants to stay in their apartments and pay the rent, without tearing up the place.

Evictions are tough and I have had some tough evictions. Landlord Tenant officers from the court have been killed trying to evict tenants. It is a stressful situation for all involved. One eviction hangs in my memory. The day began quietly enough with no real difficult task to overcome, save but one. The day was clear and sunny and bright. The eviction was scheduled for 2:00 p.m. It occurred in the first floor rear unit in a building I bought several years later in my investing life. I evicted a sick Black middle-aged woman who had cancer or some other dreaded illness just after she was released from the hospital. She was still on the gurney that she was sent home on when she was removed from the unit. Bandages were on her arms, and she wore a hospital gown that was still draped over her body.

I have always regretted that I had to evict this woman at this time, but the facts of her situation warranted the adverse action. She and her family were behind in their rent for several months and the pressure was on me to make water bill payments, mortgage payments, maintenance payments and the like. I stood outside the unit as the landlord tenant officer, with a gun on his hip, went about removing this family from their home; this was not a schadenfreude moment, pleasure felt at someone else's pain. Quite the contrary; it was a vexing moment seeing the pained and mournful look on this woman's face which clearly showed her discomfort. This look sent a signal to my consciousness that alarmed my outer door that called into question the morality of my business ethics. I took no pleasure in seeing this unfold, absolutely not, but I had to be strong even though my heart was hurting. The sheer anxiety, desperation and frustration felt by her family as they fought to find a way out of this dilemma was palpable and heart wrenching. "Just one more day Mr. Lee, just one more day," the plea was made over and over again. And after each plea, I nodded to the officer to proceed. The expression on her face was saying to me "how could you do this to me, can't you see what kind of condition I am in, what kind of man are you?"

I had to do this because it was the nature of the business. If I relented upon hearing every sob story pleading for respite, nothing would ever get accomplished and I would lose everything eventually. This eviction was not a surprise. They never are, except when the reality of it happens. Many opportunities were afforded this family to avoid this consequence but none were fulfilled. Notice in advance is always given. A stiff upper lip was required. It was my call. Did I have the toughness to stare this situation down, or was I going to shriek and fold up when courage was required? It was a wistful moment for me because I am by nature an empathetically compassionate person who feels deeply about the plight of humanity. I would save the world if I could, but I cannot. I can only try to save my soul, not an easy task with an uncertain outcome, and try to help a few family members save theirs. A fellow landlord named Gordon Ogilvy from Grenada, who bought up a lot of rental property in West Philly as well as several businesses and died of a massive heart attack trying to manage it all, once said "you cannot let their problems (meaning tenants) become your problems." Gordon was a friend but not a close friend. We had some things in common.

I had been through many evictions before and even after this one, but this one was painful. And I thought to myself as it was unfolding, how perilous it is to leave or to trust your dignity, your freedom, your welfare to the discretion of others. This is what poverty, poorness and poor decision making can result in. Even a sympathetic person such as me will end up doing what is in their self-interest. You ask yourself "did this woman deserve this?" "No! Of course not." But, in this life, do we get what we deserve? Seldom, if ever. We get what we get; pure and simple, and what you get you earn, not what you deserve. It is all based on your conduct and your decisions. Compassion is a must in this business balanced by the realities of the business.

The Department of Licenses and Inspections in Philadelphia is run by a group of egotistical, marginally educated, usually high school graduates at best, sometimes vindictive, usually inconsistent bureaucrats. They think they have some power over your property and your pocket book. They feel they have some power and they do. Nasty attitudes prevail and if you assert yourself, stand up for your rights and a personality conflict arises, forget it: you just pulled a red cape over the bull's eyes. I was virtually in a war with these people for twenty years. My father was in a war with the same type of people in Charlottesville, Virginia until he died. You've got old buildings, power crazed bureaucrats (some with an agenda) and spiteful tenants. Anybody can find anything wrong with an old building and you do not have to look too closely. In Philadelphia, when an inspector is called, he writes up a list of violations that have to be corrected within ten to twenty days. Usually there is a re-inspection without notice to the landlord except what may appear in the initial notice of violation. Most often the re-inspection date is either missed or fouled up for some other reason. If the violation is not complied with, i.e. fixed by the time of the re-inspection, you are automatically served with a computer generated court summons to appear in court. The issuance of these court summonses are automaticly computer generated and are a cost center for the department. Your failure to appear in court will result in a $5,000.00 default judgment. If you are not careful, the city ends up owning all of the equity in your building.

Trying to resolve your problem before court to avoid a court appearance is nearly impossible. You cannot get anyone on the telephone to reason with. Their attitudes were bad and they had a "don't care" approach since they knew where these matters were headed. These people add an extra layer of aggravation to an already aggravating business, so usually the matter ends up being settled in court. The department sends hearing officers, who are not lawyers to court, to resolve these matters. The hearing officers they send, think "they are lawyers" for a day; they push their weight around, trying to intimidate the hapless landlord, but I was not a hapless landlord. I was a "lawyer" landlord, rhymes with "warrior" landlord. The department's revenue source was always to get a fine and court costs even if the matter was resolved before the date of the hearing. If your name was on the court lists, you rarely if ever got out of the courtroom without some kind of financial penalty, or money generated for the city. If you advised them that the work was completed, they would schedule a re-inspection. Even if the work is "complied," many times, the department, through carelessness or negligence, would not up-date its records and remove the old violations. These old violations would remain in the system month after month as a continuing source of aggravation. It is a racket for the city to make additional money from the landlords who already are paying use and occupancy taxes, real estate, school district, mercantile, and net profits taxes to the city.

The police power of the state, to protect health and safety, delegated to the city, mandates that each city or county have a housing inspection office. The office serves a common good. The office ensures that commercial housing is fit for human habitation and that the housing facility complies with the state build-ing codes which are promulgated each year by the state legislatures. These folks should not be looked upon by landlords as the enemy; they are not. In most cases landlords who keep up with their properties already know of the repair needs, but for one reason or another, usually different priorities and other pressures, the item is not remedied. The bureaucracy of the system that lends itself to corrup-tion and abuse by the office and by counter parties originates in the misuse of the inspector's office by political power blocks in the local communities: e.g. groups of irate tenants who have gripes with their landlords, individual inspectors who hold prejudices against individual landlords and favor some over others, political hacks and wealthy property owners with clout. The inspectors lose sight of their public responsibility to be fair and impartial in the administration of their responsibility that spoils an otherwise well intended system.

For some reason I have always attracted attention. Maybe it is the way I carry myself, my height, my grey hair, but I always get noticed. As I began to mature in the real estate business, I pushed back against this system. I made enemies and I paid no bribes. I played the game square up. I fought back in court, made my deals and refused to accept the rudimentary fine and court costs protocol without challenging the basis for these money making government schemes. I was not liked "downtown" by some of the inspectors who worked in my district especially the hearing officers I dealt with in court. Usually young Black females were sent to man the hearings, and they knew after a while that I was a lawyer fighting these cases. In the scheme of things, I was "small potatoes," so it was a personality thing. Knowing I was fighting a losing game, I figured out how to survive within this slanted system—within what amounted to a "stacked deck."

In Philadelphia every principal civil or criminal issue has its own court room, time and place for its separate docket. And so it was for "code enforcement court" where housing code cases are disposed of. Just as often frequented, if not more so, was Court Room "E" on the south side of the Municipal Court building on the fourth floor; it was my home away from home.

I spent so much time in this building that the security guards knew me by name and face recognition and ushered me into the building and the hallway with-out much fanfare. Code enforcement cases were held in the afternoon at about 2:00 pm. The same procedures applied. The court crier/clerk would stand at the entrance of this quaint unremarkable courtroom, a small undecorated room by comparison with courtrooms in city hall. The seating was theater style fifteen rows deep with ten chairs in a row. As I entered the courtroom, the clerk, wearing the usual frayed dark blue blazer, with the Municipal Court yellow-gold insignia sewn onto the outside left upper pocket, dark slacks, white open collar shirt and tie, would call out my name and pull my cases to the front of the pile. All of these court officials were White men and women except for a few. The Philadelphia patronage system favored the Whites who secured just about all of the jobs available in the city court system. The court system is a solid and secure source of employment for many Whites from the northeast and south Philadelphia. The average Black was fortunate to get a job in the Philadelphia Court of Common Pleas.

In this courtroom and in many others like it in the city, cases were called in priority based upon who entered the courtroom first, and if that person was an attorney, additional priority was given to attorneys in the sequencing of the cases. One thing about Philadelphia court proceedings, they always call the attorneys' cases first. It saves the lawyers a lot of time, because some of these matters can take hours to be disposed of. The first row of chairs in the front of the court room facing the bench is usually reserved for the lawyers. I would take my place. And in sequence, I was called to the long table which spanned across the front of the courtroom and lay against a four foot high railing system that separated the bench from the court clerk's working space. This is where the advocates did their work. "Case number so and so, Mr. Lee" the clerk would repeat. After I sat down, the hearing officer would say "Mr. Lee we have a violation at 140 W. Apsley Street in apartment #3, a cracked window. Have you repaired that window?" I would reply, "Which window are you referring to, the unit has five windows which one is cracked?" "Well let's look at what the inspector says," etc. etc., and so on and so on, as she looked through her disheveled papers. After this exchange, I would say that I did not know of any cracked windows in that unit and the matter would be relisted for another court date after a re-inspection.

To end the matter, I would have to sign a subpoena to assure that I would reappear, without which they could enter a default judgment for the usual $5,000.00 if I did not come to court on the new court date. This process is designed to see if these matters could be resolved without the judge's intervention. The judge was supposed to be in his chambers, a room to the left of the bench, waiting for the distillation of contested cases from uncontested and settled cases. This process saves the court time and efficiently applies its resources to the matters that require judicial intervention. All of my cases were resolved without judicial intervention except in rare cases when my patience with the hearing officers was exhausted, and I decided to call the bluff of the hearing officers and make them try their cases before the judge. Though I always knew I had this trump card to play and that I would be playing this card from the top of the deck, my political evaluation of the pros and cons would usually dictate a course of least resistance, the settlement.

My approach was a business approach. I made it my business not to miss those hearings I was summoned to attend. But when I did, which inevitability happened, I used my lawyering skill to file motions to open the default judgments which were granted and the matters were then re-litigated and settlements reached. Because I was a lawyer, I knew how to do this with facility and economically. If I had had to hire a lawyer to accomplish these tasks, my bill would have been thousands of dollars in the aggregate. Next, I would reach the lowest settlement possible with the hearing officer, let these judgments accumulate, say up to $1,000.00, then I would gather them up and deal with the city collection attorney, usually an outside attorney who is paid a percentage to collect these and other tax delinquencies and negotiate a settlement usually fifty cents on the dollar.

I built up a relationship with a few of these fellows after a while. The city collection officer was an attorney, so I could deal with someone who knew how to get business done, not some glorified clerk trying to be more than they were in real life. And since these L&I folks had nothing to do with the collection side of their business, they knew nothing about how these matters were eventually resolved. I had the back end covered while these clerks were huffing and puffing on the front end. I had a strategy going in and coming out before the game began. I kept careful records of my settlements and saved the settlement agreements. These saved agreements would be invaluable years later when I went to sell these properties, and these same old liens appeared on title reports.

On a more sanguine note, the regulatory regime employed by the city government of Philadelphia to enforce its obligation to police the building and housing codes is an effective management approach. This is especially true when compared to other jurisdictions that criminalize infractions of housing and building codes, such as in Virginia. Everything involved in the real estate game required a strategy in order to make it work for me. I had to see the big picture: know when and where I could win and figure out a way to make the most of the winnable circumstances; and know when it was impossible to win to limit my losses in unwinnable situations of which there were many.

32

"DREAM VARIATIONS," THE LAW AND THE LANDLORD

I WAS NOW RUNNING TWO VIABLE BUSINESSES: my law practice which was growing and my real estate business which was in a growth mode. In regard to the real estate I anticipated buying more buildings. On the law side, Wendy Bee with my help continued to fight off her adversaries, but one incident almost cooked her bacon. While trying to make her payroll and to pay for other pressing bills, Wendy deposited a check into the Girard Bank, payable to her, drawn against a bank account that she controlled, for a large sum drawn on yet another bank which had not collected the funds previously deposited in a check from Wendy. The depository bank paid out against Wendy's worthless deposit. Whether or not this had been done by her before I do not know, but on this occasion it did not work. Girard Bank notified the federal authorities, and the U.S. Attorney for the Eastern District of Pennsylvania assigned the case to one of his young assistants for prosecution. Wendy received a "target letter," telling her that she was the focus of a criminal investigation for bank fraud, "kiting" checks. Scared out of her mind, Wendy called me in a panic, "Mr. Lee!" she bellowed, excited beyond belief, "I just got this letter. What does this mean!"

I left my office in a heightened sense of frenzy and went over to her office in West Philadelphia to read the letter. Though she did not know specifically what the import of the letter meant, her instincts told her she was in real trouble now, with of all people, the feds! I had handled enough criminal cases by then to know that this was a matter that had to be negotiated out if possible, to save this dear woman. Wendy had no idea what she was in for if this thing was not "handled" properly. I had to convince the assistant U.S. Attorney that, though this had happened, this poor woman was not capable of bank fraud: she was not sophisticated enough to commit fraud. Of course, that was not actually the case. The fact is that you cannot leverage your funds through a bank checking account unless you borrow the money. There is no informal borrowing. If a bank pays out on a deposit, they expect to get their money back.

This was a serious matter. I knew I needed more fire power to make this case to the U.S. Attorney, so I called my old friend Jack Myers, an old hand at the criminal law. In fact criminal law was his specialty though he practiced in other areas. So I met Jack at his office the following day and told him about my client. Jack had never met Wendy, and since I did all of her legal work I brokered the deal to have Jack work with me to resolve the matter. I told Jack how chaotic Wendy's business was and how she basically ran a "ma and pa" operation, not anything sophisticated. We told the government that her back office facility was a "shoe box" operation. And that this was a civic minded Black woman who hired a lot of Blacks from West Philadelphia, had no criminal record, was a church going woman from the South trying to make good in big city Philadelphia.

On a Friday afternoon in late summer at 6th and Market Street in the Federal Courthouse in Center City Philadelphia, we at last faced off with the Assistant U.S. Attorney. He was a young good natured White chap with blond hair who probably had bigger fish to fry. His cramped small office with cubicle dividers separating him from his colleagues belied the importance of his position and this case in our eyes. We had engaged this fellow briefly on several prior occasions, but this time we pressed in ernest our theory and made the case that this woman should not be prosecuted for this crime. She was scared to death and shivering in her boots, we told him, that the prospects of a criminal entanglement with the almighty federal government was not what she wanted and that she realized the error of her ways. We professionally begged this guy to let her go, and finally after much deliberation he relented. Perhaps he did not feel that this older Black woman had the intent to defraud or the evil mindset to warrant prosecution. We stressed that she was a pillar in her community. After all, though her act was illegal, she was not trying to run a scam; she was just trying to pay legitimate business debts.

This saga lasted for about six weeks before he sent a letter discontinuing his investigation but admonishing her that if there was a repeat of this kind of business again he would not be so forgiving. Of all my dealings with Wendy, this episode was the most threatening she encountered during my representation of her. Wendy had dodged another bullet aimed straight for her heart. I continued to work with Wendy resolving disputes with her neighbors over the renewal of her food service business license. The neighbors were complaining about the late hours of operation, the loud noises from the dance hall music and rowdy patrons who lingered outside after the hall closed. The relicensing process required that she hold community meetings to allow the surrounding community to have input on the license renewal. Work on her continuing tax problems with the city and federal government were on-going, and I was also busy defending her against civil suits filed against her emanating from the food service business.

Wendy had serious problems making ends meet especially paying the government her share of the fiduciary social security withholding taxes required of all employers, even though she operated multiple businesses. Wendy could not account for her payments or had not made the payments, and she could never settle the confusion between the two and so she could not convince the government that her numbers were correct.

This failure haunted her until her death and would not be resolved until that time. Her failure to have a cogent "back office" operation portended her financial demise. It was not that Wendy did not know how to make money. She did. She knew how to expand her business. She was sharp on a dollar, had an attractive congeniality and innate business acumen rare in most people. Most of all she had a vision that exceeded the west Philadelphia population that she served, which is the case in most successful entrepreneurial people, and she knew how to get that money from her customers. But the lack of accounting controls with competent people contributed to her undoing. This episode with the US attorney was just a signal to the observant that she was in trouble and should have served as a warning notice to change her business habits, but she didn't. It was symptomatic of being overwrought in business.

On one special occasion Wendy announced that Minister Louis Farrakhan, the controversial minister from the Nation of Islam was going to be preaching at her facility in West Philly. It was an opportunity not to be missed, one that I wanted to make sure I attended. Everyone knew that Farrakhan was a lightning rod but that he spoke the truth to Black people. Wendy made sure that I got good seats up front, and I brought along Lang who was also interested in attending. On the night of his talk, we took our seats before he entered the main assembly room surrounded by a phalanx of body guards and officialdom who flanked him and trailed him. An entourage of neatly dressed bow tied Black men all with bald heads and white shirt that glistened in the artificial light. An overflow crowd, of all Blacks, filled the room. Philadelphia has always had an active Black Muslim community, and many of them turned out to hear Minister Farrakhan. In fact one of my in-laws led a mosque in west Philadelphia several years before I came to Philadelphia when the Black Muslim movement in Philadelphia was flourishing. Jeremiah Shabazz was his name, a close associate of Muhammad Ali during his heyday. I would later represent Jeremiah in a mean child support case filed against him by his wife involving the use of bankruptcy to beat back the attack a few years later.

As Farrakhan arose to the lectern to address the assembled mass, his light brown skin and coal black hair, neatly cut, shone brightly in the spotlights gleaming on his face. He looked healthy and wore his usual gold rim glasses. He opened his mouth with a broad and inviting smile, welcoming us all into the warmth of his embrace. As he began to speak, a cameraman walked around the room with a professional size video camera taking shots of everyone in attendance, and he seemed to focus his lens on Lang and I or at least we felt that was the case.

Rapt attention was paid by the true believers. Not a creature stirred, not even for a moment of inattention, except for the cameraman. Minister Farrakhan greeted his guests by speaking in Arabic, saying "peace be upon you my brothers and sisters" and began to preach the orthodoxy of Black empowerment to the "choir" who gathered in his presence. His oratorical prowess was evident from the beginning and much anticipated. It was a magic event to be there and to listen. I could have listened to him all day because he spoke the unvarnished truth to seekers of the unvarnished truth. Those who step outside the crowd to tell the truth are truth tellers, trying as they can, to remove the ever present veil of ignorance and camouflage that prevents the truth from getting through to the people. Violence is done to those who seek to tell the truth by those who are the perpetrators of the fraud, by those who want to keep the people ignorant and have a vested interest in and who represent interest groups who profit from the fraud. Witness what happened to Marcus Garvey, Malcolm X, and Martin Luther King. Yes, his message resonated with me and was music to my ears and to others because I am and others are seekers of truth who do not dwell in the world of hyperbole and hypocrisy. I care little about what other people may say about someone who is a lightning rod such as Minister Farrakhan. I make my own evaluations about people. And since I once lived in Chicago and had eaten in some of the Nation of Islam's restaurants and seen their headquarters, I could relate to the entirety of his message.

Say what you will about the Muslims, if Black people lived their lives according their tenets, many of our problems could be remedied. Farrakhan spoke of the need for Black men to respect their women; to be independent of the White man and not to seek his favor; to start our own businesses and to embrace self-help not welfare. I was enthralled by his message and embraced his doctrine of self-help and independence. There was no mention of any of the inflammatory remarks attributed to him by his enemies in the media. His was a message of hope, inspiration and encouragement to a downtrodden people burdened by years of discouragement, deprivation and discrimination. Uplift was what he was preaching that night and those in attendance drank deep from the cup. On the late local evening news, excerpts from the speech were broadcast and pictures of the audience were shown.

I continued to do my thing. I was busy doing divorces and a lot of other legal work. I kept representing Wendy and directing her legal traffic as well as managing my real estate. Often I would pause to reflect on just what it was I was trying to do here in Philadelphia. I seemed to be blessed with the ability to succeed in spite of the obstacles that had been thrown in my path, and I was helping people as well as myself. What purpose was I serving? Was there a higher good to all of this and if so what was it? Could I identify a nobility of purpose to be served by my presence and practice in Philadelphia. Surely God had not allowed me to overcome all that I did just to meander along from one fee-paying case to another without trying to achieve something greater than self-aggrandizement. But what was that purpose?

Well, my clients needed my help. Some of them could not read, and some could but did not understand what they read. Some had no idea what this system had in store for them as they tried to remedy whatever situation they found themselves in. Many wanted the advantages of my learning to realize their dreams for their posterity. And many needed protection and basic guidance, direction and the application of good judgment to help them unravel the many entanglements life had thrown their way. There was an abundance of trust bestowed on me to do the right thing by them, and I tried my best to give a good account for that trust. The "lighthouse for the blind" continued to be the best description to describe the ministry I was delivering to my clients, *noblesse oblige*. This was a ministry built on faith. The people of Germantown were a friendly people basically, unique in their quaintness, sincere in their beliefs and trusting. After all, they were trusting me, a stranger in their midst. I was not home grown.

The evening was late and I was tired. I was about to go home when I heard this banging on my outside office door. I was in my office in the back, but I had a lamp light on in the reception area that shone through to the outside. It was Lang, anxious and distressed. He was all stirred up and in a huff and a puff. The dark brown skin of his face looked oily and greasy. Lang had a facial scar one half-inch above his left eye right below his hairline: a scar put there by his first wife "Vivienne." In the throes of a violent argument between Lang and Vivienne, she grabbed a butcher knife and cut him above his left eye leaving an unsightly gash on his forehead. The scar looked terrible. A doctor Lang knew stitched the cut together, but the cut was so new that the blood and puss that oozed from the wound made it look pink like the color of newly opened raw flesh. Reflected against his dark brown complexion, the gash made for a horrible sight. The contrast was startling and the light pink hew of his flesh made for a poignant sight, clearly noticeable by anyone looking at him, especially for a man of his bearing and demeanor, a man of the public, a gentle man. How could someone do this kind of thing to a person who earned his living in the public meeting and greeting people, not to mention the familial relationship? It hurt me deeply to see him in this condition. Lang was a good person. He had a distinguished look. His less than broad nose, thin pursed lips and small mouth made, except for the color of his skin, for a Caucasian like appearance.

Since his business was convincing people to buy what he was selling, his outward appearance was extremely important to him. When he entered an office after being outside with a hat on his head, he was so conscious about his looks that he carried a comb in his pocket that he would take out and run through his hair to get rid to the "hat hair" look before making his sales pitch to a client. He made sure he looked the part of a financial planner: dark blue suits, white shirts, nice ties and shined black shoes, his hair always in place. Lang was the consummate professional.

As the scar healed, the discolored pigmentation melded into a lighter hue than his natural skin color,leaving a permanent mark on his forehead. Exasperated Lang declared, "That's it! She tried to kill me!" Lang's vacillation about divorcing his wife was annoying. I had been down this road with him on several other occasions, so I made him a proposition to shut him up about divorcing Vivienne. I responded, "well, if you are really serious bring me $500.00 as a retainer and I will file the divorce papers." Lang was wishy-washy about divorcing Vivienne. It was an easy decision from my perspective. This was not the first time they had fought, but it was the first time blood had been drawn. Vivienne was the mother of his three daughters. Lang and Vivienne had been married for over twenty years, and they owned a split level ranch type home on a quiet street in a suburb north of Philadelphia.

Lang was decent, but Vivienne, "Viv" they called her, was a coarse woman—a ruffian by nature and bearing, a street wise woman, with a brutish temperament. She dominated Lang and pushed him around. Lang was indecisive. He had a hard time making decisions perhaps because this decision would either lead him to a new life or continue his entrapment in a world of continued low-class abuse. He knew he had out grown Vivienne, but getting rid of her was tough; it took courage and Lang was weak when it came to this aspect of his life. I often wondered about Lang. Though Lang worked among the upper classes and aspired to live like them, I questioned whether he had the value structure, innately to perpetuate it. Was there something lacking in his *modus vivendi* that left him wanting when it came to the structure and management of his household? Was there a values problems? Here was a man who had the bearing of a king but the home life of a figurative pauper. His outward trappings, the suburban home and the Volvo were possibly a facade masking deficits in his upbringing that didn't allow him to inculcate deeply enough the values, discipline, taste and virtues required not only to project middle class values, but also to live them day in and day out so that they are intrinsic to one's being. So much so, that you would demand these same disciplines of anyone who became a permanent part of your life. What was going on inside that house, behind closed doors? Was his home life dysfunctional? The morality he aspired to live was degraded to the extent that the lack of it corrupted the framework of his home life. Whatever was lacking was ruinous to him personally and limited his professional progress.

Lang always called me "coach," "yes coach this, and yes coach that," "I see your point," etc., etc. "But," he always said as a rhetorical reflex, "but not only that, but not only that" he would repeat. Perhaps this is how he used me and saw me as manifested by how often he used that handle in response. But I did not see myself as his coach I just always told him what I thought. But I used to say to myself about Lang, "that if you don't take the coaching you have to take the poaching."

During the next several weeks Lang paid me the retainer, and after some bickering with Vivienne's attorney I eventually divorced Lang, and settled his marital estate. He was finally free. After the divorce decree was issued, Lang and I met at Campbell's, a pub in Chestnut Hill near my office, for a celebratory drink. He was finally a free man.

I pressed on with my business, working every day except Sunday. I was fully ensconced in the worlds I created. And I was managing the vertiginous worlds of real estate and law that I operated every day. I decided to incorporate my practice into a professional corporation, and I incorporated my real estate management operation using the name Scattered Sites. A name I got from a Housing and Urban Development pronouncement about housing strategies in the urban core of big cities such as Philadelphia. The name caught on. I was attempting to avoid any confusion and conflicts of interest between my status as a lawyer and my role as a real estate investor.

33

※

MATURING AS A LAWYER

I N MY QUIET WAY, I was making a name for myself in certain circles. As a consequence, several unique opportunities came my way. I was asked to draft a charitable trust agreement for contributions to the Bethel African Methodist Episcopal (AME) Church in South Philadelphia, one of the first Black churches organized by freed slaves in the United States.[28] However, after many meetings and lengthy drafting sessions, and although a final draft was agreed to, the minister failed to support it and withdrew from the project.

This business came my way because of a referral and some estate planning work I did for a church official. Since I was working by myself and had no back-up, I was hesitant about getting too far out on a limb with the "exotic" when it came to the law. It took courage to press ahead on matters of this type, especially when I didn't know everything I thought I needed to know about the subject. I didn't have that "good feeling" I needed to have in order to feel confident about the undertaking. This was my perennial dilemma–not knowing when I knew enough. I found it hard to strike a balance between feeling I had a sufficient level of knowledge and worrying about what I didn't know. This was, at times, an unreasonable, self-inflicted standard and became mentally exhausting. I tried to stay on the "beaten path" because I had no one to back me up. However, over time, and through hard work, tenacity and courage, I ground this insecurity into a "bit player" in my psychological framework and pushed on. I often recalled the quote by Mark Twain that "All you need to succeed in America is ignorance and confidence." Learning from my mistakes, doing a better job every time, and doing it over and over again I became good at it after a while. Confident in what I did know.

I was asked by one of my estate planning clients, a prestigious professor of dermatology at the University of Pennsylvania, to draft an agreement between his department at the University and an allied department in the medical school. This was a unique opportunity that took me out of my usual practice disciplines into something different and challenging. Apparently, the client felt I was up to the challenge and wanted me involved. I always appreciated his confidence in me by bringing this business to me. The task was successfully concluded and the client satisfied.

Maturation was happening to me in my law practice; by now, I had been "seared on the grill." I was well beyond the novel, dilettante, and apprentice phases and well into becoming a journeyman, a connoisseur in the practice areas I knew best. I often felt that I was on a spiritual journey and was destined to do certain things because of my talents. This was ironic because, not long before this reversal of fortune, you would have thought I was incapable of any of this, looking at it from a pure bar exam point of view. In hindsight, the bar exam experience was a very poor prognosticator of my future, and I'm sure it was in the case of many others as well. Among other areas of practice, I found that I was good at transactional law: forming entities; drafting self-executing documents, such as powers of attorney, wills, deeds; trust agreements; raising estates and settling estates; transferring real property; effecting name changes; and securing contested and no-fault divorces. These were to become the mainstays of my practice.

I also developed a comfortable approach to initiating and responding to pleadings in civil litigation. I learned to love the Praecipe for a Writ of Summons, a Philadelphia civil practice that allows a plaintiff's attorney to initiate a case without filing a formal complaint. This can be especially beneficial if a lawyer is up against an expiring statute of limitations. When filed and served, the opposing party must file a "rule" on the plaintiff's attorney requiring him or her to file a formal complaint within twenty days, or the matter may be dismissed. I grew to love this mechanism because of its stealth. I enjoyed blocking complaints that were filed against my clients.

Blocking and tackling was my game. I filed numerous bankruptcy petitions to stop foreclosures and disrupt my opponents' goals and frustrate them. I enjoyed the game of law practice: the strategy, the use of legal tools as a sword and shield. I developed an affinity for motions practice, in the criminal as well as in the civil law. I would winnow down my opponent's case to its bare bones, sometimes winning a case before ever having to try it, all on motions.

On Saturdays there was standing room only in my office reception area. Some Saturdays, when I would arrive, there would be clients waiting on the porch for me to arrive and open the office. I never liked it when this happened because we would have no time to settle in before having clients hovering in the office anxiously waiting to be seen. Our business was brisk. Some weeks my take would be as much as $2,000.00 plus during a good week, from Monday through Saturday. Each month I was carrying over money in my business checking account. I would balance my account each month at the kitchen table on Sedgewick Street and ask myself, based upon the money left in the account, whether or not I was still in business? Since relocating my office to Germantown Avenue, I had been meeting a payroll every week without fail. This would continue for many years in an unbroken string of checks paid to employees working in the law office for twenty-five plus years. Most employees are only concerned with receiving their next checks, the business owner is concerned with how to pay those checks.

I had hit upon a winning formula for business success in my community: divorces via advertising; rental apartments, and consumer-law practices in the bread and butter areas that people needed help with. One of my colleagues remarked "I want to do what you are doing. You have money coming in from all directions." What he did not realize was the seamlessness of the symmetry of an urban populace hungry for what I was offering. Honest lawyering and completed assignments, value for the money, reasonable fees and an inventory of services to satisfy what this market needed, not the "high end stuff," but the basics, bread and butter—with a flair. This was all my design. I treated my clients with respect and I demanded respect from them. I valued their business and trusted in word of mouth advertising as the real sustaining influence for repeat business. I played the game for the long haul.

In one of my early Bankruptcy cases, a nice old Black woman named Viola Phillips, short in height with a kind disposition and who spoke very softly came to see me, distraught and anxious about a fix she had gotten herself into trying to help her aged mother. Viola lived next door to Mt.

Ad in The Germantown Courier, 1988, courtesy The Leader

Tabor Baptist Church on Rittenhouse Street in Germantown. She put her aging mother into a local nursing home because she could no longer care for her in her home. Viola was a nice gentle woman with two adult sons, one was living with her and the other lived in Hawaii. Viola signed the nursing home contract to be financially responsible for the nursing home fees beyond what government would pay. She was unaware of the financial consequences to her personally; she simply did not know any better. Several months later Mrs. Phillips was hit with billing totaling tens of thousands of dollars none of which she could pay. Viola only had a modest retirement income, and her small three bedroom stucco home which sat closer to Green Street on the west than to Germantown Avenue on the east. The home was modest by most standards; it was her only asset, it was her security.

I was known to Viola because I started out in the basement of Mt. Tabor when I first moved to Germantown and began practicing. Rev. Henry Floyd Johnson, a short dark-skinned balding Black man with a pushy personality, was the minister. His wife, Lois Porter, was a tall Black woman with an attractive figure. They were both from Charlottesville and had married late in their careers. Lois was one of my teachers when I attended Burley High School in Charlottesville, and Floyd, back then, was the pastor of Zion Union Baptist Church in Charlottesville. After they were married, Floyd elected to move from Charlottesville when he was offered an opportunity to succeed William Grey, Sr., then the current pastor of Bright Hope Baptist Church in Philadelphia. Bright Hope is a "big" church in Philadelphia, home to many middle class Blacks. But when the senior Grey finally "threw in the towel," his son the congressman, who had previously expressed no interest in succeeding his father, chose to succeed him and the church split. Floyd was left to his own devices to form his own church, and the son took over Bright Hope, and Floyd settled at Mount Tabor Baptist Church. Floyd and I did a lot of business together over the years. Floyd "knew everything," but he was still a decent and supportive friend. While getting my practice started, Floyd and Lois extended to me a courtesy by allowing me to use the church office to see clients in the evenings. The church knew me.

So when Viola came to see me, I was a known commodity to her via Mt. Tabor. She brought with her a copy of the complaint that had been served on her demanding judgment for over $50,000.00, which had it been granted would have put Viola "outdoors." The ravenous pace at which nursing home fees accrue would easily erode the entire value of the house in less than one year. As she sat across from me at my desk, she was forlorn and sullen. Her eyes were downcast, and as she handed me the paper her hands shook as though she had Parkinson's disease or some similar such malady. The paper vibrated with each shake of her hand: "What am I going to do Mr. Lee?" she inquired plaintively. "I don't want to lose my house! What about my mother? What am I to do with her? They did not tell me that I would have to pay this money. God knows I never would have signed these papers if I knew this was going to happen," she cried. I thought to myself "this woman is in crisis." She was visibly shaken by this experience. The nursing home had attacked her unsuspectingly. Like a vicious dog, it lunged at her from its hind legs, canines glistening heading for her neck—to induce immediate death. My job was to strike with an iron fist and knock this dog to the ground. My intent was to swish it and screw it until upon my release, it scampered away never to be heard from again.

As the burden shifted to me to assuage this woman's pain, I realized that this was what being an attorney was all about. I felt the weight of the office I represented and the responsibility that went with it. The moment epitomized what the public expects from its lawyers, why the public has come to rely on its attorneys, and why competence is so important. I tried to calm her fears and reassured her that she would not lose her house. That I would do all I could to prevent that from happening, even though at the moment I did not have a clear well-thought out solution to her problem. I pondered what the best solution to this problem was for this woman, with the view of keeping her in her home as paramount. I could have answered the complaint in the traditional way and tied the matter up in court for several years before judgment day would eventually arrive. And in the process run up her fees. Or I could put her into a Chapter 7 Bankruptcy and by doing so, cut the nursing home off at the knees and "kill it," and keep her in her home with minimal costs. But what about the equity which would be subject to the trustee's seizure and liquidation to pay off her creditors? I thought long and hard about the best way to remedy this situation.

I went home to Charlottesville that next weekend with this matter very much on my mind. We all went to my home church, Ebenezer Baptist Church in Richmond. As I sat in the pew listening to the sermon and enjoying the choir, a divine moment gave rise to the appropriate strategy. Put her into bankruptcy, and take the lowest assessed value for the home to squeeze down the equity, which is easy to do in Philadelphia where assessed values have no relationship to fair market values. Any liens such as tax liens or other dormant indebtedness liened against the house would further erode the equity cushion. Then maximize her exemptions under federal law which Pennsylvania law permitted for her equity and show that there was no equity for the trustee to go after. With the high volume of cases filed in the eastern district of Pennsylvania, the case would probably not be reviewed and get through.

It worked! The trustee abandoned the house not seeing any equity to liquidate, and the debt was discharged. As a result, Viola was relieved of any further personal liability for the nursing home debt and her home was saved. Her mother died in the nursing home, and Viola lived in her home until she died years later with her one son still living there.

My high empathy, which is always over the top, caused me to lend a part of myself to the cases that went beyond simple legal processing. And even with some of these process cases I would get personally attached. I have the peculiar ability to feel my client's pain and their need for relief, putting myself vicariously in their shoes. Winnie Mandela in her book, *Part of My soul Went With Him,* describes how part of her heart was extended and frayed when her famous husband, Nelson Mandela was incarcerated and badly treated while in detention. A similar empathy permeates my being in hard fought cases. You see, everything becomes personal. That is why it can take months if not years for a lawyer to recover from hard fought cases that end in partial or total defeat. It just takes a lot out of you. You are never the same. It has taken years for me to intellectually divorce myself from my natural tendency to lend myself to my client's cases. I have to work at being aloof. I often say to myself, remember you are not part of the family. It is because I care too much, I suppose, and because I like the uniqueness of people, their quaintness, speech patterns and personalities. I remember them all. My father was a great lover of people; he, too, enjoyed their personalities. Perhaps I get this from him.

As fate would have it, Mt. Tabor always had its eyes on Viola's house since it was next door, and they had wanted to acquire the house for some time for expansion. After Viola's death they sought my help to make this acquisition. But for the efforts I undertook to save the house years before, the house may not have been available for them to acquire. I did the deal for them which included suing the real estate agent who "went south"—took the money and ran—on the church with money the church had given him to purchase the property. I raised an estate for Viola so that title could be conveyed, clearing the title and finding Viola's lost sons. The son who lived with her all those years until she died, just up and left one day and no one ever heard from him again, and I had to track down the remaining son in Hawaii.

Bankruptcy law was an area of the law that I naturally gravitated to out of pure intellectual curiosity and enjoyment. I enjoyed reading about how financial instruments are unwound in bankruptcy. It is a lesson in how the financial and legal system evaluates the hierarchy of its financial services. Unwinding the financial "cork" gives you a perspective you do not gain when putting the "cork" in the bottle. It was fascinating to me to use this system of laws as a "sword and as a shield," as many scholars have mentioned. My estate planning background which concentrates on "winding up the cork," acquiring assets and trying to preserve them, allowed me to see the unwinding process at the other end of the financial continuum. I would stay up some nights reading bankruptcy law and falling in love with terms like "the indubitable equivalent." Great stuff, just great!

A prodigious effort of arduous work went into maintaining my law practice and running the business of the practice and running a real estate business, "keeping it all together." Solely with regard to the law practice, as in the old IBM computer commercials, I wore "many hats" trying to keep things afloat. In addition to generating the income, paying the bills, keeping the accounts, doing the accounting and banking, and paying the taxes, I also was placating clients, watching out for bar ethics rule infractions and bar complaints, managing appointments and court appearances. One must order supplies, maintain office equipment, computers and software, keep the copier going, change light bulbs, get the office cleaned, order books and updates, maintain the lawn, remove the trash, supervise employees, make a payroll, organize office files, etc, etc, etc.

As I grew in stature and confidence in my chosen areas of legal expertise, my confidence became subservient to my professional pride. At all costs, I did not want to embarrass myself, regardless of the merits of a case. I wanted to do a good job, but mainly for my own personal satisfaction. Often, it made no real difference to me whether I won or lost. Sure, the client would be happy if he or she secured a good result—and winning can gloss over many things, including your mistakes—but even when I won, those mistakes had to be examined and corrected. It was important for me to come away from each confrontation feeling good about my performance.

Aside from Wendy Bee and Lang, two long-term relationships formed from my law practice, I became counsel to the Grand United Order of Odd Fellows in America and Jurisdiction in the summer of 1986. The Odd Fellows is a Black national and international fraternal organization similar to the Masons and is headquartered in Philadelphia. The organization was founded in 1843 by Peter Ogden at a time when many Blacks, because of their exclusion from White social organizations, and as a protection from the hostilities of White society, sought to bind themselves together for their own social well-being. The Odd Fellows played a pivotal role in establishing schools for Black children after the Civil War. Often, local Black communities' nascent programs to educate their children suffered from a lack of facilities and money. The Odd Fellows lent meeting houses to leading Black educators of the day so that schools would have somewhere to meet, organize, and hold classes.

The Odd Fellows is organized locally through lodges for men and households for women. They are charted by the headquarters organization, and each local branch owns its own real and personal property and pays dues to the headquarters. The central office was run by a Grandmaster and Grand Secretary, as well as a board and executive Committee of Management. As counsel, I worked with the Grand Secretary and the Committee of Management. I followed in the footsteps of my maternal grandfather, Patrick Moon, and joined the Odd Fellows. I was initiated into a lodge near my office on Germantown Avenue and rose to become Grand Attorney within the Odd Fellows hierarchy, fourth in line to the leadership after the

Vice Grand Master and Grand Secretary. I served under four Grand Masters and six Grand Secretaries.

During one of our regular meetings, Grandmaster Gains took me for a ride around City Hall in a vintage black Rolls Royce, complete with driver. We circled the building three times before he let me out. It was a show of his status. He was dressed in his official black suit with a top hat, ready for his grand promenade—in accordance with the ritual strut of lodge members and householders, each one dressed in black and white attire with shoes to match. This was an unusual experience and full of novelty–a throwback to a bygone era when noblemen, robber barons, and patricians ruled the realm. That was what being an Odd Fellow meant in the heyday of racial segregation.

I worked with the Odd Fellows for many years and assisted them with all sorts of tasks, from lease negotiations with tenants in their headquarters building and tax settlements with the City of Philadelphia to restoring the property of defunct lodges and households to the ownership of the headquarters' organization. The latter of these assignments was the most fulfilling because it recaptured land owned by Blacks many years ago that was now valuable and would otherwise have been lost as a result of ignorance and neglect. Grandmaster Gains, a crusty old-world curmudgeon with eccentric ways, was the brainchild behind the policy. He had foreseen the huge loss of value to the organization if these lands and properties were abandoned, so he led the fight to have the bylaws of the organization strengthened and clarified to empower the headquarters' organization to acquire title to the real properties of defunct lodges and households. As counsel, I helped draft the language of the policy and to implement it.

I was particularly pleased with my work to save the Odd Fellows building in Washington, D.C., at 1851 9th Street NW. At the time, it was being sold to pay off real estate taxes. It was a valuable property in the core of the city. The lodge that owned the building had grown too weak to maintain the property and was on the verge of losing it. It proved to be a complicated legal matter to save this building. It involved bankruptcy law; a real estate sale to a charter school in Washington, D.C., that was headed by second generation illuminati; and an intricate mortgage financing negotiation that resulted in two first mortgages: one a purchase money mortgage with the Odd Fellows as mortgagee, and the other a conventional mortgage to a commercial bank, which provided construction financing. The deal was worth over $350,000; if you added in the construction financing, it was worth an additional two or three hundred thousand dollars.

The first step in my strategy for saving the property was to stop the tax sale without letting my adversaries know I was taking that track. So, prior to filing for bankruptcy, I worked out a payment schedule for the D.C. lodge with the tax sale law firm, and, of course, the defunct D.C. lodge failed to maintain it. When that failed, I put the lodge into Chapter Eleven bankruptcy. With the tax sale stayed, I worked behind the scenes to find a buyer for the building. I called my contacts in the real estate community in D.C. I knew a few since I owned a rental property in D.C, and there had already been several interested buyers seeking to acquire the property.

Once a buyer was found–the See Forever Foundation, aka the Maya Angelou Charter School—we undertook complex negotiations to put a deal together. The real estate purchase agreement was eighteen pages long. I was up against the large Washington, D.C., law firm of Wilmer, Cutler, and Pickering. It was not quite a David and Goliath undertaking because I knew where the leverage was in the deal, and I had structured such deals before, but the balance of resources between the two sides was still heavily against us.

As negotiations dragged on, my mind wandered off to the times when my father took our family to "cruise" the land he owned in Fluvanna County, central Virginia–raw undeveloped land. We would go there to pick berries in the sum-mer–blackberries and raspberries amid the thorns and thickets, with wild grass up to our hips. As we picked the berries, my hands would get nicked and pricked by the stickers and briars that grew around the berries. My trousers were filled with tics and stickers that latched onto anything that moved.

So it was with this negotiation. Though I retrieved some berries, I had to watch out for the briars and thorns. I made sure I protected my client's interest by holding out for a first mortgage on the premises, even though the bank in its usual intimidating manner wanted the only primacy in the lien hierarchy. So we did a *pari passu*, a lien structure allowing for two first mortgages, permitting both lend-ers, the seller and the bank, to occupy first positions as secured creditors against the title to the property. It was a novel, provocative, and creative approach, and also a problem solver. It was made possible because, upon renovation, the building would have enough value beyond the debt to cover both mortgages. So I saved the building for the Odd Fellows and gained much-needed capital for the organiza-tion. In addition, I saved them another $30,000 because of the ineptitude of the real estate agent, who didn't protect her interest in the deal and as a result received no sales commission.

There were several other projects, not of the same scope but involving the same principle, that I was committed to when the end suddenly came for me. My ouster was engendered by my demands to be more adequately paid, and my re-fusal to violate the ethics of my profession. I was a lawyer before I became an Odd Fellow, and I intended to remain a lawyer after my Odd Fellow days were over. That was always my mindset, regardless of my outward endeavor. I enjoyed my work because I felt I was helping Black people accomplish something for themselves; I was using my abilities to fit their needs. With all that I had helped them accom-plish, I never felt like an insider in the organization; and I was not.

When the end came, I had little support save for a phone call from the Vice Grand Master that offered some insight into my situation; other than that, no one bothered to say thank you. It's questionable whether they appreciated my efforts on their behalf. I left the organization shorn of any illusion that even "good" people will treat you right. Practicing law for the most part is a thankless job. That is why, in the end, you must make sure you get paid. It's the only measure of appreciation that speaks for itself.

Because of my varied experiences in this "laboratory" of human nature, I be-gan to reach several conclusions about people, especially Black people as they relat-ed to the use of Black lawyers, and about the general nature of people. I once saved a Black woman and her kids from being evicted from her apartment, for which she was very thankful. But when she had a personal injury case involving an automo-bile, she went to a non-Black lawyer instead of coming back to me. She didn't even inquire whether or not I would be interested in taking the case. This illustrates the point that Black people still relate to non-Black lawyers as their attorneys of choice when any money of consequence is on the table. Why is that? Because Black folks still harbor the "White is right" syndrome when it comes to the professional class. However, this may gradually be changing.

Johnnie Cochran did a lot for the perception of Black lawyers as competent professionals and Thurgood Marshall is still the icon of Black lawyering in America. Yet Black professionals still have to prove themselves every day, even to their own community, who surely should know better. There is no assumption of competence; only a presumption of incompetence, which must be overcome by sustained performance. It is hard to make believers of Black folks, but there are many exceptions, and thank God I have been the beneficiary of some of those exceptions.

34

❦

"Strong Men,"
New Properties
and Old Jacklegs

"One thing they cannot prohibit—
The strong men . . . coming on
The strong' men gittin' stronger.
Strong men. . . .
Stronger. . . ."

—from Sterling Brown's *Strong Men*

I PURCHASED THREE MORE BUILDINGS over the next five years to add to my portfolio, giving me an additional twenty-five units of rental property. I was purchasing one building a year during this time and my real estate management operation was equal to, if not beginning to exceed, my law practice in income. These were the heady days–my El Dorado. My income was now well into six figures and my net worth crossed into seven figures, which put me in "the circle of green," a local banking expression at the time. As in Voltaire's *Candide*, I had created for myself the "best of all possible worlds"–and achieved it from whole cloth.

In order, I bought 5214 and 5216 Laurens Street, two attached four-unit buildings in the Queen Lane section of Germantown in September 1984; a thirteen-unit building at 339 East Wister Street in 1988, which also had thirteen garages; and a four-unit building at 159 West Manheim Street in Germantown in 1989. I came close to buying two other buildings, but those deals didn't come together, even though I was really close to sealing them. Each of these buildings was unique. The Laurens Street buildings were dilapidated to some extent, but could possibly be saved. However, I didn't save them. I only made modest upgrades to them, which were more cosmetic than structural. The prior owner was in receivership; he had run into difficulty and wanted to shed them at any cost. I found out about his dilemma and purchased the buildings directly from the bank through their attorney. I took them over and kept them going for fifteen-plus years, until *my* gas ran out.

Dope dealers, bad decisions, obsolescence, and a worn-out, worn-down, termite-infested structure eventually got the best of me and the buildings.

I paid less than $20,000 for both buildings and, as they say in a capitalist society, "You get what you pay for." Then I did my usual thing: I separated the electricity for each unit in each building, so they used and payed for their own heat and hot water. Dad and I would joke about Laurens because it had a steep staircase going up to the third floor, two bedroom apartment. He and I both knew renting this place would be a "steep climb" for anybody who would rent it.

Entering the basement on Laurens was equivalent to taking a trip into the darkest circle of *Dante's Inferno* as described in his allegory *The Divine Comedy*. To enter this basement was to enter hell: it was dark, wet and muddy, with cobwebs everywhere, skeletons of dead rats and other vermin scattered about. I have known of some repairmen who refused to go down into these basements and neighborhoods. But this is where you must dwell if you are going to cure the ills of any building.

I got a lot out of this project: the building made money for me, but I lost the capital appreciation piece because of its lapse into disrepair. Laurens simply got away from me. I made my mistake by letting the dope dealers get in there and allowing them to stay too long. But the cash was addictive. Those guys and gals were paying me $1,000 a month for one or two units and back then that was good money. They were also an intimidating bunch and I had to tread softly in dealing with them. They knew the game, the power of that cash. But they ruined the building, driving out all the good tenants, and their presence invited other types of crime and vandalism.

When you own old buildings, it is imperative that you stay on top of them at all times. The biggest challenge came with the purchase of the Wister Street building in 1988. I rationalized the purchase of this property because Michelle found herself between jobs because of a personality conflict that developed between her and her boss. I said to her that if I bought another property it would make up for some of the reduction in income. Dad was up on one of his many visits, and we looked at this property and made an offer. The seller was in distress and wanted to unload the hulk. We got the building for less than $75,000. This humongous structure at the corner of Rubicam and Wister Streets, east of Germantown Avenue and west of the old Germantown Hospital, tested my real estate management skills like no other project. Wister Street was a stone building with a white stucco facade. The building had three floors and contained three two-bedroom units, eight one-bedroom units and two efficiencies. It took up a quarter of the block on Wister Street and three quarters of the block on Rubicam street, with long, cavernous hallways on the first, second and third floors.

I borrowed the purchase money from PSFS, Pennslyvania Savings Fund Society, a local savings and loan company, and immediately went about rehabilitating the building. Some of the units were not habitable, so I had to fix them up, paint them and put them on line, that is, make them rentable. My money was in the vacant units. The existing rental units carried the building until I gradually got the unused units in place. However, the building was inefficient and unprofitable because the prior owner had to pay for all the utilities. This was a "no-no" to my scheme of thinking. So I had to borrow a significant chunk of money to decentralize the utilities, all of them: heat, hot water, electricity, and gas.

My first task was to get estimates from several heating contractors to install thirteen heating units and thirteen hot water heaters in the building. Prior to the conversion the gas bill to heat the building and supply hot water was running seven to eight hundred dollars a month, just for the units that were habitable and occupied. After obtaining the loan from Corestates Bank, now Wells Fargo, it took the entire summer to get this work completed and organized, but in the end, the heat and hot water conversions made this project feasible financially, because if that had not been done, the building's expenses would have outstripped its income by ten-fold and destined it to a negative cash flow.

I made good use of the loan money. I had estimated the cost of decentralizing the heat at about $50,000 and borrowed that amount to complete the job. Knowing in fact, I could get it completed for less, and with the difference, I bought another building using the remaining loan proceeds and was able to decentralize the heating system in that building as well. I "doubled down," or expanded the leverage of the loan money, maximizing the reach and return on the loan. In my mind, this was a stroke of genius—a quietly kept pleasure until now.

I was really proud of this maneuver because I managed to buy another four-unit building without putting any of my own money, equity, into the deal. It was a fictional "no money down" deal. Even with all this wheeling and dealing just below the radar, I felt no pangs of insecurity, nor a lack of confidence or any kind of trepidation; I just charged ahead. This was despite my earlier experience of failure with the Kenneth Street project in Chicago. Every time I thought of Wister Street, I thought about Kenneth Street. But I was determined not to repeat that failure. In fact, that previous experience just made me work harder.

The Wister Street property was the last property I purchased in Philadelphia. I paid as I went for the repairs. The vacant units were made rentable. I had the hallways repainted and retiled. I installed new self-closing steel exterior doors, both front and back, in an attempt to improve security. I installed hot-wired fire alarm systems throughout the building on each floor. The driveway and rear parking area, that had been dirt before that made for a muddy mess when it rained, was paved over with asphalt for the first time. I also knew that I could make money if I could rebuild the thirteen wooden garages that circled the rear of the property in a half moon arc. They were all dilapidated, decayed and filled with an accumulation of junk and waste. It was mostly old tires, scrap iron, and garbage that had been dumped there over many years. I had all thirteen garages rebuilt with cinder block walls and cement floors and made them rentable and usable.

As I have often said about these old properties, I could spend a million dollars on them and still would have an old property. They absorb money like a sponge; it is unending. At its height, all thirteen rental units functioned, several of the garages were rented and the building had been given a facelift. I spent more money on Wister Street than on any other building I owned in Philadelphia.

The problems I had were many. The old stone retaining wall on the south end, the front of the building was falling apart and was constantly hit by errant motorists who struck it as they recklessly drove by. The basement flooded with sewage backup, which created a cesspool of mud and raw sewage. Also, carbon monoxide, a poisonous gas created from the burning of carbon with insufficient air, and generated most commonly in boiler and furnace rooms, was a constant concern.

No one wanted to go there unless they had to. The floor boards that supported the rear first floor unit sagged above rotting floor joists that had to be propped up on poles mounted against the floor joist in the basement to keep them from collapsing. From time to time, I checked on the stability of the jerry-rigged fix applied to keep this unit level and had to constantly ensure that there was proper ventilation in the boiler room. There was a persistent roof leak in one of the second floor units that could never be permanently fixed. It always reoccurred, just as the roof leak on Green Street could never be fixed.

Over time, tenants died in the building, got shot, used dope, set the place on fire and did everything imaginable to try to raze it to a pile of rubble. It was impossible to regulate the conduct of the people who came and went, unless I posted a security guard in the building twenty-four hours a day. I couldn't afford that, even though I often thought about it. So I monitored the property each Saturday, inspecting all the areas that I deemed needed to be checked to give myself some assurance that things were not getting totally out of hand.

About this time, the federal government changed its income tax laws limiting the amount of losses an investor could take against earned income in any one tax year. And to compound my problems the city slapped me with a $20,000 water bill for back water usage, even though I paid the water bill as it was billed. However, the city played dirty; it would bill me with estimated water usage bills then, when it got into the property to actually read the meter, it would send you an actual bill containing all the under-billed usage at once and expect it to be paid within the billing cycle. This was enough to sink a small investor and exasperated me because I never felt I got the truth about my water bills.

The water bill error caused me much angst and trepidation until it was resolved. Juggling the money from one creditor to another, piece-mealing the payments just to keep things afloat didn't do the job. The water usage remained too great and the city was unrelenting in its demand for payment. Philadelphia would not allow landlords to separate the water utility in multi-family buildings.

The city then changed its ordinance to make outstanding unpaid water bills liens against real property, so it had to be paid to transfer title unless you knew how to get around it; fortunately, I did. By the time Laurens started "going south," I was getting tired of spending money and going into further debt to save these properties. What with all these issues and having to deal with unscrupulous contractors, the end came gradually but certainly to the Laurens properties.

The weight of this water bill kept me up at night and tormented my soul because I knew that this mistake could cause the entire operation of the building to collapse. Once the city tired of my procrastination it could send letters to the tenants demanding payment, and when that happened all control by the landlord was lost. To fight this issue, I filed several petitions with the Tax Review Board, a city governmental administrative agency that has the power to adjust tax bills and water bills if they are inaccurate or if payment could not be made because of hardships, errors, meter failure or other related issues. I had practiced before this board numerous times, filing petition after petition to seek relief of one kind or another.

One thing about my practice was that whenever I found a niche that agreed with my skill level and had beneficial capability, my approach was to "work it and work it" until I wore it out or it wore me out, whichever came first. So it was with the Tax Review Board. On a few occasions, I made some headway, but on most attempts I achieved nothing. I even got slammed harshly once because the board saw no merit in my plea and was onto my strategy. They had had enough of me.

I once sought to work out a payment plan with the city water revenue department by asking a city worker for a payment plan. On one occasion, this middle-aged Black woman, who was neatly dressed and a very self-assured career bureaucrat, hardened from years of hearing pleas of the sort I was about to make, was assigned to interview me about the water bill. She said in a stern voice, "And how can I help you?"

I told her I was there to see if I could get some help on my water bill. I explained that the city had either overcharged me or had back-billed this huge amount on this property.

She looked up at me and said, "And whose fault is that?" Her tone implied, in effect, "I could care less about your problem." If her intent was to induce perturbation in me, she greatly succeeded. Her stinging rebuke still resonates in my subconscious to this day. Her lack of empathy, her meanness, her harshness to a taxpayer who helped pay her salary sent a dagger through my already punctured emotional skin. It is as though a callous psychiatrist had applied a vicious electric shock to my unwilling brain—to shock me back into reality and to bring me down.

I didn't need that kind of insensitive treatment coming from a motherly-looking Black woman who I thought would be more sympathetic. Her stance epitomized what the "city of brotherly love" was all about. I was already fully aware of the gravity of my mistake. I knew it was of my own making and that I was drowning quickly. Even so, I don't like people who are mean to me in any context and this encounter was unusually rude. I was still living in a dream world, I imagine, walking around looking for a kind word or a friend, someone who would understand my plight. "Woe is me, woe is me!" was my lament.

Before it was all over for me in Philadelphia, every utility I used in this building or in others at one time or another had been shut off. The water, electric, gas, even the telephone. Payment plans and agreements, mean customer service representatives, and harassing utility bill collectors were all part of the playing field for the average citizen and the savvy landlord. The pain of these deprivations were disconcerting but fleeting, though their sting was poignant when first inflicted.

I resolved the water bill on Wister Street a few months later by refinancing the building and paying off the bill and a few other "stragglers" that had been tormenting me as well. Wister Street was a monstrosity, but I intended to conquer it and not let it conquer me. I was not going to allow this building to drive me out of the business and to defeat me.

"That's on you," my cousin Pat had said in conversing with me one day, using an expression that summarized Philadelphia mentality. I had never heard that phrase before I moved to the City of Brotherly Love.

Problems, problems, problems–that was all the rental business ever was. Solving problems to earn your money. Most tenants care about nothing. They pay you rent and expect you to change their diapers for them. I was sued by tenants looking for a pay day based on bogus slip-and-fall claims. I won some and others were settled for relatively small sums. I had to fight a year-long court battle in the Court of Common Pleas with the city's Department of Licenses and

Inspections over a host of alleged problems. These were all problems I was addressing at the time, but the litigation kept me in court battling to keep the building operating and took up a lot of court time. Fortunately, a temperate female judge whose rulings were calibrated with justice and balance slowly caused the city's attack to waste away. The low socioeconomic demographic that I dealt with made for a tough sell when it came to behavior, values, and housekeeping. As an urban landlord, I had to fight against the "forces of resistance," decay, obsolescence, unscrupulous lawyers, numerous degenerate tenants, inflated insurance premiums, finance, nihilism, graft, quackery, shysterism, and jacklegs. It was equivalent to doing business with a "ball and chain" around my ankles–and was an exhausting, uphill battle.

I saved lots of money doing my own lawyering when it came to the real estate business. I spent many hours in court tending to my legal needs. If I had been a client, my legal fees would have been enormous. But this advantage didn't apply to the construction and maintenance end of the business. There, I was fair game to the sharks roving the waters.

When you are a small investor, you deal with small contractors, many of whom are decent, but unlicensed; some are often unscrupulous, ill-trained, mean and, on occasion, even physically threatening; indeed, some are simply thugs posing as contractors. I have had experiences with each type of contractor during my time in business. Licensed contractors charge higher fees so much so that using them, except for repairs that require licensed contractors, is often prohibitive.

Regardless of the risks involved, a maintenance operation is essential to the operation of a real estate business. Something is always breaking down somewhere in one of your units. The maintenance contractor is just as essential as the mortgage man, the insurance man, and the court system, except that they do not have liens against your property. You can't exist in this business without them. When I started doing the renovation work on Wister Street, for example, I used the friend of a guy in the building who was from North Philly. He was a rough, coarse individual who had the capacity to kill you if you wronged him, but also had a friendliness and jovial quality that made me "get on well" with him for several years. He and I did a lot of work together, and he responded well to my call for help, both in emergencies and non-emergencies.

Just about every "Joe" thinks he knows something about construction, nailing, hammering and painting. But in this business there are gradations of skill levels in carpentry, masonry, plumbing, electrical wiring, and painting. Most guys who don't go too far in school hold themselves out as "contractors" of some type, but in reality they are "jacklegs," unscrupulous, unskilled charlatans masquerading as skilled tradesmen. Society knows that these otherwise unskilled wannabes have to find some kind of work to earn a living and so this underbelly of quacks, shysters, charlatans, and thieves are allowed to lie in wait for opportunities to take advantage of unwary homeowners and landlords who don't know better, but must operate under the guise and rubric of *caveat emptor*: let the buyer beware. I had to have the money to pay these guys when I hired them, or else I could have been killed or beaten up. In fact, not far from where I lived during this time, a couple was murdered by two thug repairmen because they didn't pay them. You didn't want to owe those types money for doing work for you.

I remember a situation that developed on Laurens Street. I hired two brothers, the Blakey brothers, to do some construction work on one of the units there. The work was done in a shoddy manner and not to my liking. I hesitated in paying them and tried to tell them the work was not satisfactory. I tried to avoid them to some extent. But it was not long before violence loomed as the universal method for settling arguments in this social sphere. It appeared to me that the situation was getting out of control. And I could not reason with them; they only believed in one thing–money. These guys intimidated me and scared me to the point that I paid to get rid of them and to save myself from physical harm.

Getting references on contractors is a good thing if you can do it, but in the hustle and bustle world of complaint and response, sometimes this is impossible. You fall into situations because of expediency rather than due diligence. Money is a factor because somewhere between trying to save it and getting a problem solved is another problem. So, in many instances you try to build relationships by using the same people and building trust between them and you. You trust they will do a good job and come when you call, and they trust that you will pay them.

So for many years I relied on this tenant's friend from north Philly for most of the work on Wister Street. His name was Willaford. He was a rough-hewn, brawny Black man whose hands were as coarse as sandpaper. He was knowledgeable about a lot of day-to-day construction and maintenance jobs and stopped just short of being a "thug contractor." We worked together for a long time. He was instrumental in helping me to get Wister Street up and running, especially by renovating the vacant apartments.

Then, after several years of working together, things took a turn for the worst when we disagreed on the price of a job. I had asked him to change out a sewer pipe in the basement. I was standing with him in the basement, inspecting the work when I handed him a check I thought was reasonable, but he disagreed with it. "What's this?" he asked as he looked at the check. "This ain't enough money for the work I did." He looked up and his eyes made contact with mine. For some reason, I knew this episode was different from all the other haggles over money for past jobs. I asked him, "Well, how much do you expect to be paid for this job? It isn't that big a deal," trying to get him to be reasonable.

We were alone in the basement, the raw dirt floor of the cellar under our feet, a single dim light dangling from a pull chain light that hung from the unfinished ceiling; the raw joists above my head were my only witnesses. The space was cavernous, just like the building itself. It had several compartments, but there was no other light on and no one else there except us. We were standing six feet from a bank of electric meters arrayed against the front wall where the sewer line came in from the street. No one would hear my plea, nor would I be able to prove what in my wildest thoughts might happen.

I thought back to my encounter with John Vest, a bully I went to school with in Charlottesville when I was in the 7th grade, as I recounted. He started bullying me as we walked home alone on an isolated back street. I was stupid enough to answer him back, which sent the wrong signal and called his bluff. He immediately started punching me in my chest, and out of shock I started crying. My cries startled him and he stopped pounding me. He had proven his point. He had called my bluff and I lost. As they used to say in the street, "he bought all my wolf tickets."

There would be no repeat of that mistake. Anyway, it would be his word against mine, then credibility would decide whose story would be believed. I felt particularly vulnerable and out of my league. He made a menacing movement and a fist, as if he wanted to hit something, perhaps me–not a dramatic gesture but easily discernible. He apparently had such a thought, but may have restrained himself. In any case, I was not going to stick around to find out. I had a sense of fear for my safety for the first time around this guy. Perhaps he had gotten too familiar, or at least he thought he was familiar enough with me that he could exhibit such behavior. Dad often said "familiarity breeds contempt."

I immediately put some distance between him and me, and I left the the basement right away and quickly drove back to my office. Upon arriving, I locked my two outer doors. He followed me to the office on Germantown Avenue, arriving a few minutes later. He began yelling and knocking on the outer door asking to talk to me, but I refused to answer and would not let him in. I stayed there until I was sure he had left. I never used him again, or ever saw him again after that. After I had paid thousands of dollars to this man, our relationship had come to an abrupt end.

Many of these people are of a different class and violence is not too far from their ready arsenal of solutions to problems. Most of the workers I used were jacklegs, except for the technical jobs involving electricity, gas, heating conversions and replacements. Some of them had better skills than others, but on a whole most were of that vintage. You get what you pay for in all aspects of life. This especially applies in the maintenance world. Throwing good money after bad, having to go back and get the same thing repaired again and again is annoying and frustrating. Trying to get the thing repaired right the first time is always the objective. But in this world of cost vs. benefit, measured mostly in the short term, you have to try to blend price and quality. If you tilt too far in either direction, you could be a loser. Corners often have to be cut to make things work out. One is not always able to pay top price for the best craftsman to do the best job. You have to shop around, get several bids and find that middle ground and then bargain for favorable payment terms.

The maintenance men I used came and went. I started using this one fellow, Mason who was a mild-mannered, jovial man with light-brown skin and a gentle demeanor. How I met him is long forgotten, but just like Red Fox once said about finding one of his wives, "I just opened my wallet and there he was."

Mason had reasonably good job skills and was easy to work with. I liked him and gave him several tasks, including a ceramic tile job in two bathrooms in my home. I must have liked him to have him work in my home, which I never usually did. He had been working for a while when one day, after he had finally finished the job and had gone home for the evening, he returned unexpectedly. Mason was crying and upset.

To see a grown man cry is an unusual sight, though I have cried many times in moments of privacy. I only ever saw my father cry once during my lifetime and that was after the funeral of his oldest and dearest sister, Tobytha. I was only a little boy at the time of her death. I poked my head into Grandmother Clark's bedroom in Fitzgerald, Georgia, after returning from the funeral and there my dad sat on the end of her bed with my mother trying to comfort him, sobbing uncontrollably, a scene forever etched in my memory.

"Mr Lee, Mr Lee, I need some money, can you let me have some money?" he cried. "Can you give me some money, my wife has cancer and........." I could hardly make out his words, he was so upset. The tears streaming down his cheeks made pathways from his mental anguish to his broken heart. His supplication was earnest, his plea genuine, his need undisguised. He wanted me to give him some money.

Mason was upset because his wife, the mother of his children, and clearly the love of his life was dying, and he was powerless to do anything about it. Apparently he had just been told the grievous news and needed money for medicine or some medical expense or treatments of some kind; who knows.

However, my normally empathetic nature was challenged and counterbalanced by my business sense. I told him that I couldn't do it; I couldn't give him any money. This fellow put me in a tough spot. I liked the guy and wanted to help. I felt pressure because he was clearly in need, and I wanted to do what I could for him. But giving out money to strangers cut across the grain for me, regardless of how urgent the need. I thought to myself, if he wanted to work and earn some money, maybe I could find something for him to do to earn a few bucks. That way, both of our ends would be served, even though I had nothing pressing for which I needed to hire anyone. I told him he could work for the money if he wanted to, so I drove him over to Wister Street where there was always a job that needed to be done and put him to work.

I wanted to help him, but I was not in the business of giving money away, regardless of how ernest the supplication. There would be no such thing as a loan to this fellow. That I knew. So I tried to find a way to get money into his hands without just giving it away. I did the next best thing. I gave him a job.

After the job was completed the next day we sat in my office, and I wrote him a check. I never paid cash. I always, as a good business practice, paid by check to create a paper trail and a receipt. No sooner had I written him the check than he was off to the bank to cash it. I left shortly after him, not realizing he had gone to my bank up the street to cash the check, rather than deposit it into his own account. But there he was standing a few feet in front of me waiting to cash the check while I was in line to deposit money into the account. This was an ironic situation and demonstrated to me just how desperate many people were for money and how much pressure was on my money to perform well. Apparently, his wife had been the backbone of his life and now her demise was imminent. It was enough to make anyone panic. I never saw this guy again after this incident.

Knowing how to use people is the key, using them according to their skills and your timetable. One of my tenants on Wister Street referred me to a guy name Jimmy Ryals. Jimmy walked with a limp caused by some injury to his left leg. He reminded me, perhaps rather unfairly, of a cross between Herman Melville's Captain Ahab from his novel *Moby Dick* and the gimpy legged "Chester" from the TV western series "Gunsmoke." His limp was either the result of an old injury or a birth defect–I could never tell which. But he was a crafty old guy–a fellow who knew how to make money and how to keep it rolling in. He knew a good thing when he had it. I was his good thing.

Ryals was indeed a character. He was a caricature of an aging, semi-skilled jackleg who learned to hustle in the world of makeshift construction on the streets of Philadelphia. He was an older Black gentleman in his fifties when I met him. He was astute in many ways, knew how to make money, knew how to get along and his rules of success were adopted from the "old school."

As our relationship developed, I was paying Ryals over $1,000 a month for maintenance jobs on various properties. Rumor had it that he had married some young woman half his age and fathered a child or two by her, so he needed to work for obvious reasons. In effect, he was a hustler, but he knew what I needed done to make money: to turn recently vacated units over for quick re-rental; that was the game and he made it his business to get the job done.

Because of his physical condition, Ryals could not do the "heavy lifting," so he worked off the back of his helper Raleigh. Raleigh did all Ryals' hard work, for which Ryals paid him a portion of what he charged me. I never knew what Ryals' deal was with Raleigh. Ryals always kept him out of the picture and on the job. Raleigh was a thin, medium-height Black male with a chiseled face hardened by hard times and tough experiences. He was silent and didn't talk much; in fact, he was either slightly retarded, an alcoholic, or suffering from an addiction or afflic-tion of some kind. Something was not right with him, and he fit Ryals' strategy for making money.

The few times I saw Raleigh or spoke to him on the job he responded well enough to pass the moment, but nothing more. He was ever-present on the job site but in a non-descript sort of way. It was clear that Ryals had found a guy that needed work and had few choices, so he would do whatever was asked of him and keep his mouth shut—just right for the hustle Ryals was running. Ryals pretended to know how to fix most things, but in actuality he knew how to fix very little. His main strength was painting. He could get the units painted but not much else. He was no plumber or electrician, knew very little about dry wall repair, hanging doors or fine carpentry and he was not a mason. I used him because he satisfied my es-sential needs. My tenants didn't demand fine carpentry and they usually destroyed the property by the time they vacated the premises, so what the heck! Why spend big money when people cared so little about where they lived; there were many exceptions but this was the general rule.

Even though I barely recouped my costs for what Ryals was putting down, we went forward day after day, month after month. The centralization of my mainte-nance needs in one person helped me organize my requirements more efficiently and plan for all my costs. It also provided a monthly planning session so that my upcoming needs were spelled out and Ryals got his work orders from me once a month.

In addition to his gimpy leg, Ryals was a small-figured man, dark skinned, balding and with small eyes. When strategizing about how to cope with one Black female housing inspector who had it in for me and was giving us a problem on Apsley Street, he would put his Captain Ahab suit on and start moralizing about how this woman should be approached and how he knew better than me how to get the woman off my case. His opining religiosity about the proper "approach" conveyed an insight into the streetwise mentality of Philadelphia from a "mer-chant of the jackleg hustle." Ryals constantly schooled me on the ways of getting along with my tenants and the community, and constantly told me that his ap-proach was the better one—and perhaps it was. When dealing with the housing inspector, he would say, "Otis, we don't do it that way. I would approach her like this... You keep challenging the woman, but you got to..."

I let him do his thing for two reasons; he was less threatening to her and he was good at getting people to drop their defenses. His jivey, humble, Philadelphia smoothie approach was disarming and might have been beneficial on the site of a violation, where he could persuade her that it was being corrected. However, in court his approach lacked credibility and didn't seem to make much of a difference, and he resisted testifying when asked. The woman inspector never seemed to be affected by whatever he had said or done previously, but he bought time.

My approach, on the other hand, was confrontational and challenging. Letting Ryals run an interference game on her was a ploy I used as long he got some results or appeared to do so. Plus, using him in that way provided more value to me for what I was paying him. My usual method of payment was for him to come to my office each month and present me with a list of the repairs he had made and a price for each one. I reviewed the list to determine if the work had been completed, checked his arithmetic for accuracy, many times it was not, and made payment. However, there were times over the course of our relationship when Ryals was humbled by health issues and was unable to work. Out of respect for his dutifulness, I would send his check to him in the mail.

Whenever Ryals fell on hard times because of injury or illness he would make his "Chester" plea: "Otis, I don't have nothing coming in, man. Can you help me? Can you send me something on account?" Every time I heard him talk this way on the phone I visualized a crippled old man still trying to hustle to make ends meet with a young wife and children in need of money that was probably stretched to the limit. I thought about it, but I was not too comfortable sending him money in the mail. There was something in the mix that made me hesitate. Nevertheless, I empathized with the guy even though I knew Ryals was what he was, a slick Philadelphia jackleg.

In spite of his gimmickry, Ryals had been reliable and reasonably honest. So I sent him some money on account. Later, he would recover and bounce back and be right back out there until the end. Ryals worked with me until I left the Philadelphia rental market in earnest. He was decent and was not a thug. I could reason with him, work with him, and he rarely lost his composure. He was an urban survivor. He had to "find a way to make a way," as so many have to do who are unskilled and poorly educated. Not everyone can be an elitist. In inefficient markets such as the one I dealt in, you come to respect people, whether or not you like their style, and to appreciate the uniqueness of their artistry. If you get usable results from them and they deliver for you, are consistent, reliable and reasonable, and you can make a buck from their efforts, the relationship can be beneficial.

Decency comes in all varieties, just as indecency does. In the parade of contractors that floated in and out of my business over the years, I recall guys like Rennick Lee, who was killed in a bar room incident not of his own making. Rennick often said, "Mr. Lee, you know you ohhhh me," with his tortured English. Rennick was Jamaican. Or Mayrant, whom I sued for botching a garage rebuilding job on Wister Street. Or Mercer, the boilerman. And a host of others, most of whom were decent. The quality of their workmanship was often dubious and always varied, but I got what I paid for every time.

Fighting the insurance wars was another burden. Each year new coverage had to be obtained with various deductibles, policy limits, and exclusions. And the premiums always increased from year to year. I was always partial to insurance, almost intuitively from the time I was first introduced to it while in law school. My first introduction was to life insurance and then came casualty insurance. Insurance assuaged my ire from the anguish I felt during the malpractice litigation brought on by Elvin Pierce. I had concerns about being financially ruined if that case was not resolved favorably; fortunately it was. I was also sued several times by tenants based upon premises liability issues, slip and falls. Insurance always eased the burden, allowed me to sleep at night, and relieved my anxiety.

As my health became an issue in later years, health insurance to prevent bankruptcy became essential. The one time I failed to obtain liability insurance on a property because I was insurance weary from fighting this brutal war year after year, I had to mount my own defense to a claim. I vowed never to do that again, even though, fortunately, I won that suit as well.

Therefore, prudence dictated that I carry liability insurance if I wanted to play in the business world. "Don't go to the bank without it," whether the business is in real estate, law, medicine, or accounting. Adequate risk protection is essential. I would have been a fool to have proceeded without it. It doesn't pay in this arena to be "penny wise and pound foolish."

The key is to work with a broker who can place the coverage. After that comes financing the premium. Mortgage companies are only concerned with fire coverage to protect their investment, since their lien is already the first on any property, and they are assured of getting their investment back. Any lien on the title after theirs is of no importance to them, because in a foreclosure or sheriff's sale, all junior liens are usually wiped out. But it is of importance to you because this is where your equity is. If you are foolish enough to let liability suits that result in unsatisfied judgements eat away at your equity, you will end up with nothing when you go to sell your property. The title companies will guarantee that.

The Philadelphia market was a terrible place for inner city property owners to pay for and to secure fire and liability insurance. The premiums were so expensive. At one time, I was paying close to $15,000 dollars a year for coverage on all my buildings, and I had to pay those premiums every year. In addition to everything else, making mortgage payments, paying utility bills, doing maintenance, and defending against License and Inspection (L & I) code violation judgments, and rent collections. All prudent property owners had to make insurance payments, that can be huge at times.

"All that glitters is not gold." The Philadelphia market is particularly mean because lawyers fiendishly, with the aid of the street-wise, or even so-called "good people," are quick to file suit against a landlord in Philadelphia. They prey on insurance companies, vehicles owners, and property owners to support their lifestyles. The population as a whole is "hip" to the lawsuit mentality. This drives up insurance premiums, and for some property owners and car owners, coverage is either unaffordable or unavailable.

Typical fodder for lawyers at the time were lawsuits against asbestos insulation or lead poisoning from lead based paint in old buildings, as well as a host of other toxic torts found in old buildings. To make matters worse, this type of claim is often exempt from coverage in many policies, and if you lose, the damages could put you out of business. So you do the best that you can, but keep some coverage!

35

THE CONSOLIDATION

THE PIECES WERE ALL IN PLACE NOW. All my ducks were in a row. Between 1975 and 1989, in order of acquisition, I had acquired rental real estate on Peabody Street in Washington, D.C.; and in Philadelphia on Germantown Avenue, Sedgwick Street, Greene Street, Apsley Street, Laurens Street, Wister Street, and Manheim Street. These made for a total of seven residential apartment buildings with forty-seven rental units, not including my home on Sedgwick Street.

I was forty-two years old and had forty-seven rental units and a thriving law practice. I had met my goal to own as many rental units as my age. My equity-to-debt ratio was 3:1, or better. I was worth seven figures on my own terms and in my own right. I added value to each property that I owned: heating and hot water systems had been decentralized, utilities had been separated, driveways paved, garages built, hallways repainted, carpeted and tiled.

No one had given me anything in Philadelphia, and I didn't expect them to. Every professional experience and every borrowed dollar, every single thing had all been "hard earned." I had come to Philadelphia with only my orange Volvo and a trunk packed with business supplies that my father had given me after retiring from the Albemarle County Schools System. I credit only my mother, father and my wife for my success, as well as my own ingenuity, hard work and savvy. I had built a business from whole cloth, a business that generated in excess of a quarter million dollars in income, a cash-driven business optimally tax sheltered with appreciating assets.

Not bad for a reject and a refugee from the legal profession's "bar wars." Not bad for a Black child who grew up in the Jim Crow South and who received a less than a competitive education from its segregated schools. Although I was formally educated, my ability to practice law was mostly self-taught, I grew up in the real estate business working with and observing my father. I seemed to have some innate business acumen that aided me in my dealings in this area. I didn't feel any different and I didn't act any differently. My progression had been gradual but persistent. But at the same time I knew I had achieved financial security. I remember reading, during my Northwestern Law School bar preparation days that, "The Internal Revenue Service had nothing against millionaires; it just wanted to see a logical progression to wealth."

When I started out after high school, I was handling hundreds of dollars, then after college thousands of dollars, after law school tens of thousands, then in business it was hundreds of thousands of dollars. Where would it end, at millions of dollars? Yes, at some point! My ascent was logical. Each building block had been strategically and systematically stacked, one on top of the other for maximum effect.

Keeping it all together though was a monumental task and the stressors in my life could be measured in pounds per deciliter of blood pressure. Good judgment was critical as I maneuvered between these two businesses. And good judgment is never off duty. It had to be "on duty" 24/7 for me. Everything I did in my businesses had financial or professional consequences, whether it was in the law office or in the rental office.

I was, however, aided by my past employment experiences. At all of the jobs I have held, from Harris Bank to the U.S. Chamber of Commerce to New York Life, I have learned lessons that were then applied to my career in Philadelphia. But most of all, learning the lessons of protection, savings and growth crystalized in my mind what the fight was all about like nothing else, and it was a lasting lesson well learned from my days at the New York Life Insurance Company.

Practically speaking, there is no need to continue to have recriminations about the past. In my judgment, I did well and am still doing well. Many have done less with more and some people more with less. So I stumbled a few times getting past the bar, big deal. My stumbles didn't define my life–that's the important thing. I overcame them and worked harder because of them, in what psychologists call the "mastery orientation." The bar episode was 30 plus years ago, but it might just as well have happened 3,000 years ago. What was the difference? The past is the past; it was part of my rite of passage, nothing more. And there is no need to speculate on what might have been. What good is that? Who knows what I would have done had I entered the law on a glide path with no resistance. Perhaps this whole saga and rethinking my earlier education would never have entered my mind. You cannot consider, or dwell too much on what might have been because we don't know "what might have been." Therefore, this possibility cannot be considered. It is illogical to do so and, most of all, a waste of time. We have to live in the present; that is all we have, even though we continue to dwell in the past repeatedly searching for answers to the "reasons why." We must make the best of the decisions that are made for us when we are too young or enfeebled to do anything about them, and live with or make the best out of the choices we independently make as adults.

So why do these issues matter, if at all? They matter because, according to Elizabeth Kubler-Ross, M.D: "Life is about learning lessons." It is because of these lessons that I did a better job educating my children and reeducating myself. And it matters because "anything that stops me from being the best that I can be hurts me." In my "Walter Mitty" subconscious, I want to orate and lead Black people, just like Martin Luther King. I want to argue a case and be successful in the law, just like Thurgood Marshall. I want to play the piano, just like Rudolph Serkin and Vladamir Horowitz, and I want to write like James Baldwin.

I have an insatiable appetite to "do it all." Deep, deep down inside me is this irrepressible faith and belief in myself that sits alongside a burning desire to "win,"–not at all costs, but close to it. Accepting "no" for an answer is insufferable for me. That's why the bar experience and my related drug experiment and use, and the fallout from all of that was so affective in my case. Being a stickler for perfection but accepting the imperfection of the human experience, and, most of all, the imperfection in yourself is disquieting. It causes frustration and exasperation. I admire beauty, talent, brilliance, expertise, nature and winning. My reach has always extended beyond my grasp in everything I do. I knew then and I know now that I have a talent for certain endeavors and ability, and I want that talent to be fully developed. That is why these issues matter. A lack of vision, perspective and drive, a desire to achieve is stifling, unattractive and uncreative. I am a striver and have always thought well of myself, though I am, I hope, fully cognizant of my many deficits.

My real life's work began after school. Some people do well in school but fail in life. Others fail in school and succeed in life. A fortunate few do well in both. I fell somewhere in between. Perhaps I could have done better in school if certain things had happened, but I certainly took the "bull by the horns" after finally "finishing school." So, it is not how you start out but how you end up that counts. But when does school really end? It doesn't! Life is the school of last resort. Tenacity and determination to overcome, not accepting "no" for an answer, is what life's struggle is all about.

When I was at Jefferson Elementary School in Charlottesville in 1960, I was selected to recite the poem "The Path" by Paul Lawrence Dunbar, the noted Black poet. That poem captures the story of my life. I had no idea when I first learned it by memory and recited it many times before the class that it would later have such a direct and dramatic application to my life. I recited the words not knowing their true meaning back then, but I know what they mean now, and who would have imagined how appropriate they would be.

It is indeed passing strange how a poem learned and recited from memory by innocence can come to be reflective of the life of the declarant many years later. I cleaved "a path of my own," day after day, from Saturday to Saturday. Solving problems, "thrusting the looming rocks aside", in my life and in the lives of my clients and lending a helping hand where I could.

One afternoon, I received a call from one of my tenants. His name was Brandon Via. Brandon was a tenant who lived on the 3rd floor of Green Street for several years. He, of course, knew I was a lawyer. Via was a problematic tenant, but always managed to fall into line when the pressure was on. He had his bouts with drug use, and it was rumored that he had beaten up one of the tenants in the building during a drug-induced rage. But I got along with him reasonably well. He was a slightly built man with a light-brown complexion and closely cropped black hair, and he had an aggressive personality when he wanted to assert it.

Brandon called me because he was in the hospital with a broken jaw. The prior evening he had gone to Einstein Hospital on Broad Street to visit a friend who was hospitalized there. But while attempting to enter the hospital, he was battered and beaten savagely by a hospital guard. Apparently, words had been exchanged. Via wanted me to take the case and I did.

The convergence of the law and real estate was symbiotic and occurred on several levels. This was one of two significant cases I received from those of my tenants who chose to use my office when they had a case of some merit. The other case was a workmen's compensation case valued at about $50,000 that I received from a tenant on Wister Street. I referred that case to another lawyer and received a referral fee.

In Via's case, I was offended by the savagery of the beating. His jaw had been crushed and was broken in two places on the left side of his face. His jaw had to be wired and he had trouble eating. During the period of his recovery, he was only able to consume liquids. The left side of his face was so smashed in, it looked as though someone had taken a flat iron pan and hit him repeatedly, blackening his left eye as well.

How could one human being treat another this way, especially someone working in a hospital? I was energized by the injustice I perceived and by the desire to see justice done in this case. I played this case all the way out for Via. I filed a private criminal complaint against the guard and got a summons issued for his arrest, and later won a conviction. Then I filed a Praecipe for a Writ of Summons against the hospital for damages, a process which I loved using because of the ease and efficiency of the writ process to initiate suit.

After the hospital was served, their general counsel called and asked me in lawyer speak, "what I had." I told him I had a battery by one of his guards on a visitor to the hospital and a criminal conviction on him as well. After I sent him the medical documents and police reports, they quickly settled. Though I had pursued many smaller personal injury cases over the years, this case was the single largest personal injury case I had while practicing in Philadelphia. The case was settled for close to six figures. In one lump sum, Via got more money than he had ever had in his life. Based upon my observation of him, the money was spent as quickly as it was paid to him. He had enough money to buy a house at Philadelphia prices but his errant lifestyle caused him to run through the money. In later years, he ended up renting from me on Apsley Street.

36

⁂

WHAT A DIFFERENCE
A DAY MAKES

I N JUNE OF 1988, on one of my many visits home, to Charlottesville, Virginia, my dad, always the de facto lawyer, mentioned to me that he was being sued by the city in an eminent domain proceeding. The city wanted to take three of his properties, a duplex at 345 11th Street NW, a duplex on 4th Street SW, just off of West Main Street, and a single-family, framed house on Monticello Avenue. Presumably, the city wanted them for public use because the properties were to be converted into public housing units.

Dad showed me the court papers that had been served on him and his earnest but inartful attempt to respond. I said to him, "Look, you're not responding to these papers properly, the way you should, the way the law requires." In layman's terms, I told him that he was leaving himself open for these people to take advantage of him. Sensing his need for help and his reluctance to hire a lawyer, for whatever reason, perhaps costs, as well as his prideful determination not to ask for help, I told him I would defend him in this case. I entered my appearance *pro hac vice* and the battle was joined. *Pro hac vice* is a Latin term meaning "for this occasion," or "for this event." It is a legal term that usually refers to a lawyer who has not been admitted to practice in a certain jurisdiction but is allowed to participate in one particular case. Since I was not admitted to practice in Virginia at that time, I had to associate with a "Virginia Lawyer" to represent him in Virginia.

I did this because I loved him, I owed him, and he needed me. During his forty-year career in Charlottesville, Dad had accumulated a portfolio of more than thirty properties that contained fifty rental units. He was a big fish in a small pond and his high profile as an administrator-cum-educator in the Albemarle County Schools made him a target of the jealous, the envious, and the mean-spirited. Dad had gotten so far ahead before his competitors knew how far ahead he was, that they were left with little else to stop him with. So they decided to attack him in the press by sensationalizing any issue surrounding the management of his properties, and by so doing, to sully his reputation both as an educator and as a landlord.

I knew about his struggle, but was not living it every day, as he was. I was away doing my own thing. But, having grown up in Charlottesville and with frequent visits back home, I knew how we were viewed as a family—wealthy and foreign. Between Dad and I, we had over 101 rental units in over forty properties, spread across Philadelphia, Washington, D.C., Virginia, and Georgia. Like a malignant cancer that had metastasized insidiously, some local officials of the city government, school administration officials, the landlord tenant section of the Legal Aid Society, the press, and an envyingly resentful segment of the public had coalesced to try to bring him down.

Dad's feudatory approach to the changing demands of the market place in landlord and tenant affairs caused him much anguish during the twilight of his professional career, and he agitated this toxic brew by not putting more separation between his business affairs and his school duties, although this would not have made a lot of difference. In addition, he failed to gauge the intensity of the envy of a small cadre in a small town. Little did I know at the time that this case in Virginia, the state of my birth, would be a lagging indicator of what the future would portend for me. This case was the precursor of many legal battles I would fight for my family, and especially for my father, to defeat a conspiracy by folks who "didn't like Otis Lee" in Charlottesville.

Virginia's Rules of Civil Procedure allowed for petit juries in civil cases, so the eminent domain case would be tried by a jury of nine. I prepared for the case in Philadelphia, studying the law on my front porch on Sedgwick Street in the balmy summer afternoons and on some Saturdays and weekday evenings. There was considerable pressure on me because the total value of the three disputed properties was about $100,000, and this would be the first time my father actually saw me try a case. The city was attempting by fiat to limit the size of my father's estate. But this was not going to go unchallenged on my watch. As a staunch believer in private property rights, I was determined not to allow a bunch of what I regarded as politicized conspiratorial hacks take away land my father owned using eminent domain as a pretext.

As I entered the courtroom on High Street in Charlottesville, I felt as if I had gone from antiquity to modernity. This courtroom was up-to-date, with new furniture and benches. I had been used to Philadelphia's old rickety chairs and benches beaten down by years of wear and tear; to high ceilings and ornate court rooms that reeked of the majesty of the old world.

I subpoenaed the necessary witness to prove value and didn't contest the "public use" issue. I requested that the jury take a jury view: that they go out and see the properties at issue for themselves. This process allows the jurors to "touch and feel" the land much as a prudent buyer would do before determining value. The city relied on several precedents, one of which I reviewed and adopted as my own. I made it work against my opponents, which resulted in 345 11th Street being dropped from the suit. A quirk in the case having to do with the process of instituting eminent domain proceedings and the definition of public use facilitated the extrication of this property from the suit. Since federal funds were being used to acquire and convert the properties and their ultimate use was public housing, I doubt I would have been successful contesting the public use issue by itself. Also, it would have prolonged the trial. I went straight to value because Dad was an investor, not a souvenir collector. He was more concerned about value than anything else because he had already accepted the loss of title and possession.

The trial lasted several hours and took up most of the day. During the proceedings, the judge, Judge Pickford, ruled against the city on 345 11th St., then asked me about a specific issue that had arisen: "Mr. Lee, what are you going to do with that?" I responded calmly, in a moment of candor, "Your honor, I don't know what I am going to do with it. But I'll figure something out." The judge had no further response, sensing that he had just witnessed a lawyer who was not perturbed by surprise. Over the years of practicing in Philly, I had come to expect the unexpected.

One of Dad's "friends," a local realtor I had subpoenaed to testify, made quite a scene outside the courtroom during a break. He was a chain-smoking, irascible individual whose breath reeked of nicotine and who only spoke of nullification when it came to competition from Blacks in the real estate field. Pacing back and forth outside the courtroom, he confronted me immediately as I exited when a break in the proceedings took place. He objected to my calling him as a witness and swore out loud that, "I can't do you any good! I can't do you any good!" He repeated this phrase over and over again, yelling, "You'd be better off not calling me."

I knew this guy reasonably well; I had been over to his house many times and shared cocktails with him and his wife. Was envy, jealousy, or contempt at work here? Who knows? He was one of only two Black realtors in the city, and he was the most prominent of the two. Why was he acting this way? I couldn't imagine.

I looked him in the eye close up, taken aback momentarily by his attitude as I tried to keep my poise. His face made for an unsavory sight. It was pocked marked with pimples that had not healed smoothly and his lips were purple from the many cigarettes he had puffed on over the years. His belly extruded beyond his belt, highlighting the size of his gut. Here was a man who had pretended to be a friend to my father, but who in a time of need was finding a reason not to be helpful when, in fact, he could have been very helpful. He was someone who could have swayed the jury. But instead, he chose to be contentiously unhelpful at a climatic time. Wow! He created such a stir that I released him and didn't call him. I couldn't risk it. I thought his conduct was atrociously unfriendly and uncalled for. He could have made a huge difference to our case, but instead he chose to be an obstructionist.

In the end, I got a good result. I beat the city. I freed one property from the suit and made the city pay much more than they expected for the remaining two, and they also paid my attorney fees. That one property I freed from the "taking," 345 11th Street, NW, remained in the family for many years until we sold it for three and a half times the value in the eminent domain case. I think Dad was proud. I don't remember my father saying anything specific about my performance, but I could tell he was pleased with the outcome. I felt a gush of emotion as I fought hard to hold back the tears. It was a release of stress and pressure silently endured and I think that Dad knew nothing about this internal combustion of my emotions taking place in my soul.

After the hearing, Dad and I visited one of the jurors, George Wiley, a kindly Black, middle-aged gentleman, who was light-skinned and a native of Charlottesville. He was an acquaintance both of my dad and of me. George lived with his mother near 11th Street. In earlier years we called him "Lamb Chop" because he had an afflicted style when playing basketball down at 5th Street Park in Charlottesville. He said I had done a good job and that members of the jury had learned a lot from me during our case, mainly about such things as value and how it is arrived at.

Later that evening, I flew back to Philadelphia. Unexpectedly, this case turned out to be an auspicious beginning to my legal career in Virginia, which would commence in earnest in 1992. I didn't know at the time what lay ahead for me, but my time in Virginia would eclipse, in most phases, but not all, what I achieved in Philadelphia in law and real estate. To reconnoiter the future terrain within which I would operate in a few years was invaluable.

Upon my return to Philadelphia, I trudged along doing business as usual. My law practice was well-seated by this time, and I began thinking about how to solidify my connection with the Mount Airy community in which I practiced and lived. Jesse Jackson made a second run for president in 1988, and I thought this might be a good time for me to run as the Democratic Party candidate for Ward Committeeman. I chose to stand because the position was in my neighborhood and was low profile.

My home on Sedgwick Street was within walking distance of the office, and I felt truly connected to the people in the community I served. I remember while in law school a professor talking about the benefits of politics to a lawyer. Win or lose, it meant name recognition. After all was said and done, my campaign was all about marketing, as far as I was concerned. The extended family of the Lees had a history of running for local office in Philadelphia. My distant cousin Eddie Lee, who I met only after moving to Philly, as I said earlier, once served as Clerk of the Quarter Sessions Court, the criminal division of the Court of Common Pleas. After that, he ran for the City Council, but lost without making much of a blip on the vote tally.

The political territory of Councilman divisions in Philadelphia are broken down into districts or wards that consist of neighborhood blocks. My territory was the 8th Councilman District. No one paid much attention to ward committeemen except during elections, when it was their job to get the vote out for their party's candidate. That was my narrow view, but it was not an informed view. There was much more involved. Each party would spread money around to their committeemen to assist them in their vote-gathering efforts. The committeeman was a liaison between the councilman for that district and the voters. And, of course, he or she helped the neighborhood get their problems solved.

I figured that, if I could get this job, it would tie me even closer to the community and ground my law office firmly within the fabric of the community. I would be linked to the political system, yet still removed from it. And I would have a connection and a feeder for future business.

This *beau geste* was my highest public effort at increasing my profile in my neighborhood. In general, I eschewed politics in Philadelphia and had not made any effort to ingratiate myself with local politicians. I owed no-one anything. I only pursued this office because of its low profile and neighborhood connection to my work.

There were some issues I was concerned about in the neighborhood, like traffic, the need for speed bumps, crime, and education. But I was not about to make a big stir about any of this stuff. I would work behind the scenes and behind closed doors to get a hearing on these issues. That was my style.

I consulted no-one before embarking on this endeavor, other than Michelle, and went at it purely on my own. I printed up maybe a hundred colorful brochures with a slogan about competent leadership for our community. The incumbent, a fellow name Vanlandingham, was a neighbor who lived at the end of my block. He was an elderly, brown-skinned gentleman who wore glasses. I never really knew who he was, yet he had been in the post for years. I couldn't attest to a single thing this guy had ever done. I didn't know he even existed until I ran for his office.

I went knocking door-to-door and stuck my brochures in mail boxes and storm doors. When someone came to the door, I told them about myself and why I was running. I told them that nothing had been done for the neighborhood, and we needed new blood and a more activist committeeman. In some instances, I was greeted warmly and people said they would vote for me. But at other houses, my reception was not so warm. One woman told me, "Well, you know, we don't vote for a person just because they're Black. What experience do you have? And who are you?"

I found some of the assaults difficult to take, but I pressed on, hoping that I would be successful. I was self-funding this small campaign. Finding the time each evening after working all day to pound the pavement was not easy, but I did it. Not as enthusiastically, perhaps, as I should have done, but I got the job finished— enough to have a credible shot at the office.

The one thing that characterized my district, as well as my neighborhood, was the uneven development of the corridors. On ours, Sedgwick Street, all the homes were occupied by middle-class people who had a certain manner about themselves. One block north and southwest, it was another world, where the riff-raff indulged in all sorts of dirty tricks. There were what appeared to be some run-down houses just one or two corridors from us, whether you went north or south. Semi-detached stone and brick structures dominated the landscape, with single family residences sparsely sprinkled in between. These were old neighborhoods where families lived and died in these homes for generation after generation. That was the way Philadelphia was; a place of few recent immigrants or transients.

Election night arrived and some anxiety grew as the polls closed and the counting began. Vanlandingham was out in force, he had the machine behind him, with his wife handing out election flyers. Michelle and I were out as well, but we didn't have the inside track Vanlandingham had.

My neighbor Vince, who was Italian, of medium height, and a school teacher, was the precinct captain and he led the count. I lost by less than seven or eight votes. Vanlandingham breathed a sigh of relief. My candidacy had scared him and his wife. Perhaps he did a few favors and was able to call in his debts. After all, he had held this position for many years without challenge.

I inhaled some elements of minor disappointment that didn't last long, because I was not that emotionally invested in the endeavor. I would say the word "hypocrisy," adequately summed up my feelings about this experience. People would tell me that they were going to vote for me and then go into the voting booth and do just the opposite. But it was just as well. Maybe I wasn't really cut out for the position. Before the election, one woman came to my door complaining about some issue, and I didn't feel like being bothered. Then I asked myself, "is this what I am getting myself into?" So I reasoned that the result was a good thing for me because I didn't really know how committed I was to solving the community's problems. I needed more patience to hear people out. But the experience gave me a peek inside the political tent to see what politics at the retail level involved. Jesse Jackson carried my precinct, but, as we all know, he ultimately lost the delegate fight for the Democratic presidential nomination.

Ten years of solid law practice experience had yielded a body of knowledge and work that turned on several truths obtained through sharp lessons learned in the school of hard knocks. As I went about my business day-after-day, I often wondered what secrets those lawyers who had managed to survive for long periods knew and what did they have in common? What were the secrets of their success? So, from time to time, when I was in Center City and ran into an older lawyer tending to his business, I would ask him about his secrets to longevity in this business.

My thoughts were on sustaining what I had built. I was looking for consolidation; a way to maintain this good beginning. I made sure I obeyed the Rules of Ethics, I steered clear of the get-rich-quick schemes, the fast buck, the sleight-of-hand. I stuck with "honesty and fair dealing."

But for my brief foray into neighborhood politics, I avoided active involvement, though I was always an avid observer. I tried to build relationships, not just a client base. I continued to add value to each endeavor I had with a client and to earn the money paid to me.

On one occasion, I asked an older lawyer who was standing outside the Municipal Court one day, briefcase in hand, talking to a client of his, a question. The lawyer was nothing special. He was a short, White gentleman who hadn't shaved for a day or two, but for some reason, I was still impressed. What was his secret? The lawyer vouchsafed with gusto, "I just tell them to go fuck themselves!"

I was amazed at his candor and cynicism, but he meant it. What he was really saying about the practice of law was, try not to care too much. Keep your distance. This is how I interpreted what he was advising. Lawyers who care too much get hurt, fatigued, and dependent on opiate or alcohol. When we start out, we want to change the system, make a difference, right the wrongs, cure the ills, make everything all right. Believe me, that can be difficult, but you can have a positive impact and make a difference in people's lives. The law evolves slowly, but the effort to effect change must be relentless, consistent and continuous. If you are lucky, you may have a case that changes the law and alters the status quo.

Practicing law is a tough, mean, "no nonsense" and often thankless business. I learned to remind myself that I was not a member of my client's family, regardless of how close I thought I was to him or her, and I always kept Redmond's admonition in mind, "Every client is a potential adversary." There is so much injustice and unfairness in the world that justice barely edges ahead, if it does– and often it lags far behind. That's how the system works. Left unchanged, the system reinforces itself within and upon itself but you can change the system through the law. Most idealistic young lawyers get burned out and turn cynical, become pragmatic realists after awhile, and may grow disillusioned sometimes but never nihilists because the light of optimism—that your efforts matter—burns and flickers incessantly, but this fight requires endurance and tenacity. They're trying to attack the cape, not the bullfighter, but it is the bull most in need of help. Thank God that the overwhelming majority of people choose to do the right thing in our society, because they form the vast moral center in our society. Lawyers are the last resort, if used that way–utilized when normal human decency and responsibility break down or when properly used to anticipate a dispute or possible breakdown.

When I think about where my help came from to overcome the problems in my practice, it was mainly from White people. Blacks gave little, and they were generally snobbish, arrogant, and stingy with what they did give. Aside from the initial haphazard introduction to the practice of law I received at the hands of Redmond and McDaniel, I got most of my guidance from White members of the bar. Sure, from time to time I tried to cozy up to a few Blacks and some were marginally helpful, but I have found that you have to be "anointed" by the White man before Blacks will give you any respect.

Perhaps it is part of the White mystique that, because they have so much and are so used to having it, they are more willing to share. So is the obverse true? That the reason Blacks are so unwilling to share is because they have so little, or are used to having so much less that they fearlessly protect the little they have?

Where would Black folks be without "well-meaning White people"? So much of our progress is because of them. They were leaders in the abolitionist movement, along with Frederick Douglass, William Lloyd Garrison, and others during slavery. And they were instrumental during Reconstruction in passing the 13th, 14th, and 15th Amendments to the Constitution–the "Reconstruction Amendments" that outlawed involuntary servitude and assured that due process and the equal protection of the law applied to everyone.

When both Northern states and Southern states passed their infamous "Black Codes," forbidding Blacks from even entering certain states of the union after the Civil War and immediately thereafter, our well-meaning Republican White folks were there with the Reconstruction Amendments. Many well-meaning White brothers were also on the front lines during the Civil Rights Movement, and they were essential for the realization of the Obama Presidency, although Blacks were avid supporters during what historians may term the second reconstruction. These folks are responsible for so much that is good in this society. Where would we be without them?

I'm sure the problem I had with other Black folks lay within me, within my approach to them and my hang-ups. Blacks can be difficult to deal with professionally and as clients. The anonymity that White folks provide to Blacks sometimes operates as a cover that allows a person like me the freedom to show ignorance without paying a high price. That is why many Blacks go to White lawyers; because they do not want other Blacks to know their business. With Black folks, showing the world or admitting that you don't know something and need help, can be disconcerting and uncomfortable.

I remember having stopped at a filling station one day in Washington, D.C, and while there I saw a prominent Black judge of the local federal court system also filling his tank. With tongue in cheek, I drew up the courage to mention to him the problem I was having passing the bar. He looked at me like I was crazy. His apparent lack of empathy was penetrating to the false veneer I put forward to even broach the subject with a man of his caliber. I did so because he had lectured at my law school and I thought he might be approachable and provide some encouragement, but he didn't. Instead he looked at me with disbelief and disdain.

His reaction was bothersome but I did not let it affect me; by now I was used to the derision.

One Black lawyer who graduated from my law school, who was practicing in Philly, was so taken aback by my apparent reputation for estate planning that he hired me to draft his estate plans, in order to watch what I was doing and how I did it. He never intended to execute the documents and frustrated the process intentionally. His sole purpose was to gain access to my forms and processes. It was all about checking me out. He was taken aback at how I, a relative upstart, could have catapulted myself ahead in a complicated field of law so quickly. He wanted to find out how substantive I was, to learn how I put together my work product.

I received only one referral from a Black lawyer during my whole time in Philadelphia. One. Most of my referrals came from Blacks who were not lawyers. One prominent Black judge, in Philadelphia, the late Julian King, for whom I did some estate planning work, referred a big client to me, for which I will always be grateful. And that same judge referred me to the chief judge of the Orphan's Court who sent me work that had never before been sent to a Black lawyer in Philadelphia at that time, the audit of a trust. I worked closely with this Orphan's Court judge's law clerk and over time gained that judge's respect. I would later try a case having to do with an estate settlement issue before him to a successful conclusion, after I moved to Virginia.

I would also, over time, earn the respect of several other trial judges and received favorable reviews from them about my work. One federal magistrate judge in Virginia remarked in open court that I had conducted one of the best "detainer hearings" he had presided over in quite a while. And one local circuit court judge in Virginia wrote me a letter of recommendation for a position; in the letter, he said that I was one of the "better" criminal defense attorneys to appear before him. I always wondered about that "better" language, but on a whole, who could complain. And another local circuit court judge in Virginia, at the conclusion of jury trial involving a rape case commented to me that I and my team at done a good job on the defense. We lost the case, however.

Although I don't recall ever receiving any referrals from White lawyers either, the difference was their willingness to share their knowledge with me. Perhaps they didn't see me as competition, whereas other Black lawyers did. Perhaps they were patronizing me, helping along a Black colleague who was no real threat to them.

Lawyers are a strange breed, soldiers in America's civil wars. They can be jealous, greedy, envious, arrogant, pompous, and yet gracious to a fault. They don't give up much without looking for something in return, unless they are truly "well meaning" and really want to help you. They do a lot of good and can be very helpful, but, as Dad mused, they deserve "watching." During a visit with one of my many Jewish lawyer friends to discuss a bankruptcy case, he told me, "You don't have to be paranoid, but that doesn't mean they're not out to get you." Another lawyer said to me one day while we discussed a collection case, "All lawyers are rich—rich in problems." These aphorisms and otherwise cynical asides from lawyers, which ranged from abject cynicism to the borderline of paranoia, reflected the complicated world they traverse on a daily basis.

I hung out with a lot of these guys, especially several Jewish lawyer friends, because we just "clicked." In fact, most of my consultations were gained from my associations with them. There was a natural chemistry between us. We shared some common views about business, people, and the law. I grew to even love these fellows and admitted this to one of my closest jewish lawyer friends, who worked with me on some of my more difficult bankruptcy cases involving Wendy Bee. It was he who would always remark, "Sometimes, you bite the bear and sometimes the bear bites you," by which he meant that sometimes you win and sometimes you get your butt kicked and handed to you on a silver platter. Many lawyers are beleaguered by the world and by the system they toil in, but they persevere nonetheless. They hope for the best but know, based upon their experience and knowledge of the law, even before they take a case what the probable outcome will be. But the process must be worked through. Lawyers call this "procedural due process."

Months earlier, maybe even a year or two earlier, while I was working at the New York Life Insurance Company, I suddenly felt sharp, needle-like pains sticking me in my chest after returning to work from a lunch. It was a stickly, pricking sensation, pulsating repeatedly. I remember walking back to the New York Life office wondering what this strange new sensation was all about. I think I even went to see a cardiologist about it, but was only advised to take it easy and not hurt myself. No tests were run to determine anything. Nothing was made of the problem and perhaps the pains were just muscle contractions and of no moment, but I always remembered having what may have been ignored and misunderstood early warning signs.

Then, on 20th September 1990, I awoke from a normal night's sleep feeling odd. Not sick, but not well. I knew intuitively something was not right. I had a DUI case to try that day in Municipal Court in City Hall, and so went about my daily routine, putting on a camel-haired cashmere sports jacket and brown trousers. As usual, I walked Justin to the bus stop at the corner. He was seven-years-old at this time. As we crossed the street and ran a few steps, I felt as if I had run a mile and I said to myself, this is not normal. My chest felt heavy and weighed down. But I trudged ahead, not knowing what to make of it, or what to do. I was ever the soldier moving on.

However, my face belied my true feelings. I arrived at Courtroom 195 in city hall at about 10:00 am and took my place at the counsel table. My case was called and I began to try the case. Midway through, I experienced such terrible pains in my chest I could hardly continue with my cross examination. I didn't complain to my client or to the court. I just went ahead and finished that section of the case. When it was concluded, I went outside and tried to call my cardiologist, but as I began to talk on the phone I was overcome with dizziness, perspiration, exhaustion, and disorientation.

I remember seeing two other lawyers not far from me talking, and I tried fruitlessly to motion to them that I needed help, but everything was in slow motion and my consciousness was ebbing away. I cried just above a whisper, "help, help!" I collapsed onto the floor, dropping everything I held in my hands, including the telephone and my brief case. Like an egg mistakenly dropped on the floor, I splattered on contact. I lost control of my body as it hit the tiled concrete floor. I lay sprawled in the hallway just beyond the elevators in front of the tall, brown entry doors to the courtroom.

Wavering between consciousness and unconsciousness, I vaguely remember the two lawyers coming to my aid and someone yelling, "Call the rescue squad!" Moments later, paramedics were bending over me saying that they were going to take me to Hahnemann Hospital. They loosened my tie and collar, put an oxygen mask over my face, hoisted me onto a stretcher, and loaded me into the back of an ambulance.

As time-sensitive as I had become with court deadlines and court dates to remember, I had lost all sense of time. I don't remember how long it took for the rescue squad to arrive, nor do I remember the ride to the hospital. Fortunately, Hahnemann was just a few blocks away. In my mind, I had grown a little fat. Not obviously so, but in my vision of myself I was heavier than I liked. My self-image had always favored a slimmer profile. I had been eating everything I liked all of my life, regardless of its fat content or nutritional value: deep-dish pizza from Chicago's Uno Pizzeria via King of Prussia, a restaurant I often frequented; eggs with cheese and sausage. Everything I liked, I ate. I worked out periodically, but not regularly. I ran several miles from time-to-time, but not consistently. I was not in the worst of shape, but most importantly I was not living a healthy life style. I didn't even know what a healthy life style was! And I knew nothing about heart disease or the role that genetics might play in having the disease. My mother suffered a heart attack four months earlier; my oldest aunt, Margaret, died of a heart attack several years after my episode; and another aunt, Louise, spent the last years of her life recovering from, but ultimately succumbing to, heart disease.

At the time of my attack, I had not connected the dots. I thought it was stress. My anxiety level had been high. Once, when my mother visited me, I remember having a terrible headache. It was so bad that she became worried. I was sure it was stress. Several years before, on one of my regular checkup visits to my doctor at the Chestnut Hill Hospital, just north of where we lived and where Justin was born, the physician said to me, "You have some choices to make. What is important to you?" But I blew him off as just another doctor who knew little about me, telling me I was doing too much and should choose between one profession or the other, or get out of both.

Ironically, during those last few years, I had felt more virile and in control than I'd felt for a long time. I had felt a sense of confidence and power in my sphere of influence. I had even recently climbed up onto my roof on Wister Street with my roofer to review his work, something I never did because of the potential danger.

I was feeling empowered by my success in business and by my experience practicing law. I was getting used to trying cases, talking to judges, getting in their faces, and looking them straight in the eye. Much of the erstwhile intimidation from the bench was fading. In short, I was feeling my Cheerios. One could say I was at the meridian of my existence when the messenger of death called.

When I arrived at the hospital, there was an inordinate amount of activity surrounding me. Nurses were thrusting needles into my arm and inserting IVs. My clothes were stripped off of me. I had lost all sense of time and place. I had no idea what was going on. It all was a blurred rush, a cacophony of emergency room sounds and footsteps clamoring around trying to save my life. I'm told that I had the actual heart attack in the emergency room, but I don't know if that's true.

It was all a fuzz—an outer body experience. My soul was in a suspended state of separation from my body. It was as though my doppelganger was participating, but I was not there; and that the forces that were acting upon me had all the control. I just responded lethargically to whatever the gods of emergency medicine ordered me to do. I knew not where my watch was, my wedding ring, my briefcase, my books, my clothes, my money, or my car keys. Who would find my car, my new Volvo 740? I had driven my Volvo to work that day and parked it in a lot I discovered several blocks away from city hall. I used it because it was cheap and I believed that, if I walked a little, I could save money. But now no-one would know where it was. As I lay on the gurney in the emergency room of the hospital, none of this mattered.

I was participating in an experience that I had never envisaged for myself, a world where only a few professionals operate. The excruciating pain in my chest would not go away. It felt as if an elephant was standing on my chest and would not move. Where was this weight coming from? Why was it hurting so much? Then I heard someone yell in the background, "Call his wife!" I didn't give them the number, but later she arrived. How much time had passed in-between, I haven't the slightest idea. I saw a glimpse of Michelle leaning over the gurney, whispering something to reassure me, but I don't remember what she said. Michelle had driven all the way from southern New Jersey where she had been working, not knowing what she would encounter on her arrival. Would she be a widow before the night's end, or would God favor her and me and allow my life to be saved? No one knew the answer. I just remember her being there.

The doctors administered clot busters and sedatives to me intravenously, as well as other medicines, as they prepped me for my next procedure. I recall waking up in a room full of large, radar-shaped satellite dishes and TV monitors suspended from the ceiling. Nurses and doctors were standing about with big pieces of medical equipment all around me. I was conscious after a while and the doctors began to talk to me, asking what I felt about this or that. I responded as best I could, not really taking their questions seriously, but I distinctly remember asking them if all of this was necessary, or were they just out for the money? What a stupid thing to say in a crisis like that. But for some reason this thought predominated my thinking. Why? Because I had not remotely accepted that I had actually had a heart attack. I had not come to grips with the reality of my new situation. I had a pre-heart attack mentality in a post-heart attack body.

The doctors humored me and teased me about my accusation of their mercenary intent as they twisted my body here and there. They inserted a catheter with a balloon inside my femoral artery in my right thigh. It is a major arterial passageway to the heart and the catheter reached up into the affected chamber and the diseased artery, where the balloon was inflated and maneuvered by the physician to push the obstructing plaque against the walls, thereby creating a path for the blood to flow freely once again. This procedure is called an angioplasty and was the prescribed treatment for me. The blood vessel that had been 80 to 90 percent blocked was now reopened.

After they completed the procedure, I remember one doctor asking, "How does your chest feel?" I said, "It hurts!"

He replied in a calming voice, "It will feel better in a while."

Being both reassured and still under sedation, I dozed as I was taken to a recovery room with IVs dangling above me, my ever-present protectors filling my arteries with blood-thinning medicine to keep my blood flowing freely and prevent re-clotting in my newly opened blood vessel.

As I lay on my gurney, the nurses wrapped me so tightly in white sheets and white blankets that I felt like a mummy, with my brown head and black hair barely visible above the white linens that clothed my bed and my body so tightly. Nonetheless, I was still cold and couldn't stop shivering because my autonomic nervous system was now in control.

For the next few hours, I remained in the recovery room as I was monitored by the nurses. By this time Michelle had called my parents. She recalled that my dad was the most upset, and he told her that they would drive up right away from Charlottesville. My mother, on the other hand, managed her angst stoically. Weeks later, Dad told the Charlottesville City Council how angry he was that even during this anxious time, Jerry Tomlin, a short, balding, White, rotund man, the city housing inspector continued to torment him, "as my only son lay near to death in a Philadelphia hospital room."

I first saw my parents while I was in the intensive care unit. I was not in any condition to talk to them, but I remember seeing them through my blurred vision and also seeing my cardiologist and friend, Dr. Frank S. James. It was comforting to see him there. He was both a client and a friend. The fact that he came to see about me meant a lot. His presence and gentle manner not only gave me reassurance, but he was able to relieve some of my parent's anxiety by educating them about what was likely to happen. To this day I do not know how he found out that I was in the hospital, but he made it his business to get there. I remember seeing them gathered in the front of my room talking.

The incision the doctors made to gain access to my femoral artery and insert the catheter was supposed to heal so that I would lose no more blood. The doctors checked the incision regularly and all seemed well, but one morning my doctors lifted off the bandages covering the spot of the incision and, to their amazement and mine, there was blood oozing from the incision and a large dark spot of blood stained my sheets. Anxiousness gripped all those present as they hurriedly made several immediate medical decisions. It was decided to close the incision, since it would not close on its own. I was sedated again and wheeled out of my room into a surgical unit.

The surgical procedure was performed as soon as arrangements could be made, after which I was wheeled back into my old room in the intensive care unit. I remained there for the next several days as my convalescence continued, unremarkably from then on. I was under a cloud of fog barely able to comprehend what was going on but remember my father putting his cool hands on my forehead and gently stroking my head. His hands were like the cool mint of evergreen resting on my fevered brow. The affect was soothing, comforting and reassuring. It was a divine moment of compassion and caring between a father and a son. I knew that my father loved me: that was never ever in doubt. But that moment captured and distilled within it all the compassion and care one individual could have for another in one tender, spontaneous touch. Dad and I spoke for a moment, and I told him to "be nice to Michelle." In my weakened state, I still knew to tell him that because I knew my father. In marriage, I reasoned, the spouse only has a lease for a term of years, on condition of good behavior. The family retains the equity in that family member throughout the marriage. I knew that, in this time of crisis, my dad, because of his love for me, would intentionally usurp the immediate family hierarchy and impose his will on events.

Later, I was moved to another intensive care unit for further monitoring. The pain in my chest subsided and I felt better, but I was far from out of the woods. I was kept in this room for several days and remember the male nurse coming by each night asking me if I wanted a sleeping aid. I told him no—I was sleeping all right, for now.

The heart attack did not quell my desire to achieve all that I could. Six years later, a shocking reminder was made known to me when I was in a federal court in Virginia during a bankruptcy proceeding; I witnessed a client who was seated next to his counsel fall out of his chair with such a loud boom, so loud that it shook and shocked the courtroom, the judge, and the spectators. He died right there of a massive heart attack. He was an overweight White man of short stature and with balding hair. It was a scene I will never forget. The stress of his proceedings had caused him to die.

Many, many years earlier, Dad had lost his oldest sister, Tobytha Lee Byrd, (we called her "Bee") to an illness that still remains a mystery. Dad had loved her dearly. Bee was responsible for guiding him and encouraging him to go to college, right from their humble beginnings in Fitzgerald, Georgia. He had tried to keep Bee with him in our home in Richmond, Virginia, when she came to visit in 1955 or '56, when she was ill, but he was unable to do so. Instead, she returned to her home and family in Pittsburgh and died soon thereafter. He had always believed that, if she had stayed with him, the sheer force of his being and his personal intervention could have staved off the chain of events that caused her death.

So was this deja vu for him?

Each day brought new questions for me. Philosophical, existential questions. Why had this happened? I was just forty-three years old. But why had God put me through this, only to spare me? My college roommate, Oliver Morgan, died mysteriously in my freshman year at Howard, yet I was allowed to live. Some of my other young friends had died prematurely. Why had I, once again, been allowed to live?

A middle-aged, White female hospital cardiologist making her rounds came by my bed and we talked. I asked her. She calmly took a few moments to explain. She told me, "You are Black. African Americans have a high incidence of heart disease. Your arteries were clogged. It just happened."

But I quickly retorted, seeking absolution, that I didn't smoke, I was not obese, and I didn't have high blood pressure. So again I asked her, "Why?"

She calmly replied reminding me of my reality, as well as of my good fortuned, "We've had younger people than you in this unit, some of whom have died." She went on to say that "a woman younger than you, one room over, died recently of a heart related problem."

The gravity of my situation sank in. I was grieving over the loss I suffered, searching for some plausible explanation that would lessen the impact.

Yet I was still not dealing with the reality of my situation. My self-image had been attacked, this time from a physical point of view. I had always seen myself as strong, virile, and hearty; "Leonard" my middle name, meant "lion hearted" and that's how I intuitively saw myself, but now I realized that I was no longer a strong and vibrant young man. I was disabled, not totally, or partially, but residually, meaning I could not do what I had been doing at the same level. I had to avoid certain stressors, such as active and intensive trial practice. Was I then possibly just half a man? Dad would remark some weeks later that "half a man is better than no man at all," but that hardly reassured me. I still wanted to know why fate had singled me out. Were genetics at fault? What role had they played? Since my mother had suffered her attack several months before me, I wondered whether my genes had predisposed my body to this disease. I also debated with myself whether, even without any future lifestyle changes and the knowledge I now had to protect myself, would it be those same genetics that enabled me to survive this injury despite its severity? If that was the answer, I could accept it better because it meant that my heart condition was out of my control and my own actions were not totally responsible for my sudden debilitation.

Pondering the imponderables during each successive day, I reexamined and reassessed my mode of operation and came to grips with some truths about me and the way I worked. Finally, the reality of my situation was beginning to set in. I had suffered a heart attack. My life would never be the same. Searchingly, I noted to myself that I had never exercised consistently, though I did some running and played some basketball occasionally; my life was full of stress, from both the real estate business and my law firm; and my diet was unhealthy.

I didn't want to die in Philadelphia. Philadelphia was my home but it was not my permanent domicile. And even though Philadelphia was the *elan vital* of my professional life and had given me and taught me so much, I didn't want it to be my final resting place. This was despite the fact that my youngest son had been born in Philadelphia, I had found my wife in Philadelphia, and I continued to raise my eldest son in Philadelphia. Even though my path to economic security had been paved in Philadelphia and the physicians of this city had saved my life, I still didn't want to die there. As Thomas Jefferson once said, "I want my days to end where my days began."

I had approached Philadelphia like Julius Caesar had approached the shores of Britain: "I came, I saw, I conquered." In so doing, he avenged an earlier defeat. But instead of me conquering Philadelphia, Philadelphia had conquered me.

I had taken so many beatings in this city of one kind or another, overcome so many demons and been subjected to much rudeness, meanness, arrogance, and inconsiderate behavior by some tenants, some clients, and some citizens, both in and out of government, that I could not accept that this place would be my last chapter. I was not a native. Philadelphia began as my experimental laboratory, but had evolved into my dwelling place, a life saver and the "county seat of Leeville." I had viewed the city as a career experience, albeit a vital and pivotal one, but not as my final destination.

As I lay there, I realized that, in the future, I had to work not just harder, but smarter. I should not to be so compulsive about finishing everything every day, not so intense, use the mail rather than my feet when filing court papers, be more efficient in the manner in which I accomplished things, park closer to my destination rather than walk a mile to save a dollar, lighten up, give myself a break!

I had to realize that I was not invincible, that I was made of flesh and blood, that I was fragile and would break if pushed too far, that my mortality was real, that my "outer door" had been alarmed. As I contemplated all these factors, an angel appeared in the form of a hospital psychiatrist. His name was Dr. Goeff, and he made regular visits to the cardiac wards. He was a brown-bearded Caribbean of African descent and was both gracious and gentle. He could have been an imam the way he carried himself.

Dr. Goeff came by my room on several occasions, and we began to talk almost instantly because trust was not an issue. I instinctively knew he was my brother. I was ready to talk to him in a way that I had never talked to anyone else before. I wanted to confess, to vent, to get the venom and the poison out. Self-pity was overflowing as I tried to work myself through the stages of acceptance. I was searching for someone or something to blame, so I began with me. I told him that I wanted to have some counseling sessions after I was well enough to leave the hospital. I told him I wanted to leave some of my baggage behind. I shared with him a sampling of the things I wanted to rid myself of: my struggle against poor self-esteem, which had not been my problem historically, but had emerged from time to time and would not die; poor self-image; the color of my skin; the White school-Black school equation; the bar experience; and all of the baggage that had driven me almost to my death trying to prove something to somebody! To whom? To myself? Yes. To other people? Yes. Why? What for?

Was it the frustration of knowing that I had talent but trying to convince other people of that fact? Was that my problem? Was it not enough to know these things for myself? Was I trying too hard? What was driving me?

I was tired physically and mentally of proving myself, of trying to meet some amorphous standard of competence. The tired and worn out psychological house I had constructed for myself was full of stress and strain. It was stifling and choking the life out of me. And though the fetid and rancid by-product of my past experiences had been trampled down by trial and error and compacted until it was barely visible, remnants persisted. Metaphorically, this sewage clogged my blood vessels and was making me sick. I needed a plumber—and a licensed one at that! I was done proving myself to myself, or to anybody else for that matter; that was over. I had met the standard I had imposed upon myself and had exceeded it. Caring about what other people thought would no longer be important in my life. Either I accepted myself with all my blemishes now, or I never would.

In spite of all the psychological issues I perceived to be foils for my ills, perhaps the real blame lay with my indomitable will to succeed, to win. The pressure I put on myself was self-imposed, no White man nor his culture made me work as hard as I was working. This was me; I did it, no one else. All of that psychological stuff was just an additional gust of the headwind confronting the progress I was striving to make. It was just me and my genes.

God in the form of the Holy Spirit, in the exercise of His infinite wisdom, had seen fit not to cash my check and draw on the bank of my life just yet. He had decided to exercise his option to renew my promissory note and let it roll over until a later date. However, the attack was notice of the start of the twilight of my life; an acknowledgment that, at some point, the note would be called in and the check would be cashed. It had given me notice that my life could and would end and that I should begin to contemplate that fact now, not in a morbid sense, but in a preparatory, reflective, and thankful way.

Life will end at some point in the future. "You are going to die," the minister thundered with fervent emotion, looking everyone right in the eye at my paternal uncle's funeral. And his words rang true. This wake-up call may only last a fleeting moment or it may last for several years, but its poignant message is irrefutable. When it happens, you will know it.

It is said that luck is the residue of design. Was it luck or design that I survived? Was it the design of divine intervention that saved my life? I am more convinced than ever that there is a Holy Spirit. It does not take the form of the iconic image normally depicted in Christendom, but is a benevolent overseer. What else explains the saving graces that have been bestowed upon me?

My *leitmotif* up to that point had been to satisfy the simple needs of everyday people with basic legal services and apartments. I had served the poor, the lower middle-class, the middle-class, and some wealthy folks. Doing this had afforded me a good living. I had left the high-end lawyering to the big shot lawyers and the big real estate deals to the fat cats. Yet I had worked on enough novel issues to distinguish myself and had established a good reputation both in the law and in business. I had a field of study—estate taxation and estate planning—that was not common, especially among Black lawyers. Somebody had to serve the poor, and so I was satisfied. At least they appreciated what I did for them. They were grateful.

I had no regrets about what I had accomplished professionally or in business. My chagrin lay in the priorities I had set for myself. My health had not been one of them. I had taken it for granted. I had over-worked and over-stressed myself, and in the process, had given so much, perhaps too much, for what I had achieved.

So, what was the final medical diagnosis of my condition? The doctors told me I had suffered a moderate myocardial infarction in the left ventricle descending. The infarct, or heart muscle, dead or dying was the result of a lack of blood supply caused by the blockage in the left anterior wall of the left ventricle (LAD), which had resulted in an ejection fraction (EF) of 36%. Generally speaking the ejection fraction is a measure of how much blood is pumped out of the chambers of the heart into the rest of the body. An EF of 55% or more is normal.

The attack had been caused by atherosclerosis. Fatty substances had formed a deposit of plaque on the inner lining of the artery. Some of my heart muscle had died and would never regenerate. The question in my mind was, did I have enough heart capacity to live a normal life? Or would it be shortened by this attack?

I was assured by the doctors that I would lead a normal life, but my challenge was not to have another debilitating attack. With proper medical intervention and lifestyle changes, I could live to see my sons grow up, enjoy my grandchildren, enjoy life with my beautiful wife, help my mother and father who had given me so much, be around to properly bury both of them, and preserve my family's estate.

My recovery continued, and my caregivers were so good I was steadily falling in love with them. If my Chicago experience was apostatizing, disillusioning me of my naive belief that the system under which we all labor was in any way fair, the treatment I received at the hands of the physicians and nurses I encountered during my illness resurrected my belief in human beings and in some parts of the system.

After several more days in intensive care after the surgery on my femoral artery, I was moved to a step-down unit where I could complete my initial recovery. Things went well. But that was not the case for every other patient around me. Before I left the hospital, a new patient was moved into my room with me. He was a middle-aged White man with heart disease. One night, he moaned, hacked, spat, coughed, snorted, and gurgled from dusk to dawn. It was painful to hear him suffer so much from fluid that had built up in his lungs. It was awful and kept me up all night. The next day, I asked the nurse if I could be moved to another room. Instead, they moved him out, where to I didn't know, but that guy was in bad shape. The doctors did the best they could to remove the excess fluid from his system, but it seemed to be of little value.

The doctor assigned to discharge me came to talk to me and go over my medications. His name was Dr. Steven P. Kutalek. He was a White man of slight build, gentle, and kind, with an empathetic manner. As this whole experience had been my first introduction as a patient to the world of cardiology, I listened attentively as he went over the dos and don'ts. He required that I attend a cardiac rehabilitation program at Chestnut Hill Hospital, not far from my home in Mt. Airy, and he stressed the importance of dietary changes, of low fat, low cholesterol foods, and of lifestyle changes. He also warned me to reduce my stress level. The heart attack and my illness afterwards had caused me to lose weight. I was emaciated by the time of my release, but little did I know that I was only halfway through my recuperative process.

My mother stayed in Philadelphia the entire time I was in the hospital, except for a short period. Her presence was comforting and reassuring. She didn't say much, but her grace did all her speaking for her. Dad returned to Charlottesville to keep up with his business. Justin was not allowed to see me because he was too young to visit a cardiac ward, and it would not be good for him to see his father in such a condition. Otis visited me shortly before the attack, but he had gone back to active duty in the army. I don't know whether or not he knew of my attack, but shortly after my initial discharge he came back home. It was a blessing to have him with me during that time. The separation we experienced when he left several years earlier was healing and both Michelle and I longed for his safe return. I remember keeping up with troop deployments during Operation Desert Storm, George H. W. Bush's Iraq War. I was most worried about him during this time.

None of my in-laws visited me while I was in hospital in Philadelphia, not my mother-in-law, or my sister-in-law, or any of their kids. I don't remember even receiving a card from any of them. However, my Aunt Louise, my mother's sister did visit me while I was in the intensive care unit. She came from Mt. Vernon, New York, to visit her nephew. "Nephew," she always called me. None of my other blood relatives visited me either, though it is questionable whether or not they knew of the illness.

Philadelphia is essentially a small town and it showed. News spread like wildfire throughout the legal community that I had suffered an attack. Lang and another friend, Bryant McCloskey, came to visit. Bryant was one of three real friends I made in Philadelphia. The others being Lang and Dr. Frank James. But Bryant and I got acquainted before my days at New York Life and our relationship continued beyond my days with the company. Bryant epitomized the above average Black male Philadelphian, loquacious, street wise, a hustler with morality, a caring father and a righteous Casanova. A man who worked in business and sold others on the propriety of business products but did not excel in it himself, a stark contradiction. A man of principle who lovingly raised his two daughters by himself, yet his commitment to the women he loved never met the standards of care bestowed upon his daughters. But Bryant is a true friend, a friend I tried to help from the time we met to this day.

Wendy Bee paid me a visit. The secretaries that I busted my rear end trying to pay each week didn't visit, but they did hand me a get well card when I eventually returned to the office.

I left the hospital in a wheelchair, pushed out by hospital attendants. I went home and began my convalescence. At first, all seemed to be going well. I was put on a strict diet that Michelle tried to fix and passed several days uneventfully. Then, on a balmy afternoon I asked Otis, who fortuitously, was home on leave, to go to the office and to bring back a file. I walked around the outside of the house to the gate to await his return and to get some fresh air. It was a wonderful sunny day, but soon I began to feel strange. I had no idea what was happening, but my intuition told me to get inside because danger threatened. Hastily I walked back inside the house and up the center stairwell to the family room. Halfway up the stairs, I lost consciousness.

I was out for a few seconds, for how long who knows? I awoke to find Otis pulling me by my arms up the remaining stairs and into the small family room at the top of the landing. With Michelle's help, he laid me on the sofa. I regained consciousness within a few moments. I knew not what had happened. I was later told that I experienced an arrhythmia, a disturbance in the normal rhythm of the heart, a recoil of my frail heart to the original heart attack. It had resulted in ventricular tachycardia—the same disease that was rumored to have killed Frank Rizzo a few years earlier—a rapid, out-of-control heart rhythm, resulting in a loss of consciousness, and in some cases death.

That evening I was taken back to the hospital and placed on another gurney and wrapped in more sheets as I lay there shivering, awaiting a hospital bed. It was then that I got to know Dr. Stephen P. Kutalek and his associate, Dr. Scott Hessan, much better. Dr. K, as he was more affectionately called, was director of the electrophysiology laboratory at Hahnemann. One of his accompanying doctors informed me that I had experienced syncope, a brief loss of consciousness caused by an inadequate flow of oxygenated blood to the brain.

Late that night, I was placed in a room next to an older Black man who had a colostomy that required regular emptying and attention by the nurse. The smell from his waste bag suffused the room and made me feel queasy just thinking about what if I had to have one of those devices. The old gentleman was very matter-of-fact about it and made the nurses give him the attention he needed, oblivious to my unease.

I remember my mother coming to visit me and the doctors quizzing me about what had happened. Dr. K and his team were preparing to start a course of treatment when word was received that I was to be flown to the University of Virginia Hospital in Charlottesville for further treatment. Dad had stepped in and taken control of the rest of my hospitalization process. He had great faith in the University of Virginia Hospital and wanted me home, so he could supervise my care and have easier access to me. He was that kind of guy.

Before Dr. Kutalek and his team could diagnose what had caused the syncope, orders were given to fly me to UVa Hospital. After breakfast on the day of my trip, I was wheeled from my room and hoisted on to a flatbed in the passenger compartment of the aircraft by four attendants, as the helicopter waited with its rotors whirling and spinning on the heliport on the roof of Hahnemann Hospital. I was flown there by the Pegasus helicopter service, an air medical patient delivery service associated with UVa Hospital. The team on board, in addition to the pilot and his navigator, was composed of a nurse and an attendant, both of whom made me feel secure and comfortable.

From the helicopter pad on the top deck of Hahnemann to the helicopter pad on top of the newest wing of the hospital at UVa, took about two hours. The rotors of the helicopter were loud and intimidating, but I felt confident that the people in charge knew their business, so I didn't worry.

Upon my arrival in Charlottesville, I was wheeled into the cardiac ward and given a private room, but only because it was the only one available at that time. A Black nurse who worked this floor and was a friend of Dad's saw that I was given the room, and she advised Dad to secure the services of Dr. John Dimarco, a prominent cardiologist and head of the hospital's electrophysiology department. Dad, now in charge, made all the arrangements.

Whether or not Dad consulted Michelle before ordering the transfer was not disclosed to me either by her or him. The transfer via helicopter to Charlottesville cost my father several thousand dollars because there was no insurance coverage for that service.

This was my third time as a patient in UVa Hospital. The first time was back in 1960 when I fractured my ankle playing touch footfall in the front yard of Dickie Moon's house with a bunch of neighborhood guys not far from our home on Ridge Street. The second was when my left jaw was broken by a thug who threw a brick in my face and broke my jaw after leaving a church sponsored party at the end of Ridge Street.

UVa hospital is a modern facility and was noticeably less congested than Hahnemann. The nurses were kind and caring and one of my attending physicians was a young Black woman doctor I got to know a little.

Shortly after my arrival, I underwent a heart catheterization. I had undergone the angioplasty at Hahnemann, so now the doctors at UVa wanted to do the catheterization to determine the status of my heart attack and to know for sure whether the blocked artery was now open. Again, I was laid on the ever-present gurney, wrapped in white sheets and wheeled into a nondescript non-aesthetically pleasing room with TV monitors and large pieces of equipment that all seemed impersonal and daunting to me.

Inside the room, a cadre of hospital workers gathered around me with surgical masks covering their faces. An IV was put into my right arm, and I was told that I was going to be given a mild sedative to relax me. As the sedative took hold, a catheter was inserted into my groin and I remember seeing pictures of my heart and blood vessels displayed in color on the TV screens. After a while, the head physician told me that, "Soon you will feel like vomiting and you will feel a warm sensation. If you want to vomit, do so. The nurses will attend to you."

Not long after his advice, I had those feelings. The medicine they were injecting into me made me feel sick, and I gagged and attempted to vomit, but nothing came out. That experience was soon followed by a warm sensation as the procedure continued. I remember being hoisted up or turned around during the course of the procedure. It was not painful, just uncomfortable. After it was over, I was taken back to my room where my right leg was kept elevated for about five hours so that everything could heal and drain properly. All of this was tiring and I slept for a while. Late in the afternoon, my right leg was lowered and I was made much more comfortable.

Not long after the results of the catheterization were interpreted by the doctors, I had my first encounter with electrophysiology, to me the *bête noire* of cardiac tests.

The hospital attendants and nurses came and got me sometime after breakfast. I was wheeled into another procedure room with doctors all around. But this time they didn't have surgical masks on their faces; instead, they were dressed in their white hospital coats, some with just white shirts and ties, and they were very business-like. Machines surrounded my gurney and Dr. Dimarco gave all the instructions. I was told that they were going to give me a mild sedative to relax me and that I should remain calm–that they were going to "pace my heart."

I didn't know what they were talking about. "Pacing my heart?" What did that mean?

I soon found out when they inserted a catheter-like device into my arm or leg—which limb escapes me now—but soon I was off into a sleep of sorts and then I was suddenly jarred with a powerful force and shocked awake. The shock had been administered by an electrical current from a generator flowing through flat lead or steel looking plates that had been placed on my chest to shock my heart back into a normal rhythm. I could tell instinctively that I had been some place I didn't want to go to again.

I had lost consciousness because the doctors had simulated a form of ventricular tachycardia. Had I not been shocked back to consciousness, death would have ensued. They were attempting to trigger the arrhythmia which caused the syncope that knocked me out at home in Philadelphia. And they succeeded. The rapid heartbeat reoccurred and took me out.

It was a scary experience, one that I didn't want to repeat. I was in shock from it for a while and the force of the shock made my chest sore. I felt very unsettled for a period, until I calmed down and regained my composure. I let it be known to the nurses and the doctors that I didn't want to undergo that procedure again, but my plea fell on deaf ears.

I was wheeled back to my room and several days of calm passed, during which my sister-in-law Shelly drove down from her home in Centerville to visit me. I appreciated her efforts to pay me a visit. Her visit expressed beyond words the care and compassion she had for my wellbeing. Not long after her visit, the doctors informed me that I would indeed have to undergo another electrophysiology test. I was very dismayed and upset. I protested, but to no avail.

As I waited for the second test, I confided in my attending nurse that I wanted to take a year off and do nothing but rest. She counseled me: "Don't make any decisions now because you're too vulnerable to the affects this experience is having on you." Dad had cautioned me not to fall in love with the nurses, but I was becoming fatefully attracted to my care givers. I loved them all, not just the nurses, but also the young Black female doctor who entered my mind as she attended to me daily while making her rounds. In my many moments of vulnerability, I wanted to reach out to all of them and thank them for their dedicated care. After my release I sent out a thank you card to the nurse who was most familiar with me.

This time, before the test they gave me a mild sedative then wheeled me into the procedure room. The test was performed and the result was the same, the arrhythmia reoccurred and I was shocked out of it again. Their intent was to test for the level of medication to be used to arrest the arrhythmia and prevent it from reoccurring.

Heart rhythm disturbances are unpredictable. They can occur without warning at any time or in any place. They can be deadly if they are not corrected by surgery or controlled either by medication or by a mechanical device. It was a very serious business. Michelle and Justin remained in Philadelphia during this time, although Michelle came down during my stay at UVa.

After a day or so a big powwow took place. Dr. Dimarco came to my room. My Dad was there and we listened as the physician explained his diagnosis. A sullen atmosphere flavored the texture of our discourse. "I had a type of "arrhythmia," ventricular tachycardia the doctor said in so many words, which had caused the syncope and which could cause sudden death if not controlled by medication or eliminated by surgery. Because of my youth, my heart had rebelled and recoiled, and a short circuit had developed in my normal rhythm because of scar tissue that had grown over the site of the infarct. As he explained it, to solve these problems I could have surgery to either remove the short circuit and eliminate it, or have a defibrillator implanted under my skin near the "belly button" close enough to my heart to monitor its rhythm (and when it detected an arrhythmia it would issue a mild shock to jolt the heart back into a normal rhythm), or I could take medication.

From sullen to somber went the mood. Dad asked if Dr. Dimarco wanted to speak to my wife to explain all of this to her, but he declined. His response was unexpected. We had all expected him to say, "yes", to invite her inclusion into the decision making. Why, I wondered? It seemed unusual. This was not proceeding like the television script I was used to seeing. Was he saying, in effect, that this decision would not be affected by my spouse's input? That the decision was mine alone? In retrospect he was right, if that was his thinking. The decision was mine alone. It was my body and I had to endure whatever choice I made and live with the consequences. That's the way it is in life.

Dr. Dimarco told us that surgery in "this hospital" would be performed well and that I could expect a good result. Of course, there were no guarantees...

I was not impressed by the prospect of surgery on my heart. All I could imagine about it was horrible, not beneficial. Just the thought of these men opening up my chest—which probably would not have been required, but I did not know nor did I inquire—and all that would be engendered by that was undesirable. And my natural aversion to doctors performing surgery turned me off. So I was resigned to suffer my fate at home, which in my mind at this time was in Charlottesville. I told them both that I just wanted to go home. I hung my head in resignation and exclaimed to all that would hear my submission to my unfavorable prospects.

Why had I reached the nadir so easily? This question worried me deeply and caused me to wonder about my whole approach to life. Was it exhaustion, or exasperation with the whole heart disease endgame? Was it an inbred acquiescence to the inevitability of death that we are all trained to accept? Was it self-pity? Why had I given up hope so quickly? Where was the fight in me, the will to live?

At that moment, all of my choices appeared daunting, undesirable, uninviting, uncomfortable and filled with pain. That was my first reaction. Upon reflection, perhaps I would have opted for something less than to go home and sit in my room and let an arrhythmia consume me. But Dad had the presence of mind to urge calm and he said, "Let's talk about those options again."

Neither he nor I liked the idea of surgery and we knew nothing about pacemakers, so medication seemed to be the course of least resistance. The medicines would be harsh and strong but they would suppress the arrhythmia and taking them was the least invasive option available.

I was now told for the first time something that I had to get used to hearing: "I would have to take these pills for the rest of my life." All of this magnified, in my mind, that I was in deep trouble. My life had truly changed forever.

I was discharged from the hospital soon after I made my choice to take the medication, and Dr. Dimarco prescribed the medications for me, in addition to the beta blockers and aspirin I was already on. The new drugs made me feel lightheaded at times, off balance and not firm of foot, but other than that, I tolerated the drugs reasonably well. Liver tests and blood platelet tests had to be performed regularly on me because these medicines had the side-effect of reducing my blood platelet count and causing liver damage.

I went home to stay with my parents. I had been in the hospital for about a month between the two cities, but I emerged with the prospect of a normal life, though with some dislocation, some irregular physical feelings, reduced capacity and some restrictions on my lifestyle. My health would now be the primary focus of my life and that is as it should have been all along. I was fortunate.

37

❦

FREE AT LAST IN EARLYSVILLE

J UST BEFORE MY HEART ATTACK, I was selected for an IRS audit of my recent income tax returns. I hired Mellon Bank, successor to the old Girard Bank that I had done a lot of business with and who had made me several business loans, to prepare my income tax returns and they made a mistake that caused me to be selected for audit. While recuperating in Charlottesville, the audit was completed. It ended up costing me tens of thousands of dollars, between the accountants, lawyer, back taxes, penalties and interest that I was told to pay. I took it all in stride though, and got it behind me.

The audit was a painful experience and at times it was stressful because of the potential it had to open "Pandora's box," getting into areas that could lead to further trouble. Perhaps I had grown too quickly. But then again, there was nothing I thought unusual about my financial situation that any other budding entrepreneur would not have encountered. But the audit paled in comparison to what I was recovering from. I sued the bank that made the mistake. They paid a settlement, but this was one of the banks that I worked closely with in my estate planning practice. After the suit they quickly disavowed me and would have nothing else to do with me, even though it was "their mistake." I had had the audacity to sue a big bank and they never forgot it. Years later they would take their revenge.

I stayed around Charlottesville for a few more weeks, growing closer to my parents. They were getting used to having me around again. It was like old times, with just the three of us. Dad and I had long talks out in the yard, sitting on his white stone benches in the park-like setting he had created at "Leonard Belle Heights," the home he had built while I was a freshman at Howard University in 1970. This home reflected his ego, nestled at the top of a moderate-sized hill in the northwestern suburb of Charlottesville along "the gold coast," out along 250 west past Boar's Head Inn. This seven acre estate was the culmination of his and Mom's life's work, his little "Monticello."

In the cool of the early evenings, we talked about my future and my limitations. Dad remarked again, "Half a man is better than no man." Between the date of my discharge from UVa Hospital and my return to my old life in Philadelphia, this interstice, though reflective and pensive in its quieter moments, was a time to rethread an already tightly woven family fabric. Dad, Mother and I talked about many subjects during this time, about life, work, and the family. I told Dad that I had to change the way I did business. I tried to make him understand, but I was not always sure he got it. However, he probably understood more than I thought he did. He seemed to understand the essence of what I meant.

Each morning, Mother and I went to cardiac rehabilitation exercise classes together. She was still recovering from her heart attack six months earlier. We enjoyed going to the classes and the health foods stores, trying out all of the new heart-conscious, low-fat foods she and I now had to acquire a taste for.

But this time was fleeting because my family in Philadelphia and my businesses required my return. After another week or two, Michelle drove down to Charlottesville, as she said, "to get her husband." My mother and father were taking me over, but I was needed in Philadelphia. Before leaving Charlottesville, Michelle and I went for a walk on the downtown mall. We went into the Young Men's Shop, a local haberdashery where I used to work when I was in high school. Marshall Pryor one of the salesmen a White man, still young and aggressive, rotund but not obese with a jovial disposition greeted me and asked about my well-being. He said Otis, "You look like shit. What the hell's wrong with you?" I looked at him bemused but I did not immediately respond. Marshall would later become an owner of the clothing shop. He knew me because he started working there in the 60s when I was a junior janitor in the store.

I went on to explain my situation and he regretted having been so harsh in his assessment of my appearance. But he was right. I was feeling as well as appearing gaunt and emaciated. I had lost a significant amount of weight, just like the time after I left Delma many years earlier. Anyone who knew me could tell the difference. It would take several years before I began to resemble my old self.

Back in Philadelphia, the rustles of *a démarche*, an appeal to return, stirred beneath the souls of my feet, pointing me southward. My life was no longer centered on all things Pennsylvanian. A year or two before my heart attack, Michelle and I had contemplated moving from our home on Sedgwick Street in Philadelphia to Charlottesville. We wanted to move out of the city because of the encroachment of crime, which didn't allow us to live the quality of life our finances afforded us. So driven were we to move that we signed a contract on a house not far from where my parents were living. But I was not yet ready to move.

A local lawyer in Charlottesville filed a law suit against us, for breach of contract, but with the help of a lawyer and with some ingenuity I found a way to get out of the contract. These efforts were just indicative of the fact that we wanted to move. We looked at places to the north of Philadelphia, such as Blue Bell, Flourtown–a suburb I liked–Lafayette and as far north as Collegeville, but we weren't satisfied with anything we saw, so we didn't do anything more about it. Then I had my heart attack.

Getting back into my routine was anything but routine. Michelle did her best during my absence to keep the bills paid, my clients placated and the tenants satisfied. But it was rough on her trying to function on her job, look after Justin and keep an eye on my affairs. I also had moments of reflection that caused me to ask probing questions of both her and of myself on several levels. One night, while we were sitting on the edge of our bed in the pink room, the second floor rear bedroom overlooking the back yard, talking about nothing specific but enjoying being together again at home, I asked her directly, "Did she cry for me"? What was I looking for? Pity, an expression of my value to her, confirmation of her love? What?

The question surprised and shocked her. "What do you mean?" she responded in puzzlement.

I repeated the question again, looking her directly in her eyes. "Did you cry for me?!"

Again, what was I searching for? Toward what end was this question directed? Did she realize how close to death I had been? What did I really mean to her? Did she understand the severity of my illness and the potential loss? Was I challenging the depth of her caring? How presumptuous of me to question her love, had it not been manifested many times over? Having faced a challenging moment staring mortality in the face did my insecurities reveal themselves? Perhaps so. But in this time of deep introspection, nothing was beyond review.

"Yes," she avowed softly and sincerely, "but not the way you may have expected." Her response was without rapture or exaltation. Her approach was more reserved in keeping with her cool calm disposition.

"So in what way did you cry for me?" I asked, returning to the subject, probing for a deeper answer, looking to be reassured of her love for me. She went on to explain that she too had grieved my illness and the possible loss to the family. I got a measure of satisfaction from her response and decided not to press further, so I let the moment pass without requiring any more elaboration. I was satisfied enough. Her response was sufficient though not everything I expected. But what then was I expecting? A crying mawkishly maudlin sentimentality, a waterfall of tears, a loss of control? All of this was unrealistic and expressed perhaps more of my outsized view of my place in the family and of the love we shared. Michelle had always, possibly because of what she had overcome in her life, been reticent in the expressive side of her emotions. Her emotions nonetheless are deeply held; like still water her emotions run deep.

Shortly thereafter, we were driving downtown to Center City, about to get onto the Schuylkill Expressway when we got into a heated and intense argument about nothing. As we argued back and forth, I asked myself, why is she fighting with me so intensely? Doesn't she realize that this is stressful on me and that I just had a heart attack? What is she thinking? Her insensitivity to the nature of my condition amazed me. It was good I was on beta blockers to shield my heart from the stress of the fuss. I shouldn't have responded, but the flywheel nature of my instinct to respond added to the quarrel.

I said to myself after this incident: a vicarious appreciation of something leaves much to be desired. Since she had not herself experienced what I had just gone through, she did not know and was not capable of knowing how acute my sensitivities were during my recuperation. Nothing beats first-hand experience.

As my adjustment continued, Lang and I talked about death and I told him of my private fear that I would leave a young, attractive wife for someone else to woo, love and enjoy. I was really concerned about this subject. I didn't want to leave Michelle behind to be remarried. This thought troubled me. Lang, for his part, said it didn't worry him about the love of his life because he would not be around to be bothered by it. His view made sense but it didn't settle my unease. Not being quite dead yet, I reckoned that it still mattered to me.

Lang remarried and was living with his new wife, a much younger woman than his first wife, so he could relate to my fears. I just regretted the prospect of losing Michelle. Michelle was my prized asset, and I didn't want anyone else to have her. I took the time to review my estate plans, rereading my will and trust to make sure they represented my true intentions. All around, there was this reassessment of things essential.

Not long after my return to Philadelphia, I got in touch with Dr. Goeff. We met for several sessions. My sessions with him were cathartic and therapeutic; many tears were shared and, yes, I got rid of some of the venom, but I didn't get all the crud out. These sessions had a cleansing effect. I told him about how it seemed that I had always taken on more than I should. It started at Howard University in my freshman year when I took 18 hours and sometimes 21 hours of credits instead of the usual 15 hours, and I finished college in three years by going the year round. I always had a heavy burden, all self-imposed. No one told me to do these things; I elected to do them. My appetite was bigger than my digestive system. Heavy responsibility characterized my entire adult existence. There was always an obligation on my back. I wanted to do too much. I was constantly pushing myself to do more.

It would be a work in progress and take many years to finally rid myself, if ever I could, of the culture of White Americana and this over-sized ego that drove me to the excess that so infested my being. The cleansing I did achieve was aided by the fact that I was able to be truthful with him because he was anonymous and unbiased and was not a stakeholder in my success or failure. He was there simply to listen and offer some suggestions for repair. The sessions ended much too soon, and I later lost track of Dr. Goeff. Being the lawyer that I am, I started counseling him on the problems he was having with the power structure at Hahnemann. I long for him to this day.

I resumed my day-to-day duties and each passing day came and went. Otis returned to active duty, but we were all glad that he would be state-side and had not nor would be going to Iraq. He had interrupted his education when he enlisted in the military but was beginning to take a few college courses in the city where he was stationed. We were all heartened by that knowledge.

I gradually regained some weight and continued to see Dr. Kutalek for my regular check-ups. At one of them, he told me that he was surprised to see me looking so relaxed. I had stopped wearing suits and ties to work every day and instead dressed more casually, especially when I didn't have to go to court. Dr. Kutalek and I began to have conversations about another electrophysiology exam to see if the arrhythmia had abated. Such an abatement would alleviate the requirement to continue taking the medicines I was on. We decided, however, to give it more time and then revisit the issue. But it proved a false hope. My heart needed time to heal. Little did I know, it would be years before the doctors, in their considered opinion, would take me off of these intermittently disorienting drugs. Naiveté and ignorance had reared its ugly head again. It was a pity that I had to learn about heart disease, exercise, cholesterol, nutrition and the role of genetics the "hard way." But just like all the other lessons I have learned, am learning and will learn; if you have no one to teach you, life will teach you. You must be thankful when the price you pay to learn these vital lessons is not too high.

It was during this post-recovery period that Wendy Bee's trouble was building to a critical mass. This gracious woman, whom I so admired, was being pushed from all sides. Because of her many complex tax issues and on the advice of myself and other counsel, we put her and her investors into bankruptcy to stave off tax sales and liquidation by city and federal authorities. I had been representing Wendy Bee on a continuous basis for over five years by this time, from midway through my New York Life days. All her legal issues came across my desk and they were many. But now the die was cast. The Feds were demanding payment of long overdue taxes. The city was filing tax liens which devalued any of her properties that could be sold to raise cash, if she wanted to, and they were not in a compromising mood.

Wendy had been fighting this battle relentlessly, denying that she owed the taxes, but nothing she could do persuaded the taxing authorities otherwise. As much historical accounting as we could do didn't move the needle one notch. I referred her to several tax attorneys, but none could provide her any relief because there was none to be had. At first, I put them into Chapter 13, in order to restructure and repay their individual debts, but then their problems expanded and so their bankruptcies were converted to Chapter 11. Chapter 13 bankruptcy is a simplified reorganization for wage earners. A chapter 11 is a reorganization for businesses and is much more complex.

Even bankruptcy, however, proved fruitless because in a bankruptcy certain fiduciary taxes cannot be discharged. The vice grip was closing and this tireless soldier was running out of capacity to push back against it. Wendy, who had always been able to "pull the rabbit out of the hat," had no more tricks she could use. Magic she needed, but a magician she was not.

My office was swamped. I had four Chapter 11 bankruptcies going through my office at one time. With all of the schedules and petitions and filings, my office was clogged up tighter than a cracked sewer drain. One of my researchers remarked that I was working harder after my heart attack than before. Comments like that got my attention. I was back to doing divorces and taking a few criminal appointments. The business was back.

Wendy's problems proved insoluble. All we were doing was delaying the inevitable, doing temporary fixes, and using "lawyer's band-aids." Her tax liabilities and financial entanglements were over-lapping and defied easy resolution. And it was about then that her health issues began to arise.

I was working late one evening when I got a call from Wendy that she was to have surgery within a day or two and that she wanted me to prepare some estate plans for her. I was unaware of the extent of her health problems, but knew she worked very hard, never took a day off, and was hounded by incessant financial problems. Wendy was the matriarch of her family. She provided them with employment, paid for her grandchildren's college tuition, and put them in business. She alone was responsible for the inspiration, ingenuity and drive that created the businesses she ran. In my opinion, I was more than a lawyer to her; and she was more than a client to me, I was her confidante in business matters. We shared a tacit understanding of what she was trying to accomplish as a Black woman, and what she was up against. Wendy knew she could count on me, that I would never let her down–and I didn't.

When I arrived at her office in West Philly she was drinking a white-colored mixture from a straw-like tube stuck into a large plastic kettle. What she was drinking had something to do with her preparation for surgery the next day, she told me. I nodded in acceptance of her explanation without inquiring further.

I had put together some basic will-related documents and we went over them to tailor them more specifically to her needs. She signed the documents without further delay because there was little time to waste. It was then that she told me she was having surgery at a prominent local hospital and that the matter concerned her reproductive organs. I was taken aback. A large tumor had been detected in her uterus and had to be removed. My instincts told me this was trouble, even though I knew none of the details.

Her surgery also resulted in some disquiet. Her tumor was gone but not her disease. Her decline was predictable yet still unexpected for such a vibrant personality. The vultures were closing in and my credibility within her family, which depended upon her, began to lose its grip. I was faithful to her, though, and ever-trusting, the loyal lawyer to a good client whom I loved and respected as a person, but those cracks in her family loyalty, as her health deteriorated, were more than obvious. To my surprise, and somewhat to my chagrin, I was not the favored "go to" person anymore, others became more important to members of her family and they took my place in the business of her affairs as her life hung in the balance. As Wendy Bee's problems continued to escalate, she was no longer the undaunted champion of her family. She had been weakened by an attack from nature. Her relatives, many of whom had worked under her direction, now assumed a greater share of responsibility for running things and their true feelings about the coterie of confidantes, supporters and professionals who worked with their mother was subject to change depending upon the state of grace each occupied in their minds.

One never knows how you are really thought of by lesser known people with whom you come into contact during the course of your life—the grudges they harbor, the jealousies they carry with them—until these people rise to the top and assume some power over you. Then their true preferences are made all-too abundantly clear.

I was sitting at my desk reading my mail when I opened a letter from a law firm I had no pending business with. The letter said that they were now representing Wendy Bee and that I should turn over all my files on her business to them. My heart rate increased and my respiration quickened. I was apoplectic at the thought that I was being treated this way with no notice, not even a phone call, after so many years of loyal service. This was the thankless part of this job. All my work was now going to result in fees to someone else. As Dad often said, I had been "fattening frogs for snakes."

But this time I fought back. I rejected the letter and sent a hellfire and brimstone missive back to the lawyer with a copy to my client indicating that I would do "no such thing" without first consulting with her. I replied that, to do such a thing, in the midst of pending litigation, would be injurious to my client's best interest. I knew that this was only a stalling tactic since the rules governing lawyers required that I did turn over the files. But it did buy me some time to find out what was going on.

However, in spite of my bravura, the "die had been cast", "the handwriting was on the wall." I was out of favor and I knew it was over. What lay ahead would be only a shadow of what had gone before. Yet I still had some leverage because no one knew Wendy's business to the extent that I did. I knew everything about it–"where the dead bodies were buried and where they might rise again," so-to-speak.

Black people often played games with Black professionals. We were good enough to do the "dirty work," but not good enough to get the "good stuff." What angered me so much was that Wendy Bee and I had accomplished so much over the years and I had given her my best effort: winding up her businesses for her, fighting for renewals of her licenses, assuaging the ire of neighbors who lived adjacent to the businesses and were angry about the unruly crowds and loud music late at night, and resolving her secured liens against her real properties.

Wendy was so happy to retire the lein on her business property that she threw a mortgage burning party and danced a jig, waving the mortgage satisfaction papers in the air as she circled the floor of the building. It was exciting to see her celebrate this event. I also helped her defend several slip and fall cases, resolve contract disputes with irate clients over social events that went sour, resolve a check kiting offense, kept the tax authorities at bay as long as I did, drafted the estate plans and performed a myriad of other services. Wendy Bee's business had been an intrinsic part of my law practice.

A few days later, I got word that Wendy wanted to see me. She was in the hospital, weak and drawn with a pallor of sickness. I walked in accompanied by Michelle. When Wendy saw me, she brightened up for a moment and exclaimed, "Mr. Lee, you know my blood sugar was over 300!"

Two of her close relatives were by her bedside and then she said in her gentle but weak voice, looking me in the eye, "Mr. Lee, I had no part in writing that letter." I replied, "I know Wendy, don't worry about it. I will do all I can to help you." She also said "Mr. Lee, I don't owe these people that tax money."

I acquiesced in her plea because I didn't want to upset her further, but I realized the futility of her deathbed argument against paying her taxes. I was reinstated in my role as lead attorney for awhile after that, but the breach was there; my end was clearly visible. Another attorney had been brought in by one of Wendy's trusted friends who had backed her over the years and lent her money in times of need. He was a good guy, but now he wanted his team in there; in addition, he was named as executor under her will.

Within the next few days, steps were taken to finally pay the IRS those back taxes that had haunted this woman most of her business life. I paid them personally at an arranged meeting at the IRS offices in Center City. She raised the money with the help of her insurance agent. I wrote out a check for hundreds of thousands of dollars, and I had them sign a release satisfying the tax obligation. This would be one of the most significant acts I performed on her behalf, and it was fitting that it should fall to me since I was the soldier who had fought this battle with her in the trenches for such a long time. This part of her war was over, even though it was a Pyrrhic victory that no one could take pleasure in. I visited Wendy at her home on one or two further occasions before she finally passed. Each time I visited, I could hear gospel music playing in the background. The atmosphere in her house was surreal and elegiac. We didn't talk much. She was there, but not there,

Rosa Belle Moon Lee (Mother), circa 1993

with a nurse constantly in attendance. My visits were for the purpose of saying goodbye. My job representing her had been completed.

Almost two years from the day she was treated initially for her illness, life ceased to be for her. Wendy Bee died in February of 1993.

Dad and Mom came back to Philadelphia to spend a few days to see how I was progressing. During his stay, Dad stepped up his campaign to interest us in moving to Charlottesville again. His message this time fell on more receptive ears for many reasons. Justin was just beginning his formal education. He was in the second grade, attending a Christian day school in Roxbrough.

Dad kept hammering the point home that the schools in Albemarle County, which surrounded Charlottesville, were just like private schools paid for with taxpayer's money. He kept up this drum beat until it began to make sense. My fight to get Otis into a good high school was still vivid in my mind as well. When I thought about my illness, the fact that I was an only child, the teachers' unions, the cost of a private school for Justin and all the rest, it made sense to go forward to finally go home and move to Virginia.

However, by making this move I was forever, in my mind, closing any chance I might have had of one day being elevated to a judgeship. This was not an ambition that preoccupied my thinking, but it did cross my mind on several occasions as I observed many of my contemporaries making a play to be appointed to the bench. I had the requisite experience to make that leap as well, so why not me? I thought, vainly of course, that I would make a good judge. And the opportunity for a judgeship was especially favorable in Pennsylvania because there, judges are elected rather than appointed as they are in Virginia.

I toyed with this prospect from time to time, but it never really galvanized me enough for me to take any concerted action to do the work required to make it happen. A judgeship offered many opportunities, but it also carried with it many disadvantages. During this time, I continued to practice law on a daily basis. I received a court appointment from the Dependency Court, a branch of the Domestic Relations Court, where juveniles who are neglected by their parents are adjudicated, in order to determine if they are "dependent." If they are, the state or city will intervene to provide them with care, even housing if necessary. The city will take them from their neglectful parents and put them into foster care or the care of a relative until the parent is deemed fit to be restored to good parenting.

The case I was appointed to came to be known as the case of "The Woman Who Threw Her Baby Out of the Window." It made the Daily News and the Philadelphia Inquirer. In a fit of mental disturbance, my client had thrown her infant son out of the second-floor window of her modest two-story frame home in South Philadelphia. Such a thoughtless, brazen, heartless act by a mother aimed at the destruction of her infant son shocked the conscience of the community. The baby survived the incident without injury only through the grace of God.

I worked this case with two other lawyers, along with a child advocate for the infant. It stayed in the courts for months as we went back and forth discussing my client's mental state, her mental examinations and her compliance with psychotherapy. The District Attorney's Office considered filing charges against the mother, but a deal was worked out which allowed her to plead to something akin to reckless endangerment, so long as she received the mental help she so desperately needed.

All the parties in this tragedy were poor Whites from South Philadelphia. My client, "Mother Choley," was a thin, pale, quiet, unassertive White female with stringy blond hair who had badly lost her way–a manic depressive. She was prescribed antipsychotic medicines, which she was required to take by the court.

This case was memorable because it demonstrated how a momentary loss of mental stability, whether brought on by psychosis, delusion, a fixation, or fantasy, could cause irreparable damage both to the person and to their loved ones. If we forget for one moment the consequences of our acts, we can end up throwing ourselves "out of the window."

At the same time, Abu Jamal's case continued to wind its way through the Pennsylvania Appellate Court system. There would be no further trial of the facts. The door was closed on that. It was clear to all who had followed this case that the system, regardless of the celebrity, controversy, or notoriety of the defendant, was not going to allow Abu Jamal to walk free, once he had been convicted of killing a police officer. It was not in the system's nature to allow this.

Appeal after appeal kept Jamal from the electric chair, but he remained incarcerated with no rational hope of ever being set free. The best he could hope for was not to be executed. If truth is the final arbiter of justice, only Abu Jamal can answer the question whether or not he deserves to be set free. Here was another case where a single moment of irrationality gave rise to one person's death, a family's irrevocable loss and another's lost lifetime: of freedom, productivity, pain and agony.

Lang won a trip to Switzerland and did some skiing while there, enjoying the snow-covered mountains and the camaraderie of his colleagues. He won the trip because he was a perennial top club producer in his company and in the industry. However, when he returned, he developed a cough that he could not shake. Lang aspired to acquire the better things of life. He wanted a gentle woman. I always thought he wanted a woman like my Michelle, a cultured woman, modest and refined. I know that Lang admired Michelle and sought to find for his second wife a similar composite of qualities. He wanted to re-establish a nice home with accouterments that reflected his taste, especially his new found place as a well-respected and successful insurance salesman and financial planner. He wanted to have and to compete with the folks he sold insurance to—the professional class.

In the end, Lang married again for the second time. This marriage was to a younger woman who was decent, energetic and comely, but she had two teenage daughters. I argued against the marriage because I felt that, since he had already raised three daughters, why go through that experience again? Especially with children old enough to know that he was not their father. I didn't want to see him struggling with a household again after what he had been through the first time around. But this lady was the love of his life, the dream that he wanted to make into his reality.

Lang Dixon and I spent many good years together. We collaborated on estate plans for many of the most prominent Black doctors in Philadelphia, a dermatology professor at the University of Pennsylvania, a prominent editorial writer for the Philadelphia Daily News and Inquirer, Black businessmen and a host of lesser-known people. I met with Kenny Gamble of the Gamble and Huff songwriting team that original the "Philadelphia Sound." Access was provided by an insurance agent who had been a back-up singer with one of the singing groups working with Gamble and Huff. Mr. Gamble listened and commented as the agent and I discussed tax issues, but it was clear he was skeptical of both of us and nothing went forward after that. Lang did this same business with my counterparts in the White community, but his "trust" was with me; I enabled him and he enabled me. Between what I did with Lang and with New York Life, I was fully ensconced in estate planning during the earlier years of my practice.

Lang and I didn't always agree on the issues of race, and we had many heated and spirited debates on the subject. One that caused me to get angry with him occurred while we were seated at a bar in Center City attending some after-work get-together. The question was whether or not it was a good investment to buy a home in a predominately Black neighborhood. He thought it was, I thought it was not. My conservative real estate, professional and investment background pulled me in a different direction than Lang, even though I could understand his point. It was simply not where I would put my money. My point was that the services that would be provided to a White community would outpace those provided to a predominately Black community. On top of that were the issues of housing values and schools. I became so miffed at his attitude that I left the argument unresolved and went home early.

I often got angry with Lang, but could never stay mad at him for long. Ironically, in the end, both of Lang's post-divorce residential investments were in a White neighborhood. During this period of my life, Lang was the closest person I could call a friend in Philadelphia. We started out together in the summer of 1979, and we fundamentally saw the world the same way, despite our little spats. We understood life insurance and its role in estate planning, and since I had a sales background I intuitively understood his approach and how to help him achieve his objectives, which dovetailed nicely with mine. So I was also helping myself.

We both made money, but also wanted to help Black people move into the arena of advanced underwriting. We both saw the world as Africans—through the prism of color. I learned from my travels that many Africans, including African-Americans, see the world as black or white, there is no in between, everything comes down to race. I think this is true, and from what I observed about Lang, he thought so too. Our discussions about politics and money about family and values all had the undercurrent of race. Perhaps as Black men who were striving to make a difference, race was intrinsic to our being. It was all around us. It affected just about everything we touched or did. How could we get away from it? We could not.

Not long after Lang's second marriage, he bought his dream home. It was an overpriced house in an upper-middle class neighborhood in a suburb north of Philadelphia. It was his dream to own a house like that. Its new construction was brick and frame with a large atrium foyer, an elegant winding stairwell, four bedrooms, a modern kitchen and bathrooms that were built with ceramic tiles. I closed the deal for him on the house and was glad to see him get what he wanted.

Unfortunately, not long after his second marriage and the purchase of his new home, he was diagnosed with lung cancer. The dream he had sought to make a reality was tragically short-lived. He fought the disease bravely. He had his left lung removed and rallied strongly for a while, but within two years of his initial diagnosis the cancer metastasized to his right lung. At that point all hope was lost.

Before his final hours, his wife called me at my office and asked that I come to the hospital. It was Chestnut Hill, the same community hospital in northwest Philadelphia where Justin had been born eleven years before. As I entered his hospital room, Lang lay prostrate on his bed with the scar his first wife had inflicted upon him still visible above his left eye, his second wife seated by his bedside. We talked briefly without really saying anything. The shallowness of our small talk within the poignancy of the moment was clearly inappropriate, but not easily avoided. Life had come down "to making nice." His room was already pregnant with tributes from other people who had visited him for the same reason that I was there: to say, "goodbye old chum, job well done."

Suddenly, and without notice, I bent over and kissed him on his forehead. I don't know why I did that. It was a sudden emotional reaction to an impulse that urged me to take a part of him with me, at least momentarily. As I kissed his forehead, I could taste the salt in his skin. I didn't like the taste. It reminded me of what I had read some time ago about slave traders who tasted the skin of the slaves to see if salt was present which indicated in their minds the health of the slaves brought from Africa, a determinant of how strong they were.

Out of respect, I showed no displeasure. I endured it. Afterwards, I reasoned that I wanted to show Lang that I loved him.

He died on July 15, 1994, not long after that short hospital stay. I received a call from his wife while I was attending a Virginia Bar Association meeting in Virginia Beach. The call came in at the same time as the O.J. Simpson ride along the freeway was taking place on the TV news. O. J. was on his way to turn himself in when Lang died.

I loved Lang and respected him because he did well and was a decent guy. He made it on his own and finished in the black. He didn't have the privilege of a middle-class upbringing, or of a college education. He didn't have the firmness of a father's guidance, or the economic or moral support of his immediate family, but in spite of it all he persisted and won.

I said a few words at Lang's funeral at the request of his wife. I told the assembled congregation "that he had believed in his work, had bought what he sold, and that his work transcended the immediate gratification of just making money. He tried and succeeded in helping lift his brothers and sisters to a new level, using his knowledge of estate planning."

I drafted his will and trust and settled Lang's estate as his executor and co-trustee. I successfully managed his trust, along with PNC Bank, for the benefit of his wife and five grandchildren, as co-trustee for eighteen years after his death. He trusted me to do that for him. He had believed in what he sold. And I believed in him.

In William Shakespeare's play Julius Caesar, Mark Antony delivers a funeral oration in which he says, "Friends, Romans, countryman, lend me your ears—I come to bury Caesar, not to praise him. The evil that men do lives after them; the good is oft interred with their bones."

I pray that this is not true, that the good that men do, if it is interred with their bones, rises up from their graves with their souls in the form of a resurrection, to be used and felt by those loved ones left behind as a testament to what they tried to do while on this earth. Wendy and Lang were both good human beings who tried "to do good," and to uplift their people. I pray that their good works live after them.

— — —

Our move to Virginia began to take concrete form. We traveled to Charlottesville and looked at houses with my mother and father. Dad was the one who spent most of the time with us. We looked at several houses but since Michelle and I had been looking at houses for some time we knew what we wanted: an off-street, quiet environment with a two-car garage. When we found the home we wanted in Earlysville, a small rural community a few miles north of the city, it was a repeat of the Sedgwick Street experience. It was love at first sight. I was so taken by the verdant farmlands that surrounded the area, the absence of graffiti, the presence of farm animals, the pastoral undulation of the land, that it brought to mind the stories about the African savannahs that enriched the barren plains of that continent.

The slower pace, the quiescence, rusticity and spaciousness that my new environs held forth was a refuge from the stress of putting a life together in the asphalt jungles of Chicago, Washington D.C, and Philadelphia. The gentility of the lawyer community in Charlottesville, and the niceness and polite manners of my opponents—at least on the surface—both inside and outside the courtroom, was in stark contrast to the bullying, arrogant tactics of my former lawyer opponents.

The final realization of this move of our residence back to my home town was the embodiment of my most heartfelt hopes and dreams for a release from the pressures and strife of competition, isolation and anxieties that had culminated in my heart attack in Philadelphia. We signed the contract on the home of our dreams in the spring of 1990, but we had no jobs to come to in Charlottesville. I used to remark to my friends "that I now knew where I was going to retire, but now I had to find out how to make a living until then."

With our move now a fact, this was my valediction to Philadelphia. The halcyon days in my lair were gone. I would spend no more time in my warm and comfy office, secure in the knowledge that I had created a legal career and a real estate business sufficient to take care of my family for the rest of our lives and that would last as long as I wanted it to.

My métier was my tax orientation, small business acumen, real estate insight, financial understanding at my level, people skills, management capability, legal savvy and basic honesty. It was nothing to write home about, just a question of excelling in the basics, the fundamentals.

How do you leave these things? My minister said during one of our meetings soon after our move that it "was a good move but a big move." Being an only child, I wanted to move back to my parents' place of residence, but it was difficult with a mature law practice and a large Victorian house that we redecorated and remodeled from stem to stern that Michelle and I both loved. I didn't disclose my pending move to anyone except a select few, mostly family members. With a closing date set on our new house, I prepared myself mentally and professionally for the move to Virginia.

Most important, I had to gain admittance to the Virginia Bar. I made an inquiry as to the requirements for admission. I had become something of an expert in bar admissions from my early trials, but I needed copies of their forms and procedures. Even though I had not taken the Virginia Bar exam after graduating from law school, I was eligible for reciprocity because I had practiced law for over five years and was in good standing with the Pennsylvania Bar. I more than exceeded their requirements, and I was born, raised and educated in primary and secondary schools in the state.

There was a certain irony to all of this. Am I brave enough to say that, in the grand scheme of things, my Illinois Bar experience really didn't matter, except for the learning that took place and the growing up—the *sine qua non* of my legal education. No, of course I can't say that, because it did matter. Yet it wasn't my Waterloo, nor was it an indelible stain, nor the only possible route to my ultimate goal of practicing law in Virginia that I made it out to be. It was in Chicago that my aspiration for, and appreciation of, excellence began. In my heart I knew that it had always been my desire to practice law in Virginia, but because of my fears and my desire to "Go West," I had postponed that pursuit. I had fought the "bar wars and the practice wars" on foreign soil, saving the best and most important battleground for last.

My admission to the Virginia Bar was my "golden fleece," and it was still available to me. After twenty-six years, I was coming home to the land of my birth. My journey had taken the form of an "ear," an ear that listened to God, an ear that followed His direction as He directed my path. From Washington D.C., I had the faith to go to Chicago after law school, even though Dad argued against it, not knowing a soul, nor what lay ahead. I had the faith to go Philadelphia knowing only one family member, but otherwise having nothing but my ingenuity to help me. And now I had the faith to go home. I had come full circle. The "knight errant" mission in Illinois had been just part of my passage to where I was now. It was not, in fact, the end in itself that had so occupied my mind at the time and filled me with an erroneous notion of who I was.

Although we had found the house we wanted and I had to wind down my businesses in Philly, there were other, equally pressing matters to attend to, particularly my health. Dr. Kutalek felt it was time for me to be readmitted to the hospital to see if the arrhythmia was still there. I trusted him. He was gentle and caring. His associate, Dr. Hessan, was of the same demeanor. Together, they would see to my welfare, I was sure. I felt safe with them. So, although I feared the exam, I was willing to try again because the benefits were so enticing: a chance to rid myself of the pills that were a real nuisance to take and had several aggravating side effects. The hope that my heart had healed enough to eliminate these medicines was enough to encourage me to go forward with the test.

I was admitted to the hospital on a Tuesday to be weaned of my pills. The doctors could only perform a true test to determine the presence of my arrhythmia after all my medications had worked their way out of my system, so my test would not be until that Friday.

As I waited in my hospital bed, I worked on my Virginia Bar application. I filled out all the answers and supplied them with all the information they requested. While I was doing so, a roommate moved in. This gentleman was an elderly White man who had been on vacation with his family touring Philadelphia. He had a cardiac event that caused him to forget where he was. In fact, he apparently wandered off from his family, who were thrown into a panic in light of his condition.

I listened to his family talk when they visited him. His wife tried to console him and calm him down, but he would have none of it. He was agitated and feisty. His doctor came in while his wife was with him and told him what they were going to do. They wanted to perform some test or other and requested he take some medications. But the old man complained that he'd had enough of it all.

When they left, I got his attention and said to him, "Man, you can't give up, you have to fight back!" He responded wittily, but with a twinge of exhaustion and resignation, "I would, but they've taken all the fight out of me!" All my life up to this point I had been fighting; in Charlottesville during the high school years for my physical safety and to form a self-image; at Howard I was fighting to mature as a young adult and to learn how to study; in Chicago I fought to break into the professional ranks; in Philly I fought to be a competent professional, now I was in the fight of my life, for my health. I prayed that I still had some fight left in me. I was still young and by all accounts there should be some fight left in the tank. After all, many others had overcome greater obstacles than mine.

I often think about this incident because sometimes, after going through all that I've gone through trying to make it, life does take all the fight out of you. As each year passes, the "fight" in you declines.

I went through my third electrophysiology test without any harmful effects. The test was much milder than the ones administered at UVa, but the result was still not good. The arrhythmia had not abated; it was alive and well. So there would be no suspension of my medications, even for a minute.

Moving day arrived on August 21, 1991. The moving company pulled its long trailer in front of our Victorian house in Philadelphia and went to work. I didn't think we would ever get all our stuff out of the house, but they did over two days. Otis was there to help. He was back in town on leave from the military. His time in the army was winding down, and I could see just how much the experience had changed him. He was calmer, more appreciative of us and wanted to resume his education. In fact, he was a great help. He rode with the movers from Philadelphia to Virginia to make sure our belongings were handled with care.

Michelle and I left a day before to close on the house and make other arrangements. After we closed, my father, Michelle and I went out to the house. Once there, I ran around the periphery of the lot and touched each tree with my right hand and shouted, "Free, I'm free at last!"

My father sat on the red brick wall in the rear of our house with Michelle by his side as I ran around the periphery of the back yard giving high fives to all the tree limbs and bushes I could touch; much like an athlete slapping the hands of adoring fans as they entered or left the arena. He realized how important this day was for him, as well as for me and my family. After all, he had avidly advocated that I leave Philadelphia after my illness and had helped make the financial arrangements to make this day come true.

We were so excited that we slept on the bare floor the night before the movers arrived. My mother and Dad wondered why we wanted to do such a thing, but we were so proud of our new home and so thankful to be there. We were finally residents of, and domiciled in, Virginia! The acquisition of this property in this location was a desiderate vision and now an accomplishment. It offered the prospect of a calmer life, a rustic environment and a slower pace. I would dwell in the rolling pasture lands of rural Albemarle County, Virginia. My life in the big cities of Chicago, Washington D.C., and Philadelphia was over. Now I only wanted peace or as much of it as I could get. The death of Lang and Wendy Bee, and the death of a less-close friend, an acquaintance, who died of a massive heart attack trying to make a million dollars and my heart attack had been the low points, the nadir. But purchasing our new home in Earlysville with the promise of a new environment in which to live and work was the *ne plus ultra*. Life is a tenancy; it exists only for a term of years and as Dad often said, "we don't know what the future holds but we do know who holds the future."

I restored my soul and enlivened my vitality and, like a phoenix, I rose from ashes charred from the heat of the embattled flame. I got my second breath and embarked upon the second half of my legal career as a Virginia attorney. My Philadelphia experience had been a platform and a pallet, a large and broad base upon which to further build. In time I would apply the exact same business model and strategies this time to even greater heights where the stakes were higher and the responsibilities more acute. I would be of service to my father, conserve his estate, see to the care of my aging mother and finish the work that I began in the fall of 1969.

— — —

I was now commuting between Philadelphia and Charlottesville. This commute would later evolve into a "rotation" between Philadelphia and Charlottesville, a rotation that would last almost ten years. The transition to Virginia was a vexing, frustrating, a mean and pained experience. My association with lawyers I brought in to care-take my practice resulted in a nullity. Avarice, self-interest and jealousy characterized these relationships. Nasty fights with these lawyers ensued from my transition. These unsavory entanglements caused me to get to the point where I could no longer perforce to associate with other lawyers in my practice in-house; the emotional and professional costs were too high

The lawyers I chose to associate with during this time, though I did my best to choose the right ones, did not have my values, nor my interest at heart. They did not appreciate the hard work that had gone into building the practice they came into; hence they treated my practice with irreverence, after all, none of their blood and tears had gone into building the practice. In the end I wore them down, and beat them down and obstructed them until they realized that it was a losing proposition for them to continue to press in on me. The conflicts just faded out over time. Law cases have a life of their own. They only die when there is no longer any energy to keep them alive; they die a natural death. And so it was with the many open cases that were on the books when I moved to Virginia. I had to stick with them until they just died out.

Michelle and Justin were permanently housed in our home in Earlysville. My professional life was a Manichean dichotomy. Moving between the law, real estate and moral values was ever present in my life. But now with a law practice in Philadelphia and the start of a law practice in Charlottesville, the Manicheism was more pronounced than ever, and it would take the providence of a spiritual God to keep it all together. I was truly subject to the demands and rewards of the law, that secular god, but there was no other way for this transition to work in the immediate years following the move except for this dualism.

Michelle and I traveled to Philly for Wendy's funeral. The funeral was befitting Wendy's elegance. It was dignified, elevated and special. I was sorry to see her go, but all I could do was to bid her farewell and recall the fond memories and take satisfaction in the fact that I had served her well. Her family honored me by making me an honorary pallbearer.

As the novelty of the move to Charlottesville wore off, the reality of this region's culture became real to us. The community was inhospitable to Black professionals. Michelle who had over twenty years of experience as a health care executive had to start over as a glorified secretary. I had to resume taking court appointments which I had ceased accepting in Philadelphia five years earlier, which paid next to nothing in Virginia: the work was demanding, the expectations still high. I made more money in one week in Philadelphia than I made in three months in Charlottesville. We were so frustrated with the lack of opportunity, the culture and politics that we thought seriously about moving back to Pennsylvania. We went back and actually looked at some houses, but in the end we stayed put. Realizing that we loved our new home and the rural environment, the schools, and the lower cost of living. And I did not want to disappoint my parents who were looking forward to our being present in this community, so we stayed.

I will always be indebted to the state of Pennsylvania and the city of Philadelphia. Without the grace of Pennsylvania, I would not be where I am today and would not have grown as a person and as a lawyer and investor. Pennsylvania and Philadelphia will always have a very special place in my heart. I did not go to Philadelphia to live permanently, but I became a *de facto* expatriate of Philadelphia.

Life teaches us many lessons. What are the most important values in life? Certainly not money and not vanity or material things, though a sufficient amount of these resources are required to live well, but the essence of life is not to be found there. The essence of life, in my view, embraces those values closest to nature. Ralph Waldo Emerson said, "Adopt the pace of nature, her secret is patience." Examine nature, how it replicates life, the pace, the order, the sublime, the meditative, quietude, the reasoned, the rural; the changing of the seasons, the rainy days, the cloudy days, the sunny days. If you misconstrue a day nature brings and act intemperately, you may not live to regret it. A given day may dawn cloudy but the sun may shine before the evening. These are the values that are transcendent.

Apparently, I had that firewall buried deep within my inner being, between me and my dispair, because I didn't become a Joseph Rabearivelo, who, bereft of an adequate self image and poor self esteem killed himself because he failed to meet the standard of the French colonizer. That firewall had become an "antique" but it was still there, It needed to be pulled out, dusted off and polished up to remove as much as possible the accumulated debris of structural and institutional racism, ignorance, and benign neglect, that had piled up over years obstructing its function and obscuring its presence. The opacity that this rubble created caused the misguided perception of self and an unthinking immersion in the pound down dogma of Anglo-American and European ethnocentrism, all of which should have been thrown into an ossuary to disintegrate and degrade into the dust from whence it came. I pray, oh God! That you release me from these shackles! Release me! Release me!

In his book *Religion Explained* (2001)[29], Archaeologist Pascal Boyer defines a person as, "a life, personal identity and sentience, a breath that talks." He says that without sentience we are nothing. I agree with him. Black children and all precocious minority youngsters and even those that are not so precocious, are vulnerable and sensitive to the issues of personal identity and sentience. Dr. Kenneth Clark, the noted psychologist demonstrated this fact during the litigation of *Brown vs. The Board of Education*. And their parents had better be mindful and guardians of their children's self-image as it develops. They must make sure they protect against damage in this area.

Finally, let me conclude about my Philadelphia experience by repeating, as close as I can recall, what Paul Newman says at the end of the 1959 Warner Brothers film "The Young Philadelphians." It captures my thinking exactly: "I found out something about myself. Maybe I'm not as good or as much as I hoped I could be, but I'm not as bad as I thought I was."

38

RED CLAY OF GEORGIA

THE MAN FROM GEORGIA MADE GOOD. "Red" they called him fondly, was raised in southern Georgia. One of seven children raised by a widowed mother. He knew poverty, but not hunger; knew deprivation but did not lack for love and affection. He experienced loss, but not the loss of hope, pain but not despair. His energy for triumph over adversity was boundless, and he reinsured that his later life would not reflect his humble roots.

His face was round, his hair black with distinguished grey at the peak and closely cropped, his build rotund but not obese, his height not tall but well above short, his complexion rust colored or "red," his voice, southern with a discernible tone unique to his persona, for clarity and strength, and he wore glasses. These physical features describe the outward appearance of my father, but do not begin to describe this complex human being. My dad was far more than these physical features. Within the family he was a husband, a father, an uncle, a grandfather, a son and a brother. Professionally he was an educator and his avocation was real estate investment. Within those fields, he wore many hats: that of a trailblazer, a schoolmaster, a principal, a teacher, an administrator, a supervisor, a resource, a counselor to his colleagues, a realtor and a businessman.

Dad was diagnosed with a rare cancer two years before he passed. The rarity of its kind did not make it any less virulent. I knew from personal experience, having witnessed the progression of Wendy Bee and Lang Dixon's cancerous diseases, that he would not be around two years from that date. On one of my trips from Philadelphia, I stopped off at the hospital to visit him. And as I sat there, the nurses began his chemotherapy. I cried silently, though some water filled my eyes, because I was sitting a bit away from him he could not discern my emotions. I knew that was the beginning of the end. And just like clockwork, two years after his treatment and diagnosis the reality of his demise arrived.

Dad was determined to attend his 50th college reunion at his alma mater, Fort Valley State University in Fort Valley, Georgia. Whether to travel to the reunion was debated and even his doctor's opinion was solicited. He went. Mom and Dad enjoyed the experience, and it made him happy to go back to where his uplift began.

Aunt Dilo, clairvoyant as she was, arrived at Leonard-Belle Heights the night before Christmas on December 24th, 1998. She knew instinctively that Dad was seriously ill. She had surmised it on his last trip to Georgia, when she said to him "Red what's wrong with your head?" and he didn't reply. Dad was glad to see his youngest sister. They were close in age and had grown up together, perhaps closer than he was to his other siblings, but not by much.

On Christmas day we all gathered at Mom and Dad's home. It had snowed the night before. And the next day, the bright sun sparkled against the snow that covered the grounds; emblazoned by the glimmering white ice crystals that hung from the tree limbs and branches that accentuated the bright reflection of the snow. The affect made for a magical rustic environment. We all went outside for a walk and Dad walked over his treasured grounds for one last time. He seemed to know that this would be the last time in this life he would see his beloved Leonard-Belle Heights, his Monticello, the white house on the hill built by a Black man and his wife. He looked over the place with especial care, noticing the snow covered shrubs he and Mother had labored in the long languid hours of past hot summers to plant, having planted more azaleas than they needed which was their approach. Mother, ironically, had said previously, affirming the sanity of their approach, "we have been planting all of our lives. That's why we have what we have."

Otis, my oldest was there, and held Dad's hand as we walked down the driveway. And down to Woodberry Road to Old Ballard and back up again. I walked along side while the others trailed behind. My youngest was there, but he was still young in age and appreciation for the gravity of this quintessential moment. We all knew instinctively that this was his last panoramic view, though no one even thought to mutter an implication of that thought. God made his traveled journey ethereal especially gracious and a wonderful experience for all of us. And we all appreciated the magnitude and the significance of what we were sharing with the patriarch of the family.

After our walk on the outside we went back inside, and he gave each of us a $100.00 bill in crisp new money. He evidently had planned to do this and we all wondered, well, why Dad was doing this? He was not questioned closely; and although we displayed a quizzical look on our faces, he had no answer. He just smiled a male Mona Lisa type smile, but it was his way of saying goodbye in a manner that somewhat reflected a value that was important: giving, not always receiving, making a happy moment out of that which was innately sad, making a party out of a farewell, passing around a symbol of value. He had seen his dream home in its resplendent glory that snow-laden morning. The bright snow draped the house and the trees like a canopy of white and silver light refracted through a quiet, stilled forest on a hill, in his beloved Albemarle County. He had received the blessing he earned. His disease was a frightful nightmare, but he bore it well. A rare cancer, but virulent in its manifestation. I did all I could do to minimize any possible disfigurement that some sadistic doctors at UVA would have put him through, for I personally would not allow it. I got a referral to the Medical College of Virginia in Richmond where he was treated with a great deal more compassion. Mother and I were pleased with the way they received him and treated him. In times like these, you do what you can knowing the futility of your efforts, but you must try.

The frightful call came a day later at 2 a.m. in the morning on December 28, 1998. Mother said in a nervously strained voice, "Otis, its Lee! I cannot do any-

Otis L. Lee, Sr. (Father), circa 1995

thing with him." I said, "Mother just take it easy, we'll be right over." What she was trying to say, but could not because of the excitement of the moment, was that Dad had collapsed on to the floor in his bedroom and was unconscious and that she could not revive him. Michelle and I, as quickly as we could, scrambled to get to the house without getting stopped by the police for speeding. Since it was late at night the roads were clear and there was little traffic. It still seemed like it took an eternity to get there. When we arrived we saw Dad laid out on the left side of his bedroom floor motionless, his eyes closed. He was gone, his end had come. He faced it bravely as he had done all the adversities of his life. We all must be as brave when that "outer door" is alarmed, and it now rang for him: seventy-four years in the making. My heart was broken as well as that of mother, his grandchildren, daughter-in-law and his surviving siblings, but what can you do. Nothing. As he often lamented, "you don't know nothing! " meaning we are ignorant about what is going on in our bodies and what state of health we are in at any given moment.

In the order of the death ritual, the Albemarle Rescue Squad was called. They tried in vain to resuscitate him, followed by the police and then the undertaker. It was both eerie and uncanny to see a police officer waiting in his patrol car in front of the house with his lights on in the darkness of the early morning. It all seemed to make everything official. It was as though the police were there to make sure no crime had been committed, no murder.

His death had not come as an immediate surprise although the moment of its occurrence was unsettling. The dogged and stoic personality of this man was well known to those of us who knew him. He bore his burdens bravely and confronted his trials with valor; such was the nature of his character. To those who loved him dearly, the immutable event of death in Dad's case was an ironic blessing for him and us. The continuation of life for him at that time, suffering from the unyielding disease that attacked him, portended only more grief and suffering. I believe that Dad received God's blessing because of his virtues and devoutness. God had spared Dad from a tortuous death and instead had given him an efficient and painless end to his life that the disease would otherwise not have allowed. Dad was a proud man, and he could not accept his death in any other manner than with pride, courage and dignity.

He lay on the bier stiff, silent and still, draped in a velvet burgundy gold trimmed shroud. The trestle board of his life was embodied in the stillness, dignity and solemnity of his presence. The serenity of that moment was broken by my oldest son who remarked "that Dad looked good." The night was new and the air was cool. His flesh now cold, only thoughts of past memories heightened by the proximity of life to death pervaded the moment. He looked regal, the king we knew he was. His death occurred less than two days before I saw him again now possessed of the ages and as an indelible memory and irreparable loss for me and for those who truly loved him.

For the living, death is passage to the next stage of an uncertain existence, based upon a speculative subjective faith in the hereafter. The strength of your belief determines whether you get there or not. My dad's death meant for me the bellowing sound of a rusting alarm clock that life for me had changed forever; I was now on the spot. My muse had been silenced. All that remained were the reverberations and repetitions of the pithy remarks and sententious sayings filled with his wisdom echoing in my brain. These appellations would take the place of his physical presence as a speaking apparition, as the doppelganger directing my actions through wit and humor.

Fortunately for me, my mother survived my father and I still have her to lean on. But, the loss of Father propelled my life forward, and now I am front and center, the tower, the lighthouse, the standard bearer, the one whose judgment is relied upon. Some are made to bear this burden at an earlier age, without the bulwark of education and experience. Was I ready for this evolution? Ready or not there it was.

Dad had flair. His public life was controversial and well known by the public in this community. He was vilified by the misinformed and the malevolent, yet he earned the respect of many influential people and common folks. No one's life is one dimensional: all lives are multifaceted. On December 4, 1991, Dad was awarded an honorary Doctorate of Humane Letters degree from the M.C. Allen School of Religion at Virginia Seminary and College in Lynchburg, Virginia—the oldest Black college in Lynchburg. The degree recited his 36 years as an educator, 23 years of which were spent in Albemarle County. From that point on he referred to himself as Dr. Lee. Dad also served as the Grand Master of the local Prince Hall Lodge of Free and Accepted Masons, Inc. of Charlottesville, Virginia, culminating in fifty years of service to the Masons.

A reporter from the Daily Progress called the house before the funeral to inquire about the funeral service and to get comments from the family on a story the paper wanted to run on Dad's passing. We were put off and angry. Why would a paper that had seen to it that they castigated this man, never acknowledging any of his contributions, invade the privacy of our home to sell newspapers at our expense? I slammed the phone down on the reporter with glee. Why could they not leave us alone even at this mournful time? Instead they sought comments on a man's life they had no basis upon which to comment.

But my gesture did not stop the political hacks and other shallow men seeking refuge from nowhere from making their comments. One of whom was Blake Caravati, a former city councilman and mayor. I confronted him outside of the Charlottesville District Court when we were both there several months after Dad was funeralized. I had been looking for him to have the confrontation. The Daily Progress quoted him as saying "Lee could have done more." I asked him "how could you comment on what my father could have done? You know nothing about what he did, not to speak of what contributions, if any, he made to society, before you even came into contact with him, before Charlottesville came into his life!" He sputtered and I trembled. My upper lip nervously twitched as I got my protest out. Not because he was a leading figure in politics at this time, but because confrontations always require the effrontery to have them and confrontations require more energy. Tremble or not, I got it out. I could not let the issue rest, because in my judgment he was wrong. He should have refrained and avoided being used by the Daily Progress to sell newspapers at someone else's expense. But the lure of headlines and publicity to a politician is enticing.

On the day of his funeral, the weather was cold, snowy, overcast, grey and dreadful. Mother and I thought of postponing the funeral to another day, but she preferred to continue because we were tired and wanted an end to this phase of the grieving process. We considered the effect of the weather on those far away who wanted to attend but were amazed at those who braved the weather and showed up. We were equally amazed at those who failed to attend using the weather as a convenient excuse. Based upon who attended, we could separate the good weather friends from the bad weather friends.

We gathered at the house and were escorted to the waiting limousines, long, black and sleek. As we drove along the route to Mount Zion African Baptist Church, the local church that Dad had been a member of for all of his stay in Charlottesville, I saw a brown colored hawk with white markings perched high on an overhead electrical wire peering eerily over the procession of cars. His perch was erect as though at attention.

As I gazed upon the hawk, my mind recalled an event that occurred years before on a warm summer morning during a routine visit to my parent's home. I arose early that morning and went for a morning jog along Old Ballard Road, the country road abutting the northwestern end our home. As I rounded a curve a hawk suddenly swooped down and seized a pigeon walking several feet in front of me. The hawk placed its talons around the pigeons' neck as if to kill it or take it away. Hearing my approach the hawk turned its facile neck, gazed upon my bearing with its recessed eyes, appraising the situation. It released the pigeon and flew away. The pigeon gathered itself and later flew away.

At that time, it had occurred to me that I symbolized the hawk and my father the pigeon. My reasoning was based upon a nasty fight that had been going on between an evil clan of local officials and their compatriots and my father over some of his business dealings. And I, in the heat of that battle, entered the fray as his attorney and advocate without notice to them. After my appearance, the texture of that pre-existing fight changed. Our adversaries had not anticipated that I, the son they had forgotten about, the Philadelphia lawyer trained in the street warfare of Philadelphia litigation would assume the mantle of defender of my father. These adversaries were applying the politics of total destruction in an effort to destroy or to mortally wound him at that time. This struggle persisted for several years and was regular fodder for the local newspapers and tabloid press in the area.

Upon seeing that hawk again at this time, I felt a resumption of divine presence in my life. I wanted to make real that there was a rhyme and a reason for my existence beyond the existential, and nothing pleased me more than to exist for the purpose of helping my father who had gone well beyond the call of duty for me.

The funeral service was well attended considering the weather. My oldest son spoke movingly of his grandfather. I followed him to the podium filled with nervousness and grief. I thought of the time when we lived on Ridge St. Mother was cooking a meal, and I do not remember exactly what we were talking about, but during that conversation I said to her, "at Dad's funeral I am going to speak." Mother in her usual sharp wit replied, "are you sure you will be in any condition to do that?" I was too young to know of the emotional depth about which she spoke. I had no response.

I spoke about my dad at the funeral, as I viewed his casket lying there beneath the stage. I looked out into the audience, their eyes transfixed on me, and I wondered what they were thinking. Was it of me or of him? Did they expect me to get through this or was I expected to breakdown in tears and uncontrollable grief. Either way, each set of circumstances could have been expected.

Before I left the podium I saw a diminutive man slip into the back of the sanctuary and take a seat. I recognized him. A snake in the form of a well-known Black Charlottesvillian, he was a part of the evil cabal. Why was he there? Was it out of curiosity or a begrudging respect? Or was it to confirm in his own mind that Mr. Lee was dead? He left before the service was over to avoid, in my opinion, being seen by the family.

We imported a preacher to preach the eulogy because Dad had little regard for the ministers that pastored the local churches. Dad was a devout Christian, though far from being a saint. He took his religion seriously, but made room for the charlatans and the fraudulent. He hardly missed a Sunday service and he held strong feelings about the order and processes of religion. Dad had been used to a "silk stocking" church in Richmond, but had to settle for the "country church" level in Charlottesville. I was a strong advocate for not using any local preacher. Dad and I shared a common disdain for fake religiosity and the purveyors of the con. Though fraught with delay, inconvenience and tribulation, our minister of choice was Dr. G. Daniel Jones of Grace Baptist Church of Germantown, in Philadelphia, Pennsylvania, my former pastor, who agreed to eulogize him. Dr. Jones made it into Charlottesville on that blustery, inhospitable day, overcoming many travel inconveniences flying from Philadelphia to Charlottesville. I will be forever grateful for his service. We were gladdened by his appearance on the podium when we entered the church. It was as though, through all of this sorrow, the Lord's blessing had again shone through.

The church service ended, the funeral procession made its way to the burial grounds. After a brief grave-side service, my father was entombed in a mausoleum. The snow and the wind continued to howl, and the bitter cold betokened a harshness to the reality of his death. No solace could be found in the comfort of the weather. I thought of it all as pure unadulterated reality—a "dog's breakfast," so to speak—the theater of the death ritual alarming my outer door, letting me know along with the others who were thoughtful, that at some appointed time in the future a similar ritual would await them.

Is this what it had come down to, the last sad act? Where was the life after death? The essential dogma of the religion so dominant in his life and the lives of all the other Christians gathered to funeralize him. The *raison d'etre* of the Christian faith. I have yet to see it after my father's death, or in the death of those who went before him, that I also loved except in the quotidian remembrances and loving memories we carry of them each living day that we go forward. If life after death is somewhere else, I have not seen or witnessed it. Is the resurrection inside each of us? As we carry the treasured memory of our departed loved ones? That is the closest I, in my humble, vacillating and meager knowledge of the Christian faith, can come to.

In Masonry we are taught that in the end, all we have is the "delight in the happy reflection of a life well lived in piety and virtue." We all must make ready for the "narrow house" we all one day will occupy. What did it all mean to Dad? I will never know. He lived well and as far I know he lived a virtuous life. Not a perfect life but a decent, noble, upstanding life. He knew success, and from what I could observe he found contentment. Coming from his humble roots to the plateau he last occupied was a long and tortuous journey straight upward. He out-lasted and out-maneuvered many who claimed to be smarter, those who were more cunning—the evil doers and the sanctified.

Am I changed by the experience of his death? Yes, sure. I am both changed and chastened. No, life will never be the same. I had the good fortune to have him in my life actively for 51 years, enough time to grow up and mature. God can work it out that way for some. Others less fortunate must find a way forward without the longevity of fatherhood in their lives. I am changed because I no longer have his wisdom, and the anima, the core of his character, of his being, available to me through his invariable presence. I am left with the spiritual reassurance of his love. I am chastened by and fortunate to have had the responsibility to inherit my father's "throne" or that which is left of it, with a responsibility to live up to the labor he put into making and leaving a legacy worth inheriting. Dad set the stage for us to "win," my job is to see that we keep on winning. Figuratively, I lost my right arm when my father died and when my mother expires I will have lost my left arm. All that will remain of my upper body will be the torso, that includes my heart which I bequeath to my children and my wife.

"Don't give up," was his mantra which he restated more in the later years than when I was younger. I seemed to be blessed with a strong will to prevail. I can think of only a few worthwhile endeavors that I quit on. I strove to embody Dad's advice, and I still think of it often when tested whether to throw in the towel or not. Winston Churchill is quoted as having said "Never, give in, never, never, never give in on nothing great or small, large or petty. Never give in except to convictions of honor and good sense."(sic). I have fallen short of that standard, but I have not given in on many things that were really important.

"All you gonna get in this life is a living and a killing," was another one of his oft quoted mantras. I think about this expression often, especially when the futility of striving wears thin. And the wear and tear of life makes you wonder whether or not it's all worth it. The reasoning is that you just as well get the "living" because the "killing" literally is inevitable. Life as he saw it came down to the basics, life or death. It seems to me from my experience that life cuts with a jagged edge, its blade is not rounded and smooth, it tears as it cuts.

There were issues talked about while I was being raised, and there were issues that were not discussed. We did not discuss Black history, academic competition, though Dad, more so than Mom, got angry when my report card was not good; we did not discuss the importance of reading as an academic exercise and we did not discuss sex or *Brown v. the Board Of Education*. What was discussed was vocabulary building, college attendance, people, Black and White politics in general, the Albemarle County School System, The Charlottesville School System, many of the individual personalities in Charlottesville, the church, piano playing (mine especially), real estate issues, the extended family, and the old sayings he loved to quote.

He also said about me that "I was too nice." What he meant was that he thought I was soft. That I gave folks too many breaks, but he didn't really know me, because if he did, he would have known of my sterner side. The difference is that I have tried to be decent, not a pushover or mean person, just civil and decent. My mother always advised me, even in the midst of strife, "be civil, that's all you have to do, be civil." Dad was less forgiving than me, he was harder.

Mother was always in there, pitching, though her style was much softer, more understanding and I could always get her to see my point of view. Mother has truly loved me, and I her, all of our lives together; we are inseparable actually.

Dad while teaching me to drive on route 250 west, the Old Richmond Road, before route 64 west was opened and available, said to me as I drove along: "You know the car now. You are in the driver's seat. Just keep the car in the middle of the road." I had been driving for a while and apparently not scaring him to death in the process, such that he felt comfortable when he uttered these remarks. He knew I wouldn't take these words literally.

I have applied this statement to much more than driving because its application is broad and his meaning went well beyond driving an automobile. He was always talking in parables to make a point.

I am truly my father's son. It seems that I become more like him every day. His imprimatur is so impressed upon me that perhaps this is what is meant in the Christian tradition of "life after death." My dad lives on within me every day.

As Dad got more into retirement, he played more golf. He was good at it. And sometimes when he was having fun he would say, "Lord don't take me now, I'm just beginning to live." On one of his happier days at his home, after a few drinks, which he enjoyed, he declared with much bravado: "it all belongs to me! It all belongs to me!" as he took another swig of whiskey from his favorite drinking glass. In this moment, he was really feeling it: pride, accomplishment, power and command. After all, in a certain kind of way, it *did* all belong to him. He created his estate. Though I was my own man, I belonged to him, and he was a significant part of my success. He liked to run the whole show and dominate everything and everybody if you let him. He was that kind of guy. He had made it the hard way. Affirmative Action had not been invented when he took on the system. Jim Crow was the perverted black bird he made paradise out of. He held that bird in his hand most of his adult life. But by witnessing the success he achieved, you would not have known it. Before he passed, Dad established and endowed the Otis and Rosa Lee Scholarship Fund at the Mt. Zion Baptist Church in Charlottesville, the first such fund established in the history of the church, still in existence today.

Lee Family residence, 1970's to present, Albemarle County

39

❦

WAXING PHILOSOPHIC

W HAT IS LIFE ALL ABOUT? It defies explanation. But, can it be summed up briefly and simplistically as breathing, eating, sleeping, gratifying, weeping, procreating and dying? In many respects life can be likened to a "deed" to a parcel of real estate. Each of us owns the deed to our lives. But the estate granted in the deed is a tenancy for a term of unknown years. When that term is determined, the estate ends and the remainder, your soul, if you believe in such things, ascends into the world beyond. There are no exceptions: no ifs, ands, or buts, regardless of your station in life or your wealth. When the estate ends you must vacate the premises through death.

There is no "why," just "is." Seldom can you answer why unless there is some scientific cause or effect, then you may be able to come up with a plausible explanation. But most of the time you will be stuck with "is."

Neither Blacks nor any other race, for that matter, should give up their lives for what they do not receive in life, but it happens all the time. Life vs death: in the law of contracts we say there must be mutuality on both sides of the contract. In mathematics we look for equality on both sides of the equation. Balance, equality and mutuality are essential elements in any formula for fairness; it's as simple as that. Black life is equal to White life in any context! But it has been devalued historically in the American scheme of things. For example, military service requires that one be willing to die for his or her country. If we are willing to die for our country, then we should receive from our country the fullness of its bounty, its liberty, unfettered or undiminished in any respect. After all, death is perfect, all-consuming leaving nothing behind, nothing to be gained or aspired to.

But we, as a people, Black people, do not receive that unfettered liberty. In effect our country is not willing "to die for us," figuratively speaking. We have not and still do not receive the full measure of its liberty, yet those Blacks in the military continue to sacrifice their lives for this unrealized gain. There can be no, inequality between the sacrifice expected and the benefit received. If the two are not equal, it is an unfair exchange. Blacks for generations have been volunteers and conscripted into this bargain. Is it fair? Is it just? Does it make sense? Why are our lives, the only thing we truly own, worth less than our liberties? After all it is with the payment of our lives Black and White that we have secured our liberties. Why should we not receive the best and the most that life has to offer in the country for which the ultimate sacrifice is made? Can you answer this question? Does the proposition make sense? I think it does. In America Black folks have always been over-charged, receiving less in return than the price paid. I am conflicted by this un-equivalent exchange in value, and it gives me pause. Blacks have always paid a high price for what they have gotten out of America.

Our family has been enormously blessed, and we have profited from the bounty of America. So the question is complex and requires careful thought. Life is unfair. There is no justice. Richard Pryor, the late comic use to say "there is no justice, just us," meaning we are the ones, Black people, who populate the jails and the penitentiaries. There is no fairness, don't even look for it. And, as I have said earlier, "you get what you get" in this life, not what you think you deserve. And do not confuse what you think you deserve with what you can afford. Because what you "think" you deserve you may not be able to afford. The two are mutually exclusive; they have nothing in common with one another.

America is the last bastion of republican capitalism, capitalism based upon people driven demand and entrepreneurship in its truest form though modified to provide safety nets for some essential needs that the public requires. Essentials such as healthcare, housing, education and some social services. The founders of America subjugated the Indians to take their land. The founders expropriated labor from Africans through slavery and built a "colossus" as W. E. B. Dubois has described America. In spite of its imperfections, in my opinion, America is still the best hope for African Americans. America has done much good in the world. This country has been a force for good even though it has perpetrated much evil and death as well.

At the end of my junior year at Howard University, I stood in the center of the courtyard on the main campus deciding what career path to take. The new classroom building at my back, Frederick Douglas Hall in front of me, the School of Religion diagonally to my far right and the law school diagonally across from the School of Religion. I decided to go into law rather than religion because I did not want to be a hypocrite. Knowing the type of person I was, enjoying a drink, loving women and all the "sins" of the world, I did not feel I could live life on the straight line that I innocently perceived the life of "a man of the cloth" should symbolize. I had been active in my church back home and many thought I was destined for the ministry. Perhaps I was too sincere during those days, but I do not regret the decision, although religion would have been a better match for my temperament and some of my talents. But the law is my love and has utilized all of my abilities fully.

Hypocrisy is a phenomenon that applies to individuals as well as nations. It is interwoven in America's foreign and domestic policies, which is to be expected. It is important to understand and decipher the nuances and logical inconsistencies. But on balance America is still the best hope for mankind, if enlightenment prevails. The western world has been "branded" for the White man; his standards, culture and political system are in place and it will stay that way. His is the image of beauty, including the image of God. Many races including ours dislikes its "own kind" and embraces the "other kind," the White kind. What are we to make of this?

American hypocrisy is as American as apple pie. It has been around a long time, and I see no hope of it fading anytime soon. Hypocrisy perhaps is an essential ingredient in governing, and we know that it is endemic to politics because most people do not read or analyze anything and do not require logical consistency. Though progress has been made, this hypocrisy manifests itself in the justice system, in education, in religion, in health care, in business, in domestic politics and in foreign politics and in so many facets of life—not the least of which is race—the most pronounced hypocrisy of them all.

Trying to maintain a linear logical consistency in life is difficult, if not impossible. Trying to do so is just as difficult as applying the Hegelian Dialectic, a complex syllogism that revolves around the formulation of a thesis, an antithesis and a synthesis. This approach is thought to have application to many situations in the world. Hegel's philosophic theory is a pattern of thought that requires the thinker to think outside of traditional values. Seekers of truth require other methods to ferret out the real truth, as opposed to the false-truths so often propounded by self-interested egocentric politicians, demagogues, racists, and self-promoters. Another way of thinking must be explored whether directly applicable or not. At best, I have only seen true logical consistency exhibited in nature, mathematics, science and in legal theory, but not in the application of the law because there, the consistency can become blurred by subjectivity and politics. Neither nations nor people have been able to achieve complete logical consistency objectively, because it is extremely difficult if not impossible to achieve. And perhaps it is not even to be expected; self-interest will always prevail in the business of people and nations. The old Redmond thought comes to mind. "No permanent friends, just permanent interests." People *are* nations, their cultures and institutions. Hypocrisy is in the nature of things like life, it finds its way. It exists as an expedient to achieve other goals and objectives.

Why was my real estate endeavor different than the law experience? Because the real estate business didn't define me. It didn't penetrate to the core of my personhood. My work in real estate came naturally almost as second nature. I was raised on this stuff, brought up in it. There was no psychological trauma from past setbacks. Setbacks and bad business deals were a part of the game. That is the way I saw this business even though people have killed themselves because of failed business schemes, botched deals and economic insolvency.

The law, on the other hand, had become the definition of who I was. It defined my identity. The law and my matriculation within it had gotten all entangled up in "me." That was a false and flawed construction that I had concocted in my own mind. There was and is no correlation between who you are as a person and your secular external achievements. These vanities have nothing to do with your self-worth as a person, the goodness or evil that makes up your worth as an individual.

They are adornments, trappings, not expressing the essential nature of the person. It is not how many houses you own, how much cash you have in the bank, or how many degrees you have that defines you , though these things do make life easier to bear. It is not these secular things that we remember about our loved ones who have passed on. We remember their sense of humor, how they talked, their laughter, their idiosyncrasies, their goodness, their values. There must be a "firewall' between how you see yourself as a human being and your external achievements and failures. You must prevent the flames of the fires of the world from penetrating the barrier separating one from the other, and if it does, the wall gives you enough time to "get out" to save yourself. Maybe that is why I didn't jump out of that window on the 21st floor of my apartment on that awful day of my despondency in Chicago ten years earlier.

Janet G. Vaillant in her wonderful biography *Black, French and African* (1990)[30] tells the true story of the African Leopold Sedar Senghor, who became the first post-colonial president of Senegal, one of my heroes and whose home outside Dakar I visited on one of my trips to Africa. She explains how, around 1935, Sengor failed his exams several times before he attained his doctorate in France and finally became a member of the prestigious Academie Francaise, and how his friend from Martinique, Aime Cesair, co-originator of the doctrine of Negritude with Sengor, had a nervous breakdown trying to measure up because of the competition he encountered studying for his entrance exams to gain entry into the prestigious Ecole Normale. And finally, of Joseph Rabearivelo, mentioned earlier, another immigrant student, a Malagasy, who committed suicide because he could not make peace within himself, a torn would-be intellectual trying to live up to French standards from an African background and yet still respect his African heritage and his Blackness. Passing and failing exams is just a part of the passage.

When you are young you have limited vision. You depend upon your parents for direction and it is the quality of their vision that initially shapes the direction of your life. Up to this point in my life I reflected upon the fact that I had really been playing a series of "games." The games of life. So over time, through trial and error, I assembled a hodge podge of rules of *my* game that have served me well as I have played at the game of life. The best focus that I bring to the games is to see life through the lens of a lawyer. It is through this prism, perhaps a distorted one depending on your perspective, that games come alive with vibrancy and real life consequences. The law teaches one to "look for the issues." Thinking like a lawyer brings a certain perspective to each situation and demands that you see and evaluate other points of view and ponder opposing views critically in search for the elusive "truth", if that is what you are searching for; balancing tests characterize the law.

In some games I did well but in others, for example, the "bar admission" game I did not fare so well initially because of a poor and flawed strategy. Gamesmanship, naiveté and strategy are metaphors for decision making in life based on individual experience or tutelage. As I have come to say, if you keep doing what you do, you are going to get what you got! Then as before and since, to play any game successfully you must first understand and know the rules of that game. You play any game better if you know the rules of that game. Do not play a game if you do not know its rules. You enjoy the game and get more out of playing the game if you know the rules. The game of life is fraught with traps, tricks, schemes, pot holes and rules of the game that the unwary do not know and can only learn by going through and surviving the school of hard knocks. That is of course, unless someone pulls you aside and schools you on what you need to do to avoid the pitfalls. Even then, there is no such thing as "smooth sailing."

The New York Life game I played well. I came out on top. The chamber of commerce game was played well. My strategy was good, honed by years of being the "grey haired boy." Finding Michelle and bringing her into my orbit was handled well, again the experience of having been in the social marketplace for years had taught me to recognized quality, a "flight to quality," and to seize an opportunity to settle a vital component of my life. The game of academic excellence was not played so well, initially, not because the innate talent was not there but because my parents did not play this game well. Perhaps they did not know the rules of this game as well as they should have, but few do, unless exposure is gained from your own experience or tutelage. Many factors kept me from doing better at this game, but the proverbial "light bulb" did eventually go off years later.

I strive to do everything better the next time if I do it over again, to ultimately master the job, to become facile in its execution because efficiency is money. Learning from mistakes, uncompromising self-critiques to ascertain the truth of the effort expended to obtain the favored result. "To thine own self be true," don't play games with yourself about the reality of your work ethics or actions. I have found that any activity can be made into a game, be it a job interview, a date with a girl you like, a case in the law, a real estate deal, whatever. Gamesmanship, the game within the game is important to perceive. You have to see it to perceive it, and you must perceive it to play it. You have to see the pieces on the chess board moving each one to accomplish the particular objective. Like pawns on a chess board, if you can, maneuver the people into the position that best suits you.

As my experience grew I began to play the money game reasonably well at my level and found that I had a certain talent for it. I am a great believer in stratagems and tactics, "a theory of the case," so to speak, about how you intend to win or succeed. I am an inveterate competitor and I like to win most of all. That surging and insatiable desire to win, to be the victor, "to be the best" permeates my whole being, striving for perfection though falling woefully short. I see competition in almost everything. Either "it yields or I break," as was the case in the bar exam competition. Where did this desire, this drive to be the best come from? Possibly it all started at 5th Street Park in Charlottesville in one on one basketball games I played as an adolescent. I enjoyed beating each opponent that I played, using my own homespun moves created many times out of whole cloth, but there was no transference of the competition to other facets of my young life. I play to win in everything I do. I observe successful people and adopt their approaches, imitating those attributes I find attractive. I am a discriminating counter-culturalist personality, a demanding individual, so much so, that I cannot even meet my own demands. As the actor recites in the movie, There Will Be Blood, "I have a competition in me, I do not want anyone else to win." This is my mind set, though it is perhaps a neurotic position.

When I get involved in something I go all the way; halfway is seldom satisfactory and usually results in a poor outcome. I eschew "half-ass and half-hearted" work and desultory work efforts. I have a high regard for men or women with high levels of expertise because that is what I am striving to attain. I usually am fully committed when I finally get geared up which usually occurs gradually, it is a slowly building process with me but when critical mass is achieved I get totally committed to the task. Like a knot tied into the tread of a piece of fabric, I become imbedded in the cloth of the endeavor, realizing that every endeavor will not result in a "pure" victory. I look for the "win," and you must define what a win is to you. It is somewhere in the result or in the experience, realizing that in the end none of us will finish the game alive. We will all succumb to the call of nature, this surrender is not a loss but a given in the game of life.

Learn and master the game of leverage. Know when you have it and when you do not. And always know where the leverage is in every pursuit. In an old book, a favorite of mine from my Chicago days, *Winning Through Intimidation* (1976)[31], the author, Robert J. Ringer, talks about intimidation and how to win using it. Intimidation and leverage are two very important components for effecting wins.

I do not view myself as a big time player by any means. That is a ludicrous proposition. I am "small potatoes" in the scheme of things. I just want to be a "player." My view is that I like to keep winning at small deals and let them accumulate, keep my head down and when I look up I'm there. I believe in "gradations," i.e. there is a size for everything commensurate with where you are in life and the needs that must be satisfied. For example, I cannot compete with men like Warren Buffet and Bill Gates, few people can. I'm not in their league but, in the realm I work in, in the "small" small business level, and at the individual entrepreneur level, I like to think that I can compete and win. You see, I believe that a small business consistently and persistently well run can be a financially successful and a rewarding enterprise regardless of size, because all businessmen are faced with the same problems. The small business individual is just a microcosm of the bigger business reduced by scale.

"You are the director," a law professor uttered during a continuing legal education seminar. Mike Smith from my Chicago days said, after he passed the bar and began to practice law, "I got him right where I want him," speaking of an adversary he was pursuing. Vision is required. The problem with most people, Blacks especially, is that they do not learn the rules of a game until the game is over. Learn the rules of the game first, then play! Not after the game is over and you have lost and wonder why? As this White dentist from Illinois told me as he waited for me to board a tour bus while on a vacation, "you are so far behind you think you are ahead." Stand outside of yourself and see the context within which you are dealing, and know that your opposite number is thinking his or her way through each and every encounter with you. Play your cards "close to the vest," do not let the right hand know what the left hand is doing and always play your cards when played "above the table." Never telegraph your pass as they say in basketball. Trickery and subterfuge are of little value except for internal mental exercises. If ever implemented and unsuccessful all credibility is loss never to be regained again. In the words of the German philosopher Friedrich Nietzche, "I am not upset that you lied to me, I am upset that from now on I cannot believe you."

Whitey Bulger, the Boston mobster of infamous repute, was credited with saying about communications many, many years ago before he went on the run that, "if you can say it rather than write it, say it; if you can gesture it rather than say it make the gesture." In other words, limit your communications to what is absolutely essential. This approach does not work too well for lawyers in most of our dealings but a paucity of language is always beneficial. The less spoken the better. Be a man or woman of few words, but when you speak have something to say. The Albert Carr book *Business as a Game* (1971)[32] makes the point about when to talk and when to keep your mouth shut. Remember the old saying "it is better to remain silent and be thought a fool than to open your mouth and remove all doubt."

Know that things do not happen without action, karma, or force behind them. Remember, there is reason and logic to everything under the universe. A better strategy makes for a better result. Think things through before getting involved and visualize in your mind's eye how the end should pertain, if you cannot you will end up on the wrong side of a good result. Spend your time on substantive pursuits. I have never frittered away my time or my resources on illusory or wild schemes promising something for nothing, it does not exist!

And finally, remember that everything costs. If whatever you want does not costs you something it usually is not worth anything. There is no such thing as a "free lunch." Don't expect it, it too does not exist. There is a price to be paid for everything. The "price" system is alive and well. If it is "free," it is probably not worth anything and if the item or thing you want does not *cost* you something *you* do not own it. You get what you pay for in this life, no room for a sinecure in this order of things. Get used to paying, expect to pay because that is where you are headed. Dad remarked many times around the house, "if you live like the White folks you have to pay like the White folks."

I have always spent my time on substantive pursuits regardless of the apparent difficulty, pursuits that either had a monetary payoff or a cultural benefit. And I have always eschewed the cult of personality, not buying into any man, except my father, but so much. A healthy dose of scepticism helps to season the "pie in the sky" fantasy from reality.

One last item, goal setting. It is important to always set goals for yourself. Let your reach extend beyond your grasp. I read somewhere that the best way to achieve an important goal is have a bigger goal. When the larger goal is achieve the lesser included goal—as we say in the law—is achieved. Goals and projects keep you going moving in a positive direction.

40

PAYING THE COST
FOR THE FUTURE

E CONOMISTS VIEW THE PRICE SYSTEM within the macro economy as a
function of supply and demand and market share, and that government has
a role to play in establishing prices. Price can be defined as that which is
charged to make something available to another person so they can own it. Prices
can be determined by particular producers who exercise price leadership in a particular industry or in a particular product or commodity. The allocation of resources and their scarcity is also a factor in determining price. A market mechanism
normally is required to determine prices. The Webster's dictionary definition of
price is "the amount of money needed to purchase an object; the cost at which
something is obtained, or that which must be given, done or undergone in order to
obtain a thing." Price can also be defined phychologically and sociologically as the
expenditure of mental and physical pain that one 'pays' in anxiety, suffering, etc.

Closely related to price are the words "cost", "charge", "expense" and "value."
Webster's defines these related terms as follows: "The cost of something is the
total amount spent including all prices and charges. A charge is the sum asked for
rendering a service. Expense suggests cost plus incidental expenditures. Value is
defined as the worth in usefulness or importance to the possessor; a fair price or
return for goods or services; to regard highly; prize; esteem; to rate according to
relative estimate of worth or desirability"; hence value encompasses elements of
price, cost, charge and expense.

Leaving aside economics and dictionary meanings for the moment, but focus-
ing on the human price of these similar, yet distinguishable terms; price and value
go well beyond the strict definitions of economists and linguists. Government is a
willing and sometimes unwilling co-conspirator in the price people have to pay for
things they acquire. Human beings have been and will continue to be, the beneficiaries of sacrifices paid by their ancestors. The price demanded and the price paid
for progress is a prerequisite in all human endeavors of lasting value; this cost can
be seen and detailed in everything we do.

Loving America is difficult at times, but love her we must. It is all we, as African Americans, have. We are hybrids as Baldwin notes. Our Black forefathers,

such as W.E.B. Dubois, Carter G. Woodson, Booker T. Washington and Marcus Garveyites, the Jamaican from Queen Anne's Bay which I visited; debated during their times whether Black folks should leave America and go back to Africa, specifically Liberia and some other West African countries or to stay where racism abounded in heavy handed proportions. However, the better judgment, by our thoughtful forefathers, was for us to stay and fight it out. After all, we paid for it by working for "nothing" for four hundred years, getting beaten and culturally eviscerated in the process. We have paid the price, earned the equity, we earned it the hard way, the old-fashioned way, and we have a superpriority lien against the title to America, and we cannot be dislodged; no Affirmative Action given here. America is our home.

DuBois talked about the complexity of this issue in his discussion on the "duality of the Black soul, loyalty to Blackness and loyalty to this country," in his book *The Souls of Black Folks* (1903). James Baldwin in his piece entitled *Notes of a Native Son* (1955) recites, "Negroes are Americans and their destiny is the country's destiny. They have no other experience besides their experiences on this continent and it is an experience which cannot be rejected, which yet remains to be embraced." The fact that America has changed and is evolving means that there is hope, there is a brighter future, but we must be vigilant, realizing that the game has changed. It is not about abject slavery and legal discrimination as we knew it. It, the game, is about economics, education, class and values and the price to be paid to be successful within the existing environment.

Sometimes war is a price for peace. It is the price for the achievement of political objectives unachievable by other means some would argue. Christians postulate that a life of obedience followed by death is the price for salvation and life after death. Great men and women such as Mahatma Gandhi, Martin Luther King, Abraham Lincoln, Nelson Mandela and Jesus Christ all paid a price for the causes they believed in. Men and women of lesser prominence within our individual families and outside of our families have also paid a price to advance their family's status and freedom. I have recounted my family's story about our first home in Richmond and how upset I became when I recall what my parents had to do to make ends meet, but that is the price and the struggle for success. White folks also have innumerable stories of suffering and struggle and "up from the boot straps" strife and conflict; in fact that is the "American Story" with one major exception, race. Drawing upon Nell Irvin Painter again: "White folks have only had to face competition from other Anglo-Americans and European immigrants, and prejudice among Anglo-ethnicities to distinguish the degenerates from among them."

This is one contributing reason why White folks are so unwilling to do anything to help Blacks because they feel that they have had to struggle and do without, so why should there be any exception for Blacks? Obviously, there are many reasons why this limited narrative does not apply. Here again, a price demanded, a price paid, the sacrifices made to live a better life. My father worked two and sometimes three jobs to make ends meet. He worked in a dairy, he waited tables; my mother worked as maid and housekeeper in White folks' houses to support the family. Where would we be without the sacrifices of our forefathers who paid a price for our current well-being? The whip, the lash, the shackles, the rape, the separation, the degradation. The price our ancestors paid cannot be measured in market share, or in supply or demand. But it can be measured in voting rights, public accommodations, integrated schools and hospitals. We measure the price and appreciate the value that people of color have given and acquired through the accomplishment and progress for themselves and for their posterity.

The Indian people of southern Asia struggled for generations to rid themselves from the ravishes of English colonialism. But for the sacrifices of Jawaharlal Nehru and Mahatma Gandhi, the Indian nation would not have been born into permanent freedom and emancipation. Out of this struggle came the nation of Pakistan and later Bangladesh. A succession of leaders have nurtured and managed these nations toward an Indian democracy. The Indian people are free today because of the price paid by their forefathers.

No success is attained without the payment of a price, the bearing of costs. An honor roll student pays the price of delayed gratification and discipline. He or she stays home or goes to the library and reads books and studies while others go out and play. And for that price the honor student receives the accolades of academe; recognition and promotion; access to special opportunities, not to mention the personal strengthening of growth and development that come with self-discipline and hard work and the knowledge that goes with it; and perhaps admission to the college of his or her choice rather than having to settle for what is left.

A first generation businessman pays the price to establish a business, pay down debt and fight off regulators to build a business. And for that sacrifice, he is rewarded with economic security and his family is able to live a financially secure life. He has self-determination and control of his economic destiny. He learns through trial, as I have learned, that you do not chase dollars, you chase value. Because it is value that counts most of all. It is value that endures. And that it costs money to maintain wealth once wealth is accumulated. I have related my story of the price I paid to become the first lawyer in the Lee family clan and the value I derived from that effort.

The correlative of price is benefit or detriment. As the saying goes, "the burden of potential is the expectation of performance or success." The price paid for crime is punishment. Regardless of the endeavor, whether it is good or bad, the price system is always at work, always exacting an exchange for the bargained for behavior or goods delivered. There is no "free lunch;" there is a price for everything. The price for poor judgment is a poor result. As Alan Greenspan, the former Chairman of the Federal Reserve said during one of his interviews, "the free lunch has not been invented yet." America pays a price for its racism, the underutilization of its people of color, the waste of human capital in a global, competitive economy. Can America afford to continue with such polices? I think not. We need everybody's shoulder to the wheel.

Price is the effort, the work, the hardship. Webster's further defines price as the energy in "anxiety and suffering" that is expended. The result is the end product, the consequence of a particular action. The old adage never rang more true than today, "you get what you pay for." If you don't pay anything, you don't get anything. "Nothing ventured, nothing gained," the old truisms still ring true. To go on with the clichés, "you can't get something for nothing." Anything worth having costs: if it does not cost you anything it usually is not worth anything. You don't own it until you pay for it.

Price is also an entry fee. Price though not defined as "sacrifice," shares some common relationships with sacrifice. Sacrifice is the correlative to price or vice versa, whichever you prefer. Again according to Webster's, sacrifice is defined as "to dispose of without profit," "a loss incurred in selling something below its value." There are many qualities of sacrifices. So price and sacrifice both involve payment of some kind. Giving up something to get something, an exchange of unequal value in the case of a sacrifice. A value that may be postponed or unrealized at the moment; an investment in the future. The premium paid to have access to certain things. For example, if you want to live in a certain neighborhood so you can send your child to a certain public school and be away from the immediate encroachment of crime, you must pay the "price" to gain entry. Perhaps to pay that price you might have to sacrifice going out to dinner as often to pay more for a house than you expected. If you want to drive a certain car you must pay the price. The correlative is obtaining value for your choice and going without in some form or fashion to get what you want.

Price is used by the political system and by those with economic power as an artifice and a substitute for overt racism, for racial separation, for example. White folks of a certain ilk "will always" find a way to separate themselves from the Blacks or from those they perceive as less desirable, and they do it by upping the price. When overt racism is no longer in vogue, the economic system becomes the tool. Barriers are constructed with price tags instead of signs reading "for colored only," "for Whites only," "no Blacks allowed." With laws against discrimination now on the books, standards are set to bar people from access.

Jesus Christ, in the Christian world, is said to have paid a price for the salvation of mankind. That because of his death, men and women can look forward to a new life after death redemptive of their sins on this earth. "Jesus paid it all, all to him I owe" so the Baptist hymn goes.

There are layers of prices to be paid by each generation. Each preceding generation had its price that it paid to advance American culture: the World War One Generation, The World War Two, Generation, The Vietnam Generation, The Civil Rights Generation and on. The race to advance society proceeds apace. Each generation can either fail to make the sacrifices necessary to pay the price or suffer the regression of falling behind and delaying the inevitable cost to be paid.

There is even a price or cost for good health. You must exercise and eat from a proper diet to achieve the best health available to you. Take good care of yourself, visit the doctor regularly, and take control of your health rather than letting your health take control of you. Go on the offensive against poor nutrition, lack of exercise and bad habits. A discipline to achieve a healthy psychological balance between work and play may result in better health, a less restricted lifestyle, and extend your life. As one of my friends, who was also a client, Dr. Frank S. James, a cardiologist in Philadelphia remarked to me one day in my office, "you can either die healthy or you can die sick."

That is why you should be careful about the decisions you make because you are a beneficiary of and a prisoner of your choices and decisions. Each of us must decide what price, if any, we are prepared to pay to achieve a specified result. We must reconcile the inequalities and inequities and decide what he or she is willing to die for, if anything. What are you willing to die for? What sacrifices have you made lately? What price have you paid thus far to accomplish something out of the ordinary? And are you willing to keep paying? That is the question. Get used to it. Paying and receiving is what life is all about. This is why it is senseless and a waste of time to be envious and jealous of what someone else has or what they have achieved because you have no idea what sacrifices that person has made to be where he or she is.

There is a price for sex. It has never been free. Why men, and for that matter women, have ever thought it was free is beyond me. Poor people pay a higher price for sex than rich people. The more babies you have, the more it costs. The more mouths you have to feed, clothes you have to buy and all that goes with it, not to mention really doing a "good job" raising the kids and providing them with the exposures and opportunities they need to excel, the more time is consumed and the more sacrifices it requires. To do a good job at anything requires giving of yourself without limits, making a commitment. Rich people have large families; they can afford them in more ways than just economically. Poor people who have large families just make themselves poorer in the economic sense and in most cases are unable to give their kids the opportunities they need to thrive, not just survive.

Nature exacts a price for sex through procreation intended or not intended; as well as the contraction of disease for indiscriminate sexual acts, acts that could otherwise be prevented by careful and responsible conduct. Sex cannot be treated whimsically, though in our modern world we often do, or we think we are getting away with doing so, when in reality we are not. With each act of intercourse we get drawn in further and further. Into a world of our own creation, filled with fantasy, expectation, commitment and nature's designs. Women do not allow access to their bodies without a price, usually in the form of a commitment to a relationship. Sex for women is an investment in the male and they know it, so sex is usually not cavalierly given. Many men are expedient, exploitive in intent, unthinking and aggressive when it comes to sex because they view the sexual conquest as some sort of trophy, driven principally by lust. It is postulated by people who have studied this question, that women trade sex for a relationship whereas men will commit to a relationship in exchange for sex among other things. Unless prostitution or absolute immorality is involved, most women do not freely engage in sex without some machination, calculation or expectation in their minds that the investment of their bodies will be rewarded with some beneficial return subjectively determined on the basis of *their* values. I once had a highly educated woman I was seeing in Chicago say to me that "a woman's morality was determined by how she controlled access to her vagina." This is harsh but real. The old saying has some application. "Women are the last to fall in love and the first to fall out." Women know this issue far better than men, for they are the repository of the nexus: they are raised to see it coming.

In the family in which I was raised as I said before, we did not discuss sex. It was only obliquely alluded to. What I learned about it, I learned by trial and error. But for the grace of God and some good instincts, my child bearing life could have been more prolific. If we had had these discussions frankly and honestly much grief for me could have been avoided. In my household I did not discuss the subject much at all with my oldest son, Otis. If I had done a better job with that, it may have saved him some grief. I did discuss it more intensively with my youngest son,

Justin, realizing the error of my ways. His mother and I saw to it that he received some sex education outside of the home, but we did not teach him everything he should have known before leaving home. This is a complex issue and I am not attempting to dispose of it here.

What is the price for me to die for America? Answer: undisguised, bare bones unmitigated fairness and equality unfailingly applied in all aspects of American life—untainted by color and applied transparently, intrinsically embedded in the fabric of the culture: in the bedroom, in the board room, in the dining room, in the classroom and in the historicity of the sub-Saharan African as written by White historians, in the hospital, in politics, in the church, in the neighborhood, in the bank, in the police station and in the courts, in Hollywood where the European ethnocentric cultural dogma is propagated. In my heart I want to be a patriot.

I am, however, willing to consider dying for my immediate family and to fight for America to defend the values symbolized by America and the benefits my family has received from this country in spite of the hypocrisy about race, not to mention the discrimination. I will not die for the application of those values when it comes to race. I do not want to be killed in the process of fighting America's wars until the bargain is equal for me and my descendants. Are you willing to die for an unfulfilled promise, for pie in the sky, for something you have not fully received? Something that is inchoate at best and at times illusory?

As we know, Abraham Lincoln paid with the price of his life on April 14, 1865 for his political position that The United States of America should be one nation undivided by slavery. The United States paid a heavy price for its racist views that Africans were inferior to Whites. That we were animals, chattel to be bought and sold like a piece of livestock; furniture to be used and to decorate with at the whim. More than six hundred thousand men lost their lives because America could not agree that Africans should not be enslaved. These men lost their lives over the role of racism in society. The perpetuation of a false proposition—social, political and economic White supremacy. Even after the monumental sacrifices in blood and treasure, post-Civil War segregation carried with it the price of under-utilization of a valuable human resource; productive people in our society were sidelined and marginalized because of racism.

On April 4, 1968, over 103 years later, Martin Luther King paid with *his* life to complete as much as he could the process begun by Lincoln, assuring that American Blacks could live in dignity and freedom. Without his sacrifice and the sacrifices of many others, including Fannie Lou Hamer, Mary McCleod Bethune, and Dorothy Height, the *Civil Rights Acts*—including *The Voting Rights Acts* and The *Public Accommodations Acts*—would not be law today. *Brown v. Board* would not be law today without the sacrifices of Thurgood Marshall and his battery of lawyers who spent endless hours working to perfect the legal arguments that made the case against segregated schools. Without these sacrifices and prices that were paid in money and human sweat and tears, segregation and Jim Crow would still exist. As George Wallace, the notorious southern governor remarked during one of his clamorous orations, "segregation today, segregation tomorrow and segregation forever." Without the price of sacrifice, would these conditons still exist?

Prices are demanded and must be paid for the sacrifices to live a better life. We must understand that as Blacks trying to survive in this culture and in this economic system that we do not have "indemnity" in the system. Blacks cannot fail and count on repeat opportunities. We usually get one shot and that's it. Whites who operate and own the system get repeat opportunities after failing. You must plan for that unsafe landing: This fact motivated my parents.

By analogy, Blacks in America are somewhere between being orphans, step-children, and adopted people, especially for those among us who know that Africa is our "ancestral and biological" mother. But after knowing who our biological mother is, we must go back and live with our "step" mother, not our "adopted mother," who *should* be a nurturing substitute, because we have not been fully adopted in either the legal or social sense by America—the one who raised us—and perhaps we never will be. It is to America we have become accustomed. It is to her we have given the best of our lives. It is to her that we have earned the "equity of redemption, the right to repurchase" our rights. It is her whose values have become inculcated into our values. It is the homogeneity of America in the production of goods, products and commodities in the rendition of services that we have come to expect and upon which we rely. It is her system of government, albeit imperfect, that offers us the constitution, a structure, for the surest course for the protection, execution, and emancipation of our rights. In short, America, I have concluded, is the "best deal" a stepchild can hope for.

Bishop John Shelby Spong writes in his book, *Resurrection: Myth or Reality? A Bishop's Search for the Origins of Christianity* (1994)[33], in Chapter 21 entitled "Life After Death," I say by analogy, and speaking metaphorically about America, "As for me and my house," meaning my family, we will honor to the extent we can, accepting and recognizing the hypocrisies and imperfections that exist in America, dwell in the house of America. As you can and will see I am very much persuaded by Bishop Spong—by his teaching and precepts. John Shelby Spong, when I followed him was the Episcopal Bishop of Newark, New Jersey.

Leopold Senghor, one of my heroes, the elocutionist of French who was rumored to have "taught French to the French," urged African people to acculturate where appropriate, spoke of this approach in his origination of the concept of "Negritude". We as a people must look deep within and emulate our ancestors; they are a rich repository of excellence. Blacks especially must realize that this society is largely inimical to our essential needs. We must compensate for that factor, by respecting, learning and embracing our ancient history and present culture, for we do have one.

Finally, White folks have put forward the guilt-trip trap of the "angry Black man" as though we are not supposed to be angry about what we as a people have endured and continue to endure from their misdeeds to put it kindly Shelby Steele in his book *A Bound Man* (2007) discourses on this subject. His thesis is that "Obama could not win," talking about Obama's run for the presidency of the United States of America, because he would be unable to convince or relieve White people of their fear of or guilt about the "angry Black man." This concept is a "fiction," as we say in the law, a trap for the unwary, designed to make us behave and feel guilty about *their* guilt for the wrongs *they* committed against people of color. We have a right to that anger—our anger is justified. Anger is healthy just like laugher is healthy. We must not be fooled by these contrivances, fictions put forward to stifle true emotions and to suppress what is natural. Fictions can be used as tools and devices to limit the correct perception we should have of our history and the people responsible for the creation of a portion of that inglorious past. It is what we do with that anger that is important, not the fact that anger exists. There is more than enough cruelty to support that anger. Clearly Mr. Steel's theory did not apply to President Obama. Where we channel the energy that flows from anger is the probative question. We need to use the energy of discontent to positively effect change, making sure these atrocities and the not-so-subtle residue of it never reoccurs, and that the truth is revealed on all levels.

This memoir is not a tirade against White people, quite the contrary. But rather this is a discussion of the impact of the system of Whiteness on me. This memoir represents the world as I see it, my passage. This memoir is about how the culture of mediocrity, the veil of naiveté and cultural ignorance shaped my struggle to reach my goal—of becoming a competent lawyer. This triple threat, this three legged stool, this tripartite of blindness, had to be overcome in order for me to succeed. I opened my eyes, however painfully, to see how these three phenomena, all insidious factors though not innocently occurring, affected my best self. These factors had to be destroyed; they had to be extricated from my being. Having done so, I was at last free to exist in this world on my own terms, terms more befitting the person I truly am. As a consequence I became an actualized man.

All during my formative years there was no discussion, that I can remember, at home or at school, about the beauty and the worth of the virtues of our African ancestry, the culture of Africans that embraces discipline, hard work and scholarship, the contributions of Africans to Black Americans through the experience of colonialism and its aftermath. I passed through those years in a fog, ignorant of my heritage and the significant place of that African heritage in the history of the world. Saddled only with the images of Black people as portrayed by White America, I was half baked.

Before going to Howard University, I knew nothing about Leroi Jones, a.k.a Amiri Baraka; Haile Selassie, the Lion of Juda; Kwame Nkrumah, liberator and President of Ghana; Leopold Sedar Senghor, the poet and philosopher of "Negritude"; or DuBois, the quintessential academic. I knew nothing about Alexander Sergeyevich Pushkin, a Russian of African descent who is the father of Russian poetry, who wrote that "a lack of respect for one's ancestors is the first sign of barbarism and immorality." I knew little about Thurgood Marshall, an inspiration to all who labor in the courts for justice, or Langston Hughes and a pantheon of others throughout the African diaspora. Howard University allowed me to come into my own. It was an incubator for me. My appreciation of the Black professional and the seeds of awareness of African History began at Howard University. It was there that my eyes began to open, that my first opportunity to embrace self-actualization occurred. Imperfect as it was, the onus was on me, the *onus probandi*, not the school. I lamented about the missed opportunity to attend the Milford School many years ago, but the "specialness" that I sought or that I thought I would have attained would not have come by attending a private White school but from self-pride from within—from an internally driven specialness and externally affective specialness. No one can give that to you, only you can give that to yourself. That's why I say it's not about "acting White" when it comes to academic achievement, it's about "acting Black" in the cultural traditions of African people; it is there, we just have to draw upon it.

In one of his memorable speeches given the night before he was assassinated, Martin Luther King spoke of the desire to live a long life if he were fortunate to do so saying, "Like anybody, I would like to live a long life. Longevity has its place. But I am not concerned about that now. I just want to do God's will." It is not how long you live, but how you live long, the richness and purposefulness of the life you live. The experiences, the depth of your commitment to doing well, achieving something, however you define it, is vital to the life you live long. This is what King was talking about. He was not afraid about what his premonition revealed to him about his fate because he had a higher calling, a higher mission to get something out of the life he was given; making an historic contribution to people of color everywhere in the world and to America in particular. In the words of Dr. Kubler Ross, "life is a responsibility," and Dr. King knew this.

When I viewed the video of that speech, which I have seen several times, his delivery was so filled with the rhapsodic energy of a man possessed with a rapture and emotion that I am always moved to tears by the sincerity and earnestness with which he spoke.

Dad had his many mantras, but one that he used in the latter years was "show your love." This one baffled me. But Mother had hers too, and it was repeated to me over and over again, "do the right thing." Mother was a believer in doing the right thing by people and in life's challenges. What you do in life and how you treat your fellow man matters.

The deeper meaning in this memoir is that education must not be taken for granted by middle class Blacks just because they live in a good neighborhood. Being middle class is more than having a certain amount of money, sending your child to a better school than the one in a lower class neighborhood. And just going to White schools is not enough. Black families must ensure that their kids get the rigor and competitiveness that is required to "win" in this society in the spirit of W.E.B. DuBois. We must pride ourselves in "beating them" at the academic game and to achieve that we must embrace competition, run toward it not away from it. We not only have the capacity to win, but we also have the history and the cultural heritage. Poverty of the mind does not discriminate on the basis of race or economics.

Although there are many exceptions, some Blacks have a pathology of suffering from a lack of vision and economic disadvantage: That was not completely my problem. My problem was a lack of cultural enlightenment. Being middle class means more than a nice house and a White school, to me it means knowing "how to do things the right way," all the way, in all aspects of life. Eat the whole loaf not just a slice. Thoroughness in education, competition in education, not being satisfied with what is thrown off, used up, crumbs from the table, White leftovers. We must embrace the entirety of middle class life not just the fringes, the pretense. Demand the best and except nothing less! Keep your standards high and look to high culture for inspiration.

We are reminded by Leopold Sedar Senghor, that our challenge as a people of African descent is not to abandon our historical culture and substitute in its place European culture and Anglo American culture. But to assimilate the parts of White culture that will enhance African culture and African American culture. We are reminded by Baldwin that "everything done by Negroes in this country is, in a way, done in imitation of White people." Culturally, we are a hollowed out log with no center. That vacant center must be filled by ancestral culture and assimilation as it must be by necessity and by choice. But in spite of this fact, once we, as a people begin to fill that center with more knowledge of our own ancient and ancestral culture, we should lean more heavily toward acculturation, a blending of cultures rather than a rejection, disrespect and illiteracy about our own. We should not want to be White or to unthinkingly emulate all that they do. What we must do is incorporate those aspects of White culture that we find accommodation with and eschew the rest, safeguard and retain above all else what is innately African.

Baldwin makes a similar point in his writings when he says in *The Fire Next Time* (1963)[34], in the chapter "Down at The Cross", "The only thing White people have that Black people need, or should want, is power—and no one holds power forever." Baldwin also opined that the objective should be for "the Black man to walk upon the earth just like a White man."

Having meandered through the barren plains of the cultural breach, ignorant of the ancestral self, torn and tormented by the negative stimuli of race debasement and caricature for 55 years, I finally tasted the sweet savoring fruit of cultural renewal and wholeness. I traveled thousands of miles from my home in Jeffersonian Virginia to Goree Island two miles to the east of Dakar, Senegal and to Cape Coast Castle and Elmina Castle at Cape Coast in Ghana, 149 kilometers west of Accra. I went back to and through "the door of no return," reentered that door and closed the circle. A warm breeze swept away the clouds that had occluded my view of my self-image made opaque by the distortions of ignorance and half-truths. Blue skies were now overhead, an epiphany occurred, a satori.

The ancestral soul of the average American of African descent sails upon the sea with an anchor that extends only to a shallow depth and lacks the weight sufficient to penetrate the deep waters of the inner soul from which springs a value system rooted in antiquity incapable of exploitation and usurpation. Many young Blacks act the way they act because they know nothing of their ancestral heritage, they are spliced and diced, whipped and thrown, from one fad to the next with no centrality of rooted values, transcendent to every whim and caprice the pop culture throws at them. There is confusion and a misunderstanding, among some of us, about the difference between high culture and pop culture. Many of our people don't have a clue about the richness of their heritage and continue to view themselves through a glass colored Whitely. If we can transfer higher cultural ideals to our youth perhaps, they will be less inclined to reject each other and those among them who strive for excellence. The White model of excellence is extraordinary, but it is not by far the exclusive example. If we are successful, our youth will be compelled to embrace the beauty within that is welded deep in the recesses of their ancestral souls. The gifts of our antiquity are theirs for the grasping.

These ideas are not new. Some would say that these ideas are just warmed over Afro-centric rhetoric. The issue is not the timeliness of these ideas, but their application.

41

A WATERSHED WEEKEND

WATERSHED WEEKEND began on January 22, 2011. A weekend that held within its grasp the pinnacle of beauty and the nadir of sickness and potential death. My youngest son, Justin, the Harvard Lawyer, recently brought to our home in Charlottesville, Virginia, a Nigerian woman with the Ebo name of Ofunneka Chude, "Perla" is her nickname, whom he was seeing and had been involved with for several months prior to the visit. Intending, according to him, to advance the relationship beyond just friendship. We had met Perla on two prior occasions and was impressed with her. Her charm lay in her quiet unassuming diminutive style, cat-like in her quietness, smart and intelligent with chiseled sharp features. A beauty, an African beauty, hence her nickname Perla. Perla is about 5'6" and comes from the Ebo tribe from the town of Onitsha, and the village of Umudei located in Anambra State in Nigeria.

Curiously, I felt the irony that our son, who had eschewed everything African—even the African clothing we bought him on our trip to the motherland—would be attracted to an African woman and not a Black American woman whom everyone in our family expected him to pursue. In fact, he had pursued such a female several months earlier but found her values to be lacking and the relationship did not last. It is amazing what love will overcome.

So Perla's visit to our home would be different this time. It would extend beyond the small talk, not that that was the only kind of talk we had exchanged before, but the talk this time would be even more substantive. After all, we wanted to get to know her better. And I was especially interested her African roots, culture and traditions, and her perspectives on North America and Europe. Especially since all three continents had played a role in her background.

Perla, born in Italy to Nigerian parents, was partially reared in Italy but attended high school in California where her parents settled the family. She attended and graduated from a college in Virginia. Her parents are well educated holding advance degrees in their chosen fields. One could say that Perla is of Italian-African descent, if there is such an ethnic designation. From my experience, I have found that it is not uncommon for elite African families to educate their children in western countries and to settle themselves there to take advantage of opportunities both cultural and economic.

Our weekend began uneventfully. I swam in the early morning had a great swim; attended a lecture at the Miller Center, a public affairs research and lecture forum associated with the University of Virginia. Later that evening we all assembled, including my mother and my wife Michelle, to have Perla's birthday dinner and drinks at Bonefish Grill, a fine restaurant north of the city in Albemarle County. The evening at our table was festive and filled with glee. We all joked with one another, laughed out loud and had to be shushed by Michelle in her usual capacity as the sheriff at these events. But Perla was the center of our attention. We felt a sense of honor to play host to her in our town. We wanted our town to make a good first impression. She visited Monticello with Justin during the day but kept her reactions close to her vest. However, Justin and I decried the hypocrisy of Thomas Jefferson, whose eloquent espousal of human rights for mankind in the Declaration of Independence excluded the Africans he enslaved and wrote disparagingly about in his *Notes on the State of Virginia*. This founding father, after his wife died, maintained a concubinage relationship with Sally Hemings, a Black woman of notable beauty on his exclusive hilltop estate, according to Annette Gordon Reed, author of *The Hemingses of Monticello* (2008). The slaves were good enough to be bedded down but not good enough to be freed and treated with dignity as citizens, despite the fact that "5,000 African Americans, and even more slaves would serve in the Continental army."[35]

Mother sat at the far end of the dinner table that abutted other tables on her right and left. I first sat at the other end of the table opposite Mother that was adjacent to the aisle. But it was so busy in that restaurant that night that I was forced to move to a seat to my left to keep from being side swiped every couple of seconds by the traffic going back and forth in the aisle. I moved to my left and sat directly across from Justin. The restaurant was busy and bustling with diners, waiters and hostesses and the like. Perla sat on Justin's left and Michelle sat directly across from Perla. The mood remained cheerful and funny with jokes being told. I thought about my oldest son, Otis, who, though serious most of the time, enjoys a good laugh once and a while, a joke of his own liking. I thought he would have enjoyed this evening along with his lovely wife April. But they were not there on this occasion, an occasion that was spontaneous and effervescent, sparking like a good champagne. It was turning out to be a whale of a special evening for a special person who had come into our lives bringing a refreshing perspective on all the taboos, contradictions, hangups, mislearned stupidity that dwells so commonly among Black people and White people about Africans and people of color.

The highlight of the dinner was the presentation to Perla of her birthday cake. Justin had asked his mother and me to secure the cake from a local bakery. His time schedule, as usual, was "pushed," but he wanted to surprise Perla with a cake, and we stepped in to help. He wanted to surprise Perla because she was not expecting a birthday cake at the dinner. Justin wanted this night, and in fact their birthday weekend together, to be special: he was taking his best girl to visit his home town and to visit his parents in their home, a big move, usually indicative, but not necessarily of further things to come, maybe. Justin is the young lover lawyer trying to make an impression and he did, it seemed.

Michelle and I arranged to have the cake baked, a 10-inch yellow cake with butter cream frosting. We handed the cake to the waiter as we entered the restaurant out of Perla's sight, so she would not be tipped off. After the main meal was served and everyone had finished eating, Perla was completely surprised when the waiter brought out the cake with candles lit, just two, and sat it on her left side. She had turned her head slightly to the right to talk to Justin just as the waiter approached, so she had no time to disguise her surprise before the waiter brought the cake. "OOh! OOh! OOh!" she exclaimed, "is this for me?" The innocence of the exclamation would be admitted in court as part of the *res gestae*—circumstances, so spontaneous, representing true emotions expressed at the time of an event, denoting truth unfiltered by artifice.

"Yes!" we all said in unison "it's all for you." Her smile was infectious, grinning from ear to ear, exposing her smooth ivory colored teeth all so perfectly aligned. Her glow shimmered as she blew the two candles out and made her wish silently to herself. The cake was decorated with pink lettering that said, "Happy Birthday Perla." We chose not to put her age on the cake since women of all races are usually sensitive about their ages, and we did not want to offend. Some of our dining room neighbors turned around to notice, if only momentarily, what the fuss was about. At that moment, when Perla first saw the cake, what I saw was chimerical. I took a mental picture of her that reflected the beauty of an African dawn as the fog and mist from low hanging clouds stirred by the moisture of a neighboring river, ebbing and flowing, was burned off in the early morning light, with Baobab trees with their large trunks and clusters of leafy green limbs extending from the trunk in round clusters resembling rounded green buds silhouetted against the surrounding lush savannahs.

This was the scene that came to my mind. That which was reflected in recollections of long road trips through the African countryside as Michelle and I rode along the roads of Senegal and Ghana on our way to one city after another, driven by a driver who feared no evil. The soft yellow and gold illumination gently bounced off of Perla's smooth quartz like complexion. A beam of artificial sunlight found its way into the prism of the refracted light, creating a soft dim light that made her pearl beauty glow and sparkle. Her face became a piece of ebony chalcedony, a precious dark wood made of solid salts and stone. She was indeed at this moment a "Pearl," a daughter of Mother Africa. The sub-Saharan tone of her color radiated, making me, the old man who had labored long when "Black was seen as not beautiful," see the beauty of Blackness once again in its physical, not philosophical manifestation. It wasn't that I was realizing the beauty of Black people for the first time, quite the contrary, I love Black people and appreciate the rainbow of our colors, the shades of hue that we come in. But this moment, as in any special moment, poignantly reflected a resurrection, a reaffirmation that "Black was indeed Beautiful," sublime, elegant, gracious and exquisite. That is why this color is treated so elegantly in this culture as a color, but not its culture. If you can see it and appreciate it, all other colors as well as cultures emanate from it.

The theoretical possibility that this union could produce children is a profound thought especially when one considers that the maternal ancestral string of these children would extend all the way back to the village of Umudei in Nigeria and not end at some court house in America whose records only extend to the records of White slave owners who were thoughtful enough or who even cared enough, which so many did not, to prepare and probate wills and deeds and kept records of their slaves, their children and their families. Any children of this union would grow up knowing more about their heritage than 99% of African American children born in the United States save for that very few who also can trace the string of their ancestral origins to its natural African beginning; to be able do this would be a defeat for the historical doctrines and their underpinnings that reverberate in the politics of White America.

After such a festive Saturday, I had a restful Sunday, January 23rd, watching, as I usually do, sports events on television and reading my favorite paper. At this general time I take pride in my athletic activities built around swimming. I had completed that Monday another 30-minute freestyle routine without interruption and had completed the rest of my routine; 2 laps of butterfly, two laps of breast stroke, two laps of back stroke, two laps of side stroke and ten laps of what I called round robin, a combination of all the strokes except the side stroke. So on that Sunday I felt as good as usual with no early warning of any impending trouble. The Friday before Perla's birthday affair, I swam early but completed my modified program which consisted of only 15 minutes of uninterrupted freestyle. I did the swim routine this way so as not to over tax my body, I thought. Around 11:00pm I closed up the house and went upstairs, put on pajamas and got into bed.

As I lay there awake, I expected my heart to beat in its usual unorthodox manner but that it would settle down in the usual course, and I would fall asleep as I had been doing for years. But this time I noticed my heart beat was fast and getting faster. In a weak voice, I said to Michelle, "I don't feel well." I knew instinctively that my heart was not acting the way it usually did at this time. Without notice, before Michelle, who was sitting in a recliner several feet in front of me, could turn around to ask me what was going on, I was unconscious—for about one, two or maybe three seconds at most. It was my old nemesis syncope, brought on by the return of ventricular tachycardia, VT, the trigger. I could not get my breath and I had no time to cough, which had been mentioned to me to do if I felt threatened by the tachycardia, all to no avail. I had not had an incident since September of 1990, a week or so after being released from the hospital following my heart attack. I instinctively knew what had happened to me. When I awakened, Michelle was standing over me asking "what was making me feel bad," and I explained to her I had been "knocked out" during those fast and fleeting moments before she had even realized it. But for the grace of God I could have been gone then, but only through his grace did my heart return to a normal sinus rhythm immediately after the episode. Unlike in the past when, in my judgment, insignificant aberrant cardiac events had occurred, I told her that this time "we must go to the hospital." I did not waver or procrastinate about the decision because I knew something dangerous was up.

Michelle and I had spoken just a few days back about whether or not, if one of us had to go to the emergency room, we should go to Martha Jefferson or to UVa. Martha Jefferson was less crowded and they were building new facilities and we pondered whether I would be treated more kindly, but not necessarily more competently. There was no issue this time because I knew instinctively that I had to go to UVa when the "chips were down." All of my cardiologists were there, and without question I was going to be treated by the most competent physicians in Charlottesville by going to UVa. So we dressed and drove frantically to the emergency room. I knew some of what I was in for when I got started with cardiac medical treatment. The IV's, the needles, and the endless repetition of telling the doctors what brought me to the hospital. I must have told my story 15 times as each new doctor wanted to know my story again. I said to Michelle, "why don't I just record the story so each doctor can listen to it, and I would not have to repeat it until I was tired of telling it." The emergency admittance process was problematic. The intake clerk was new on the job and did not know how to input my information. We were nervous that while he fiddled and asked his supervisor questions I could have had another event. Patience was at a premium.

As the process took hold, the cardiologists on duty all made their way to my bedside in the emergency room all asking the same questions. I felt as though I was a criminal defendant trying to tell a consistent story so that I would not be caught in inconsistencies and be arrested. Black folks sometimes always think the worst, even though that was far from what was happening. My lawyer mind never stops working. A bed was not yet available and we had been there since midnight on the 24th. It was not until the next morning, sometime after 10:00 am that I was moved to the cardiac ward. Before then I had to lay on a gurney with its thin mattress that became ever more uncomfortable as each hour passed. Michelle became upset because, even though I had been admitted to the hospital, I was still in the emergency suite. We even foolishly thought about leaving, because I thought that all the doctors would do would be to observe me for a few hours and I would be back home. But that was far from the reality of what was in store for me.

Finally, a regular hospital bed was brought in so that I could rest more comfortably before being moved to a Post-Anesthesia Cardiac Unit, PACU room. These rooms were single rooms with glass sliding doors, and it felt good to be in a room like this, but I wondered what was the cost of such a room, but kept my curiosity to myself. The day passed uneventfully and later in the evening I was moved to a regular cardiac ward room, sometimes referred to as a "step down room." My heart was being monitored constantly by the doctors and nurses, and I was wired for sound all the way. In fact, I could hardly move around in my bed without pulling some electrical cord or monitoring apparatus.

But all was well, and my new nurse Donna, a veteran of the cardiac ward, came in to check me in formally. "You are a lawyer I hear, therefore you don't have no trouble reading or writing or understanding," she implored with a southern drawl that was both rustic and quaint. The other nurse asked "how do you best understand things, by someone telling you, reading or showing you pictures?" No one had asked me that before and certainly not in a hospital. I said to her "usually if someone tells me something or I read it I do pretty well with it." She nodded her acquiescence, finished her routine of checking me into the ward and left. I immediately liked Donna, because she was matter of fact, and clearly knew what she was doing. She had been a cardiac nurse for 15 years before I got there and probably had seen it all. She was the real deal. A White, small statured blond haired woman who wore her hair in what seemed like a bowl cut. She walked with a slight limp because of her ailing knee. She assured me that everything would be alright, that she was planning, in the not too distant future to have her knees operated on, and she had just accepted it for what it was. She lamented "don't feel bad, cancer has destroyed just about all of my family, but I'm still here." She was reassuring.

I could identify with her and her knee procedure because Michelle, several years earlier, had both of her knees operated on and I knew it was painful. But she said it was a procedure that had to be done and that was it, and she wanted it over with. Medical people often think this way because they are accustomed to medical procedures and do not make a big deal about them. Us lay-people get scared to death when doctors and nurses start talking about surgery and grue-some sounding procedures. All I could think about was the pain and the agony, and life and death. In my experience, both doctors and nurses under-sell the pain and discomfort associated with medical procedures because many of them have not undergone the procedures themselves. I was scared half the time I was in the hospital to begin with, because it usually meant high medical bills, sickness, pain, bad news and recuperation. I wanted to avoid all of this if I could. I had said to my doctors, Michelle and my mother that at age 63, I only had 2 more years before I could make it to Medicare. My doctor had even assured me that, by the way I was taking care of myself, I should make it with ease. Well it did not happen that way, especially the "with ease" part. Something happened on my way to age 65.

The afternoon and evening were normal and uneventful. I went to sleep. The nurse had given me something to help me sleep because I asked for it. So I slept and was in a deep sleep, when all of a sudden all of these nurses and doctors came to my room and awakened me. It was about 9:00 pm. I was surprised to see them all. There was a clamor, and much excitement. The doctor explained to me that my heart rate had dropped to 30 beats per minute and that my blood pressure had dropped to 106. I was unaware of this since I had been asleep. The lead doctor, an attractive White female with long flowing auburn hair, seemed to me like she could have been a model or something other than a doctor. She said as she looked at me in a compassionate, yet disciplined way that she "did not know what to make of what was happening to me." She was excited and animated and so were the other nurses. They were all baffled by what was causing this deterioration in my condition.

The female doctor said, "in an abundance of caution we are going to put these electric pads on each side of your chest just in case" because if something hap-pens we won't have to waste time putting them on if we need them. The nurses peeled off two large oval shaped white with silver backing sticky tile-like plates and stuck them on both sides of my chest. The leads from the pads were attached to a machine, which I later discovered was a defibrillator seated next to the right side of my bed. I had not paid any attention to the device during the excitement of the moment. The doctor had been clairvoyant. I was still somewhat underwhelmed be-cause I felt no discomfort and I knew that a slow heartbeat was called bradycardia. I did not equate that with harm because I had never experienced it before, and did not know enough to be concerned. "Ignorance is bliss," the saying goes.

The female doctor had a handful of EKGs, electrocardiograms, taken immedi-ately upon their arrival at my bedside. And from what I could see my heart rhythms seemed like they were all over the place. I did not know how to interpret them in any way; they just looked ominous to me. PVCs, premature ventricular contrac-tions, characterized my heart rhythm anyway. As my cardiologist once said, "I just have a crazy heart beat," a result of the initial heart attack. After they all left, I went back to sleep for several hours. Between 5:30 am and 6:00am the next day there was another sudden rush to my bed. I heard Donna running to my room panting out of breath. I could see her limping, trying her best to get to my bed which was the second bed over from the door. I heard her say, loudly and with authority, "Do it now! Do it now!" she demanded of the doctor, who was an Asian fellow, standing in front of the defibrillator. He apparently was to operate the machine if required. All of a sudden POW! was the sound I heard and felt. I rose from a flat position to an upright position as though a spring had suddenly been activated in my bed to push me forward. I said "Ouch! Oh, Oh! Ah, ah!" in a mournful tone without much exuberance. The scene was surreal, my curtain was drawn and these medical people were all standing around me shouting at one another trying to work together to save my life in that excited and exigent moment. The electric shock shook me, but it did not hurt. I was surprised that I did not feel any pain, but I knew I been shocked. Donna yelled excitely, "He's out of it! He's out of it!" she ordered. Giving notice to the doctor that no additional shock was required.

Apparently I had gone into a storm of ventricular tachycardia. My galloping heartbeat, probably set loose by the ventricular node, had sent an electrical impulse that bounced off of the scarred muscle tissue from the previous attack racing my heart beat at over 100 bpm, possibly as high as 400 bpm. Life cannot be sustained at that pace. A heartbeat of about 60 to 100 bpm is normal. I was partially awake, but I was powerless to speak, taking breaths was impossible, as though something had captured my speech and channeled it elsewhere similar to an alarm system you have in your home that takes control of your phone system to notify the police of an unwanted intrusion. The best I could do was to communicate with my head only momentarily that all control was lost. The nurses, there were now three, all excitedly rushed about doing one thing or another: fixing IV's, taking EKGs and checking my drips and making other adjustments when several other doctors on duty came to my room and said "we are moving him first thing in the morning to the critical care unit where he can be monitored by the nurses over there right across the hall who only have two patients to tend to at a time.

Nature left to its own devices had death as my destination in the early morning hours of January 26th. The panicked nurses asked whether one of them should "call his wife." I initially said no, always undervaluing the state of affairs, but upon immediate reflection said "yes, call her." Several hours later, after I had been moved to the critical care unit, my primary cardiologist, Dr. Robert S. Gibson, a man whom I like and the physician who has followed my case for over 20 years, told me that "but for the grace of God, I had survived the initial black out at home. And that only because I was in the hospital when the second attack came, I survived." Words from a man whose cardiology judgment I trust.

The second VT had been more vicious and had more energy intended for moribundity than the Sunday attack. The defibrillator, with 60 joules of power impacting my chest wall was sufficient to halt the "Secretariat" of galloping rhythms racing to the finish line of my Kentucky Derby intended for my demise. Were it not for the supervening power of that machine, the intercession of God in the exercise of his divine wisdom, who gave the nurses, the technicians and the doctors the knowledge, judgment and experience to use it appropriately, Secretariat would have won this race. My heart was irritated and contemptuous of me during this time. Irritated with me perhaps for not having taken better care of my health early on in my life. My naiveté about heart disease, exercise, eating healthily had been lessons hard-learned only after the fact. But God, through his graces gave me a second chance to do better. And do better I certainly tried, but as I ponder the whys and wherefores of this latest attack, I have to wonder if it's something that I did that triggered this event. Did I over-do it with swimming so many laps. I thought at one time I would be the "poster child" for cardiac rehabilitation the way I was swimming and my assiduity in maintaining my routine, twice a week without fail regardless of the weather or where I was in the world if a pool was available. I thought I was doing well, but maybe it was "too" much. I had not taken the old medication for over six years, possibly longer, and had not had an incident that went this far. Just as in the past, I may have tried to do too much, bitten off more than I could chew; always pressing, striving, overreaching, competing and trying to win. It's just my nature and maybe that nature is incompatible with, as one of my doctor's remarked, "with the way I'm wired." Perhaps I just need to realize that I've won and just quit!

On the other hand, the heart is an essential muscle that pumps oxygenated blood throughout the body to nourish our vital organs. The heart does not think or feel anything: it is controlled by the autonomic nervous system that pretty well does what it wants. We are the ones who care, that try to alter nature because nature does not care, is unthinking and left alone destroys as much as it creates. We equate God with nature, maybe the two are not equivalent, perhaps they are, I certainly do not know, do you? But be that as it will or may, I say that God, in combination with nature, has allowed me to live to raise my children, to see them educated and receive some of the highest degrees that can be awarded in education. Allowed me to have the love of a beautiful and classy woman for over 30 years and to have amassed enough wealth to live and have the lifestyle many people would envy. Yes, I have been blessed. After one moderate heart attack, two syncopes, three heart catheterizations, and one potentially terminable VT, I am still here, thank God. These events though significant in their own right, on a scale of 1 to 10 with 10 being the highest, still fall at about a four or five. There are many other more serious and daunting heart procedures and illnesses that make my situation pale in significance. But each of us deals with his own fortunes, good and bad. As the gospels ask: "must Jesus bear the cross alone? No! Pick up your cross and bear it, there is a cross for me and there is a cross for you."

After the VT, the doctors recommended that I have an implant of a device known as a cardioverter/defibrillator in the left wall of my chest, right below the left clavicle. The device is about the size of a cigarette lighter. As I told you, the news handed out by doctors can be most distressing. A young but experienced Hispanic physician Dr. Lopez, with a heavy but clear accent, working the floor during my stay was the purveyor to me of the news, what the cardiology team was recommending. I no longer was under the burden of proof about the syncope. It had happened on their watch. I was a kind of cardiac hero, if there is such a thing, because I had gone through the shock treatment. All of the doctors were apologetic because they felt they should have been able to intervene to prevent the VT from going long enough to the point that an electric shock had to be administered. But everyone knew that regardless of the missed opportunity, if there was one, my life had been saved. So who was complaining? No one, especially not me. It was either the implant or a procedure called an ablation where they try to track and find the errant short circuit and fix it. A more complex and uncertain procedure. Twenty years ago I had resisted having the older generation of a cardioverter device implanted because it seem too dreadful to entertain, so I opted for medication as I mentioned before. This time though, the technology had advanced and my uneasiness had turned into thoughtful consideration. Just the thought of having a foreign mechanical device in my body was repugnant to me. It violates a spiritual rule of mine about nature, what God has given you is sacred, that man's mechanical and synthetic devices are antithetical to that creation. I had always thought of myself as a good physical specimen, proud of my physical shape but not especially the look. This new recommendation conjured up thoughts of debilitation and decline but this time it was clearly necessary. But I still resisted it, albeit reluctantly.

But I accepted the surgery. Michelle said to me over the phone with her usual pragmatic approach, "Otis you have no choice!" I knew she was telling me the truth. As I said to myself many times lately as the years have passed on, no one knows their situation better than the person whose situation it is. I knew in my heart of hearts that I had to have the surgery to have the implant inserted, after all, it could, if this event occurred again, save my life. But I wanted the device implanted by the best in the middle Atlantic region and that guy was Dr. John Dimarco, MD, Ph.D, head of the Electrophysiology Lab in the cardiology department at UVa. Dr. Dimarco had diagnosed my original arrhythmia and prescribed the medication I had been taking until the decision was made to discontinue the medication, so he knew me, or at least I thought he should have, but he may not have, for many years had passed since he last treated me. I trusted that the job would be done right. He has a national reputation in his profession, and he is the guru around the cardiology department in the hospital.

As I lay on the gurney as the anesthetic slowly took me out, I said to Dr. Dimarco that I was writing a memoir and that he was in it. He replied with a wry sense of humor, "is that a threat?" How could he have thought that? "No! It was an honor!" I replied just audibly enough for him to hear me, but I do not know if he actually did. He implanted the device.

I cried a lot during this hospital stay. My feelings were really hurt by the thought of dying, self-pity, the dislocation that this was causing my family and my business: the realization is that, knowing me, life would change again. As is stated in the prayer of Saint Francis of Assisi "all things pass but God never changes." I had to accept the reality that I was being sent another signal that my death was clearly going to happen; that I was weakening albeit gradually. I had faced the reality of my death during my first heart attack and slowly worked myself through it, though the thought never ever completely ever left my mind.

But all the fuss being made over me, which I normally try to avoid, if at all possible, bothered me. To those closest to me I had revealed my vulnerabilities, my frailties, and my fragility, my weaknesses under the pressure of sickness and the possibility of loss. I could not stop the tears regardless of how hard I tried. What was wrong with me? Why can't I stop crying? "What is the reason," I asked myself again. There was a hurt deep within, admitting to the fact that this proud Black warrior, this fighter who innately thought the world of himself, regardless of what the world thought or had thrown at me thus far; up through all the battles that had been fought, win lose or draw, was being hobbled by forces beyond my control, and even though I had done all that I could, I could not prevent it. But one lesson that has come to me is: summon up the courage to LIVE, fight to live! In spite of the hardships, perceived or imagined—I don't know which ones are worse—the pain, the disappointments, the failures, the fear, the timidity, or the discouragement, one must find a pathway to summon up the will to fight to live. You must find that encouragement somewhere in your soul, in your being. As the old heart patient who was in my room at Hahnemann years ago said "they have taken all the fight out of me." I innocently replied to the old man, "you got to fight on!" I did not know what I was talking about then, even though I had fought some significant battles up to that point. But I had just started on my road of learning *how* to fight to live when you feel there is no fight left in you. "Find it!" as Dad often said, in a context not befitting these circumstances, but still applicable, "don't give up, don't give up!" There is still much work to do, and I must be about my father's business.

42

"THE ONLY LIGHT WE'VE GOT IN ALL THIS DARKNESS"

"For, while the tale of how we suffer, and how we are delighted, and how we may triumph is never new, it always must be heard. There isn't any other tale to tell, it's the only light we've got in all this darkness."

—from James Baldwin's *Sonny's Blues*

COLOR AND CULTURE, the twin giants of human interaction. I am sub-Saharan in color and so are and were my parents and many of my other relatives. Yet when confronted with accepting an African whose color is richer and more dark, I, and some of my relatives, had an unexpected and moderately unaccepting reaction. We, myself included, opined many times about how color does not matter, "Black is beautiful" goes the rhetoric, but do we really mean it? Do we really feel it, have we internalized it, embraced it so that our skin color is nothing else but skin color: the outer presentation, the veneer, offering only a peek into our cultural past having nothing to do with our character. It carries no denotation one way or the other. As Perla remarked during one of our conversations, "back in my country (Nigeria) color does not matter." I welcomed that statement whole heartedly as one who has tussled with the issue of skin color and all of its connotations in American life most of my life until enlightenment prevailed.

Color is not intrinsic to who we are; it is but an adornment, an accessory for purposes of race identification. It is only a part of who we are and nothing else. Color is the drape that covers the window into our souls. It is part of our persona, the public side of who we are not our anima, the spiritual part of our humanness, our soul, as described by the prominent Swiss psychologist C.G. Jung and W.E.B. DuBois. Color has no substance to denote any substantive differentiation, in intelligence, capability or talent; environment and values are the determinants. Enlightened Black people should judge people based on their character not their color, or race. Do you really know what the color struggle is all about? This color thing is hard to shake; it is so ingrained in the culture of America and North

415

America, Europe and some parts of Asia that it takes strong discerning intellectual breadth, depth and reasoning to overcome the "whitewash."

Race scientists and the eugenicists of the dominant European and Anglo-American culture sought to establish White paragons of beauty, as represented the *odalisques*, White women. Regardless of the harm committed to people of color by the propagators of this flawed theory of color-related intelligence and beauty, some people have not been swayed by the dogma. Hierarchal racial beauty as represented by the *odalisques*, has long been discredited. In the Western world, race is a rigged social construct, a fiction, as I said before, brought on by a hegemonic implementation of racial hierarchy; the system of Whiteness. As Nell Painter notes in her book *The History of White People* (2010)[36], a fabricated unsupported standard of hierarchal racial beauty is nonsense:

But the question we have to ask ourselves as enlightened and free Black people who have fought to throw off the shackles of White indoctrination even in the age of Obama is: Are we really proud of our color, have we really gotten past it, or has the White color culture captured our imagination, won out, even among thoughtful educated Black people? Do we see the beauty in our women if they do not straighten their hair? If they do not pat themselves down with makeup to try to brighten their skin to resemble Whiteness? When they wear their hair in its natural form rather than imitate the White model?

I want to quote some Baldwin here. James Baldwin is one of the authors I most admire. Baldwin states the case and makes the point in his piece entitled *Color*, written for Esquire Magazine in 1962, and reprinted in *James Baldwin, Collected Essays*:

> "Everything done by Negroes in this country is, in a way, done in imitation of White people, but everything depends on the manner and intention, and the degree of hardheadedness......... (sic) Girls who have ceased doing whatever it is that American Negro girls do to their hair and allowed it to resume its natural texture are very strongly admired in some circles, but looked on with nervousness in most. Such a girl is no longer merely colored, but "somewhere else," (sic) and she poses in her presence, by all that triumphantly kinky hair, the great problem of just "who" (sic) the American Negro is, and what his future is to be [...] But Negro men are intimidated in another way altogether, having despised women with kinky hair for so long. And they are told, 'You been so brainwashed by the White man, you even wanted your women to look White!'(sic) [...] And toward what standard of beauty ought Black people now turn, especially as they exemplify, in themselves, so many different standards [...] Color, for anyone who uses it, or is used by it, is a most complex, calculated and dangerous phenomenon."

Nell Painter's *The History of White People* cited above, states the biological facts of the case:

"skin color is a by-product of two kinds of melanin: red to yellow pheomelanin and dark brown eumelanin in reaction to sunlight. And several genes interact to make people light or dark, reddish, brownish, or yellowish. Ancient scholars were wiser than they knew when they related skin color to climate. Today's biologists concur. Sunny climates do make people dark-skinned, and dark cold climates make people light skinned. How much of which sort of melanin people have in their skin—and to what degree it is expressed—depends entirely on exposure over time to the sun's ultraviolet radiation.

Our species originated in Africa some 1.2 million years ago, evolving from primates like chimpanzees, which like most other animals have light skin under dark hair. Shedding that thick coat of hair, humans quickly developed dark skin, and they stayed dark until leaving Africa for cloudier territory about 100,000 years ago, when residence in dark wintry regions like northern Europe and Northern Asia required another color change, this time from dark to light-skinned. Europeans and light skinned Asians lost pigmentation through different genetic processes in Europe and Asia. The Fundamental Black/White binary endures, even though the category of Whiteness—or we might say more precisely, a category of non-Blackness—effectively expands. As before, the Black poor remain outside the concept of the American as an "alien race of degenerate families." Nonetheless, poverty in black skin endures as the opposite of Whiteness, driven by age-old social yearning to characterize the poor as permanently other and inherently inferior."

From Countee Cullen's *Heritage*

> *What is Africa to me:*
> *Copper sun or scarlet sea,*
> *Jungle star or jungle track,*
> *Strong bronzed men, or regal black*
> *Women from whose loins I sprang*
> *When the birds of Eden sang?*
> *One three centuries removed*
> *From the scenes his fathers loved,*
> *Spicy grove, cinnamon tree,*
> *What is Africa to me?*

On the question of Africa: we say we love Africa but are we really talking about real Africa, or the romantic ideal of Africa. Do we love all that Africa entails and is? Most African Americans, in my opinion, could not make it in Africa, I mean live there on a daily basis, even if they had to today. African Americans complain about their condition here in America but fail to take advantage of the many opportunities available to them in America that would not be available to them in African countries. For example, a public primary and secondary education supported by tax paying real property owners.

Do we know enough about Africa to say whether or not we truly love it or not? All most folks know, both Black and White, is that we were taken from somewhere in Africa, West, East or Central, and enslaved against our will in America, South America or the Caribbean, but that is not the complete story. Did you know for example, that we are descendants of Egyptians, Nubians. That our history sprang from Upper Egypt which was called Nubia, and Kush? That our culture was integrated with Egyptian society and extended to land south of Egypt as well as in Egypt itself in a land that is now called the Sudan? That many of the Pharaohs of Egypt were Nubian, Black, the color of ascendency? That there are many scholars who have documented and discredited White historians' purposeful misinterpretations of our real culture and history?

When I was in Egypt, I visited a Nubian village and made sure to research, as much as a non-academic could, the cultural nexus between Americans of African descent, Africans and our sub-Saharan culture to debunk the racists' theories that we have no past and no culture, theories promulgated by western historians for political purposes. Contrary to these theories, Africans themselves were complicit in our ancestors enslavement. Africans and Arabs took slaves as a normal course of activity as early as the 8th and 9th centuries—during internecine wars and while trading among themselves and other groups—continuing through the 19th century. Arabs owned slaves among varied racial and ethic groups including many millions of Africans during this time. This was the culture during those periods but, it was the White slave traders who made a business out of it, purposefully destroying cultural and family connections to create literally a "door of no return" hence the African slave trade. Some Africans, especially tribal chiefs profited from our capture and enslavement; it was not the Africans who terminated this barbarous trade but the English wizened in part by the torment of the enormity of the immorality that their greed, avarice and competition engendered, which the Portuguese, Spanish, French and Dutch set in motion.

This shame, along with other considerations, caused the English to end the traffic in mercantile Black slavery which profited the South in America more than any other region except Brazil, in South America. Brazil ended external slavery in 1830 and was the last country in the Western Hemisphere to end domestic African slavery in the Americas on May 13, 1888. It is postulated by some authors that Britain did not end the international traffic in African slavery for the good of the African but because of the effect that increased competition from Brazilian sugar plantations operated by Portuguese and Spanish colonizers had on their profits.[37] The American Civil War was fought over the continuation of the inhumane institution and to keep the profits flowing. Did you know that in post-revolutionary America that Congress agreed, in compromise with the South over other issues, to end the traffic in international African slavery by 1808, but not its domestic slavery? Professor Klarman, whom I have mentioned previously, I am sure would agree that this compromise, ending the traffic in capturing Africans and enslaving them in America, was a "side benefit" incidental to larger and greater political and economic issues in bargaining with the South during the post-Revolutionary period, which it was.

Historians have shown that the Japanese started World War II, not only over the fight for oil and energy supplies, but also because of their ethnocentricity.[38] They believed that their culture was superior to that of the Whites and the West and they sought unsuccessfully to prove it. Non-White civilizations thrive in modernity and in technology driven environments seldom shown in Western media. This is what I enjoy seeing, the myth debunked, that the Black man—the animal as he was once seen—the African that has no history and no culture. That we were all heathens unsaved by Christ, living only in jungles, swinging from trees, in poverty, naked, ignorant, in rape, in robbery, in chaos and in ignominy. That we should be grateful, get down on our knees and thank whatever and whoever our God is, that the White man "saved" us, from our own backwardness through slavery in America, Brazil and the Caribbean to endure 400 years of barbarity. For this we should be forever beholden to him, forever grateful. Perhaps, there are many things we can be grateful for as a people living in America, but slavery and its aftermath is not one of them.

Why is it that the United States contributes more money in foreign aid to the country of Israel than to the continent of Africa? A conservative estimate of annual direct foreign aid from all sources to Israel is almost 114 billion[39]. Estimated foreign aid to sub-Saharan Africa, over the past 4 years has been approximately 3.2 billion with the United States proposing to triple its aid to 7.2 billion. The Congressional Research Service determined that between 2009 and 2011, U.S. foreign assistance totaled $23.19 billion[40], aid to one country compared to 49 countries in the African continent. Why is this allowed to happen? Why is Africa the dumping ground for the debris of the West? Why was the massacre in Rwanda allowed to fester until hundreds of thousands of people were killed and slaughtered because of inter-tribal rivalries between the Hutu and the Tutsis engendered by European colonial political decisions? The Rwandans were responsible for this genocide themselves and should not have needed the White man to come to their rescue and end the carnage.

And why was Africa divided into nation states and not allowed to develop along its traditional boundaries by regions and with communal living? Instead it was divided into individual states where everything had to be owned, fueling feuds and killing that might have been avoided. And finally why were the buildings in Haiti so poorly constructed that when the recent earthquake occurred over 200,000 thousand Haitians died compared to just tens of thousands in other earthquake sites such as in Australia and Japan? The answer lies in color politics, racism, apathy and the self-interest of the United States and European foreign policy.

Basil Davidson, the African historian, espouses these truths in his book entitled *The Black Man's Burden, Africa and the Curse of the Nation-State* (1992)[41]. Race is the key that unlocks the door. It's not what we allow; it's what we get, for we are powerless, as individuals to some extent, to change the power balance as it exists because of the political realities we face. James Baldwin again iterates this concept in an appropriate passage in his *Notes of a Native Son*, in the chapter "Encounter on the Seine":

> "The African before him has endured privation, injustice, medieval cruelty; but the African has not yet endured the utter alien-

ation of himself from his people and his past. His mother did not sing 'sometimes I feel Like a motherless Child,' and he has not, all his life long ached for acceptance in a culture which pronounced straight hair and White skin the only acceptable beauty. They face each other, the Negro and the African, over a gulf of three hundred years—an alienation too vast to be conquered in an evening's good-will, too heavy and too double-edged ever to be trapped in speech. This alienation causes the Negro to recognize that he is a hybrid. Not a physical hybrid merely: in every aspect of his living he betrays the memory of the auction block, and the impact of the happy ending."

How many of us would actually move to Africa to live permanently? Some African Americans have done so, but I would not. Because having visited on an extended tour, and I plan to return again, there are too many deprivations that I would have to endure that would make my life uncomfortable at my age and in my state of health. I have an "out." What is yours? For example, I need quality health care, potable water and sewage treatment facilities as well as other necessities and amenities I have become accustomed to. I need statesmen instead of tyrants and dictators who loot the peoples' money for their own pockets. I need justice not vengeance and cronyism. I need consensus for the good of the country not wars over egos and the maintenance of graft. I need educated and informed leaders not strong military men who know nothing about governance but who may be in love with the opportunity brought on through "might" rather than the vote! I need self-interest to be subjugated to the public interest, and I need respect for the sanctity of human life. Much of these needs can be satisfied in many African countries but is strikingly absent from many others.

So for me, it would not work long term. Besides, the African elite, of which I am not, and the political elite control the towns and cities, the bureaucracies of government, education, politics, and industry, areas I would be interested in. In Africa, I would be as removed from the inner workings on that continent as I am from the inner workings in Washington D.C. On the outside looking in, looking for something that does not exist, looking to reconnect but finding out just how disconnected from Africa I really am. So, I should just as well be comfortable in my dreams of Africa, back home, dreaming of the ideal about Africa, the mother land; it's better for me that way. There is comfort in the dream, and in the fantasy, just like there is comfort in the dream of the Christian heaven and the Egyptian promise in the afterlife.

Africa is a beautiful continent to visit, but living there, at least for me, is another story. I do not mean to dissuade any Black person from moving and living in Africa; it can be done and is being done, very successfully by many enterprising African Americans, but for me the greatest benefit is to go and visit, soak up the culture, enjoy being Black and in the majority and trying to find ancestral roots. Finding the ancestral root, or as close to it as one can come, and bridging the cultural divide arbitrarily imposed upon us by the greed and avarice of the slave traders: that is what I enjoy most. Seeing sophisticated Africans doing sophisticated things, living in modern urban and rural homes and apartment buildings, doing business in business centers, with skyscrapers, traffic jams, good restaurants, nice hotels, seaside resorts and with good governance, fine universities and libraries: in effect, in "civilization."

James Baldwin opined in his book *No Name in the Street* (1972), in the chapter "To Be Baptized": "A civilized country is, by definition, a country dominated by Whites, in which Blacks know their place." Civilization must, if it exists at all, be under his rule, his culture, his mores and his branding. But if you can pull yourself away from the television—and the indoctrination that goes with it—the greatest propaganda tool in the history of mankind used to perpetuate hegemony, political indoctrination and control and cultural ethnocentricity—read some relevant books and travel, you will find that civilization exists "outside of his rule" and it thrives not only in Africa but in Asia as well. All that being said I still prefer the Western standard of living. Even though we know how these standards were obtained, through the subjugation of minorities and people of color.

In Basil Davidson's book *The Lost Cities of Africa* (1987)[42], he notes that

> "it is this probable fact of their major movement (Africans) and migration and settlement in the fifteen centuries or so before the coming of European trade and penetration that gives this long historic period it greatest significance. This is why the definitive history of African peoples, when finally it gets itself beyond the hesitations of the learned and the speculations of the unlearned—when finally it is fully written—will have to explain the course of the discovery and growth of agriculture in continental Africa, and even more, the course of the discovery and growth of the use of metals, but principally of iron. [...] Yet the record is very far from one of stagnation. These were pioneering peoples. They tilled where none had tilled before. They mined where there was none to show them how. They discovered a valuable pharmacopoeia. They were skillful in terraced irrigation and the conservation of soil on steep hillsides. They built new and complex social systems. They transformed whatever they could borrow from other and technologically more advanced social systems to the north, added and adapted and experienced and invented, until in the course of time they acquired a range of technique and a mastery of art, philosophy and attitude and temperament and religion, that were unique to themselves and make the "Negro-ness" the negritude, they have today."

This African metal age of the last fifteen or twenty centuries, in short, is the formative period of modern Africa. It possessed its own dynamic of growth and change. It produced its own cultures and civilizations, uniquely African.

Making the cultural and ancestral connection is what it is all about for me. If that can be achieved, that will enhance with great pleasure my Blackness, reveling in being Black and of African ancestry, palin-genesis, biologists call it: a rebirth and regeneration of me as an American of African descent. Knowing where you come from and visiting the motherland to bridge the chasm, the cultural ancestral chasm, is a requirement.

I said to myself, as I wrote the following words on September 4, 2002 flying to Accra: "I am an admirer, a devotee of something I know little about in reality, of the continent of Africa and its people. But my desire for knowledge of the African diaspora is insatiable, my love for my people unyielding, despite the onslaught of misinformation and the torrent of intentional disinformation, falsehoods and ambiguity about the motherland. The chasm in my cultural self may never be bridged, never be fulfilled, never satisfied, yet I must acquiesce in my present plight. I must accept the world as it is, but I journey forth resolutely in search of Nubian love and truth."

A few days later on September 7, 2002, while visiting Elmina in the central region of Ghana close to the south bay of the Atlantic Ocean, it came to me that on the question of justice and reconciliation, which we are all looking for, we need look no further. But we must see. In spite of all the crimes and atrocities committed against us, God has granted justice. God has given the Black man a continent, a big slice of the earth called Africa that the White man does not own, possess or control, though he has worked hard to do all these things, albeit with little lasting success. Compare what the Blacks have in Africa to what the Jews have in the Middle East, in Israel. There is no comparison.

In my view, Americans of African descent, like the devoted Muslim who must make a hajj at least once to Mecca during his lifetime, should make the pilgrimage to Africa at least once in his or her life, if it is within their financial means. I believe such a journey would enlighten that person and provide a balm to the wounds. It would also provide appreciation for what they have in America and a greater appreciation of African cultural underpinnings.

Additional thoughts came to mind while flying out of Johannesburg, South Africa en route to Cape Town on September 10, 2002: "The Blackman has already won. The problem we have as Black people is that we must realize that there is no distinction between the culture of the slave master and that of the colonizer. They both were and are White men and women individually, and in corporations and institutions, bent on perpetuating European and Anglo-American ethno-centrism; closely followed by Asian ethnocentrism." It took several days after being in Africa for me to begin to feel relief from the oppression of White culture. I thought the relief would come immediately but it took a while. However, after a few days I began to feel that the darkness of my skin color was no longer a line of demarcation, but a gateway into a majority Black culture. Everybody looked like me. In essence the message was "the darker you are the more authentic your African pedigree." This feeling coupled with seeing for the first time White people being in the minority, including Asians and South Asian Indians was an intellectual breath of fresh air. Black majority status, rule, and authority, without considering all the corruption and incongruities with governing was emboldening psychologically and therapeutic.

43

"WITNESS THAT DEEP WATER AND DROWNING WERE NOT THE SAME THING"

Failure should be our teacher,
not our undertaker.
It should challenge us to new
heights of accomplishments, not
pull us to new depths of despair.
Failure is delay, but not defeat.
It is a temporary detour, not a
dead-end street.

William Arthur Ward

S WIMMING, before the advent of the latest cardiac event was for me both therapeutic physically and psychologically challenging. Health wise I took up swimming to ensure, as much as I could, that I would not get diabetes. I reasoned that when I had my heart attack in 1990 I was ignorant about the causes or how to prevent heart attacks, not knowing that genealogy played a role as well. But now I was more educated about heart disease and related diseases. Mother suffered from diabetes, and I knew the pain she endured and I did not want to exacerbate my present condition with another preventable condition, such as diabetes since I knew generally how to prevent it. I was also concerned about my endurance level which before I began swimming was limited. I felt winded when walking or engaging in moderate exercises and yard work such as mowing the grass. I was out of shape. I had worked on the treadmill consistently but that was not doing the trick. Also I was looking for something to do, something to fill the vacuum in my time since I was retiring from the practice of law and Michelle was fully occupied with her doctoral studies. I felt empty, hollow and without purpose or focus—a male mid-life crisis.

Most of all I wanted to finally overcome my fear of the water and learn an exercise I could do for the rest of my life, since playing basketball was getting beyond my capacity. I was also tired of not knowing how to swim. I had avoided this sport because of my fear of water. This flaw typified the view of some Blacks and White folks as well, but I have never been one who dwelled in, wallowed in, accepted or tolerated stereotypes; they are anathema to me. I wanted to get over this bugaboo. I was a runner to some extent both in Philadelphia and in Charlottesville, but none of these exercises had the confluence of benefits that could be achieved by swimming. Before I began to swim, because of my heart condition and lack of conditioning, I could not push a power mower 100 feet without being exhausted. I knew then that something had to be done to improve my endurance and overall health.

So I took up the challenge of the sport and committed myself whole heartedly to it. At one time I could not swim half way up or down a 25 meter lane without stopping and turning on my back to rest and recover. I had taken a beginners swimming course at Howard as I said earlier, but I did not learn how to swim; all I did was fake it. I still had the fear which prevented me from swimming, and I did not even have a rudimentary foundation in proper technique. But now I was fortunate to have come under the tutelage of a good, compassionate White female swim coach who is the aquatics director at the local athletic club I attend. She swam like a dolphin in the water. She set a high example, so graceful and fluid in her strokes. I marveled at her proficiency, technique and skill in the water and of course, as usual, I wanted to swim like her. So I worked and invested hundreds of dollars in swimming lessons at the club over six years and I practiced two sometimes, three days a week for an hour at each session.

I also like swimming because it is a solitary sport for those who swim this way, which lends itself to my sense of isolation and reclusiveness. I like the seclusion, the individuality, the contemplation, and feel of the cool waters on my body, and I had no one to compete with except the clock and myself. The serenity and quietude of finding the pool unoccupied was finding a moment in heaven for as long as it lasted. I made sure I learned all of the strokes and worked to gain a proficiency in each. Not to be an expert in each stroke, but to swim each of them with some measure of proper technique and style: the freestyle, the back stroke, the breast stroke, the butterfly, the side stroke. The elementary back stroke was the only existing stroke I could do before the lessons began. Now, after years of consistent swimming, I am swimming to the extent that swimming is an exercise, not just a recreation for me. Through those lessons, I became a fitness swimmer. In other words, I could swim well enough to get an aerobic benefit from the exercise. For me, I could not be satisfied with going half way. It is all the way or dissatisfaction.

Of course I read a book on the subject after a while, because it bothered me that I had taken all these swim lessons and never read anything formally about the techniques for swimming, beyond what my coach had taught me. I bought specialized goggles, fins and caps and ear plugs to defeat the aspects of swimming that were distasteful, such as water in my ears and up my nose. I found a way through equipment experiments to limit these aspects. I learned how to do flip turns and open turns and practiced them until I developed a technique suitable for my style and level that facilitated my strokes. Now, when I swim I can compete well with the above average swimmer in my age class and health condition who may also have learned how to swim late in life. That is because I have been there and paid the price to conquer a fear, and in the process took control of my health, increased my endurance, lowered my blood sugar to the point that diabetes was no longer an immediate threat; improved my overall health and enhanced my self-image. I became a swimmer, all because of a burning desire and I paid the price demanded.

When we traveled, I made sure I swam. I swam in Xian, Beijing and Shanghai, China; I swam in Istanbul, Cappadocia and Antalya, Turkey. I swam in Dakar,

Senegal. I was prepared to swim in Russia but the opportunity did not present itself. Like golfers who enjoy playing on the links around the world when they travel, I sought to do the same thing with my swimming. I became a competitor against myself, setting higher and higher goals and trying to mimic swimmers that swam better than me by observing them and learning from their techniques, the same approach taken to learn how to practice law competently. But in the end, I can only go so far. Age, training and health have stymied my progress. Ironically, my over-exertion, with longer and longer endurance stretches in the freestyle to 30 minutes in a 25 meter pool without interruption with flip turns at each end, along with continuing my regular routine, may have led to my latest heart rhythm disturbance. It is posited by one of my friends who is a cardiologist, that by pushing myself so hard and stressing myself to these higher levels I may have unleashed an enzyme in my heart that may have triggered a dormant tachycardia impulse. We do not know this for sure; it is only speculation. After all, I had begun to do this longer routine over a period of several months but only periodically when all the factors, my mental state, the quiet of the pool, etc. existed. There is no evidence to support the theory; in fact some of my doctors have said that the swimming had nothing to do with the rhythm attack. I was taken off the old arrhythmic medicines years ago, before I began the swimming, so I had no protection. I traveled around the world and had no problems, thank God! Who knows? Perhaps the stressors involved with building the Fitzgerald Company over the last 12 years may have contributed. I just do not know. In any event, no more over-achievement for me! No more vigorous competitive exertions. Henceforth I will, in more ways than one, do what I can and forget about the rest. No more competition, against myself as well as others, no more comparisons. It will be what it is. This may be easier said than done for me, but I am going to make a concerted effort to pull back from these competitive instincts

To be finished with my father's business is to finish my business because his business is my business, and my business is his business. The linkage cannot be broken; there is an intergenerational transfer of values and materiel: to satisfy my duty to the children I produced, not to be solely a friend but a father, a dad, a light, an inspiration and a helmsman for the example of what manhood should attempt to embrace. Not perfection but, decency, civility, truth and honesty in the attempt. To care for my widowed mother to make her last days as gratifying as it is within my capability to do, realizing the frailties of age and the limitations us human beings have when doing battle with nature. And to my wife, to see that her faith in the man she entrusted with her future is validated with a good return on her mental, spiritual and physical investment and to be there for her as her friend foremost, her lover always, her guardian as needed and her protector until the end, as long as God enables me to be capable. And of course to myself. I have to finish the job of living this life to its fullest as best I envisage it to satisfy the trust reposed upon me by my profession and to those members of the public who put their trust in me; to have gotten all I can get out of myself within my true capability and strengths, in spite of the imperfections, foibles, and complexities that nature imposes. If I can do these things and do them well or even come close, I will finish this life in good standing with those that matter most in my life.

44

THE DOOR OF NO RETURN

I VENTURED OUT onto a short stone ledge underneath the transom of the door of no return in a fort near Cape Coast in southern Ghana. At my back stood the rear of a labyrinthine complex of dark concrete rooms with little light or ventilation, at the end of a winding dark tunnel twenty feet above the shore line. Flashes of light staccato in sequence beamed upon my face as I gazed upon the glimmering blue sheen of the Atlantic Ocean and imagined the horrible scenes of my ancestors with shackles on their ankles, arms tied behind their backs, being led from the dungeons of the barracoons from which they had been kept: waiting to be loaded onto slave ships anchored off shore to be packed like sardines for transport to an alien land for further subjugation, humiliation, and deprivation. Tears welled up in my eyes.

I traveled on "the grand tour," half way around the world, to many places including Egypt, Russia, Finland, India, China, England, France, Turkey, Brazil and to the continent of Africa to find the holy grail of race pride, just to realize that it was right there in my DNA, of all places, ever present. As the old folks would say, "if it was a snake it would have bitten me."

On the question of DNA, I took those tests, through African Ancestry, a firm associated with Rick Kittles Ph.D., to determine—as much as these tests can determine—what my African lineage shared genealogically with the samples of DNA available from tribes in Africa, contained in the firm's sample. Sure enough, without much surprise, my paternal linkage came up with ancestry as measured by the Y-chromosome DNA markers: a shared paternal genetic ancestry sequence similarity measure of 100% with the Ewe people of southern Ghana close to the south eastern fringe of Togo.

Using standard techniques but dissimilar biological factors for genetic analysis of mitochondrial DNA to determine my maternal African linkage, the study disclosed that I share with my maternal ancestors DNA traits with a sequence similarity of 99.7% with the Bubi people, inhabitants in Bioko Island, Equatorial Guinea today.

Before this, I acquired my African name "Nana Yaw" drawn from a dialect of the Asante tribe in Ghana, meaning, "chief born on Thursday." The name was bestowed on me during a naming ceremony held outside of our hotel room in Accra. I was impressed by the new *nom de guerre* particularly because the nomenclature was from the Akan people from the Ashanti region of Ghana. When I arrived and traveled through Ghana, I had a sense that I shared a connection with these people. It just seemed so natural. We traveled to Kumasi a city in the south of the country and visited a military museum. While looking at the pictures on the wall of some of their officers, I saw a picture of a man, an officer in the Ghanian military, who looked almost exactly like my father. I was awe struck by the resemblance so much so that I asked our guide to return to the museum to take a picture of that man because the similarity was so striking. The irony is, of course, I did not know then that I have an ancestral link, not only to the country of Ghana, but to that region as well, since the Ewe people inhabit the southeastern region of Ghana.

African names are complex. Usually within the name there is a definition of where the child was born geographically within the country, the designation of his tribe and the day of the week on which he or she was born and his father's surname.

Two questions are raised by this event. What in reality is the significance of a name? And what affect did this naming event have on my being? I was not then nor am I prepared today to discard the patronymic I've known all my life. My father toiled and labored to make his name mean something to stand for something good and positive. And he thought well enough of himself to give his name to me, albeit a name he knew not from whence it came, though it can easily be imagined that the name is of slave master origin. Consequently, I have labored hard to give the name meaning and honor. Is all of this work and toil to be disregarded solely for the sake of an ill-defined only partially discovered African ancestry? I think not. But how did this new name make me feel? It bridged a psychological gap, contributed to the healing process and made the African experience have deeper meaning and wholeness.

When you boil it all down to the "pot liquor" as my father often said, these experiences make you feel better, lifts the human spirit, elevates self-respect, bolsters self-esteem and the abstract African heritage you know is in your blood more real.

My father, on many mornings before I would leave the house would ask me "whose son are you?" I often would reply "come on Dad, do we have to go through this again?" "Yes," he would affirm, "whose son are you?" he would repeat, but this time looking more sternly, as if to say I am serious about this. "Otis Lee's son" I would say sheepishly. His point was to make sure that I knew that when I left his home my behavior had better be up to the standard of his name, and I knew that my dad would not let me soon forget it, not once, if it was not.

An attempt to eviscerate a proud and ancient cultural history was only partially successful. Blood proved to be thicker than mendacity and meanness. The vestiges of the cultural past that remained after the middle passage were debased and caricatured to sever the remnants from their tenuous moorings on which they clung. With the onslaught of adverse Americana directed at the tenuous moorings that held the waning cultural roots together, those flimsy roots began to whither and even became the object of scorn as generations of hitherto Africans became Americanized. The Africans of the middle passage clung to what they had and their successors must work hard to stitch together the cultural twill that will withstand any attack. That fabric must be strong enough to connect the past with the present and make it live again.

African people, the whole diaspora, must view ourselves from a millennium perspective. The world is the way it is because of the present allocation of power. But the arc of time is long and enduring and will once again at some future time restore mankind to its natural balance. The poet William Cullen Bryant wrote: "truth crushed to the earth will rise again," and Baldwin iterates, in *The Fire Next Time*, "Time catches up with kingdoms and crushes them, gets its teeth into doctrines and rends them; time reveals the foundations on which any kingdom rests, and eats at those foundations, and destroys doctrines by proving them to be untrue."

Making the "connection," that's what it is all about. Knowing where you come from and visiting the motherland to bridge the chasm, the cultural ancestral chasm is a necessity for those to whom these issues matter. Years ago I knew nothing about the great African leaders. In Accra, I visited Senghor's awe inspiring monument and the memorial of Kwame Nkrumah. I was attracted to Senghor by his brilliance, simply through my own inclination to gravitate toward people of substance who were notable and Black. I was ignorant of many of his contributions, and I had the pleasure of visiting his hometown while in Senegal, traveling to Joal, a small coastal fishing town outside of Dakar, and touring the museum in his honor.

While visiting Goree Island, one of the most notable of the many slave depots off the coast of Dakar along the West African coast. The curator of Goree, a Black man with skin as black and leathery as fresh raw hide put through a tanner, exclaimed in a bellowing voice how this slave place was the staging area for slaves bound for the Americas; that the "Jews complained of the holocaust which took place over a decade or two at most but, that the Africans had been enslaved for 400 hundred years." The curator was not diminishing the severity of the Holocaust, but putting that tragedy in perspective when compared to what the African had endured; expressing sympathy but dealing with the reality of history. Sympathy for the Jews is in order, but so is sympathy for the Armenians, the American Indians, the Timorese, the Palestinians and other repressed and suppressed groups all around the world. No race has a monopoly on oppression, but Black oppression ranks high if not the highest in its severity, duration, and cruelty. Twenty-five million or more were killed or died in passage; and over eleven million lived to be enslaved. These are not exact numbers, I'll leave that to the academicians, but the numbers who were killed, who died in transit and who were enslaved are in the tens of millions. After the curator finished his oration, he presented us with the visitors book to sign, you could write whatever statement you felt was appropriate and each person was given a certificate of attendance witnessing that we, a few of the fortunate, had been blessed to visit this sacred site in the history of Africans; "the fortunate" few African Americans.

What is more, having studied the career of W.E.B. Du Bois, another of my heroes, the quintessential academic, having read several volumes of biographies about him and several of his books, most notably The Souls of Black Folk, I visited his museum and home outside of Accra while in Ghana. In South Africa, Michelle and I visited Nelson Mandela's home, in Soweto, visited Robben Island where Mandela spent 27 years of his life, twelve kilometers by boat off the coast of Cape

Town. I sat in the prison yard and looked into the prison cell where he was incarcerated, and I tried to imagine just for a fleeting moment what that could have been like, unimaginable!

I have been to Atlanta to visit Martin Luther King's memorial, another one of my heroes, and studied the writings of King and Malcolm X as well, and the list goes on. Alexander Sergeyevich Pushkin, whose home we passed by while cruising on the Neva River in St. Petersburg, Russia several years ago, was another one of my favorites.

As the years passed, I reasoned that perhaps the fault lay within, not without. Ohh! stop whining man! Forget about it! How important is this cultural thing anyway? To be reconnected with the mother country, to bath in the bosom of kindred spirits. You made it in spite of the real or imagined, perceived amorphous or not so amorphous beast of racism. What does it matter in the end? I crawled into the belly of my deficits and laid claim to the heart of my latent genius and fought to free myself of this scourge—to exorcize from my being those demons fabricated for political, sociological and exploitative purposes. By returning to Africa, I tossed overboard the demons I carried and vowed never to carry them again. A scab grew to cover the festering wound and dried up the oozing puss that seeped from the psychological contusion.

The transformative experience of exiting the dungeons from the doors of no return and turning around and reentering that door was for me the receipt of the "Balm in Gilead." I had been released. I had bridged the gap, crossed the divide and in the process personified for myself the origins of my beginnings. I reveled in the beauty of my Blackness, the dominance of Black, the pearl of ebony, no longer a minority but in the majority. That moment of transcendence was exaltation.

The truth is that there are many doors of no return through which we leave and never return, some by choice, others by circumstance, but the power of knowledge to face these travails is determinative. Thousands of doors of no return exist in every soul untutored, in every ghetto of the mind, every broken home and in every dream deferred. A healthy self-image and a good dose of self-esteem are essential building blocks for a run at a successful life.

There is peace in the valley of my soul these days. The wanderings of my mind have been stilled. All questions have not been answered, but the essentials needed for a reconciliation with my essence are in place.

An old swimming friend, named Frank Featherstone, a career Navy man and a graduate of the Naval Academy, once responded to a question I asked him about what he thought it took to be successful in this world: "moderation," he said, "use it in everything you do, and be comfortable in your own skin." His perspective, from the White point of view, was especially poignant both figuratively and physically, but however one took that statement it rings true, and finally he said, "smell the roses as you go along".

I would add not only "smell the roses" but put your nose down in the blossom and inhale deeply.

Whether you have no need for the twine that ties you to your ancestral fabric, or you feel that you are threatened without it. What and who you came from matters, it matters greatly. It matters because it means respect for yourself, when others treat you with disrespect or you forget to respect yourself when feeling low.

Self-esteem, which is not easy to get and much more difficult to maintain, pride in who you came from, and respect for the price paid by your ancestors so that you can live a life, whether to your liking or not, which in all likelihood was better than theirs, are essential to how you live today. And, it provides an assist to help you live up to the sacrifices made by your ancestors whether they are related to you or not, because it is upon their shoulders that we stand. It is the ability to separate the noise of life from the music of life: that is the *sine qua non*, the *elan vital* of living a successful and balanced life in a culture filled with challenges.

It was recounted in a biography of Nelson Mandela how knowledge of his lineage, that he had been sired by a king and knew his roots sprang from a line of kings, sustained him and kept him from being broken during his 27 years of captivity in South African prisons. Some say writing about this stuff is cathartic, redemptive, and therapeutic. Maybe so, but maybe, for African-American generations removed, it really is something less easily obtained—maybe it is emancipation.

Epilogue:
My Journey from
South Boston to Cambridge

S O HERE I SIT IN HARKNESS COMMONS, the student center at Harvard University Law School in Cambridge, Massachusetts on a sunny, cool spring day in April 2005. This is a modern red brick building with polished stainless steel and smooth dark hardwood finishes, marble stone bathrooms, ceiling to floor panoramic windows and state of the art dining facilities, everything here is "first world." The law school campus pulsates with the history of scholarship, high learning, arrogance and entitlement. This institution is one of the pinnacles of academic achievement: this place houses a vast repository of law, philosophy, literature, science and numerous other areas of academic inquiry.

I am here accompanying my youngest son, Justin, the third generation of the Moon, Penick/Lee, family to labor in the halls of the academy. I am here with him during "admitted students weekend." He is nervous, not knowing what to expect, yet proud that he is among the privileged few to be feted at this event. I have reflected on how I got here to Cambridge, Massachusetts from my family's beginnings in South Boston, Virginia and Fitzgerald, Georgia. My story is nearly complete, but my son's story of education and achievement is just beginning.

A Word About Historic Smithville, N.C.

After many years of waging a fight yet unfinished and after four years of searching and a ten-day adventurous sea coast tour from southeast Virginia down to southeastern North Carolina, I found a place in a small seaside hamlet called Smithville Township, North Carolina, surrounded by ocean's, rivers, creeks and streams that, long ago, changed it's name. I view the acquisition of this property as a piece of paradise, an El Dorado, a piece of heaven here on earth; my place of tranquility, but in reality there is no absolute peace, except in the habitation of the dead. As literal payment for my tribulations, those self-inflicted and those externally administered. It matters not.

God blessed me to have acquired this cottage, in a resort community that I call my chateau by the ocean. A quiet place to contemplate, to read, to write, to have a place of solace and quietude, to simply do nothing. A momentary respite from the cares and unpleasantries of other communities; to quietly prepare for the final chapter—which I do not expect anytime soon, but that will surely come when nature and God see fit—of my life. When I think of all the needless trash that I endured, the filth and the disquieting encounters, both physical and mental, and the psychological wasteland that I traversed, which I admit probably pales in significance to the travails of others, despite all the hurt and pain of life's ups and downs, I feel that I finally have payment, some recompense for my anguish, payment for this part of my life's journey.

EXEGI!

Spiritual Afterthought:
Faith of Our Fathers
Living Still

I believe in religion because I choose to believe in religion. I do not accept the Christian pathway or dogma or for that matter, the dogma of any other faith system. To me they are all flawed in one way or another. There perhaps is no "perfect" religious belief system. I find myself, therefore, most closely associated with believing in Deism—one who believes in a benevolent holy spirit, a spiritual force for good in the world without accepting the superhuman, supernatural events recited in religious dogma. I am a spiritualist. As the old Negro spiritual says "his eye is on the sparrow and I know he watches me." I believe because I refuse to accept that my world is limited to that of man with his many faults and foibles. I need to believe in something greater, something more generous, something grander, more caring, more powerful, and more equitable. From a purely psychological standpoint, what makes you feel better about your prospects, the religious view or nothingness, oblivion? For me, religion is more comforting. I have been saved by the intercession of an inexplicable force for good in my life, which I define as God. I would not be here but for, his or her or its intervention, his or her or its design, his or her or its omnipotent vision for my life. That's why I must believe.

I believe that superstition, God or Deity worship, over millennia have evolved into a bureaucracy of those whose power and wealth increased because of their fictional affinity to the unknown, i.e. holy men, witch doctors, soothsayers, medicine men, shamans, mythologists, mystics, prophets, priests, bishops, popes, pastors, ministers and Imams. Those who sought to explain the inexplicable evolved their beliefs and practices into the bureaucracy of religion. A body of subjective sophistry, and polemics and theological academic doctrine so dense and developed which encloses the mysticism surrounding the rituals and practices, policies and principles well beyond what the average person can grasp or for that matter understand. The advocates and promoters of religious doctrine realize that people are gullible, naturally fearful of the unknown, ignorant, therefore easily led to follow a system of beliefs that will assuage their angst and remove death as the ultimate extinction. They are then caused to believe any ostensible plausible direction and explanation.

Religion is an institution that exits to perpetuate itself. People profit from the institution. Some of the best jobs people have ever had have come from being "a messenger of God." I eschew the quacks, the charlatans, the fakers, who feign piety for profit and social status, the opportunists, the screamers and sanctimonious politicians posing as preachers who use histrionics instead of reasoned thought to convey the precepts of a faith. These are not men called from divine inspiration but men who called themselves because of what they can make out of espousing a dogma they have contrived to sell to the public in the name of a job and religion.

From my reading on the subject, I know that many Christian religious scholars see God as an abstraction, that God had no beginning or end, a force unapproachable by ordinary men such as me. That he must be approached, in the Christian tradition, through an intermediary, his agent, his representative.

For Christians, it is Jesus Christ who represents, the word incarnate, the Logos, the trinity; Father, Son, and Holy Ghost. I know from my research that the divinity of Jesus Christ was the source of the division in the Christian Church between East and West. And just as the Roman Empire was divided between East and West, so is the Christian Church. Each sector has its own Pope; in fact in the Eastern Christian church it has more than one.

Very briefly and without elaboration, there developed in 319 A.D. between factions in Alexandria, Egypt and thereabouts advocating the priest Arius' Christological subordinationist view, that God did not have a beginning, but the Logos did, meaning the divine word or reason incarnate in Jesus Christ. Athanasius, of Alexandria, probably one of the most influential Christian leaders after the death of Jesus Christ, urged the opposing view, that faith should take priority over reason and that the Son of God was one and the same as the Holy Spirit and God the Father. The debate over this subject was first officially deliberated and voted on in the First Ecumenical Council assembled at Nicaea in 325 A.D in Brithynia between Arius and his supporters also of Alexandria and Athanasius. Athanasius won the argument that resulted in the Nicaean creed which we recite today in Christian Churches. Subsequent councils were held over the years to continue the defense of the divinity of the Holy Spirit, the human soul of Christ and Christ's divinity. And prepared the groundwork for the orthodox doctrine of the Trinity as we know it today. Battles over these issues continued for a long time. Athanasius was responsible for selecting the 27 books of the New Testament included in the Bible. Athanasius is described as "a pillar of the church, his doctrine the rule of the orthodox faith."

Terms like Theotokos or Godbearer, speaking of Mary; homoousios, Christ is one in essence with the father; eschatological, meaning final, judgment, death and future state; ontological, an argument for the existence and perfection of God; Monophysitic, Miaphysites Dyophysites, and hypostasis and consubstantiation are all terms defining either the two natures or one nature of Christ, but are not terms commonly encountered by the lay public. But each term defines even more closely the essence and nature of Jesus Christ and helps explain the controversy over this subject in ancient times. At the Council of Chalcedon in 451 A.D, the Eastern church split from the Western church over these issues.[43]

Gaining an understanding of all this dogma is beyond the capability of most parishioners and congregants. Some of these religious doctrines are so abstruse and nuanced that deciphering them requires studious discipline and determination. I have gained a simplistic understanding as a layperson that has helped inform the basis of my decision to believe, not the truth or falsity of any of it, just simply an understanding of how the dogma came to be—the basis for it all. I do not accept blindly following or believing in anything or anybody. Everything in my view must make sense and have some empirically logical underpinning.

Having visited some of the great museums of Europe, I have come to recognize that the artists who painted images of Christ and other important religious figures from Western theology have painted and portrayed these images as White men and women. If logically one is to accept the definition of the Trinity, that Christ is God in incarnate, then it is the position of the religious hierarchy both in the east and the West—based upon the works of many White artists and portraitists, some of whom are very famous, not the least among them being Michelangelo, and Leonardo Da Vinci, who were commissioned by religious leaders of their day—to paint these images, along with many others: that God is a White man. The depiction of Jesus Christ as a White man when in fact he was Jewish and swarthy in complexion points to nefarious intentions on behalf of the power structure to indoctrinate the people in the belief that Jesus Christ was White. Certainly those in the religious bureaucracy in the west are responsible for these images and this iconography, further evidence of the "branding" of the world in the White image. This is unacceptable to seekers of a higher truth, a higher salvation, a higher elevation to the divine. This is a convenient and useful position for the state, the system and for imperial cultures, who want the White brand to predominate the entire culture of the Western world including life after death the most significant tradition of Christian religious belief. That is why some of the Eastern religions such as Islam are actually more appealing because some of them, Islam in particular, prohibit iconography and image making of the prophet or supreme spirit. At one time Christianity forbade the same thing. This is especially comforting and appealing to me in my state of mind. I cannot accept God, incarnate in Jesus Christ as my God being represented as a White, blond haired, blue eyed man. Just as I cannot accept the movies and some historical portrayals of Egyptians as being White which they were not, the cradle of it all.

W.E.B. Du Bois is quoted by one of his biographers as saying that he, Du Bois, saw no evidence of the Christian dogma. And that he, Du Bois, was of the opinion that "all art was propaganda." Edward W. Said, the noted Palestinian scholar and a former professor at Columbia University, puts forth his thesis in his book, *Culture and Imperialism* (1993), that European imperial powers such as America, England, Italy, Spain, Portugal, France, Germany, the Netherlands, and others, through the works of artists, composers, and portraitists promote the subjugation of perceived lower cultures in non-White societies and seek to impose their imperial cultures upon them, making these cultural products images of themselves and representative of their "superior" society. I perceive this to be correct, like metadata in computer usage these messages are hidden and insidious.

All of the above is good for gaining an understanding of what it is you believe in. All of it written by mortal men who studied these subjects, had opinions and took a proprietary interest in promoting their view of Christianity. But in my view their theories did not elevate them any higher toward approaching God than the most ignorant, simple believer in a higher being. Why must God or his image be anthropomorphic? This, in my view, is purposefully contrived for the aforementioned purposes. For me, I do not need all of this body of theological erudition that enabled the formation of the religious bureaucracy in the world. What I need is less formality, but reverential respect, dignity and seriousness of thought, no icons, no gimmicks, no hyperbole, just intelligent cogent thinking about the need to have a respect for the almighty, the high spiritual force, to acknowledge his or her presence in the world and in the events of our lives, albeit not fully comprehensible.

For years I was tormented because I kept questioning the logic and science of the Christian dogma. I was haunted by perceptions that having these curiosities was an apostasy, was blasphemous. But the more I kept reading and gaining clarity, history and knowledge and more education about religion and what it was that I was being led blindly and unintelligibly to believe in, the less I believed blindly. Hence, I formed my beliefs more intelligently with a focus on what was important, in the purpose for religion, filling that inexplicable gray area in our lives; assisting us to deal more effectively with the sacred and the profane, and the positive effects it promotes individually and in society. I became less focused on the people or the personalities, but more on the spirit. When I was in the throes of depression and drug use, I sent away for a Surgeon General's Report on the harmful effects and dangers of smoking marijuana. The more I read about its harmful effects, the more my inner voice kept gnawing at me to leave it alone which I did. And so it has been with me and religion. The more I have inquired, the less I believe in the dogma of most religions. But this has not dissuaded me from believing in the "Great Spirit." For me it is impossible to reconcile the injustices, inconsistencies, empiricisms, realities, and the unfairness that exists in the world and have been allowed to persist through the centuries, with the underpinnings promises and dogma of religion: Notwithstanding the flawed messengers that step forward to sell and represent religion of one faith or another.

Mahatma Gandhi believed that God was truth. Some have espoused that God is our inner voice speaking to us in our sleep and in moments of quiet consciousness when we listen. Some say God is nature, that the two are one and the same. That God is reality. That God is the anthropomorphisation of Nature. Elizabeth Kubler Bryant believes that "God is the source, the beginning and the end." Perhaps God is all of these things. Put a label on all of these definitions of the spirit and call them God. But I continue to listen to that inner voice to lead me. If it's God, which I think it is, I gladly give him the praise, but I follow it and when I do I seldom have been wrong about the course of actions I have taken as a result. And this is where faith comes in. Religion does not change reality; only reality changes reality.

Throughout the journey of my life thus far, I have followed that inner voice. And the older I get, the more carefully I try to heed the directions of that voice. I was raised in the Christian Church, I went to Sunday school every Sunday and memorized all the names of the books of the Bible, though I have not yet read the Bible completely, but I have read several books that explain the history and teachings in the Bible. People thought I was going to be a minister because of my proclivity toward religion when I was growing up. I know more about Christianity than any other religion though I do not exalt it above any other faith. I could not accept being an atheist, and I am not a secularist, nor a literalist. I have bordered on being an agnostic at times but, essentially I believe in making room for religion in my life to give balance and wisdom and respect for the unknown power which I believe exists in the world, though not scientifically proven. The plausibility of a Holy Spirit makes it presence known throughout life and through people, and gives us hope about tomorrow. Dad's saying has application, "we do not know what will happen in the future, but we know who holds the future."

But I do not understand how God can allow the injustices which predominate in the world: that is why my search has been to understand, as much as I can, why things are the way they are. "Lean not upon thine own understanding," the Bible says. From my adventures in Chicago, where I knew no one except my wife and child, to my trials after struggles with the bar exam in Illinois, to my sojourn in Philadelphia, through my heart attack in Philadelphia and related heart illnesses, to my resurgence in Charlottesville, Virginia; I have always been mentally alone for the most part trusting the direction of my God. I can only attest to what God has done and been in my life and that he, she or it has intervened to save me time and time again. "Nobody knows the troubles I've seen," the Negro spiritual goes, except for my wife Michelle since we were married and of our immediate family. As an only child, I have had to chart my own journey, which has been based on my God inspired decisions alone.

I have postulated that man, even prehistorically, has always worshiped a force greater than himself because he cannot explain all of the events that occur in his world and the greater world outside of him. Pascal Boyer in his book *Anthropology of Religion: Religion Explained, the Evolutionary Origins of Religious Thought* (2001) demonstrates that peoples in all parts of the world, even in the most primitive of environments have worshiped a deity of their own definition and within their own traditions and cultures. The problem is, of course, because of the ethnocentrism of the powerful elite, we know who they are, they are not hard to define. They have determined what is good and evil. They have denigrated these unfamiliar other world beliefs, and relegated them to heathenism and irreligiousness. I believe this is wrong. Just because you do not understand something does not mean it is worthless or of less value than what you are familiar with and believe in.

Christopher Hitchens in his book *god is Not Great, How Religion Poisons Everything* (2007), put forth the view that it is almost criminal to inculcate children with religious beliefs. You are using gullible minds, easily led into believing a dogma they don't understand, that is not scientifically based that will attempt to control their lives for the rest of their lives without empirical substantiation. And extract from them in the process money, guilt, conflict, doubt and confusion. By analogy, cigarette manufacturers seek to hook the kids when they are young so they will be life-long inhalers of nicotine smoke. Religious dogma, through institutional propagation, seeks to do the same thing.

I was on a cruise to Greece celebrating my parents' 50th wedding anniversary, with some close friends along with my Aunt Louise, when I was confronted by a White college professor from Santa Clara, California. I was reading a book on Christianity, entitled *A History of God, the 4000 Year Quest of Judism, Chrisitiany & Islam* (1990), by Karen Armstrong. The professor walked right up to me unannounced; I guess she assumed that there was no need for formality, since we were all on this relatively small cruise ship together. So, she asked me "Excuse me, how could Black people believe in Christianity?" I thought for a second and said hesitantly, "because it was all that they had." The implication of her question was, in light of how Christianity was used to rationalize Black subjugation and certain sects within the faith stood by and allowed it to happen, how could we as a people accept this dogma?

My answer was not complete, nor was it a good one, for I had not read enough to give a more cogent and thoughtful answer. A better answer would have been that the slaves had their own religion but were not allowed to practice it. They were considered heathens for having the religious practices they brought with them. Many of them were possibly Moslems or followers of other religious practices that were seen as threats and shrouded in mysticism to their slave masters. Christianity was the only religion permitted, and even that was restricted. People must have hope, some solace from their degradation. So don't blame the slaves for adopting Christianity; blame the slave system and those who promoted and profited from it.

Call him or her or it what you will: Yahweh, Jehovah, Allah, Vishnu (one of the three principal Hindu Gods, including Shiva and Brahma), Krishna, Ganesh the lesser Gods or Buddha, or Nirvana. Whether the holy book is the Koran, Bhagavad-Gita, the Bible, Vedas, or Upanishads, Hindu holy texts, it all points in the same direction—a higher or greater force than man.

— — —

Intrinsically a part of religion is the concept of faith. Athanasius believed that faith should trump reason. Perhaps he knew that if faith did not overcome reason religion was lost.

"O God our help in ages past and our hope for years to come," "I will lift up mine eyes unto the hills from whence cometh my health and strength." "Faith of our fathers living still in spite of dungeon, fire and sword, O how our hearts beat high with joy when e'er we hear that glorious word! Faith of our fathers, holy faith! We will be true to thee till death." So goes the first stanza of the words of a favorite Baptist Church hymn, "Faith of Our Fathers Living Still" written by Frederick W. Faber. Faith, as defined in the American Heritage Dictionary, is "a confident belief in the truth, value, or trustworthiness of a person, idea or thing; belief that does not rest on logical proof or material evidence; belief and trust in God and in the doctrines expressed in scriptures or other sacred works; religious conviction."

The tradition of faith as I have defined the concept has existed in mankind for millennia. It can be seen as an essential ingredient in perseverance, steadfastness and in overcoming the obstacles of injustice, misfortune and inhumanity. It is embedded through religion, moral values and ideology. In one form or another, faith is utilized by people for many purposes.

Could the forces of evil, inhumanity, misfortune, etc., be overtaken by sheer endurance void of the idea of faith? Does faith somehow empower the individual to overcome his situation? Can the power of faith be divorced from religion, or is it purely a religious concept that cannot exist in a simply secular context, i.e. drive, will, endurance, speculation and hope?

When we speak of faith, what is it that we have faith in? Is it faith in tomorrow, that tomorrow will be better than today? Faith that our God will deliver us? Faith that we will get through whatever situation we are in? Or faith that all things will come to an end; that whatever it is, it will not last forever? Is this "faith" nothing more than the expectancy of an optimist or the knowledge that as long as the earth keeps spinning on its axis, things will evolve.

What is the essential difference between faith and hope? To me, faith is religiously based, hope is its secular counterpart. Is there any evidence that faith in a religious context has ever in reality lastingly changed anything? These are not rhetorical questions, but queries that go to the essence: what exactly is the source of this "faith"? Is it innate in human beings to be optimistic and to believe in a better tomorrow, or is it a religious concept inculcated and adopted when we are young and reinforced throughout our lives by the occurrence of random and expected and unexpected events attributable to a higher force than ourselves? Does faith in God explain the inexplicable? A substitute for no other answer?

A complete analysis along with detailed answers to these questions extend beyond the limits of this monograph but do represent the lens through which I will try to discuss the derivation of the value of faith and its use by people to survive in a world often inimical, and hostile to the tranquility and peace we all seek.

When the traffic in slavery began in the middle fifteenth century, Portuguese traders seized Africans from their villages in West Africa without concern, knowledge or appreciation for their culture, traditions, family structures or adaptability. No thought was given to whether or not these people would or could survive in this new world. Whether or not the newly enslaved people had a system of beliefs that would enable them to withstand the ordeals that lay ahead did not concern their captors. The captured African people were thought to be heathens since they were not Christians and left to their own devices to survive or not. They were thought to be too ignorant to have what Christians call faith. Were they religious? Yes, they had their own belief system. It may have been Islamist, pagan or some other form of belief. Did they have a system of rituals which normally characterize a faith system? Within their culture, yes. Was faith a component of that belief system? Perhaps not as the Judeo-Christians know the concept of faith, rather a belief system composed of Islam, tribal cultures, mores and a regional system of governance; the interwoven mixture of indigenous religious belief and self-preservation.

The American Indians are another example of a people beset by heinous crimes of injustice and genocide. Do they attribute their present day circumstances to the results obtained from unfettered faith in whatever gods they worship or to the magnanimity of their conquerors? Or to the deeds they hold to American lands and the indigenous rights they hold as the original inhabitants of the lands called America, negotiated through treaties and law? They too were thought to be heathens because they were not Christianized, but they had their faith and a belief system of their own culture that existed well before the White man set foot upon these lands.

After slavery was abolished in 1865, followed by racial segregation and Jim Crow, African-Americans continued to struggle for freedom and equality. For over one hundred years people of color were discriminated against and down trodden. What source enabled them to have faith that their future would be different? Was it the faith of religion, or was it simply the indefatigable human will to survive? It was, I believe, a combination of the two.

The Jewish people suffered through the holocaust during the German Third Reich, a political party in a Christian nation from 1933 through 1945 until Europe was liberated from the horrors of Nazism. The Jewish religion is full of principles of faith to enable people to hold on and to have hope for tomorrow and as a refuge from the inexplicable. In sum, the Jewish community believes what is said in Matthew 7:12 NIV, "Do to others what you would have them do to you." For those Jews that survived, was faith the bridge over which they walked to endure, or was the intervention of the militarily allied nations who joined to defeat Hitler the cause of the survival of some of the Jewish people?

In the Baptist hymn, *Strong Son of God, Immortal Love* by Alfred Tennyson, the third and fourth stanzas recite,

> "we have but faith, we cannot know, for knowledge is of things we
> see; and yet we trust it comes from thee, a beam in darkness let it
> grow; let knowledge grow from more to more, but more of rever-
> ence in us dwell; that mind and soul according well; may make
> music as before."

Tennyson is saying by these verses that faith is separate from knowledge but that both can coexist in harmony.

Therefore, it can be reasoned that faith, or whatever you call "belief in something," is not derived from Christian dogma and should be contrasted with the reality of knowledge. That faith is not restricted to any one people, sect, tribe, clan or ethnic group. The former dwells in the world of the supernatural and the latter is finite and is within known reality. Faith is metaphysical, abstract, incorporeal, intangible and subtle. Faith and reality are opposites yet they are a requisite for mankind to succeed. One must have faith to press on when reality stares you in the face and says this is not possible. One must believe that the impossible is possible without any proof of that "possibility's" existence, except within your own consciousness.

The German philosopher and political economist Karl Marx opined that "religion is an opiate for the masses," a balm to soothe the pain of reality which for many is unbearable. Life is full of hard lessons, sprinkled with heartbreak and disappointment. Life can be a trying experience on many occasions for a lot of people. We must all swallow hard the bitter taste of life's volatile mixture. Religious scholars have often spoken of the role religion plays in assisting people to cope with pain and suffering in their lives; to help people attain hope and as a way to explain trials, as a path out of difficulties; a method for lifting burdens. For many, when the extreme of reality has been confronted and limits of human understanding exhausted, the last resort is religion. The "will" to continue is summoned from faith, in the Western world, from the Christian "God who we deem is in control." There is an old saying that "God does not put on anyone more burdens than they can bear," a self-satisfying prophecy.

What impact do drive and determination have on the results achieved by faith? Do these character traits play a role in faith? I believe they do.

Faith is intrinsic to people who believe in religion. Without it there is no religion, hence the emphasis on this essential element. Belief and conviction are endemic to mankind. Faith is not the sole property of religion, however faith exists independent of religion. The secularists call it the human will to achieve: determination, perseverance, the natural order of things, evolution, all of which account for the forward movement of human progress. The natural force of human evolution is inevitable and infinite, it will happen whether we believe it will or not. The crux of the matter is the "state of mind" of the believer or non-believer. Faith makes it easier to bear the burden of human existence. If practiced it removes from the human being the pain of his predicament and places the burden upon a higher force, it exposes the helplessness of the human reach, the powerlessness over events we wish we understood or even better, that we wish we could control. Religion makes faith more accessible and comforting to the individual, it is a balm to the central nervous system. It is a passage through which we travel to acceptance and relinquishment to overbearing forces. Faith is derived from the human will to endure. After all, self-preservation is the first law of nature. Faith is the province of those who make good decisions and those who do not but are eager to find a way out.

Often what comes to mind is the old African-American spiritual, *There is a Balm in Gilead*. I first heard this hymn as a child attending Ebenezer Baptist Church in Richmond, Virginia, and its joyful melody has always been a part of the music of my spiritual being. I find myself humming it almost unconsciously. There is a history to this song just as there is a history to everything but I need not elaborate on that; just focus on the lyrics and the rest takes care of itself.

> "There is a balm in Gilead, To make the wounded whole; There is a balm in Gilead To heal the sin-sick soul. Sometimes I feel discouraged, And think my works in vain, But then the Holy spirit revives my soul again. If you can't preach like Peter, If you can't preach like Paul, Just tell the love of Jesus, And say He died for all."

In Hebrews 11:1, faith is defined as the "substance of things hoped for, the evidence of things not seen." Ray Palmer sums up the quest for explanation in his hymn *Jesus These Eyes Have Never Seen*:

> "Jesus, these eyes have never seen that radiant form of thine; the veil of sense hangs dark between thy blessed face and mine. I see thee not, I hear thee not, yet art thou oft with me; and earth hath ne'er so dear a spot as where I meet with thee. Yet though I have not seen and still must rest in faith alone; I love thee, dearest Lord and will, unseen, but not unknown. When death these mortal eyes shall seal, and still this throbbing heart, the rending veil shall thee reveal all glorious as thou art!"

James Baldwin makes the point in his piece *White Racism or World Community*:

"It is important to bear in mind that we are responsible for our soul's salvation, not the Bishop, not the priest, not my mother, ultimately it is each man's responsibility alone in his own chamber before his own gods to deal with his health and his sickness, to deal with his life and his death."

So let me conclude, not with my own words for you have read enough of them by now, but rather by quoting John Shelby Spong's book *Resurrection: Myth or Reality?* (1994):

"Yes to Jesus—my primary window into God; Yes to resurrection-which asserts that the essence of Jesus is the essence of a living God; Yes to life after death-because one who has entered a relationship with God has entered the timelessness of God. [...] Out of these affirmations I will live, I will love, and I will enter life deeply, I will scale life's heights and explore its depths. I will seek truth without fear, and when I find it, I will act on it regardless of the cost. I will never rank peace above justice or the unity of an institution ahead of the integrity of that institution. [...] I will treasure those persons with whom my life is emotionally bound today, and I will enjoy the expanding privileges of their friendship. When they die, I will grieve at the loss that my life will experience. I will not speculate on how, if, or in what form I might see them again. That is not my business. My business is to live now, to love now, and to be now. [...] so let us live, my brothers and sisters. Let us even eat, drink and be merry, not because tomorrow we shall die but because today we are, and it is our vocation to be alive-to be alive to God, alive to each other, alive to ourselves. [...] "Choose ye this day whom you will serve!" As for me and my house, we will serve the crucified/risen one who said, "I have come that you might have life and that you might have it ABUNDANTLY," and I will live in expectant hope that where he is there will I someday be. That is quite enough for me."

ENDNOTES

Chapter 1

1   A genealogist from South Boston, Faye Royster Tuck, researched the record and provided documentation for much of what is known about the family history of Patrick Moon and Helen Penick. The absolute historicity of all that is recounted here cannot be guaranteed, but much care has been taken to recite credible facts related by the genealogical record and oral history from surviving family members.

The genealogist determined that Parham Moon also had a slave named John Moon, born 1829, died November 1, 1865 of pneumonia. It is indeterminable whether John Moon and Patrick Moon were related.

2   According to genealogist Faye Royster Tuck, Tabitha Rudd, a White woman, was the daughter of Thomas Rudd of Chesterfield County, Virginia. Tabitha Rudd was born in 1771 and died in 1845. Tabitha obtained slaves from her father in Chesterfield and brought them to Halifax County, Virginia.

On May 2, 1795 in Chesterfield County, Virginia, Tabitha married Nathan Penick, a White man, born in 1771 and who hailed from Halifax County, Virginia. Nathan died on July 27, 1853 in Halifax County. At his death Nathan Penick owned Helen Penick's materal grandfather, Armistead Penick. It is unclear whether Nathan Penick owned Armistead separately or whether he obtained ownership of Armistead from the estate of his wife Tabitha.

Burwell Penick, born 1828 was the brother of Armistead Penick, they lived near each other in Halifax County. Their parents were Peter Penick and Mildred. Burwell married Isabella Johnson on December 31, 1874 in Halifax County, Virginia. Isabella Johnson's parents were Raleigh and Martha Johnson. Martha's sister, Elizabeth Johnson had married Patrick Moon in 1867.

443

The Penicks were known to be mulatto.

Armistead was the son of Peter and Milly Penick. Armistead Penick was born a slave of record in Halifax County in 1820. Armistead married "Susan" who was born in 1825. Helen's mother was Margaret Sue Penick a child of that union who was born in 1861, Margaret married a "Johnson" but the date of the marriage is unknown. By the will of Nathan Penick, probated in Halifax County Court on August 22, 1853, Armistead was bequeath to Nathan Penick's son William Penick. William Penick in settlement of his father's estate purchased Armistead for $875.00. Elizabeth "Lizzie" Johnson Moon, Isabella's sister was my grandfather's (Patrick Moon's) mother.

Chapter 2

3	Tramezzino, Michele. *The Three Princes of Serendip*. Venice, 1557.
	This ancient story depicts the adventures of the three sons of a Persian King, that through happenstance and fortuitous events and judgement they deal with unexpected events.

Chapter 5

4	*Shelly v. Kraemer*, 334 U.S. 1 (1948).

5	*Corrigan v. Buckley*, 271 U.S. 323 (1926).

6	*Oliver Brown, et al v. Board of Education of Topeka, et al*, 347 U.S. 487 (1954).

Chapter 6

7	Tippy Rhodes: See *http://faculty.virginia.edu/vafolk/ffv1a.htm*.

8	Lassiter, Matthew. *The Silent Majority: Southern Politics in the Sun Belt South*. Princeton: University Press, 2006.

9	Governor James Lindsay Almond, Senator Harry F. Byrd, the Byrd machine, his son, Harry F. Byrd, Jr., and Mills E. Godwin were prominent statewide and regional advocates of segregation. They and many others in the not so "silent majority," were ardent enforcers of the 1857 United States Supreme Court *Dred Scott* decision, authored by Chief Justice Roger B. Taney, which ruled that Blacks were chattel, i.e. personal property, could not be a citizen and were not protected by the constitution, and had no rights that the White man was duty bound to respect. Dred Scott was a slave born in Virginia. Nor was that all, the Supreme Court decision in *Blyew vs. U.S.* (1871), held that a Black man could not testify against a White man in a civil or criminal case, this case prevented Blacks from achieving or having any expectation of any kind of fairness or justice in the court system was just as appalling as the Dred Scott decision, hence the expression Dad always asserted "race clouds justice". The Blyew decision though overruled by later legal precedent reflected the legal community's disdain for Blacks; the weight it gave our problems or protection of our rights. These decisions along with the 1896 Supreme Court ruling in *Plessy v. Ferguson*, which upheld the separation of the races in transportation and education, put into the culture by law that which was the prevailing view in custom, and practice, that Blacks were inherently inferior to Whites. Together, this trilogy of racial caste cases established a "Maginot line" that separated the races and delineated the boundaries for Black people in everyday life. This portraiture of judicial mandates was the painting that I lived in, grew up in, and which framed my world as a Black youth in north and south Georgia, South Boston, Richmond and later Charlottesville, and that of my parents. These court decisions operating in tandem formed a slipstream for the myriad of maladies that afflicted Black people, both mental and physical, then and that persists to some extent today. Later judicial precedents such as the *Brown vs. the Board of Education* decision handed down in 1954, and the passage of federal civil rights legislation enacted by Congress in 1964, began to "gradually" change the culture, but not necessarily the mindset of the Whites as well as the Blacks, and slowly lifted the veil.

Chapter 7

10   According to Lassiter, "in the early months of 1959 federal and state courts invalidated the school-closing legislation, and Black students peacefully broke the caste barrier in Virginia's secondary school system." It was the VCPS, the Virginia Committee for Public Schools, that triumphed over the hard core segregationists, and the rural diehard black belt White politicians that resolved the conundrum that the Whites found themselves in of "desegregation or no public schools," quoting Lassiter. Moreover, as Lassiter asserts, and as I recollect and experienced personally, "municipalities of urban and suburban Virginia proceeded to implement a bad-faith gradualist formula based on one-way individual desegregation limited by residential geography, avoiding the structural measures required to disestablish the dual school system."

The Virginia segregationists were determined not to comply with Brown unless made to do so, kicking and screaming all the way. These failed politicians were dead serious about not doing anything to upgrade Black education, and everything to enforce state sponsored systemic mediocrity all in accordance with Plessey.

11   See *http://www.vqronline.org/articles/1998/autumn/lechner-massive-resistance-virginias/*.

12   *Charles W. Baker v. et al v. Joe V.Carr et al*, 369 U.S. 186 (1962).

13　Jones, Judy, Wilson, William, Estate of. *An Incomplete Education*. New York: Ballantine Books, 2006.

Chapter 11

14　*New York Times Company v. L.B. Sullivan*, 376 U.S. 254 (1964).

Chapter 14

15　Klarman, Michael J. *From Jim Crow to Civil Rights, the Supreme Court and the Struggle for Racial Equality*. USA: Oxford University Press, 2006.
The proper designation for Black Americans is Americans of African Descent.

16　According to *Emancipation, The Making of the Black Lawyer 1844-1944*, by J. Clay Smith, who served as acting dean of the law school during my attendance at Howard University School of Law, "the first Black lawyer admitted in Charlottesville was reported in the New York Globe to be R. C. O. Benjamin, sometime prior to 1891. For in that year people came from miles around to witness the admission of Harrison H. Ferrell as the second colored admitted on court day in 1899" Clay also quotes another Black lawyer during this era as saying that "the only way out for my people is to get education and own property."

17　All of the schools I attended from Albert V. Norell Elementary and Baker Upper Elementary in Richmond, to Jefferson Elementary and Burley High School in Charlottesville were all Jim Crow Schools. Marginally uncompetitive, warm and fuzzy but lacking in rigor, bastions of systemic mediocrity. I was working well below the "level playing field" often talked about as the ideal place we all should get to. Allegorically "climbing Jacobs Ladder" that was what our challenge was. Trying to get to that "level playing field" to "launch our boats" down the "mainstream" of American middle class life. Once afloat we usually did well, but getting to the launching dock was problematic. The tragedy is that most of us never get to the top of "Jacobs Ladder" and never reached that level playing field, falling off many rungs below. Elementary and secondary schools are the most important because if the right lessons are learned there the climb is less steep.

18　Jeffries, Stuart. "Was This Britain's first Black queen?" *The Guardian* (March 12, 2009).

Chapter 16

19　The difference between terms "Black" and "African American": to me, Black is used more generally and African American is used when being more specific or elevating the speech.

Chapter 19

20 Translated by Haxton, Brooks. *Fragments: The Collected Wisdom of Heraclitus*, New York: Viking, 2001.

Chapter 21

21 DuBois, W.E.B. *The Philadelphia Negro, A Social Study*. Philadelphia: University of Pennsylvania Press. 1899.

22 Webber, Ross A. *Management, Basic Elements of Managing Organizations*. Homewood: Richard D. Irwin, 1975.

Chapter 22

23 It is an example of the Second Empire mode of French Renaissance Revival architectural constructed in the late 19th century. City Hall is the nation's largest municipal building. See *http://www.nearchitecture.com/buildings/pa/ philadelphia_city_hall.html*

24 Hitchens, Christopher. *god is NOT Great, How Religion Poisons Everything*. New York: Twelve Hatchet Book Group USA, 2007.

Chapter 24

25 In reality, this was my third building. The Kenneth Street building in Chicago had failed, but many lasting lessons had been learned.

26 Horatio Alger was an author who lived between 1832 and 1899. Alger wrote books about people who gained wealth and middle class stability by leading morally straight lives, struggling valiantly against poverty and adversity and achieving success against the odds.

Chapter 25

27 See *www.thiscantbehappening.net/node/47*, also see *www.Fantompowa.net/ Flame/hougland_move_massacre.html*

Chapter 33

28 Richard Allen, an 18th century leader of the Black independent church movement, organized the Bethel AME church in 1794.

Chapter 37

29 Boyer, Pascal. *Religion Explained The Evolutionary Origins of Religious Thought.* New York: Basic Books, 2001.

Chapter 39

30 Vaillant, Janet G. *Black, French, and African The Life of Leopold Sedar Senghor.* Cambridge, Massachusetts: Harvard University Press, 1900.

31 Ringer, Robert J. *Winning Through Intimidation.* Canada: Fawcett Crest Books, New York: Ballantine Books, 1984.

32 Carr, Albert H.Z. *Business as a Game, A Knowing guide for Executives on the Way Up.* New York: Signet, 1971.

Chapter 40

33 Spong, John Shelby. *Resurrection, Myth or Reality?* San Fransisco: Harper, 1994.

34 Baldwin, James. *The Fire Next Time.* New York: The Dial Press, 1963. See "Down at The Cross," for elaboration and his take on the subject.

Chapter 41

35 Ferling, John. *A Leap in the Dark: The Struggle to Create the American Republic.* New York: Oxford University Press, 2003.

These soldiers of color fought in a war for freedoms they were denied, freedoms that they and their progeny would not fully achieve for some 524 years, measured from when the first slaves were taken by "Portuguese seamen on the decks of a half dozen hundred-ton caravels, the new sailing ships [...] This cargo consisted of 235 slaves." until the last of the civil rights acts were passed in the United States of America in 1968. See, Thomas, Hugh. *The Slave Trade, The Story of the Atlantic Slave Trade: 1140-1870.* New York: Touchstone, 1997.

Chapter 42

36 Painter, Nell Irwin. *The History Of White People.* New York: W.W. Norton & Company, 2010.

37 Meade, Teresa A. *A Brief History of Brazil, Second Edition.* New York: Checkmark Books, 2009.

Ferling, John. *A Leap in the Dark: The Struggle to Create the American Republic.* New York: Oxford University Press, 2003. Also see Meade, Russell. *God and Gold: Britain, America and the Making of the Modern World,* New York: Vintage, 2007.

38 Yergin, Daniel. *The Prize: The Quest for Oil, Money, and Power.* New York. Simon & Schuster, 1991.

39 According to a Washington Report on Middle East Affairs for November 2008. See *http://wrmea.org/component/content/article/245-2008-November/3845-con.*

40 See *www.fas.org/sgp/crs/row/RL33591.pdf.*

Dagne, Ted. "Africa: U.S. Foreign Assistance Issues." *CRS Report for Congress* (September 15, 2011).

41 Davidson, Basil. *The Black Man's Burden Africa and the Curse of the Nation-State.* New York: Three Rivers Press, 1992.

42 Davidson, Basil. *The Lost Cities of Africa.* Boston: Little Brown and Company, 1987.

Spiritual Afterthought

43 Meinardus, Otto F.A. *Two Thousand Years of Coptic Christianity.* Cairo: The American University in Cairo Press, 2010.

GRAPHICAL INDEX

PHOTOS:

HISTORICAL DOCUMENTS, PHOTOS, AND GRAPHICS:

INDEX

General Topics and People